Justice and Reform

Justice and Reform

The Formative Years of the OEO Legal Services Program

Earl Johnson, Jr.

RUSSELL SAGE FOUNDATION   NEW YORK

PUBLICATIONS OF RUSSELL SAGE FOUNDATION

Russell Sage Foundation was established in 1907 by Mrs. Russell Sage
for the improvement of social and living conditions in the
United States. In carrying out its purpose the Foundation conducts
research under the direction of members of the staff or in close
collaboration with other institutions, and supports programs
designed to develop and demonstrate productive working relations
between social scientists and other professional groups. As an integral part of its operation, the Foundation from time to time pub-
lishes books or pamphlets resulting from these activities. Publication
under the imprint of the Foundation does not necessarily imply
agreement by the Foundation, its Trustees, or its staff with the
interpretations or conclusions of the authors.

Russell Sage Foundation
230 Park Avenue, New York, N.Y. 10017

© 1974 by Russell Sage Foundation. All rights reserved.
Library of Congress Catalog Card Number: 73–83890
Standard Book Number: 87154–399–0
Printed in the United States of America

This Book is Dedicated to
My Parents, Earl and Doris Johnson,
and My Children, Kelly Ann and Eric

Contents

Preface

When the thought first occurred to write a book about the Legal Services Program of the Office of Economic Opportunity (OEO), it was 1967 and I was still the Program's director. For several years I had been living through the creation of this new and unique institution. Constructed by a coalition between some of the most conservative and the most innovative elements in American society and powered by ambitious but apparently conflicting goals, the Program seemed an interesting vehicle for a case study of political process. However, it has become much more than that.

By 1973, the Legal Services Program comprised 250 community-based agencies staffed by more than 2,600 full-time lawyers manning 900 separate law offices. Funds were provided by the Federal government through annual grants exceeding $60 million. Program lawyers had served over five million low income clients and argued a hundred appeals in the United States Supreme Court. They were winning over 70 percent of their cases and had obtained hundreds of millions of dollars for the poor. Their legal challenges struck down oppressive statutes and curtailed unfair practices in every section of the country. But this vigorous representation also incurred vetoes of legal services grants by governors in California, Arizona, and Connecticut, and led the vice president of the United States to attack the Program in public speeches and coerce its lawyers in private meetings. Their work even moved one especially conservative member of the Republican administration to complain that "legal services lawyers have had more influence on public policy than President Nixon. . . ."

Actually some sort of national legal aid program was overdue. In England and most of Europe, governments long ago assumed responsibility for furnishing lawyers to those unable to afford their own. These nations view publicly supplied legal counsel as integral to the administration of justice. Yet it was not until 1965 that the United States government took its first step in this direction. Founded as part of a militant "War on Poverty," the Legal Services Program had a different genesis than its European cousins. And in many ways it also was a bolder initiative than its antecedents either here or abroad.

None of the European systems have experienced so many dramatic accomplishments or such violent official criticism. Praised and condemned, a survivor that has been in jeopardy almost from birth, the OEO Legal Services Program stands as a unique phenomenon not only among legal aid schemes but also as a vestige of the original reform fervor of this nation's "War on Poverty."

Justice and Reform only touches on this drama of congressional confrontations and veto controversies, Supreme Court victories and other well-publicized events of recent years. The book concentrates instead on the formative era of the Program. It is a study of the personalities and forces, the decisions and negotiations that set the course which eventually carried Program lawyers to the Supreme Court and inevitably into collision with reactionary political elements. The study also sets forth some hypotheses about the real impact of legal services on American society and the possible shape of future developments.

1

Part I explores the two precursors of the Federal Program: the legal aid movement and the neighborhood lawyer experiment. It was primarily the official and unofficial leaders of these two pioneering efforts, rather than Congress or government administrators, who shaped the OEO Legal Services Program. Their divergent philosophies provided both the motivation for the Federal investment and the measure of its success. The first chapter examines the decades old legal aid movement, its focus on due process justice, and its general aversion to Federal funds. Chapter 2 discusses the several foundation-sponsored neighborhood lawyer experiments, their successes and tribulations, and their diverse prescriptions for curing the common enemy of poverty. In each chapter we touch on history, but only as it provides background for discussion of the goals and attitudes of the leadership group.

Part II is a study of process rather than philosophy. Chapter 3 traces the decisions and negotiations that implanted a national administration for legal services in the Office of Economic Opportunity. Chapter 4, in turn, describes the hectic 18-month campaign that produced the operating arm of the Legal Services Program, a nationwide network of Federally-funded law offices. How the goals of both legal aid and neighborhood lawyer were presented to an essentially conservative constituency are discussed in this account, as are the concerns expressed and tactics employed by particularly determined opponents of the OEO efforts, and the critical role of the American Bar Association.

In *Part III* the emphasis is again shifted. While Part I is concerned with the origins of the Legal Services Program and Part II is concerned with how it was established, Part III inquires into how it was managed. For this purpose any attempt at chronological presentation of events is abandoned. Instead, the OEO Legal Services Program is treated as a case study in the administration of a Federal grant-making agency. Each chapter in this section examines a different function common to government grant-makers, especially in their formative years. The subject of Chapter 5 is policy formation and legitimation. Chapter 6 delves into the vital question of bureaucratic survival. And in Chapter 7, the problem of inducing grantees to further national goals and policies is analyzed.

Part IV asks whether it was all worth it, and where we go from here. Returning to the original purposes of the men and women responsible for the creation of the Federal Program, Chapter 8 seeks to assess the Program's contribution to due process, justice and social reform. In Chapter 9, the emerging policy issues are appraised and some tentative proposals are offered for future movement toward the fundamental goals which found institutional expression in the OEO Legal Services Program.

2

In recounting the Program's history, I sought to steer a middle course: on the one hand, I shunned the formal, generally technical style of the law review article. At the same time, the book is not written in the breezy prose of popularized history. In the historical sections, the actual words and events are recreated wherever possible, including the underlying motives and emotional flavor.

The book may be of interest to general readers. I hope that it will be. But it succeeds in my expectations if it provides some useful information and insights to three special audiences. First, the study will be of value to students of governmental behavior as an example of how individuals and institutions translate complex, competing goals into specific action through the awkward mechanism of a Federal grant-making agency. Second, social welfare planners may find the discussion of historical developments, social-economic effects and cost effectiveness an aid in their own appraisal of legal services and similar programs. Finally, bar association leaders, poverty lawyers, government officials, and others with a particular interest in the Legal Services Program may gain a greater understanding of the context of the Program's philosophy, policies and performance.

Addressing in a single book these diverse audiences presents a special problem to the writer. The lawyer, the sociologist, the political scientist, and the economist possess specialized vocabularies and bring different perspectives to the subject. It is not easy to create a discussion that will be meaningful to each of these professions, yet understandable to all. One approach is to make liberal use of technical terms, laboriously defining each word and the underlying concept for readers lacking the necessary background. I have chosen instead, wherever possible, to purge the book of legal and social science jargon and to use words familiar to the general reader. I hope in doing so I have not distorted the meaning or oversimplified the analysis so much as to offend the experts.

3

Researching and writing this book was a full-time occupation for one year and a part-time preoccupation for an additional four. I am indebted to many individuals and institutions who made the work easier, and hopefully, better. But it was Russell Sage Foundation and the Walter Meyer Research Institute of Law that made it possible. With their backing I was able to spend a year at the Center for the Study of Law and Society at the University of California, Berkeley, assembling the documents and conducting the interviews which constitute the raw materials of the study. Consequently, I feel a special debt to Orville Brim and Stanton Wheeler of Russell Sage Foundation, Maurice Rosenberg of the Walter Meyer Institute and Philip Selznick and Sheldon Messinger of the Center for their advice and encouragement during this period. Chapters 8 and 9 also profited from preliminary research performed in connection with National Science Foundation Grant GS–33823, "Social-Economic Impact of Legal Practice," a study commenced while Fredrick Huszagh was director of NSF's Law and Social Science Program.

Assembling the data for this book was not a one-man task. During 1968 and 1969 I was aided by two very able research assistants, law students at the time, but now lawyers, Susan K. Fisher and Nancy Lenvin. In later stages, I was helped by Maureen Drummy, who kept me abreast of relevant developments in Washington. I also was blessed with three secretaries, Gaundzale Dixon, Billie McClellan, and Charlotte Simmons who could perform many research functions as well as type manuscript with accuracy and dispatch.

Literally hundreds of individuals and organizations contributed information important to the study and I am grateful to all of them. Unfortunately, I only have space to single out a handful for mention. The American Bar Association (ABA) opened its files to us. Three of its past presidents—Lewis Powell, Orison Marden, and William Gossett—were generous with their time and personal papers. Other officials of the ABA and the National Legal Aid and Defender Association were equally cooperative, among them Junius Allison, Lowell Beck, John Cummiskey, Bert Early, William McCalpin, Philip Murphy, John Robb, Maynard Toll, Theodore Voorhees, and Howard Westwood.

Many of the early pioneers in the legal services movement shared their information and insights. E. Clinton Bamberger, Jr., Gary Bellow, Edgar Cahn, Jean Cahn, William Pincus, A. Kenneth Pye, Edward Sparer, and Elizabeth Wickenden were especially helpful. Various pieces of the history also were supplied by legal services lawyers, local bar association leaders and other individuals, many of whom are cited in the notes.

An extra note of appreciation is due several of the men and women interviewed during the research phase who consented to review parts of the manuscript as well. The final manuscript also profited from the suggestions of others who read draft chapters, including economists Charles LaFave and Robert Levine, political scientist Victor Rosenblum, sociologist Jerome Carlin, lawyers Arthur LaFrance, Joseph Harbaugh, and Robert Spangenberg, and most of the staff of the Center for the Study of Law and Society. Their insightful recommendations are reflected throughout the book. I am especially indebted to Jean C. Yoder of Russell Sage Foundation's publications department for her editorial skill and the many improvements she suggested.

At this point it is customary for an author to thank his wife for her patience and understanding. But I have much more to acknowledge, for my wife, Barbara, herself a former OEO staff member and legal services lawyer, has contributed in many other ways. At various times she has been researcher, typist, and critic. Especially considering her own full time career, this seems to be a contribution above and beyond the call of matrimony.

Earl Johnson, Jr.

Manhattan Beach, California
November 1973

Part I: The Roots

Chapter 1: The Legal Aid Movement and the Goal of Equal Justice

Chapter 2: The Neighborhood Lawyer Experiments and the Goal (s) of Social Reform

Most European legal assistance schemes can trace their origins to a constitutional or statutory provision guaranteeing appointment of counsel for indigent litigants. Though government funds have become available only in relatively recent years, the legal right to a free lawyer has existed in these countries for decades or centuries. This is not the case in the United States. As late as 1972, the Supreme Court refused to consider whether the Constitutional principles of due process and equal protection embrace a right to counsel in civil litigation.[1]

In Part I we pursue answers to several intriguing questions. Among them: Why was the United States so tardy in recognizing a governmental role in legal assistance to the poor? Who provided that help in the past, and why? What was the source of the ideology that eventually made this country's legal assistance program so productive and so controversial?

1: The Legal Aid Movement and the Goal of Equal Justice

This is a book about a political invention of the mid-twentieth century—the Legal Services Program of the United States Office of Economic Opportunity. But, in a real sense, this invention owes much to concepts incorporated into the philosophy of Anglo-American society during the mid-thirteenth to mid-fifteenth centuries.

From the pledge of the *Magna Carta,* "To no one will we sell, to no one will we refuse or delay, right or justice,"[2] extracted out of King John in 1215, early English justice evolved a principle that free counsel should be provided to litigants too poor to employ their own.[3] This common law development culminated in the inclusion of a written guarantee in the Statute of Henry VII enacted in 1495:

> . . . [T]he Justices . . . shall assign to the same poor person or persons counsel learned, by their discretions, which shall give their counsel, nothing taking for the same; . . . and likewise the Justices shall appoint attorney and attornies for the same poor person or persons. . . .[4]

These early provisions in the English law arose during a period when that nation was wrestling with some of the fundamental issues of the relation between man and the state. Many of the notions that found their way into the United States Constitution originated in the minds of Englishmen who were deciding under what terms they would surrender their personal sovereignty to another authority. It is significant that a guarantee of counsel in court proceedings apparently was deemed an essential part of this social contract. If a man were to give up his right to take or protect property by force of arms, he needed assurance that he would have an equal opportunity to prevail in the substitute arena for deciding these disputes, the courts. To the English subject of the fifteenth century, equal opportunity in the courts entailed the assistance of legal counsel and, when necessary, counsel supplied by the government.

In the centuries that followed, actual practice began to fall short of these early *in forma pauperis* provisions,[5] although the goal of equal justice implicit in the *Magna Carta* and the Statute of Henry VII was never extinguished. Ultimately the gap that had developed between the ideal and reality so disturbed the collective conscience of the British electorate that Parliament enacted a comprehensive statutory right to counsel in 1949, backed fully by the government treasury.[6]

The historical right to counsel that had existed in English legal proceedings was not imported into colonial America. Unlike the mother country with its complex and technical courtroom rules, practice in the frontier society was straightforward and inexpensive. In a majority of cases, both litigants could and did proceed without the assistance of lawyers.[7] As a matter of fact, several colonial legislatures passed statutes barring lawyers from lower courts.[8] Consequently, at the time this nation was shaping its political philosophy and in the era when its founders were contemplating the same issues of personal sovereignty and social contract that occupied the English nation-makers between the thirteenth and seventeenth centuries, legal counsel was not perceived as a necessary requisite for equal opportunity in the judicial proceedings most relevant to the poor.

The implications of this temporary happenstance were profound and long-lasting. The written Constitution of the United States contains a commitment to the principle of justice[9] but no explicit guarantee of the legal help essential to that goal. The Bill of Rights is premised on concepts of "due process" and filled with provisions designed for the protection of the individual and the regulation of government, yet the only right to counsel explicitly endorsed is for Federal criminal cases.[10] Even as civil procedures and proceedings became more complex in the decades after approval of the Constitution, omissions derived from a simpler age persisted, and counsel was denied to the poor in cases only a trained lawyer was capable of conducting.

One result of the momentary simplicity of life in the foundation years of the Republic is that no sustained effort was undertaken to help people unable to afford their own lawyer until fully 100 years after the Declaration of Independence.[11] The motivation for this initial venture in legal assistance came not from a conviction that counsel is a matter of right, but rather indignation over the abuse of the legal process by those able to retain their own lawyers. It was March 8, 1876, when the German Society in New York City established the first legal aid organization—*Der Deutsche Rechtsschutz Verein*[12]—in order to discourage exploitation of newly arrived German immigrants by "runners, boardinghouse keepers and a miscellaneous coterie of sharpen."[13]

The second legal aid organization in the United States also was originated out of indignation, in this case over "the great number of seductions and debaucheries of young girls under the guise of proffered employment" in Chicago. Formed in 1886 under the auspices of the Woman's Club, it operated under the name of The Protective Agency for Women and Children.[14] It is unclear how many seductions or debaucheries were averted by Chicago's

"Protective Agency" lawyers. But they evidently established the need to provide legal help for the poor in that city, because in 1888 the Bureau of Justice, the first true legal aid society open to people of any nationality or gender, was set up by the Chicago Ethical Cultural Society.[15]

In each of these cases, the organization furnishing legal assistance was a private, not a governmental, agency. The financial support came from charitable donations rather than the public coffers. And the services rendered were perceived as a gratuitous dole, not a matter of legal right.

By the 1960s, the Chicago and New York legal aid societies had been joined by hundreds of similar organizations and criminal-defense agencies.[16] (A full account of the intervening 72 years would occupy several volumes.[17]) I propose to briefly summarize that history only as a backdrop for making a more complete investigation of two issues of special relevance to the development of the OEO Legal Services Program: first, the ideals and goals motivating the leadership of the legal aid movement; and, second, the attitude of participants in the movement toward public (especially Federal) subsidization of legal assistance.

A BRIEF HISTORY OF THE LEGAL AID MOVEMENT

Until 1920, legal aid was provided by a loose, unorganized collection of independent organizations located in a few of the country's larger cities. After that year, it emerged as something that could be called a movement, with a measure of organization and a unifying national mission.

The legal aid movement was largely the creation of one man and one book. In 1914, Reginald Heber Smith, a 25-year-old graduate of Harvard Law School, accepted an offer to take over the reins of the newly formed Boston Legal Aid Society. This was not a great honor, since the BLAS had only two lawyers at the time, but in this, his first job upon graduation from law school, Smith became appalled by the miserable way the law treated his clients. This, in turn, aroused him to seek a grant from the Carnegie Foundation to write a book about the current legal system and what it meant to America's poor.

Starting in 1916, Reginald Heber Smith toured the legal aid societies and the court systems of the nation uncovering the facts and writing the book that was to be the first definitive treatment of inequality in the administration of justice. His book, *Justice and the Poor*,[18] pulled few punches. Smith had taken a hard look at the state of justice in America and found it wanting.

The first section of *Justice and the Poor* marshals case histories and statistics demonstrating that America did not live up to her rhetoric about equal justice. Smith found barriers to justice in 1918 that still exist over 50 years later—court fees, litigation expenses, the cost of getting a lawyer. He summed up the situation in these words:

The essentially conservative bench and bar will vehemently deny any suggestion that there is no law for the poor, but, as the legal aid societies know, such is the belief today of a multitude of humble, entirely honest people, and in the light of their experience it appears as the simple truth.

• • •

In that direction we have imperceptibly, unconsciously and unintentionally drifted. The end of such a course is disclosed by history. Differences in the ability of classes to use the machinery of the law, if permitted to remain, lead inevitably to disparity between the rights of classes. . . . And when the law recognizes and enforces a distinction between classes, revolution ensues or democracy is at an end.[19]

Then as now, virtually the only encouraging sign was the existence of a handful of dedicated lawyers on the payroll of legal assistance organizations. Smith's book recounted the history of legal aid in the United States from the inception of *Der Deutsche Rechtsschutz Verein*. It was with some pride that he noted the "enormous growth" of legal aid societies after the turn of the century. By 1917, there were actually 41 cities with some sort of legal aid organization.[20] This represented an annual investment of $181,408[21] in legal assistance to the poor of the nation. There were 62 full-time legal aid attorneys at that time and 113 part-time attorneys[22] who spent from one-half to one-third of their working day on legal aid. The 41 legal aid organizations handled a total of 117,201 cases that year.[23]

Reginald Heber Smith's primary recommendations for the future concerned the means of opening up courts to the poor and finding more money to support legal aid. The keystone of his proposed strategy was the formation of a national association of legal aid offices.

The need for some union of legal aid organizations that will rationalize the work and provide a central responsibility and authority is obvious. . . . For the future, the work is too great to be conducted in a slipshod way, and its extension into new fields is too important to be left to a hit-or-miss policy . . . matters of policy should become uniform as rapidly as possible. . . . Some initiative must be manifested in establishing societies where they are needed. There must be some central body authorized to represent and speak for the organized legal aid movement in the councils of the bar, at the meetings of charities, and in the law school conference. . . . If their voice is to be heard, as it has not been heard in the past, and if their opinions are to carry weight, they must present a united front, having clearly formulated their aims and speak with singleness of mind to a definite . . . purpose.[24]

Smith's book ended on the hopeful note that:

These suggested future developments are all practical and capable of achievement. Once these matters are given proper presentation, the loyal support of the bar, the assistance of the courts, and the sustaining interest of the public may be confidently expected. The ends which they seek to attain are of direct concern not only to the fair administration of justice, but to the well-being of the nation.[25]

It would be practically impossible to find a critic of Reginald Heber Smith's book at the present time. But when it was first published in 1919, *Justice and the Poor* caused a storm in the legal profession. Smith had exposed the inequity of the American legal system, which alienated many lawyers and judges. As Henry W. Taft, president of the New York Bar Association said:

> [*Justice and the Poor*] has evoked public criticisms of the administration of justice which are unfortunate, particularly in this period of unrest. . . . Its author . . . is not free from some blame for this, for his generalizations have been frequently made for rhetorical effect. . . .[26]

Even the officials of the American Bar Association were upset. They refused to turn over the membership list when Smith said he wanted to send a copy of his book to every member of the profession. However, despite the carping, Smith's book stirred the conscience of some of the leaders in the American bar, particularly Charles Evans Hughes, former presidential candidate and future Chief Justice of the Supreme Court. And largely as a result of his interest the entire sixth session of the 43rd Annual Convention of the American Bar Association, held in 1920, was devoted to a panel on legal aid. Reginald Heber Smith, Charles Evans Hughes, Ernest Tustin, and Judge Ben Lindsey all delivered speeches about the general problem of poverty and the administration of justice.

Smith's own speech summarized the arguments he had made in *Justice and the Poor* and closed with a ringing call to action.

> If we were to take command of the moral forces which are now stirring throughout the nation, we shall find public opinion ready to fight staunchly at our side. Let us assume that leadership by declaring here and now that henceforth within the field of law the mighty power of the organized American Bar stands pledged to champion the rights of the poor, the weak, and the defenseless.[27]

At first, it looked as if the "mighty power of the organized American Bar" was going to make equal justice for the poor its primary mission in life. At the 1920 ABA meeting a Special Committee on Legal Aid was created and no less a personage than Charles Evans Hughes was named as chairman.[28] A year later the Special Committee was converted to a Standing Committee on Legal Aid,[29] and Reginald Heber Smith was named chairman (a position he held until 1937). In 1923, Smith's recommendation for the establishment of a national organization of agencies and persons interested in legal aid, a point he urged so strongly in *Justice and the Poor,* became a reality when the National Association of Legal Aid Organizations (this organization was later to become the National Legal Aid and Defender Association) was formed.[30] Shortly thereafter a number of state and local bar associations formed committees to promote legal assistance to poor people in their jurisdictions.

The decade of the 1920s was an era of promising growth for legal aid. During the ten years immediately after the formation of the Standing Committee on Legal Aid by the ABA, 30 new legal aid organizations[31] came into existence and the total financial resources available for legal aid more than doubled.[32]

With the onset of the Depression, the members of the American Bar Association, and private attorneys everywhere, had a new concern—their own livelihood. Corporations were going bankrupt, people were broke, and those clients that were not either bankrupt or broke were out to trim expenses. The legal profession was shocked to find out that when people began to trim expenses, lawyers were one of the first services to be eliminated. Only the legal aid societies found their client rolls burgeoning; the rest of the profession was in a pronounced decline.

The legal aid caseload swelled from a total of 171,000 new cases in 1929 to 307,000 in 1932,[33] almost a doubling in the workload during the first three years of the Depression. But financial support for legal aid did not keep pace. In fact, it dropped off. As an example, in New York City—where the legal aid movement started—only 229 lawyers out of the 17,000 practicing in the city made contributions to the legal aid society in 1934.[34] As a result, the number of cases confronting legal aid societies so outstripped legal aid facilities that clients became tired of waiting and tired of inadequate service. For the rest of the decade, the caseload actually declined.[35]

From the beginning, legal aid leaders worked through local bar associations to establish legal aid societies. Occasionally, they attempted to set up societies through local charitable organizations or other community groups. But as Harrison Tweed said while serving as NLADA president, "We have found, however, that this procedure does not succeed. The absence of leadership and approval by the bar association . . . renders it all but impossible to establish a new office or even to materially strengthen an existing one."[36] Not that Tweed and his associates found every local bar to be an ally. As Tweed complained sarcastically, "Anyone who has had anything to do with legal aid knows that local bar associations do not always rally to a man in a fight to the finish for the establishment of adequate service to the poor."[37]

Emery Brownell, longtime staff leader of the NLADA, was even more critical of local lawyers. In his 1951 definitive study of legal aid, written for a survey of the legal profession, Brownell wrote, "Whether due to unfounded fear of competition, inherent lethargy, or mere lack of interest, the failure of local bar associations to give leadership, and in many cases the hostility of lawyers to the idea, have been formidable stumbling blocks in the efforts to establish needed [legal aid] facilities."[38]

The legal aid movement was dependent on local bars for support but, as Harrison Tweed, Emery Brownell, and other legal aid leaders were frank to admit, unfortunately the bars tended to be apathetic or hostile when initially approached about establishing legal aid facilities; it is surprising that anything was accomplished. The men who went out in the field to sell legal aid to the local bars soon learned that flowery speeches about equal justice and the moral responsibility of the bar did not produce new legal aid societies. What sold lawyers were documents that stressed practical advantages of the legal aid office: a legal aid society will keep undesirable, nonpaying clients out of the private practitioner's office; a legal aid society will secure back wages for a discharged employee or support funds for a deserted wife, thus keeping people off the relief rolls; a legal aid society will educate people who have not used a lawyer before about the value and necessity of lawyers, which will increase the business of private attorneys; a legal aid society offers an opportunity for younger members of the profession to gain valuable experience, and, a legal aid society builds the public relations image of the bar with the general public.[39]

After nearly two decades of stagnation the legal aid movement received an assist from a totally unforeseen source. In 1950, Great Britain instituted its so-called Legal Aid and Advice Scheme.[40] The threat of a similar government-financed plan in the United States spurred many formerly apathetic state and local bar associations to establish private legal aid societies.[41] By the end of the 1950s, Emery Brownell, NLADA executive secretary, could report: "The fact is that there has been a breakthrough. Whereas in 1949 . . . 43% of the large cities were without offices, the percentage . . . was reduced to 21% by the end of 1959."[42]

Despite its comparative prosperity, the movement entered the 1960s far short of meeting the need for its services. True, there were 236 legal aid organizations of various descriptions and 110 defender offices.[43] But in 1962 the combined budgets of all the legal aid societies in the entire nation totaled less than $4 million.[44] This amounted to less than two-tenths of 1 percent of the nation's total annual expenditure for the service of lawyers[45]; two-tenths of 1 percent of the nation's legal resources to provide representation for the more than one-fourth of the nation's population unable to afford a lawyer when they needed one. Expressed in other terms, the equivalent of 400 full-time lawyers were available to serve almost 50 million Americans (a ratio of one lawyer for 120,000 persons) as compared with almost 250,000 full-time attorneys to take care of the remaining 140 million (a ratio of one lawyer for every 560 persons).[46]

In the 1960s the legal aid movement continued to depend almost entirely on charitable contributions for sustenance. Staff attorneys were woefully underpaid and carried unrealistic caseloads.[47] The characteristic failings were catalogued in an earlier Russell Sage Foundation study.

Three out of four accepted applicants for legal aid receive only a single brief consultation; only a minimal amount of time is given to the investigation of fact, to legal research and drafting of legal documents, and to court work. Many offices, in fact, are incapable of handling cases that require extensive investigation or time-consuming litigation. The situation is further aggravated by low salaries, high turnover in personnel and inadequate direction "by disinterested or inactive boards of directors." There is little time or incentive to enter into a contest over legal principle, to make or alter a law, or to combat institutionalized sources of justice.

The effectiveness of Legal Aid is also limited by its vulnerability to pressure from local bar and business interests which are its principal financial supporters. . . . Pressure from local businessmen has led to the exclusion of bankruptcy cases in many Legal Aid offices, and it has resulted in a reluctance to pursue claims against local merchants, landlords, and others whose interest would be threatened by more vigorous representation. The tendency, therefore, is for Legal Aid to become a captive of its principal financial supporters.[48]

In part, the movement leadership was innocent of the flaws in legal aid. Much that was wrong was the product of things beyond their control, such as an attitude of apathy among local bar associations and from the general public. Legal aid leaders tried, but their persuasion and might yielded only thousands of dollars where scores of millions would have been insufficient. Legal assistance simply was not high on the agenda of community chests, bar associations, and the like. And even when they got the money, it often came with strings. It was scarcely the fault of the legal aid movement that landlords and merchants lacked the public spirit to finance lawsuits against their interests.

But legal aid decision makers also were captives of the movement's own philosophy. Their horizons were limited, their range of policy options circumscribed by unconscious acceptance of shared goals and attitudes. In this they are not unique. I think it is fair to say that for most policy makers the scope of objectively feasible alternatives is much broader than the choices subjectively considered as possible courses of action. Sometimes consciously but more often subconsciously we write off perfectly reasonable, and sometimes optimal, alternatives because they do not fit our mental set.

In the next two sections we trace the evolution of the most relevant attitudes shared by policy makers in the legal aid movement.

THE MOTIVATING PHILOSOPHY OF THE LEGAL AID MOVEMENT

For all practical purposes, the philosophy of the legal aid movement originated where the movement itself started, with Reginald Heber Smith and his book, *Justice and the Poor.* This is not to deny a certain debt to philosophers as ancient as Socrates and Plato. But the goals and rationale of the American legal aid movement were derived principally from the writings of Smith.

And what were those goals and rationale? After specifying the injustices of the American legal system as it existed in 1916, Reginald Heber Smith spelled out the mission of the fledgling legal aid movement:

> We can end the existing denial of justice to the poor if we can secure an administration of justice which shall be accessible to every person no matter how humble. . . . .
>
>   •   •   •
>
> In vast tracts of the civil law and in all of the criminal law related to the more severe crimes, equality in the administration of justice can be had only by supplying attorneys to the poor. . . . . [T]he legal aid organizations must extend themselves into all of the large cities, and must triple their staff and undertake a three-fold increase of their work. If these things can be done, that part of the denial of justice which is traceable solely to the inability of the poor to employ counsel will be eliminated, and it is only in this way that the great difficulty of the expense of counsel will be completely overcome.[49]

Smith's statement of goals was echoed many times by subsequent leaders of the bench and bar. In 1926 Chief Justice Taft wrote:

> [T]he real practical blessing of our Bill of Rights is in its provision for fixed procedure securing a fair hearing by independent courts to each individual . . . but if the individual in seeking to protect himself is without money to avail himself of such procedure, the Constitution and the procedure made inviolable by it do not practically work for the equal benefit of all. Something must be devised by which everyone, however lowly and however poor, however unable by his means to employ a lawyer and to pay court costs, shall be furnished the opportunity to set fixed machinery of justice going.[50]

Fifteen years later, Associate Justice Wiley Rutledge spoke to the same goal, "Equality before the law in a true democracy is a matter of right. It cannot be a matter of charity or of favor or of grace or of discretion."[51]

Academic supporters of legal aid sounded the same theme. In 1926 Professor William Vance of Yale Law School summarized:

> The process of setting the machinery of the law in motion involves effort and expense. Those very weak economically . . . cannot bear this expense. What does it profit a poor and ignorant man that he is equal to his strong antagonist before the law if there is no one to inform him what the law is? Or that the courts are open to him on the same terms as to all other persons when he has not the wherewithal to pay the admission fee?[52]

In a similar vein, Dean Arthur T. Vanderbilt of New York University Law School wrote in 1938, "In the process of improving the administration of justice, legal aid work challenges our attention. It is the only practicable method, thus far discovered, to guarantee no person shall be denied equal protection of the laws because he is poor."[53]

American Bar Association leaders with varying degrees of enthusiasm have reiterated the goal of equal justice. At the founding of the legal aid movement in 1920, Charles Evans Hughes said,

> The legal aid society is an agency of justice—doing what it is not practicable for lawyers to do individually on any large scale. The legal profession owes it to itself that wrongs do not go without a remedy because the injured has no advocate. . . . Does the lawyer ask, who is my neighbor? I answer—the poor man deprived of his just dues.[54]

The leadership of the legal aid movement itself never wavered from the central theme. One of the most influential, Harrison Tweed, an eminent Wall Street lawyer who served several terms as NLADA president, expressed the urgency in 1951, "Every lawyer and every layman should help with mind and money, heart and soul, until the objective of justice for all has been attained. Then, but not until then, we can all go fishing."[55] And the longtime executive secretary of the National Legal Aid movement, Emery Brownell, reinforced the view, "If law is to fulfill its important mission, the facilities of Legal Aid in the United States must be materially strengthened, for here is the tested and exclusive means of assuring that every citizen stands equal before the law."[56]

Reginald Heber Smith, who maintained a position of leadership in the legal aid movement through the 1950s, warned that equal justice was not merely a goal for the legal aid movement but a prerequisite for the survival of American democracy. As he said in 1951:

> It is a fundamental tenet of Marxian Communism that law is a class weapon used by the rich to oppress the poor through the simple device of making justice too expensive. According to this view, lawyers are simply the mercenaries of the property class. The danger of this attack lies in the fact that it awakens a response in all those who feel they have been denied their rights. Nothing rankles more in the human heart than a brooding sense of injustice. The illness we can put up with; but injustice makes us want to pull things down.
>
> This has always been true because it is human nature. In 1901 Lyman Abbott, Editor of *Outlook,* said in his address at the 25th Anniversary Dinner of the Legal Aid Society in New York, "If ever a time shall come when in this city only the rich man can enjoy law as a doubtful luxury, when the poor who need it most cannot have it, when only a golden key will unlock the door to the courtroom, the seeds of revolution will be sown, the firebrand of revolution will be lighted and put into the hands of men, and they will almost be justified in the revolution which will follow."[57]

It is difficult to detect much sympathy for the social and economic deprivation of the poor in the writings of the leaders of legal aid, but their sensibilities as lawyers clearly were shocked by the deprivation of due process caused by poverty. An abiding concern with the integrity of the legal system and threats to its survival pervade the pronouncements of the movement. Each man, rich or poor, deserves his day in court; that is what this country is all about; and besides, if we do not insure that access, the masses will revolt and tear down our system of government. Entirely missing is an evident stake in the outcome of the poor man's day in court and its implications for his other social and economic problems.[58] Legal aid discharges its responsibility and satisfies its ultimate goal if a poor man is provided reasonably qualified legal counsel. Apparently, lawyers must bear the guilt for inequality in the administration of justice but need not share the guilt for the existence of poverty. These attitudes generally were not a product of insensitivity on the part of those who supported legal aid but rather the result of a failure to appreciate any close connection between a denial of equal justice and the perpetuation of economic inequality.

In line with this attitude (or possibly contributing to its existence), Reginald Heber Smith, while damning inequities in the procedural law, found that:

> The body of the substantive law, as a whole, is remarkably free from any taint of partiality. It is democratic to the core. Its rights are conferred and its liabilities imposed without respect of persons. . . . [I]t is instantly apparent that the legal disabilities of the poor in nearly every instance result from defects in the machinery of the law and are not created by any discriminations of the substantive law against them.
>
> • • •
>
> On examination and on authority, the statement is warranted that the substantive law, with minor exceptions, is eminently fair and impartial. In other words, the existing denial of justice to the poor is not attributable to any injustice in the heart of the law itself. The necessary foundation for freedom and equality of justice exists. The immemorial struggle is half won.[59]

Whatever its sources, this philosophy was reflected in the policies of legal aid organizations. The Standards of the National Legal Aid and Defender Association, for instance, deemphasized the taking of appeals "to establish *useful* principles," stating that, unlike other appeals, they should be undertaken only "when costs are available."[60] Similarly, "actions to create legal machinery" for the "social betterment" of the low-income community were not even accorded the status of required standards by the NLADA. Instead they were characterized merely as "recommended policies" to be implemented by local legal aid societies "as far as local conditions permit."[61] Consequently, those legal actions probably best calculated to improve the social-economic status of the poor[62] were subordinated in the official national standards of the legal aid movement. As a further consequence, apparently no civil legal aid lawyer ever brought a case to the U.S. Supreme Court in the 89 years that legal aid was provided before 1965[63]; in fact, only a handful of civil appeals were lodged in any court.

Because of its commitment to a goal of equal justice justified in terms of perfecting and protecting the legal system, the legal aid movement concentrated thought and energies on a specific task. ABA President Jacob Lashley defined that mission in 1941:

> The goal is as obvious as it is essential. We must so plan it, and organize it, and build it, that there is a nationwide network of legal aid offices. Every city or every county must have a definite office well known publicly as the courthouse itself, to which poor persons in need of advice and assistance can apply.[64]

The emphasis on maximum coverage resulted in the processing of over eight million legal aid clients from 1876 through 1948, at a total cost of only $20 million.[65]

Considering this goal of equal justice and its contemplated implementation through opening legal aid offices the length and breadth of the nation, it might have been expected that bar leaders would have been lobbying every session of Congress for the monies necessary to make their ideal a reality. Government funds already support legal assistance in England, Scandanavia, Germany, France, Switzerland, and apparently soon will be in Italy and Austria.[66] But American proponents of legal aid did not petition their Congress. For the reasons why they were reluctant, we must examine another phase of legal aid history.

FOUR DECADES OF DEBATE ABOUT GOVERNMENT FINANCING OF LEGAL ASSISTANCE TO THE POOR

By the 1960s, the legal aid movement was almost exclusively a privately financed undertaking. Local legal aid organizations derived their support from community chests (60 percent), bar associations (15 percent), individual lawyers and special fund-raising campaigns.[67] There was almost no governmental support—Federal, state or local—and a philosophical preference among the members of legal aid societies that things remain that way. But this was not always the case. In 1919, when Reginald Heber Smith wrote *Justice and the Poor,* he reported that 28 percent of the cities with a legal aid organization were served by municipal government agencies[68] and that this type of legal aid was on the increase.[69] Smith's own evaluation of these public bureaus was generally favorable.

> Certain direct advantages have resulted from the fact that a legal aid bureau was a public undertaking. St. Louis affords an excellent illustration because, during its history, it has been both a private and a public organization. The

investigator reports that since the society came under public control her position has carried with it much greater dignity and power, enabling her to use channels formerly closed and to do more efficient work. . . . Even more important, the public bureaus are unquestionably better known, they reach a wider field, and they are answering the demand for legal assistance with a nearer approach to completeness than the private societies. . . . It may be here noted that since the Hartford society became a public bureau on January 1, 1917, its work has more than tripled. In St. Louis the work has likewise made a substantial increase.[70]

In fact, Smith viewed government-financed legal assistance as the wave of the future:

> Inasmuch as the legal aid organizations are rendering an essential public service, it is likely that ultimately their work will pass under public control. This fact should never be forgotten by those who are, or may become responsible for the future of organized legal aid, and they will do well to shape their plans with this end in view. There is no need to hasten this process of transferring the responsibility to the state, the ideas which must precede it are imperceptibly but steadily taking possession of men's minds, and the change will come about in its own good time.[71]

This was consistent with Smith's basic concept that legal aid should be an integral part of the administration of justice. Since judges, court clerks, and other elements of the justice system were paid out of public funds, he felt legal aid lawyers also should be part of the government obligation.[72]

The 1962 statistics reveal that Reginald Heber Smith's predicted drift toward government financing of legal aid did not materialize over the succeeding four decades, in part because state and local governments were slow to assume their responsibilities for the financing. But most members of legal aid societies were equally reluctant to press public officials to supply tax funds for legal assistance to the poor.

The issue of government versus private financing of legal assistance surfaced at the very moment the ABA gave legal aid its endorsement and support. At the 1920 meeting of the American Bar Association, Ernest L. Tustin advocated publicly financed municipal legal aid bureaus. The recognition that legal assistance was a public responsibility made such organizations "superior to private organizations in the psychological results produced." It also would contribute to confidence in the law and its administration.[73] But Tustin's line of argument was not persuasive to Charles Evans Hughes. In his address, the future Chief Justice argued that, "Unfortunately, the administration of municipal government in this country has not been so successful as to justify at present its extension to this field. The service is one which politics would ruin."[74]

This debate over the respective virtues of public and private financing of legal aid continued at a quiet, gentlemanly level for the next three decades.

In 1926, Chief Justice William Howard Taft expressed a more tolerant attitude toward public support than had Charles Evans Hughes just six years earlier.

> Without expressing a final personal conclusion on the subject, it seems to me that ultimately these instrumentalities will have to be made part of the administration of justice and paid for out of public funds.[75]

Proponents of legal aid were as divided during the 1920s as the profession's leaders, Hughes and Taft. Generally, representatives of societies along the eastern coast were suspicious of public involvement while west of the Alleghenies, most felt that government help was necessary and desirable.[76] The leading private organization, the venerable New York Legal Aid Society, proved its disdain for public support by refusing to touch a $25,000 municipal fund specifically appropriated for its use.[77]

Opponents of public provision of legal aid seized on some flagrant examples of political interference to document their case. A newly elected mayor in Dallas, Texas attempted to replace the attorney for the city's legal aid bureau with a personal friend and political ally. When this move created a public outcry, the mayor did away with the bureau entirely. The same fate befell municipal legal aid in Portland, Oregon, where the legal aid attorney had made the political error of campaigning against the successful mayoralty candidate.[78] The main admitted disadvantage of private financing, however, was the fact that there was never enough of it. Seldom articulated was the "political interference" to which privately funded legal aid attorneys also were subject.[79]

Whether welcomed as the preferable approach or tolerated as a necessary evil, municipal financing of legal aid was increased throughout the 1920s.[80] But the Depression reversed that trend dramatically. With tax revenues shrinking, many municipal governments found themselves in deep fiscal difficulties. Since legal aid bureaus were among the last services to become a municipal responsibility in most communities, they were the first to go when funds ran short. Several were abolished; some had their budgets drastically reduced; a few were converted to privately financed legal aid societies.[81]

Contrary to the Smith thesis, the municipal legal aid bureaus never recovered from the forced retrenchment of the Depression years. As Emery Brownell later observed:

> At one time it was considered that public bureaus held a distinct advantage in the important matter of securing financial support. There appears to be no reason why this should not be so, since the cost of legal aid service is extremely small compared with its direct and indirect benefits and must appear as a very small item in a city budget. Prior to 1932 this proved to be the general experience. Since then, however, the societies, especially those participating in Community Chests, have proven themselves better able to secure funds for the service.[82]

By 1962, there were only five municipal legal aid bureaus still in existence —four fewer than in 1919, seven fewer than in 1932. Where municipal bureaus had constituted 28 percent of the total number of legal aid organizations in 1919, only 4 percent were municipally funded in 1962.

As municipal funds dried up during the 1930s, some in the legal aid movement began to look to higher levels of government for the needed financial support. Under the leadership of Land Summers, the Seattle Bar Association in 1938 lobbied a plan for state government financing of legal aid through the Washington legislature. A statute[83] was passed that authorized the state bar association to administer a statewide system of legal aid. The Board of Governors of the State Bar was considered a public body (Washington had an integrated bar) and thus eligible to receive and administer state tax monies. Unfortunately for the course of legal aid in Washington state, this provision languishes on the statute books. In the more than 30 years since its passage, the Washington legislature has never seen fit to appropriate funds for the system it authorized in 1938.

The Depression also spawned the first proposal for Federal financing of legal assistance. In 1937, Pelham St. George Bissell, a justice of the municipal court in New York City, conceived a plan which would use Works Progress Administration (WPA) funds to open a branch office of the New York Legal Aid Society in the Bronx. The office would be manned by unemployed lawyers, of which there were many in those days, and administered with the "advice and assistance" of the Legal Aid Society. Interestingly, this proposal earned the stamp of approval of the Legal Aid Committee of the Association of the Bar of the City of New York. However, before the office could become a reality, the WPA appropriation was cut by Congress and the agency withdrew its offer of support.[84]

This whole experience, however, had made the Legal Aid Committee of the New York Bar aware of the possible use of Federal funds. Its 1937 report said, "It would be well for this committee, next year, to make further investigations along this line with a view toward extending legal aid to other parts of the city, with the aid of funds supplied by the Federal, state, or municipal authorities, but under the general direction of the Legal Aid Society."[85]

Although public financing—and especially Federal financing—of legal aid was always considered to be relatively controversial in some quarters, until 1950 it remained a respectable alternative, one that could be urged before any bar association or legal aid society. Then, two events converged to throw public provision of legal aid into disrepute. In 1949, England adopted a comprehensive nationwide system of legal aid—the Legal Aid and Advice Act of 1949.[86] This is a government-financed system which compensates private attorneys for any cases they handle on behalf of people who cannot pay a fee. The subsidy is available to persons who are unable to afford legal help or who can only pay part of the fee.

At almost the same time, Senator Joseph McCarthy of Wisconsin launched the attacks that began the era that was destined to bear his name. "Creeping socialism" became the great evil, the insidious enemy of American society. And anything which smacked of Federal government action was equated with "creeping socialism." Every loyal citizen and every patriotic organization became alert to Federal encroachments, especially in their own backyards. To many leaders in the American bar, anything patterned on the British system constituted "socialization of the legal profession."

Only the National Lawyers' Guild among legal organizations in the United States came out for a system of Federal support for legal aid. The 1950 Convention of the Lawyers' Guild received and endorsed a report from its Committee on Professional Problems entitled "The Availability of Legal Services and Judicial Processes in the Low and Moderate Income Groups and Proposals to Remedy Present Deficiencies."[87] The rather conservative recommendation of this report envisioned creation of state legal aid commissions to be administered by the state bar associations. These commissions would receive and disperse Federal funds to local commissions, which, in turn, would screen applicants for legal assistance and refer impoverished clients to private attorneys. The entire program—like the British system—was to be financed by government but controlled by bar associations.

Despite the conservative nature of its recommendations, endorsement by the National Lawyers' Guild did not make the average lawyer favorably disposed toward a program of Federal support based on the British model.[88] The reaction of Robert G. Storey, Dean of Southern Methodist Law School and former president of the American Bar Association, was typical:

> What are the trends toward regimentation of our profession? To me, the greatest threat aside from the undermining influence of Communist infiltration is the propaganda campaign for a Federal subsidy to finance a nationwide plan for legal aid and low-cost legal service. . . .
>
> It is obvious that certain members of the bar and particularly the National Lawyers' Guild are spearheading the organized effort to obtain a federal legal assistance act. It is true that they represent a minority of the bar; yet the previous illustrations [the methods by which Hitler and Lenin secured their revolutions by taking over the legal professions in their respective countries] emphasized that an organized minority with ruthless methods has been responsible for the downfall of many governments.[89]

Suddenly the legal aid movement was America's savior from "socialization of the legal profession." The 1950 report of the ABA Standing Committee on Legal Aid leaned heavily on this argument: "The private legal aid office, operated and supervised by lawyers, . . . is, we believe, the American way to meet the need."[90] And Orison Marden, president of the NLADA at the time, cited as one of the primary values of legal aid societies to the legal profession the fact that legal aid is the prime buffer against the socialization of the profession.[91] In 1950, the ABA General Assembly passed a resolution condemning any government role in providing legal aid and reiterating the principle of interest and control by bar associations.[92] (In retrospect, it seems ironic that the British system of legal aid incurred the violent opposition of most members of the American Bar when it first came to the attention of the profession in this country. Fifteen years later many rank-and-file lawyers were to embrace this approach to legal assistance as the "savior of the legal profession."[93])

As the 1960s began, the organized bar and the legal aid movement still were firmly committed to the advantages of privately financed and controlled legal aid. They were only a few years past the ABA resolution condemning government influence. Thus, it is not surprising that no bar leaders rushed forward to testify when Congress conducted its hearings about the war on poverty. In an earlier time—the 1930s, for instance—proponents of legal aid might have embraced the opportunity to obtain government funds. But the rhetoric and experience of the 1950s had turned the leaders of the legal aid movement completely away from a consideration of Federal financial support. Even after the war on poverty came into existence, it was unrealistic to expect the initiative for Federal involvement in legal assistance to come from the American Bar Association or the National Legal Aid and Defender Association.

2: The Neighborhood Lawyer Experiments and the Goal (s) of Social Reform

The OEO Legal Services Program was woven out of many threads. Although legal aid formed the gray central core, the strands of color and texture that made the new program unique were spun by men and women unconnected with the legal aid movement during an unusually creative period in the early 1960s.

I. NEW HAVEN—THE DESIRE TO DECENTRALIZE AND THE CONSEQUENCES OF CONTROVERSY

The first of the new initiatives originated with some foundation executives in New York City. In the early 1960s, a former government administrator, William Pincus, was responsible for grants related to the law at the Ford Foundation. His early interests were in the fields of legal education and representation for indigent criminal defendants. Pincus helped produce financial support for pioneering efforts to establish law school clinics and organized defender systems.

The interest in criminal representation led Pincus to establish relations with the National Legal Aid and Defender Association. As a result of this experience, Pincus began to develop a concern for providing legal assistance not only in criminal cases but in civil cases as well. He was particularly disturbed by the tendency of legal aid societies to concentrate their resources in a single downtown facility far removed both geographically and psychologically from the urban ghettos which housed the poor.[1]

Paralleling Pincus' concern about legal aid, others in the Ford Foundation had become dissatisfied with the systems currently utilized to provide the entire range of social services. Paul Ylvisaker, who was in charge of the Foundation's Law and Government section, conceived an ambitious experiment for improving life in the ghettos. Under this so-called gray areas program, Ford contemplated pouring several million dollars into selected low-income urban neighborhoods to establish decentralized service centers which would offer residents the assistance of consumer education specialists, social workers, health services and similar aid.

One of the urban neighborhoods considered for the "gray areas" program was New Haven, Connecticut. Led by a dynamic, progressive mayor, the home of Yale University, and in the midst of an ambitious urban renewal effort, New Haven seemed a logical candidate for the sort of social experiment the Ford Foundation desired to initiate.

In November, 1962, Ylvisaker traveled to New Haven to meet with a small group of social planners and local leaders. Among those attending this meeting were Edgar Cahn, a young Yale law student who already had earned a Ph.D. in political science, and his wife, Jean Cahn, a recent Yale law graduate. The Cahns had been invited because of a paper Edgar had written about urban social-service systems.[2]

During the discussion of services to be offered by the neighborhood centers in New Haven, Ylvisaker reflected Pincus' views and suggested that the group consider including lawyers. Since it was already envisioned these centers would offer medical services, consumer education services, and psychiatric services among others, this seemed a natural suggestion to round out the team. It met ready acceptance. Professor Joe Goldstein from Yale Law School and Jean Cahn were assigned the task of preparing that section of the proposal.[3] The result was a one-paragraph description stating that two neighborhood centers would have teams of social workers and lawyers to "diagnose, refer, and coordinate" the legal problems of the poor.[4]

On January 2, 1963, Jean Cahn and Frank Dineen opened up law offices in two of the newly opened neighborhood multiservice centers. They had no affiliation whatsoever with the New Haven Legal Aid Society but were employees of Community Progress, Inc. (CPI), the nonprofit corporation which was running the Ford sponsored gray areas program in New Haven. In the early weeks, they established some promising relationships with black groups and started work on several civil cases. But the honeymoon was short. Soon after the two neighborhood lawyers settled into their offices, Jean Cahn received a request from the worried parents of an accused rapist to handle the defense of their son. When Mrs. Cahn began working actively on the case, her employer at Community Progress, Inc., became nervous. It had not been anticipated that the attorneys actually would take criminal cases. The CPI management approved only with the understanding that the neighborhood lawyer would be a relatively inactive co-counsel to the public defender responsible for the defense. CPI did not want its employee asking questions or speaking up at the trial itself.

But shortly thereafter Mrs. Cahn's co-counsel stepped out of the case and she was left in charge. The neighborhood lawyer asserted her client's claim that the white girl had consented to the sexual advances of the black defendant and took this defense to the newspapers. It was not long before irate New Haven-ites, stung by the accusation that one of their young white girls may have submitted to a Negro, shifted their anger from the accused rapist to his defender, Jean Cahn, and her employer, Community Progress, Inc. The pres-sures proved too powerful for the infant antipoverty agency. On February 27, 1963, barely seven weeks after they opened, New Haven's neighborhood law offices were ordered to suspend operations.[5] Thus, the Ford Foundation's first legal services experiment collapsed virtually before it began.

II. MOBILIZATION FOR YOUTH—THE PROMISE AND PERIL OF STRUCTURAL REFORM

The equivalent of Community Progress, Inc., on the lower east side of New York was called Mobilization for Youth. However, while CPI had been begun under the auspices of the Ford Foundation, Mobilization for Youth (MFY) was started as an anti-delinquency program sponsored by the President's Committee on Juvenile Delinquency. MFY's purpose was "to advance the understanding of juvenile delinquency and to combat the social problems of juvenile delinquency and youthful crime on the lower east side of New York."[6]

As might be expected, it was much more difficult to establish that juvenile delinquency would be prevented by providing people with legal services than it was to justify inclusion of lawyers in New Haven's multiservice neighbor-hood centers. In fact, the initial MFY proposal did not contemplate any legal assistance. But experience during the first several months of MFY's operations suggested that juveniles and their families had a definite need for the help of lawyers.[7] Accordingly, in March, 1963, MFY contracted with the Vera Foun-dation, a Manhattan-based institution that designed and sponsored bail reform projects and similar programs, to draft a proposal for a staff to provide legal services. In May, 1963 the Vera Foundation recommended creation of a legal unit to be operated by the Foundation and performing three functions:
1. direct service and referral;
2. legal orientation for MFY staff members who were not lawyers, clients and community leaders; and
3. the achievement of social change primarily through legal research and the persuasion of governmental administrators to change their policies.[8]

The MFY Board approved the recommendation that a legal unit should be established, but decided against having the Vera Foundation supervise the lawyers. Instead, MFY moved to create the legal unit under its own auspices in cooperation with Columbia University. Professor Monrad Paulson of the law faculty organized an advisory committee and Edward Sparer, a 33-year-old labor lawyer, was employed as director. Sparer spent the months of Sep-tember and October 1963 conferring with the MFY staff and with community residents concerning the legal needs of the neighborhood. Sparer's thinking also was influenced by Elizabeth Wickenden, who is neither a legal aid leader nor even a lawyer but a social welfare planner. Mrs. Wickenden, who came to Washington in the New Deal years and occupied top staff positions in the public assistance administration, had left government and become a consultant to the National Social Welfare Assembly located in New York. She was intrigued with the possibility of using lawsuits to change the welfare system in the same way civil rights lawyers furthered desegregation through the courts. By 1963, she had spoken and written several times on the subject. She had even described several areas where the legal structure of public assistance seemed especially vulnerable to attack.[9]

In November, almost nine months after the demise of the New Haven neighborhood office experiments, the President's Committee on Juvenile Delinquency made a $50,000 grant to support the MFY legal unit through June, 1964. On the basis of his discussions in the fall of 1963 and research performed by legal unit staff members in early 1964, Sparer refashioned the priorities of the legal unit. He found the initial proposal to be "largely devoid of significant and concrete direct representation suggestions," primarily because the "personnel drawing the proposal were not lawyers and were not themselves sensitive to the wide scope of need."[10] Dismissing the functions of referral and orientation training as relatively unimportant, Sparer recommended to the MFY Board that the resources of the unit be focused on "a demonstration of the value of legal service to the poor in those very basic areas where the [legal aid] society was not presently giving service."[11] Sparer urged that the MFY legal unit direct its resources toward achieving social change, primarily through the use of test cases.[12] Moreover, he further sharpened the focus to emphasize reform in the areas of public housing, housing code enforcement, unemployment insurance, and welfare.[13] Sparer put together a four-member staff, each of whom was assigned to one of the chosen fields of concentration. With the MFY unit specializing on major test litigation in select fields, "all traditional civil law problems which cannot be settled by immediate negotiation will be referred to the Legal Aid Society."[14]

Shortly after the MFY legal unit began operation, it faced a crisis very similar to that which had caused the New Haven law offices to be closed a year earlier. Their first series of test cases challenged the Welfare Department and its arbitrary application of welfare abuse laws. When Sparer advised the MFY leadership of his intentions, they recommended he approach department officials about his plans. Sparer complied and the Welfare Commissioner originally said he supported the test cases. But when served with the complaints, the Commissioner changed his mind and warned MFY leaders that these legal actions might cause withdrawal of the Department's support for their politically sensitive agency.

Pressure from the Welfare Department prompted representatives of public agencies on the MFY Board to demand an investigation of the legal unit. The issue was assigned to MFY's Committee on Direct Operations, chaired by Henry Cohn, then the Deputy Administrator for the City of New York. Sparer contended this committee, and MFY in general, lacked jurisdiction. In April, 1964, he countered with a memorandum approved by the legal unit's Faculty Advisory Committee, recommending that the legal unit have independence over policy making and censuring any interference by staff or board members of MFY.[15]

In June, 1964, the MFY Committee on Direct Operations met to determine whether it had power to investigate the handling of specific lawsuits. Columbia Professor Marvin Frankel,[16] who had succeeded Monrad Paulson as chairman of the legal unit's Faculty Advisory Committee, argued that the attempts of the MFY Board to question the judgment of the attorney staff constituted a violation of the relationship between a lawyer and his client, which was protected by the Canons of Legal Ethics. He pointed to the court order authorizing the legal unit and its prohibition against "interference in the conduct of particular cases by lay members or officers [of] MFY."[17]

Deputy Administrator Cohn and the Welfare Commissioner responded that the type of cooperative effort envisioned in the original MFY proposal required that all professions and disciplines participating in the program subordinate their professional standards to the common interest. To insist that lawyers must pursue their clients' cases even when that jeopardizes relationships vital to the total MFY effort would defeat the purpose behind the MFY concept. But Judge Florence Kelley, who had been brought in by the city officials to balance Frankel's legalistic arguments, upheld the importance of maintaining the purity of the relationship between a lawyer and his client.

Undercut by their own advocate, the MFY Committee on Direct Operations eventually approved the legal unit committee's policy statement by a 4 to 0 vote,[18] a position which was accepted by the full MFY Board without discussion. Thus, the MFY legal unit avoided the pitfall that had forced the New Haven law offices to be closed and in the process obtained a permanent recognition of the lawyers' independence by the MFY Board. They soon were engaged in an imposing agenda of test cases.

III. THE SECOND NEW HAVEN PROPOSAL—AN ALTERNATIVE DIAGNOSIS OF POVERTY

In 1964, New Haven's Community Progress, Inc. again incorporated legal services in its proposal to the Ford Foundation and HEW. This time the one-paragraph description was expanded to a 49-page exposition of a "neighborhood social-legal program." The analysis departed substantially both from

Sparer's call for structural reform and Pincus' desire for more ready accessibility to legal services.

The New Haven proposal diagnosed poverty almost exclusively in terms of weaknesses in the individuals who were poor. As stated in the CPI application:

> The legal problems of the financially and educationally incapacitated citizen are closely related to social, economic, and psychological factors. Criminal assault and juvenile delinquency may reflect underlying domestic problems. Personal bankruptcy may hide family budgeting or psychiatric difficulties. Wage attachments may indicate economic credit abuses and chronic unemployment. Social, psychological, and educational factors may make the client unable to cooperate effectively with legal and social services.[19]

The solution emphasized a team approach aimed at "curing" the deficiencies of the individual poor.

> Any long-term solution to the needs of the deprived urban citizen requires coordinating social, economic, educational, and legal services for the individual family as a unit and for the neighborhood with high concentrations of families in crisis. The permanent solution to a bankrupt family may, for example, be the legal procedure of bankruptcy, an opportunity for job retraining for the unemployed husband and parent, . . . and a psychiatric opportunity for the juvenile delinquent son about to be released from the Chesire School. . . .[20]

This coordinated team approach was to be provided to a few selected families and would include "education, training, employment, youth work study, youth development, leisure time and cultural arts, neighborhood services, and coordinated social service programs."[21]

The underlying assumption that people are poor primarily because of their own inadequacies—psychological, educational, physical, and so on—broke sharply from the Wickenden and Sparer analysis which conceived poverty as a phenomenon attributable in substantial part to the existence of laws and practices that discriminate against the lower classes. This different diagnosis led the New Haven proposal writers to recommend a different kind of staff than the litigation specialists hired for the MFY program.

> We propose to meet the social-legal problems of the inner-city families through the Neighborhood Social-Legal team. . . . This neighborhood staff, consisting of a neighborhood coordinator (social worker), a lawyer, a neighborhood worker, and a social investigator, is planned in three inner-city areas. The Neighborhood Lawyer will be a member of the Neighborhood Staff. Therefore, unlike other neighborhood legal programs the lawyers' activities will be coordinated with a wide variety of community services. An integration between social and legal services is planned. The team's approach to Social-Legal Services differs fundamentally from traditional cooperation between legal and social agencies in that a mechanism for intensive effective cooperation is made possible by the grouping of lawyers and social workers into a team.[22]

In order to assure that the lawyers on the team understood their role and the limitations of the law in dealing with problems of the poor, the New Haven proposal provided that the neighborhood attorneys "will be supervised by the Neighborhood Coordinator in carrying out the day to day social-legal duties in the neighborhood. . . ."[23]

The concept of neighborhood social-legal teams was never implemented in its pure form even in New Haven, mainly because the CPI proposal itself was never funded. Because of the furor over the rape case which caused suspension of the earlier neighborhood lawyer program, William Pincus of the Ford Foundation came to think it was important to separate legal services from the rest of the CPI program. As a consequence, a new entity—the Legal Assistance Association (LAA)—was formed by some leading members of the New Haven bar and professors from Yale Law School. The LAA proposal, which received Ford Foundation backing, was much more traditional. It called for neighborhood law offices supervised and staffed primarily with lawyers; other personnel operated under the supervision of staff attorneys.

The underlying notion remained very much alive during the developmental period of the Washington, D.C., Legal Services Program and even in the first year of the National Legal Services Program.[24] Though the proposal that CPI had made on January 24, 1964, was never funded, it profoundly influenced the opinion of members of the organized bar and old-line proponents of legal aid. The prospect that attorneys might be controlled by social workers bothered even those in the legal establishment who generally supported innovation and expansion in legal assistance to the poor.[25]

IV. WASHINGTON, D.C.—PREVIEW OF THE PROBLEMS OF THE NATIONAL PROGRAM

The third of the early neighborhood lawyer programs was funded by the Ford Foundation for Washington, D.C. It is notable primarily for three reasons. It was the largest; it was the only one able to capitalize on experience gained in New Haven and New York; and, it was located in the nation's capital and, consequently, was the most influential on those who shaped the national OEO program of legal services to the poor.

The initial proposal for the Washington program was prepared by Washington Action for Youth (WAY), an organization sponsored by the President's Committee on Juvenile Delinquency. WAY, like MFY in New York, had been formed for the purpose of developing and operating programs to combat juvenile delinquency in the urban ghetto. The proposal for legal services, prepared in late 1963, was almost a duplicate of the MFY application both in objective and structure. However, before either the Ford Foundation or the President's Committee could take any action on the proposal, WAY was supplanted by the United Planning Organization (UPO). The latter was formed by the Ford Foundation to accomplish a broader mission—the development and operation of a full-scale gray areas program in the Cardozo area in northwest Washington. UPO soon was preoccupied with the exhausting political task of establishing three neighborhood service centers, a system of advisory councils, planning groups, and all the other paraphernalia of a major antipoverty effort.

In May, 1964, the UPO policy makers decided to consider adding legal services to the package of programs offered in their neighborhood centers. William Grinker, a young attorney serving as special assistant to the Director of UPO, was charged with the responsibility of developing these legal services. Grinker resorted to a consultant, Gary Bellow, who was then deputy director of the Public Defender Office in the District. Bellow spent most of the summer of 1964 preparing his first draft.[26]

While working on the proposal, Bellow met Edgar and Jean Cahn, who had moved to Washington, D.C., and were in the process of drafting a law review article analyzing Mrs. Cahn's frustrating experience as a neighborhood lawyer.[27] Bellow drew two lessons from the story related to him by the Cahns—first, the importance of decentralizing legal services in neighborhood offices and, second, the necessity for insulating the lawyers from UPO so they would not be terminated the first time one of their cases proved controversial. From the MFY program, Bellow borrowed the idea of specialization. His draft proposal also emphasized teamwork with other disciplines; representation of organizations located in poverty neighborhoods; preventive law; and education of poor people and social workers about legal rights.[28]

In order to shield the lawyers from the political pressures that doomed the initial New Haven experiment, Grinker and Bellow sought to cultivate support in the local legal profession. Fearing that the District of Columbia bar association might reject the new ideas embraced in their proposal, they approached the more liberal Judicial Council,[29] which was composed of the Federal judges in the District.

In September 1964, Judge David Bazelon, chairman of the Judicial Council, appointed a special committee to review and report on the UPO proposal. Led by Judge Skelly Wright, the committee included many persons not on the Judicial Council.[30] Among them were Howard Westwood, senior partner in the city's largest law firm, Covington and Burling; Patricia Harris, then a professor at Howard Law School and later Ambassadorix to Luxemburg; and Ken Pye, associate dean of Georgetown Law School. Virtually all were Democrats, and liberal ones at that. Consequently, Bellow and Grinker shook their heads when the committee refused to approve the proposal and assigned a subcommittee chaired by Westwood to oversee a redraft. In part, the rejection was due to matters of style. The committee members faulted the sociological jargon liberally sprinkled through the proposal. As Westwood later said, "We were appalled by the fancy semantics. Obviously, it would have been laughed out of court had it been generally exposed."[31] But beyond that, the committee objected to some of the concepts expressed and even to the innate criticism of provision of legal assistance through existing methods.[32]

Though handpicked by a judge who supported UPO aims, this was a pragmatic committee. Howard Westwood, one of the few members previously involved with the D.C. Legal Aid Society, accepted the bypass of the existing organization only because "If the characters with money wanted some new organization that would make them feel as though they were discovering a new world, that was okay with me. I knew damned well there was no new world. . . . If, to get the dough, we had to have an organization separate from the old, limping society, so what?"[33]

Bellow's redraft did not represent a wholesale retreat from the goals articulated in his original proposal. However, he did abandon most of the sociological terms introduced in the initial draft and replaced them with the writings of judges, bar leaders and legal aid lawyers which articulated the need for the kinds of innovations he proposed. The committee approved the new proposal unanimously and it was forwarded by UPO to the Ford Foundation and the President's Committee.[34] Thus, the proponents of innovation in the area of legal assistance learned a lesson in sophistication from their first confrontation with the organized legal profession. This lesson would serve them well when they moved from the local scene to negotiation with the national bar leaders.[35]

In November, 1964, UPO received funds to establish a program with fourteen attorneys and three offices, to be called the Neighborhood Legal Services Project (NLSP). Insulation was guaranteed by delegating policy making and administrative control to a separate board of directors composed entirely of local lawyers.

As the initial large, multi-office program, NLSP was the first of the new efforts to confront some of the major management and philosophical issues. (At least, it was the first program to commit these policies to writing.) The deliberations of the NLSP Board of Directors are especially significant because, for the first time, practicing lawyers attempted to grapple with the new goals and new concepts and translate them into operating policy directives. The New Haven proposal was conceived largely by welfare planners; the MFY program had been developed by a think tank and was supervised by an advisory panel of law professors. The NLSP project, in contrast, was dominated by establishment lawyers from major corporate law firms[36] and individual practitioners from the black community.[37] Only the Board chairman, Georgetown associate dean Ken Pye, and Jeanus Parks of the Howard Law School faculty came from the academic community.

In the most significant of early policy decisions, the NLSP Board attempted to establish "criteria to be utilized in the selection of . . . categories of cases which are to be handled directly by the NLSP staff." A written directive promulgated to all NLSP staff, articulated the criteria as follows:

(a) The extent to which a given category of cases is related to non-legal programs which are a part of the United Planning Organization effort against poverty in the District of Columbia. . . . It is the opinion . . . that progress can be enhanced by close coordination of the legal and non-legal efforts in these areas.[38]
(b) The extent to which the given category of cases is not being handled by other legal services or cannot be handled adequately by such services because of statutory limitations, shortage of funds, or other factors.
(c) The extent to which it appears that the given category of cases is within an area of law where especially difficult legal issues with significant impact upon the poor could be raised.[39]
(d) The extent to which assumption of responsibility for directly handling the given category of cases would not so inundate the staffs of the NLSP offices that they would be unable to provide quality legal services to their clients. . . . [N]o matter how qualified the attorneys on the staff, the legal service will not be of the desired quality if the quantity of cases to be handled is overly burdensome. Thus, it is recognized that most cases within categories which bring large volume but do not meet the previously discussed criteria should be referred to other available services.[40]

The NLSP Board applied these criteria to and chose to focus the project's resources on consumer credit practices, housing problems, public assistance and veterans benefit programs, juvenile problems, and representation of adult criminal defendants in certain matters.[41] Domestic relations cases were to be automatically referred to the existing Legal Aid Society.[42]

Other fundamental policy issues first committed to written policy by the NLSP Board later appeared in the basic guidelines of the National Program. These included a method of referral of non-indigent applicants (to be sent to the local lawyer referral panel);[43] registration fees for clients (not to be charged);[44] eligibility standards ($70 per week to a family of four but with flexibility allowed in the case of outstanding debts, illness, recent unemployment, etc.);[45] outside practice by staff attorneys (not allowed);[46] and representation of groups of poor people (to be provided when the group's resources were insufficient to afford counsel).[47]

The more or less practical problems of delivering legal services were resolved much more easily than the philosophy of the program. The NLSP was an intellectual descendant of the theory that underlay the New Haven program rather than MFY. In the summer of 1964, while preparing the original NLSP proposal, Gary Bellow and Edgar Cahn had journeyed to New York and met with MFY leader Ed Sparer. Sparer played down the importance of decentralizing legal services in neighborhood legal offices and social-legal treatment of the "whole man." Instead he argued that all available resources should be focused on strategic legal actions that would create new legal rights for the poor. Bellow and Cahn rejected this "narrow" definition of the role of the new legal services lawyer in favor of the expansive catalog of goals outlined in the NLSP proposal and the emphasis on close collaboration with other disciplines to "treat" low-income families.[48] The result was a charter for NLSP containing a long agenda of possible objectives beyond the reasonable capacity of 14 lawyers scattered among three neighborhood offices. This meant the staff and Board of Directors, who had not designed the proposal, were compelled to make the real choices concerning the scope and priorities of the program.

Shortly after NLSP began operating, pressure was put on the staff and the Board to concentrate on two problems. First, Howard Westwood and other members of the Board wanted NLSP to establish quickly the extent and depth of the unmet need for legal representation among individuals in the ghetto communities. They felt it was important to justify the neighborhood program by proving that the existing downtown legal aid society was failing to help thousands of potential clients. They wanted the statistical evidence of unfulfilled need. And they got it. During its first month of operation, NLSP served 27 clients; in the second month 84 clients; and by only the fifth month after the first office opened, NLSP served 445 new clients, an annual rate of over 5000.

While the NLSP Board sought to prove that many individuals in the ghetto communities were not receiving legal aid, the UPO staff pressed for forming interdisciplinary teams to "rescue" poor individuals and families from poverty. UPO even employed a consultant, Don Michaelis, author of a book about "Synergy" and its application to social welfare programs. ("Synergy," a term borrowed from chemistry, describes a process where the whole exceeds the sum of its parts.) Michaelis argued that if several different social services acted together, they could lift more families out of poverty than if each service acted autonomously.

Some UPO officials went so far as to suggest they included legal services in their proposals to the Ford Foundation and the Federal government only to provide the lawyers who could make this fundamental approach work. In their view, the lawyer was essential because many poor people would not take their basic social problems to anyone else. In order to seek out other professionals working with the poor, such as social workers and psychologists, a disadvantaged person had to view himself as somehow ill or weak. But that same individual could go to a lawyer with a "legal" problem without implying a confession of personal inadequacy. The lawyer's role was to then draw in all of the other helping professions to treat the social, psychological, and economic dimensions of a poor person's situation.

To the disappointment of UPO staff members, NLSP attorneys never really were used successfully. The other services did not start working as quickly as NLSP, and by the time they were in operation the neighborhood lawyers were absorbed with other priorities. Moreover, the clients often remained reluctant to accept assistance from the staffs of the social services even when advised by their attorney to do so.

At the same time that external pressures were pushing NLSP to accept a large number of legal cases and to become involved extensively in the individual social and psychological problems of their clients, the NLSP staff was groping almost unconsciously toward yet a third goal—effecting major social change through test case litigation. NLSP established a training program offering over 50 hours of instruction and produced more than a thousand pages of written materials stressing the various legal attacks that might be made against laws and practices affecting low-income consumers, tenants, and welfare recipients.[49] Meanwhile, over 20 law students were employed to research possible innovative legal theories that might be employed to change the legal structure then impinging on the poor.[50] This foundation eventually contributed to a series of landmark decisions in the District of Columbia.

V. THE CAHN THESIS—A CIVILIAN PERSPECTIVE FOR THE AGENCIES OF REDISTRIBUTION

During the early development of the neighborhood lawyer experiments the various approaches were expressed almost exclusively in the form of grant proposals and speeches. Not until Edgar and Jean Cahn prepared an article for the *Yale Law Journal* was there a cohesive, published statement.[51] The central thesis of the article also provided its title, "The War on Poverty: A Civilian Perspective."[52] The Cahns maintained that neighborhood lawyers were necessary to the forthcoming antipoverty programs because they could provide a voice for the poor in the design and implementation of those programs.

The Cahns envisioned the neighborhood law office as a response to the overly "military" approach embodied in both the foundation-sponsored experimental efforts and the nation's recently enacted war on poverty legislation. They admitted:

> Wars require recruitment, mobilization, internal discipline, a careful assessment of objectives, and a comprehensive strategy for victory. The War on Poverty is no exception.[53]

But this coordinated, comprehensive approach had inherent problems. It implied a "monopoly on all the opportunity and assistance available to the urban poor" and this monopoly would be under the control of professional social workers and the local political establishment.

The pattern of aid is one of a donee's unquestioning acceptance of an expert's dictation of what is "good for the client" and of an administrator's unchecked and unreviewable authority to terminate assistance. That power defines a status of subservience and evokes fear, resentment and resignation on the part of the donee.[54]

The Cahns also feared that the social service monopoly which the Community Action Agencies of OEO were designed to be possessed many of the traits of monopolies in other fields of endeavor.

Monopolies are characterized by a tendency to expand, to perpetuate themselves and to operate at less than optimal efficiency. These tendencies do not disappear when the market monopolized is the market for social services or when the product is social change.

• • •

In effect, "coordination" and "comprehensiveness" become the trademark of a monopoly created by an association of independent agencies. The result is often better public relations with no compelling necessity for a commensurate improvement in services . . . and risk avoidance is . . . likely to play a particularly important role.[55]

The Cahns' portrayal of the typical Community Action Agency (CAA) was not a pretty one. It would be a monopoly of local social services, dedicated primarily to its own survival and "prosperity," subservient to local political interests, afraid of its own shadow, controlled by social service administrators and local politicians, and demanding the obedience and subservience of its employees and its "beneficiaries." In the words of the Cahns, "It neglects the poverty of the spirit in ministering to the needs of the flesh."[56]

With this prognosis about the future character of the war on poverty it is not surprising that the Cahns searched for some institution which could operate as a countervailing force by responding to the "civilian" population of the poverty neighborhoods and could effectively insert this "civilian perspective" in the private and governmental institutions that most affect the lives of the poor. What they sought was someone who took his orders from "civilians" rather than social service monopolies or local politicians but who could exert influence on all the institutions in the local government and private sector. Having defined the need, the solution seemed obvious to the Cahns. The traits they had described were those traditionally associated with the legal profession —at least the lawyers serving business entities, labor unions and wealthy individuals. An attorney is warned by the canons of his profession to listen to his client and could, by his own monopoly status over access to the courts, exert a unique, powerful influence over the decisions of local antipoverty agencies. It is not surprising that the Cahns recommended neighborhood law offices as the social mechanism for bringing the civilian perspective to the war on poverty.[57]

The Cahns provided some theory for the experiments being conducted in New York and Washington. Their article also formed the basis for a dialogue between social activists and poverty fighters on the one hand and legal aid proponents on the other. And it furnished a rough blueprint to other communities that were contemplating a neighborhood law office program with foundation or government financing.

Many of the themes developed in the Cahn article concerning the role of the neighborhood law office merely reflected what neighborhood lawyers already had done in New Haven, New York, and Washington, D.C., as well as the ideas of Gary Bellow and others involved in designing the new programs. The unique contribution of the Cahns was to present the concept of a neighborhood law office which would serve as the powerful voice through which a local poverty community could exert influence over the agencies responsible for distributing income and opportunity to that community.

VI. THE PHILOSOPHY(IES) OF THE REFORMERS

There is a tendency to think that the ideology behind the neighborhood lawyer experiments was monolithic. Actually, the architects of the new wave were far apart in their analysis of goals and especially means. Even at this early stage, three schools of thought could be isolated: the social rescue theory embodied in the 1964 New Haven proposal, the law reform strategy pioneered by Wickenden and Sparer, and the Cahns' "civilian perspective."

It may be useful to analyze these three basic theories in terms of the ends they sought to achieve and the means through which lawyers were to assist in reaching these goals. The objective contemplated in the New Haven proposal was treatment of the social, psychological and educational deficiencies of persons who are poor in order to make them capable of competing for a share of the nation's affluence. Multidisciplinary teams were to be formed that would be capable of simultaneously diagnosing and treating all of the defects. The lawyer's role was to work on the legal problems faced by the family but only in close coordination with the other members of the team.

Wickenden and Sparer wanted to modify rules and practices that seemed to divert income and opportunity away from whole classes of poor people. Their primary method of attack was test case litigation.

The Cahns sought to make the local agencies charged with redistributing income and services, especially the local Community Action Agencies, more responsive to the desires of the recipients of that income and those services. This responsiveness was to be achieved through neighborhood law offices situated close to the consumers and staffed by lawyers who maintained a traditional obedience to their clients' wishes.

There were other important differences. The New Haven model placed lawyers under the domination of social workers; the Cahn model made the clients' wishes supreme; and the Wickenden-Sparer model suggested lawyers should perform a planning function and, thus, to a large extent, set their own priorities. The three also differed sharply over who or what to blame for poverty. To the designers of the New Haven proposal, it was the poor person himself and his inability to compete that made him poor; to Sparer, it was the legal structure that prevented poor people from realizing a fair share of the nation's affluence; and, to the Cahns, the chief villains were the institutions responsible for redistributing income and opportunity.

Although the ideological gulf between reformers was immense at this early stage, virtually no one cared, or even accurately perceived that differences existed. Circumstances favored unity. They were a minority seeking change confronted by an 89-year-old establishment that embodied a status quo that none of these divergent groups approved. At this stage, their own disagreements could be ignored.

All three did share a commitment to a fundamental social and economic goal—the reduction of poverty. Unlike most supporters of legal aid, leaders of the neighborhood lawyer experiment were not neutral about the dollars-and-cents effects of what their lawyers did. They were after something more palpable than procedural due process. This was the shared interest that distinguished theirs from the prime aim of the legal aid movement and it is what bound them in common enterprise during the years the National Legal Services Program was being shaped.

Another attitude shared by these reformers is worth noting. Unlike the leadership of legal aid, neighborhood lawyers bore no antipathy, residual or otherwise, to government financing. In fact, with the exception of the abortive New Haven program, all the experiments were funded at least partially with Federal money. Thus, the proponents of the neighborhood law office approached the prospect of an expanded government role from an entirely different perspective than did the legal aid movement. At the same time, they did not have a unified, prepackaged product to sell a Federal agency. They represented a series of experiments that, as we have seen, varied widely in ideology and approach. The goals and philosophy of the Federal Legal Services Program were yet to be shaped.

Part II: The Establishment of the Program

Chapter 3: Birth of the Federal Program

Chapter 4: Development of Local Legal Services Organizations

The Federal legal services institution, almost two centuries in coming, took a little more than three years to construct, from early 1964 through June 30, 1967. The establishment of Legal Services did not follow a traditional course. Most Federal programs are created by Congress, their dimensions spelled out in statutes. Not so with Legal Services. Over half the lawyers were funded before any specific legislation was passed.[1] Moreover, private individuals outside government profoundly influenced the creation and operation of the Program. In fact, their role was virtually unique both in its intensity and its visibility.

The institution-building actually occurred in two stages. Chapter 3 describes the first, the almost two-year process that produced governmental and bar association support at the national level and culminated in the founding of a Federal Office of Legal Services. Chapter 4 reports the personalities, issues, conflicts and tactics of the second phase. This quasipolitical campaign installed a network of community-run and OEO-financed lawyers in more than 200 separate localities.

3: Birth of the Federal Program

By the end of 1964, there were two legal assistance movements in the United States. One was almost 89 years old, a child—or at least step-child—of the American Bar Association, charitably financed at a level of about $4 million a year, led by middle-aged establishment lawyers, and concerned solely with the goal of equal justice. The other movement was two years old, unaffiliated with the organized bar, financed by the Ford Foundation and the Federal government at about half a million dollars, conceived and led by youthful lawyer-politicians and dedicated to some vaguely conceived goal of social reform. Over the next 18 months these two divergent movements were fused into a single crusade. That, in turn, led to a Federal program of legal assistance to the poor. In this chapter, we will explore the people and events that produced both the merger and the Program.

I. A PARTNERSHIP IS FORGED

The emergence of the OEO Legal Services Program is partly accounted for by the presence of certain individuals in certain key positions at just the right time. The progressive wave that suddenly enveloped the country in the mid-1960s (and as quickly subsided) also helped. But the precondition that made the individual decisions for merger and expansion feasible was the advent of the Office of Economic Opportunity and especially its Community Action Program.

A. The War on Poverty Is Declared

Sometime in late 1963, the United States discovered poverty. At least the government in Washington did. President Johnson, who had inherited a long agenda of pending legislation from his assassinated predecessor, sought a domestic initiative to call his own. He found it in a "War on Poverty."[2]

With enthusiasm, President Johnson energized the Federal government to design, build, and launch his antipoverty warship in record time. In February, 1964, he gave Peace Corps director Sargent Shriver the job of chairing the task force on poverty. Drawing staff and consultants from throughout government and academia, the task force held a whirlwind round of hearings, produced reams of study papers and in a matter of weeks prepared its legislative proposal. With strong Presidential backing, the proposal became a statute on August 20, 1964.

The war on poverty legislation created an entirely new agency, the Office of Economic Opportunity (OEO). Lodged in the Executive Office of the President, OEO was responsible for operating some of the antipoverty programs and coordinating the rest. The President put Shriver in charge.[3]

Of the several components of the OEO the Community Action Program (CAP) was the largest and most innovative. Based principally on the Ford Foundation's gray areas experiments, discussed in Chapter 2, this part of the legislation envisioned Federal financing of community-based and community-designed antipoverty efforts. Virtually any type of proposal was eligible for funding with the hundreds of millions available under this title of the act. It was as if the task force, lacking time to draft creative legislation, hoped that creativity would surge during the implementation stage of the act.

In any event, CAP's flexible mission opened up unparalleled opportunities for trying out pet ideas and expanding undernourished programs for the poor at Federal expense. It might have been anticipated that legal aid leaders would be near the front of the line. After reading Chapter 1, it should come as no surprise that they were not. Proponents of the traditional movement were wary of Federal money;[4] they also saw no connection between their services and the avowed goal of OEO, the elimination of poverty.[5]

B. Planning the National Legal Services Program

The idea for a National Legal Services Program financed by the Federal government actually originated before the OEO legislation was enacted. In the summer of 1963, while working at the Department of State, Jean Cahn showed an early draft of the *Yale Law Journal* article to her supervisor, Abram Chayes, at that time the legal advisor in the department. Chayes was very interested in the concepts expressed in the Cahn article, but even more intrigued with the possibility of converting those ideas into a major Federal program. Chayes showed the article to his wife, Antonia, who is also a lawyer. She was equally intrigued. As the Cahn article circulated for comment, the circle of people interested in a national program expanded. Adam Walinsky, later to serve as top speechwriter and idea man for the late Robert Kennedy, was an early recruit. Dr. Len Duhl, a psychiatrist at the National Institutes of Mental Health, became interested because he foresaw a role for legal services in the total package of assistance given to inmates of mental institutions. Gary Bellow, deputy director of Washington's public defender's office, supplied practical experience about the rendering of legal assistance to the poor. Other close friends and professional associates of the Cahns soon followed. Edgar and Jean Cahn were reaping a double benefit. They were receiving helpful suggestions about their article, and a powerful and creative group was being assembled.[6]

The first issue to concern the group was finding a source of Federal funds for the contemplated legal assistance program. By early 1964 the poverty program legislation, then being drafted by the Presidential task force under Sargent Shriver's leadership, appeared to be the most likely possibility. The Cahns persuaded Associate Justice Arthur Goldberg to send letters to President Johnson and to Shriver asking that a section on "Justice for the Poor" be included in the legislation. However, this idea was ignored, probably because of the bias for *economic* betterment of the poor.

The next opportunity to persuade the Federal government to take an interest in legal services resulted from Edgar Cahn's reputation as a speech-writer. At the time, in the spring of 1964, he was working at the Justice Department and was asked to prepare a Law Day speech for Attorney General Robert Kennedy. Cahn's draft featured the need for equal advocacy for the poor.

> The poor man looks upon the law as an enemy, not as a friend. For him the law is always taking something away.
>
> It is time to recognize that lawyers have a very special role to play in dealing with this helplessness. And it is time we filled it.
>
> • • •
>
> Lawyers must bear the responsibility for permitting the growth and continuance of two systems of law—one for the rich, one for the poor. Without a lawyer of what use is the administrative review procedure set up under various welfare programs? Without a lawyer of what use is the right to a partial refund for the payments made on a repossessed car?
>
> What is the price tag of equal justice under law? Has simple justice a price which we as a profession must exact?
>
> Helplessness does not stem from the absence of theoretical rights. It can stem from an inability to assert real rights. The tenants of slums, and public housing projects, the purchasers from disreputable finance companies, the minority group member who is discriminated against—all these may have legal rights which—if we are candid—remain in the limbo of the law.[7]

The speech provoked some press comment about the legal problems confronting the poor. But more important, it resulted in Cahn being assigned to Adam Yarmolinsky, Shriver's top aid in the poverty task force. It was not long before Cahn's speech-writing gift put him in a key position as special assistant to Shriver himself. This meant a strong advocate of legal services was in a position to influence the man who was about to become the director of the war on poverty. Shortly after the "War" became an agency, Shriver created a special task force to assess the potential role that lawyers might play in the antipoverty effort. Most of the persons already associated with the Cahns' informal group were appointed to that task force.

With Federal funds for a legal services program at least a possibility, the task force focused on the mechanics of putting the program across in local communities. Thinking on the committee about this question ran on a continuum. At one extreme were those who favored giving the money to newly formed corporations composed of poor people, concerned citizens, and liberal lawyers and ignoring legal aid and the local bar associations entirely. This faction did not even want to talk of the program in terms of law and justice but purely as an instrument of social change. At the other end of the continuum stood those who argued that the support of local bar associations was essential. They stressed the use of existing legal aid institutions wherever possible and favored phrasing the goals and methods of the program in language familiar to lawyers —equal justice, due process, and the like. In between were those who wanted control shared by local bars, the poor and the general public.

Abe Chayes, with more experience than the others in practical politics, strongly urged the necessity of wooing the local bars. He pointed out that the local bar and local judges could defeat a legal services program by harassing it with grievance actions and denying program lawyers any break in the courtroom or in negotiations. Chayes urged that the OEO staff talk to members of the legal profession in their own language and get them involved. He forecast that if a local bar viewed the local legal services agency as its program they would stand behind it and protect it when one of the lawyers had to sue the power structure.[8]

Largely because of their bitter experience in New Haven, Edgar and Jean Cahn agreed with Chayes. Jean Cahn argued that she could not trust nonlawyer organizations such as the community action agencies that would be running the local antipoverty programs. Citing New Haven's Community Progress, Inc., as the prime example, the Cahns argued that CAAs simply did not understand the lawyer's role and would not protect poverty lawyers when they undertook controversial cases. The Cahns said they would choose the bar association over the Community Action Agency every time.[9]

The opposing view was upheld primarily by Adam Walinsky and Gary Bellow, who feared that by involving the local bar associations, OEO would be "watering down the legal services organizations with conservative lawyers." Bellow and Walinsky stated they could not imagine a local bar association allowing legal services lawyers to represent rent strikers, for instance. They were especially concerned about the South, where it seemed doubtful that a Southern bar would support a local program that undertook a civil rights case, or any other meaningful legal action.[10]

The discussion continued for several weeks with little progress. The task force members were articulate and each of them was firmly convinced of the rightness of his position. Then Gary Bellow went through an experience that caused him to reconsider his stance on the issue. As you recall from Chapter 2, Bellow prepared the draft proposal for the Washington, D.C., Legal Services Program. It was couched in exactly the language and expressed the very aspirations Bellow had argued for in the task force deliberations. As you also remember, that draft was rejected by a committee whose liberalism and social concern would be difficult to match anywhere in the country. If any group of lawyers anywhere were to place a stamp of approval on the kind of language and thinking Bellow was expressing, this was the group. But they refused to accept the plan; they reported they liked the idea of a neighborhood law office program, but they were concerned about the stress on social goals and sociological terminology that permeated the document.

Although he changed the language and the form of argument much more than the actual substance of the proposal—fitting the new goals and functions into familiar categories and demonstrating that bar leaders had been advocating these changes for years—the experience modified Bellow's own views about the proper approach that should be taken to initiate a legal services program in a community. He began to see the importance of organized bar support. When the Westwood committee unanimously endorsed his redrafted proposal, Bellow came to the view that local bars might support the essence of what he and the Cahns wanted to do. The key was to make the organized bar understand that all they asked for was that legal services lawyers be granted the freedom to do for poor people what private lawyers already did for their clients. The view that Chayes and Cahn held soon prevailed in the task force deliberations and local bar support became an essential ingredient in the proposed national program.[11]

C. The American Bar Association Appears

During the early months that the task force deliberations were being held, neither the Cahns nor anyone in the planning group had considered the possibility of enlisting the support of the organized bar at the national level. They tended to distrust the legal aid movement and its official embodiment, the National Legal Aid and Defender Association. Moreover, they were concerned with the creation of local legal services projects. Consequently, their attention was riveted on local bar associations not the American Bar Association. But events were soon to shift everyone's interest to the national scene.

In October, 1964, Lowell Beck, assistant director of the American Bar Association's Washington office, read a short feature about Edgar Cahn in the *Washington Post.* The newspaper described Cahn as a special assistant to Sargent Shriver who had prepared a law review article about something called a neighborhood law office. Cahn purportedly was intent on convincing Shriver that the poverty program should sponsor a nationwide legal assistance program based on the type of office outlined in his article.[12]

Beck's interest was aroused. He called a personal friend, Jules Pagano, at Peace Corps headquarters, who arranged a luncheon between Beck, Don Chanel, another ABA staff member, and Edgar Cahn.[13] At their meeting Cahn described the neighborhood law office idea and the experimental programs the Ford Foundation and the President's Committee on Juvenile Delinquency had started in New Haven, New York and Washington.[14]

Beck observed that he thought the organized bar should have a vital interest in the proposed program. The legal profession had been involved in legal aid for decades and probably could either help or hinder OEO's efforts in this field, depending upon how the bar leadership chose to view this new initiative. Beck ventured his own personal support for the idea of close cooperation but was cautious in his estimate of ABA reaction.[15] Cahn and the ABA representatives parted with a promise to meet again after conferring with their respective supervisors.[16]

At an October 21, 1964, OEO staff meeting, Cahn reported on the tentative interest of the American Bar Association. Shriver was encouraged enough about the prospect to request Cahn to arrange a meeting between President Johnson and the bar leadership.[17] The OEO director also employed Jean Cahn as a special consultant on legal services.

Shortly after undertaking this assignment, Mrs. Cahn concluded that the Presidential meeting should be preceded by a White House conference on law and poverty.

> . . . At the end of that conference a report to the President would be made and hopefully he would respond with an appropriate statement on the place of the legal profession in the War against Poverty. It is considered desirable that if the President is involved, it be at the request of leaders of the bar concerned over the role of the bar in the War on Poverty and that a request for a meeting with the President should be initiated by the bar itself rather than by Mr. Shriver. The request would be sent to Mr. Shriver for him to present to the White House. Therefore, we look toward the establishment of a top-level steering or planning committee of the legal profession that will generally oversee the design of the conference and which will request that the conference end in a meeting with the President.

While OEO was rushing forward with plans to involve the leadership of the national bar in a high-level meeting, the ABA was approaching the issue gingerly. After the meeting at the Lawyer's Club, an opportunity arose for the bar leaders to learn more about the new legal assistance movement. The Department of Health, Education and Welfare was sponsoring a conference on legal services to be held in Washington from November 12 to 14, 1964. The HEW Conference was conceived by the staff of the Office of Juvenile Delinquency and Youth Development (OJD), successor to the President's Committee. The purpose was to bring together the people involved in the three experimental legal services programs OJD financed—New Haven, New York, and Boston,[18] for it had been discovered that each program was proceeding down a different track, experiencing different problems, and meeting with varying degrees of success.

John Murphy, a young associate from Washington's largest law firm, was employed on a consultant basis to run the conference. Murphy had no prior knowledge of or experience in legal assistance, so he relied heavily on advice from Gary Bellow, Edgar Cahn and Ed Sparer.[19]

By oversight, Murphy failed to invite anyone from either the ABA or the NLADA, because he visualized the HEW meeting as just a "simple little conference about New Haven, Boston, New York, and a few other programs."[20] In fact, John Cummiskey and William McCalpin of the ABA leadership requested invitations to the conference and were refused.[21] The conference was never intended as a "sell-job" to persuade bar leaders or anyone else that these experimental programs should be the basis of a national effort. The purpose was merely to "explore what was being done and ask some questions about it."[22] Considering the narrow function of the HEW Conference, it is understandable that the ABA was rebuffed.

But Lowell Beck was disturbed. He felt he was losing a perfect opportunity to educate the ABA leadership about the emerging concepts in legal assistance. Fortunately, Beck's knowledge of Washington quickly led him to call Ken Pye, then associate dean of Georgetown Law Center. Pye was able to obtain two invitations to the HEW Conference from his friend Jack Murphy.[23]

The two men chosen to attend the HEW Conference were Junius Allison, executive secretary of the NLADA, and William McCalpin, chairman of the ABA Standing Committee on Lawyer Referral. Allison was a veteran of over 25 years in full-time legal aid work, seven of them at NLADA headquarters in Chicago. McCalpin's previous experience with legal aid was minimal. The Conference proved to be interesting to McCalpin and insulting to Allison.

On the afternoon of November 12, conference participants turned their attention to the topic "New Legal Services for Economically Depressed Metropolitan Areas," and by implication criticism of the old forms of legal assistance in metropolitan areas—the legal aid societies. Charles Grosser, deputy director of Mobilization for Youth, led off the discussion.

> In his history of the New York Legal Aid Society, Harrison Tweed, a former president of the society states:
>
>> No appraisal of the services of the society can ignore the fact that the number of applicants for help on the civil side has not increased over the last

40 years, during which there has been such a vast increase in the population of Greater New York.

Mr. Tweed suggests that this is a result of a lessening of legal needs of the poor caused by a decrease in immigration, the existence of claims procedures which do not require a lawyer to be present, the increase in the provision of direct and indirect legal services by unions and political clubs, the improvement of business practices, and the redistribution of income. The argument can be made, however, that the legal needs of the poor have not decreased, but that alienation and self-selection, identical with those experienced by other professional institutions, are the cause of the phenomenon.

The existence of unmet needs, or of numbers of unserved eligible recipients is a mandate to seek new organizational forms by which to provide service. Reaching out into the local community, located in informal congenial settings (storefronts, apartments), making services readily available to all, and avoiding prejudgments as to appropriateness of service requested are ways in which the neighborhood idea can overcome the inadvertent selectivity of the large central service organization.[24]

The criticism of existing legal aid practices was continued in a speech by Charles Parker, a prominent private attorney who was president of the board of New Haven's second and surviving experimental program, the Legal Assistance Association. If unmet needs disturbed Grosser, Parker's complaint focused on the poor quality of legal aid service.

My impression is that the New Haven bureau has been most frequently used by residents of the inner city slums and housing projects, mostly Negroes, many of whom are fairly recent arrivals from the South, for superficial relief in legal emergencies such as wage attachment and evictions.

In common with the other traditional social agencies, public and private, neither legal aid nor the public defender in New Haven seemed to have any capability of dealing creatively with the problems of the deprived citizens at the core of the city, the multiproblem families, in short, the people described in Michael Harrington's "The Other America." In New Haven, and I suspect elsewhere, legal aid services have been characterized by repetitive work for the same clients such as continuous wage attachment modification, interrupted service, incomplete referrals, repetitious arrest, continual inability to meet bail, repeated incarceration. An illusion of service for these clients has taken the place of constructive social therapy.[25]

In her speech about the ethical problems involved in legal assistance to the poor, Zona Hostetler, a young lawyer formerly with Covington and Burling, attacked the established legal aid movement from another direction.

Through the years this struggling legal aid activity has at least been permitted to exist with a minimum of opposition. When the legal aid activity has become too competitive, however, I am sorry to say, that the opposition has increased. Such opposition can often be very intense and very effective.

Again, existing legal aid societies, somewhat cowed by the barratry rules, have been timid in inviting the poor to partake of their legal aid fare. Thus they have waited for clients to come to them—clients who (1) know they need a lawyer; (2) know that there is a legal aid; (3) can overcome their fear, ignorance or distrust of lawyers and the law; and (4) have the carfare, shoes, or baby sitting help to get there. Obviously, as others throughout this conference have told most eloquently, many of the poor most desperately in need of help are never served.

However, any kind of aggressive neighborhood activity has thus far been es-chewed by the traditional legal aid offices for fear of condemnation under the long-standing rules governing improper solicitation of legal business. Indeed, even the most bland types of advertising have often been avoided. Here in the District of Columbia, for example, you would hardly know there was a legal aid office. If you look in the yellow pages of the telephone directory under "Lawyers," you won't find any reference to it. If you look in the white pages—and you're clever enough to look under "Legal" and not "Lawyer" you'll find in the smallest type possible, the words "Legal Aid Society."

In contrast, the lawyers referral system, which charges a fee for services, appears in the telephone directory in both the yellow and the white pages, and in fact has an advertising box (the only one in the lawyer section) proclaiming in large black type: Lawyers Referral Service—Referral if you have no lawyer.[26]

Edgar Cahn closed the afternoon's formal presentations with some remarks that gave the earlier criticisms real significance. He announced that OEO had decided to inaugurate a national legal assistance program and that his wife, Jean Cahn, had been appointed by Sargent Shriver to develop and coordinate the program. He left unanswered the question of what kinds of organizations were to be funded by OEO to render these services.[27]

When the meeting was opened for discussion, several legal aid lawyers rose to defend their movement and to propose that any new or increased legal assistance should be provided through the existing legal aid societies. Mary Tarcher, assistant attorney in chief of the New York Legal Aid Society (by far the largest of the existing legal aid organizations, with 20 percent of the total national budget for legal aid) made the case for the established legal aid movement in these words:

> Why is it necessary in a place like New York where they have a legal aid bureau that is almost a hundred years old with a competent staff that is trained and educated and experienced in the problems that legal aid is familiar with—why is it necessary when other projects are commenced in which legal aid problems are part of the program—why is it necessary to go outside of legal aid and organize separate groups of lawyers to handle these problems when there is an agency existing for that purpose?
> We all know that one of the major problems of legal aid, wherever it may be,

is the lack of funds, and sometimes it is difficult to do everything that we legal aid lawyers think we have to do because we can't get the money. Now if these other agencies have the peculiar ability to raise the money that we can't raise why don't they join with us and ask us to do the job that we have had the experience, the training, the interest and the knowledge for lo, these many years.[28]

The response from the legal activists was made by Ed Sparer, and Nancy LeBlanc of the MFY Legal Service Unit that operated in the same city as the New York Legal Aid Society. Among their points, as summarized in the conference proceedings, they distinguished the thrust of the neighborhood lawyer programs from the legal aid approach:

> . . . The work with administrative agencies which affect the lives of the poor in a crucial way goes beyond counseling the client and dealing with the welfare workers on the departmental level. There is the additional focus on 'law to be developed' towards which legal intervention has been geared.
>
> • • •
>
> Legal Aid lawyers have become good technicians, while . . . comprehensive, community action structures require generalists who can work with community groups, labor, business, etc. . . .[29]

Sparer and LeBlanc concluded with an argument that aggravated the legal aiders.

> Experimentation in the social area frequently requires a new organization because of hostile attitudes and rigidities in established services.[30]

The HEW conference ended without bringing the two groups any closer together or healing the injured feelings of the legal aid attorneys. In retrospect, however, the meeting was notable for two reasons: It exposed the professionals in the competing legal assistance movements to each other's philosophy and problems; and it had a profound impact on two very influential people who had been there—Junius Allison and Bill McCalpin.

Allison and McCalpin returned from the HEW conference with completely different messages for their respective organizations—the NLADA and the ABA. Allison and the other proponents of legal aid in attendance were upset by many of the speeches and comments of the upstart neophytes from MFY, LAA, and academia. The conference itself was by implication an insult to the legal aid movement. How could anyone hold a conference on legal services to the poor without featuring the accomplishments of the 246 existing legal aid societies? (As we have seen, many of the speechmakers had emphasized the deficiencies of those societies. Time and again, the legal aid movement was compared unfavorably with the experimental HEW-funded programs.)

The HEW conference and the impending OEO effort in legal assistance were at the top of the agenda for the December, 1964, monthly meeting of the

NLADA Executive Committee. Allison reported on the conference and stressed the hostile attitude of some of the participants toward the existing institutions. He expressed serious concern that the established legal aid movement would be shut out of the contemplated OEO program, which, from all indications, was likely to bring a massive Federal investment in the legal assistance field.[31] Edward Carr, director of the New York Legal Aid Society and a member of the NLADA Executive Committee, also expressed his fears based on what his staff members had told him about the conference. He stressed that from what he understood the OEO funds might be available only temporarily on a demonstration basis. Carr speculated there was a very real danger OEO would establish competing legal assistance organizations and dry up legal aid's sources of charitable support. Then, if the Federal government should later withdraw, the poor would be without any legal help.[32]

After some more discussion, the NLADA Executive Committee passed a resolution that some of its members later were to regret.

> The Executive Committee of the National Legal Aid and Defender Association has received reports that throughout the country legal assistance for the poor will be a part of the so-called Anti-Poverty programs under the Economic Opportunity Act.
> . . . With ample funds, traditional legal aid and defender organizations can be broadened to meet the full legal needs of indigent people in metropolitan centers.
> The creation of separate, duplicating agencies to offer legal services under Economic Opportunity programs will be more costly and less effective than will the proper use of existing facilities, and serious ethical questions will be raised where nonlawyers attempt to practice law.[33]

Whatever its long-run implications might be, this resolution had a crucial short-term effect. The NLADA had eliminated itself as an effective negotiator with OEO.[34]

D. The ABA Decides

After the HEW conference, Allison attempted to persuade McCalpin, and presumably the ABA, to "fight back" against the threatened Federal intrusion into legal aid.[35] McCalpin, however, was skeptical of Allison's stance and the general reaction of supporters of legal aid to the HEW conference. He had not been involved at all in legal aid affairs before ABA president Lewis Powell assigned him to attend the HEW meeting. Thus, McCalpin felt no personal affront when the real and imagined deficiencies were pointed out by conference speakers.[36]

But before McCalpin could forward his report on the HEW conference to the ABA leadership, another event thrust the war on poverty to the top of the Association's agenda. On November 17, 1964, Sargent Shriver, in Chicago to address an Eleanor Roosevelt Memorial dinner, announced the inauguration of a new network of "supermarkets of social service" for the nation's cities. Among the services to be offered at these "supermarkets" was legal assistance for the poor.[37] The idea of being part of some "supermarket of service" was repugnant enough to the professional image of the lawyer. But Shriver's speech contained an allusion to the use of laymen as "homework aides, recreation aides, . . . health aides, . . . and *legal advocates for the poor.*"[38] These aides would undertake jobs "which we have assumed could only be served by professionals, but which cannot wait for the professional to get to them."[39] This raised the dangers inherent in the unauthorized practice of law by nonlawyers. Within a few days, ABA headquarters was inundated with letters from lawyers urging Association president Lewis Powell to counterattack against the government threat to the profession.[40]

The day after the account of Shriver's "supermarkets of social service" speech appeared in newspapers around the country, Don Hyndman, ABA's public relations director, drafted a memorandum to Powell and ABA executive secretary Bert Early.

> Evidence is piling up that the administration in Washington is looking toward direct government legal aid as a part of the "war on poverty."
>
> The enclosed *Chicago Daily News* story on a speech here this week by Sargent Shriver is one late clue. Another was the three-day "Conference on the Extension of Legal Services to the Poor" held in Washington November 12–14, under the auspices of the Department of Health, Education and Welfare. The thrust of that conference seemed to be that existing private agencies are not meeting the need. . . . It could be that the HEW Conference was intended to lay the groundwork for a new federal program embracing legal aid.
>
> This obviously raises important questions for the organized bar, it seems to me. (1) What will be the effect of a government *on private legal* aid? (2) On traditional private legal services? (3) *Will existing agencies be brought in,* or will the government's program be a parallel effort? What should be the bar's attitude?[41]

Powell realized the ABA leadership could not afford to postpone a full consideration of its posture toward the OEO's lightly veiled intentions to mount a legal services program. Powell was under considerable and increasing pressure from ABA members who had heard about Shriver's speech or the HEW conference to take an immediate and strong stand against the incipient Federal program. But Bert Early and Jim Spiro, his top ABA staff members, were urging a different course. Powell wanted the counsel of ABA's own experts on legal assistance. Accordingly, he summoned his key advisors—including Bill McCalpin and John Cummiskey—to a meeting at ABA's Chicago headquarters in late November.

McCalpin presented the group his version of the HEW conference, which was much less negative than the general reactions Powell had been receiving.

McCalpin felt there might even be some room for cooperation between the ABA and OEO. Then Cummiskey, chairman of the Standing Committee on Legal Aid and Indigent Defendants, reminded everyone of the ABA's long-standing advocacy of expanded legal assistance for the poor. He argued that the Association could not retreat from that 40-year-old, very public position merely because of some unfavorable mail from irate lawyers. The possibility of an immediate campaign against OEO and its plans for a legal services program was soon ruled out. At a minimum they needed to find out more about OEO's intentions and whether ABA could fit into those plans. Three questions seemed especially important to the ABA leadership.

1. What kind of program was OEO intending to inaugurate?
2. Who in the OEO hierarchy was really making the decisions about legal services?
3. How much participation would OEO allow the ABA? It was generally agreed that the ABA did not desire to administer the government-financed legal assistance program the way the Law Society does in England. They did want "meaningful participation" in policy making.[42]

Someone suggested that Powell should arrange a personal meeting with Sargent Shriver and secure the answers to these questions. This tactic was abandoned on the grounds that they really did not know enough about OEO's general objectives as yet. It seemed ill-advised to commit the ABA's most powerful and prestigious figure to the negotiations without some clearer conception of the broad parameters of the Federal government plans for legal assistance to the poor. They finally settled on a low-keyed approach. Lowell Beck was assigned to set up a meeting with Edgar and Jean Cahn. John Cummiskey and Bill McCalpin were designated to represent the ABA leadership group at this initial confrontation with the OEO.[43]

A few days before Christmas, 1964, Lewis Powell telephoned Cummiskey and McCalpin to advise them the meeting had been scheduled for 11:00 A.M., the Monday after Christmas. It was to take place in ABA's Washington office. Those who would attend, besides the Cahns, McCalpin, and Cummiskey, included Barlow Christensen of ABA's headquarters staff and Don Chanel and Beck from the Washington staff.

As the meeting began, it was fairly obvious each party was wary of the other. The Cahns began the meeting with their interpretation of OEO's current thinking. The agency was interested in creating a program that would have a meaningful impact on the problem of poverty. As far as they could determine, the ABA and the established legal aid societies had never demonstrated an interest in anything more than a band-aid operation. The existing societies were deficient in manpower, quality, and philosophy. They had not done anything to bring their services to the people in the neighborhoods. It was not that OEO did not want to work with the organized bar; in fact, wherever possible they contemplated some form of participation by the local bar. But in view of the past record of the existing national legal aid movement and the ABA's partnership with that movement, the Cahns expressed serious doubts about the feasibility or desirability of any cooperative effort between ABA and OEO. The mood was restrained, but the language was tough.[44]

John Cummiskey, an experienced labor negotiator, began by reminding the Cahns of the difficult job they faced, should the ABA oppose the OEO program. As an example, he advised them there were hundreds of letters at ABA headquarters from lawyers who were irritated by Shriver's "supermarket" speech. The ABA could take an obstructionist approach and present these views to Congress.[45] Cummiskey then defended the ABA from the charge that it did not care about effective legal assistance for the poor. He began by admitting most of the faults of the established legal aid societies. "We've been saying those same things for years. Have you ever read any of the reports of the ABA Standing Committee on Legal Aid?" The Cahns owned up to the fact they had not. Cummiskey argued that the ABA leadership wanted to see neighborhood law offices come into being; they sought higher quality service; they thought preventive law and community education were good ideas. But there simply had not been enough money in the past to accomplish everything they wanted.[46]

The Cahns contended that OEO had not yet instituted a national push for legal services. At this stage OEO was merely reviewing applications from local community action agencies that wanted legal services. Moreover, the agency was insisting that the local bar approve any such application.[47]

The discussion continued for over two hours with almost no visible concession from either side. However, Cummiskey felt he and McCalpin had begun to overcome the Cahns' initial distrust of the ABA and its motives. He was certain they were becoming convinced the ABA wanted to support the basic OEO objectives for the expansion and improvement of legal assistance.[48] But actually the Cahns left the meeting still uncertain about what the ABA was planning to do next. They felt there was yet a possibility the ABA would forward the negative letters to Congress.[49]

All in all, it was not a friendly meeting nor did it appear to be a very promising beginning for a relationship between OEO and ABA.

Despite the apparent inconclusive character of this meeting on December 28, it actually was the foundation of an eventual partnership between the bar and the war on poverty. Neither side was sure about the other's intentions, but each of the participants reached a decision about what he wanted to happen. Cummisky and McCalpin felt it was imperative the ABA participate in the OEO program if the agency would concede them a reasonable role.[50] At the same time, the Cahns decided that OEO needed ABA support if it could be gained at reasonable cost.[51]

ABA staff member Barlow Christensen summarized the crucial December 28 meeting in a revealing "staff report."

> Though the meeting might be characterized generally as successful and quite encouraging, such characterization would have to be qualified by reference to three relevant and important factors about which we still lack much information.
>
> First, we are not entirely sure, even yet, just what position the Cahns occupy in the OEO scheme of things. Indeed, we don't know who in the agency—if anyone—even knew that they were meeting with us. . . . Both of the Cahns occupy essentially advisory positions outside these operational divisions. Mr. Cahn, a special assistant to the Director of the agency [Mr. Shriver], functions as a general advisor and speech-writer. His wife is employed as a sort of high level "thinker" on the subject of legal services. . . .
>
> Second, we know relatively little about the extent to which the Cahns' ideas have been accepted by the policy-makers of the agency. It would appear that they are the principal source of the OEO's interest in legal services as a part of the "War on Poverty" program. . . . Beyond this, we still cannot say how extensively the policy-makers within the agency have adopted, or will adopt, the Cahn ideas and attitudes.
>
> Third, we do not know how firmly the Cahns may be committed to the attitudes they expressed at our meeting. They appeared to be sincere, but this sort of thing is almost impossible to evaluate, even at first hand. . . .
>
> Some observations about the meeting might now be appropriate, with the warning that they are to be interpreted in the light of the three factors discussed above:
>
> • • •
>
> Plans for OEO activity in the legal service field do not appear to be nearly so far advanced as Mr. Shriver's speeches have seemed to suggest. Thinking and planning seem really to be in the very beginning stages.
>
> Prospects appear, at this time, to be excellent for the bar to participate and to make its views felt in "War on Poverty" programs.
>
> • • •
>
> Mrs. Cahn stressed her commitment to the idea that legal services under such comprehensive programs should, wherever possible, be provided through existing institutions, and that the bar should play an important role in planning such programs at the local level. Indeed, it may be that local bar participation will come to be a requirement for OEO approval of legal service elements in any proposed community action programs.
>
> To the extent that we can assume Mrs. Cahn's statements to be representative of agency policy, there would appear a present opportunity for the bar to participate actively in planning the legal service elements of local community action programs, and thus to insure that the programs developed will be ethically acceptable to the profession and in the best interests of the public. But even though these attitudes may represent present agency policy, we can surely expect the agency to take more direct action should it be found that the bar is failing to rise to the opportunity.[52]

The Cahns had more than one reason for embracing ABA support. Certainly the national organization would be extremely helpful in gaining local bar association approval for OEO-funded legal services. But less obviously and more important, the Cahns needed ABA prestige within OEO itself. The time was December 1964. The concept of prepackaged so-called "National Emphasis" programs (Headstart and Upward Bound among others) was still unknown to the infant war on poverty.[53] All decisions, all priorities, all programs were handcrafted in the local communities by Community Action Agencies. According to the Cahns' own theory of legal services[54] the primary function of the neighborhood law office was to inject a "civilian perspective" into the strategies and policies of the local Community Action Agencies. This implied that legal services offices represented a potential threat to the smooth functioning of local Community Action Agencies. In that state of affairs, it was not too realistic to expect that very many CAAs, if left entirely to their own devices, would submit proposals for legal services offices as part of their comprehensive antipoverty campaigns. Accordingly, unless OEO could be persuaded or pressured into granting legal services a special status, neighborhood law offices would become a reality in only a few especially tolerant areas. The Cahns perceived that the ABA could provide just the muscle needed to persuade OEO to affirmatively promote legal assistance for the poor.[55]

McCalpin and Cummiskey sensed OEO's almost religious deference to community wishes (at this early stage in OEO's development) from their conversation with the Cahns on December 28, 1964. On the very next day, McCalpin sent a memorandum to the members of his lawyer referral committee with copies to Lewis Powell and other bar leaders:

> I think it is fair to state that the Cahns presented a view of OEO presently playing a passive and receiving role with respect to community action programs. They say that the initiative must rest with the local community to evaluate its needs, formulate a comprehensive program within the meaning of 202 of the Act and submit the same to OEO for approval expressed in the form of financial underwriting.[56]

McCalpin expressed the opinion that the initiative—or at least the opportunity to seize the initiative—had shifted from OEO to the ABA.

> If my estimate of their current outlook is accurate, then it seems that we must be considering a change in our approach. Up to now our attitude has largely been one of reacting to something we thought was being pushed at us. Perhaps it is now time to realize that the War on Poverty presents an opportunity to improve existing and inaugurate additional facilities for providing legal services and perhaps to create new vehicles for this purpose. The question is whether the Bar wishes to take advantage of the opportunity offered. If it does, we must then begin to ask ourselves what changes and improvements we want to make and what form or forms we believe the rendition of legal services should take in the future. If we

decide not to seize the opportunity then we must either accept continued rendition of legal services at present levels or their improvement outside our professional organizations.[57]

It is revealing to note the contrast between the reaction of the NLADA and ABA to the new legal assistance movement. Where the NLADA resolution sought to restrict OEO funding to existing legal aid organizations, McCalpin mentions as a positive feature the "opportunity to . . . create new vehicles" for "providing legal services." McCalpin had posed the question facing the ABA succinctly. Lewis Powell studied the critical paragraph closely, then wrote "well expressed" in the margin.

After digesting the information Cummiskey and McCalpin had brought back from the December 28 meeting, the ABA leadership undertook a serious in-depth appraisal of the entire OEO legal services question. The consultations took place by memorandum, telephone, and included one meeting at ABA headquarters in Chicago. Bill McCalpin, John Cummiskey and Bert Early were the chief advisors. But, in essence, it was one man's decision; the others were merely helping Lewis Powell.

The American Bar Association and its president, Lewis Powell, did not come to make this big decision about OEO's proposed legal services program entirely unprepared. By coincidence, Powell had chosen the availability of legal counsel to all as one of three top priorities for the Association during his term. As early as August 14, 1964, during his inaugural speech, Powell announced:

> On the civil side, the bar has no less responsibility to see that legal services are available for those who cannot afford them. For years, the Association's Standing Committee has been a leader in this effort, working with the National Legal Aid and Defender Association. There are now 246 legal aid offices across the country, but there are still some voids as well as areas where the quality and scope of established legal aid service must be improved.
>
> The importance which the officers and Board of Governors attribute to the work of the Standing Committee is evidenced by a budget appropriation for the new year of $39,000. This is more than double that of last year and is the largest single net appropriation for any one Committee.[58]

After describing the Association's expanded effort to provide legal assistance to the poor, Powell told the House of Delegates about the need to make lawyers available to the lower middle class whose incomes were just above the legal aid standards. Interestingly, his description of the attitudes among this class of persons closely parallels that which activist spokesmen were saying about the poor.

> Unfortunately, this type of person is more likely to encounter legal difficulty than persons in higher income brackets. Garnishment of wages, repossessions resulting from default on installment purchases, evictions for non-payment of

rent, bankruptcies, the failures of husbands and fathers to provide support and maintenance—these are but a few examples of the type of legal involvement familiar to every lawyer, so commonplace to the citizen in the low income bracket. . . .

It has been correctly said that respect for the law is at its lowest with under-privileged persons. There is a natural tendency for such persons to think of the courts as symbols of trouble and of lawyers as representatives of creditors and other sources of "harassment."[59]

What Powell said next was directed to the problem of legal assistance for the lower middle class; but it foreshadowed his approach to the OEO Legal Services question: "Our profession must face up to this problem and find more effective solutions. Unless we do so others—far less interested in the profession of law and also less competent to devise reasonable solutions—will undertake this for us."[60]

Powell's emphasis on broadening the client base served by the legal profession was not an overnight inspiration. Nor did this goal, which generally is identified as a liberal notion, spring naturally from the essentially conservative stance of this Virginia lawyer. It was instead the product of thoughtful reflection about some specific problems facing his profession.

The image that emerges from an examination of Powell's speeches and interviews with him and other ABA leaders is that of a visionary realist. By that, I do not mean that Powell necessarily possesses a dream of what the world ought to be, but rather that he comprehends the long-run consequences of the trend of events—a view of what the world actually will become. McCalpin described it as almost a prescience.[61] During the year before he assumed the ABA presidency, Powell and Bert Early, the ABA's executive secretary, engaged in a dialogue about the future problems and prospects of the legal profession. As McCalpin described it, Powell and Early were "educating and moving" each other. On May 17, 1964, the Supreme Court pushed that education along with *Brotherhood of Railroad Trainmen* v. *Virginia, ex. rel. Virginia State Bar.*[62] In that case, the Supreme Court ruled that a state bar association could not prohibit labor unions from reducing legal costs for their members by arranging referrals to a select panel of cooperating attorneys. Powell viewed this case as the precursor of societal pressures that soon would diminish the prerogatives of lawyers and restructure the delivery of legal services.[63]

Over the year before Powell assumed the presidency, he and Early worked out a long-range strategy for modernizing the legal profession. They were convinced that lawyers either make some drastic changes in the way they marketed their services or change, in forms less welcome and beyond the control of lawyers, would be thrust upon the profession by outside forces. The plan that Powell and Early devised was not a detailed blueprint for a revamped legal profession, but they did possess a general notion of the ultimate configuration. Probably there would be increased specialization, more extensive utilization of nonlawyers, group practice, "Blue Cross" style insurance, and similar arrangements for the middle class and lower middle class. It probably also meant that there would be increased financing of legal assistance for the poor.[64]

After Powell became ABA president, he and Early set their strategy in motion. The first step was the inaugural speech at the ABA annual meeting —to afford the membership the tiniest glimpse of Powell's concern for the future of the profession. The second move was made shortly thereafter as Powell and Early broadened their base of support, gradually exposing ABA leaders like Cummiskey and McCalpin to the ideas they had nurtured over the previous months. Later on Powell was to establish a special study group—the so-called Select Committee on the Availability of Legal Services, chaired by McCalpin—to consider the entire problem in depth and report back to the House of Delegates. But at the time the OEO question burst upon him, Powell had only reached step two bringing key ABA leaders into his confidence. Suddenly, far out of sequence, he was forced to consider taking one of the ultimate issues to the entire ABA membership. Not even his own thinking had carried him to a decision about what the role of the Federal government should be in the provision of legal services. But Powell's reflections over the past year on the entire problem of which this was a part gave him a perspective no ABA president before or since could have brought to this question.

Another phenomenon that helped shape Powell's decision about Federal financing of legal services was the decade-long struggle over Medicare. The ABA's sister professional organization—the American Medical Association— had fought against the enactment of the Medicare legislation with every resource at its command. Tens of millions of dollars had been committed to the doctors' campaign to prevent this Federal incursion into the health services field.[65] The most sophisticated public-relations techniques, the most heavy-handed lobbying efforts, the subtlest person-to-person persuasion all were brought to bear. Scores of influential groups—including interestingly enough, the ABA itself[66]—had been enlisted to back up the AMA position. But this enormous expenditure of money, time, and effort at best only delayed the passage of Medicare legislation for a few years. And when the final defeat was administered to the forces opposed to Medicare, organized medicine lost much more than a single legislative battle. The bitter struggle damaged the AMA's credibility with Congress and distorted its public image as the guardian of the nation's health almost beyond recognition.[67]

Powell was aware of the fate of the AMA for resisting Medicare and realized the OEO Legal Services Program presented problems for the legal profession much like those that Medicare had posed for the medical profession.[68] Resistance to legal services could result in loss of public image, a precious asset. Like doctors, lawyers could lose their monopoly to provide and to receive income from providing certain important services. This monopoly position exists at the sufferance of the general public. If sufficiently aroused, the electorate could change the laws to allow anyone to appear in court, write a will, draft a contract, or handle an appeal. The monopoly would be broken; the prices— and presumably the quality—of legal services would tailspin, and lawyers would be driven out of business. Even if nothing this drastic were done, the state legislatures are constantly enlarging or contracting the scope of the legal profession's monopoly by allowing or disallowing others to perform certain functions like handling trusts, title searches, and so on. Accordingly, the profession could not afford to tarnish its public image through blind opposition to progress.

On the other side of the issue, Powell knew it would be much easier to lead the ABA membership in a crusade against OEO than to obtain even grudging tolerance for the Federal Program. His mail told him that. Only with a determined time-consuming campaign could he hope to produce ABA endorsement of the Program. Even then it was a gamble, for the ABA was basically a very conservative organization. For reasons explored in Chapter 1, 15 years earlier the Association had taken a firm stand against Federal funding of legal assistance to the poor. The war on poverty was especially unpopular.

Taking a stance in favor of OEO was a gamble from another point of view as well. In effect, the proposed Legal Services Program was an unknown quantity. What if Powell placed his personal prestige on the line to gain ABA support only to see the OEO program develop into the monster its critics within the Association had predicted, run by "social workers," stealing middle-class clients from private attorneys and engaging in massive violations of the Canons?

In order to minimize this particular risk, the ABA staff, Cummiskey and McCalpin engaged in delicate negotiations with Edgar and Jean Cahn. On January 11, 1965, Mrs. Cahn traveled to the ABA's Chicago headquarters to meet with Bert Early and other Association staff members. They were joined by Edgar Cahn on January 12. These negotiations culminated in a series of understandings about the role of the ABA in the future operations of the OEO Legal Services Program.[69] These understandings included a promise of ABA participation on a permanent advisory committee which would provide policy guidance to OEO on legal services matters.[70]

Reassured that OEO would be reasonably responsive to a reasonably supportive ABA and convinced by his own examination of the question that Federally supported legal assistance was inevitable, Powell announced to a small group at ABA's Chicago headquarters, on January 22, 1965, that he was committed to a policy of securing ABA endorsement of the proposed OEO Legal Services Program. This official support could not be given by Powell alone. It required a vote by the ABA House of Delegates—the chief legislative body of the Association.

E. Persuading the House of Delegates

The decision to introduce a resolution in the House of Delegates came less than a month before the Association's midwinter meetings scheduled between February 4 and 10, 1965. Powell felt success depended upon a carefully drawn resolution and a proper indoctrination of the opinion leaders in the House before it convened. He assumed personal responsibility for the preparation of the first draft of the resolution. On January 24, Powell forwarded a copy of this draft to Bert Early, John Cummiskey, and Bill McCalpin. Obviously, he was far from confident at this stage of their preparations. His cover letter to the draft resolution said:

> There will, I am afraid, be a good deal of suspicion with respect to any government intervention in the rendering of legal services. Thus, I am by no means positive the House will approve anything at this time and in the present state of understanding.[71]

Powell's apprehension about eventual passage had guided his draft of the resolution. The cover letter continued:

> For the moment, I think all that we can do is try to frame a resolution which salutes the problem, authorizes cooperation with OEO, and makes it clear that we will insist on legal services being performed by lawyers in accordance with ethical standards.[72]

Powell's draft resolution was modified only slightly by McCalpin, Early and Cummiskey. It was then forwarded, as Powell instructed, to Wayland Cedarquist, Edward Wright (chairman of the committee that was then revising the ABA Canons), Theodore Voorhees of the NLADA and the ABA's Administrative Committee. Powell was beginning to try to increase the support for his resolution.

Over the next two weeks, Powell's supporters telephoned or personally spoke with almost every member of the top structure of the American Bar Association. This included past presidents such as Whitney North Seymour, president-elect Edward Kuhn of Tennessee, and former NLADA presidents Orison Marden and William Gossett (who incidentally were to become ABA presidents in 1967 and 1968). All of these leaders agreed to support the resolution. Several were enlisted to deliver seconding speeches after it was introduced. Powell intended to let the delegates know that the OEO Legal Services Program was favored by a very broad spectrum of ABA leaders. He calculated that any doubter would be swayed by the prestige of the group supporting the resolution and that even an out-and-out opponent would be reluctant to oppose such an awesome combination publicly. By the time the ABA convention started, Powell and his helpers had unified the top ABA opinion-makers behind passage of the resolution in favor of OEO.[73]

As the ABA convention approached, OEO officials remained skeptical, most of them feeling that ABA endorsement was an impossibility. They looked upon the ABA as the keystone of the "establishment" and most unlikely to become a supporter of an antipoverty program. The Cahns, with superior knowledge and greater faith, were taking bets on the outcome.[74]

During the final week of January, Powell and his advisors laid their plans for the forthcoming midwinter meetings. Seldom has a single ABA resolution been the subject of such careful planning. Barlow Christensen drafted a seven-page memorandum of recommended strategy which outlined several options. This document was circulated for comment and ultimately refined to a final two-page battle plan.

1. *Sunday, February 7, 1965, Gold Room, Roosevelt Hotel, 10 a.m.*
   a. Presentation by selected speakers of different facets of overall problem.
   b. Discussion by all persons in attendance.
   c. Introduction of draft resolution by John Cummiskey, Chairman, ABA Standing Committee on Legal Aid and Indigent Defendants. Presentation of resolution will emphasize it as the result of consideration by the various elements of the problem presented in the morning's discussion, many people participating in such discussion, and with the belief that the resolution incorporates appropriate authorization and procedure for the ABA to deal with the problem.
   d. Voting on the resolution with Messrs. Kuhn, Murane, Cummiskey, Voorhees, Gossett, McCalpin and Gayle actively supporting the resolution.
2. *Sunday, February 7, 1965, Wildcatter Room, Roosevelt Hotel, noon.*
   Special meeting of ABA Board of Governors to consider approval of resolution as passed by session described in No. 1 above.
3. *Monday, February 8, 1965, ABA House of Delegates.*
   a. The subject of expansion of legal services will be a special order of business at 3 P.M. Monday afternoon in the House of Delegates. This is to be arranged by Mr. Gayle in cooperation with the Chairman of the House, Edward Murane.
   b. First, John Cummiskey will present the report of his Standing Committee on Legal Aid and Indigent Defendants.
   c. Second, William McCalpin will present the report of his Standing Committee on Lawyer Referral Services.
   d. Next, John Cummiskey will rise to state the problem of the expansion of legal services was considered at a special session Sunday morning resulting in the adoption of a resolution which was considered and approved by the Board of Governors at a special session. He will then ask the Secretary to read the resolution to the House of Delegates, copies of the resolution having been distributed to members of the House in advance.
   e. Mr. Cummiskey, after the reading of the resolution, will move on behalf of his Committee and Mr. McCalpin's Committee on Lawyer Referral that the House approve the resolution. Messrs. Voorhees, Gossett and Kuhn will be counted upon to second the resolution and to speak in support of it.[75]

ABA conferences are fluid affairs. There are scores of section breakfasts, committee luncheons, programs, law school reunions, parties, dinners, and meetings over a week-and-a-half schedule. ABA members come and go (thousands attend), some staying only for the day their section or committee meets, others remaining for the entire conference. During the midwinter meeting, the ABA House of Delegates convenes for four days, but their meetings do not start until the convention has been underway for several days. What this meant in February, 1965, was that Powell, Cummiskey and the others had three or four days to lobby individual delegates before the House met to consider resolutions. John Cummiskey was especially effective in this role. He is a gruff, husky, plain-spoken man, who likes to "lay it on the line." His background as a negotiator in labor disputes (on behalf of management) stood him in good stead.

At one point during the convention, Cummiskey had to respond to a real emergency. Someone ran up and excitedly related that the Young Lawyer Section, consisting of all ABA members under 36 years of age, was considering a resolution that condemned the proposed OEO Legal Services Program. Cummiskey rushed to the room where the Young Lawyers were meeting and requested the opportunity to speak. He told them about the resolution that was to be considered by the House. He gave them the names of the many prestigious bar leaders supporting the resolution and reminded them of ABA's longtime support of legal aid and also that legal aid was starved for funds. After Cummiskey's impassioned plea, the Young Lawyers withdrew their proposed opposition.[76]

On Sunday morning, February 7, 1965, at an informal brunch meeting, Powell's forces began to implement their carefully conceived strategy to gain the support of the second level of the ABA leadership. Present were the Board of Governors (all of whom are members of the House of Delegates as well), chairmen of certain important committees and some other especially influential delegates. The proposed resolution was distributed to everyone and the presentation began. After discussion of recent developments in the legal assistance field by several speakers, Bill McCalpin summed up the challenge.

> It is a rather sad and at the same time an exhilarating fact that the past 60 minutes have constituted the most concentrated, the most broadly based and the most constructive consideration of the basic question, How can the legal profession best serve the public? in a quarter century. What we are here considering is no less fundamental than the reason for and the justification of our existence as a profession.
>
> It would be more encouraging if these questions arose in our midst *sui generis.* What we cannot ignore is that this self-examination has been *forced* upon us by the public whom we are sworn to serve. It is well to remember that it is this public

which has given us our status and our position. It is this same public who, if we fail them, will dilute or extinguish that status and position.

• • •

Two broad paths lie before us. One is the well-trodden road of obstruction, reaction, opposition—limited or total. . . . It is a negative approach—the road to oblivion.

The alternative is to meet the challenge head-on, frankly, with the penetrating analysis and the restless curiosity of a lawyer addressing himself to a legal problem. To admit the problem and seek constructive solutions. To put a positive face on our profession. This course I submit is in our best tradition. How can we follow it?

• • •

An early course of treatment obviously must be the enlargement and improvement of present forms of extending legal service to the public—Lawyer Referral Services and Legal Aid. This is the opportunity as John Cummiskey has said which is presented by the War on Poverty, if we will but take it.

• • •

It is not entirely by accident that I have undertaken to describe our present situation in terms of analogy to a medical problem; for our problem is not unlike that which has confronted our brother profession the past few years. It now seems clear that whatever their ability to diagnose and treat the ills of the body, they did not recognize the symptoms, nor diagnose their social ailment and apply corrective treatment in time to forestall a massive assault on the problem by forces outside their profession. I would hope that we can learn and profit from their present vicissitudes. Let us recognize and handle our own problems or surely they will be handled for us.[77]

A full airing of problems and questions followed. Lewis Powell made his support clear. At a propitious moment, John Cummiskey moved that the informal group pass a resolution asking the House of Delegates to adopt the resolution in favor of OEO. From the discussion that followed this motion, it was clear the group was in agreement. But it was decided that the Board of Governors was the appropriate body to enact that kind of resolution.

The informal meeting then adjourned, and the Board of Governors immediately convened as a formal body in an adjoining room. Their first item of business was to adopt a resolution unanimously endorsing the resolution that was to be submitted to the House.[78] As a result of this vote, Powell moved into the House of Delegates debate with a solid phalanx of support from the men to whom other delegates looked for leadership. In order to forestall any claims of insufficient time to study the resolution, printed copies were placed on the desks of all delegates a full day before the resolution itself was to be introduced.

On Tuesday, February 7, 1965, John Cummiskey, in his capacity as chairman of the ABA Standing Committee on Legal Aid and Indigent Defendants, introduced the resolution before the ABA House of Delegates. He gave a brief supporting speech stressing the Board of Governors' unanimous endorsement of the resolution. Ed Kuhn, the president-elect of the ABA, Bill Gossett (who was to become ABA president in 1968), and Ted Voorhees, president of the NLADA, were ready with speeches to answer every conceivable objection any delegate could possibly raise. But no one had anticipated what followed. A voice seconded Cummiskey's motion; another moved the previous question; and there was no objection to an immediate ballot. The vote was taken and the resolution passed . . . *without a single dissenting vote.* Its essential provisions proclaimed:

WHEREAS, the organized bar has long acknowledged its responsibility to make legal services available to all who need them, and this Association has been a leader in discharging this responsibility; and

WHEREAS, despite this considerable effort of individual lawyers and the organized bar over many decades, it is recognized that the growing complexities of modern life, shifts of large portions of our population, and enlarged demands for legal services in many new fields of activity warrants increased concern for the unfilled need for legal services, particularly as to persons of low income, and that the organized bar has an urgent duty to extend and improve existing services and also to develop more effective means of assuring that legal services are in fact available at reasonable cost for all who need them; and

WHEREAS, the Economic Opportunity Act of 1964 provides for cooperative programs with state and local agencies through which various services, including legal services, may be rendered to persons of low incomes who need advice and assistance; and

WHEREAS, freedom and justice have flourished only where the practice of law is a profession and where legal services are performed by trained and independent lawyers;

NOW, THEREFORE, BE IT RESOLVED, that the American Bar Association reaffirms its deep concern with the problem of providing legal services to all who need them and particularly to indigents and to persons of low income. . . . .

FURTHER RESOLVED, that the Association, through its officers and appropriate committees, shall cooperate with the Office of Economic Opportunity and other appropriate groups in the development and implementation of programs for expanding availability of legal services to indigents and persons of low income, such program to utilize to the maximum extent deemed feasible the experience and facilities of the organized bar, such as legal aid, legal defender, and lawyer referral, and such legal services to be performed by lawyers in accordance with ethical standards of the legal profession. . . .

Lewis Powell's victory was complete. Bernard Segal, a member of the House of Delegates in 1965 and the man elected to serve as ABA president in 1969, said, "That vote was the proudest moment I experienced in the House of Delegates since the decision to oppose packing of the Supreme Court back in 1937." Within hours, Sargent Shriver sent a telegram to Lewis Powell, thanking the ABA for its support and pledging OEO's cooperation.

In retrospect, it is not unusual that the ABA House of Delegates passed the resolution. An ABA president has tremendous power to influence a vote in the House if he chooses to focus his time and resources on the issue involved. Certainly no president could have worked any harder or more artfully to influence a decision than did Lewis Powell. But to achieve a *unanimous* vote was much more difficult, given the social and economic views of many members of the ABA House of Delegates. John Cummiskey later indicated why he thought a unanimous vote was won.

> The majority of the delegates favored the resolution because they knew legal aid required more money for much-needed expansion. The rest of them knew that if the Federal government was set on starting a legal services program, the ABA had better be involved in the formulation and administration of the program. It was a bit of the carrot and the stick. In effect, they had no alternative.[79]

Lewis Powell ventured the opinion that some of the more conservative members—especially those from the South who were the most likely delegates to cast a negative vote—were swayed by the strong support that he and ABA president-elect Edward Kuhn had given the motion. "They knew that Ed and I were both Southerners and basically conservative. I guess they felt that if we were satisfied this was the best course for the ABA to follow then they wouldn't oppose."[80]

II. THE UNCERTAIN ROAD FROM PARTNERSHIP TO PROGRAM

It was generally assumed that with an endorsement from the American Bar Association, the OEO Legal Services Program was firmly on track and would be in full operation by early summer. A steering committee chaired by Sargent Shriver and Lewis Powell was formed that included over 20 leaders from the Bar Association, legal education, and the judiciary. It convened in mid-February to plan a major conference that would launch the national effort. It was decided to schedule the conference for June, 1965. Although there was discussion about possible White House involvement, the ultimate sponsors decided upon were the American Bar Association, the Department of Justice, and OEO. Almost every leading proponent of legal aid in the nation was invited, both paid staff directors and board members. The platform was to be shared by spokesmen for the legal aid movement and theoreticans for the new neighborhood law offices, in effect, a symbolic public handshake between the proponents of equal justice and the advocates of social reform.

While planning moved forward rather smoothly for the June conference, inside OEO the program was soon bogged down by bureaucratic infighting and inertia. Jean Cahn, Shriver's special consultant on legal services, attempted to create a separate office for legal services within the OEO structure. She even began to gather a small staff consisting primarily of Mrs. Kitty Chayes (State

Department Legal Advisor Abe Chayes' mother) and a George Washington law student, Ron James. Mrs. Cahn was bitterly opposed by the Community Action Program (CAP), one of the three major sub-bureaucracies within OEO.[81] The CAP staff viewed legal services as merely one of many services to be delivered locally through Community Action Agencies and thus logically should be operated at the national level by the CAP administration.

Deeply suspicious of Community Action Agencies and the Community Action Program,[82] Mrs. Cahn insisted legal services could not be subordinated to "nonlawyer" control at either the local or national level. She supported her stand with the ABA resolution of endorsement and the deep concern expressed by ABA leaders that the OEO Legal Services Program be operated in a professional manner from top to bottom.[83] In the meantime, CAP leaders were arguing to Shriver that their efforts to generate a locally planned, comprehensive, coordinated assault on poverty would be defeated if the administration of each type of service reposed in a separate office within the OEO bureaucracy. They pointed out that inconsistent policies and goals would result, of the same type that characterized previous governmental efforts to aid the poor and which OEO was deliberately instructed to avoid.

In late March, 1965, less than two months after the ABA endorsement, Mrs. Cahn tried to force Shriver to a decision. She demanded the establishment of an administrative system that, at a minimum, gave her rather than the CAP director final authority over legal services grants. Failing that, she threatened to resign from her position as special consultant on legal services. When her resignation deadline came and passed without response from Shriver, Mrs. Cahn followed through on her threat. The date was April 1, 1965.[84]

The American Bar Association did not complain strenuously to Shriver about the loss of Mrs. Cahn. For one thing, they did not view Mrs. Cahn as "their" proponent within the OEO bureaucracy. The ABA had not participated in any way in her selection as special consultant to the agency director. Moreover, they did not perceive Mrs. Cahn as the director of the Legal Services Program but rather as Mr. Shriver's personal assistant whom he was free to retain or discharge.[85] But Mrs. Cahn's resignation did throw the incipient Legal Services Program into disarray, complicating what might have been a relatively easy transition to a permanent director holding a solid position within OEO.

During the ensuing months, responsibility for policy formulation and grant making passed through several hands as OEO experimented with a series of ad hoc arrangements while searching for a permanent director. First came William Downs, a forty-fivish lawyer who had been active in the administration of Catholic charities in Michigan. He was employed as an interim consultant, on a basis similar to that of Mrs. Cahn, a relationship which lasted less than a month.[86]

Shriver then turned to Bruce Terris, a lawyer in OEO's General Counsel's

Office.[87] Terris took this assignment very seriously, developed some draft policy guidelines, performed much of the staff work for the June 1965 conference and commenced a file of all pending proposals or letters of inquiry relating to possible legal services grants. Sensing again that they might be losing control over legal services, the CAP hierarchy sought to dislodge the program administration from the General Counsel's Office. They argued, and probably correctly, that it was inconsistent for the agency's lawyer to operate a part of the agency's program. Clearly, they urged, a conflict of interest might arise when the General Counsel, as a lawyer charged with rendering objective legal opinions about the propriety of agency policy, was himself the developer and proponent of a part of that policy.

As a result of CAP's objections, formal responsibility for grant making was transferred to CAP, and B. Michael Rauh[88] was assigned as a special assistant for Legal Services Programs in the office of the CAP director. However, Terris in actuality retained a role in establishing legal services policy within the agency.

The date of the June conference on law and poverty arrived and still there was no permanent director for legal services and, in effect, no Legal Services Program. The conference itself generated interest and controversy, but no demand for legal services in local communities. After that convention it was even more apparent that a major Federal program of legal assistance to the poor would come about only if OEO itself provided the push. The search for a permanent director was then moved to the top of the agenda both in the ABA and at OEO.

Within OEO there was a sharp split over the kind of qualifications the director of legal services should possess. In large part, the dispute reflected differing conceptions about the responsibilities and power of the legal services director. CAP officials perceived the job as a middle-management bureaucratic position within the CAP structure.[89] Accordingly, they searched for someone with substantial administrative experience but were indifferent to prior legal aid involvement or reputation in the legal community. Shriver, on the other hand, saw the need for a man who could provide strong leadership for a major new program. He wanted to retain the support of the legal profession and thus sought a private attorney with an established name in the organized bar.

During the summer of 1965, Shriver offered the legal services directorship to William McCalpin, Chairman of the ABA Select Committee on Availability of Legal Services,[90] and John Cummiskey, Chairman of the ABA Standing Committee on Legal Aid.[91] Both reluctantly demurred because of the impossibility of extricating themselves from their law partnerships for a temporary period. Shriver's search continued without success during the remainder of the summer.

In the meantime, Theodore Berry, the new CAP director, was conducting his own quest for a legal services director. Maintaining lesser standards, he had easier success. In early August, Berry submitted his candidate, a middle-aged black woman lawyer from Missouri who had occupied some lower- and middle-range positions in state government. She met Berry's specifications for the legal services director perfectly. Fearing that Shriver in his desperation to fill the job would yield to the CAP director's pressure, Bruce Terris leaked word of this candidacy to the ABA. The bar leaders were alarmed and advised Shriver this appointment would doom efforts to involve the local bar associations and legal aid societies.[92] At this time, Shriver promised that no appointment would be made without ABA concurrence. Beyond that, he invited the ABA leadership itself to choose some suitable candidates and submit their names to OEO.[93]

Lewis Powell responded to Shriver's challenge, enlisting the help of NLADA President Ted Voorhees, ABA president-elect Orison Marden, his legal services advisors McCalpin and Cummiskey, and the NLADA's recently retained Washington Counsel, Howard Westwood.[94] Like Shriver, the ABA president articulated the need to find someone well-known to people involved with legal aid and organized bar associations, whose nomination would allay suspicions from local bar associations and legal aid staff attorneys. Westwood responded with a letter disagreeing with Powell's specifications. Admitting the need for someone with establishment credentials, Westwood urged that prior legal aid or organized bar experience should not be a prerequisite. Relative youth and immense energy seemed more important to NLADA's Washington adviser. In his letter, Westwood summed up the ideal candidate as "a Scandinavian boy scout."[95]

By the time the annual ABA meetings were held in Miami in August, neither Shriver nor the ABA yet had found a promising candidate to head the Legal Services Program. The OEO Director previously had agreed to make a major address at the convention. He had expected to be in a position to recount the successes of a full-blown OEO Legal Services Program; instead he had to deliver a speech, fully six months after the ABA endorsement, in which he apologized for the delay in mounting the program. The OEO Director personally accepted blame and promised early action. He also publicly pledged the organized bar a prominent policy-making role in the agency's legal services effort.[96]

The audience for Shriver's speech included E. Clinton Bamberger, Jr., a 39-year-old Baltimore attorney. Bamberger had come to the August 1965 meetings to learn something about these new neighborhood law offices he had been hearing about because he had recently been assigned the task of chairing the Maryland State Bar Committee on Legal Services. After listening to a panel discussion, Bamberger approached one of the speakers, Ken Pye, and extended a luncheon invitation. Pye had other plans and pointed out Howard

Westwood, who, he said, knew as much about Washington's neighborhood lawyers as anyone.

While Bamberger was learning more about Washington's law offices at their luncheon meeting, Westwood was sizing up the young Baltimore attorney. As he recalled later, "Something about Bamberger appealed to me. He was establishment. He was a nut. He looked like a Scandinavian Boy Scout. Perfect. And he was young, and, apparently, restless."[97] As they left the dining room, Westwood startled Bamberger with the suggestion, "You know what you ought to do, you son of a bitch? You should take that job as Director of the OEO Legal Services Program."

Taken aback, Bamberger rejoined, "Like hell I'll take that job. You have a lot of nerve asking that after telling me what a lousy job it would be."

"I wasn't asking whether you would take the job; all I want to know is whether you'd be interested in thinking about it."

"I'd be willing to think about it," Bamberger replied, "but that's all I'm willing to do."[98]

Immediately upon returning from the Miami convention, Westwood checked with friends in Baltimore. He found that Bamberger was a partner in Piper & Marbury, Baltimore's largest law firm. He was a trial lawyer specializing in the defense of insurance claims. He had been moderately active in local bar association affairs, serving as chairman of the Young Lawyers Section of the bar at one time, but more involved in community activities, including chairmanship of the Baltimore Blue Cross. He was a liberal Democrat and former finance chairman for Senator Joseph Tydings' 1962 election campaign. From his luncheon conversation, Westwood had gleaned that Bamberger was very articulate with a deep, moving orator's voice, an independent thinker with virtually no previous exposure to legal aid, its philosophy or performance. To Westwood, this seemed like an ideal combination of traits: a background conservative lawyers could scarcely impeach, yet possessed of youth, vigor, and an independent judgment which should appeal to the new activists in the neighborhood lawyer camp.

Satisfied with Bamberger's credentials, Westwood sent letters to Powell, Voorhees, and Marden, suggesting Bamberger's name and urging Bamberger's candidacy in the strongest terms.[99]

In the meantime, others had come up with two additional names for the legal services directorship, A. Kenneth Pye, associate dean of Georgetown Law School, and Jerome Shestack, partner in one of Philadelphia's largest law firms. Both were Democrats. At the time, Pye was board chairman of Neighborhood Legal Services in the District of Columbia and Shestack had played a leading role on the board of the Lawyer's Committee for Civil Rights, which supplied lawyers in support of desegregation litigation in the South. Shestack also was deeply involved in committee work for the ABA.[100]

In late August, 1965, the ABA submitted the names and resumés of Bamberger, Pye, and Shestack to Sargent Shriver as nominees for the position of Legal Services director. Interestingly, the ABA did not consult with the three individuals to ascertain their willingness to serve. They counted on Shriver's renowned persuasive powers to convince the anointed. Shestack was flattered but begged off, asking to make his contribution to the Program through membership on the National Advisory Committee that Shriver had promised bar leaders he would establish. Pye could not accept because he was committed through the end of the next academic year.[101] With Bamberger, Shriver used a different approach. Shriver asked him to come to Washington for personal interviews with him and others on the OEO staff. Bamberger consented and on September 6, 1965, journeyed to OEO headquarters for a full day of conversations with the leaders of the war on poverty. By the end of the day, he found that without saying yes he was committed to become Legal Services director on September 24.[102]

With Bamberger's appointment, an agonizing period of indecision and doubt about whether OEO was to have a legal services program came to an end. The remaining issue was to determine what kind of program it was to be. However, even the answer to that question was partially predetermined by Bamberger's personality and perspective. We have already described something of what he was like. Probably even more important, though, we should note what he was not. Bamberger was not a long-time supporter of legal aid, steeped in the goals and methods of that movement. Yet Bamberger also was not one of the new lawyer-reformers, who were deeply antagonistic to legal aid and all it stood for in the past. He was not a conservative in political philosophy unsympathetic to social change and the reformist objectives of the overall war on poverty. Nor was he a bar politician or a career bureaucrat ambitious to ascend within some hierarchy. Possessed of the credentials of an establishment lawyer, Bamberger was no tool of the establishment. He brought a fresh, open mind capable of embracing the reformers as well as the proponents of legal aid, the concepts of due process justice and social-economic reconstruction.

There is a common notion that the course of human events is determined by impersonal historical forces and that individual human beings only appear to maneuver the rudder. But in subsequent chapters, as we learn more about the program that Bamberger initiated, it might be interesting to speculate how different things would have been with a leader from the establishment bar or, at the other extreme, one of the more radical of the legal activists at the helm.

Other than the man in charge, there was little about the new Federal Program that was set at this point. The ABA had not insisted that OEO adopt some narrow definition of the lawyer's role in the war on poverty. Instead the bar leaders bargained for, and received, a role in policy making, a function they understood would take place in the future. There even appeared to be a willingness to experiment with new concepts and approaches, especially in the reports and speeches of Bill McCalpin.

For their part, the proponents of the neighborhood lawyer experiments likewise settled for future influence rather than an ironclad guarantee that the Program would implement any of their innovations. Some seats on the National Advisory Committee and an open door to Bamberger were all they could be sure of in late 1965.

In effect, a merger had been consummated and a new Federal program launched without any resolution of the philosophical differences. Actually these issues were not fully worked out until well after the OEO Legal Services Program had become a multimillion dollar endeavor with over 250 local agencies. Nor was that eventual resolution to be a simple choice of one ideology over the other.

Later I will devote a chapter[103] to a consideration of policy making in the Legal Services Program, including the development of ultimate goals and priorities. But, at the time Bamberger was hired, a complete consensus was unnecessary. The feeling of interdependence was enough and the excitement of participating in possibly the greatest adventure in the history of the legal profession more than enough to encourage everyone to rush forward into the next stage, the creation of a network of local law offices across the entire nation.

4: Development of
Local Legal Services Organizations

In an 18 month period—from January 1, 1966 through June 30, 1967—the nation's investment in legal assistance for the poor was increased eightfold over the level it had taken the legal aid movement 90 years to reach. During those 18 months, 300 Legal Services organizations—many of them new—were given OEO grants. An annual total budget level of $42 million was reached. Over 800 new law offices and almost 2000 new lawyers were funded. By the conclusion of this burst of activity, OEO had constructed a system of law offices and lawyers about the size of the United States Department of Justice and all its U.S. Attorneys' offices.

I. THE PRELIMINARIES: ORGANIZING THE NATIONAL SUPPORT

On September 24, 1965, when Clint Bamberger became the first director of the OEO Legal Services Program, the agency was not equipped either to promote or process any substantial number of legal services applications. There was no professional staff, secretaries, telephones, or even desks. Moreover, beyond a handful of bar leaders that maneuvered the February ABA endorsement, the legal profession was uninformed, skeptical, apathetic, or hostile. Thus, Bamberger was confronted with major organizational and public-relations tasks as well as policy-making responsibilities[1] if he hoped to achieve his target of 75 legal services grants before the end of the Program's initial fiscal year, June 30, 1966. In those hectic months, Bamberger and his staff operated simultaneously to line up national support in legal aid and organized bar circles, stimulate interest in local communities, formulate policies and procedures, negotiate with various community interests, and process grant applications through a bureaucratic maze.

A. Organizing the Office: Staff and Priorities

Bamberger recognized his weakness, virtually no knowledge or background in legal aid, old-fashioned or new. He sought a deputy director who compensated for that lack. Internal OEO support divided into two camps. Even before he accepted the position, Bamberger was taken to lunch by OEO General Counsel Donald Baker for the evident purpose of hearing the virtues of Bruce Terris, at that time a lawyer in Baker's office.[2] Shortly thereafter, Community Action Program (CAP) director Theodore Berry, the number-three official in the agency, indicated his strong support for B. Michael Rauh, 30, the special assistant who tended legal services affairs in the months prior to Bamberger's arrival.[3] (Rauh, incidentally, was the son of Joseph Rauh, AFL-CIO General Counsel and chairman of the District of Columbia Democratic party.)

In part because he was reluctant to antagonize either the General Counsel or the CAP director, Bamberger chose to go outside the agency. After interviewing several candidates, he bypassed the legal aid movement and chose me. At the time, I was deputy director of the Neighborhood Legal Services Project in Washington, D.C. and, thus, clearly representative of those who had participated in experiments with neighborhood lawyers rather than legal aid. But it is also true I had been endorsed by Howard Westwood, NLSP Board member and Washington counsel for NLADA. Obviously, I was not thought of as a radical or an enemy of legal aid.

At headquarters and in OEO's regional offices, the new Legal Services director favored a different type of person, in effect, "baby Bambergers," recruited from high-calibre, high-priced private law firms. He calculated that young associates from such firms would be most persuasive with the legal establishment. However, in the winter of 1965 there were very few promising associates who were interested in Legal Services and even fewer law firms that were willing to grant leaves of absence to their bright young men. An intense campaign among private firms yielded only one prize, Charles Edson, a 1959 Harvard graduate, from the largest law partnership in St. Louis.[4]

The rest of the headquarters staff came from a variety of sources and possessed an assortment of backgrounds:

Kalman "Buzzy" Hettleman, 29, was a former amateur tennis champion from Bamberger's hometown, Baltimore, who had graduated second in his class from the University of Maryland in 1964.[5] *Nira Long,* who at that time was one of the few black graduates of UCLA Law School, transferred from the Agency for International Development.[6] *Susan Fisher,* an ex-airline stewardess married to a young lawyer in the Washington office of a San Francisco law firm, was loaned to Legal Services on a two-week temporary assignment by the Headstart division in early 1966. (Eighteen months later she was still with Legal Services.)[7] *Dawn Gale,* another nonlawyer on temporary assignment from Headstart, stayed with Legal Services for three years. *Barbara Yanow,* a lawyer borrowed from another part of OEO, was a former staff member to a Michigan congressman and later for the Democratic National Committee.[8] *Kitty Chayes,* mother of Legal Services strategist Abram Chayes, was the only carry-over from the pre-Bamberger period.[9]

The personnel recruited for the regional offices were equally diverse in background.

William Greenawalt (Northeast Regional Office, New York), 32, was a tough, sometimes high-handed, former Wall Street lawyer who was a perfect match for the tough, sometimes high-handed Wall Streeters who ran the New York City Bar Association as well as their kin in Boston, Springfield, Providence, and other Northeastern cities.[10] *Don Stocks* (Western Regional Office, San Francisco), 34, was a black honor graduate of the University of Pittsburgh Law School.[11] *Henry McGee* (Great Lakes Regional Office, Chicago), 33, had been the first black member of the Student Governing Board at Northwestern University in 1954 and the first black editor-in-chief of the law review at Loyola Law School.[12] *Theodore Mitchell* (Southwestern Regional Office, Austin), a 30-year-old Harvard graduate, was recruited from the legal aid office on the Navajo Indian Reservation in Window Rock, Arizona.[13] *James Cordell* (Southeast Regional Office, Atlanta), 40, from Columbia, South Carolina[14] and *William Barvick* (North Central Regional Office, Kansas City), 30, a Kansas City native, came from private practice.[15] *Herman "Tex" Wilson* (Mid-Atlantic Regional Office, Washington), 31, was virtually stolen from the Justice Department's Tax Division. Wilson, the third black among our seven regional directors, had been the marshal (that's the same thing as president) of his senior class at Harvard Law School in 1961.[16]

In retrospect, this staff was notable for three reasons. *First,* the small size, 15 professionals, compared unfavorably with many other program areas in the Office of Economic Opportunity. For instance, VISTA, with a smaller budget to administer, had a staff exceeding 300 employees.

Second, as suggested by their achievements before and after serving with the Program, the original Legal Services staff was unusually talented. It seems unlikely that very many other government programs have commanded this degree of intelligence and judgment at the *operating* level during the critical formative period of their development. Without this highly qualified group, it probably would have been impossible to adopt the decentralized, "common law" policy-making process that characterized the early years of the Program.[17] Moreover, persuasion of local bar associations and other community groups would have been much more difficult.

Third, the entire staff was short on bureaucratic experience. They were mission oriented and had joined OEO temporarily in order to achieve a goal they all considered important, rather than being government careerists. This common characteristic made the Legal Services office impatient with bureaucratic channels, flow charts, and delay. Staff members also were almost completely immune to the typical methods of enforcing governmental discipline. Thus, there naturally was some tension between them and the middle-echelon OEO managers who tended to be career government administrators drawn from other Federal agencies.[18]

It was necessary not only to select a staff but to outline an agenda for the initial effort. A November 10, 1965, memorandum recommended concentration on urban areas with the highest priority accorded the ten largest cities because "Our notions as to what . . . is worth funding in rural areas are not sufficiently developed." The memo recommended experimenting with separate trial and appeal staffs to handle cases "with broad legal significance," programs based on referrals to compensated private counsel (soon known as Judicare) and, in rural areas, circuit-riding attorneys and lawyermobiles. Finally, the proposed agenda called for emphasis on funding research and supportive programs.[19] With only slight modifications, this became our game plan for fiscal year 1966.

B. Mobilizing the Legal Aid Movement

The path from ABA endorsement in February 1965 to widespread acceptance of the Legal Services Program in local communities was longer and more treacherous than either the Cahns or the ABA leaders had envisioned in early 1965. By November, the problem was further aggravated because the momentum generated from passage of the February resolution had long since been dissipated by the long delay in mounting the Program.

The most direct way—and Bamberger was in dire need of shortcuts if he were to create 75 local agencies by June 30, 1966—was to engender enthusiasm for the new program among the existing 242 legal aid societies. Already organized, and with boards, staffs, and clients, these societies were ready-made to receive OEO's funds, if only they could be persuaded to accept terms that promised the Legal Services Program a reasonable return on its investment.

The first opportunity to find out if a mutually profitable bargain could be struck with local legal aid societies came with the annual meeting of the NLADA scheduled for November 18, 1965, in Scottsdale, Arizona. The top leadership of the NLADA, including its president, Theodore Voorhees of Philadelphia, its executive director, Junius Allison, and its Washington counsel, Howard Westwood, were committed supporters of the OEO Legal Services Program by this time, but the rank-and-file members were far from convinced of the virtues of Federal financing. Less than a year earlier the NLADA executive committee had passed an ambivalent resolution about OEO.[20] Moreover, many of those who had been active in legal aid for several years recalled that the Legal Services Program was conceived by critics of the existing movement and born of low regard for the capacity of its personnel.[21] This insulted the staff members of local legal aid societies, who made up 60 percent of the convention audience. The rest were board members from the local societies, as a whole a conservative lot, and thus even more distrustful of the Federal government. As a consequence, in November 1965, the NLADA was peopled primarily by skeptics and opponents of the OEO Program.

Bamberger was more concerned about the NLADA meeting and the reaction of the legal aid societies than I was. He was convinced that unless the existing local organizations could be persuaded to become part of the OEO Legal Services Program it would be impossible to mount a major national effort. I was more sanguine about our ability to find other community groups to sponsor local legal services agencies if the legal aid societies refused to cooperate. In retrospect, Bamberger probably was right.

Voorhees made the new Federal program the central topic for the 1965 convention. The first full day of meetings was to be devoted to speeches by Bamberger, Julian Dugas (director of the Washington, D.C., program), Westwood, and myself. Each speech was to be followed by questioning from the audience. We knew it would be a risky business to open up the entire program to audience discussion, but it was a necessary risk. We could not leave the impression that any issues had been suppressed or that any doubts had gone unanswered.

Bamberger led off before the packed auditorium of over 300 vitally concerned legal aid attorneys and their supporters. He deliberately chose to make it absolutely clear that the OEO Program embraced the goals of the reformers as well as the legal aid movement.

> I believe that the idealism of the Legal Aid concept is the fulfillment of the obligations of lawyers to serve all—poor as well as rich—without qualification; but I also believe that the practice has sometimes fallen short of the ideal.
>
> • • •
>
> Lawyers must be activists to leave a contribution to society. The law is more than a control; it is an instrument for social change. The role of [the] OEO program is to provide the means within the democratic process for the law and lawyers to release the bonds which imprison people in poverty, to marshal the forces of law to combat the causes and effects of poverty.
>
> Each day, I ask myself, How will lawyers representing poor people defeat the cycle of poverty? This is the purpose of the Office of Economic Opportunity, and, unless we can justify our contribution to that purpose, the program I direct is not properly a part of the War on Poverty.
>
> • • •
>
> As I prepared this speech, I sensed that I said too much and yet not enough. I would be more pleased if I could not just talk to you, but talk with you for the

whole day. It would take me that long to review with you all of my thoughts about the evolving policy of the Legal Services Program of the Office of Economic Opportunity. When we continue this discussion this afternoon, ask the hard questions. If I can answer, I will. If I cannot, I may ask you what the answer is.

If you will accept bold ideas, new theories, courageous innovation, and disputed principles with an open and inquisitive mind and a renewed commitment to make the law an instrument of advantage for disadvantaged people, we will be a significant generation. I challenge you to disturb me with proposals of great magnitude and bold concepts.[22]

I knew we might be in some trouble when the applause failed to approach the eloquence of Bamberger's speech. After the Westwood and Dugas speeches, the floor was opened up to half an hour of questioning before lunch. The first question was from a legal aid society director from the Midwest.

We heard a lot of stuff this morning about new ideas and new challenges and new things in general. But I didn't hear anybody cite any authority for any of this. Nobody mentioned Reginald Heber Smith, the founder of this legal aid movement, or any of the other great men that have helped keep this thing going through the years.

Bamberger had scarcely finished answering that "question" when the late Ernest Schein, at that time the chairman of the board of directors of the Washington, D.C. Legal Aid Society, asked for permission to come to the rostrum and make some remarks. He read from a typewritten statement:

By this time, your hearts and minds should be filled with the virtues of the antipoverty program as it relates to legal services to the poor. Nonetheless, I respectfully suggest that there is a further point of view which it is imperative to consider now.

Other authorities, grown old in the service of Legal Aid, still are skeptical about the takeover by public and political authorities of the civil Legal Aid institution. Many of you are genuinely concerned about the implications of support by public funds of an enterprise essentially the responsibility of the community and specifically of its members of the bar.

This is not the occasion for emphasizing the intricate procedures which develop in publicly financed projects administered by government employees. With your permission, however, I present the problem of the District of Columbia with which I am most familiar.

The United Planning Organization inaugurated an entirely distinct neighborhood law office project with its own board of directors, its own operations, planning, and personnel recruitment. Seven such neighborhood law offices, as has been pointed out, are now in operation, with one more in immediate prospect.

No foundation funds or government antipoverty appropriations have come to the Legal Aid Society. . . . . .

Without wishing to belabor the subject, I shall outline some of the hazards which we see in the publicly sponsored Legal Aid program. In an article in *Look* (July 27, 1965), Sargent Shriver, whom we all love and greatly respect, lumps all the proposed antipoverty projects together, pre-kindergarten classes, child care, job training, health services, and legal services. He said, "These local programs are gambles." He further wrote in his article, and repeated in Miami, that OEO does not know whether every single one of the projects will work; and frankly stated that his office did not know very much about running a Legal Aid operation. . . . .

The combination of social worker and lawyer has always been a difficult one. We try to confine ourselves to legal services as, of course, affected by social conditions and welfare conditions in a community. It is naive to expect that the administration of government-sponsored Legal Aid, with its pattern of over-staffing, overpaying, and overadministering, will not create problems.[23]

My concern grew even more when Schein's statement drew much greater applause than had Bamberger's. It looked as if the gamble had been lost. An open question period, designed to quiet all fears about the Program, instead had given the opponents a platform for well-planned attacks.

We broke for lunch with the issues still very much in doubt. For the moment, it appeared we may have come all the way and obtained the endorsement of ABA's establishment lawyers, only to have the professionals actually working for legal aid revolt against the Program. Bamberger, Westwood and I met during the lunch hour period. We went over my speech in fair detail and made some changes.

I began the afternoon with a reference to the first issue that had been raised in the morning questioning period.

I believe someone this morning stated that he hadn't heard any authority cited by any of the speakers. So, let's begin this afternoon's session by citing some authority. I'd like you to hear a quote:

No one doubts that it is the proper function of government to secure justice. . . . Nor can anyone question that the highest obligation of government is to secure justice for those who, because they are poor and weak and friendless, find it hard to maintain their own rights.

Now these are not the words of some law school theoretician—although they could have been. Nor was this statement made by Clint Bamberger at this morning's session—although it could have been.

No, these are the words of Elihu Root, one of the foremost lawyers in American history, writing in 1919. The statement is from his foreword to *Justice and the Poor,* by one of the grand old men of Legal Aid, Reginald Heber Smith. Much has happened to Legal Aid since those words were penned. The number of clients served by Legal Aid organizations numbered only in the thousands in 1919. They are counted in the hundreds of thousands today. At the same time, this growth has been stunted because government has been slow in accepting its obligation to justice, the obligation Elihu Root so clearly recognized over forty-six years ago. Now, belatedly, the Federal government has taken a tentative step toward meeting the government responsibility.

With that belated recognition of obligation has come a challenge to those charged with administering the government program. That challenge is to tele- scope four decades of development into a short span of years. The development which Legal Aid organizations might have undergone had they not been underfi- nanced and understaffed through the years.[24]

I then spelled out some of the new goals and innovative approaches the neighborhood law offices had introduced and ended the speech with an invita- tion. When I finished, Allan Fisher, the staff director of the Washington Legal Aid Society, raised his hand and asked permission to come to the microphone. Like the chairman of his board, Fisher brought with him a typewritten state- ment. In a voice quivering with emotion, he delivered a bitter attack:

You have heard that there are seven neighborhood offices in strategic parts of Washington and that too rapid expansion—and that is what it amounted to—has brought down upon our heads a lawsuit in the Federal district court. Two defen- dants were named: the Community Action Program—we call it the United Plan- ning Organization—and the Legal Aid Society itself. Some lawyers serving per- sons almost indigent felt that their livelihood was being imperiled and hence undertook to challenge the very existence of both these organizations.

The neighborhood lawyers have fine paper records, but they are young men, and they are inexperienced. Now these zealous young men walk into court and give the judges such an argument that the judges themselves burn up. They will ask you for reports and explanations, why we did this and why we did that, and hold you accountable.

Clients are using both organizations. When we dispose of a matter and send a client off, some of them go to the neighborhood offices and say, "Legal Aid Society ain't doin' nothin' for me." The neighborhood man tries to deal with the situation.

This is not the breed of the traditional Legal Aid lawyer who for years has accepted pauper pay in order that a cause might be promoted and continued and who in some instances drew upon his own private resources in order that he might stay and do that job.[25]

The only thing encouraging at this point was the fact that Fisher's attack did not draw nearly the applause that Schein's speech had received in the morning.

What followed was one of the most grueling experiences of Clint Bamber- ger's professional life. For three and a half hours, he stood at the podium and answered questions. He took on all comers—the friendly, the probing, and the antagonistic. As a trial specialist, Bamberger was used to cross-examining witnesses, but this was something new. He was now in the position of a witness with 300 cross-examiners. There is an old saying that lawyers make poor witnesses. That adage certainly did not apply to Clint Bamberger. On the stand, he was forceful, candid, energetic, and sometimes witty. It was as if he had been born to play this precise role.

Bamberger began to exercise some of the techniques that he would employ time and time again in the ensuing months as he faced similar groups of skeptical lawyers. One of the NLADA questioners asked a long, complex, detailed question about whether a practice advocated by some neighborhood lawyers constituted a violation of the canons of the legal profession; whether the basic philosophy of the Legal Services Program violated the canons; and on and on. Bamberger paused significantly, leaned over toward the microphone, and then slowly, precisely, and emphatically uttered one word, "Noooo." The entire audience broke out into chuckles and applause. This simple, straightforward answer to a complex, hostile question had made a big hit with friend and foe alike. Bamberger filed this interesting finding away and used it many times at future meetings.

Time and again questioners attempted to lead Bamberger away from one of the positions he had taken in his morning speech. They tried embarrassing him, "Now, Mr. Bamberger, you really didn't mean to say so-and-so. . . . Did you?" This was usually met with the reply, "That's precisely what I meant to say. And furthermore. . . ."

And when a questioner offered a veiled threat, "Now you don't *really* expect the legal profession to go along with . . . ?" Bamberger would reply, "I do because I'm a lawyer and that's what I think our profession is all about." Any weakness Bamberger displayed in this kind of confrontation was a tendency to get red-faced angry about questions that appeared to be particularly inane and vicious. Fortunately, the NLADA group were skeptical and fearful, but not obnoxious or Neanderthal. Only once during the long day of questioning did Bamberger's temper flare, then for only a moment. His answers, his honesty, and style began to get over to the audience. You could almost see the respect for Bamberger and the Legal Services Program developing in the auditorium. The questions and the questioners became more and more respectful, more and more friendly, more and more positive as the afternoon wore on.

By the time Ted Voorhees closed off discussion in the late afternoon, most NLADA members accepted the Program and many were enthusiastic. The next two days Bamberger and I were hard-pressed to see the scores of delegations from legal aid societies around the country. They all wanted to find out about getting Federal funds.

C. Educating the Local Bar Associations

Mobilization of the rank-and-file supporters of legal aid was an essential first step. However, it seemed a relatively simple assignment compared with gaining the allegiance of the remainder of the legal profession. Those involved in the legal aid movement, after all, shared a commitment to the clients of the Legal Services Program and accepted the basic tenet that poor people need legal assistance. This was not so for many state and local bar associations and individual lawyers.

During the remainder of 1965 and the early months of 1966, Clint Bamberger was to participate in over a dozen confrontations similar to that he faced at the NLADA conference. In each, he spoke to an audience composed largely of the ignorant, the neutral and the skeptical. And in each he was pitted against a few hostile questioners who were attempting to sway the audience against him.

In December, 1965, at the meeting of the American Association of Law Schools in New Orleans, he was questioned sharply and in detail about the prospective policy that all boards of directors of local Legal Services agencies must contain representatives of the poor. A New Orleans judge finally asked, "What can poor people possibly tell lawyers about legal services?" Bamberger replied, "Judge, when it comes to providing legal services to the *poor,* I'm not sure if *lawyers* have much to contribute. Our past performance hasn't been anything to brag about. But I have no doubt that poor people have something to say. They've been there before." Two years later, the judge admitted even he was impressed with that straightforward answer.

At the January, 1966, midwinter meeting of the American Bar Association in Chicago, Robert Kirk Walker, president of the Tennessee Bar Association, challenged Bamberger by stating, "When they get into the matter of social revolution . . . then there is where we part company."

Bamberger stood his ground with an answer that made all the newspaper wire services, "I believe there is going to be a social change in this country and if lawyers want to stand by and watch it happen and not participate in it . . . and shape it. . . . this is their choice."[26]

Although Bamberger's many speechmaking trips kept him out of the office much of the time during a critical period for the Legal Services Program, it was more than worthwhile. His verbal parrying and thrusting with the critics and the doubters were beginning to pay off. It was a necessary job, and no one handled it better than Bamberger. True enough, the Cahns and their helpers had persuaded the ABA leadership that the OEO Legal Services Program was a good thing. True enough, the ABA leadership in turn had convinced the ABA House of Delegates of that same thing. And true enough, in one very tough afternoon, Bamberger had converted almost everyone that counted in the legal aid movement. But that left about 249,000 of the 250,000 practicing lawyers in America who knew nothing of the Legal Services Program or had serious doubts.

Bamberger did receive a lot of help. ABA president Ed Kuhn, president-elect Orison Marden and supporters of legal aid like John Cummiskey made many speeches to local and state bar associations. And once the NLADA squarely acknowledged the Legal Services Program, its leaders actively campaigned not only with its constituent legal aid societies but beyond in the general profession. NLADA Washington counsel Howard Westwood distributed hundreds of copies of a six-page memorandum that dispelled most of the reservations bar members harbored about the Federal Program. NLADA president Ted Voorhees was especially active on the speechmaking circuit. In a typical hard-hitting address, he said:

> It is comforting for us, as lawyers, to see a spreading of legal aid, higher salaries to our underpaid staff members, and better service to our clientele. But to concentrate our attention on only the traditional legal aid aspect of the Legal Services Program is to miss perhaps the major point.
>
> If anyone should boast of the accomplishments of Legal Aid, it should be the president of NLADA, but I can only say that our annual measure of accomplishment has never come up to more than a fraction of the community's need. Because of shortage of funds and apathy within the profession, we have done little more than dent the surface of assistance to the poor.
>
> For the first time in history a truly resourceful, imaginative and novel approach has been developed to eradicate poverty and the indignity of inequality that are a part of it.
>
> The heart of the new program has to be the providing of legal services. Whether we are talking in terms of a man's right to an opportunity for employment, or to receive welfare that is legally due him in the absence of a job, or to live in an inhabitable dwelling under the minimum standards of the rent and housing laws . . . , the whole bundle of rights that the poor ought to share with the rest of us are utterly meaningless to them unless legal representation is provided to give those rights reality.
>
> We would assuredly give it that backing if its beneficiaries were our own rich clients. It is unthinkable that we should do less, simply because the service is designed to help the poor.[27]

The organized bar support was also reflected in many ABA publications. Scarcely an issue of the *ABA Journal, ABA News* or *ABA Washington Letter* was published during 1966 and 1967 that failed to mention developments in Legal Services. And in March, 1966, the Association distributed to each of its 30,000 members a 30-page pamphlet describing and promoting the OEO program.

ABA support helped and in places was critical. But to my mind Bamberger deserves most of the credit for a minor miracle. Lawyers are, fortunately, and at the same time, ironically, generally not only among the most persuasive, but among the most easily persuaded people there are around. Possibly because they earn their living and spend their days trying to convince others through written and oral argument, they develop a connoisseur's respect for sound, artfully presented reasoning. They would immediately reject the cheap tricks that I have seen some politicians and demagogues use with less sophisticated audiences. But they admired and could be swayed by the sharp intellect, quick reactions, and witty style of a good trial lawyer. And Bamberger excelled in this very area. Not that all the lawyers who heard Bamberger became firm supporters of the Legal Services Program. But many did, both conservative and liberal. And just as important, virtually no one remained a firm opponent of the Program.

II. THE MAIN EVENT: TRANSLATING AMORPHOUS SUPPORT INTO LEGAL SERVICES GRANTS

The NLADA and bar association campaigns created a favorable atmosphere. It made it respectable for a legal aid society or local bar to accept Federal funds. But the only result that counted for Bamberger and the Legal Services Program was to see actual grants made to local communities. That required hard work at the local level, which also tested Bamberger's philosophical commitment in a way the missionary effort among bar associations never could. It is one thing to rhapsodize about new, vague approaches at pleasant luncheon meetings. It is another to make tough choices and alienate powerful people in order to implement your rhetoric.

The campaign on the local level involved far more than the tiny staff of the Legal Services Program. It absorbed scores of ABA officials and staff members and occupied the time of literally thousands of local bar leaders, community action workers, and poverty representatives during the months their local communities were forming Legal Services agencies.

Each grant was the culmination of a difficult, often prolonged, political process. If the funds were given to an existing legal aid society, fundamental structural changes and reforms had to be negotiated. If not, an entirely new political entity had to be created. In either case, it took a political feat of some magnitude. In the next section I will attempt to convey some understanding of how this was accomplished in over 250 separate localities during the 18 months from January, 1966 through June, 1967.

A. The Usual Scenario

An application for a Legal Services grant almost always reflects a compromise among some of the most diverse elements present in an American community. The policy of the Legal Services Program requires that such organizations as the local bar association, the local community action agency, poverty representatives and the minority bar be allowed to participate in the drafting procedure. In many places, other groups also were drawn into the process.

These ranged from interests like the ACLU, the NAACP, and SNCC to normally conservative elements including the municipal administration, public prosecutor's office and the welfare department.

The initiative for preparing a Legal Services application could be taken by any of the groups mentioned above. As a practical matter, in communities with existing legal aid societies, the board and staff of the society ordinarily took the lead. However, there were exceptions. In some cities—Detroit is the prime example—the legal aid society opposed the principle of Federal financial support for legal assistance. In others, the society was unwilling to accept some essential requirement imposed by the policy of the Legal Services Program. The New Orleans Legal Aid Society, for instance, could not stomach the requirement that representatives of the poor should participate on the society's board.[28] Elsewhere, Los Angeles and Miami among them, community groups merely stole a march on the legal aid group and put together their own grant proposal. But where the Legal Aid Society was willing to be the vehicle for a Legal Services Program—and after the intensive educational campaigns by the ABA, NLADA, and OEO, most societies were interested in the Federal funds—its leadership ordinarily seized the initiative.

In communities without existing legal aid societies—generally Southern cities or towns and rural areas anywhere in the nation—either the community action agency or the local bar association usually prepared the formal proposal. However, more often than not, the process was set in motion by an individual attorney or handful of attorneys who heard of the Legal Services Program at some conference or read about it in an ABA publication.

The sponsoring group—whether the legal aid society, bar association, CAA or some other—usually arranged for an OEO staff member or consultant to explain the Program to bar and community leaders. Often with the help of the staff member or consultant, a draft proposal was prepared and then circulated among other community groups for their approval. If the OEO suggestion that all interested segments of the community participate from the beginning in Program development had been followed consistently, this stage could have been relatively painless. But for varying reasons, proposals tended to be prepared by a single interest group which only passed it on for approval on a take-it-or-leave-it basis.

After the application received "community" approval (which usually meant bar association and CAA approval), it was forwarded to OEO. This was the stage at which the real bargaining ordinarily began. At its best, this was when the Legal Services staff became the champion of the poverty groups and ethnic organizations that heretofore had been powerless to affect the program design except through their diluted influence in the CAA. It was thus at this stage that OEO's traditional deference to the supremacy of local decision making came most directly into conflict with the Legal Services Program's goals of high quality and *effective* participation of the poor.[29] The Legal Services staff was caught between competing policies, and its performance reflected this ambivalent position as the staff shifted its basic approach from community to community. Sometimes it would impose the staff's own solution on a local situation; at other times it adopted a "hands off" attitude toward the internal community struggles.

No matter the OEO role, in the clear majority of communities the ultimate resolution was acceptable to all pertinent local interests. However, in a substantial minority, a powerful element was sufficiently dissatisfied to seek to upset the negotiated settlement and sometimes to block the grant. How these local factions maneuvered and why, and especially why they met with a general lack of success formed a determinative part of the first 18 months of the history of the Legal Services Program.

B. The Anatomy of Conflict

Where there was conflict, it followed no single pattern from community to community. The best I can do is convey some understanding of three dimensions that characterized these situations: the contesting parties; the issues that divided them; and, the tactics employed by the contestants to influence the resolution of the controversy.

1. The Contestants

In most communities, parties lined up in one of the following ways:

A. COMMUNITY ACTION AGENCY VERSUS THE BAR ASSOCIATION OR LEGAL AID SOCIETY. In some cities, including Miami, New York, and New Orleans, community action agencies contended with the bar-sponsored legal aid societies or the bar itself over issues of program design and control. In these early years the average CAA board was dominated by middle-class liberals; the local bar, of course, by well-to-do, moderate to conservative lawyers. Although frequently the conflict represented a split between liberal and conservative ideologies, in some places it sprang from the reluctance of the CAAs to surrender control to a separate governing body as required by OEO policy.

B. POVERTY COMMUNITY VERSUS THE BAR ASSOCIATION OR LEGAL AID SOCIETY. In San Francisco, and a few other localities, representatives of the poverty community attained enough power to play a dominant role in the application process. Their demands tended to revolve around the issue of control, especially over personnel selection. Bar associations not only resisted demands for outright control but in some places objected to any of the poor participating in agency administration.

C. LOCAL GOVERNMENT VERSUS THE BAR ASSOCIATION OR LEGAL AID SOCIETY. Chicago provided the most dramatic example of a struggle between a city government (which operated the CAA) and a legal aid society backed by the bar association. Local government was motivated by fears about the kind of lawsuits poverty lawyers might file. The legal aid society and its bar association sponsor wanted to be free to sue whomever they liked, even city hall (and if they did not persist in that position, OEO did).

D. ESTABLISHMENT BAR LEADERS VERSUS RANK-AND-FILE LAWYERS. The citizens of Philadelphia, Baltimore, Albuquerque, and several other communities witnessed a strange contest, pitting the bar association establishment against its membership. The association was split because bar association activities tend to be dominated by members of the larger, more prosperous law firms who in turn counsel the major financial and industrial interests. In contrast, the rank-and-file lawyers—individual practitioners and small partnerships, for the most part—make their living from representing small commercial interests and middle-class individuals. This brought the bar leadership into conflict with its membership in several cities where the leaders favored a Legal Services application. The rank-and-file revolted because they feared a Legal Services agency would take away some of their clients and harm others, especially landlords, credit companies and collection agencies. In bar association affairs, the big firms control the structure, but the rank-and-file have the votes. As a result, these turned out to be among the hardest fought of the local contests over Legal Services grants.

E. MINORITY LAWYERS VERSUS ESTABLISHMENT BAR ASSOCIATION OR LEGAL AID SOCIETY. A variation of the contest between establishment members of the bar and the rank-and-file lawyers surfaced in a few communities such as East St. Louis, Illinois. The minority lawyers who practiced in low-income neighborhoods sometimes feared they would lose business to poverty attorneys. They also distrusted the establishment middle-class bar to set up a system that would give them a fair share of the clients turned away by neighborhood law offices because they could afford to pay for their own counsel. However, minority lawyers seldom expressed outright opposition because the chief beneficiaries of the planned Legal Services agency were of the same race as they were. Thus, the conflict was subdued, and usually was concluded with an agreement granting minority lawyers membership on the board and creating a special referral panel. In a few Southern communities, notably Baton Rouge, the minority members of the bar actually initiated the Legal Services proposal and contested with the white majority for control of the program.

F. OEO LEGAL SERVICES STAFF VERSUS ONE OR MORE COMMUNITY INTEREST GROUPS. In several communities the dominant interests were able to suppress local dissent. If the proposal was not to its liking, the OEO staff found itself in direct conflict with the official "community" position. Usually a suitable compromise could be negotiated. One exception occurred in San Bernardino County, California, where the local bar association was able to induce the CAA and other community groups to approve a program design—Judicare

—deemed unacceptable by OEO. The association could do this because it did not have to deal with any groups that might have proposed alternative plans to the OEO, and, with no alternatives, the OEO had to assert national policy directly over local desires. The result was a standoff because, without any opposition, the bar association also saw no reason why it should fashion a program its members did not favor.

It is notable that many of the interest groups that years later reacted against the lawsuits brought by poverty lawyers had no voice in the negotiations carried out before grants were made. Landlords, credit merchants and welfare administrators seldom knew of the plans for a local Legal Services agency and, if they did, scarcely imagined the consequences for their own practices.

2. The Issues

Virtually every conceivable issue was raised in one community or another. However, most disputes centered on one or more of the following:

A. WHETHER THERE WAS TO BE A LEGAL SERVICES GRANT AT ALL. If the CAA wanted a Legal Services grant badly enough it held the ultimate power to submit an application despite objections from other community groups. If the CAA did not, it was difficult, but not impossible, to fund a Legal Services agency over its opposition. Except for some CAAs that preferred to invest their resources in other types of programs, however, the only opposition to the principle of seeking a Legal Services grant came from local bar associations or rank-and-file lawyers.

B. THE SIZE OF THE PROGRAM. The CAA sometimes was concerned about budget considerations, a worry that evaporated when the funds for Legal Services were made independent from other OEO grants to the community. But local lawyers, fearful of competition, often sought to limit the number of offices and attorneys.

C. WHO WAS TO CONTROL THE AGENCY? Control of the Legal Services agency involved two issues. The first was the composition of the Legal Services board, especially the representation to be afforded to the client community.[30] This question frequently brought the CAA or poverty organization into conflict with the legal aid society or the bar. The second issue of control had to do with the CAA's role in the administration of the Legal Services agency. Legal Services policy dictated that poverty lawyers were to be supervised by a board that was independent from the CAA. This rule did not sit well with CAAs in several communities and they tried various strategies to retain some hold on the Legal Services attorneys.

D. ISSUES OF PROGRAM DESIGN.

1. The delivery system: How the services were to be made available. OEO, the CAAs, the poverty communities, even the legal aid societies favored the

provision of services through salaried staff attorneys. But some local bar associations and dissident rank-and-file attorneys advocated paying private lawyers with Federal funds to handle low-income clients.[31] This system, called Judicare, provoked discussion and controversy throughout the legal profession.

2. *Eligibility criteria: Who was to receive the services?* There were a number of skirmishes between CAAs and bar associations to determine how poor an applicant had to be to make him eligible for legal services. Usually the CAA favored a more generous standard than the bar association. But occasionally the antipoverty agency sought to bring the criteria the Legal Services lawyers applied into line with the standard used by their other programs. This move ordinarily would have made fewer people eligible for legal services than the prevailing legal aid criteria.[32]

3. *The scope of representation: What kind of cases were to be taken?* Many legal aid societies historically had refused to handle certain categories of cases. Divorce and bankruptcy were typical examples, and they remained surprisingly resistant to expanding their services in these directions.[33] CAAs and poverty communities frequently were more concerned about other issues. Thus, a confrontation arose between OEO and the local legal aid society.

4. *The salaries of staff attorneys.* The problem of determining salaries erupted in dozens of communities. Legal Services policy[34] insisted that neighborhood lawyers be paid salaries comparable to lawyers of similar experience in the area. But this often meant the legal services staff received higher compensation than CAA personnel received. The legal aid society and bar association usually pushed for better pay than the CAA wanted to approve.

3. Tactics of Resistance.

Most conflicts were resolved by negotiations among the competing community groups. OEO sometimes interceded to favor one position over the other but usually waited for the application to come in before judging the merits of the case. However, the losing party—whether it was the CAA, local bar association, dissident lawyers, or any other faction—did not always accept defeat either at the community level or within OEO. Local bar associations and dissident lawyer groups were especially adept at conceiving ways to seek reversal of decisions they did not like. The most common means of opposition were to appeal to the OEO senior staff; appeal through the organized bar either to the ABA or state associations; appeal to local or state government; appeal to the judiciary and appeal to Congress.

A. APPEALS TO OEO SENIOR STAFF. When a Community Action Agency was frustrated by a decision of the Legal Services staff, the usual recourse was to OEO officials who had power to review those decisions. In a later chapter, we will describe the complex procedure applying to Legal Services fundings.[35] For now it is sufficient to know there were almost a dozen checkpoints outside the Program's staff through which such an application was required to pass. Any one of those OEO staff members in effect could activate an appeal to higher authority within the agency and possibly overrule the decision made by the Legal Services Program. Most officials of major CAAs had relationships with some OEO staffers who possessed review power over Legal Services grants. Thus, here is where they lodged their own complaints.

Actually, since CAAs, at least those outside the Southern states, held most of the cards in local community negotiations and, moreover, favored most of the positions promoted by Legal Services staff, they seldom had cause to appeal. However, a number of objections were lodged against Legal Services policy in Michigan, over the issue of salaries for poverty lawyers. These were made because the salary sufficient to attract a decently qualified attorney exceeded the compensation paid to CAA staff leaders in many of these communities. CAAs resisted submitting salary schedules for Legal Services grantees which dwarfed the CAA's own compensation levels. Meanwhile, the OEO Legal Services staff insisted on the higher pay for local poverty attorneys if a grant was to be made at all. Usually, the CAA yielded and submitted the application with the requested salaries, then asked other OEO officials for a reversal. The resulting negotiations produced some of the more heated disputes within the OEO bureaucracy during the spring of 1966. Because of time pressures and the apparent pettiness of the issue, all the salaries were established at a level midway between what the CAAs paid and what the program staff wanted, without appeal to Shriver or the top echelons of command. In retrospect, the compromise salary levels proved to be too low in most of the communities and, as a result, the overall quality and performance of those agencies was impaired.

B. APPEAL WITHIN THE ORGANIZED BAR.

1. Appeals through the American Bar Association. During the first year of the OEO Legal Services Program, dissatisfied bar associations usually took their appeals to the ABA. Knowing of the Association's role in the Program and often on a first-name basis with its leaders, the dissidents selected what appeared the natural channel for effective protest. In most instances the local bar leaders attempted to reach some ABA official who sat on the National Advisory Committee to the Legal Services Program, the body Shriver created to provide policy advice to the OEO staff. John Cummiskey, the ABA's legal aid committee chairman, probably ended up with the majority of these complaints.

On the whole, this tactic proved ineffective because many local bars were seeking relief from the enforcement of clear policies. Because they had participated in the formulation of those policies,[36] ABA leaders were unsympathetic to requests that they urge exceptions on the Legal Services staff. Also, NAC members were reluctant to jeopardize their influence with OEO on major policy questions by exerting pressure on behalf of some individual local bar. They felt it would have been a poor expenditure of the bar's limited political capital. Finally, the NAC members felt constrained by the Committee's own ground rules that it consider the general policy of the Program only and not meddle in decisions about individual grant actions.

On three or four occasions, the NLADA's Washington counsel, Howard Westwood, interceded for a legal aid society involved in a confrontation with OEO. But his approach was low key; he merely asked for a review by the headquarters Legal Services staff. In one such instance, Minneapolis, a compromise was struck because of the persuasive argument made by the society's director, but in all the remaining cases no changes were made in the OEO stance. Cummiskey's infrequent contacts with regional and headquarters personnel also were low key and seldom affected the OEO decision in any way.

When it became apparent that the national leaders of the legal profession would not "knee jerk" to the aid of local bar associations who were displeased with OEO positions, the disappointed lawyers sometimes turned to other pressure points outside the profession. However, the San Francisco bar threatened to appeal their case another step within the organized bar structure, taking it over the head of the ABA leadership to the House of Delegates. This ploy was averted in a meeting between Bamberger, Cummiskey and the leaders of the San Francisco delegation at the February, 1966 ABA convention. The Legal Services director agreed to certain compromises that satisfied the local bar and they dropped the resolution.[37]

2. *Use of the power of the state bar.* State bar associations vary widely in their responsibilities and influence. Many are merely voluntary social organizations to which only a minority of the jurisdiction's lawyers even bother to belong. At the other extreme, some so-called integrated bars (those where bar membership is a prerequisite to practice law) in effect administer the legal profession in their states. The typical state association falls somewhere in between, maintaining some policy-making and supervisory functions but lacking the influence of the major local bars.[38] Rarely could the organization on the state level do more to affect a Legal Services grant than the local bar itself. Consequently, dissidents seldom took their case to a state association.

Almost the only appeal to a state bar association, and by far the most dramatic, was made in North Carolina. Early in July, 1966, local bars, antagonized by Legal Services grants made in Charlotte and several rural areas, appealed to the executive secretary of the North Carolina State Bar. Long an opponent of the OEO Program, the state secretary conceived a plan to halt the newly funded agencies before they could open. The state bar, an integrated body, simply invoked its power over the right to practice law in North Carolina and promulgated rules disbarring any attorney who worked in a law office that complied with Legal Services policies.[39]

There was only one flaw in the strategy used by the members of the North Carolina Bar. Their rules applied statewide and thus impinged on an existing Legal Services agency that had been established a few months earlier in Winston-Salem. Founded and led by the most prominent lawyers in the state, the board of the Winston-Salem program refused to submit. Instead, they quietly drafted a Federal lawsuit to enjoin enforcement of the state rules, then threatened to file it unless drastic changes were made which would legalize the Winston-Salem operation. This was enough to bring the North Carolina Bar to the conference table. In March, 1966, a series of negotiations between the Legal Services staff, state bar officials, and Winston-Salem board members culminated in an agreement that allowed all the agencies in North Carolina that had received grants to begin operation.[40]

C. LEVERAGE THROUGH LOCAL GOVERNMENT. Sometimes a dissident community group had a measure of influence in city government. This was especially true of lawyers, who tend to be deeply involved in local politics as councilmen, campaign managers, party officials, and lobbyists. Thus, in communities where municipal government occupied a strategic position in relation to the filing of a Legal Services application, dissatisfied lawyers might block a grant they found obnoxious.

In 1966 and 1967, local government usually was only remotely related to the Community Action Agency and its activities. But in some areas, like Philadelphia and Chicago, city governments actually operated the antipoverty programs. Elsewhere, the mayor or council chose many of those who served on the CAA board, and in a few other cities government officials gripped a less direct but equally effective lever. They supplied public funds to pay the 10 percent local contribution required to match all OEO grants.

Dissident lawyers in Philadelphia found they had less influence with the city than did the poverty community and minority groups. And, as in most other cities where local government had the requisite power over the process of applying for Legal Services, everything went smoothly. The major exception was Baltimore, where rank-and-file lawyers persuaded the city council to hold up its contribution to the local CAA until the latter withdrew an ambitious ten-office Legal Services application approved by the bar association's executive committee. With this lever, the dissident lawyers were able to reduce the eventual grant to a two-office program.

In Chicago, where the mayor *was* the CAA, the agency held up submission of the Legal Services application for months while seeking an agreement that poverty lawyers would refrain from suits against municipal agencies. The regional OEO office gave in to the mayor but was overruled by the headquarters Legal Services staff. A compromise ultimately was approved that required all such suits to be brought by the downtown legal aid facility rather than the neighborhood offices.[41]

D. INVOKING POWER OF STATE GOVERNMENT. In most communities, state government was not a formal party to the negotiations over legal services. Nevertheless, it retained one potent power—the gubernatorial veto. Under the Economic Opportunity Act, a state governor could veto any antipoverty grant he found objectionable.[42] True, the OEO director was empowered to override the veto, but he seldom did so. Without doubt, a gubernatorial veto placed a powerful lever in the hands of state governors.

In the one instance where a dissident lawyer faction vigorously registered its views with a governor, the result was a veto. The North Dakota State Bar Association had sponsored an application for a statewide Legal Services agency. But many rank and-file lawyers opposed any program for the state. When the grant was announced in April, 1966, the opponents managed to reach the ear of North Dakota chief executive William Guy. He vetoed. Shriver pleaded with the governor, a fellow Democrat, to rescind the action. But when Guy did not yield, the OEO director refused to exercise his own power to override the veto.

Interestingly, disaffected groups almost never took their grievances to their state government prior to the initial funding of a Legal Services agency. It is especially noteworthy since this is precisely where most complaints have been lodged by interests adversely affected by poverty lawyers after the grants were made and the programs in operation. Several factors may account for this phenomenon. First, in 1966 and 1967, dissidents seldom could expect a friendly hearing in states where the executive mansion was filled by a liberal. Second, in the opposite situation with a conservative—especially a Republican governor—in office, the chance of an OEO override was very high. Thus, the state chief executive was reluctant to veto, since it appeared a futile, and possibly politically embarrassing, gesture. Finally, where the Legal Services Program was part of a comprehensive antipoverty grant, the governor had to veto the entire package to quash the neighborhood lawyer segment.

E. RESORT TO THE COURTS. Lawyers are gifted (or cursed) with a natural instinct to take their grievances to court. Not surprisingly, a disgruntled local bar association in Stanislaus County, California[43] and dissident lawyers in Orlando, Florida,[44] Philadelphia,[45] Houston,[46] and Washington, D.C.[47] brought lawsuits to enjoin Legal Services operations. Usually filed after one of the other routes of resistance had failed, these cases were premised on several grounds. First, it was sometimes claimed that Legal Services agencies violated state laws banning the practice of law by corporations. Second, it was alleged they violated ethical rules guaranteeing the sanctity of the relationship between the attorney and his client and prohibiting solicitation of clients and "stirring up" litigation. Third, it was asserted that neighborhood law offices deprived low-income clients of the freedom to choose their own lawyer and, more to the point, deprived private attorneys of some income. The Florida suit raised an even more fundamental issue, the constitutionality of the Legal Services Program and the war on poverty itself.[48]

The courts proved to be the least rewarding route of appeal for bar associations and dissident lawyers, for all the legal challenges were thrown out at one stage or another. Preliminary injunctions were denied in the Washington, D.C.,[49] California[50] and Houston[51] cases and the lawsuits subsequently dropped. The Orlando complaint was dismissed outright because the lawyer-plaintiff and intervening bar associations lacked standing to challenge the Economic Opportunity Act.[52] The Philadelphia case went through a four-day hearing and resulted in a 54-page opinion, a ringing exoneration of the Legal Services Program which ended in these dramatic words:

> The sum of the matter is that the role of the legal profession is critical in the struggle against poverty to which the national effort is firmly committed. The public interest surely demands that role go forward with all possible speed and without delay. Let it begin—Now.[53]

Only in New York City did judges throw some obstacles in the path of the Legal Services Program. The bar was not the moving force because state law mandates that the courts automatically must review the proposed charter for every new legal aid program.[54] In late 1966, months after the first fiscal year ended for the Legal Services Program, an appellate court rejected the proposed charter for our largest program, New York City. Funded at an annual budget level exceeding $4 million, this agency actually consisted of an umbrella corporation that administered ten sub-corporations serving different sections of the metropolitan area. The court's principal concern, and the major reason it cited for turning down the application, was the complexity of the arrangement and the fact that the umbrella corporation would operate some law offices itself as well as overseeing the offices of the other ten. However, in its written opinion the court ranged far beyond this central issue, delivering itself of several observations about the proper goals, functions and philosophy of a Legal Services program.[55] The judges appeared to be especially skeptical about organizational representation by neighborhood lawyers and noted:

> [i]t would be one thing to allow neighborhood law offices to handle poor men's credit unions. It would be quite another to have them handle, advise, and represent political factions or organizations of social and economic protest, however worthy.[56]

Any encouragement the New York decision may have offered to opponents of Legal Services elsewhere in the country was short lived. A few months later, on October 10, 1967, the Appellate Department approved a new application filed by the New York agency, one which contained only minor revisions dealing primarily with program structure.[57] Representation of groups, test cases and legislative advocacy clearly remained permissible.

In sum, dissident bar associations and lawyers found their forays into the courts completely unrewarding. If the ABA was an undependable recourse because of its alliance with OEO, the courts were a complete dead end, principally because judges are bound by the law, and the Legal Services Program apparently was on a sound legal footing.

F. PRESSURE THROUGH FEDERAL LEGISLATORS. It was very late in the first fiscal year before dissatisfied parties began to complain to their local senators and congressmen. But during the summer of 1966, four programs— the Albuquerque legal aid society, a multi-county agency for Florida migrants, and two Michigan programs—became enmeshed in the snare of "congressional concern."

At the time, OEO was on a short leash and knew it. The agency's very existence was a year-to-year thing, dependent on passage of an annual authorization bill. Shriver expected his program heads, Legal Services included, to minimize friction with the legislative branch. This did not require capitulation to every demand merely because it was uttered by someone on Capitol Hill. It did mean explanation, negotiation, and sometimes compromise.

In several instances, a House member was mollified merely by a letter replying to allegations made by one of his constituents against OEO. In another case, the two disputed Michigan grants were settled by a personal meeting at the legislator's office between the Legal Services director, the complaining parties, and the congressman. None of these situations required concessions of any kind, merely a detailed rational defense of OEO's position.

The grant to Florida Migrant Legal Services, Inc., marked the first significant intrusion of the legislative branch into the affairs of the Legal Services Program. In late June, 1966, just days after the funding of the new agency, several small county bar associations prevailed on a majority of the Florida congressional delegation to urge suspension of the grant. Confronted by a powerful and pivotal bloc of House members, especially Tampa's Sam Gibbons, a leading Democrat on the committee with jurisdiction over OEO, Shriver complied. He then ordered the Legal Services staff to seek to work out a resolution that would satisfy the congressmen.

Negotiations over the Florida Migrant Legal Services grant lasted almost a year. Of course, the local bar associations were really the interested parties, and, as a first choice, they preferred the Program to be run through the county bars with their members being paid to render the assistance. However, they would be willing to settle for being permitted to select the majority of the board members of the regional agency.

Negotiations included meetings between the Legal Services director and the state bar president and his aides, several sessions with local bar officials, both in Washington and Florida, and frequent conferences with concerned congressmen. The ultimate compromise was accepted by all parties, with the notable exception of five of six local bar associations in the area ultimately served by the Program, and one of the three congressmen from that area. That was good enough for Shriver and he released the funds.[58]

Not every dissatisfied party could activate congressional pressure against OEO, for a congressman might realize that a majority of his constituents supported OEO projects, or he himself did, or he did not have much influence with the administration.

Even acknowledging the limitations, pressure through the Federal legislature was the single most effective form of resistance available to most groups unhappy with the outcome of a community confrontation over a Legal Services grant. If all the dissidents had succeeded in activating their senators and congressmen, the program's momentum would have been slowed down considerably. As the Florida migrant episode demonstrated, the time involved in negotiating out a score or so similar situations would have tied up at least half of the staff resources.

The salient fact is that during the first year most opponents did not take their appeals to Congress. Instead, they were drawn to one or more of the other alternatives discussed above. This presented the Program with the gift of time ... time in which to build momentum and establish a base of support in scores of communities represented by their own senators and congressmen.

C. The First Year Results

By April, 1966, we began to turn the corner. The opponents of Federal support for legal assistance were fresh out of arguments. The "Judicare" champions were on the defensive. The American Bar Association's power and commitment began affecting attitudes in scores of local bar associations. Possibly more important, we broke the internal OEO bureaucratic log-jam that had been holding up the processing of Legal Services applications.[59] Thus, in April, OEO was able to make 34 grants totalling over $6 million for Legal Services —more than the combined budgets of all then existing legal aid societies in the entire country. In May 1966, another $6 million was granted for Legal Services.

On June 28, 1966, Clint Bamberger completed his last day as director of the OEO Legal Services Program. After three weeks of agonizing introspection, Bamberger had decided to take up an offer to run for Attorney General in Maryland. By then we knew that the spring campaign had borne fruit far beyond our expectations. On June 30, the last day of the fiscal year, another 70 grants were signed, adding another $11 million to the nation's investment in legal services.

Our original goal for the first fiscal year had been 75 grants. But by that date fully 130 communities had received OEO funding for legal assistance programs and another 25 grants had been made to law schools, bar associations and similar groups to provide research support and training assistance to the operating agencies. Financial support for legal assistance to the poor had been increased from $5 million a year in 1965 to better than $25 million.

D. The Aftermath: Quelling Backlash in the Legal Profession

For several months before Bamberger resigned, a counterattack had been brewing against the Legal Services Program in several areas of the legal profession. Stifling this incipient movement became my initial challenge upon taking command of the program on June 29, 1966. I was originally appointed only as acting director. It soon was clear that my permanent status was closely tied to how well I handled these dissident elements in the organized bar. In the meantime, Shriver and the ABA were searching for another Bamberger—a 40-50-year-old lawyer from a prestige law firm. At 33 and with no private practice experience, I was perceived as probably too young and non-establishment to deal effectively with bar associations.

As early as December, 1965, the Tennessee State Bar Association had passed a resolution condemning the Legal Services Program and instructing its local associations not to participate.[60] Not much later, the Florida bar voted a similar resolution against the Program.[61] And in the summer of 1966, the North Carolina bar took the most radical stand—threatening to disbar any attorney who went to work for the newly founded Winston-Salem or Charlotte Legal Services projects.[62]

But the most dangerous threat to the national Program emanated from Al Cohn, the president-elect of the American Trial Lawyers Association (ATL). Cohn toured the country in the spring and summer of 1966 preaching about the horrors to be visited on the profession by the OEO Legal Services Program. Creating the illusion of documented fact through the use of charts, Cohn predicted a dismal future: the socialization of the legal profession, lower income for lawyers, a Federal dictatorship over legal assistance, and much more.[63] Ironically, he called for the substitution of "Judicare" for the OEO Program, despite the fact that "Judicare" meant putting every lawyer in the country on the Federal payroll, a questionable solution to the problem of socialization of the profession.[64]

What made Cohn's opposition so dangerous was his eminent position in the American Trial Lawyers. The ATL was a strong, national organization of some 25,000 lawyers—at the time about one-fifth as large as the ABA. Most of its members earned their living as plaintiff's counsel in personal injury litigation, representing people who have been hurt in accidents.

Since many of their own clients were poor, the ATL lawyers naturally feared competition from the OEO Legal Services Program, even though poverty attorneys did not take personal injury cases. They were a good audience for Cohn's innuendoes.

Al Cohn submitted a resolution condemning the OEO Legal Services Program to be voted on at the August, 1966 meeting of the ATL. If Cohn could mobilize his Association (he would be its president by the end of the summer) into wholehearted opposition to the Program, it was very likely to spark a national revolt among rank-and-file lawyers. There was no guarantee even the ABA leadership, or the precious resolution passed by the ABA in February, 1965, could survive.

Al Cohn's campaign and the growing state bar opposition in the South represented a real threat to the Legal Services Program. The staff of OEO decided to meet these challenges, first by means of a regional conference for bar leaders from the seven Southeastern states on July 15, 1966 in Atlanta. Then I asked the ATL for permission to address its board of governors at the August, 1966, convention prior to the decision on Al Cohn's proposed resolution.

The Southeastern Regional Conference attracted 200 local and state bar leaders—some interested, some inquisitive, some suspicious, and many very hostile. After the peaceful morning panel discussion was over, I began answering questions and was still doing so when the meeting broke for dinner that night. As it turned out, so much of the opposition and so many of the doubts sprung from a lack of information, inadequate information, and false information, that the conference produced a surprising number of converts to Legal Services.

Some of the rumors that passed for fact during the summer of 1966 included:

1. OEO lacked the congressional authority to fund Legal Services because it was not specifically listed in the Act. (Actually, the Community Action title used language broad enough to embrace legal services and the committee report made explicit the congressional finding that legal services was a permissible activity for OEO funding.[65])

2. The Legal Services Program was about to be ruled illegal by a court in Philadelphia. (As a matter of fact, the court decision came down shortly before the Southeast Regional meeting. As we observed earlier, the judge not only sanctioned the Program, he endorsed it.[66])

3. The Legal Services Program was a threat to the private bar because it gave free services to anyone earning less than $5500 a year, which would include most residents in many Southern communities. (In reality, eligibility standards were set individually for each community. Only in large Northern urban areas were those making around $5500 served. The national average was $3600 for a family of four.)

The president-elect of the Tennessee bar was startled by what he heard on the first day of the conference, for it bore no resemblance to the "facts" used to persuade the bar to pass that resolution against the Legal Services Program in 1965. As a result, he called the man who was president at the time and asked him to fly to Atlanta for the second day of the conference. The two of them then repeated some of the questions that had been vital to the deliberations surrounding the enactment of the condemnatory resolution. In October, 1966 the Tennessee State Bar explicitly rescinded its former position and came out in support of the OEO Legal Services Program.[67]

Shortly after the Atlanta conference, the Florida bar mellowed and most of the major cities in the state soon had programs.[68] And a few months later, the North Carolina Bar also reached an accommodation with the OEO Legal Services Program.[69]

The most important convert at the Atlanta meeting was Jack Travis, the president-elect of the Hines County (which includes Jackson), Mississippi Bar Association. Travis also happened to be on the Board of the American Trial Lawyers Association. He was one of its solid, conservative Southern members. As such, Travis became a key figure in future negotiations with the ATL leadership.

My speech to the ATL board was deliberately short, about fifteen minutes, followed with an hour of questions. As was true at the Southeastern conference, I was aided greatly by my opponents. Many of the erroneous rumors again were paraded before the board. When it was claimed that there had been no mention of legal services in the congressional debate on OEO, I could refute them by quoting directly from congressional reports. When opponents objected that the Legal Services Program was using unethical advertising, I could show that legal aid societies had been "advertising" for years and with the express sanction of the ABA Ethics Committee.

But the issue was not finally resolved by the discussion with ATL board members. Serious negotiations began that evening when Jack Travis, conservative Mississippi lawyer, sat down with Dean Robb, prominent Detroit trial lawyer who was a member of the National Lawyers Guild, Jack Fuchsberg of New York, and William Colson of Miami. (Both Fuchsberg and Colson had been presidents of the ATL and still wielded considerable influence in organization affairs.) When this group finished drafting a resolution endorsing the OEO Legal Services Program, Robb and Travis agreed this was the first time they could recall being on the same side of an issue confronting the ATL.

They showed the resolution to me; I agreed. Then the four sat down with Al Cohn and asked him if he would accept this and withdraw his own resolution. At first Cohn protested, arguing this statement was directly contrary to his proposal. But finally, he turned to Travis and said, "If even you aren't with me, I guess I can't win this one."

On June 24, 1966, with only one dissenting vote, the ATL Board of Governors passed a resolution endorsing the OEO Legal Services Program and asking for a seat on the National Advisory Committee.[70] A few months later, Jack Fuchsberg was appointed by Sargent Shriver as the first ATL representative on the Committee.

While the Legal Services staff pacified the Southern bar associations and the American Trial Lawyers, Shriver and the ABA had been scouting candidates to replace Bamberger. The bar association actually tendered a former state bar president to OEO. However, his personal interview with Shriver did not go well. A former ATL president fared better with the OEO director, but the ABA balked because of long-standing animosity toward the rival organization. This might have precipitated a critical test of the ABA's influence in Legal Services administration. It was averted, however, when personal problems unrelated to the Legal Services position compelled the ATL leader to withdraw his candidacy.

At the August, 1966, ABA convention in Montreal, John Cummiskey approached me about the Legal Services directorship. On the strength of my work over the summer, the ABA leaders had decided I could negotiate effectively with state and local bar association leaders, and shortly after the convention, Washington staff member Lowell Beck communicated to OEO the ABA consensus that my appointment should be made permanent.[71] But Shriver hesitated. He still wanted a private attorney with solid establishment credentials.

Then in late September, the White House sent over its own candidate for the position, a thirty-four-year-old Texan only recently graduated from law school. His major credential was a wealthy wife who had been very generous to the President's campaign treasury. Shriver was dissatisfied and, with some difficulty, he managed to avoid hiring the Administration nominee. The leaders of the ABA, however, were appalled, for they now saw the continuing vacancy was an open invitation to drag the entire Program into partisan politics.

With greater urgency, the bar leadership renewed their support for my candidacy. On October 2, on the eve of the annual NLADA convention, Shriver asked me to assume the permanent directorship of the Legal Services Program. I accepted and remained in the position until mid-July 1968.

The most significant aspect of these events was not that Shriver heeded the views of the ABA. He had done that when Bamberger was hired. What was important was the fact that the leadership of the association was willing to support someone clearly aligned with the neighborhood lawyer experiments rather than legal aid or the establishment bar. They would not have been a year earlier during the search for a new director. But Bamberger's tenure provided a transition. The leaders of the legal aid movement had seen someone like themselves, a lawyer from a major firm, absorb and advocate the rhetoric of reform. He had given the new concepts some respectability. My selection as Bamberger's replacement was the clearest evidence thus far that many ABA leaders had begun to acknowledge a broadened mission for the Legal Services Program.

III. THE OUTCOME: DIMENSIONS OF THE OEO LEGAL SERVICES PROGRAM

With the opposition of the American Trial Lawyers Association and state bar associations suppressed and a new permanent director finally installed, the OEO Legal Services Program resumed its energetic development and funding of new agencies. During the fiscal year between July 1, 1966 and June 30, 1967, OEO increased the number of Legal Services grants made during the first year from 155 to 300 agencies and the annual budget level from $25 million to over $40 million.

The following year, the financial drain of the Vietnam war and the unpopularity of the antipoverty war combined to slash the OEO budget. From that point forward, the Legal Services Program struggled merely to maintain its existing local agencies. It succeeded even while OEO was compelled to cut back most of its other operations. But as a result of the continuing budget problem, only a handful of new Legal Services agencies were established from mid-1967 at least through 1972.

A. Primary Characteristics of Grantees Funded in 1966–67

The three hundred grants had been spread over two hundred-ten separate communities. Nine of the ten largest cities had OEO funded law offices as did forty-six of the fifty largest. By mid-1967, every state except North Dakota and Alabama had at least one Legal Services Agency.[72]

1. Size and Delivery Systems

The agencies ranged in size from those with one lawyer, in places like Philadelphia, Ohio, to forty in Washington, D.C. Some individual agency budgets were as low as $30,000, and the largest single grant was made to California Rural Legal Assistance at an annual level of $1,200,000. But ten separate subagencies in New York City received $4,500,000, six in Los Angeles County were funded at over $1,500,000 and four in the San Francisco Bay Area at almost $2 million.

There were over 800 neighborhood law offices provided in the 210 communities. The New York City area alone included over 30 offices. Philadelphia had a dozen and Washington, D.C., had ten. But the median agency fit the following profile: an annual budget of $177,000, three neighborhood offices, a staff of seven attorneys, three clerical personnel and one community worker.[73] The average salary of staff attorneys was approximately $9500 and of agency directors about $12,000. These were modest incomes compared with earnings available in private practice, but they were approximately 45 percent higher than the salaries paid to lawyers in pre-OEO legal aid societies.

In most areas, service was delivered through neighborhood offices. But in a rural section of Oklahoma, a lawyer drove a van containing his secretary and library from one crossroad to another on a regular schedule. Legal Services attorneys in Hawaii flew to the smaller outlying islands on scheduled jets; those in Alaska took bush planes to remote villages. In rural Wisconsin, a New Haven neighborhood and a suburban area near Oakland, assistance was supplied by paying fees to private attorneys who lived in those communities. Lawyers on Indian reservations sometimes confronted unique problems. On the largest of these preserves, the huge Navaho reservation that spans parts of four states, only Indians were allowed to appear in tribal court. So the Legal Services Agency created a whole new career line for Navahos—lay counselors—who doubled as interpreters in the law offices and advocates before the tribal courts.

2. Eligibility Criteria for Free Legal Services

Only persons unable to afford private attorneys were eligible for help at Legal Services offices. These eligibility criteria were negotiated individually with each grantee. The standards tended to reflect factors such as the local cost of living, the fees charged by private attorneys, and the size and location of the community. In some rural areas, especially in the South, a family of four had to earn less than $2200 a year to be eligible for legal assistance. Yet in some Northern cities—Philadelphia, New York, Washington, D.C., for example—a family could earn $5500 and be deemed needy for free legal services. The median standard for a four-member unit was close to $3600 per annum.[74]

3. Composition of the Governing Bodies of Local Agencies

The local agencies, of course, were governed by boards of directors. On the average, about a third of the members of these boards were representatives of the poor. About 55 percent were lawyers, but not all of these were chosen by the organized bar. Many were picked by law schools, or liberal legal groups such as the ACLU. The remaining 10 percent of the Legal Services boards tended to be middle-class laymen representing the Community Action Agency, ethnic organizations such as the NAACP, local government, and liberal volunteer groups.[75]

B. Policy Implications of Funding Policies During 1966 and 1967

In an early decision, the Legal Services staff determined to establish a national system of law offices in the shortest possible time. This choice was not based on any lack of regard for careful hand-crafting of local Legal Services agencies.[76] But we felt it essential to capitalize on the favorable climate created by the official ABA endorsement and the intense commitment exhibited by the reigning leaders of the organized bar. If it took the OEO Program three or four years to establish outposts in the most important communities, the aura of the ABA resolution might fade and the association leadership certainly would turn over. Thus, we foresaw a definite risk that opposition would drown the Program before legal services could be brought to the poor people of the nation.

Money was an even worse gamble. In fiscal 1966, local communities already were asking for more funds to support various antipoverty programs than the total appropriation OEO had received from Congress. Even this early, it was clear that in the future, most of the poverty agency's budget would be absorbed by the needs of refinancing existing grantees. Thus, the only money the Legal Services Program could count on after June 30, 1966 was what it took to re-fund the grantees it had in place on that date.

It was our estimate that if a nationwide Federal legal assistance movement was to be mounted, we must seize the moment.

One important implication of this decision was the advantage it gave to pre-existing organizations, usually legal aid societies that were ready-made vehicles for operating a Legal Services program. There seldom was time to create a new institution in a local community. As a consequence, over forty percent of the 1966 OEO grantees were established legal aid societies.[77] The proportion went down only negligibly in 1967.[78]

The urgent eighteen-month drive to institutionalize Federally assisted legal services for the poor did more than favor existing legal aid societies and bar-sponsored entities. On the plus side, it built a broad political base for the Program. Virtually every sizable city, state and congressional district was covered by poverty lawyers. Hundreds of bar associations, community action agencies and poverty organizations were actively involved in the Program. When opposition mounted against a controversial agency like California Rural Legal Assistance or when the entire Federal effort came under assault as it did in 1967, 1969, 1970 and 1972, influential supporters involved in local programs throughout the nation rallied to the defense. Even otherwise mediocre legal aid organizations frequently performed admirably to help shield the more vigorous agencies from political attack.[79]

In retrospect, it also is clear that without the intense pace of the 1966–67 funding campaign, few communities would presently offer any Federally funded legal assistance for the poor. Our worst fears about the OEO budget were realized. The first eighteen months, in fact, turned out to be all the time we had to plant the agencies that now comprise the Legal Services Program.[80]

On the other hand, there is no doubt the Legal Services staff paid a price for its rapid development of the Program's operating structure. We were committed to building a national institution overnight and could not afford to screen grantees through a fine mesh. As a result, many agencies were funded that lacked the philosophical orientation or personnel to carry out the antipoverty mission embodied in the experimental neighborhood lawyer programs described in Chapter 2. This fact has been noted by several commentators,[81] and a subsequent survey confirmed that only 23 percent of the Legal Services boards supported the use of agency resources to achieve legal change.[82]

In point of fact, at this early date the Legal Services Program possessed no specific priorities and goals for implementing its general aspiration to reduce poverty. As discussed in Chapter 2, the neighborhood lawyer programs had not produced a unified philosophy or a single prescription for eliminating poverty, but rather a portfolio of themes, many contradictory.[83] Without some template to superimpose on the sponsor's promises, motives and design features, it would have been difficult to accurately predict which agencies would effectively carry out the full mission of the OEO Program.

Nevertheless, the Legal Services staff was aware that many of its grantees were risky investments from the viewpoint of the war on poverty. We were confident, however, that we could work with these agencies in some still undefined ways to make them effective instruments of social progress. The institution-building phase was complete. The institution-shaping process was yet to begin.

Part III: The Management of the Program

Chapter 5: The Policy-Making Process
in the Legal Services Program

Chapter 6: "Up the Bureaucracy":
Preserving Policy and Program Integrity
within the OEO Administration

Chapter 7: Implementing National Goals:
Affecting the Management
of Local Organizations

In describing the history that preceded and birthed the OEO Legal Services Program, I have presented events chronologically. But in Part III, each chapter traces the entire development of a discrete aspect of program management. Together these measures largely shaped the ultimate philosophy and performance of this new institution.

In Chapter 5, we consider how policy was made in the OEO Legal Services Program. We also discuss what those decisions were and evaluate some of the more important ones. Chapter 6 recounts the strenuous conflict within OEO over who was to control the Program, its policies and grants. We learn why Legal Services advocates and OEO officials alike cared so much about this issue, the tactics employed and the adverse effects of this constant warfare on the smooth administration of the Program. Finally, in Chapter 7, we examine the most crucial problem facing the Federal grant-maker: how to attain a reasonable level of performance from local agencies.

Since all three chapters span both Bamberger's administration and my own, it may be confusing to the reader as to who was in charge when a given decision was made. Just remember that the first director served from September, 1965 through June 28, 1966, and I occupied the position from June 29, 1966, until July 5, 1968.

5: The Policy-Making Process in the Legal Services Program

The Economic Opportunity Act—the statutory framework of the war on poverty—afforded broad discretionary powers to the administration of the Office of Economic Opportunity. The OEO could provide or withhold financial assistance to local antipoverty organizations on almost any basis it desired. Although inherently limited in its ability to determine grantee performance,[1] OEO certainly could shape their promises. It could choose to favor certain poverty cures and program features and deny financial aid to others; it was in a position to set minimum standards and establish high goals. But this power was seldom employed. For the most part, OEO deferred to local Community Action Agencies to set their own priorities and design their own solutions to poverty.

The reluctance of the staff of OEO to establish strong national policies was derived from the local orientation of the community action concept. Some OEO officials held an almost religious reverence for the preferences of local Community Action Agencies. This stance often was taken at the expense of the poor (who usually were outvoted in the councils of local CAAs) and the effectiveness of the antipoverty effort (because CAAs tended to stress low-impact, uncontroversial programs and to repeat the errors of other CAAs).

The Legal Services Program represented not the first—but probably the most pronounced—departure from the theory that antipoverty programming had to be determined entirely at the local level. Many issues that in other programs would have been left to the local agencies were resolved instead at the national level. Why? The motivation can be traced primarily to the legal profession's distrust of local Community Action Agencies and the OEO Legal Services staff's concerns about local bar associations. The ABA sought guarantees in the form of national policy that OEO-funded attorneys would adhere to professional standards and that they would not compete with the private bar. The Legal Services staff wanted assurances that poverty lawyers would undertake all types of cases, and that the poor would have a meaningful voice in agency management, among others. Thus, there was a common interest in the formulation of a strong statement of national policy.

In this chapter, we consider the development of national standards and goals during the first 20 months of the OEO Legal Services Program (from November 1965 to June 30, 1967). By the end of this period, the basic issues were resolved, the goals established, the course set. Moreover, at least through the end of 1973, these policies remained almost unchanged and nothing fundamental had been added.

National policy making went through two phases in the period between 1965 and 1967. The first took three months, from November 1965 through the end of January 1966, when a formal statement was published. From then on, policies were generated through an informal process that will be described later. In many instances, these latter positions touched issues more crucial than those covered in the printed document.

The first phase culminated in a booklet entitled *Guidelines for a Legal Services Program*. The *Guidelines* were to present the principles the government would follow in funding proposals forwarded to it, and to give applicants the limitations and goals to be adhered to if they were to receive favorable consideration. The drafting, review and approval of this publication absorbed the attention of the Legal Services staff and the National Advisory Committee for much of the first three months of the Program's existence.

I. FORMULATION OF LEGAL SERVICES GUIDELINES

Shriver had promised the ABA a policy role in the Legal Services Program through membership on the National Advisory Committee.[2] The preparation of the guidelines for the Legal Services Program was to be the single most important policy-making event. Thus, it was only natural the National Advisory Committee was to be included in the process of creating the basic document. All of this was decided before Bamberger arrived at OEO to become the first national director. He was skeptical about the entire concept of a national advisory committee and worried about its role in the formulation of the *Guidelines*. "It was my neck on the line, my professional reputation at stake," Bamberger observed later. "I didn't want to release control of the Program to that group, or anybody else."[3]

Confronted with the reality of a National Advisory Committee (NAC) and a meeting of that body to consider a draft of the *Guidelines*, Bamberger decided to appoint himself as chairman of the NAC, to avoid resolutions and votes, to promote a full panoply of non-policy roles for NAC members, and otherwise to divert the committee from exercising an independent voice in policy making.[4]

Bamberger discussed his plans for the National Advisory Committee with Edgar Cahn, at that time still a special assistant to Shriver. He fully expected

Cahn to agree with his strategy. But Cahn surprised the new Legal Services director by stating he felt that Bamberger should be more willing to share his authority with the NAC in a meaningful way. Bamberger was impressed both with Cahn's specific advice about the NAC and his underlying rationale—the desirability of sharing power. This led Bamberger to approach the first NAC meeting with a more open, although still somewhat cautious, view of its role.[5]

The National Advisory Committee to the OEO Legal Services Program was not as monolithic as Bamberger initially feared. Its membership did include ABA president Ed Kuhn, ABA president-elect Orison Marden, ABA past-president Lewis Powell, NLADA president Theodore Voorhees, and several others from the hierarchy of the organized bar. But there also was representation from the neighborhood lawyer experiments: Jean Cahn, Gary Bellow, and Bruce Terris (the Attorney General's representative). Their viewpoint was shared by Soia Mentschikoff, a New Dealer turned law professor, and Elizabeth Wickenden, whom you will recall as an originator of the idea of using test cases to attack economic problems. The middle ground was occupied by Jerome Shestack, a partner in a major Philadelphia law firm. He was a key influence in committee deliberations because of his impeccable establishment credentials (his senior partner, Bernard Segal, became ABA president in 1969) coupled with a progressive attitude on most issues facing the NAC.

Actually, several important policies were incorporated in the *Guidelines* without provoking any controversy between the two camps on the NAC. The principal ones included:

1. Legal Services grantees were to accept all categories of civil cases, a departure from prevailing legal aid policy which excluded most divorce cases and bankruptcies. (*Guidelines* at p. 11)

2. Representation was to be provided in felony cases only on a temporary demonstration basis and even in misdemeanor cases only in jurisdictions where the state government fails to provide adequate services. (*Guidelines* at p. 13)

3. Legal Services grantees were to be governed by separate boards of directors rather than the CAA's. (*Guidelines* at p. 7) This policy reflected the concerns of both legal aiders and neighborhood lawyer exponents that legal services be free of the interests typically reflected on CAA policy-making bodies.[6] It is an example of a concession the Program staff could never have extracted out of the OEO bureaucracy without the leverage provided by the organized bar.

4. Offices were to be accessible, which in most cases meant decentralized neighborhood law offices (*Guidelines* at p. 21), and attorneys to be paid salaries comparable with lawyers in the community who possessed similar levels of experience. (*Guidelines* at p. 23)

The NAC deliberations on the Legal Services *Guidelines* centered on two issues. One of these divided the committee members; the other brought them together. (Another critical policy question was resolved, but without dispute.)

A. Representation of the Poverty Community on Legal Services Boards

The first meeting of the National Advisory Committee was held on November 11, 1965, and the draft *Guidelines* were submitted for discussion. The most crucial and controversial provision sought to implement the general statutory requirement that poor people be afforded "maximum feasible participation" in the operation of programs aimed at helping them. In the draft it was suggested that "meaningful participation of the residents of the areas served may be secured in several possible manners." The possibilities included representation on the boards of Legal Services agencies; creation of advisory boards; and, employment of the poor on the agency staff.[7] There was a latent ambiguity in the draft *Guidelines,* however. Were the several possible manners alternative methods for satisfying the "maximum feasible participation" requirement? Or were they all mandatory?

Bamberger knew the provision suggesting representation of the poor on agency boards was a fearsome prospect to existing legal aid societies. They would be required to restructure their boards and thereby disrupt long-standing relationships. He also knew it was a sore point with many local bar associations who resented the idea of laymen—especially impoverished laymen —sitting in a management capacity over members of their profession. He fully expected the representatives of the ABA and NLADA to express these fears and prejudices. Thus, Bamberger introduced the topic gingerly.

> Now I throw this out and *I'm willing to have the idea discarded.*[8] I am not personally convinced that representation of the poor on the board is always the best way to get this. . . .
>
> It would seem to me that in some instances you might really get a better involvement of the poor by creating effective advisory bodies, providing them with the kind of support they need to say what they want to say, and to guarantee that it must be heard by the policy-making board, that the policy-making board must act on it, and that there be some way that all of this evidence is documented.[9]
>
> . . . Now that's why on the fifth page we—having set out the objective—then set out four ways . . . in which we thought that this kind of, in my mind, absolutely necessary participation of the poor in the policy-making and evaluation of legal services programs must be accomplished.[10]

If Bamberger's tone sounds hesitant, consider that he was proposing what was still unthinkable by most of the legal profession. It is easy to forget— almost within minutes after they are accepted—just how unacceptable some ideas once were. At the time Bamberger introduced this provision, there were no Legal Services agencies in existence that actually had poverty representatives on their board of directors.

Orison Marden, president-elect of the ABA (and a former NLADA president) was quick to seize upon the equivocation in Bamberger's statement:

... I agree with your philosophy a hundred percent. I think that the poor should be involved, but they can be more effectively involved really through advisory boards. . . . You would be getting closer to the situation that way than you will having three or four so-called representatives who would be sitting like dummies on the board, in all probability. It's like putting laymen on a medical board. They can be an advisory board for a hospital. . . . But so far as the technical operation of the profession, you don't put laymen on. I don't see much harm in it, but I don't think it does much good. I think your idea is much better.

Bamberger moved quickly to clarify his position.

Well, that "and"—I never say "and/or." I always say either "and" or "or," and I said "and" there deliberately, because I'm concerned with saying—if we say the "or," there will never be a proposal for poor on the policy-making board."

Another ABA representative then expressed his fears about the reaction of legal aid societies and local bar associations.

[T]he Legal Aid bureaus with which I'm familiar have a continuing problem of raising funds. Their boards, in the main, are made up of people who have demonstrated an ability to go out and get money, plus a few lawyers who provide a little policy-making know-how for them in providing legal services.
. . . But I would be mightily afraid that if you had to break down an existing legal aid board and add three or four people who properly could be regarded as representatives of the poor who are going to be served, . . . that you create a very real difficulty for the continuation of the existing program of any given legal aid organization.
Now, when you come to the Bar Association, it would be impossible.
You may have real difficulties not only in initiating local programs but in getting them adopted and processed.

Other members of the ABA and NLADA supported this point, and representation of the poor began to look more and more like a very unpopular, impractical concept. Finally Bruce Terris spoke out.

This is a subject I feel quite strongly about and . . . I don't think I'm in agreement with any of the people who have talked up to now.
I must say that I really think that people would have quite a different view if they'd ever sat through some meetings of advisory committees in which the poor participated.
[T]hey're smart enough and we're smart enough to know that there's a difference between advisory committees and the guy that makes a decision. I think we all realize the difference here between you [referring to Bamberger] who make the decision and we who can give some advice. They recognize it just as well as we do.
I think you have got to make a very clear choice, and that is whether you're going to consider the poor as a real integral part of the program, or are you going to continue the system . . . we've run in this country in the past—legal services

and others the same—of giving services to the poor. We give them; you receive them; we'll listen to your advice.

It was obvious Terris was advocating a harder line than contemplated in the draft *Guidelines* provision. Bamberger probed to find out just how far Terris wanted to go: "Well then, are you speaking for the proposition that there ought to be an absolute requirement that they, the poor—the people to be served—be on the policy-making boards?"

Terris replied, "Absolute may be too strong. You never know when there may be some justification. But I would put the burden of justification on the proponents who said, 'we have some special circumstances.' "

Gary Bellow then backed up Terris.

> There is a notion that, one, it doesn't make any difference, and, two, that it wouldn't be helpful. . . .
>
> Last night in the UPO [local community action agency of which Bellow was then Deputy Director] advisory committee meeting there was a discussion about how much power the advisory committee had in UPO. And after a great deal of argument in which they felt they didn't have any power, one person stood up and said, "Well, we've got ten votes on that 40-man UPO board, and if we can get ten other people to go along with us, then we have real power."
>
> I wouldn't feel so strongly about that if I hadn't begun to see the kinds of contributions the poor can make. Poor people have told me that lawyers tell them that they don't help them because they don't want to aggravate some judge. That's a very useful thing to hear, and not one you usually hear from anyone but the people who are affected.

Then, from an unexpected source, came a suggestion that one category of Legal Services agencies—those run through existing legal aid societies—be relieved of any requirement that the poor be represented, at least for a period of time. Jean Cahn made the proposal in these terms.

> I have a feeling that there are two separate problems. One is what do we do about the old-line agencies that have been in existence all this time. . . . If you try to get them to adopt the program . . . they won't adopt the program usually, rather than come in with poor people on the board. Or will you go along with them, say, for a year with the program on the condition that the second year, poor people go on the board? . . . Now, that, I feel, is a reasonable kind of alternative for these agencies that have been in existence.

In what was to become a familiar role, Jerome Shestack, the man who lived in both camps, began to draw the ABA representatives and the legal activists together. He started by soothing the fears of the bar leaders.

> Just to share with you Philadelphia's experience, when we were first given the impression that they had to have actually four members of the community on the board, . . . the board didn't resist it too strongly because frankly the leader of

the Bar didn't think any of those poor people were going to make any difference, and there are going to be eight people from the bar association represented, and they would control the policy-making. So they figured that . . . if that's what you need to get money, okay, we'll do it. It wouldn't make any difference.

Now I suspect that in time the eight members of the Bar Association will have the same experience that Mr. Bellow mentioned, . . . and then there won't be any resistance in the future and it won't be merely a token acceptance of the principle but an acceptance of the idea itself.

With the issue of practicality apparently resolved, Robert Ming, a black lawyer from Chicago, surfaced the problem of elitism. "What lawyer worth his salt is going to let a group of laymen, poor or rich, tell him how to utilize his legal services?"

To this point, Mrs. Cahn retorted, "With all due respect to you, these boards have been sitting with lay people on them for years and years and years." (She was referring to the common practice of appointing wealthy or influential laymen to the boards of legal aid societies.)

As the meeting wore on, the opponents of representation of the poor seemed to be running low on arguments. One of them finally elaborated on Ming's point about lay control of the lawyer's professional performance.

Well, Mr. Director, I want to raise a technical legal question. We've got a lot of law around the United States about the practice of law by people other than members of the Bar. . . . And from the discussion that I'm listening to I'm wondering if a legal program that satisfied these statutory requirements wouldn't violate some state law about who may practice law in the state.

By this stage of the meeting, Bamberger had moved from a position of tentative support to wholehearted advocacy of representation of the poor on Legal Services boards. He artfully threw this question to John Cummiskey: "Well, I don't think that Legal Aid Societies which have existed with lay people making policy on their board have violated any of those statutes and I think frankly there have been adjudications about that. Is that right, Mr. Cummiskey?" Cummiskey replied: "Yes."

Then Professor Soia Mentschikoff's calm voice settled the issue.

. . . I assume that if a board of *lawyers* began to tell me how I should represent a particular client, I would tell the same thing to them that I would tell a bunch of poor people. So I don't think you're even talking about a board which could interfere with the lawyer-client relationship. . . .

You're dealing with different kinds of problems, what kinds of cases they represent in a general way, what kind of people that they choose to serve.

Bamberger nodded, "That's what I mean."

With Bamberger's response, the discussion of the issue of representation of the poor on Legal Services boards was concluded. There was no vote, but the proponents clearly had carried the day, primarily because they were able to counter conjecture with fact and smother fear with reality. Attempts to frame it as a practical impossibility or illegal proposal simply failed. Bamberger, who entered the meeting with his own serious doubts about the wisdom of requiring representation of the poor, emerged with a strong conviction of its necessity.

The *Guidelines* provision was redrafted to remove any ambiguity about the requirement that representatives of the poor must be included on the policy-making boards of local Legal Services projects.

> Policy for the legal assistance program must be formulated with the participation of the "residents of the areas and members of the groups served." As explained in the preceding section of this pamphlet, the legal services program will have in most instances an autonomous policy-making board separate from the governing body of the community action agency. The poor must be represented on the board or policy-making committee of the program to provide legal services, just as they are represented on the policy-making body of the community action agency.[11]

In subsequent months, the participation of poverty community representatives on Legal Services agency boards turned out to be the single most controversial guideline (though not the most controversial policy).[12]

It may be debatable whether these representatives contributed much to board deliberations. But even if they did not, the importance of this particular guideline cannot be overestimated. As often happens, a basic philosophical stance developed out of a decision on a peripheral issue.

Board membership for the client community was not a central tenet of the neighborhood lawyer ideology, a fact tipped off by Jean Cahn's flexibility on the question. None of the existing programs even had poor people on their governing bodies. But the policy became significant because it represented a major departure from traditional legal aid thinking. It marked the OEO Legal Services Program as something new and different. From the very beginning, it confronted legal aid societies interested in acquiring Federal funds with the necessity of reorienting old structures and existing patterns of doing things. Undoubtedly this prospect turned some societies away from OEO. But many others accepted the bargain and thereby became more receptive, flexible institutions.

B. Avoidance of a National Means Test

The second meeting of the NAC was held on January 4, 1966, and considered a guideline that had not been incorporated in the earlier draft.

During December, Joseph Kershaw, OEO's director of research and planning, lunched with Bamberger several times, building a case for a single, uniform eligibility standard for Legal Services clients. Kershaw, along with the general counsel's office, wanted to bring all OEO programs into conformance with the official government definition of a family that would be considered poor, at that time an urban family of four that had an income of $3155 a year. His arguments sounded persuasive. To maximize its impact, OEO should concentrate its resources on the lowest income group. Too many government programs originally designed to benefit the poor eventually had diluted their efforts, serving the near-poor and even the middle class. More than any earlier social agency, OEO's focus was the poor. We have a definition of our target community, let's stick to it.[13]

Impressed by Kershaw's logic yet not totally convinced, Bamberger agreed to submit a draft guideline on the subject to the NAC. But he did not promise to personally endorse or argue for the agency position. Anthony Partridge, OEO deputy general counsel, was chosen to present the draft guideline to the committee meeting.

After reading the proposal and listening attentively to the Partridge justification, the NAC almost to a man (and woman) raised their hands for recognition. The legal activists did not want to accept the government definition for poverty as a guide. Neighborhood lawyers had charged that legal aid societies had turned away many who were needy because they set their criteria on income very low. To restrict the OEO Program in the same way would thwart one of the reforms the lawyers hoped to achieve.

The proponents of legal aid were equally upset. NLADA president Voorhees recounted the long-term campaign waged by national leaders to persuade local legal aid societies to raise their eligibility standards. "And now, when we've finally gotten reasonable standards in some cities,[14] OEO threatens to set us back decades." Other bar leaders backed up the Voorhees position.

The legal activists and supporters of legal aid had found a common cause. They maintained the pressure. After hours of parrying with Partridge,[15] a resolution condemning the proposed guideline was introduced and passed unanimously. Kershaw and the general counsel's office relented and withdrew the uniform national means test.[16] In its stead, the Legal Services staff promised to prepare a statement of "principles."[17] Specific criteria concerning client eligibility were to be negotiated separately with each agency that was to receive a grant.

To a student of group dynamics, the January 4 NAC meeting would have been fascinating. For the first time, the diverse elements on the committee coalesced around an issue and with that unity moved OEO decision makers. More important, perhaps, the NAC membership had become a true group, with inward loyalty as well as commitment to their outside constituents. Thereafter, they emphasized issues on which the committee could reach a consensus and refused to be drawn into divisive controversy.

C. Advocacy of Reform and Representation of Poverty Organizations

During the year preceding Bamberger's employment as Legal Services director, OEO had prepared several sets of "tentative" guidelines for the Legal
Services Program. But the draft guidelines submitted to the first National
Advisory Committee meeting were not merely a rewrite of these earlier versions. Martin Wolf, a consultant from Los Angeles, was assigned the responsibility of producing a new rough draft. By design, this draft constituted a new
start at the task of stating the basic policy of the Legal Services Program. In
the main, this proved a wise strategy because it dissipated most of the opposition that had crystallized around some of the specific language used in earlier
drafts without, in most cases, disturbing the underlying concepts. But it did
result in one drastic—almost disastrous—omission.

All drafts of the guidelines that had been prepared before Bamberger became
director had included a powerful endorsement of two specific phases of advocacy—the reform of laws and practices unfavorable to the poor and the
representation of groups and organizations of poor people (as distinguished
from limiting representation to individual poor people).[18]

Inadvertently, Wolf omitted any reference either to reform or representation
of groups. Since we deliberately were disregarding earlier versions, Bamberger
and I did not spot this in our review and rewrite of the Wolf draft. Nor did
any of the National Advisory Committee members mention it either in written
comments or during the detailed discussions of the guidelines at the November
and January meetings.[19]

In mid-January 1965 the final draft of the guidelines had been completed
and was about to be sent to the printers when Ken Pye, associate dean of
Georgetown Law Center, stepped into my office. "I have something I'd like
to check out with you, Earl," he said, handing me a thick manuscript. "I know
you don't have time to read the whole thing. But this is an article I've been
writing for *Law and Contemporary Problems.* Will you take a look at this page
and the two or three following it, and let me know if it's still true. The article
is overdue already. That's why I'm in such a rush."

I then skimmed the relevant parts of Pye's manuscript.

> . . . In the spring the [draft] Guidelines had stressed the desirability of providing
> representation for "organizations of the poor such as credit unions, cooperatives,
> and block clubs" both in organizing and litigating.
> [In the draft guidelines Bamberger submitted to the NAC] no mention was
> made of law reform or group representation. While it was again made clear that
> one of the criteria for evaluating the program would be the contribution that it
> has made to eliminate the causes and effects of poverty, it was not suggested how
> any long range effect could be accompanied without substantial involvement in
> law reform or group organization and representation.

• • •

However, there certainly has been no emphasis placed upon achieving institutional change through group organization and representation and efforts aimed at law reform. It seems to have been assumed that these objectives can be achieved by a program in which principal emphasis is placed on providing lawyers to those in need. The result may be an unintended de-emphasis upon action aimed at the elimination of the causes and effects of poverty.[20]

Pye's analysis of the successive drafts of the guidelines picked up the omission no one had found. I told Pye his statement was still valid—the current draft of the guidelines contained no references to law reform or representation of groups of the poor. But I assured him the omission was inadvertent. To bolster that statement I showed him a publication I was preparing at the time —a booklet entitled "How to Apply for a Legal Services Program." This was a detailed set of instructions and a format for grant applications. Sections in the draft *required* the members of a local organization to specify precisely how they proposed to reform the laws and practices injurious to the poor and to provide for representation of groups. But I could not dispute that these were vital concepts that should have been introduced in the guidelines.

Bamberger and I worried over Pye's article for several days. With the guidelines expected at the printers imminently, it was an awkward time to insert such basic—and potentially controversial—language. Time was running out on the 1966 fiscal year. If the guidelines were not published and in the hands of potential applicants within a few more weeks, there would be no chance of funding a significant number of Legal Services projects before June 30. Thus, we could ill afford an uprising of National Advisory Committee members that would result in a demand for yet another committee meeting. At the same time, if we published guidelines that did not require advocacy of reform and representation of groups, we could undercut our efforts to reshape the legal aid movement, for it would be much more difficult to insist on compliance if these requirements were omitted from the basic policy statement of the Program.

Bamberger elected to risk delay. We drafted sections for the guidelines that required Legal Services attorneys to engage in these two special forms of advocacy. To reduce the chance of opposition, we attempted to couch these sections in language that would answer the more obvious and legitimate concerns of bar members.

> Free legal services should be available to organizations composed primarily of residents of the areas and members of the groups served. However, the services should not be provided if the organization is able to retain an attorney for the type of representation it seeks. By pooling their resources, a group of individuals may be able to afford counsel in cases where an individual could not. At the same time, the combined resources of the members of an organization may be insufficient to

retain an attorney to handle the particular legal problem in which the organization requires representation. A flexible standard should be applied. The factors to be considered include the size of the organization, the relative poverty of the members of the organization, and the cost of the legal assistance which the organization desires. . . . .

Advocacy of appropriate reforms in statutes, regulations, and administrative practices is a part of the traditional role of the lawyer and should be among the services afforded by the program. This may include judicial challenge to particular practices and regulations, research into conflicting or discriminating applications of laws or administrative rules, and proposals for administrative and legislative changes.[21]

The *Guidelines* were sent out for one more round of comments from National Advisory Committee members. Fortunately, no one challenged the new language or the need for an expression of the necessity of advocating reform and representation of groups.

Shortly thereafter, the *Legal Services Guidelines* was issued. It was a relatively progressive statement of the minimum program requirements and reasonably ambitious goals[22] that had the support of the organized bar (which, as we saw in Chapter 4, was of inestimable value in persuading local bar associations to embrace Legal Services programs).[23]

II. "COMMON LAW" POLICY MAKING IN THE LEGAL SERVICES PROGRAM

Once the *Guidelines* and *How to Apply for a Legal Services Program* booklets were issued, policy making for the Legal Services Program entered a new phase. Deliberately, we chose not to issue detailed binding regulations to elaborate on the basic principles laid down in the *Guidelines.* Instead, drawing on our experience with a process familiar to all lawyers—the common law system—we treated each application as a separate case. Policy evolved in the same way legal principles evolve, through decisions in individual cases. The *Guidelines* book was our constitution; the regional Legal Services personnel lower court judges; and the headquarters office the appellate court.

This approach to policy formulation seemed appropriate to the demands of the Program in its beginning stages. Clearing the *Guidelines* and *How to Apply* booklets through the OEO bureaucracy had exposed that as a time-consuming procedure. A formal policy pronouncement was likely to be irrelevant or even outmoded before it could make its way through the OEO maze and be issued as a so-called *CAP Memo*—the designation given OEO regulations. (An example: the proposal to raise the amount credited to local programs for the contributed time of private attorneys took over 18 months from the initial draft until its ultimate issuance.)

The "common law" process also minimized the possibility that certain unproven approaches would be frozen prematurely in published regulations. With so little known at this early stage about which program characteristics were essential to a successful Legal Services project and which features were relatively unimportant, we felt ill-prepared to create a complete system of detailed policy pronouncements. The process we adopted promoted flexibility and facilitated experimentation. We could approve a certain type of program in one community and refuse to fund it someplace else.

As experience began to validate some particular general principle, the headquarters staff would be advised to apply the "rule" to every application submitted for approval. If a regional Legal Services director desired to ask for an exception for some community, he could make an "appeal" to Bamberger or myself. Almost like an appellate court we would hear his argument attempting to distinguish the present case from the communities out of which the "rule" had evolved. Few rules were held to be absolutely binding in each and every case. There always was the possibility of granting an exception if the circumstances justified.[24]

The "common law" process was not without its price. The reverse side of flexibility is inconsistency. In the absence of written policy regulations, regional Legal Services personnel had unprecedented latitude—particularly with respect to the details of local projects. The headquarters staff reviewed and modified each application to make it conform to a relatively loose standard of uniformity. But some considerable and sometimes undesirable variations crept into Legal Services policy—in part because of the absence of a detailed "code" dictated from the national office.

The normal process of policy formulation I have described was sufficient for most issues. But sometimes the question was of such consequence that we were compelled to create binding, publicly announced principles. Even then, we avoided the internal OEO bureaucratic process wherever possible. And here again, the National Advisory Committee proved of value. Once there was a consensus of NAC members on a given issue, a speech by the Legal Services director was the equivalent of a formal OEO policy pronouncement as far as our constituencies—the Legal Services agencies and bar associations—were concerned. This phase of policy making and legitimation is illustrated by the handling of the Judicare question.

A. The "Containment" of Judicare

Before the formal *Guidelines* booklet was even returned from the printers, the state bar association of Wisconsin raised a question that the published policy statement did not consider. Philip Haberman, executive secretary of the Wisconsin Bar, proposed a program called Judicare and asked for a million dollars in Federal funds.

Judicare, like its namesake Medicare, relied on compensating private practitioners to provide the professional service. This contrasted with all legal aid offices and the new generation of neighborhood law offices which used full-time or part-time salaried attorneys. The basic idea of paying fees to private counsel for their representation of the poor was borrowed from the British Legal Aid and Advice Act of 1949. But the Wisconsin Bar had given its version a uniquely American flavor by incorporating a "credit card" feature.

Under the Judicare plan, a cardholder could go to any participating private attorney and receive services from that attorney on the same basis as a fee-paying client. When the attorney completed his services for the Judicare client, he was merely to forward a bill to the Federally-financed Judicare fund for payment.

Even before the Wisconsin State Bar Judicare proposal was actually received in the Legal Services office, Bamberger was bombarded with telephone calls from Wisconsin congressmen urging the immediate funding of this "important program."[25] The intense congressional interest alerted us that this was not to be a routine proposal. In a memorandum to Bamberger, I raised several questions about the Judicare concept: the private lawyer's lack of expertise in the legal problems of the poor; possible conflicts of interest between the poor and wealthy present or potential clients of these lawyers; and the inability to identify patterns of abuse or to carry out a legal strategy to remedy those abuses. On this basis I suggested we reduce the Wisconsin program to a small experiment, fund it along with two or three other Judicare proposals and postpone consideration of further Judicare programs until these could be evaluated.[26]

Bamberger readily concurred. He already sensed support for Judicare welling up among state and local bar associations around the nation. He had learned that the Connecticut state bar was preparing an application involving a Judicare proposal and other associations were considering that step. Bamberger could foresee that "We won't see anything but 'Judicare' ever again unless we do something about it."

Bamberger decided it was imperative to make his position on Judicare public at the earliest moment. He sounded out several leaders in the ABA and NLADA on the issue. To a man, they were wary of a compensated private counsel system. This attitude might seem anomalous, especially on the part of the hierarchy of the organized bar, whose primary constituency consists of the private attorneys of the nation. On closer examination, it is not so surprising. Bear in mind that at this particular moment most ABA leaders had been part of the legal aid movement. They had long fought to convince local bar associations of the virtues of providing legal assistance with paid staffs as opposed to loosely constructed volunteer panels of private attorneys.[27] To proponents of legal aid, Judicare appeared almost indistinguishable from the panel system. Their own previous analysis made them suspicious of any system which relied exclusively on the ad hoc efforts of private attorneys and fearful of a strong Federal initiative in this direction.

Other bar leaders had other, more personal reasons for opposing a heavy investment in Judicare. They harbored a low regard for the calibre and motives of the practitioners most likely to represent the poor under such a system. They envisioned an unseemly scramble for the Judicare dollar among thousands of marginal lawyers, a spectacle that could inflict untold injury on the image of the profession. Since preservation of a good image was one of their prime reasons for backing the OEO program in the first place, it made little sense to risk a public relations debacle. That might be worse for lawyers in the long term than outright opposition to the war on poverty. Beyond that, a few bar leaders also could remember that this proposal in essence was the same "English system" they and the most conservative elements in the bar reproached so mightily in the 1950s. Thus, without even considering the weaknesses of Judicare as an instrument of reform, lawyers in favor of legal aid had ample independent grounds for opposing Federal sponsorship of compensated private counsel.

Convinced he was on firm ground with the National Advisory Committee on the issue, Bamberger took advantage of his next major address to articulate the OEO policy on Judicare. In a speech at the 1966 midwinter meetings of the ABA, he told the National Conference of Bar Presidents:

> Specifically, I think it is important to point out my concerns about the so-called "English System" and its variations. These are programs whereby some branch of the state or local government or some other organization certifies the indigency of a potential client, who may then consult the private attorney of his choice at the whole or partial expense of the government.
>
> At first glance, the "English System" seems attractive. With only a relatively minor change in our present system of legal representation, it would permit many more people to consult a lawyer. It would also make every lawyer in the community available to the poor, instead of just the small group which may be practicing in a firm of "free" lawyers. This is the so-called "freedom of choice" argument. And finally, the lawyers who perform the services are guaranteed payment, a virtue which needs no further explanation.
>
> But these apparent advantages are, unfortunately, more advantageous for lawyers than for the poor we are committed to assist. Indeed, for the poor, such a plan has at least one major deterrent. The contemplated certification of indigency would require them to submit themselves to another means test by the welfare authorities or their counterparts. It is a certainty that vast numbers of poor people would be too frightened or too proud to place themselves voluntarily in the gears of another bureaucracy, with the result that they simply would not participate in the program at all.
>
> The "English System" is also disadvantageous for another reason that I consider even more important. It clearly can achieve no other goal than the mere

resolution of controversies. The Legal Services Program of the Office of Economic Opportunity and the Legal Aid movement have far greater ambitions.

We cannot be content with the creation of systems of rendering free legal assistance to all the people who need but cannot afford a lawyer's advice. This program must contribute to the success of the War on Poverty. Our responsibility is to marshal the forces of law and the strength of lawyers to combat the causes and effect of poverty. Lawyers must uncover the legal causes of poverty, remodel the system which generates the cycle of poverty and design new social, legal and political tools and vehicles to move poor people from deprivation, depression, and despair to opportunity, hope and ambition. I do not believe that an "English System" which parcels out the legal problems of the poor to lawyers engaged not because they have a singular dedication to assist poor people but because they are members of a bar association or a lawyer referral panel and somehow "chosen freely" by the poor will ever provide the necessary concerted and thoughtful legal analysis and challenge which must occur if the OEO program will be more than a chain of legal first-aid clinics. Twenty lawyers selected by twenty poor clients on twenty different days to defend eviction notices will never have even the opportunity to learn that every eviction was retaliation for the tenant's complaint of housing code violations and so look for the test case to challenge the consequent perversion of the administration of justice. But three lawyers in a "poor man's law firm" would soon see the common thread and seek the legal remedy to prevent the continued proliferation of the same legal crises.

I also entertain the presumption that an "English plan" is more costly than the provision of free legal services by salaried attorneys. Given a fixed sum of money, I speculate that I could obtain more lawyer assistance by employing a lawyer's full-time for a definite period than by dispensing the same money to numerous lawyers in specific fees for services rendered.

But I admit my concerns are speculative. We will approve a very limited number of "English System" applications, evaluate the costs and the results carefully and assess the comparative success of such an approach. We have several preliminary applications for this method; I doubt that we will approve all of them, and I am certain that there is little likelihood that additional applications will be approved. However, we may approve such plans in sparsely populated areas where there is no other reasonable method to provide free legal assistance for the poor.

My attitude about the "English System" is best described by the remark a judge once made about my argument before him: "Mr. Bamberger, I have an open mind about that point—but not necessarily an empty one."[28]

Because Bamberger's address in Chicago was consistent with the majority view on the National Advisory Committee, it carried almost the same weight as if a published guideline had been promulgated on the topic of Judicare programs. However, his speech did not quiet the supporters of Judicare completely. In literally scores of communities, the local bar association continued to propose some variation of the Judicare theme. But the ABA and NLADA leadership maintained a solid front in support of OEO's Judicare policy,[29] and the Legal Services staff enforced that policy. In line with Bamberger's announcement, we funded experimental Judicare programs in a rural area in Wisconsin, an urban neighborhood in New Haven, Connecticut, and a rural-suburban area near San Francisco. We also established a program combining the use of a full-time staff and some private attorneys in Riverside County near Los Angeles. But then we drew the line. No more Judicare funds were granted until the experimental programs had run their course.

The unswerving refusal to extend OEO assistance to any additional Judicare program was not a popular decision among many local bar associations, but they soon came to believe we were serious. As a result, in community after community, Judicare proposals were converted to applications for programs using salaried staff lawyers.

B. The Evolution of a Policy: Lawyers as a Majority on the Boards of Legal Services Agencies

Sometimes policy was made deliberately in response to some particular incident such as Judicare. But at other times, a general pattern evolved slowly, quietly, almost subliminally through the course of a hundred uncontested cases. Then unexpectedly, it might become an issue of vital practical concern; and usually the general pattern was elevated to announced policy thereafter binding, for better or worse, on the Program.

All debate in the National Advisory Committee about the composition of Legal Services boards of directors had revolved around the question of including representatives of the poor.[30] This issue was settled for practical purposes by the *Guidelines.* But the NAC deliberations left unresolved, undebated, and unnoticed another equally vital issue—the composition of the remaining two-thirds of these local boards. Were all other members to be chosen by local bar associations? Were they all to be lawyers? Which other community groups could appropriately be asked to select members?

With the exception of requirements that the poor and the minority bar be represented on Legal Services boards, the national and regional OEO offices would approve virtually any proposed board structure that was submitted from a local community. The effect of this attitude was to delegate policy making with respect to this important set of questions to local communities. It thus produced a pattern which reflected the power relationships in those individual localities. Most—but by no means all—of the pre-OEO legal aid societies were creatures of their local bar associations. Consequently, where the grant was made to one of these agencies (about 40 percent of all grants) the local bar usually occupied at least a majority of the seats on the board of directors. Newly created entities, on the other hand, tended toward a more cosmopolitan combination of community interests. The local community action agency, ethnic organizations, labor unions, law schools, local governments, and the ACLU were among the types of organizations that succeeded in gaining representation on Legal Services boards.

Until the late Spring of 1966, Bamberger's efforts were directed toward the preservation of the policy *void* at the national level. There were forces seeking to compel the national office to *require* that a majority of the board members of each local Legal Services project *must* be selected by the local bar. Bamberger resisted because such a rule probably would have doomed effective legal services in communities where the local bar was antagonistic to the OEO program. Moreover, it would have alienated many CAAs and poverty organizations.

The Florida State Bar Association was the primary institutional voice advocating a guarantee of local bar control. As early as October 1965 the Florida bar submitted an application to OEO which sought funding for a program to stimulate Legal Services projects throughout the state. In many respects, it was a promising venture, a perfect entree for Legal Services into the inhospitable South. But negotiations broke down over one element of the proposal. The Florida Bar Association insisted, as a condition of its assistance, that no Legal Services program would be funded in the state unless a majority of its board was selected by the local bar. The application also provided that the state bar would have the right to veto any application from a local community.

Marshall Criser, chairman of the Florida bar's newly created Legal Services committee, traveled to Washington in October to urge early funding of the proposal. He argued that without state bar support OEO could not begin any local programs in Florida. After some early vacillation, Bamberger decided bar cooperation came at too high a price and rejected the application.[31] On March 19, 1966, the Florida State Bar Association retaliated by enacting a resolution which stated:

> The Florida bar determines that it will oppose—and recommends that local organized bar associations oppose—any application for federal funds to provide legal services which does not provide representation of the organized bar in not less than a majority of members of the governing board, which will locally supervise and administer the legal services program.[32]

Other individual lawyers and entire bar associations took up the cause, but Bamberger was not to be moved. He successfully resisted all attempts to force a national policy pronouncement requiring or even favoring local bar domination of Legal Services boards.[33] (At the same time, Bamberger was approving many grants which, in fact, did give the local bar association the right to select a majority of the Legal Services board. But this was consistent with the earlier decision to allow local communities to work out their own board structure.)

In May, 1966, a related policy issue involving board composition was thrust to the fore. It was posed initially by an application from the neighborhood poverty councils in San Francisco.[34] This was the first application (other than a handful from sparsely populated areas)[35] requesting a board of directors on which *lawyers* constituted *less* than a majority. Under this proposal the poor selected over 50 percent of the board, all of them nonlawyers. Bar associations, law schools, the ACLU and other legal groups elected lawyers, but these representatives were in the minority by a substantial margin. The issue in San Francisco was not *local bar association* control but something more fundamental—*lawyer* control.

There was ample precedent—of a sort—on which to base a decision about the board composition embodied in the San Francisco application. By this time, over 100 applications had been received in Legal Services headquarters. Without any national requirement, in every populous community the conflicting interest groups had uniformly concluded that lawyers should constitute over 50 percent of the board membership. In some places, this lawyer majority was dominated by the local bar association; in others lawyer representatives chosen by the ACLU, law schools and other more liberal organizations exercised substantial influence. But whether liberal or conservative, one thing remained constant. Lawyers formed the majority.

Bamberger's decision was also rendered easier—as a practical political matter—because of the ABA's long-term concern over "lawyer control" of Legal Services. Not *local bar association* control but *lawyer* control had been one of the rallying cries since the national bar leaders first became involved in the OEO Legal Services alliance. In any event, Bamberger negotiated a compromise with the neighborhood poverty councils in San Francisco. They still would select a majority of the board. But a lawyer majority also was insured through an OEO imposed requirement that a number of the representatives chosen by the poor must be lawyers. The San Francisco compromise was the first step in the elevation of the principle of "lawyer control" from a matter of accidental uniformity (or collective wisdom) to firm national policy.

One month later—on June 16, 1966—Bamberger was scheduled to have a public confrontation with the Florida State Bar Association, the leading proponents of bar association control of Legal Services, when he addressed the annual convention of the state bar in Hollywood Beach. Bamberger chose this occasion to announce for the first time in a public forum that OEO required a majority of lawyers on Legal Services boards. In this speech he distinguished between control by lawyers and bar association control.

> I would love to believe that all of our apparent disagreements could be cleared up by a simple explanation of the actual facts (and I do believe that most of them can be) but I cannot deny that every once in a while I encounter an actual

difference of opinion. In paragraph three of the June resolution, I believe there is such a difference of opinion, for that paragraph states that 'no federal program should be initiated without controlling representation of an organized bar association.' OEO has not promulgated such a regulation, and it is not our intention to do so.

Let me quickly add that the disagreement is less than it appears on the surface. Although there is no formal requirement that the governing body of a legal services program be controlled by the organized bar, we have made it clear to all applicants that our overwhelming preference is to fund programs in which the board does have a majority of lawyers. Of the 122 programs we have funded to day, fewer than 10 are governed by boards which do not have a majority of lawyers, and several of these are in rural areas in which there simply are not enough lawyers *present* to be able to make up a governing board.

Our rule might be stated as follows: we require a majority of lawyers on the board unless we are persuaded that it would be impossible to obtain such a majority, either because of a paucity of available lawyers or a refusal of lawyers to serve, or we are persuaded that a majority of lawyers would destroy the effectiveness of the program. I should note that we have yet to encounter the latter situation anywhere in the country.[36]

With this speech to the Florida State Bar, Bamberger codified a rule that had evolved from hundreds of individual decisions in more than a hundred different communities. In August 1966, two months after succeeding Bamberger as director, I promulgated a memorandum to all Legal Services staff based on the Bamberger speech.[37]

Since the announcement that lawyers must constitute a majority on Legal Services boards, there has been considerable criticism of this particular rule. Critics complain that most lawyers are conservative on economic and political questions and tend to represent wealthy interests. Thus by guaranteeing them a majority of the seats on Legal Services boards, OEO allegedly did a disservice to the goals of the program and to the clients of poverty lawyers.

I submit the issue is not that simple. The employees of a Legal Services agency are in the business of advocating frequently controversial causes on behalf of often unpopular clients. The staff lawyers need independence from board interference and protection from pressures emanating from the outside community. Subsequent history has suggested both the independence and the protection usually are found in the ABA Canons of Ethics and the Code of Professional Responsibility. Provisions in the Canons and the Code guarantee all members of the profession, poverty lawyers included, the right to exercise their independent professional judgment in handling clients' cases,[38] and prohibit anybody, including boards of directors, from interfering in any way with that exercise.[39] Lawyers have the duty to represent unpopular clients and causes.[40] Simultaneously, these ethical requirements instruct an attorney to follow his client's wishes[41] and to pursue his client's best interests by any lawful means.[42] Under the new Code, all such protections and duties explicitly apply to lawyers paid by the government as well as those retained by the client himself.[43]

Members of the legal profession are sworn to obey the ethical commands of the Canons and the Code. Beyond that, a hierarchy of local, state, and national disciplinary committees are available to enforce these provisions.

The ethical code under which attorneys live sets them apart from other board members of a Legal Services agency. They are not free to vote their personal political and economic philosophies. Lawyers owe fealty to a higher, or at least different, set of goals—the preservation of the integrity of the profession. In theory, and surprisingly often in practice, this means voting to support the right of a Legal Services lawyer to bring lawsuits inconsistent with the personal philosophy of the lawyer board member or the best interests of his own clients. Not only is an attorney who is a board member *morally* bound to protect the independence of his fellow lawyers on the agency staff, he commits an ethical violation if he votes to strip another attorney of the shield of the profession's Code. Thus, a board member who is a lawyer—unlike other directors on the agency's governing body—is under threat of disciplinary action to uphold the poverty attorney's freedom of action on behalf of his low-income clients and to support the representation of unpopular clients and causes. Since these principles form the underpinning of effective legal services, there appears to be some virtue in mandating that a majority of board members come from a class of persons who are duty-bound to preserve the profession's ideals regardless of personal economic and political views. In the recent past, some of the sturdiest and most persuasive support provided Legal Services programs imperiled by powerful political opponents has come from conservative attorneys sitting on their policy-making boards.[44]

Of course, requiring that a board be composed of a majority of lawyers may have negative effects as well if it increases the probability of placing control of the legal services in the hands of persons unsympathetic to the goals of the poor. Many critical problems the board must decide on—the selection of a staff, for instance—are beyond the ambit of professional ethics. Thus, lawyer members may be duty-bound to permit a staff attorney to file a controversial class action, but nothing in the Code requires them to vote to hire attorneys who in fact will undertake such actions.

It is unclear that OEO's rule requiring a majority of lawyers on boards encouraged conservatism on Legal Services boards. Many board members who are lawyers have turned out to support vigorous legal representation on behalf of the poor while many nonlawyers have not. Moreover, as previously observed, national policy was relatively uninfluential in this area. Most communities appointed boards with a majority of lawyers before the rule itself was formulated and doubtless most that filed applications after that date would have followed the same pattern in the absence of a Federal regulation. But whether this is attributable in part to the rule or not, over half the Legal Services boards initially funded by OEO were dominated by members unsympathetic to using the law to advance the economic position of the poor.[45] This caused difficult management problems for the Legal Services staff[46] just as the ethical commitment of lawyers on the boards made the political problems easier to handle.

III. NECESSITY MOTHERS A PRIORITY GOAL FOR THE LEGAL SERVICES PROGRAM

The most important policy that was decided upon during the formative period of the OEO Legal Services Program was also the last. It set the management focus that dominated agency policy for several years. It also finally resolved some of the issues about philosophy and direction left open when the proponents of the legal aid movement and those who conducted the experiment with the neighborhood law offices agreed to merge to support a Federal legal assistance program in 1965, questions also kept open during the preparation of the *Guidelines* and the succeeding year of "common law" policy making. Principal among these questions were: Which goals were Legal Services lawyers to pursue—the wider distribution of due process justice favored by the legal aid movement or the various reformist prescriptions emanating from the neighborhood lawyer experiments?

If the agenda was to encompass both sets of objectives, how were resources to be allocated among them?

And, assuming reform was to be one of the ultimate objectives, which of the several analyses of poverty and its solution (identified in Chapter 2) should be followed?

These policy questions might have gone unanswered by OEO for years, and possibly forever, were they resolved satisfactorily, as they might have been, by the day-to-day performance of Legal Services grantees. Government agencies are natural procrastinators, especially about difficult, controversial issues of fundamental policy. The Legal Services staff was no different, especially when it came to philosophical matters that threatened to divide the Program's two major constituencies. However, very quickly, further procrastination was out of the question. Events reached the point where no decision would itself be a decision; a policy void at the national level would be in effect equivalent to a choice in favor of one of the competing policy alternatives. Before discussing what went into the decision itself, however, let us first consider the forces that made that step an urgent necessity.

A. Too Many Clients and Too Many Goals: The Early Crisis in Legal Services Management

From late 1965 to June 30, 1966 OEO invested over $20 million in legal help for the poor. During the next fiscal year, the annual budget rose above $40 million. Those who were trying out the neighborhood law offices thought this would give them the wherewithal to cure each and every failing of the legal aid movement. But it was a miniscule amount; in 1965 the American population spent a total of $5.2 billion on lawyers.[47] Thus, before the infusion of OEO money, the better than 20 percent of our population that cannot afford legal assistance received one-tenth of 1 percent of the nation's investment in legal services (two-tenths, if budgets for public defenders are included). The investment of $40 million still left the poor with only eight-tenths of 1 percent of the nation's legal assistance. This meant that in 1967 the poor man's share of the total outlay for lawyers remained six times smaller than his share of the national income. In percentage terms, *the bottom 20 percent on the income scale received about 5 percent of the nation's goods and services*[48] *but less than 1 percent of its legal assistance.*

Oblivious to the continued poverty of legal assistance programs for the poor, OEO and many of its agencies set out to accomplish a vast assortment of goals and to cure legal aid of an almost inexhaustible accumulation of real and imagined deficiencies.

We soon began to learn the price of this shotgun approach. In July 1966 evaluation teams had begun examination of the Legal Services projects then in operation. By October and November a fairly standard portrait was beginning to emerge. Within a few months after a legal assistance organization hired the lawyers and opened the offices made possible by OEO funds, those offices and attorneys were swamped by more needy clients than they could properly represent. In effect, the entire Legal Services Program was drifting steadily toward complete preoccupation with the "processing" of caseloads. The more progressive and innovative goals of the Program were being buried under an avalanche of cases. Evaluation teams could only recommend to the agencies that they simultaneously handle an overwhelming caseload, improve the quality of representation, educate the community about their rights, work with other disciplines on all the legal, social and economic dimensions of their clients' problems, undertake test cases, create new economic entities and pursue all the other goals of the Legal Services Program.

It was relatively easy to reach the conclusion that there was no hope of curing all the shortcomings of legal aid, broadening the scope of its services simultaneously in all directions, and yet handle any significant number of clients. At the same time, it seemed even less desirable, politically and philosophically, to provide comprehensive assistance to a few and turn away the many

—which was the only way to accommodate all the new goals envisioned by the architects of the neighborhood lawyer experiments. At the least, that would have torn the Legal Services coalition asunder because the prime objective of the proponents of legal aid, the wider distribution of due process justice, would have been abandoned. The rationale for the support given by the organized bar to the OEO Legal Services Program would disappear and with it the powerful backing so vital to the Program's survival[49] and expansion.[50]

The theorists of the neighborhood lawyer experiments had been unusually astute in detecting weaknesses in the legal aid movement. They had been even more imaginative in proposing new goals for the Legal Services Program. But now it was time to cull, for not all the new directions that had been recommended were of equal importance. If any were to be salvaged, priorities would have to be established.

B. Surveying the Policy Options

The four most-heralded new initiatives and thus the leading contenders to become the top priority for the Legal Services Program were:

1. Social rescue—participation in coordinated social services efforts designed to "rescue" low-income family units from poverty.
2. Economic development—the creation and operation of credit unions, laundromats, co-op grocery stores, housing projects, and other business enterprises designed to bring more money into the low-income community.
3. Community organization—a concerted drive to organize poor people into groups that could exert pressure in the political and private economic spheres.
4. Law reform—test cases, legislative advocacy and other techniques directed toward causing changes in the laws and practices which formed the social and economic structure of poverty.

Three criteria were most relevant in choosing between these alternatives. *First,* the comparative effectiveness of each strategy in providing benefits to the largest number of low-income people. We were aware that only a small fraction of the persons needing the help of an attorney could be served at Legal Services offices. Somehow, the benefits poverty lawyers conferred would have to be extended beyond the relatively few poor people they could serve directly as clients. *Second,* the relevance of a lawyer's special skills and training. If a lesser trained, lower paid poverty program employee could perform the same function essentially as well, concentration of Legal Services resources on that objective would be wasteful. *Third,* the political feasibility of the alternative. Political feasibility was measured largely by how acceptable a given priority would be to Congress and to the boards and staff leaders of local Legal Services agencies.

1. The easiest of the four possible priorities to eliminate was the "social rescue" strategy. As you will recall, the genesis of this option is found in the New Haven proposal analyzed in Chapter Two.[51] Although noncontroversial and thus eminently feasible as a political matter, this approach, of necessity, reduced drastically the number of poor people aided by Legal Services lawyers. It called for comprehensive treatment of the legal-economic-social-psychological problems of a few thousand families in place of less intensive help to hundreds of thousands of families.

The major premise of the social rescue theory—that the structure of society is equitable and the poor merely need help in negotiating that structure—also seemed suspect. Subsequent experience on an experimental basis suggests social service teams are not very effective even with the relatively few families given this intensive assistance.[52] But at the time of the decision, we were unaware of the empirical evidence on this question. We were willing to assume a high degree of success with the chosen few. That still did not meet one of the primary criteria—to benefit the millions who could never receive even cursory assistance in Legal Services offices.

2. Economic development was a more attractive possibility. Never mentioned as a primary antipoverty strategy during the pre-OEO era of the neighborhood lawyer experiments, the idea was adapted from the work that major private law firms frequently perform for establishment businessmen. As envisioned, Legal Services lawyers would use their expertise to develop new business entities owned and staffed by the poor. Again, this alternative avoided controversy. In fact, it sounded like an Adam Smith favorite. And potentially this approach could benefit indirectly—as owners, employees and consumers —many persons who never entered a neighborhood law office. But beneath the surface appeal, economic development appeared less convincing as a candidate for the top priority target of Legal Services attorneys.

First, economic development required massive infusions of capital from the government and the private sector if enough businesses were to be established to benefit many poor people. In early 1967, there were virtually no funds available for investment in economic organizations assembled by poor people.[53] Thus, to divert the efforts of hundreds of Legal Services lawyers to the creation of new economic entities appeared likely to produce more frustration than income for the poor.

Second, assuming funds were available for economic organizations operated for the benefit of the poor, which skills were most needed to make these businesses succeed? A lawyer obviously is useful on many occasions—at the time of incorporation and when dealing with local regulatory bodies. But accountants and knowledgeable managers are more crucial to business survival. Moreover, within a short time after commencing operation, a new business should be able to afford to pay for necessary legal advice. Thus, the role of the Legal Services lawyer in economic development may be peripheral and should be temporary. It seemed incongruous to convert a peripheral and temporary function into the primary objective of Legal Services lawyers.

Third, there was a very real danger that economic development would aid the middle-class blacks and businessmen of all races much more than the hard-core poor. There was, and still is, a tendency to confuse economic development for blacks with economic development for the poor and aid to individual businessmen with aid for low-income people.[54]

For all the above reasons, it was relatively easy to find that economic development was not yet a mature approach to the poverty problem.

3. Community organization could have been rejected on purely political grounds, because by 1967, it was anathema to most congressmen.[55] To them, community organization meant two things: first, encouragement of civil disorder and, second, development of a political base for opponents of present officeholders, like the congressmen themselves. To have announced that poverty lawyers henceforth were to spend a substantial part of their time organizing community groups would have signed the death warrant for Legal Services.

But there also were valid nonpolitical reasons for de-emphasizing the organization of community groups as a primary role for Legal Services lawyers. For one thing, there were too few Legal Services lawyers—at the time less than 1000 scattered over the entire nation—to organize enough viable community groups to help very many poor people. Imagine a political party with fewer than 1000 precinct workers nationwide and you gain some appreciation of the problem. The handful of tenant unions, welfare organizations, and consumer action groups that the Legal Services Program might be expected to assemble over a two- or three-year period would lack the political muscle to move Congress or a state legislature and, in most cases, would be unable even to generate the economic power needed to bargain effectively with a landlord or merchant.[56]

Disregarding the problem of numbers, poverty attorneys probably would have constituted the highest paid, best educated, least effective organizational force in history. Success in community organizing probably is a function of traits like personality, identification (including ethnic) with the group to be organized, a certain degree of animal cunning, a touch of demagoguery, and a number of other characteristics not related to law school education or, for that matter, to formal education at any level. Local community action agencies had several thousand such organizers on their staffs, employed at about one-quarter to one-third the salary of a Legal Services lawyer. It seemed a poor allocation of Legal Services resources to divert them from tasks only attorneys can perform in order to increase by a few percentage points the community organization forces already in the field.

4. Law reform describes a bundle of techniques—test cases and legislative advocacy are the most prominent examples—aimed at changing statutes, regu-

lations, rules and practices that are unfavorable to the poor.[57] In essence, it is an amplification of the strategy urged by Elizabeth Wickenden and Edward Sparer during the pre-OEO era.[58] But the roots go further back, because for decades major law firms have engaged in this form of advocacy on behalf of corporations and other wealthy clients.

Law reform possessed several advantages. To begin with, it offered the possibility of benefiting many of the poor who could not possibly be served directly at Legal Services offices. A single test case or legislative change or modified administrative regulation can benefit thousands of individuals.[59] Moreover, law reform is a function that fully employs the lawyer's skills and training. Nobody else is in a position to prepare and file test cases and only a very experienced, knowledgeable and probably well-educated individual is serious competition to the lawyer in legislative advocacy.

Politically, law reform was bound to be somewhat controversial, but less so than other methods that have been used to generate fundamental social and economic change. Law reform—unlike "community organization," "social reform," and similar concepts—has deep roots in the ideals of the legal profession. The recently enacted ABA Code of Professional Responsibility, which supplanted the Canons in 1970, contains explicit language imposing the duty of law reform on every member of the legal profession:

> Changes in human affairs and imperfections in human institutions make necessary constant efforts to maintain and improve our legal system. This system should function in a manner that commands public respect and fosters the use of legal remedies to achieve redress of grievances. By reason of education and experience, lawyers are especially qualified to recognize deficiencies in the legal system and to initiate corrective measures therein. Thus, they should participate in proposing and supporting legislation and programs to improve the system. . . .
>
> Rules of law are deficient if they are not just, understandable, and responsive to the needs of society. If a lawyer believes that the existence of a rule of law, substantive or procedural, causes or contributes to an unjust result, he should endeavor by lawful means to obtain appropriate changes in the law. . . .[60]

Thus, the ideals of the legal profession offered a pre-existing, conservative, well-accepted rationale for law reform. Opponents in the political arena figured to find it more difficult to challenge the right of lawyers to pursue their clients' interests in the appellate courts or legislative chambers than to dispute the merits of social revolution, community organization, and the like.[61]

Law reform appeared to hold out another type of political advantage, because it was where the goals of the legal aid movement and the neighborhood lawyer experiments intersected. To those steeped in the ideals of legal aid it was implicit in the concept of equal justice that a client should have the opportunity to challenge the legality of laws and practices in circumstances where a well-heeled litigant could do the same. Meanwhile, the antipoverty mission of the neighborhood law office experiments likewise was served because law reform offered the opportunity for significant social and economic change. Since law reform tended to satisfy simultaneously the two major constituencies of the Program, it apparently would be easier to implement than most other possible strategies that might have been named as the priority function of poverty lawyers.

C. Law Reform as the Priority Management Goal for the National Legal Services Program

Applying all three criteria—political feasibility, breadth of impact and relevance of legal expertise—law reform appeared to be the best choice for the highest priority function of the Legal Services Program.

This involved an election among the several antipoverty strategies advocated during the pre-OEO period.[62] In effect, the Wickenden-Sparer diagnosis of poverty and its solution had been chosen over the social rescue theory behind the New Haven proposal and the Cahns' emphasis on using lawyers to guarantee accountability among institutions redistributing income and opportunity to the poor.

Having settled on the goal, the next step was to turn the law reform priority into official policy. There already had been dialogue with the National Advisory Committee about the case and goal overload problem our evaluators were finding among local grantees. Finally, at the January 14, 1967, meeting Maynard Toll, the new NLADA president, suggested a resolution expressing the committee's concern and urging the staff to insure that ample resources were committed to major actions that might attack fundamental community-wide issues.[63] Seconded by the ABA legal aid chairman, John Robb,[64] the resolution was favorably received during the ensuing discussion.[65]

On March 17, 1967, I was scheduled to keynote the Harvard Conference on Law and Poverty. Since the NAC shared our concerns about the urgency of the caseload problem, we decided to use that speech to announce the choice of law reform as the priority mission of the OEO Legal Services Program. With over 400 in attendance, including several ABA officials and representatives from almost every Legal Services agency in the country, the Harvard Conference seemed an ideal opportunity to address all the relevant constituencies at the same time in the same place.

The speech itself was a rearticulation of the considerations that originally led us to select law reform.

> Almost all of you here know from firsthand experience the kinds of problems legal services programs are having today, the massive caseloads, the need to develop imaginative techniques to reach the unsophisticated audiences, the ability to maintain the dynamic quality of the program. . . .

I think the time has come when we must officially acknowledge that it is not possible to achieve fully all of the goals of the Legal Services Program. We cannot at the same time provide every indigent with a lawyer, treat all his problems legal and personal, work devotedly to change the statutes and court holdings that have placed our clients in a disadvantageous position, and develop the theories to win the battles of tomorrow as well as today. In the 18 months since the beginning of the Legal Services Program it has become apparent that the estimated $400 million to $600 million necessary to provide services to every indigent is not going to be available today or in the immediate future. . . .

My purpose in speaking with you this evening is to state that the primary goal of the Legal Services Program should be law reform, to bring about changes in the structure of the world in which the poor people live in order to provide on the largest scale possible consistent with our limited resources a legal system in which the poor enjoy the same treatment as the rich . . . I believe law reform is vital because it is the means by which we can provide more for the poor than in any other way with less expenditure of time and money. Law reform can provide the most bang for the buck, to use an OEO phrase.[66]

To assure the legal aid supporters that OEO was not suddenly abandoning their primary goal of extending due process justice to the multitude, I added,

When I emphasize law reform I am not suggesting that we abandon our many, many services to hundreds of thousands of poor people. What we are talking about is priorities . . . In a number of our programs staff attorneys are working full-time almost exclusively with individual clients . . . The lawyers' days are entirely devoted to services: going to court, making telephone calls and attempting to reach settlements. I am *not* suggesting that these services be terminated. I *am* suggesting that directors of projects faced with such situations devote their attention to changing the structure of their office to make time for work on law reform available.[67]

A few months later, we testified about law reform in Congress,[68] and the Senate report gave official endorsement to our policy:

[T]he legal services program can scarcely keep up with the volume of cases in the communities where it is active, not to speak of places waiting for funds to start the program. The committee concludes, therefore, that more attention should be given to test cases and law reform.[69]

Of all the decisions made during my tenure as director of the Legal Services Program this one—right or wrong—was the most significant. At the same time, I suspect the most important part of that decision was *not* the selection of law reform as opposed to one of the other competing goals. What was crucial was the decision to set *some* priority as official policy and then attempt to direct energies and money toward achievement of that objective.

Too many government programs—and human endeavors in general—are drowned in their own multiplicity of goals. It is not as disastrous to rank your priorities incorrectly—if you are at all close—as not to choose at all. Without this decision and the concentration of resources that ensued[70] the Legal Services Program probably still would be wallowing around, perhaps achieving a bit of community organization, a touch of economic development, a minimum of law reform; a few families would have been subjected to the multidiscipline team treatment and tentative steps would have been taken in twenty or so other new directions. But nothing would have been done on a sufficient scale to have any impact on the problem of poverty or even to determine whether it had a potential to make a difference.

6: "Up the Bureaucracy": Preserving Policy and Program Integrity within the OEO Administration

Whenever a new program is undertaken by a government agency, you can be assured a power struggle will not be far behind. Legal Services was no exception. While the program was still but a dream, its place within the bureaucracy already was a topic of prime concern to many OEO officials. In this case, the ultimate structure soon became an issue of relevance not only to OEO but also to the American Bar Association and the lawyers serving in local Legal Services projects.

I. PREDISPOSITION FOR INDEPENDENCE: THE EXPERIENCES OF LEGAL SERVICES ADVOCATES BEFORE OEO

As discussed previously, the OEO Legal Services Program was derived in part from the experiments with neighborhood law offices funded by the Ford Foundation and the President's Committee on Juvenile Delinquency in New Haven, New York and Washington, D.C. By the time negotiations commenced between OEO and the American Bar Association, experience in these pilot programs had made the Legal Services advocates extraordinarily sensitive to issues of bureaucratic power relationships both at the national and local levels.

The first neighborhood law offices were funded as part of Community Progress, Inc., in New Haven. CPI was the forerunner of the CAAs funded by OEO and, in fact, became New Haven's CAA after the advent of OEO. Under the original CPI program, the lawyers were hired and fired by the CPI management and were subject to day-to-day supervision by that management.

It is significant for the subsequent history of the Legal Services Program that one of the original neighborhood lawyers in New Haven was Jean Cahn.[1] As you will recall, CPI closed its law offices and discharged the attorneys when a controversial case endangered the agency's public acceptance. Understandably, this experience made an indelible impression on Jean Cahn and her husband, Edgar, one which generated the theme of their influential article in the *Yale Law Journal* and shaped their advice during the formative stages of the Federal program.[2]

The New Haven debacle also profoundly influenced the design of other experimental neighborhood law office programs. Although New York's MFY Legal Services unit was funded as a direct operating arm of the overall anti-poverty agency, the unit had a separate "advisory committee" of law professors and practicing attorneys with exclusive jurisdiction over issues of professional responsibility.[3] The Washington, D.C., program, which started later than MFY, had more time to digest the New Haven experience; consequently, the Neighborhood Legal Services Project was controlled by its own board of directors composed entirely of lawyers. The local CAA delegated to this separate board the power to select the staff director, to hire and fire other personnel, to establish policy and generally to administer the program.[4]

Virtually every attorney who worked in the early neighborhood law office programs experienced situations that reinforced their urge for independence from the community action agencies. While serving as deputy director of Washington's Neighborhood Legal Services Project (NLSP), I was confronted with one of these conflicts in understanding. In early 1965, the operations director of the Washington Community Action Agency summoned me to his office and demanded that an NLSP attorney retract a letter he had written to the police department on behalf of a client. The CAA was engaged in delicate negotiations with the department, and police officials had threatened to break off those talks unless the NLSP attorney withdrew the complaint discussed in the letter. In the CAA's estimation, the negotiations were much more important than a single individual's complaint of police misconduct. At the same time, the legal profession's code and the lawyer's traditional allegiance to his client's cause prohibited him from abandoning the individual's interests even to further the CAA's noble efforts to benefit the entire community. We were able to resist pressures from the Community Action Agency to withdraw the claim, but only because of the protection provided by NLSP's semi-autonomous board.

From this sort of confrontation, the architects of the neighborhood lawyer experiment decided the only way to guarantee low-income clients the same unswerving loyalty enjoyed by those capable of hiring their own counsel was to place power over Legal Services administration in the hands of persons absolutely committed to that ideal. As a practical matter, that appeared to require lawyer control.

The representatives of the organized bar had other reasons for seeking an independent administrative status for Legal Services at the local level. They were concerned about economic issues such as eligibility standards, referral of ineligible clients and the treatment of fee-generating cases. A CAA board dominated by poor people, local government officials and middle-class "do-gooders" was unlikely to establish realistic criteria for determining who should qualify for legal services or to understand the various categories of fee-generating cases that private attorneys are willing to undertake without requiring a retainer from the client. The organized bar also was interested in guaranteeing that Legal Services lawyers complied with the Canons of Professional Ethics. Legal assistance for the poor raises a whole range of difficult issues involving the application of specific canons.[5] A CAA board composed primarily of nonlawyers often would not even realize that these canons existed. More than that, there was no guarantee they would be sympathetic to the profession's viewpoint even when they perceived the problem. Thus, local bar associations and the ABA alike wanted a lawyer-dominated, bureaucratically independent structure to supervise Legal Services operations at the local level.

II.   THE OEO BUREAUCRACY

From its creation in 1964 until 1969, the staff of the Office of Economic Opportunity was divided into three major departments responsible for the administration of VISTA, the Job Corps, and the Community Action Program (CAP), all funded by the Economic Opportunity Act. VISTA administered a domestic peace corps, the Volunteers in Service to America, which accounted for slightly more than 3 percent of the total OEO budget. The Job Corps office administered a residential retraining and employment program modeled on the CCC camps of Depression days. Approximately 25 percent of the OEO's funds were expended on the Job Corps centers. The remaining 70 percent of OEO's budget was allocated to the Community Action Program (CAP).[6]

A.   The CAP Commitment to Local Initiative Programming

CAP's original statutory mandate was "to provide stimulation and incentive for urban and rural communities to mobilize their resources to combat poverty through community action programs."[7] Community action programs soon became known as Community Action Agencies (CAAs) to differentiate them from the Community Action Program administration in OEO. Generally, CAAs were newly created, nonprofit private corporations founded specifically to expend funds received from OEO. Other sections of the original Economic Opportunity Act required that the CAAs be "developed, conducted and administered with the maximum feasible participation" of the poor; and that 10 percent of the total program cost come from sources outside the Federal government.[8]

CAP's basic management philosophy was to defer to local CAAs all decisions related to the design and implementation of local antipoverty plans. Instead, CAP personnel tended to concentrate their attention and effort on structural and budgetary issues. In their review of local applications they asked questions such as: Is the board of directors of the CAA broadly based? Does the membership of the board carry out the statutory mandate of maximum feasible participation of the poor? Is the CAA director's salary out of line?[9]

The organization of the CAP bureaucracy reflected the commitment to what soon became known as "local initiative" programming. Its staff was divided on geographical rather than functional lines and staffed with "generalists" rather than specialists. Each CAP generalist was assigned to the CAAs located within a given geographical area and to review applications and monitor the programs conceived by his assigned CAAs irrespective of the nature of the applications or programs. Thus, the "CAP generalist" might expect to appraise the merits of a health program one day, a job training program the next day and a recreation program the third. This system did not promise meaningful review of the possible effectiveness of a program, but it eliminated any chance that CAP generalists would become bored.

Shortly after OEO came into existence, the agency began to establish regional offices in New York, Washington, D.C., Atlanta, Austin, Texas, Chicago, Kansas City, and San Francisco. The purpose was to place the "CAP generalists" and other administrative personnel closer to the local agencies whose applications they were reviewing and whose operations they were monitoring. In early 1966 OEO delegated grant-making authority to the directors of these seven regional offices, which tended to reinforce the geographic basis of OEO's lines of administrative authority. It also further encouraged dependence on staff generalists as opposed to specialists and the tendency to defer to local CAAs for programmatic decisions.

B. The Coming of the National Emphasis Programs

OEO was still in its infancy when its top leadership partially abandoned dependence upon the "local initiative" concept. There were several reasons for this. For one thing, local communities often displayed almost no imagination in devising solutions to local poverty. For another, many CAAs were bogged down for months considering problems of board membership and staff selection and were in no position to even think about planning to overcome poverty. Finally, in early 1965, just halfway through its first fiscal year, the staff of OEO realized it was in great danger of committing the supreme bureaucratic sin: failure to spend the agency's total appropriation. The agency, with the strong endorsement of its director, Sargent Shriver, hurriedly decided to experiment with a new approach to antipoverty programming—standard pre-packaged components that a local CAA could elect to "buy" if it desired, the first being

Headstart. It was designed by experts in early childhood development to overcome the cultural deprivation suffered by most children from low-income families. Ten million dollars was set aside in the total OEO budget for July 1, 1964 to June 30, 1965 to fund applications from local CAAs that met the standards of the Headstart concept.

OEO was not far along with the development of its Headstart program when it realized that the existing CAP staff of generalists was oriented toward administering locally initiated and designed programs; it was unequal to the task of promoting a highly specialized program or of evaluating its implementation at the local level. Educational experts, not CAP generalists, were needed to prepare the program guidelines and application forms, to review incoming proposals and to monitor compliance with the detailed conditions under which a grant was made.[10] Moreover, although only a few months old, CAP already was encrusted with flow charts, concurrence points, and other bureaucratic entanglements that were not necessary for the administration of a straightforward program like Headstart.

The OEO leadership solved this problem by borrowing a management concept pioneered by the Defense Department. When the latter faced similar problems in launching major new efforts such as the Polaris submarine, it created so-called Special Project Offices, charged with the single mission to develop a new weapons system and put it in place. Until that mission is achieved, the special project office is virtually a self-contained unit within the general bureaucracy, empowered to perform all the functions necessary to completion of its specific task. Then, when the weapons system is finally in place, it is turned over to the regular bureaucracy and the special project office is dissolved.

In early 1965, OEO established a modified version of a special project office to develop, promote, fund, and evaluate Headstart programs. This office remained a part of the CAP bureaucracy. But it had its own staff of specialists in child development that performed most of the functions that were distributed among several levels in the administration of "local initiative" programs.

The Headstart office exceeded Shriver's expectations. In its first six months of existence, which was the last half of OEO's first fiscal year, Headstart attracted enough interest from local CAAs to account for grants totalling $80 million. This was *eight times* the original allocation for Headstart fundings and took over 20 percent of the total CAP budget for that first fiscal year. With its streamlined organization and well-packaged product, Headstart quickly absorbed millions of loose dollars that inexperienced CAAs lacked the capacity to spend on programs of their own design.

The "Headstart" experience convinced Shriver of the worth of pre-packaged, OEO-promoted programs. It also persuaded him that special project offices were a useful management technique. OEO even coined a new term—"National Emphasis Program"—to describe this concept in CAP programming.

At the same time, the CAP administration had taken some lessons of its own from the "Headstart" success. They had seen this single program divert 20% of the total CAP budget during the first fiscal year of operation. (In OEO's second year "Headstart" absorbed almost one-third of CAP's total appropriation.) They could see the funds available for "local initiative" programs dwindling and their own power eroding before the onslaught of "national emphasis" programming.

III. NEGOTIATIONS OVER THE POSITION OF THE LEGAL SERVICES PROGRAM WITHIN THE OEO STRUCTURE

In September 1965 Sargent Shriver brought Clint Bamberger to OEO headquarters to convince the Baltimore attorney that he should accept the directorship of the Legal Services Program. Beforehand Bamberger was advised by ABA leaders to seek assurances that the Legal Services administration would enjoy substantial autonomy, and he accordingly pressed for a commitment of independence from CAP.[11] But Shriver was unwilling to go that far. He responded that the community action concept required a coordinated effort in the local community and coordinated management in Washington. Thus, the Legal Services office must be under the CAP administration. However, he was willing to promise Bamberger the new program would enjoy a preferred status within CAP. It would be a national emphasis program as was Headstart. Bamberger would have his own staff and primary authority for the approval of Legal Services grants. Although Bamberger normally would report to the CAP director, he was guaranteed direct access to Shriver whenever he felt the need.[12]

In the bureaucratic tradition, the simple pact between Bamberger and Shriver soon evolved into an extraordinarily complex, hybrid administrative setup. By this time, the CAP leadership had seen Headstart absorb one-third of their total budget and were wary of any similar potential "upstart" national emphasis program, which Legal Services looked as if it might be.[13] In a series of meetings with Bamberger, CAP officials insisted on a procedure at both the regional and headquarters levels which required every proposal that came from a local community to meet the approval of nine reviewers outside the Legal Services staff before it was submitted ultimately for Sargent Shriver's signature.[14] If an application was found unacceptable by anyone it was to be returned to the Legal Services staff for appropriate modification. If the change was deemed objectionable, the only recourse was to appeal to a higher level in the bureaucratic chain. As a practical matter, short of Shriver himself, there were few who felt sympathetic toward the objectives of the Legal Services staff on most disputed issues. If the CAP administrators sought to ensnare the Legal Services national emphasis program in a web of red tape, they had succeeded.

On November 11, 1965, at the first meeting of the National Advisory Committee, Bamberger and CAP director Theodore Berry described in very general terms the compromise the Legal Services director had reached with Shriver and CAP. Bamberger began,

> I know from some conversations that you are interested in knowing of the relationship of this office to Mr. Berry's office and to the office of Mr. Shriver, and we have had some discussions about this and there is a [proposed] document which has not been approved that spells it out.
>
> Now it spells it out in the language of management people and not in my language. . . . I'll read that to you:
>
> "The Director of Legal Services is the chief proponent in OEO of legal services programs for the poor and ultimately responsible for the execution of the program within the annual program parameters approved by the Director of OEO.
>
> • • •
>
> "Legal Services, although separately identifiable, is an integral part of the CAP organization, as are other special national projects such as Headstart and Upward Bound.
>
> "The line of reporting authority of the Director of Legal Services is through the CAP Director to the Office of the Director of OEO.
>
> "The CAP Director is responsible for the development and submission of an integrated national CAP program including all special projects to the Director of OEO.
>
> "The Director of Legal Services and the regional directors will jointly select the legal services representative to be employed in the regional offices.
>
> "The regional legal services representative will have the same organizational relationship to the regional CAP manager as the Director of Legal Services has to the CAP Director.
>
> "The formalized reporting channel from regional legal services representatives to OEO headquarters is through the regional CAP manager, but the communication line for program purposes is always open between the Director of Legal Services and the regional legal services representative."[15]

Considering the obscurity of internal bureaucratic issues, the deep interest of many Committee members was surprising. Bruce Terris, the Justice Department representative asked:

> In the past there's been considerable discussion that we're going to have, with perhaps one or two or three other programs within OEO, particular importance and emphasis. And part of that importance and emphasis was going to be separate high-level staff and a staff with greater independence and decision-making power than perhaps some other things that weren't considered of such importance. I'm not at all sure after listening to the description that that continues to be so.

Terris was followed by Martin Wolf, a Committee member from Los Angeles.

> I personally think it's perhaps the most inefficient type of setup that we could provide. And I would like the Advisory Committee to address itself to perhaps two or three specific problems.
>
> One: Will there be a separate budget for Legal Services on a nationwide scale, or are Legal Services still to be within the general CAP-assigned budget for each community?
>
> Secondly, as far as legal analysts in the regions are concerned, how much responsibility do they give to the local CAP director in that region, and how much to Mr. Bamberger? Are they to serve two masters?
>
> And thirdly, how much power and authority does Mr. Bamberger have? For example, if a [CAA] decides that they want a certain type of legal service component, does Mr. Bamberger have the power to veto or override that decision?

This query prompted several minutes of discussion between Berry and several NAC members. Finally, ABA president-elect Orison Marden raised the issue that was to hang over the Legal Services Program for three years: "I'm embarrassed to ask this question because it betrays the abysmal ignorance I'm afraid is mine, but is it essential in the OEO program that the Legal Services part be tied in administratively as far as nationally and locally, with the CAP program?"

But Berry, the CAP director, held firm, "We think it is. We're going to maintain the integrity of the community action concept as it's spelled out in the statute."

Later in the discussion, several committee members concentrated on the recruitment problem raised by the ungainly bureaucratic structure. As Bruce Terris observed:

"Having had a little experience in OEO trying to attract first-class attorneys, in this case to the General Counsel's office, it seems to me your chances will be materially hurt by the setup which doesn't have responsibility entirely to other attorneys. . . ."

Terris was interrupted by Shriver's entrance for a courtesy visit with the Committee members. The OEO director was met with an unforeseen barrage. Philadelphia lawyer Jerome Shestack began:

> [T]here's been a strong feeling among the members of the Committee that the Legal Services Program is administratively so much under the CAP that it's going to hurt what I suppose is the two-fold objective of the Legal Services Program. One, to obtain the best type of legal services possible for the local community and two, to obtain the best type of lawyers possible to run these programs. . . . And I think I say correctly the consensus of most of the people here is that you would materially strengthen the success of the program if you could provide a separate budget and relieve the Legal Services Program from the administrative setup that it presently seems to be working under.

Shriver responded,

Well, let me say that I think you are addressing yourself here, Jerry, to one of the really difficult problems of organization with which we have been struggling, because community action by its nature encompasses many of the most fundamental aspects of human life, of which justice is obviously one. The medical services are another. Education is a third, and so on. And every community action program in every city does have components in these fields or soon will have components in this field.

The medical profession feels very much the way you [do], representing the legal profession. . . . They feel that in the medical profession the bringing of health services to poor people is so essential a part of any war against poverty that . . . administrative problems or difficulties mean that you can't get the right kind of doctors or other medical personnel.

The idea of legal services, its present structure . . . is the same as, let's say, the Polaris Missile Project in . . . the Defense Department. The people who run those things are called program directors. Rickover is the Program Director for Polaris. What he does get . . . is a budget which we expect him to be responsible for. . . . He gets the authority to establish the standards, the policy, et cetera. But the Program Director—let's say Rickover building the Polaris submarine—has to report to at least one or two people above him who have two jobs: one of them is the allocation of funds across all potential . . . new weapons. Because when you start Polaris, Polaris is competing with Minuteman or . . . with something else for the total budgetary capacity.

The most penetrating response to Shriver's argument was made by the soft-spoken but articulate Soia Mentschikoff, probably the leading woman law professor in the country.

Legal services are not in the same category as education, building of Polaris missiles, rendering of medical services, and the like. And they [are] not, really, for two very basic reasons: first, what they involve is representation of a particular interest and a particular client. Representation of that interest and that client may involve warfare with the medical services, the educational services, the entire political structure of the city which is involved, and with every social service agency in that city.

Secondly, legal services connote not only the representational aspect but the planning and organizational aspects as well, and I would hope that part of the scope of legal services would be that. . . . What that means is that legal services cannot, should not and must not rest on an integration of general community programs. And as it is now envisaged this is supposed to be an integrated part of a general community action program. The general community action program really doesn't have any relationship with legal services. It could be the very function of the legal services that may be performed [to] damn everything in the community action program. Now I think this is what you really have to face.

Do you want legal services that are truly going to be independent, that are going [to] ride free, that are going to say to CAP as well as every other governmental organization, "You're wrong. You're doing the wrong thing. This isn't what you're to do." Or do you want a legal services program which is always getting the bottom of the barrel because the people in CAP are the people who do have the educational interest, the medical interest, the social welfare interest and the like—there are, after all, limited resources. And if they're to evaluate the situation, for them legal services has bottom priority, not top. . . . I think the real issue that has to be faced here is, do you want a first-rate Legal Services Program? If you do, it must run independently. If you don't that's a different question. That's the basic policy issue.

A few minutes later, Shestack narrowed the discussion to the issue of Bamberger's independent access to Shriver. "And if we're going to have the flexibility that seems to be an inherent element of this program, we would be a lot more comfortable if we knew that there was really an open door between his office and yours, so that these decisions could be made on the level where he would approach you without having to write memos that would go via and through and so on. I'm sure Admiral Rickover has that kind of access."

Shriver responded,

> You all, I'm sure, agree about the fact that this is an administrative shambles. The reason, generally speaking, that it's considered an administrative shambles is because I do what you just got through describing, and I do it as a matter of principle and philosophy at the beginning of a new venture, because I don't think there's anybody bright enough . . . to sit by and know exactly [what] should go through channels. . . .
>
> So, on my desk, for example, there's a battery of what they call "hot lines" where I have telephones . . . for maybe 20 or more people in this agency. Now that's considered heretical. As a matter of fact, all you have to do is go up to the Princeton School of Public Administration and you'll find out it's impossible. . . . Well, what I'd say is that the head of Headstart is right on that thing; the head of Upward Bound is right on that box. I don't know—Clint's on that at the end of the month. . . . It is because of my propensity for talking to people down the line without asking permission of the guy who might be a problem—that's one of the reasons why people say that there's a certain amount of chaos around here.

A Committee member interjected, "Constructive chaos." Shriver laughed, "I call it constructive chaos but that's self-serving."

But ABA leader Marden was not about to allow Shriver to jest his way off the hook so easily.

> [A]s you know, lawyers more than doctors or anyone else are terribly preoccupied with language and the way in which you go about describing relationships. . . . [I]f you go to the American Bar Association leaders who see the need to sell this program to the Bar, you'd want to be able to assure lawyers candidly that there is direct access from this program to you, without their being answerable to and subordinate to the social workers. [T]here's a real value to rephrasing the memorandum of authority here so that instead of saying that this organization

of legal services is an integral part of CAP and reports through the CAP director to you, it ought to be phrased in terms of the Director of this program who can report directly to you after consultation and coordination with CAP, but not being answerable to CAP.

Shriver perceived he was being forced into a commitment that he was unwilling to make.

I sat in this room six months ago and everything that was said here today subsequently was said by the doctors—but not as eloquently, that's all. . . . Now, Clint, for example, in this organizational structure, is much closer to the head of this operation than the Assistant Secretary of State for Latin America is to the Secretary of State. The Assistant Secretary of State for Latin America is in an extremely high and important policy-making position in the State Department. He has to go through not only the AID Director but through two Under Secretaries to get . . . to the Secretary of State. So, in Washington terms, [Bamberger is] anything but layered over, as the phrase goes.

Bamberger finally closed the discussion, "Maybe we can try it for a while. We can see how our actions work out after three more months when we'll be back here."

John Cummiskey then reminded Shriver he may not have heard the last of the issue concerning the relationship between CAP and Legal Services: ". . . I think the real answer is, we get back and keep pressing to get these proposals in here, and if we have administrative troubles, I'm sure from the conversation you've heard today that we'll bring it up again."

There were many issues to concern the National Advisory Committee during the next few years: the Legal Services *Guidelines,* budgetary levels, legislative attacks against the program and many others. But if there was a theme to the deliberations of this Committee, one to which the members returned again and again, it was the unworkable relationship between CAP and the office of Legal Services.

Less than a month after the National Advisory Committee meeting had been held, a major reshuffling of the OEO administration further complicated the management task which confronted the Legal Services staff. In early December, Shriver delegated his authority for approving grants under $500,000 to the seven regional OEO directors. Headquarters personnel did not see a program proposal until after it had become a grant. Consequently, it appeared as though the Legal Services director was to be stripped of his primary source of power before the Program he headed was even underway.

On December 5, 1965, Bamberger hurried a one-page memorandum to the CAP director.

When Sargent Shriver spoke of delegating his authority to the regional directors, he may not have realized that in almost all instances he would be delegating authority to approve Legal Services Programs and that only a very few of those would be crossing his desk. I think he ought to be made aware of this.

At this stage of building this program, I am not willing to delegate to either my people in the region or the regional [OEO] director the final authority to approve applications for Legal Services grants. The suggested procedure should be modified to provide for approval by me before approval by the regional [OEO] director.

The reasons for my position are:

(1) We are beginning a new program without inflexible guidelines and a program which will probably never evolve to the point where we are funding a fixed kind of program. Legal Services Programs will not fit a mold. We must encourage different approaches and methods to find the most effective.

(2) We are dealing with a limited amount of money, and we cannot afford to have all of the expenditure concentrated in limited areas.

(3) We are dealing with an extremely sensitive program about which there is considerable criticism and opposition. National guidance and responsibility is necessary to counter this.[16]

The veiled hint that this was an issue about which Bamberger felt strongly enough to lodge an appeal with Shriver was not lost on the CAP hierarchy, and they quietly agreed to an artful compromise. The regional OEO directors and the national Legal Services director would share the authority in making Legal Services grants. Applications for such programs would undergo simultaneous review by the headquarters staff for Legal Services and regional OEO personnel. A grant could not be made without the signatures of both the regional OEO director and the national Legal Services director. Thus, each possessed a veto power that could be overridden only by Shriver himself.

IV. EXPERIENCE UNDER THE "SEMI-AUTONOMOUS" LEGAL SERVICES STRUCTURE

After this second compromise between Bamberger and CAP was converted to management instructions[17] and flow charts, it came out a masterpiece of complexity with as many checkpoints within the regional offices as there originally had been in the headquarters review process. Predictably, all the pending Legal Services applications, of which there were seventy-five at the time, soon were trapped in this maze. From December, 1965 through March, 1966 almost no grants emerged from the review process.

This laggard performance became the prime topic at the March 6, 1966, meeting of the National Advisory Committee. The NAC members were told that, during the first nine months of fiscal year 1966, the Legal Services Program had obligated less than $3 million in grants. CAP director Berry unintentionally confirmed their suspicions of bureaucratic sabotage by announcing that the Program would have to be satisfied with only a few demonstration projects rather than the nationwide network of neighborhood law offices the organized bar had expected ever since the ABA had endorsed the Program in February 1965.[18]

Whether deliberate sabotage or not, it was known that scores of Legal Services applications languished on the desks of CAP personnel in regional offices across the nation. The problem for the Legal Services staff and the National Advisory Committee was to dislodge the stalled proposals and make the seemingly unworkable bureaucratic machinery work. It was fairly obvious the way to accomplish this was not to appeal to the CAP leadership. Rather, the case had to be made to Shriver himself. Therefore, on March 8, NLADA president Theodore Voorhees sent a letter to the OEO director, pleading on behalf of the National Advisory Committee.

> I would like to review the background of some of the causes of the uneasiness we expressed to you last week. . . .
>
> At the November meeting of the Advisory Committee, we tried unsuccessfully to persuade you that Legal Services should not be engulfed in the Community Action Program, but it was not until our January meeting that our present fears began to arise. . . .
>
> . . . Mr. Berry told us on Thursday, March 6, that we could only look forward to the funding of a limited number of programs, and these would have to be good. . . . [T]he fact remains, that twelve months after the ABA resolution in New Orleans there are only 17 Legal Services funded, with a total allocation of less than three million dollars. Whatever the reasons, the statistics can only be interpreted by your Advisory Committee as establishing that some of the key people in OEO do not have their heart in the Legal Services Program.
>
> . . . [W]e of the Advisory Committee are not prepared to abandon at this early date the idea that the Legal Services attack on poverty must cover the whole country nor are we yet willing to accept retreat to a few enclaves.
>
> I sincerely trust that you have not been persuaded to take this defeatist view, i.e., that OEO will accomplish at most some demonstration programs that may be worthwhile. We in Legal Aid have fully committed ourselves to our Legal Service War on Poverty, and if OEO is going to adopt a detached and skeptical view of the worth of this program, we, who consider ourselves your faithful allies, will soon find ourselves high and dry. . . .
>
> Please do not interpret this as an indication that we mistrust your sincerity. We know that you fully share our conviction that legal services are a powerful weapon in your war. But we feel that your agency as a whole is less than fully enlightened and that without your strong intervention to protect this program, it is in danger of being wrecked.[19]

Shriver responded by summoning Bamberger and asking how the applications might be brought up for approval. The Legal Services director said he needed Shriver's backing to prod disinterested or recalcitrant regional personnel. They finally settled upon a plan—a press conference strategy.[20] In early April, Shriver would schedule a press conference for April 25, at which he and several bar leaders were to appear to announce the funding of 25 or 35 Legal Services grants. Shriver's instructions to headquarters and regional personnel were that *at least* 25 Legal Services applications must be forced through the review process before the April 25 deadline.

The Legal Services staff then supplied Shriver with a stream of detailed status reports that revealed the precise location of the 35 grant applications that could feasibly be signed in time for the press conference. These reports named the persons on whose desks the applications currently rested. As the target date approached, Shriver began placing personal calls to staff members who were delaying the flow of these grants.

These tactics may have irritated the CAP bureaucracy but they also made it produce. On the scheduled date, April 25, Shriver, surrounded by ABA leaders, announced that the 35 grants had been approved. This $6-million package totaled more than the combined annual budgets of all existing legal aid organizations. Shriver then passed the word internally that he was scheduling a press conference on May 26, for the sole purpose of announcing another 25 to 35 Legal Services programs. The status reports, telephone calls, and prodding continued, and on May 26 it was announced to the media that 32 grants, totaling over $7 million, had been made. The same strategy was employed a third time to gain approval of another 52 grants worth over $10 million dollars on June 30, the last day of the fiscal year.

The intervention of Shriver and the success of the press conference strategy apparently upset CAP's plan to contain OEO's new national emphasis program—Legal Services. On April 15, in the midst of the drive toward the initial target date, CAP director Berry had promulgated a memorandum reducing the Legal Services national budget allocation from $20 million to $15 million and setting maximum figures for each region on that basis. Bamberger reacted by sending a memorandum addressed to Berry but also forwarded to Shriver, complaining about the unilateral action.

> This reduction contradicts and impairs our current efforts to have as many legal services programs as possible funded in FY '66. In addition, the allocation of the $15 million through the regions, which to my knowledge was done without our participation, creates problems in some if not all regions. For instance, the allocation for the Great Lakes Region is $2,145,000 and, if all of the grants scheduled for approval are finally approved for the Monday, April 25 sign off, we will have $2,061,530 approved in that region with only $83,000 left for the remainder of the fiscal year. We already have pending applications in the region which will far exceed that amount. One result of this is that Bill Downs is now saying that we must stop encouraging applications and make judgments about the few additional applications we will approve in the Great Lakes Region.

... It is unfortunate that the memo with the $15 million allocation was ever sent out without asking me what was going to be funded within a week. .... We now have the contradiction of my being pushed and pushing to get more programs approved and the regional directors concerned with staying within their allocations.[21]

Shriver returned the memorandum to Berry with a handwritten note:

Please change this situation immediately, especially by telling Bill Downs. We want these programs.
Sarge.

And if there were any doubt about his displeasure with CAP, he included a marginal note:

Ted Berry,
not just unfortunate
it's ridiculous.

The allocation of $15 million was immediately returned to $20 million and before the end of the fiscal year was increased to $25 million.

In its first fiscal year, the OEO Legal Services Program made more grants and committed more funds than its most enthusiastic supporters had expected.[22] However, this was accomplished despite the bureaucratic arrangements created to house the Program. Only by subverting, circumventing, compromising and pressuring the regional offices and the CAP administrators was the Legal Services staff able to overcome the inherent delays and complications of the formal procedures.

Moreover, these stresses and strains carried over into subsequent years. The National Advisory Committee and Legal Services staff continued to press for a completely independent program while CAP sought to assimilate the Legal Services office into its own structure. The competing pressures resulted in a stalemate and the perpetuation of the status quo, a complex, conflict-ridden and inefficient compromise.[23]

V. THE REGIONALIZATION CONTROVERSY

In mid-1967, even the leaky bureaucratic vessel in which the Legal Services Program had ridden out its first 20 months was placed in peril. It appeared for a time as though the Program would be swallowed up by CAP and, even after the ultimate threat of extinction was thwarted, the buffeting continued at a lessened pace until the entire OEO bureaucracy was reorganized by the Nixon administration in 1969.

This threat had its origins in June, 1966 with the appointment of Bertrand Harding as the new deputy director of OEO. A career civil servant, Harding had risen through the ranks of the Federal establishment to become deputy director of the Internal Revenue Service. By coincidence, he also had chaired a special Task Force that examined OEO's administrative structure and its problems in late 1966.[24]

Harding was not selected for the OEO job by Shriver but by the White House. Rightly or wrongly, the White House had diagnosed the war on poverty's ills to be largely the result of administrative inefficiency. Shriver was well known for his low regard for neat bureaucratic pigeonholes and channels. His willingness to tolerate—and even encourage—direct access by the Legal Services director, rather than requiring adherence to a pattern of reporting through the CAP director, was symptomatic of Shriver's general management philosophy.[25] Harding was sent to straighten out OEO,[26] and thus Shriver was in a difficult position when confronted with Harding-initiated (and by implication White House-backed) changes in his "administrative (or creative) chaos." Since Shriver was the official who had promised the organized bar an effective role in policy making and that lawyers would run the Legal Services Program, his diminished power over management questions accounts, in no small measure, for what happened to the Legal Services Program during this period of rapid administrative reorganization.

A. The Management Consultant's Report

Bertrand Harding is an experienced, astute government official. It is not his style and it was not his intent to launch sweeping changes, disrupting entrenched bureaucratic power relationships, without building a convincing case and assembling a powerful internal consensus for change.

One of Harding's first actions was to engage a prestigious management consultant firm—McKinsey and Company—to undertake a comprehensive study of OEO's internal management.

After analyzing the agency's existing organizational structure,[27] McKinsey issued a report discussing the feasibility of two alternative theories of management for large-scale organizations—decentralization versus regionalization. Each of these management concepts presupposes a headquarters office and several regional offices. Under the decentralization approach, individuals in the regional offices are extensions of their respective divisions at headquarters. They generally are chosen and promoted by the headquarters division, report directly to the chief of the headquarters division and receive instructions and policy guidance from the same source. Any power they possess is delegated to them from their division manager at the national level.

Under regionalization, on the other hand, virtually all power and responsibility are transferred to an overall regional director who, in turn, delegates to other personnel in that office. The regional director—not the headquarters division leader—selects and promotes staff and it is to the regional director—

not the headquarters division—that the regional staff member reports. In effect, regionalization divides a single national program into several separate regional programs. The headquarters is confined to an advisory role except for certain centralized functions such as congressional relations.

After a very brief analysis of the suitability of these two management theories for the OEO organization, the McKinsey report recommended full-fledged regionalization. This proposal accorded with Harding's own predispositions. During his tenure at the Internal Revenue Service, he had been one of the architects of the reorganization of that agency, incidentally one of the most thoroughly regionalized of all government agencies.

The implications of the report for the Legal Services Program were profound, for it recommended dissolution of the semi-autonomous status of the Program. The national Legal Services director was to be stripped of his power to approve grants.[28] Nor would he participate in the selection of regional personnel. Moreover, the regional Legal Services staff members also would be deprived of most of their existing authority, which was to be transferred to CAP generalists.[29] The regional Legal Services personnel were to function strictly in an advisory capacity to the CAP staff and then only when their advice was requested. Thus, with one deft stroke the McKinsey report recommendations threatened to excise lawyer control from the Legal Services Program.

B. The Decision to Resist Regionalization

The McKinsey report was merely a proposal to OEO, and the first thing the Legal Services staff had to do was determine whether OEO's administrators were likely to accept those recommendations and especially those relating to the Legal Services Program. The staff also wanted to find out when Mr. Harding was planning to decide these issues.

From conversations with several individuals close to Harding, we ascertained that he favored the extreme form of regionalization recommended in the McKinsey report. I was told he was very experienced in this type of bureaucratic strategy. The McKinsey recommendations would not be implemented instantaneously, but only after a consensus was developed through a series of meetings with program heads, regional directors and other concerned OEO officials that might stretch over the next six months or longer. But Harding was determined to regionalize OEO completely—and along with it, the Legal Services Program. We were advised to accept that fate and accommodate our thinking to the revised structure.

That was not an encouraging prospect for some of the very basic goals of the Legal Services Program. There was little support for many of those objectives elsewhere in the agency. Two examples illustrate the problem.

. . . One Regional OEO Director—the man who under full regionalization would have exercised sole ultimate power over the Legal Services Program in better than twenty percent of the nation—said he did not believe it was appropriate for Federally-supported Legal Services lawyers to sue local government agencies.[30] On this ground he had approved a restriction on the Chicago Legal Aid Bureau precluding its neighborhood attorneys from filing suits against city agencies. Only the power of Legal Services headquarters to withhold concurrence from such a grant restriction prevented that policy from going into effect and thereby emasculating the Chicago legal assistance effort.

. . . OEO's General Counsel echoed the sentiments of many nervous OEO officials when he argued at the May, 1968 meeting of the National Advisory Committee that law reform—the announced top priority of the Legal Services Program—was too dangerous politically.[31]

Almost as debilitating as the philosophical differences were the administrative weaknesses of the structure into which the Legal Services Program was to be merged under the McKinsey and Company recommendations. Legal Services policies, lawyers and clients would pass into the hands of inexperienced generalists and be subject to inappropriate procedures which might be more costly to the goals of the Legal Services Program than any deliberate opposition to those goals. Edwin Kepler, director of the Bridgeport Community Action Agency in a May 26, 1967 letter to Sargent Shriver provided firsthand testimony.

. . . The contrast between the administration of the prepackaged [national emphasis] programs and community action [local initiative programs] is the difference between day and night.

. . . To a greater or lesser extent, the prepackaged programs administered by OEO appear to me to be competently run. In making application for a Legal Services Program, for example, a CAA finds itself dealing with qualified legal specialists who know what is to be done and who are eager to minimize delays in getting the program underway. . . .

In stark contrast is CAP's service to community action. Here we find (to use Connecticut as an example) one person charged with responsibility for reviewing in onerous detail all the original (non-prepackaged) programs of more than a dozen different CAAs. These programs necessarily treat with a variety of local problems and, for proper review, require not only an acquaintance with the local scene but also familiarity with a greater range of disciplines and professional and technical fields than any one person is likely to have. Merely to spell out the matter in this fashion is enough to excuse the person assigned to this responsibility for his failure to meet it. The requirements and conditions of the job are impossible, and this situation has been permitted to exist without correction for the past two years.

. . . At a recent meeting of Connecticut CAA directors, I heard the observation made that if OEO were deliberately trying to sabotage community action in a subtle, covert way, it could hardly do better than to adhere to the present practice of discouragement, delay, obstruction, and ignorance of local conditions that now characterize OEO's field operations.[32]

Full regionalization also would violate the gentleman's agreement OEO had made with the ABA—the agency's guarantees of lawyer control, a national office, meaningful policy input by bar leaders and all the rest. These were very real commitments upon which the ABA had relied and because of which it had nursed the Program through its delicate infancy. This added a moral dimension to the McKinsey recommendations.

Despite these problems, we already had learned enough to know there was no chance of persuading Harding to exempt Legal Services from the general regionalization order. An appeal to Shriver also appeared to be futile. First, Shriver was absorbed in a heated congressional struggle over OEO's survival as an agency. Second, he had delegated full authority over internal administration to Harding and for that reason would be reluctant to override his deputy director in that area. Third, we suspected that Shriver was under severe pressure from the White House to support Harding's efforts to reorganize OEO, regardless of his own opinions. And finally, it was well known Shriver would be leaving the agency in a few months. Thus, any commitments he did make would be short-lived in their effect. Only three alternatives were therefore left: to carry out Harding's regionalization decision, resign my position, or go outside channels to attempt to mount political pressure that would compel the OEO's second-in-command to except Legal Services from his decision. Either of the first two alternatives would have guaranteed the full regionalization of the Legal Services Program.

This was something I talked over with Damon Holmes, Harding's special assistant, on several occasions. The basic issue was the loyalty owed by a Federal bureaucrat to his superiors in the agency and to the policies they favored. Holmes took almost a military view of civilian government agencies. According to his thesis, each bureaucrat owed allegiance to the decisions of the bureaucrat above him in the same sense that an army lieutenant follows the orders of his captain, the captain takes orders from his major, the major from his colonel, and on up the chain of command. Holmes said that, if I considered the McKinsey and Company recommendations this serious, there was an honorable recourse even in his conception of bureaucratic responsibility. I could resign as Legal Services director. This would wash my hands clean of any stigma attaching to what I conceived as immoral conduct toward the ABA. It likewise would remove me from responsibility for whatever befell the policies, attorneys and clients of the Program when they passed into the hands of those I felt were not always sympathetic to the lawyer's unique role in the war on poverty. But the resignation alternative would have only hastened rather than forestalled implementation of full regionalization. Although it may have been personally satisfying, it appeared that move was suicide for the Program as a program and eventually would visit real harm on the lawyers and clients. For that reason, I elected to remain and attempt to mobilize outside pressures to affect decisions of my superiors in the OEO hierarchy.

C. Making the Bureaucracy Respond

To bring outside pressure, we alerted certain key leaders of the organized bar to the McKinsey and Company report in the summer of 1967. Their reaction was almost violent. The leadership of the ABA viewed the recommendations themselves as a prospective breach of OEO's contract with the Association, which, as I have said, had bargained for a semi-autonomous office of Legal Services administered throughout by lawyers. This was the realization of the deepest fears the organized bar had harbored about the OEO Program from its inception. Without lawyer control, they feared for the independence of the lawyers serving disadvantaged clients; they were concerned about adherence to the Canons of Professional Ethics; and less altruistically, they probably were bothered by a possible lack of sensitivity to some of the economic problems of the bar.

Richard Nahstoll's reaction was typical. He was a former president of the Oregon State Bar and had served on a team that had toured the nation promoting the Legal Services Program during 1966 and 1967. Though Nahstoll was a liberal Democrat and ACLU member, he was just as upset as the Republicans who occupied most of the leadership positions in the ABA. "If that McKinsey thing goes through—or anything like it—I'm going to barnstorm this country from one end to the other telling lawyers that the ABA was double-crossed and that they should fight the OEO Program tooth and nail."[33]

The organized bar began to act at the ABA's annual convention which was held in Honolulu in early August, 1967. Vice President Hubert Humphrey was the featured speaker and Orison Marden, the ABA president (and incidentally a former NLADA president) was Humphrey's official host. He capitalized on the opportunity to acquaint the Vice President with the threatened implementation of the McKinsey report and its implications for the Legal Services Program. Humphrey agreed this was not a wise administrative change and promised to investigate.[34]

The following day, Marden telephoned Sargent Shriver in Washington. He advised the OEO director of his conversation with the Vice President and detailed the reasons for the ABA's deep-felt opposition to the McKinsey recommendations. Shriver's response was somewhat vague about the long run. But he was unequivocal about the immediate future. He promised there were no present plans to implement the recommendations with respect to the Legal

Services Program. And further, that step would not be considered until there had been a full airing of the issues with the NAC.[35]

At the time of the ABA convention, however, many of the McKinsey recommendations already had been put into effect in several regional offices. For instance, in the Great Lakes (Chicago) and Southwest (Austin) regions, regional Legal Services officers were barred from contacting Legal Services projects directly or responding to requests from communities interested in applying for this type of grant. Thus, we sought to follow up the Marden conversations with some affirmative action which would nullify these administrative changes. From Hawaii, I telephoned Washington and requested the preparation of a memorandum for Shriver's signature. The memo was addressed to all regional OEO directors and ordered reinstatement of the status quo in the administration of the Legal Services Program while the McKinsey and Company recommendations were under discussion at headquarters.

It then became apparent that Shriver was not a completely free agent in making decisions about the internal administration of OEO. That memorandum remained on his desk—unsigned—for weeks. Although it stated no more than he had orally committed to Orison Marden in August, Shriver procrastinated over the memorandum through August and September. He asked for the views of CAP director Berry and OEO deputy director Harding. Predictably, they opposed his issuing the statement on grounds the recommendations about Legal Services were sound, and probably would be implemented. That meant the proposed memorandum would merely confuse the regional offices.

In the meantime, the situation in the regional offices was drifting steadily toward the McKinsey recommendations, because the OEO regional directors sensed the growth in power those recommendations entailed. By late September, 1967, there was a very real possibility that the Legal Services Program would become regionalized without any formal consideration or decision in OEO headquarters. It was in this state of affairs that the National Advisory Committee came to Washington for its regular quarterly meeting.

On the night before the September 21 NAC meeting, I had dinner with several key ABA leaders, including its new president-elect, William Gossett. Another former NLADA president, Gossett was a prominent corporation lawyer who had served formerly as vice president and general counsel of the Ford Motor Company. A cool, hard negotiator, he was determined to use the NAC meeting as an occasion to extract some sort of firm commitment from the OEO administration.

We also discussed the longer range problem of how to protect the integrity of the Legal Services Program after Sargent Shriver departed. By this time, it was obvious that Shriver's tenure would not extend far beyond the conclusion of the struggle to gain congressional approval of OEO's 1967 legislation. Any promises he personally made to the NAC would not bind OEO after that date.

For that reason, it was concluded that the members of the National Advisory Committee should concentrate on Harding, who probably would influence OEO administration more than anyone else after Shriver's departure. But what if Harding would not agree to any meaningful commitment? Then, it was agreed the organized bar had no recourse except to approach Congress.

John Robb, chairman of the ABA's Standing Committee on Legal Aid, and John Tracey, assistant director of the ABA's Washington office, reported they already had made some preliminary inquiries of a few congressmen on the crucial House Education and Labor Committee. Although uniformly supportive of the ABA position, these congressmen were pessimistic about the prospects of passing a statutory provision prohibiting the full regionalization of the Legal Services Program. The issue was too narrow and the change too technical to attract support.

Congressman James O'Hara of Michigan suggested the same purpose might be accomplished by inserting some appropriate language in the final report which was to be submitted by the Education and Labor Committee in a few weeks. Federal agencies—especially those as politically vulnerable as OEO— treat the language of committee reports with almost the same respect as the statutes themselves. Bureaucrats know that next year they must appear before those same congressmen sitting on that same committee with the same power to modify, curtail, expand or emasculate the powers and responsibilities of the agency. They know they must account for every policy and decision they have made during the preceding years. Any departure from the clearly expressed intent of the committee itself will be almost impossible to justify to the satisfaction of the members. Thus, Congressman O'Hara's suggestion of using the committee report to restrain OEO from altering the Legal Services Program's administrative relationship offered a feasible political alternative almost as effective as legislation itself.

No decision had yet been made to deploy ABA's strength in Congress, for that depended on the outcome of the National Advisory Committee meeting the following day. Robb had drafted appropriate language for the House report if that meeting proved inconclusive. The draft was passed around and approved with only slight modifications. That crumpled piece of paper in John Robb's breast pocket was the ABA's ace-in-the-hole—or more aptly its ante for the next game—as president-elect Gossett and his associates sat down at the table with OEO's top officials on September 21, 1967.

Shriver appeared at the morning session and discussed the reorganization issue in general terms. He adhered to his position that the McKinsey report would not be implemented until there had been full consideration of the problems. But as anticipated, he referred all questions about long-term policy to Harding, whom he promised to deliver for the afternoon session. Consequently, the NAC was willing to release Shriver from the witness chair with a pair of lighthearted poems summarizing their concerns.[36]

The afternoon exchange with OEO deputy Harding and CAP director Berry
was not nearly so friendly. ABA president Orison Marden recapitulated the
Committee's position.

[M]ay I just make one or two general observations, perhaps to show you why
we are so concerned about the whole picture. I don't want to make any invidious
comparisons with other professions, but when the Legal Services Program was
first born within the agency, we had one terrific job to get the organized bar and
lawyers generally interested in it and behind it and supporting it. [W]e had to
represent to lawyers and we did represent to the lawyers . . . that this was going
to be a professional program, run by lawyers. Lawyers were going to be on top
of it, Canons were going to be enforced, and there would be a National Advisory
Committee to supervise and help the director with his guidelines and so forth.
And, up and down the line, lawyers would be running the Program.

Then along comes McKinsey and we hear that laymen are going to be in charge.
. . . Then we hear that in fact . . . without McKinsey [actually being approved
by OEO headquarters] the professional operations of these lawyers are being
sabotaged in large part by paperwork, by taking telephones away, by taking
secretaries away, all sorts of little things that in effect are attempts by . . . regional
CAP people to assert authority over the Legal Services Program.

Now, we regard as one of the most important parts of this program the power
in the director of Legal Services to sign off these programs, because we have had
instances of very poor programs coming out of the region that would have been
approved regionally if they had not been stopped here in Washington.[37]

Harding responded by pressing regional Legal Services personnel to state
specific complaints about treatment of the Legal Services Program by CAP.
Several NAC members attempted to summarize some of the testimony they
heard from Legal Services staff members in the morning session. But Harding
was able to refute or obscure their hazily remembered points, until finally
William McCloskey, the forty-two-year-old black lawyer who served as regional Legal Services director from Chicago took the floor.

I am from the Great Lakes region. [The Director of] the Great Lakes regional office opposes the control of Legal Services by the national office, and
the status quo that Mr. Shriver, Mr. Harding, and Mr. Berry . . . described as
a schizophrenic, cockamamie system. . . . When two programs were funded
on June 30, without the knowledge of the Legal Services Program, when I
was informed about it on July 5, I was told that it was done because the Director wants to have a showdown as to who is going to run the Legal Services Program, whether Earl Johnson is going to run it in Washington or
whether Alan Beals [the Regional OEO Director] is going to run it in
Chicago.

McCloskey then recounted several other examples of the attempts of the
regional office to usurp his authority or that of the headquarters Legal Services
office.

Now, in each of these instances, what was done to hamstring the Legal Services Program was not because of a shortage of funds or an attempt to improve the service. But it was specifically stated that it was to show who was boss. . . . I think whatever this word 'schizophrenia cockamamie system' means, it describes the attitude of the region toward the Legal Services Program. And that is the only way I can explain it. . . . And if I, as a lawyer, were required to do some of the things that [the Regional OEO Director and the regional CAP office] want, I would have to either resign or face disbarment, because their conception of what a Legal Services Program is doesn't meet with our guidelines. They don't meet with mine as a professional lawyer.

Gossett saw an opening to seek the firm written commitment from Harding that was the minimal objective he wished to achieve at this NAC meeting.

Mr. Harding, you wonder why these things are done. I think with some time we could persuade you that they are being done and that they are being done deliberately, and that they represent tactics that are harassing. But the thing that gives us concern, and the reason we are here and the reason we are speaking so candidly, is that we are fearful that those things would not be done if they didn't have support from this office.

Now—

Harding, taken aback by Gossett's accusation, broke in, "Which office—my office?"

"I am talking about it this way—the OEO office," Gossett replied, then returned to the attack.

You say that the instructions from here are that the status quo is to be maintained. Now, the thing that gives us concern is why those instructions have not been put in writing. . . . [W]as there objection from others in this office to signing such a memorandum as was prepared by Mr. Johnson for Mr. Shriver's signature?

Harding's response to that question prompted a lengthy exchange between himself and several NAC members about the respective merits of oral versus written directives. Dissatisfied with Harding's replies, former National Bar Association president Revius Ortique broadened the discussion, "I agree . . . that this whole issue goes deeper. . . . Our concerns really grow out of the possibility that this understanding that we were willing to accept, based on our beliefs in what they were saying to us, is now slowly trickling away. And before it gets away completely, this Council is disturbed enough to adopt a resolution."

CAP director Berry began to worry aloud about the implications of the NAC comments.

[W]hat seems to emerge here is a restlessness with being part of the administrative organization for the ongoing Community Action Programs, to move further and further to the right or left, I don't know which, for establishing for this bureau independence and autonomy, separate, distinct from Community Action and completely de hors Community Action. I hope that wouldn't be the eventual result. We are willing to address ourselves to every measure that will effect good administration and at the same time protect all of the things that this Advisory Committee first addressed itself, from the very beginning, as to both the integrity of the program and the quality of the program.

"Well, we have some uneasiness and restlessness, Mr. Berry," NLADA president Maynard Toll responded, "in view of the history of written communications on this subject."

Gossett joined the heated discussion, "You tell us that the status quo is going to be maintained—we are uneasy about it. I think there is reason for us to be uneasy, because you seek to . . . brush it off on the ground that this is a concern about nothing, and that really this thing is going on just as it has. If it is going on as it has, why don't we put it in writing?"

With time running out, John Robb put the underlying fear squarely on the table:

> This concerns this problem that we have raised and that hasn't really been answered by either of you, that there seems to be some feeling in the regions that the reason why Legal Services is being subjected to this extra-special pressure is because there is some support from the top, at some high level in the agency. Which would suggest that we have simply sidelined the McKinsey report temporarily until maybe the appropriations bill is out of the way, or the heat is off, and then renewed efforts are going to be made to put it into effect. May I ask each of you directly, is there any such support being given to these programs from your offices?

Berry paused—then answered, "No."

"My answer to that," Harding said, "is that we are—I am giving earnest, careful thought to the best way to effectively strengthen the regionalization concept without doing violence to the quality of programs—certainly Legal Services and Health. And we are going to have the same issue when it comes to the question of regionalization of the comprehensive Health Program."

Harding's equivocal reply discouraged John Cummiskey. He looked squarely at Harding as he warned,

> I honestly think that you are unrealistic if you think you can accommodate this conflict. I believe that the conflict is now arising again because the Legal Services Program has proved itself, has seen the possibilities of creative law, and is beginning to show its muscle, which may eventually go into a kind of revolt. And I think we would be well advised if at some point we reexamined this whole relationship between the Legal Services Program and the OEO. It may mean that you have to have an amendment of the law, but I don't think the conflict is going to subside, I think it is going to get worse.

No one on the National Advisory Committee was satisfied with the responses made either by Harding or Berry. Bill Gossett had not received the ironclad commitment he sought. With scarcely a wave of the hand, he authorized John Robb and John Tracey to proceed with the strategy of placing restrictive language in the House committee report. That very afternoon they spoke with Congressman James O'Hara of Michigan and Congressman Lloyd Meeds of Washington. Both were liberals and members of the House Education and Labor Committee. O'Hara, in fact, was chairman of the Democratic Study Group—a coalition of over 150 liberal congressmen. As a major spokesman for the forces favoring OEO in Congress, he was in a unique position to advocate a proposal which tended to curtail the authority and freedom of the agency's staff. It was akin to the special credibility a Southern conservative carries in arguing for civil rights legislation.

O'Hara and Meeds promised to see the paragraph was inserted in the working draft of the committee's report. With good fortune, it would not be questioned by other members and emerge unscathed in the final report as a unanimous committee recommendation. If not, they would undertake to obtain majority committee approval of the language the ABA approved or its equivalent.

A few weeks later, the report of the House Education and Labor Committee was issued in final form. It contained the following provision:

> Within OEO, primary responsibility for the direction and administration of the Legal Services program has been lodged in the Legal Services Director and the lawyers on his professional staff. This has included primary authority respecting the initiation, supervision, evaluation, funding and refunding of individual local projects. The approval of the Legal Services Director has been required before any such individual project is funded or refunded. These aspects of the overall program have been largely responsible for its success, for its close adherence to professional guidelines and standards and for the unprecedented vigor with which it has been supported by the legal profession. The committee expects the continuance of these features of the program's administration.[38]

This was John Robb's precise language as it was supplied to Congressmen O'Hara and Meeds.

The appearance of this directive in the committee report startled the top OEO hierarchy. For a time, Harding and the General Counsel's office toyed with the idea of asking the Senate Committee staff to insert a contradictory directive in the report of the Senate Labor and Welfare Committee, which had jurisdiction over OEO in the upper chamber. But this thought was soon abandoned. Assuming it could be accomplished in the face of opposition from ABA lobbying, the conflicting language would tend to confuse and divide the liberals on the relevant committees in the two houses of Congress. These were the very legislators that OEO was counting on to preserve the agency's hide.[39]

In order to reaffirm the determination of the ABA's resolve, Gossett wrote a long official letter to Shriver and sent copies to Harding and Berry.

> If at that meeting we seemed to speak bluntly, and if the discussion sounded somewhat acrimonious at times, it was because the subject of the meeting was a matter of deep concern to all of us. We assume our full share of responsibility for the tone of the meeting. . . .
>
> And let me add that the singular success that the Program has enjoyed to date is attributable to a large extent, we think, to the support of the organized bar and to the centralized control of the Program, its standards and its objectives from Washington.
>
> If, therefore, it were contemplated that the Program should be controlled by laymen; if the regional legal service officer were to be no more than a technician who might be consulted periodically by CAP officials but would have no determining voice in the establishment or operation of community legal services facilities, if the direct lines of communication between the regional legal service officer and the local bar leaders on one side, and the Legal Services officer in Washington on the other, were to be terminated; and if the local head of the CAP, and not the legal services lawyer, were to be the decisive voice in establishing and directing local legal service facilities, all as recommended by the McKinsey Report, then we think the whole program would be in serious jeopardy.
>
> But we need not contemplate or even suggest the possibility of failure. For the Program now has the strong support of the bar, and *will continue to enjoy that support if the present arrangements are continued, as we hope and expect that they will be.* . . .[40]

Meanwhile, several influential congressmen called Shriver and expressed their displeasure over the trend toward regionalizing the Legal Services Program. Shriver pledged to restore the original arrangements. He further promised that no changes would be made without full prior consultation with the organized bar and Congress.

The pressures orchestrated by the ABA in cooperation with the Legal Services staff proved overwhelming. Harding capitulated and reversed his own carefully plotted campaign. He expressly excepted the Legal Services Program from the regionalization orders then engulfing the rest of OEO. The program's semi-autonomous status was guaranteed at least for the life of the Democratic administration.

Having halted the drift to regionalization, the staff of the Legal Services Program returned to the normal level of conflict which accompanied its hybrid position in the OEO structure. The question of improving the administrative relationships between Legal Services and CAP was delegated to a joint subcommittee made up of NAC members and CAP staff. Co-chaired by New York lawyer Jacob Fuchsberg and CAP deputy director William Bozman, this subcommittee wrestled with the problem for months without developing a mutually acceptable formula. The Legal Services advocates were not really satisfied with anything short of independence from CAP while the OEO representatives were not pleased with any resolution other than that of submerging the Legal Services Program into CAP.

The deliberations of the subcommittee did serve the function of forestalling any thought of implementing the McKinsey recommendations during the months after Shriver's departure. By the time the subcommittee reported it had reached an impasse, the presidential election and possible change of administration was in the offing. It made no sense, politically or pragmatically, for the acting OEO director, Harding, to order a reorganization of Legal Services that might be countermanded in a matter of months.

This standstill in relations between CAP and Legal Services remained in effect until June 1969, when the first Republican OEO director, Donald Rumsfield, refashioned the antipoverty bureaucracy by abolishing the CAP administration and elevating the Legal Services Program to the status of an independent operating division reporting directly to him. Legal Services advocates had seen the program through a scrape with bureaucratic extinction and were able to revel, momentarily at least, in President Nixon's announcement:

> The Office of Legal Services will . . . be strengthened and elevated so that it reports directly to the [OEO] Director. It will take on central responsibility for programs which help provide advocates for the poor in their dealing with social institutions. . . . This goal will be better served by a separate Legal Services Program.[41]

7: Implementing National Goals: Affecting the Management of Local Organizations

Distributing grants has become the way of doing business for the Federal government. In earlier days, when Congress desired to provide some service or product to the nation's citizens, it usually established a Federal agency staffed entirely by Federal employees to dispense that service or to create that product. The nation's mail is delivered by Federal employees. Its social security checks are issued by Federal employees. Its parks are patrolled by Federal employees.

But beginning on a substantial basis in the 1950s, the national government has shifted more and more away from direct operation of its programs. Instead of hiring its own employees to dispense the service or create the product, Congress establishes only a grant-making apparatus at the national level. The grant-makers supply Federal funds to state governments, cities, universities and private organizations which, in turn, offer the desired service or product to the nation's citizens. This has become the prevailing pattern for most new Federal initiatives, especially in the field of social welfare.[1] The nation's public assistance system, employment and job-training efforts, educational and scientific research endeavors are essentially Federal grant-making programs.

Like the rest of the war on poverty, the Legal Services Program also was a Federal grant-making program. The lawyers actually rendering the legal services were not Federal employees. They were neither hired nor fired by Federal employees. Nor did they take their orders from the national government. Rather these attorneys were the employees of a locally controlled organization which incidentally received all or a part of its financial support from the Federal government. Moreover, the philosophy of the OEO legislation and its administrators conferred an unusual amount of power and discretion on the local organizations that received grants. As administered by CAP, it was the grantee, rather than the Federal government, which designed as well as operated the services to be rendered to the poor.

These factors carried profound implications for the staff of the Legal Services Program and its ability to determine the direction and quality of the representation offered by Legal Services attorneys. In the following section we will explore some of the limitations inherent in the grant-making approach to the operation of the Federal programs and the special limitations imposed by the philosophy underlying community action. This will aid in understanding why and how the Legal Services staff sought to enlarge its authority beyond the powers exercised elsewhere in OEO.

I.   RESPONSIBILITY WITHOUT AUTHORITY: THE DILEMMA OF THE AGENCY MAKING A FEDERAL GRANT

The core of the grant-making agency's problem rests in the allocation of powers important to operating a program between the agency making a grant —the Federal government—and the agency accepting the grant—in this case, the local Legal Services Agency. Which are the most important powers?

1. One of the powers involves the right to *hire and fire* the *director* of the local agency that is rendering the service. The staff director, more than anyone else, is responsible for the fundamental stance of the agency on all the operational issues of relevance to its clients. If he is conservative or overly cautious or easily intimidated, the agency will tend to be conservative, overly cautious or easily intimidated. In most agencies, the director either hires and fires the other staff members or at least screens applicants for consideration by the board and recommends discharge of employees he deems undesirable. He establishes priorities; encourages or discourages, rewards, punishes or ignores conduct by agency employees; interprets OEO policy, local board policy, and the Canons of Professional Ethics for agency employees (the power to interpret is the power to distort); and otherwise guides the staff in one direction or another. Questionnaire returns from persons who have evaluated Legal Services agencies suggest that the single most important factor in the success of an individual agency is the orientation and ability of the director of that agency.[2] Common sense and experience in the business world tend to bear this out.

2. Another power involves the right to *hire and fire* the primary *operating personnel* (the staff attorneys in the case of a Legal Services Agency). The operating personnel—their intellect, orientation, commitment and experience —ultimately determine the quality and impact of the services received by the agency's clients. The individual or group with the power to select the staff attorneys in a Legal Services agency thus can largely control the quality and impact of the agency's product. And the individual or group holding the power to discharge staff attorneys can enforce conformity with their philosophy and priorities.

3. Another power is the ability to *reward* and *punish* agency personnel for

their performance of agency functions. Once an attorney is employed, his behavior on the job can be influenced by a variety of incentives. Salary increases and promotions at one extreme and demotion or discharge at the other are obvious examples. But more subtle rewards and punishments often are just as effective. A word of praise or a sharp reprimand, special mention to a possible future employer and similar actions can provide the psychological reinforcement to insure compliance with desired policies. The individual or group in a position to administer a reward or punishment—subtle and otherwise—can rein in any but the most independent employee.

4. There is the power to *supervise* agency personnel in their day-to-day decisions and conduct. The operating personnel do not make all relevant decisions themselves. Others can influence these choices either through advice, persuasion, or by countermanding the staff attorney's own decisions. These decisions can range from where to file extra copies of letters to whether to file a suit against the governor.

Any sensible manager would insist on holding these powers before undertaking responsibility for the success or failure of an enterprise. Yet each and every one of these powers is denied to the leadership of a Federal grant-making agency. It is the board of directors of the agency that receives the grant, and the staff director of that agency, who possess all these powers. This is a satisfactory arrangement only if there is a willingness to accept whatever product a random assortment of agency boards is interested in delivering. But if Congress, the general public, the consumers of the government-financed service, or anyone else is interested in a specific result, then the Federal grant-making authority must be given, or itself assume, some influence in the areas described above.

Particularly in a program aimed at institutional reform, or seeking national impact, or requiring sophistication or creativity, or involving a potential for controversy, it is seldom that any substantial number of local agency boards will employ the director, hire and supervise the staff, and otherwise manage their agencies in a manner to produce satisfactory results. The administration of the OEO Community Action Program—possibly because of its interpretation of the underlying philosophy of the statute and possibly for other reasons —was generally unconcerned with the basic management decisions of the agencies receiving grants. Their approach was to rely upon the more traditional powers of the grant-making agency—the power to influence the structure of the agency's board of directors and the overall design of the agency's planned projects. As we shall discover later, the staff of the Legal Services Program found it necessary to go far beyond these measures.

The management philosophy of the CAP administration was grounded in its interpretation of the phrase "community action." In fact, the meaning of that term underwent a drastic transformation between 1965 and 1967.

In the early months of OEO, community action equated almost precisely with "community organization." *"Real* community action" meant substantial power—in essence control—for the poor in the antipoverty efforts of the community. To guarantee *"real* community action," the Federal government was to deal firmly with other elements of the local community—to insist the poor be given a strong voice in the community action agencies and to insure that they receive meaningful programs.

Sometime in 1966 or 1967, I observed a subtle change beginning to infiltrate the term "community action." Before long, community action translated to local control (and as a practical matter this was usually local government control). Under this definition, to insure *"real* community action" the Federal government was to keep hands off the local community action agency. The local government, local businessmen, and the local establishment in general were to be free to plan and carry out their own version of an antipoverty program. In the interests of community action, OEO officials should *not* interfere to insist on meaningful participation by the poor or that meaningful antipoverty efforts were planned and carried out in the community.

Thus, at the very time the Legal Services Program staff was pondering the general weaknesses of local agencies operated under the principle of total local autonomy, the CAP administration was drifting toward an even more deferential attitude toward local decisions and control.[3]

It would be a mistake to infer there was unanimous agreement among the supporters of Legal Services that the Program should depart from the prevailing CAP approach of total community control. Local autonomy versus national direction was raised as an issue at the very first meeting of the National Advisory Committee. John Cummiskey posed the question in these terms:

> Well, it seems to me that there's one basic inconsistency that runs through all of our conversations including the guidelines because you start out by talking about local initiative and innovations, and if you come up with something at the local level, this is what we want. We want you to use your discretion to capacity. Because every place and every community is different. What's good for Chicago isn't going to be good for Podunk.
>
> But then we always have this little squiggle at the tail end that has to conform with the policy of OEO. And we have had some incidents where programs have been presented at the local level that have been held up because of policy problems.[4]

Cummiskey was referring primarily to the effect of national guidelines on the scope of local autonomy. But his comment raised the broader question of whether the Federal government should be allowed any meaningful role in the management decisions relevant to the success of Legal Services agencies.

Yet despite an occasional query, the National Advisory Committee seemed undisturbed about the insertion of national influence into the management of local agencies on a scale never attempted by other elements of the Community Action Program. The boards of local Legal Services agencies, the local CAAs, and local bar associations were another thing, however.

II. "BALANCED FEDERALISM": NATIONAL MANAGEMENT PARTICIPATION IN SUPPORT OF NATIONAL GOALS

By March, 1967 we had developed a fairly precise management goal for the Legal Services Program—to focus substantial program resources on law reform.[5] The very fact that the Legal Services Program staff had settled on a well-defined priority put it a long stride ahead of the rest of OEO's Community Action Program. March 1967 was, after all, only 14 months after the first National Advisory Committee meeting, 11 months after the first major funding of local Legal Services agencies, and only six months after most of the existing agencies actually began operation. OEO's Community Action Program, in contrast, had been in existence for almost 30 months and it was another year before they even *began* a serious attempt to define any specific national program priorities and goals.

But this long stride ahead of CAP was only a small step toward achievement of our management goal. As observed earlier, the Legal Services Program was not a self-contained Federal agency. The lawyers who worked in Legal Services agencies were *not* Federal employees; agency directors and boards that gave them direction were *not* Federal employees; their selection, promotion and psychological rewards were *not* Federally determined. All the inherent limitations of a Federal grant-making agency which were detailed earlier in this chapter and all of the special limitations applicable under the statutory and philosophical framework of the CAP section of the OEO legislation stood between us and effective management of the Legal Services Program (and maximization of the impact of that Program on the legal-economic-social structure that promoted poverty).

Over the succeeding months, the staff of the Legal Services Program experimented with a series of stratagems for circumventing these obstacles. Almost simultaneously, we tried:

(A) To persuade Legal Services agency board members and others in the legal profession of the legitimacy of our management objectives.

(B) To compel adherence to national priorities through evaluations and the sanction of potential or actual discontinuance of Federal financial support.

(C) To create a system of countervailing incentives that could be offered to employees of legal assistance agencies that would transcend the rewards, punishments, and limitations which might be imposed by the board or staff leadership of a local agency.

(D) To substitute the judgment of a single national hiring authority for local agency leadership in the selection of a substantial proportion of the operating personnel.

(E) To create a national superstructure of special agencies staffed by talented lawyers who could plan and carry forward law reform activities, enlisting local agency personnel to assist in these projects.

A. Persuasion of Local Agency Management

The persuasion of those responsible for fundamental management decisions in the local Legal Services agencies, like the original campaign promoting the OEO program, was undertaken with the assistance of the national leaders of the organized bar. These national bar leaders had been convinced by the Cahns, Sargent Shriver, Clint Bamberger and especially by one of their own, Lewis Powell, to embrace the concept of Federal financing of legal assistance to the poor. There had even been a clear warning in the writing of the Cahns and the rhetoric of Bamberger's speeches that more was to be expected of legal assistance lawyers in the future—that somehow they were to make a major contribution to the elimination of poverty. But until 1967 most bar leaders appeared to view this as an incidental by-product of the expansion of the legal aid movement and the usual activities of legal aid lawyers.

Experience proved to be a surprisingly quick and convincing teacher. It exposed the National Advisory Committee to the actual problems facing Legal Services agencies. At several meetings of that committee during 1966 and early 1967 members heard reports from evaluators and agency personnel describing the caseload problem and its crushing effect on innovation.

The motion made by Robb and Toll, discussed in Chapter 5, prompted the creation of a special NAC subcommittee to investigate the various methods of maximizing the effect of Legal Services attorneys.[6] The report of this subcommittee which was submitted to the April, 1967 meeting of the National Advisory Committee did not present a panacea for the caseload problem. But it confirmed the dedication of the NAC to the other goals of the poverty program, and especially law reform.

Within a short time, the leadership of the national bar was promoting the newly announced management goal of the Legal Services Program. By November, 1967, William Gossett, then president of the American Bar Association, was justifying law reform in public speeches to local bar associations. Typical of his powerful advocacy, Gossett told the Chicago Bar Association:

> [W]e need also to move on to new approaches on a new scale. . . .
> Justice is at best an elusive ideal. But it is a powerful one—capable of profoundly changing the hearts and minds and lives of men whatever their lot. To achieve this metamorphosis, however, the law—the only avenue to justice known to men—must constantly battle through to new frontiers of concern and interest.

The Legal Services Program of the Office of Economic Opportunity (with 800 offices and 1,800 lawyers in 47 states) has charted some of these frontiers that are today in crying need of penetration. They are: tenant-landlord relationships; consumer protection, particularly in installment buying; welfare law; and due process for juveniles, usually the unwanted children of the ghetto.

As every lawyer knows, there are appalling injustices in the laws governing the relations between landlords and tenants. . . . So in most states, legislative changes in landlord and tenant laws are long overdue. And there are other pressing needs. . . . [T]he whole nation—must face up to the need for social and economic innovation in our cities, and do it now![7]

Possibly the most convinced and convincing advocate of law reform as the highest priority for the Legal Services Program was John Robb, chairman of the ABA Standing Committee on Legal Aid to Indigent Defendants. Because of his position, he was more deeply engrossed in the actual performance of legal aid lawyers. Almost monthly he became more persuaded of the importance of law reform to the effectiveness of the Legal Services Program and its role in American society. By May 1969, he was testifying before Congress in these terms:

Many of these people will never see the inside of a law office. They will suffer indignity in silence.

But if you can see a regulation changed at the source, at the jugular, where it is being promulgated, thousands of people will benefit, who would never have an opportunity to pursue these results, because many of them considered that the law is their enemy, and that lawyers will tell them the same thing they have been hearing from other people. Law reform is therefore absolutely essential to the program, and one of the main things that the Murphy Amendment, as I understand it, would be directed against.

I would say that in discussing legal services without a law reform program, what you are doing here, it is much like an eight-cylinder car that is running on two cylinders. You are chugging along, making a lot of noise, but not going anywhere.

A legal services program without law reform will never get to the place where it is intended. It will never bring equal rights for people, it will never stand out, it will never bring dissidents into our system in feeling they have some stake here, and that problems can be solved within the system, as many of the gentlemen, including the deans, have so eloquently testified here before.[8]

In July, 1969, in an effort to insure continuing national support for the law reform priority, Robb, as chairman of ABA's Committee on Legal Aid, wrote to the incoming ABA president-elect, Edward Wright:

In accordance with our earlier discussions, I am sending further information about Legal Aid and Defender matters, including some of the serious problems which we face. . . .

The second great need is for a vigorous law reform effort. Legal Aid Agencies can achieve only limited although gratifying results on a case-by-case basis. Band-aids can't do much to attack deeply rooted infections. The real challenge for Legal Aid and for the bar is in achieving basic changes in the law so as to attack the underlying conditions which contribute to poverty, crime and the problems of our ghetto areas. Lawyers have always been in the forefront in effecting needed changes in archaic laws or in the development of new laws which are made necessary by changing circumstances. The American Assembly last year under-scored the obligations of lawyers and bar associations in this area. A major emphasis on law reform is currently under way among Legal Aid Agencies in such fields as housing, welfare, consumer credit and the like. The bar and lawyers in private practice must stoutly support these efforts for the voiceless unrepresented poor in the same fashion that they advocate changes in the law which unfairly afflict their own clients. . . .[9]

Neither Bill Gossett nor John Robb are radicals. Both are Republicans; both make their living representing some of the wealthiest and most powerful interests in American society. But for some reason, they and many others in the national leadership of the legal profession became advocates of law reform. This contrasted with prevailing attitudes at the local level. It was rather rare for essentially conservative elements on local agency boards to support this form of advocacy as wholeheartedly as Gossett, Robb and other national leaders.

The reasons for this apparently are based on differences between the national leadership of the organized bar and local leadership in that same profession, which are difficult to fathom. It may be that those leaders with a broader perspective are the ones who tend to rise to positions of national power. Or it could be that as any relatively sensitive person ascends toward national office, the parochial interests associated with his own clients gradually dimin-ish and then disappear in the shadows of the problems of the total society. Or, possibly, there was more time and opportunity for national bar leaders to educate themselves about the need for an antipoverty priority. Even more important, however, may have been the kind of law these bar leaders practiced. Law reform and all its techniques—test cases, legislative lobbying, advocacy before administrative agencies and the rest—are commonplace to the major firms out of which the ABA leaders came. They do this for their corporate and trade association clients all the time. Thus, it was easier for this type of lawyer to conceive law reform as a natural part of equal justice than it was for the typical private attorney who spent his time handling personal injury cases and drafting wills. Whatever the cause, the leaders of the American Bar Associa-tion and other national leaders of the organized bar were soon far ahead of most local agency board members and remained so at least through 1972.

Complementing the efforts of men like Bill Gossett and John Robb, the

Legal Services staff attempted to further the cause of law reform with local board members through our own speeches and writings. We recognized that many agency boards were dominated by politically conservative lawyers, but since we never viewed law reform as a radical proposal, it seemed natural to speak to them of the conservative roots of the concept. In a speech originally prepared for delivery at the University of Kentucky and repeated before many local and state bar associations, I argued:

> [A]n aspect of our program which seems daring and bold to many people is the emphasis we have placed on law reform. "Law reform" and "test cases" are phrases which give some lawyers an uncomfortable feeling. A few even interpret these phrases to represent something radical and sinister. But what is a "test case"? It is simply a lawsuit to which you devote enough time and effort to present your side of a legal issue in the best possible light with knowledge that you probably will have to carry the case to the appellate courts. Ordinarily you know beforehand that precedents do not exist on the key issue involved in the case, or that the existing precedents are against your client. But bringing test cases is not a subversive tactic; it is a lawyerlike method of offering the courts an opportunity to think about new issues or rethink old issues.
>
> I suspect that the reservations some of you may have about law reform stem from a belief that the present law is fine—that the status quo should not be tinkered with. I am sure there are lawyers who approve of laws that prevent a person from receiving welfare until he has been a state resident for a year, or two years, or three years and, as in some states, even six years. And there are lawyers who approve of court decisions that allow a landlord to evict a tenant merely because the tenant has reported housing code violations to the proper local authorities.
>
> I am sure there are lawyers serving as members of boards of directors of local legal services programs, and even as staff members, who feel that many of the laws and court decisions which the poor want to challenge are good laws and good decisions. It is to be expected and it is healthy. I am not concerned about it . . . so long as these lawyers fully appreciate the duty of lawyers serving clients, rich or poor—the duty to use every argument and every ethical stratagem, to raise every non-frivolous issue and to raise it artfully and argue it persuasively.
>
> We have no loyalty oath in the Legal Services Program—no oath that a board member or staff attorney must believe in the ultimate virtue of every legal change and every legal advantage the poor desire to achieve. But I submit the poor do deserve the same unquestioning devotion as the clients of other lawyers. I know a lawyer in Chicago, for example, affiliated with one of the largest, most prestigious firms in the city, who handles the tax work for some of the most powerful corporations and wealthiest individuals in America. This lawyer does *not* believe in the policy justification for oil depletion allowances—but no one is more artful in the use of these statutory provisions to save his clients' tax monies than he. He does not believe in the special tax break afforded capital gains. But no lawyer constructs more imaginative, better reasoned briefs for extension of this tax break

to other forms of income. This lawyer understands his role as a member of the legal profession, and I respect him for it. And I respect him even though I do not believe in the desirability or merit of many of the issues he raises. And yet, the more imaginative the argument he develops, the more persuasively his argument is presented, the more respect I have for him as a lawyer. The Legal Services Program asks no more than this: that even though staff attorneys, board members and other lawyers do not favor the changes which the poor demand, nevertheless, they make certain that those changes are presented to the courts and presented with as much imagination and persuasive skill as able lawyers can muster. The lawyers making those arguments, and the Legal Services Program which supports those lawyers, deserve the respect—and assistance—of the most conservative lawyers in America.

• • •

If it is possible in 1968 to invent a more conservative approach to the problems that face our country, I would like to hear what it is. The absence of a worthwhile answer to that challenge probably accounts for the broad support the Legal Services Program has received from conservative, as well as liberal, members of the bar. I submit that every member of the bar, conservative and liberal alike, has reason to embrace this program and that every citizen of this nation, conservative as well as liberal, has reason to pray for its success. It is our last, best hope to achieve essential change within a framework of law and order and to preserve law and order amid the turmoil of a tide of rising expectations.[10]

This same message was reiterated in one form or another time and again in the monthly newsletter of the Legal Services Program, *Law in Action.* Distributed to every agency board member, agency director and agency attorney, this publication also was sent to several thousand local bar association members. Its role was illustrated when some governing boards sought to suppress Legal Services attorneys who had brought controversial and meaningful legal actions on behalf of the poor. A *Law in Action* column reminded board members the Canons of Professional Ethics prohibited this sort of interference with the independent judgment of a lawyer.[11]

The speeches by national leaders of the bar, my own efforts and those of other staff members probably had some influence on local agency boards. It did make outright opposition to law reform a less respectable position for a local agency board member. There were isolated instances where a speech or *Law in Action* column was used to change the mind of a local board member who sought to suppress agency attorneys. But the resistance of many board members ran so deep that they would not yield to persuasion either from OEO or the leaders of their own profession. A sampling of the impressions of evaluators of Legal Services agencies in 1969 revealed that in over 62 percent of the projects, the agency boards actively suppressed or, at best, tolerated efforts at law reform on the part of their attorneys.[12] Clearly it was not easy to convince local boards and bar associations that Legal Services lawyers should champion the cause of the poor in a manner and with an intensity that might risk the wrath of the wealthy and powerful in American society.

B. Evaluations: The Effort to Compel Adherence to National Goals and Standards

As well as campaigning to persuade local agency board members and directors of the legitimacy and importance of law reform, Legal Services was endeavoring to compel at least minimal compliance with that goal through the evaluation mechanism. These evaluations were conducted annually. On the average, a three-man team spent three days in each community assessing the performance of the local Legal Services Agency. They interviewed staff and board members, local judges and lawyers, CAA personnel, representatives of the client community and anyone else who might provide information about the agency and its activities. According to the manual prepared by Charles Edson of the Legal Services staff, each evaluation team was to forward a report to Legal Services headquarters containing its findings and recommendations about the evaluated Legal Services Agency. In practice, the teams which were composed of some combination of Legal Services staff members, private attorneys, law professors and other very busy individuals, did not always submit these reports. On other occasions, when reports were prepared, they were sketchy and inadequate. In any event, on the basis of these reports, a Legal Services staff member was to prepare an evaluation letter, to be signed by myself and sent to the director of the Legal Services Agency. Again, because of a shortage of staff, these evaluation letters were not always prepared and sent. But these limitations did not bar a more important use of the evaluation technique; that is, the accomplishment of major surgery on clearly deficient grantees. A single example should suffice to demonstrate how evaluations were used to reorient certain local Legal Services agencies.

In a city of 300,000 located in the industrial Midwest, evaluators found an expanded legal aid society whose director discouraged law reform and deliberately structured his program to frustrate it. He scattered his ten attorneys among a like number of offices and insisted that they take all cases that crossed the threshold to insure that this staff would be too swamped for time-consuming test cases or legislative reform. He encouraged settlement of all cases and demanded the right to approve all cases brought against city agencies, an authorization seldom granted. The staff recruited by this director appeared to agree with this policy.

The evaluation report recommended extensive changes in personnel and structure. The director and half the staff should be replaced. A law reform office should be started in conjunction with a nearby law school. The remaining offices should be consolidated and several repressive policies should be rescinded.

Recognizing the agency board probably was no more sympathetic to law reform than the director it had hired, we decided to send Hugh Duffy, one of the evaluators on the OEO staff, to explain, justify and negotiate what seemed harsh demands. The formal evaluation letter threatened that the grant would be terminated unless the recommendations were implemented. After a stormy meeting with the board at which Duffy adopted the stance of mediator between Legal Services headquarters and the members of the agency board, a compromise was hammered out. The law reform office would be set up in partnership with the law school. The number of offices would be cut in half. Several restrictive policies would be abolished. Staff members would be encouraged to be more vigorous in their handling of certain categories of cases, especially welfare. However, the board balked at firing personnel, including the staff director. Duffy promised to seek a reprieve from Legal Services headquarters. This was granted, but only with the condition that the agency was to be reexamined in three months to determine its compliance with the promises made by the board.

Three months later, Duffy returned and found that the law reform office was nearly ready to be opened, several offices consolidated, and a few significant test cases actually underway. Satisfied that an honest effort was being made, we granted a further extension. A year later almost all our recommendations had been realized, including those pertaining to staff.

Even more drastic changes were made in several communities. After informal negotiations had been held with the bar leaders in a large Southwestern city, the staff director and his deputy were fired and the Federal funds were given to an entirely different agency. And in a metropolitan area of one million population, the veteran, but timid director of the legal aid society was replaced by a young, aggressive black lawyer whom OEO helped to recruit. The key elements remained the same. Not the evaluation itself, but the follow-up stage was critical: a firm recommendation for change, delivered orally or in an official letter, coupled with a threat of grant termination, then a series of personal negotiations by an OEO staff member, and a final settlement between the Legal Services office and the agency board. Although it was a time-consuming process, it usually worked relatively well, and, as a result, almost a dozen weak directors were replaced between January 1, 1967 and July 1, 1968. Restrictive policies discouraging law reform were abolished in a score of agencies, and other significant modifications were made in several others.

The process did suffer two shortcomings, however. First, the shortage of staff personnel made it impossible to subject many agencies to an intensive follow-up. During this period the total Legal Services staff, headquarters and regional, still consisted of only 15 professionals. Moreover, they were occupied with many other tasks, not the least being annual evaluations of all 300 of those who received Legal Services grants. That left only a few days a year for follow-up, not nearly enough for the scores of agencies that merited this intensive attention. (In retrospect, we probably could have made better use of the few staff members we had by doing away with the automatic annual evaluation of all grantees and substituting a system of selective review and follow-up concentrated on agencies with substantial problems.)

The second problem was more difficult to overcome. Reluctant board members can be compelled to make drastic program modifications only if they think the pressures from OEO are potent and real. But the only leverage possessed by the Federal grant-maker is his theoretical ability to refuse to re-fund an agency that is providing low quality services. The loss of Federal financial support might embarrass a conservative Legal Services board, but the real punishment would be inflicted on the agency's clients who would lose their sole source of legal help. Usually the community's poor prefer mediocre legal assistance to none. In effect, the only way we could discipline a delinquent agency was to beat some innocent clients over the head. Thus, in reality, we were extremely reluctant to actually carry out the threat of grant termination that was our only sanction at the bargaining table. Some boards realized this and steadfastly resisted OEO pressures for change. At best, the Legal Services staff was compelled to bluff its way through most negotiating sessions with grantees.

In addition to those situations where OEO staff members negotiated the replacement of a Legal Services agency director or engineered other major surgery, evaluations had other uses. None of these involved the threat or actuality of a fund cut-off and thus were more readily employed.

First, the prospect of an evaluation visit provided an agency director who himself wanted to engage in law reform some persuasive ammunition to use with a board of directors reluctant to undertake that kind of activity. The staff leader could urge that "If we don't file some test cases and do some work on legislation, we are not going to look very good to the OEO evaluators." However, conservative boards of directors rarely select vigorous staff directors,[13] and thus the evaluation mechanism seldom could be used this way.

Second, the "reward" of a good evaluation or the "punishment" of an unfavorable evaluation could motivate a reluctant agency board or staff to undertake actions—law reform in particular—that would please the evaluation team. In 1967 and 1968, findings and recommendations of evaluation teams were used to make the basic refunding decisions. A good evaluation could result in a bigger budget for the agency, as well as approval of a higher salary for the agency director or his management level staff. A bad evaluation could, and often did, result in a reduced budget, denial of salary increases, and other cut-backs in projects that meant something to those responsible for the management of the local agency.[14]

Third, through the evaluation process it was sometimes possible to identify local agencies that were willing to engage in law reform but lacked the necessary skill and sophistication. As early as November, 1966, a panel of experienced agency directors was assembled to work with inexperienced personnel from other agencies. As a practical matter, the members of this panel were so occupied with responsibilities in their own agencies that they were seldom available when called upon to render assistance, and there were few others that could help.

Fourth, evaluations provided the raw data upon which the Legal Services staff could base a reallocation of its limited funds among the existing local Legal Services agencies. Upon refunding, Legal Services staffs often increased the budgets of agencies receiving favorable evaluation reports at the expense of reductions in the budgets of local agencies that were not furthering national goals. Accordingly, the productivity of the total Legal Services investment tended to improve somewhat as superior agencies gradually drew a larger and larger proportion of the national budget.[15]

C. National Incentives in Support of National Goals

Everything described thus far was calculated to influence the attitudes and performance of agency boards and staff directors, those charged with the primary management decisions at the local level. These techniques sought to convince or compel the local leadership to select and motivate the operating personnel to carry forward the principal objectives of the national Legal Services Program.

At the same time the Legal Services staff initiated several steps aimed at achieving results irrespective of the attitudes held by board or staff leaders of grantees. In effect, we sought to exercise directly or indirectly some of the prerogatives that ordinarily repose solely in the management of local agencies.[16] In the first of these steps, we attempted to superimpose an independent system of incentives that would pull staff attorneys and other operating personnel of the local agencies toward the national goals of the program. These national incentives were designed to build allegiance among staff attorneys toward the national program that would transcend the rewards and punishments administered by the local agency leadership.

1. A national newspaper—*Law in Action*—was founded and published monthly between March, 1967 and July, 1968. It featured law reform successes and the attorneys responsible for those successes.[17] This newspaper was mailed to almost 40,000 subscribers each month. Thus, it afforded neighborhood lawyers the opportunity for national recognition. In fact, it was about the only way of acquiring a reputation outside your community or the respect of one's peers in the Legal Services world.

2. A national clearing house of legal memoranda and pleadings in law

reform cases was established. A *Clearinghouse Review* published summary accounts of its recent acquisitions and the lawyer responsible for the case. The clearing house also stimulated law reform by providing lawyers ready access to the ideas and professional work of innovative attorneys elsewhere in the nation. A looseleaf reporter, *Poverty Law Report*, was established to further knit together a national program and create a new field of law.

3. A national training program was instituted to orient and motivate staff attorneys toward the reform of laws and practices that harmed the poor. The training sessions exposed the participating lawyers to new legal theories and new techniques for accomplishing change rather than merely giving them familiar material about traditional approaches and existing legal principles. They also had the opportunity to meet attorneys who had been successful with reform efforts in other communities and states.

4. A Project Advisory Group was founded. Two-thirds of the members of this body were agency directors and the rest were staff lawyers actually serving clients on a daily basis. The PAG met to advise the national leadership of the OEO Legal Services Program (and also to select three members to the National Advisory Committee). It gave a few staff attorneys a direct voice in Federal policy making and provided others in local agencies some measure of participation in and loyalty toward those national policies.

5. One by-product of the national law reform centers, which will be discussed in greater detail in a later section,[18] was motivation for agency attorneys to engage in law reform. These centers distributed information about possible reform issues and made their services available to assist interested local attorneys in carrying such cases through to a successful conclusion. In effect, they encouraged reform by doing the groundwork research, sparking the imagination, and otherwise making it easier to engage in test cases and legislative advocacy.

All five of the measures discussed in this section were designed to make neighborhood attorneys feel they were part of a national program rather than merely employees of a local agency. *Law in Action,* the *Clearinghouse Review,* the *Poverty Law Report,* the training conferences and all the rest were constant reminders that the national program had national goals and recognized local attorneys who wanted to work toward those goals, that it offered them assistance in that work and gave them a role in the formation of Federal policy. Thus, enthusiasm was generated among rank and file Legal Services attorneys that could only be suppressed by the most determined and explicit efforts of local agency directors and boards unsympathetic to the national objectives. The most dramatic example of this commitment among staff attorneys surfaced in late August of 1969, when one hundred experienced neighborhood lawyers meeting at a training conference in Vail, Colorado, demanded that the newly appointed Legal Services director take steps to guarantee their freedom from interference by local agency directors and board members. Shortly thereafter he issued a strong statement supporting their position.

D. The Reginald Heber Smith Fellowship Program: National Recruitment of Operating Personnel

Of all the decisions made by the director of the board of a local agency, none ranks in importance with the selection of the staff attorneys—the operating personnel who deliver the service to the consumer. The ability and orientation of these men and women largely determine the effectiveness of the local Legal Services agency.[19] Boards of directors naturally seek to recruit and hire lawyers who are likely to carry out their conception of a legal assistance program. In 1966 and early 1967, since many Legal Services agencies still had a narrow perspective about the proper role of legal assistance, they seldom sought out high calibre attorneys. Moreover, that kind of lawyer frequently would not accept employment with such an agency even if he were offered a position.

It was clear that if the Federal staff could upgrade the qualifications of attorneys working in the neighborhoods, it would immediately and profoundly enhance the quality and direction of the legal services rendered to the poverty community. The obvious way to accomplish this objective would have been for OEO to assume the responsibility for hiring for all local agencies. But, of course, this was legally and politically unfeasible, for the community action title of OEO confers only grant-making authority on OEO administrators, not the power to operate local agencies or to recruit for such agencies. Even if OEO were given that authority by statute, the American Bar Association, local bar organizations, Legal Services agencies, and Community Action agencies, among others, would have protested. Aside from that, the idea of "Federal attorneys" was anathema to virtually everyone responsible for the creation and maintenance of the OEO Legal Services Program.

In order to avoid the stigma of Federal government control and yet achieve the objective of central recruitment and selection of high-quality lawyers who possessed a broad conception of their role, we resurrected an idea contained in a November 1965 memorandum.

> . . . We best solve our recruiting problems by funding a law school or law schools to establish a one year fellowship program. . . . After a brief training program, they would be placed in local programs. . . . There are good reasons, political and otherwise, for calling them Reginald Heber Smith Fellows. . . . This gives us a central recruiting authority possessing the highest standards and the prestige of a law school-related fellowship as a drawing card. It should give us a much better class of lawyers than the ad hoc decisions of a host of independent legal services programs.[20]

In early 1967, after considering applications from several law schools, a grant was made to the University of Pennsylvania to operate the "Reginald Heber Smith Community Lawyer Fellowship Program."

The first-year plan for the fellowship program called for recruitment of 50 lawyers, including graduating seniors as well as those already in practice. From the beginning it was contemplated that if the program proved successful *and* sufficient funds were available, classes would be enlarged in succeeding years until almost all new attorneys entering employment with local agencies would be selected through the Reginald Heber Smith program. (The program was, in fact, enlarged to 100 attorneys the second year and 250 attorneys the third year of operation. By 1971, almost 25 percent of all Legal Services attorneys then employed had been recruited through this program.)

Recruitment of the first 50 attorneys was not begun until February, 1967. Despite the late start—most law firms make their hiring decisions in December or January—the response was encouraging. Over 275 lawyers and graduating seniors applied before the March deadline. The 50 Fellows chosen for the charter class, were evenly split between graduating seniors and experienced lawyers; six of these came directly from Wall Street law firms, and several others from other major firms around the country. Another half dozen had clerked for Federal or state judges. One had graduated first in his class at the University of Chicago Law School, another was third at the University of Pennsylvania, another seventh out of a class of 500 at Harvard. Several others stood in the upper 10 percent of their graduating classes. One-third of the original group had qualified to serve on the law review at their respective institutions. The quality of the Reginald Heber Smith Fellows appeared to justify the underlying assumption that there was an untapped pool of high-calibre legal talent interested in serving in local Legal Services agencies.

The 50 lawyers selected to participate in the Reginald Heber Smith Fellowship Program underwent five weeks of specialized training at the University of Pennsylvania during August, 1967. This training featured topics unfamiliar at that time in the curriculum of most law schools—welfare law, consumer protection, housing code enforcement, and test case litigation. In the course of this orientation phase of the program, the Fellows were exposed not only to academicians but also to practicing poverty lawyers, community organizers and ghetto residents. They were reminded constantly of their unique role in the Legal Services agencies to which they were to be assigned.

In September, 1967, the 50 Fellows were assigned to 39 separate Legal Services agencies. They remained employees of the University of Pennsylvania rather than the local agency during the period of their year-long internship. The Fellows' mission was to undertake activities calculated to have a broad effect on the problems of poverty instead of taking a regular caseload of routine legal problems affecting only the individual client. The contract letter with the local agencies explained this special role.

The suggestion that a Reginald Heber Smith Fellow be assigned under these terms provoked some lively discussion on a few of the more conservative local boards. In Albuquerque, for instance, it took an impassioned plea from a representative of the poor to convince the governing body to sign the contract letter with the University of Pennsylvania.[21] But every local agency that was offered a Fellow ultimately accepted.

In February, 1968, the Fellows returned to Philadelphia for a week of seminars. At that time, they compared notes about their experiences with the local agencies. Certain generalizations emerged from these discussions that guided future use of the national recruitment strategy.

First, the more experienced Fellows, of course, generally were more successful than the recent graduates in improving the performance of local agencies that were performing poorly. Those who were inexperienced usually lacked the maturity and confidence to operate effectively in a hostile environment which required at least as much tact and political savvy as legal expertise.

Second, all the Fellows tended to be more successful in lifting mediocre agencies toward excellence than rescuing the obstinently deficient.

Third, they had more success in upgrading local agencies when they were assigned in pairs rather than singly. This allowed them to reinforce each other and better solve the delicate political problems inherent in such an assignment.

Fourth, as might have been foreseen, the Fellows achieved more improvement in law reform performance than in the overall quality of local agencies.

Finally, almost all of the Fellows felt they were "making a difference" in their agencies. Several of the experienced lawyers among the Fellows said they had never felt as useful in their professional lives.[22]

Despite frequent complaints and occasional frustration, 85 percent of the Fellows elected to continue with the Legal Services Program when their one-year internships expired in August, 1968. This was, in part, due to the fact that they could report a 500 percent increase in agencies classified as "very active" in law reform during the year of their internships (September, 1967 to August, 1968)[23] and over 80 percent said the Reginald Heber Smith Program had made a significant contribution to the general increase in law reform.[24]

E. Supplementing Local Agencies with National Law Reform Offices in the Initiation and Prosecution of Law Reform

All the management strategies discussed thus far were aimed at increasing the effectiveness of the OEO Legal Services Program as an antipoverty strategy by sharpening the focus and improving the performance of individual local agencies. As a matter of logic, there was at least one other basic approach— to establish special *national* agencies funded solely for the purpose of bringing test cases and advocating legislative change. Those agencies obviously would not be accountable to local boards of directors.

The prototype for these national law reform centers already existed at the time the staff of the Legal Services Program began its search for means of enhancing the Program's impact. Created in early 1965 by Edward Sparer, the Center for Social Welfare Policy at Columbia University operated for almost a year on Ford Foundation money before OEO had developed a national program of legal assistance. Sparer's Center was chartered for the specific purpose of reforming welfare law in the United States. This was to be accomplished largely through test case litigation and legislative proposals. The Center staff researched possible legal theories, planned the litigation and prepared the briefs but relied on cooperating private attorneys in local communities to file and litigate the cases. In May 1966, Columbia submitted an application to OEO for funding which would enable the Center to continue and enlarge its program. This grant was approved in the spring of 1966 without any thought of the role this type of effort might play in the future of the Legal Services Program.

In mid-1967, most local Legal Services agencies were still lagging in their efforts at law reform and the management strategies devised to improve local performance were barely underway. (The first class of Reginald Heber Smith Fellows, for instance, did not arrive at their assigned projects until September, 1967.) At the same time, the small amount of funds invested in the Columbia Center—less than $200,000—was beginning to pay off handsomely. Lawsuits conceived, briefed and sometimes argued by Center attorneys already had produced some notable gains for the poor, including Federal district court decisions striking down welfare residency and man-in-the-house restrictions in several states. Using less than one-tenth of 1 percent of the Legal Services total budget, Sparer's organization was responsible for an inordinate proportion of the OEO Program's national impact on the economic and social problems of the poverty community. Consequently, the Legal Services staff decided to attempt to emulate the success of the Columbia Welfare Center in other fields of the law.

In the next few years, a dozen national law reform centers were established by the Legal Services staff. Some of the principal ones are:

1. A housing law center at the University of California, Berkeley.
2. A consumer law center at Boston University Law School.
3. A juvenile law center at St. Louis University Law School.
4. An employment law center in New York.
5. An education law center at Harvard Law School.
6. A health law center at U.C.L.A. Law School.
7. An elderly law center at the University of Southern California Law School.

The national law reform offices magnified the economic and social impact of the Legal Services Program in several ways.

First, they could *initiate* lawsuits and legislative proposals in communities and states where the managers of local grantees were unwilling to undertake law reform. Generally, the national center could link up with some neighborhood lawyer who would be willing to act as co-counsel in the matter. The agency leadership would be less resistant because they did not have to commit any substantial amount of their own resources to the effort. Moreover, even a conservative board or staff director usually was reluctant to ask an attorney to withdraw from a case he already was handling even though they might have adopted policies which would make it difficult for him to plan and initiate that same case.

Second, national law reform offices also could increase the *possibilities of success* in litigation filed by agencies that are short of time, legal talent or special expertise, although they might have been more than willing to undertake meaningful reform. The national office personnel were able to concentrate on and master the relatively narrow legal specialties to which they were assigned. By comparison, the members of law reform units in large local programs of necessity could not. At best a local law reform unit could only allocate one attorney to each broad field of law—to welfare, consumer affairs, and so on. A national office, on the other hand, could assign one man to food stamp programs, another to welfare residency issues, and another to old-age assistance programs. Outside the largest metropolitan areas, the support the national law reform office provided the local agencies became even more important. The average size local Legal Services agency consists of seven attorneys. Typically, only one of those seven lawyers would be specializing in reform activities. That attorney relied upon the various national offices to supply the detailed expertise he could never hope to cultivate in the several complex fields of law relevant to the poor.

And finally, the national law reform offices could furnish *training and research materials* that would enlarge the law reform capacity of attorneys in local Legal Services agencies. Not all issues relevant to the poor are sufficiently complex or monumental to merit the direct attention of national office personnel. With 50 separate jurisdictions, there are literally thousands of different rules and practices in the United States which discriminate against the poor. The national law reform offices could not themselves hope to handle the litigation or advocate the legislation that would raise each and every one of these thousands of issues. But they could multiply their own effectiveness by sharing some of their own expertise with the 2000 local poverty lawyers.

III. THE FEDERAL GOVERNMENT'S PROPER ROLE IN MANAGING GRANTS

In this chapter we have explored the assortment of strategies employed by the OEO Legal Services staff to regain some influence over the output of the local grantees to which it distributed Federal funds. Of the five management tools used, the first two are fairly standard. Federal grant-makers have been cajoling and threatening the managers of local grantees for decades, usually with little success. If there was innovation in anything the Legal Services staff did, it was to concentrate on operating personnel—their recruitment and incentives—and to establish national centers committed solely to the national priority. Thus, even though board members and staff directors continued to oppose legal reform after being pressured to support the Federal goal, it was still possible those same agencies would participate in their fair share of law reform. For one thing, many of the lawyers working in these agencies are or have become committed to the national aim irrespective of their superiors' views. The proportion of active poverty lawyers who had been recruited through the Reginald Heber Smith Program rose steadily from 3 percent in 1967 to almost 25 percent by 1972. Hundreds of other neighborhood attorneys evidence a similar commitment by membership in Poverty Lawyers for Effective Advocacy (PLEA), an organization formed in 1969 to preserve freedom to engage in meaningful activity for the poor. Similarly, the national law reform centers, constantly looking for good issues, often involve neighborhood lawyers in test cases or legislative reform even though the board or staff director is unsympathetic to the Federal policy.

One of the central tenets of our management philosophy was this emphasis on affirmative enforcement techniques as opposed to negative ones, the reliance on the carrot more than the stick. We sought to reward good law reform efforts and to recruit attorneys interested and capable of achieving that national mission. We had much less faith that fund cutoffs or other threats would convert recalcitrant boards or staffs to our thinking.

These precepts led the Legal Services staff away from the more traditional path of promulgating comprehensive, detailed regulations implementing the national goal, strictures which all funded programs were expected to obey.[25] The decision to try something new was grounded in a dissatisfaction with the old way. Grant-making agencies have been issuing performance goals and regulations for years. Results depend either upon voluntary compliance from willing grantees or the grantor's ability to coerce the resistant ones. Given the number of Legal Services agencies skeptical about law reform, there appeared to be doubt about the utility of promulgating precise guidelines defining the objective and expecting every agency to concentrate energies on its accomplishment. Certainly what we had found out about the tendency of state

184 • THE MANAGEMENT OF THE PROGRAM

welfare departments to disregard HEW regulations was not an encouraging sign. Even more critical, the Legal Services staff lacked truly effective sanctions to enforce compliance. The big lever was grant termination but, as observed earlier, that was little more than a bluff.

To the extent formal regulations might have performed an informational function, putting grantees on notice about the law reform priority, this was more than accomplished by the speeches, *Law in Action,* training programs, conferences and other elements of our management campaign. More grantee staff and board members heard or read about law reform in these sources than would ever peruse a booklet of regulations.

All in all, it seemed to make more sense to invest our time and resources in affirmative management strategies rather than writing detailed regulations, negotiating them through the OEO administration, and hoping their very existence would convert reluctant boards and staff leaders in local agencies.

A clue to the outcome of this course of action is found in the final report of a consultant firm hired to evaluate over 100 Legal Services grantees during 1970. The evaluators concluded that for the Legal Services Program, the whole exceeds the sum of the parts.[26] A possible explanation of this phenomenon is found in the accomplishments of hundreds of talented, committed staff attorneys working in mediocre local agencies. Marching to a different drumbeat than their reluctant leaders, these individual lawyers can produce substantial results without really upgrading their employers' overall reputations. Adopting the consulting firm's language, the "parts" of the Legal Services Program—its grantee agencies—may simply not measure up to the program's "whole"—its total impact on the problem of poverty. If so, this reflects the strength—and the weakness—of the management strategy used by the Legal Services staff in the mid-1960s.

Part IV: An Assessment

Chapter 8: The First Seven Years: Testing the Potential of Legal Services to the Poor

Chapter 9: Toward Justice and Reform

In this final Part, we attempt to evaluate the past and appraise the future. Over five years have elapsed since the decisions, policies and management strategies described in the first seven chapters. Thus, we are in a better position to trace some of the effects of the forces set in motion during the formative half-decade of the OEO Legal Services Program, the years from 1964 to 1968.

In Chapter 8, we attempt to determine how well the Legal Services Program has satisfied the aims of its basic political constituencies, as well as its clients. The measuring tools include statistics, subjective questionnaires, a survey of social impact actions and even a rudimentary cost-benefit analysis. Along the way, we have occasion to draw comparisons with other evaluations of the Program's contribution.

Chapter 9 looks ahead to the prospects of equalizing justice and minimizing poverty. Some of the political and practical problems standing in the way of a costless or low-cost legal system are addressed. We also seek to articulate the lawyer's role in social change and outline institutional arrangements that might maximize his effectiveness. Finally, we consider the interdependence between justice and reform and what this convergence of goals means for the future of government-subsidized legal assistance.

8: The First Seven Years: Testing the Potential of Legal Services to the Poor

One yardstick for measuring the success of a governmental program is how well it satisfies the express goals of its basic constituencies. For the Legal Services Program, the original constituencies were prominent lawyers supporting the legal aid movement and the reformers who created the neighborhood lawyer experiments. The former sought the expansion of due process justice. A lawyer for every poor person with a legal problem is probably a fair characterization of their ultimate goal.[1] The architects of the neighborhood lawyer programs on the other hand, for all their differences over ends and means,[2] were united in their commitment to a basic objective, the reduction of poverty.

It is important to note that these aspirations are not inherently inconsistent. Assuming unlimited resources, the philosophy of "a lawyer for every poor person" embraces representation of individuals or groups with claims that will restructure the economy to reduce poverty. Thus, if there were lawyers enough to afford a full scope of legal services to all needy persons and groups—in other words if the legal aiders could achieve their ultimate goal—social change would come about merely as a by-product. The test cases would be filed, the legislative proposals drafted and advocated, the administrative agencies kept in line without any deliberate emphasis on law reform.

Unfortunately, the resources are not unlimited.[3] Individual poverty lawyers, local Legal Services agencies, and the national program itself must make choices among cases and clients. If guided solely by the original dominant goal of the legal aid movement, the decision probably would be to provide a narrow range of services to a maximum number of clients. In a lawyer-scarce situation, the most legal services for the greatest number of people translates into handling as many simple problems as can be undertaken in the course of the attorney's day. Total commitment to the goal of social reform, on the other hand, would lead Legal Services lawyers and administrators to take only those cases which promise a major quantum of social change. Maximization of economic and social dividends rather than maximization of clients served would be the criteria applied in all resource allocation decisions. As will be established shortly, neither the legal aiders' initial goal nor the legal activists' goal has been pursued to the exclusion of the other. The Legal Services administration, some individual agencies, and many Legal Services lawyers endeavor to satisfy both of these fundamental objectives.

In the years since the founding of the program, other constituencies have been added, principally poverty lawyers and organized client groups.[4] But the aspirations remain the same. New elements of the coalition line up behind one or another of the original goals, or more commonly behind both. Thus, the measuring rods remain the same despite passage of time, expansion of resources and the advent of new constituencies: What has the program done for the quantity and quality of due process justice in America? And, what has been its impact on the social and economic dimensions of poverty? How well the Legal Services Program has succeeded in this dual quest is the subject of this chapter.

I. THE LEGAL SERVICES PROGRAM AND THE QUANTITY AND QUALITY OF JUSTICE FOR THE POOR

In part, the contribution of the OEO Legal Services Program to the primary goal of the legal aid movement can be measured in plain numbers. For instance, in 1965, the last year before the substantial Federal funding was begun, the combined budgets of all legal aid societies totaled $5,375,890.[5] By June 30, 1968, the OEO Legal Services Program was operating at an annual budget level in excess of $40,000,000 a year (including training, support, research and experimental programs).[6] And by 1971, the contribution of OEO to civil legal assistance reached $56,176,052.[7]

In 1965, staffs of all legal aid societies in the country made up the equivalent of 400 full-time lawyers.[8] By June 30, 1968, OEO had augmented this by 2000 positions,[9] and in 1972 there were 2660 staff attorneys.[10] These lawyers manned over 850 offices in more than 200 communities. Nine of the ten largest cities and 46 of the largest 50 had OEO-funded law offices by mid-1968. As of July 1, 1972, only one of the largest 50 cities was still without a Legal Services program.[11]

The statistics demonstrate an increase in output as well as finances and lawyer resources. In 1965 NLADA reported legal aid societies processed 426,457 applicants for legal assistance.[12] By 1971, this figure had risen to 1,237,275.[13] There was some change in the kinds of cases handled: a much higher percentage of welfare problems and some reduction in the proportion of domestic relations cases.[14]

It is fairly obvious that the tenfold expansion in the financial investment from 1965 to 1971, and the five-fold enlargement of the lawyer force did not result in a commensurate increase in the number of clients served. Thus, if case volume were the sole measure of the goals of the legal aid movement, the OEO program served them only moderately well. However, most legal aid leaders were interested in improved quality as well as numbers. On this score, the evidence of progress is dramatic.

The caliber of the lawyers attracted to the OEO-funded programs generally surpassed the professional quality of staff attorneys who had worked in the pre-1965 legal aid societies. Apparently this was partially the result of a better than 40 percent increase in average salaries.[15] Probably more influential, however, was the activist image projected by the OEO program[16] and its attraction for young lawyers in the late 1960s. It was reinforced by the Reginald Heber Smith Fellowship Program which actively recruited throughout the nation. The payoff from that program was not merely the 800 Fellows signed on from 1967 to 1972, but hundreds of others drawn to Legal Services at the local level by this national recruiting campaign. Before the OEO program, it was almost unheard of for a high-ranking graduate of a major law school to accept employment with a legal aid society. By contrast, as we have already seen, Reginald Heber Smith Fellows brought legal talent the most affluent corporation law firm might envy[17] and in the single year of 1968, seven *Stanford Law Review* editors took employment with Legal Services agencies, along with scores from other law reviews across the country.[18]

Assuming one measure of improved quality is more vigorous defense of their clients' interests, the trend is definitely upward. While legal aid societies only litigated 6 percent of their clients' cases in 1959,[19] by 1971, Legal Services lawyers were taking 17 percent to court.[20] The NLADA did not maintain statistics about appeals; however, they were rare. Legal Services lawyers, on the other hand, now average well over 1000 appeals every year.[21] Possibly the most revealing statistic is the apparent fact that in the entire 89-year history of the legal aid movement from 1876 to 1965, not one legal aid staff attorney had taken a case in the United States Supreme Court.[22] Yet in five years—from 1967 to 1972—219 cases involving the rights of the poor were brought to the high court, 136 were decided on the merits, and 73 of these were won.[23]

Outside evaluators have given most Legal Services grantees high marks in those phases of performance related directly to the prime goal of the legal aid movement. Out of a sample of 110 local agencies appraised in 1967 and 1968, 35 percent were rated "excellent" or better in their handling of routine service cases, and fully 63 percent "good" or better.[24] A consultant firm responsible for evaluating most Legal Services agencies in 1970 and 1971 reported similar results.

> Both the quantity and quality of the individual services rendered by Legal Services projects far exceeded that generally offered by their predecessors [i.e., charitably financed legal aid societies]. Moreover, the quality of individual services provided

by Legal Services programs in most instances at least equals that provided by private attorneys to paying clients.[25]

As might have been anticipated from the facts recited above, most of the legal aid leaders interviewed during the preparation of this book exhibited a high degree of satisfaction with the performance of the OEO Legal Services Program.[26] They had seen their movement, for many of them a pet project, suddenly take a great leap forward. With ten times the money, five times the lawyers, almost triple the caseload, and a dramatic improvement in legal talent, the impact of the Federal program on legal aid seemed almost entirely positive. Even some of the policies they originally opposed, especially the involvement of poor people on local boards, had not proved nearly so mischievous as expected.[27]

The most conspicuous deficiency of the OEO Legal Services Program in the eyes of the legal aid movement was its failure to achieve a real breakthrough in areas of the country, most notably in the South, where legal assistance was still unknown. Bar leaders harbored the hope that the lure of Federal money would succeed where the moral blandishments of national legal aid leaders had failed.[28] Yet the South, with the highest proportion of poor people and the fewest charitably financed legal aid lawyers, received only a dribble of Legal Services resources.[29] Instead the OEO Program invested most heavily in the Northern industrial states and the far West. This pattern of funding arose from a combination of factors: two parts deliberate planning, one part error in judgment and one part pure chance.

The initial funding plan for the fiscal year ending June 30, 1966, emphasized urban areas and communities with proven receptivity to legal assistance programs.[30] With seven months to stimulate, develop, and process 75–150 local grants worth $20–$25 million, this appeared not just sound, but possibly the only feasible policy. As an inevitable consequence, the first year monies went almost exclusively to those communities already geared up for a Legal Services Program, most of which already had an ongoing legal aid society. OEO thus reinforced the pre-existing pattern of development. Where the legal aid movement had been able to gain a foothold, the Federal government provided the funds for expansion. Where legal aid had been frozen out in the past, OEO seldom had the time to cajole.

During its second fiscal year, between July 1, 1966 and June 30, 1967, when the Legal Services Program doubled the number of grants, the South was made an explicit priority, and most of the money that was invested in that region was disbursed during this 12-month period. However, in a major error of judgment, the staff of the Program relied for too long on the tactics that served well in other parts of the country. Elsewhere we had been able to count on a natural tension between generally conservative bar associations, rather more liberal community action agencies, and often anxious legal aid societies and radical poverty organizations to generate an application for a Legal Services grant. OEO usually had to mediate among these groups and frequently had to modify the program submitted. But at least the drive and sponsors for some sort of effort to provide legal services were present.

In most communities in the South, however, this pre-condition simply did not exist. With some notable exceptions, Community Action Agencies in the South were dominated by elements as conservative as the local bars. Often, in fact, the same individuals controlled both. Even where the CAA was relatively liberal, it usually was afraid to take on the bar association, a powerful group in many Southern communities. Nor were there independent radical poverty organizations in most areas of the South. And charitably financed legal aid societies were virtually unknown. As a result, unless the bar association wanted a Legal Services Program, there was no one willing to trigger the application process. Even if a proposal did come forward from a Southern CAA, it usually was withdrawn if the local bar raised objections.

Since the legal profession in most Southern communities had long resisted the concept of charitably financed legal aid, they were not good prospects to support a Federal system. Consequently, their lockhold on local decision-making effectively blocked submission of Legal Services applications from the South. And OEO's continued reliance on local initiative doomed most of the Southern poor to do without lawyers.

By mid-1967, the Legal Services staff realized the error of depending on traditional elements in local communities. We then turned to the approach pioneered in rural California and Florida, statewide or regional Legal Services organizations unrelated to any CAA or local bar. These independent agencies drew support from whatever liberal groups existed throughout a large geographical area, and thus were in a much better position to ignore the opposition of local bar associations. However, it took patience and a heavy investment of OEO staff resources to assemble such a statewide or regional organization. Unfortunately, by the time we developed this strategy, it was fiscal 1968 and funds for new grants had evaporated. Since then, OEO has succeeded in financing regional organizations at modest levels only in Appalachia and south Texas.

The stagnant national budget foreclosed the opportunity to open independent Legal Services organizations in the South. When the money was there, the applications were not. When the applications finally came in, the money was gone. Had we started to form regional organizations sooner, the South undoubtedly now would have hundreds of poverty lawyers instead of a few score.

II. THE LEGAL SERVICES PROGRAM AND ITS CONTRIBUTION TO SOCIAL REFORM

In his book evaluating the war on poverty, *The Great Society's Poor Law,* Sar Levitan drew the following conclusion about the Legal Services Program:

> By and large, the Legal Services Program has operated much like traditional legal aid. The additional objectives of the newer program—legal reform, education, representing organizations of the poor—have not been ignored, but the overwhelming press of cases has forced the Legal Services attorneys . . . to spend their entire time on usual Legal Services. . . .[31]

Levitan's book was published in 1969. But it was based upon research performed mostly in 1967.[32] The quoted text appears to give a fair appraisal of the contributions of the OEO Legal Services Program in 1967. In fact, it squares with the findings of OEO's own evaluations during that period, the very reports that prompted the decision to invoke management pressures to upgrade the performance of the Legal Services Program in the area of law reform.[33]

But there is evidence suggesting Levitan's conclusions may have been out of date by the time they appeared in print. As reported in Chapter 7, while only *12* percent of the Reginald Heber Smith Fellows rated the local agencies to which they were assigned as "very active" in law reform at the time they joined the Legal Services Program in September 1967, just a year later the Fellows reported more than *60* percent of these agencies to be "very active" in law reform activities. Conversely, over one-third said their assigned agencies were undertaking "no activity" or "little activity" in the field of law reform in September, 1967. But by August, 1968, this dropped to 5 percent.[34]

There is further support for the proposition that the management pressures applied during 1967 and 1968[35] brought about a significant shift in agency priorities and performance. A compilation of returns from a random cross-section of almost 50 Legal Services attorneys reveals that as of October, 1968, these attorneys reported an average of eight cases each with significance beyond the client served.[36] Assuming this sample is typical, the figures project to a total of *16,000* such cases for the Legal Services Program as a whole. This statistic does not appear out of line when one considers that in just four years Legal Services lawyers managed to fill three volumes of the CCH publication, *Poverty Law Report,* with synopses of their more significant law reform cases.

Evaluators participating in the appraisal of over 100 local Legal Services agencies reported that 43 percent of these agencies were "good" or better in the category "effectiveness in Law Reform."[37] Among larger programs, 60 percent achieved this rating.[38] Furthermore, fully 278 of the 320 Legal Services agencies have had cases reported in the *Clearinghouse Review,* 127 of these had four or more reported, and 47 had eleven or more,[39] even though that publication contains only the most far-reaching of the cases submitted by local agencies. Not overwhelming statistics, yet a bit more encouraging than Levitan's conclusion.[40]

An involuntary confirmation of the thesis that poverty lawyers have made material gains for the low-income community is furnished by the individuals and institutions that experienced those successes firsthand—the landlords, merchants, welfare administrators and government officials who have opposed the poor in their major litigation. Three times—in 1967, 1969 and 1972—representatives of these groups introduced bills in Congress designed to inhibit actions by Legal Services attorneys. Senator Murphy, chief sponsor of the 1967 and 1969 legislation, explained his reasons in the following words:

> Legal services attorneys are not only working as defense counsel, they will also bring a cause of action as well as defend an indigent in a suit. They will do one thing more. They will institute test cases. Recently, in this manner, they have begun to challenge our laws all too often. . . .
> There are too many cases for legal services to handle without involving themselves in these test cases.[41]

Both "Murphy Amendments" failed largely because the American Bar Association followed up on the commitment of its leaders and threw its power behind the Legal Services Program.[42]

The reactions of other individuals and agencies indicated that the Legal Services Program was taking effect. Governors vetoed Legal Services refundings in California, Florida, Connecticut, Arizona and Missouri. In 1970, NLADA reported that community chests in St. Louis, Albuquerque, New Orleans and half a dozen other localities had withdrawn support from local OEO-funded legal aid societies because of their involvement in controversial cases. The University of Mississippi Law School threw out its OEO-sponsored Legal Services Agency because it had begun to undertake meaningful litigation. In Philadelphia, the police commissioner announced department personnel would refrain from giving to the Community Chest because it supported the legal aid society. The police chief in Los Angeles denied use of a municipal communication facility to the University of Southern California merely because that institution co-sponsored the law reform unit for the Los Angeles area—the Western Center on Law and Poverty.[43]

All this evidence may counter the mediocre rating awarded the OEO Legal Services Program by evaluation expert Sar Levitan. But does it conclusively prove that a significant contribution has been made to the social and economic betterment of the low-income community? For one thing, much of the proof is subjective, depending on the impressions of evaluators and the reactions of those who have felt its impact directly: landlords, credit companies, welfare administrators. The only hard data are statistics, admittedly pretty impressive, about the numbers of test cases filed, Supreme Court victories won, and the like. But it is important that we not equate big lawsuits with social-economic payoff, for it is not the number of class actions filed and won that counts for the poor, but the dollars received or other tangible benefits conferred.

What this means is that the question of the Program's contribution to the antipoverty goal cannot be answered nearly as easily as its role in due process justice. The analysis must be more sophisticated than what sufficed for the legal aid goal; and much more so than the testimony and statistics assembled thus far. The law and what lawyers do with the law must somehow be linked with real changes in social, political and economic conditions surrounding the poor. At least one observer believes that linkage does not exist. In a provocative law review article,[44] Geoffrey Hazard, former director of the American Bar Foundation, argues that while Legal Services lawyers can contribute to civil justice for the poor, they can do almost nothing to promote social justice for that class. We shall have occasion to examine Hazard's thesis shortly.

Those who conceived the neighborhood lawyer experiments shared a belief in an implicit hypothesis, a very general assumption, to the effect that what lawyers do could help to reduce poverty. They expected the operation of the Program to prove out that hypothesis. Seven years later we lack the data to establish that finding conclusively. But we are at least in a position to refine our analysis and spin out a series of smaller, tighter hypotheses suggesting with some precision not only that lawyers reduce poverty but how they reduce poverty and by how much. To that task, we devote the remainder of this chapter.

The elements of our analysis are: (a) a survey of social-economic effects produced by Legal Services lawyers and (b) a rudimentary evaluation of the cost effectiveness of the Legal Services lawyer as an antipoverty investment.

A. A Hierarchy of Social-Economic Effects

Poverty in America is a more complex problem than elsewhere in the world. And by that, I do not mean to merely underline the common notion that it is a paradoxical social fact in a nation of general affluence; nor am I merely referring to the prevailing diagnosis that American poverty has many complex causes. What I am suggesting goes beyond these oft-repeated statements. Poverty has become a shorthand expression for a whole bundle of current social problems. Thus—rightly or wrongly—the "War on Poverty" has been forced to carry the freight for a number of related social goals. One of these is racial discrimination. In fact, one reason poverty is such an explosive issue in our country follows from the racial composition of the low-income group.

A black American has a much better chance of being poor than a white citizen. But it would be entirely possible to totally eliminate racial discrimination and give each *individual* minority person as good a statistical chance as a white to be above the poverty line without reducing the total number of people who are poor by even one. In other words, we could alter the racial composition of poverty drastically without doing anything about poverty itself. For every black who is moved out of poverty by obtaining a steady, well-paying job, a white may slip below the line because he lost that job, or at least lost out to the black in his bid for the position. It is important to bear in mind there is a very real difference between equalizing opportunity for the individual to escape poverty and the elimination of poverty itself.[45]

The fact the war against poverty is used to refer to all these problems and goals complicates our inquiry into the potential impact of the Legal Services Program. We must examine not one but several possible social-economic effects, related not only to poverty itself but to the special characteristics of the individuals who happen to comprise the lower economic class in late twentieth-century America. These effects are:

1. Increase in goods and services received by lower income individuals and groups.
2. Equalization of opportunity among racial, economic, and geographic groups.
3. Enhancement of the personal freedom enjoyed by lower income individuals and groups.
4. More participation by low-income individuals and groups in decision making in the private economic sector and among government agencies.
5. Peaceful, orderly resolution of grievances held by lower income individuals and groups.

This catalogue does not purport to exhaust all the possible social-economic effects of the nation's antipoverty campaign. But it is enough if we have succeeded in identifying the most important ones to which the law and lawyers can make some contribution. In the succeeding sections we take each effect and determine whether and how it relates to the legal structure and what Legal Services attorneys do.

In describing the social and economic impact of cases taken by poverty lawyers, I do not mean to suggest that these attorneys deliberately set out to achieve such results. Undoubtedly, the vast majority of cases were brought or defended by counsel bent only on serving a specific client and his or her goals. Even where a test case was filed or a legislative measure advocated, the long-run impact on the overall poverty community was only vaguely perceived. In the words of Howard Westwood, "[Legal Services lawyers] would be fighting to establish the doctrine of unconscionability in contract law whether or not it were to result in redistributing one penny of wealth."[46] Yet for purposes of planning, policy and evaluation, we need to know whether the Legal Services Program in fact improves the economic and social lot of the poor, and by how much.

1. The Increased Distribution of Goods and Services: The Core of the Antipoverty Strategy

In most countries, poverty means nothing more than that a segment of the population, usually the vast majority, does not receive sufficient income to maintain a decent standard of living. It is the result of an inadequate total gross national product in the poorer nations or the relative inequality of distribution of the national product in wealthier ones.

A. THE DIMENSIONS OF INEQUALITY. In the United States, the wealthiest of countries,[47] it is commonly accepted that poverty is a phenomenon of unequal distribution, not insufficient means. In 1966, when the OEO Legal Services Program was barely underway, the bottom 20 percent of the population on the income scale received about 5 percent of the gross national income.[48] By contrast, the upper 20 percent received over eight times that amount—more than 40 percent of the national income.[49] And the disparity was more pronounced as we descend further into the depths of poverty. The bottom 10 percent of the population was left with 1 percent of the income[50] while the upper 5 percent received almost 20 percent.[51]

Contrary to some popular opinion, things have *not* been getting better for the poor, proportionally speaking, in recent decades. While the bottom fifth's share of national income did climb during the 1930s and 1940s,[52] it actually declined from 1947 until the 1960s, when the war on poverty began. In the year 1947, the lowest quintile received 5.0 percent of the nation's income. By 1962 this had fallen to 4.6 percent.[53]

Since the war on poverty was begun, we have become accustomed to defining the poor by recourse to a fixed income standard, a so-called poverty line. Anyone with an income below that line is deemed poor, those above are nonpoor. The definition is based on an estimate of the income required to sustain a minimal standard of living in the United States.[54] In 1965, it was drawn at $3155 for a nonfarm family of four.[55] By 1970, reflecting inflation, the line was moved up to $3970.[56] Applying this gauge, poverty will be eliminated if and when every person receives an income above the arbitrary level.

A different measure conceives of poverty as a failure to participate fairly in the nation's total affluence and not as a matter of achieving certain minimum standards of shelter, diet, recreation, and so on.[57] Under this definition the poverty line is set at some percentage share of the nation's total goods and services, whatever the total is, rather than a fixed dollar income level.[58] Some authorities have suggested the appropriate standard should be one-half the median income.[59] Thus, poverty would be abolished only when the poorest person in the nation received one-half the amount received by the average individual.[60]

By either of these definitions, the reduction of poverty entails distribution of a larger quantity of goods and services to persons on the lower end of the income scale. However, the choice of one concept of poverty over the other has two crucial policy implications.

First, there is the matter of how much the income of the poor must be increased in order to abolish poverty. It is estimated that it would have taken another $15 billion to lift everyone over the $3155 poverty line when OEO started.[61] By our second definition, a shift of approximately $35 billion would have been necessary to give people in the lowest fifth of the population one-half the median income.

Second, the choice of which definition to use affects whether poverty can be overcome by increasing the nation's total income rather than redistributing income from the affluent to the poor. In other words, can we bake a pie so large that the smallest slice will be sufficient so no one lives in the condition called "poverty"? Applying the minimal standard of living concept, it is at least conceivable that at some point in the future our gross national product might reach a level where even ditch-diggers and migrant workers earned enough to afford decent shelter and a healthy diet, and in that sense no longer were poor. In contrast, the fair share of affluence standard can never be satisfied by expanding the total national income. To advocates of this definition of poverty, a 5 percent share is never ample for 20 percent of the population no matter how large that share is made in absolute terms.

Economists have adopted a term, the "poverty-income gap,"[62] to express the difference between the dollar income currently received by the poor and that which could elevate them out of poverty. It provides a handy measure of the degree of poverty at any given time. However, as we have seen, the size of this income gap depends on one's definition of poverty, especially whether it is based on a minimum standard of living or an adequate share of affluence.

It also is important to note that the distribution of goods and services among different economic classes depends in part upon factors other than the allocation of dollar income. It is related as well to what a dollar received by the poor will buy in comparison with what that same sum will buy for other income groups. If the poor must pay higher prices for goods and services, then an increased share of the dollar income may become illusory. Studies of pricing policies followed by merchants catering to the poverty community are not encouraging.[63] It is not impossible to imagine a situation in which the bottom fifth doubled their share of the nation's total dollar income to 10 percent, yet saw their actual share of goods and services lag behind at 6 or 7 percent.

In summary then, it probably is fair to say that the dollar income gap stood somewhere between $15 and $35 billion when the war on poverty was launched. Moreover, the real income gap (in terms of goods and services received by the poor) was substantially greater than that. We now turn to an examination of the reasons those gaps existed, and especially the role of the law in their perpetuation.

B. THE LAW AS A MECHANISM FOR DISTRIBUTION OF GOODS AND SERVICES. In a pure laissez-faire economy, the distribution of goods and services among individuals and groups is determined by the purely economic laws (or natural principles) of the market place. Supply and demand set prices. Supply and demand establish the wage structure for different occupations. Supply and demand apply an automatic brake to profit margins. Political law—the decisions of legislators, administrative agencies, and courts—although important to the common defense and domestic tranquility, has no influence over who gets what, who prospers and who starves in the laissez-faire world. That is the business of *natural economic* laws, not *man-made political* laws.

But the laissez-faire world is no more—if it ever was. In modern America, the distribution of goods and services is as much a function of man-made political law as the natural operation of impersonal economic forces.[64]

1. Laws determining the tax structure. The most obvious way a part of the legal system can affect the distribution of income is through the tax laws. Approximately 28 percent of the nation's gross national product is taken out of the private sector through taxation, Federal, state and local.[65] This revenue then is returned to the economy through various general benefits (national defense, police protection, and street cleaning, among others) and individual benefits (farm subsidies, welfare payments, and so on). Thus, the laws establishing rates, exemptions, deductions, and the rest of the tax structure are extremely influential in determining the distribution of goods and services among various individuals of various income levels in society.

Progressive levies, for instance, take a higher percentage of the income received from the marketplace by upper income groups and a lesser percentage out of that received by lower income groups. Even if the bottom groups were to receive no more than their per capita share of the benefits paid out of these taxes, an important redistribution will have taken place. Upper income individuals will have been taxed more than their per capita or proportional share of income but receive back only their per capita share of public benefits. Lower income persons, in contrast, will have "purchased" a per capita share of benefits without paying their per capita, or even proportional share of the total cost.[66]

The Federal income tax is a progressive levy.[67] Potentially it is a very effective instrument of redistribution to the lower economic classes. But its redistributive effect has been nullified by the regressive character of Federal social security taxes and state and local taxes.[68] These latter revenue measures

—sales taxes, personal property taxes, and the like—impose a higher proportional burden on lower income than higher income groups. As a consequence, the net effect of the total tax structure, Federal, state, and local, is that the lowest strata pays nearly as large a proportion of its income in taxes as the middle class and upper middle class.[69] Some studies indicate even the wealthy pay a percentage only eight points above the poor.[70] But that fact does not detract from the power of tax laws over the distribution of goods and services or their *potential* for bringing about a net gain in the income received by many low-income people.[71]

2. *Laws determining the distribution of government benefits.* The corollary of the tax structure is the government benefits structure. These legal rules determine who receives which type of benefits in what amounts when the government spends its tax monies. For redistribution purposes, so-called transfer payments[72] are the single most influential part of the government benefits structure. Transfer payments go to specific individuals in the form of social security, Medicare, subsidies for farmers and other economic groups, welfare payments of various types, and similar substitutes for individual "earned" income. In contrast, most other government expenditures are designed to provide services to the general public—everything from national defense to garbage collection.

Many transfer-payment programs are constructed for the express purpose of providing money or services to those who need the aid, especially individuals whose earned income is insufficient. Welfare assistance for the blind, the disabled, and fatherless children are examples of this category of income transfer. But there is another type of program, equally important, that redistributes tax revenues to certain individuals or groups in the name of some independent social or economic goal. Usually termed subsidies, these payments are made to farmers to encourage them to restrict food production[73] or to Lockheed to maintain a national defense manufacturing capacity. Subsidies may be motivated primarily by society's desire to improve production, conserve resources, and the like. But as a by-product these transfer payments have as profound an effect on the share of the total income of many individuals as if they were in the form of direct welfare aid from the government.[74] The majority of subsidies are directed to middle-class and upper-class recipients. However, a significant amount is given to the less affluent, especially via farm subsidies.

At the time the war on poverty was being started, approximately 16 percent of the nation's gross national product was redistributed through transfer payments of all types.[75] Unlike the existing tax structure which, as we have seen, is almost neutral in its effect, transfer payments have a powerful redistributive influence.[76] In the mid-1960s, the bottom fifth obtained less than 3 percent of the "earned" income paid out by our economy. But that same class received

30 percent of the transfer payments.[77] Thus, the laws that create different categories of transfer payments, establish the levels of payments, and so on, play a significant role in the distribution of goods and services, especially to the share allocated to the poor.

3. *Laws distributing competitive advantages among participants in the economic contest.* Less obvious than the laws governing our tax and government benefits structures, but much more important, are those that establish the rules of competition in the marketplace. The law handicaps certain participants and assists others. It also restrains nearly everyone, but in varying degrees. Although these rules often are enacted for other reasons—to stimulate production, conserve resources, and the like—they nevertheless have a substantial impact on the distribution of income among individuals, economic entities, and classes. For instance, laws guaranteeing licensed medical doctors a monopoly over the diagnosis and treatment of disease may be designed to save lives, but they also have the effect of distributing a larger share of the nation's gross national product to the individuals in that profession than they otherwise would receive. (A similar observation could be made about lawyers, architects, public accountants, liquor store owners, and scores of other professions and enterprises.)

Government intervention in the distributive processes of the economy is by no means limited to laws creating special monopolies for certain producers. Antitrust statutes, rate regulations, prohibitions against usury, collective bargaining provisions, and analogous "rules of the marketplace" influence directly and indirectly, sometimes profoundly, sometimes slightly, who will be allowed to compete and how much they will take away from the economic contest. As an example, Federal labor relations legislation guarantees collective bargaining rights for most industrial workers but not farm workers. This pattern almost insures that organized industrial workers will be able to wrest a proportionately larger share of the national product from their employers (and ultimately the consumers of industrial products) than individual farm workers can beg from growers and the consumers of agricultural products.[78] Similarly, provisions banning monopolies and unfair trade practices, at least to the extent they are enforced, encourage competition. This in turn tends to allow consumers to buy more with less money, to reduce the profit element in the total cost of the product, and to spread profit income among several producers. Conversely, statutes sometimes sanction so-called fair trade pricing, that is, an enforcible minimum price that all dealers must charge for certain brand name products. This virtually guarantees that the preferred manufacturers and retail outlets will enhance their shares of profit income at the expense of the consumers. Thus, the real income of many individuals is affected by the existence and the degree of enforcement of such laws.

C.   EXAMPLES OF LEGAL ACTIONS AFFECTING THE QUANTITY OF GOODS AND SERVICES DISTRIBUTED TO THE POOR.   From the general proposition that the law is a principal influence on the distribution of goods and services in American society, let us now turn to an examination of how Legal Services lawyers have affected the share received by the poor. Potentially these lawyers can influence both the amount of income distributed to the poor and the purchasing power of that income, in other words, the number of dollars the poor receive and how much those dollars will buy.

1.   Legal actions affecting the distribution of dollar income to the poor. Income for the poor comes in almost equal amounts from two primary sources —earnings and transfer payments. The law is intimately involved in both. Earnings, of course, refer to any form of compensation—wages, profits, and so on—obtained for work performed by the recipient. Transfer payments, as previously discussed, embrace various types of distributions generally made to individuals from tax revenues and not as compensation for current contributions to the economy.

(a)   Laws affecting the earnings structure for low-income occupations. The poor are profoundly affected by laws that regulate the bargaining situation for occupations in which they are employed. In fact, 30 percent of the persons below the $3155 poverty line in 1965 worked full time but at jobs that simply did not pay a living wage.[79] Another 40 percent were wage earners a substantial period of the year, many of them in seasonal occupations such as farm work.[80]

Most of the jobs performed by the poor are important, some absolutely essential to the economy. Yet for a variety of reasons—historical, economic, and legal—they yield only a tiny financial reward. As an example, it appears difficult to argue that an assembly-line job in an automobile plant demands any more intelligence or ability than fruit picking. But factory workers are paid three or four times as much as migrant farm workers. Nor is ship loading any more strenuous than potato harvesting. Yet a longshoreman's annual income may be five or six times higher.

In a completely free and competitive labor market, the earnings structure presumably would be a function of the supply and demand for the services of various occupations. Government laws and actions would be inconsequential. In present day America, however, much of the labor market is not characterized by open competition. Supply and demand are manipulated by unions (and equivalent employee associations[81]), large employers (and employer associations), and the government. Even some of the apparently free labor market such as agricultural work is influenced by the law. In California and other border states, Federal immigration statutes and regulations determine the supply of farm labor by controlling the influx of temporary workers from Mexico during the harvest season. Thus, in one of the few Legal Services actions that improved the competitive position of low-income wage earners, poverty lawyers in 1967 filed a suit that stopped the importation of foreign workers.[82] The smaller labor pool, of course, increased competition for local help and thus raised their pay. It is estimated this added over $2 million to the income of domestic farm laborers that year.[83]

The impact of the legal system on the earnings structure is seldom so direct as that manifested in the California farm labor situation. But the indirect influence of the law is pervasive and important. In an era where most wage levels (and hence most production costs and consumer prices) are negotiated over a bargaining table in response to the power of organized workers, the laws governing the availability and rules of collective bargaining are instrumental in setting the earnings pattern. Of special importance is whether a given occupation is covered by the National Labor Relations Act. Without that protection, it is difficult for workers to unionize effectively. But once organized under the NLRA, a group of workers is surrounded with enforcible legal guarantees. These give the union members bargaining power with which to obtain higher wages from their employers. As a consequence, the average annual income for organized workers is from 30 to 50 percent higher than the average for the unorganized.[84]

It appears that certain occupational groups are discriminated against largely because they are shut out of the collective bargaining process. Farm workers and employees in some service industries, among others, are denied coverage under the National Labor Relations Act. Thus hampered in their ability to organize, these employees have been doomed to low wages (and high prices for goods produced by organized workers) in a society where most occupational groups are able to extract a larger share of the gross national product through the coercive effect of collective action.

Another attempt at legal manipulation of the earnings structure—minimum wage legislation—has more debatable effects on unorganized employees. These statutes seek to place a floor under the income of workers. Presently, however, many occupations are excluded from such protections and the statutory minimums seldom are adequate even to guarantee that employees covered by these laws will avoid poverty. Through litigation, Legal Services lawyers have begun to expand and enforce minimum wage laws. The most notable success was a case raising wage levels for 200,000 California farm workers by 25 cents an hour, thus increasing annual earnings for that group by almost $100 million.[85] Other actions have sought to extend the coverage of minimum wage laws to new classes of employment.[86] However, the long range efficacy of this strategy has been questioned. Many reputable economists contend that legislated wage floors merely cause employers to discharge marginal workers rather than increase their total labor costs.[87]

Thus far, it appears the actions of poverty lawyers have had only a moderate effect on the earnings structure. They have yet to change the laws that exclude low-income occupations from the NLRA and its armament of bargaining advantages. Other than unusual situations such as limiting the import of workers from Mexico and their work on minimum wage coverage, there is little that lawyers have done that offers much promise of increasing earnings for low-income occupations.[88] However, before we conclude the $100 million a year of increased wages represents the sole contribution of the Legal Services Program to the economic betterment of the poor, it is necessary to examine the other principal form of income that sustains the poverty community.

(b) **Laws affecting total dollar income distributed through government transfer programs.**   Transfer payments of various types now account for half the total income received by those below the poverty line.[89] Of that group, approximately 30 percent presently receive some form of public assistance (representing over 20 percent of total income to the poor).[90] Another 30 percent derive transfer income in the form of social security (18.7 percent of total income for the poverty community).[91] And 9 percent receive unemployment compensation some time during the year.[92] The remaining one third of the poor are not paid any direct financial aid by the government.[93]

The law governing transfers is a hodgepodge of Federal statutes, state statutes, Federal regulations, state regulations, local ordinances, regulations, and practices. This characterization is especially true for the administration of public assistance. Everything from the amount of aid to the recipients' rights upon termination is controlled by one or more of these statutes, regulations, rules or practices.[94]

Many of the laws determine in a substantial way the total income distributed to the poor. Obviously, the rules establishing the amount of assistance to be paid individuals found eligible for aid have the most direct bearing on the total going to the poor. If one million people are receiving $1000 a year and you raise the level of payments to $1500 a year, you will have generated a half-billion dollar redistribution of income to the poor.

But other parts of welfare's legal structure likewise have a substantial impact on the total income received by the poor. The total income received by the poor also is a function of the rules establishing eligibility for individuals to receive aid. Thus, if there is a program with one million recipients each receiving $1000 for which the standards are altered enough to make another 500,000 people eligible, you will have generated a half-billion dollar increment in the total income received by the poor. Moreover, that half-billion dollar increment will be as real as if the level of individual payments had been raised from $1000 to $1500.[95]

In this country, the eligibility criteria for transfer payments—public assistance, in particular—have not been noted for their liberality.[96] Until recently, between 300,000 and 400,000 poor people were not granted aid because of just two restrictive rules, the substitute parent rule[97] and the residency requirement.[98] When the Supreme Court overturned these limitations in legal services lawsuits filed during 1968[99] and 1969,[100] HEW predicted a $300 million to $400 million increase in public assistance income.[101] At the time of the Court decisions, that translated to a potential 3.5 percent to 5 percent increase in the welfare dollars distributed to the poor,[102] a 2.5 to 3.6 percent reduction in the income gap,[103] and a 1 percent increment in the total income received by the bottom fifth of the population.[104]

Some social planners think our system of transfer payments should stipulate a minimum income which every American should be guaranteed.[105] Currently, millions of the needy do not make enough to rise above the poverty level and cannot receive aid because of restrictive eligibility rules. If we could change these requirements, billions of dollars could be transferred to the low-income group.[106] Thus, as we have seen, eligibility requirements do affect the share of the nation's dollar income which ends up in the hands of the poor. But there are other laws that affect the poor as well.

The laws influencing benefit levels in transfer programs: As stated earlier, the most direct way to enlarge the total amount of transfer income for the poor is to increase the size of individual payments rather than the number of people receiving those payments. In most welfare programs, the amount of these payments is set by state or local authorities. The Federal government agrees to supply a given percent of the total cost no matter how generous or stingy the individual payments turn out to be.

In a series of Supreme Court tests, poverty lawyers sought to outlaw certain common devices used by state and local governments to hold down benefit levels for certain classes of poor people. These practices included "maximum grant" provisions limiting the total sum that would be given to one family unit, irrespective of the size of that unit[107]; smaller benefits for disfavored classes of welfare recipients, such as children of dependent mothers, than for politically popular ones, such as the blind and the totally disabled,[108] and percentage reductions from the minimum standards of need required by the Federal government.[109] However, unlike the efforts to liberalize eligibility standards for welfare, these court challenges were largely unsuccessful.[110] Although legal rules clearly structured benefit levels, they were rules that generally could not be (or at least were not) changed in the courts. On the other hand, in a different sort of lawsuit, one Legal Services agency used existing law to constrain a state governor from exceeding his authority to reduce medical payments to the poor.[111] In the process, the poverty attorneys restored over $200 million in benefits to low-income residents in that single state.[112]

The laws determining whether local governments must make Federal transfers available to their low-income citizens: Many Federal benefits are administered through state or local governments. Some of these programs, most notably those involving food stamps, failed to provide benefits for everyone who was eligible simply because county authorities elected not to participate.

In the late 1960s over one-third of the poorest jurisdictions refused to join.[113] As a result, millions of dollars worth of goods earmarked for the poor never reached them.[114] Then in 1969, lawsuits were filed in 26 states. Poverty attorneys claimed that counties were legally bound to administer the Federal food program and, further, that the Agriculture Department was required to furnish the food itself in jurisdictions that refused to comply.[115] Two years after this legal thrust began only eight counties still held out.[116] It is estimated the low-income sector secured an annual dividend of hundreds of millions of dollars in additional food as a result.[117] Similar efforts to force local participation in school lunch programs have met with substantial, but less universal, success.[118]

The laws that structure the distribution of general public services: Education, police protection, garbage collection, street maintenance, and other similar services theoretically are supplied to the general public on an equal basis roughly approximating per capita distribution. But in many states and communities, the poor are not provided their share of these necessities.[119] In other jurisdictions, low-income people must pay higher tax rates for the same level of public services.[120] As a result, several lawsuits have been brought to demand that the costs and benefits of education, municipal utilities, and so on be fairly distributed. Apparently some of these legal actions promise to produce millions of dollars of public services for the poor (or at least the same services at less cost).[121]

The laws that create benefits that may be distributed to members of more than one economic class: In recent years, the Federal government has created a number of programs—principally in the field of subsidized housing—that can benefit either middle-class or lower-income citizens. The proportion going to each tends to depend on their relative sophistication and aggressiveness (or that of their advisors) in pursuing the government aid. Encouraged and assisted by the OEO-funded National Housing Center,[122] Legal Services lawyers have been actively pursuing a share of these benefits for the poor.[123] As a result, several million dollars of Federally financed housing, and some economic development funds have been channelled to the low-income community.[124]

2. *Legal actions affecting purchasing power of dollar income received by the poor.* The amount of goods and services the poor obtain depends on more than their dollar income. As observed earlier, there is every indication that they not only receive fewer dollars but that each dollar they spend buys a smaller quantity of goods and services than middle-class and upper-class consumers can purchase with the same sum. There are many reasons for this, but the law lurks behind, or at least aids and abets, almost every one of the factors contributing to this reduced purchasing power.[125]

An FTC study in Washington, D.C., established the average markup for appliances was two or three times higher in stores catering to the poor.[126] David

Caplovitz' book, *The Poor Pay More*, documented in depth and detail the assertion of its title.[127] And the files of Legal Services lawyers are replete with cases of consumers who paid two to four times the manufacturer's suggested retail list price for television sets, freezers, stoves, and other major household goods.[128]

In part these prices may reflect a higher cost of doing business with low-income consumers. But beyond the legitimate considerations, price levels for durable goods frequently are inflated by one or a combination of the following factors.

(1) Some merchants tell outright lies about the price, quality and other terms of the purchase.[129] Fraud pays off for the seller in the high percentage of sales transactions that go unchallenged in the courts.

(2) High pressure tactics and sleight-of-hand are used by smooth salesmen dealing with undereducated, unsophisticated buyers.[130] The customers are induced to sign blank contracts[131] or to waive all the promises made to them orally,[132] or pay much more than they intended.[133]

(3) Usury laws are avoided when the law allows a "time-price differential." This means a merchant avoids a 6% interest limitation by raising the price on a $100 item to $200. He can then charge the legal 6% interest rate on the $200 "time-price" price and receive a return on his money equal to better than 100 percent interest on the $100 "cash price." The law explicitly permits this time-price differential—a different and higher price for credit sales than the price charged for cash sales.[134]

The poor also pay more for the basics like food and shelter. Food costs them more because grocers located in the ghetto generally impose a higher general price structure.[135] The poor man's rent dollar does not go very far either. Minorities, in particular, find themselves paying substantially more than middle-class whites for an equivalent amount of space.[136] Since many poor people are compelled to spend 40–50 percent of their total income for rent, higher rentals alone can reduce their total purchasing power by 10 percent.[137] The housing dollar is further depreciated because the shelter it purchases is typically a dilapidated, unsafe, unhealthy apartment in a dirty, overcrowded neighborhood.[138]

A common thread runs through all these transactions that rob the dollar of its purchasing power. Whether buying food or a refrigerator, borrowing money or renting an apartment, the poor suffer because of an inferior bargaining position and lack of sophistication about the market and how it operates. Correctly or incorrectly, they perceive their choices of suppliers and terms as sharply circumscribed. They are easily confused about interest rates, time prices, add-on security, balloon payments, and all the other subterfuges available to hide the true cost and value of purchases.[139]

The law is closely intertwined with all transactions affecting the purchasing power of dollar income. In fact, it inevitably intrudes in a sense and on a scale not true of transfer payments or the earnings structure. Merchants, creditors and landlords are themselves compelled to go to court to collect debts or regain possession of property. Thus, the legal system can readily influence the comparative bargaining strength of the parties. The courts or legislature need simply stipulate the circumstances under which they will enforce the affluent person's claim against the poor. As a general rule, the low-income consumer-tenant gains from any law that sets outside boundaries on the permissible terms of a sale or rental, since the stronger party ordinarily prevails in these transactions to the extent the law allows. For example, if the legal system warns it will not honor purchases where the price extracted exceeds 1½ times the prevailing market value, it tends to neutralize some of the advantage enjoyed by sophisticated sellers in their dealings with impoverished, often uneducated, customers.

Much of the work of poverty lawyers is based on the assumption they can make a major difference in the purchasing power of the dollar income distributed to the poor. The hypotheses include the following:

—If time-price differentials are disallowed and usury laws enforced, the 50–300% above market prices charged for durable goods will be curtailed.

—Fraudulent sales practices—which lead to poor people being stuck with inferior merchandise, higher prices, meaningless warranties, and all the rest—can be enjoined through class actions against offending merchants.

—The recently emerging doctrines of unconscionability and adhesion contracts can nullify unreasonable prices and other unfair terms in installment contracts.

—Outlawing or modifying certain collection practices, such as deficiency judgments, add-on security, garnishments, repossessions, etc., can protect debtors from still further losses and costs.

—Vigorous enforcement of housing codes can enhance the livability of rental housing. Effective housing code enforcement, in turn, depends upon encouraging tenants to file complaints with public officials by outlawing retaliatory evictions; and providing tenants with some legal means of compelling the landlord to comply with the code where housing authorities fail to move either through sanctioning the withholding of rent or authorizing affirmative suits by tenants against their landlords.

In one jurisdiction or another, actions undertaken by poverty lawyers have begun to test each of the above hypotheses by changing the legal rules.[140] But the more important questions remain in doubt. Have net prices fallen? Is the quality of the product or housing improved? In other words, have new legislation and court decisions raised the purchasing power of the poor man's dollar income?

These issues are complex. As an example, while on the surface there appears to be a clear cause-effect nexus between legal changes promoting housing code enforcement and more value for the housing dollar, the logical chain has several questionable links. The threshold question, of course, is whether the code requirements in fact will be enforced. In other words, will public officials or courts obey the legal rules and effectively impose them on landlords? That, at least, is a variable that can be measured readily. But more critical is the landlord's response. He may make the mandated repairs but pass on the cost to the tenant in the form of higher rents. In that case, the tenant has not enhanced the purchasing power of his housing dollar. Value may have gone up, but so has price. But even that may seem preferable to another course of action usually open to the landlord—taking the apartment off the low-income market. If the cost of compliance with code conditions is perceived as too high, the landlord may elect to abandon the building, demolish it or convert it to completely refurbished high rent apartment units.

Some authorities argue that rigorous housing code enforcement will lead inevitably to higher rents, abandoned buildings, and apartment conversion outlined above.[141] However, another observer contended recently that local economic conditions frequently dictate that slum owners repair their buildings when ordered by housing code authorities or the courts. Moreover, these same financial circumstances may require landlords to absorb the renovation costs.[142]

The dispute over the efficacy of housing code enforcement is symptomatic. Legal changes that might increase the purchasing power of dollar income usually stir up complex forces and reactions. Dropped in the middle of a fluid market, a new rule may generate unintended, even counterproductive economic ripples. Potentially, at least, abolishing wage garnishment or some other collection device might induce merchants to deny credit to low-income customers. Strict enforcement of usury limitations also might cut the credit supply to the poverty community. Similarly, merchants barred from charging unconscionable prices may lower quality, quantity, or services.

In theory, sellers, landlords, and creditors can accommodate to new legal restrictions in almost endless ways, and it is conceivable that they will always be able to manipulate quality and price variables to perpetuate their advantage. And if they succeed, low-income consumers will not experience any net gain in purchasing power. Professor Hazard, in fact, bases his conclusion that lawyers cannot measurably reduce poverty almost solely on his wholehearted acceptance of this rationale. In a law review article he writes:

> [S]pecific wrongs as violation of housing codes or usury laws are . . . misleading as indicators of an anti-poverty strategy. If there were compliance with the housing code at higher rents, the tenant would still be poor—better housed but worse fed or clothed. If there were compliance with the usury laws, the poor would

simply go without credit. . . .[S]uch a remedy is not responsive to the wrong of impoverishment as such.[143]

We already have observed that the dollar income gap apparently has been reduced by several hundred million dollars through the actions of poverty attorneys.[144] This appraisal is not touched by Hazard's reasoning. It in no way depends upon market conditions or comparative bargaining power. Thus, no matter what studies eventually show about the capacity of legal action to enhance purchasing power, Hazard's ultimate conclusion that Legal Services lawyers are ineffectual in reducing poverty is still suspect. At best, it is a generalization induced from a small sample of experiences. Moreover, the entire sample comes from a single, comparatively narrow class of cases involved with the legal system's attempt to manipulate certain consumer markets.

Upon closer examination, Professor Hazard may even have underestimated the contribution of the entire legal system to the dynamics that determine what the poor get for their money, for merchants, creditors, and landlords might not be able to adjust to new constraints in every situation. Only empirical research can establish what actually happens to prices and quality in various market circumstances when a statute or court decision strikes down a collection tactic, or lowers the effective interest rate, or bars unconscionable prices and terms, or compels a landlord to make repairs. For the most part, that research is yet to be performed. But in the interim, there are several reasons to question the validity and universality of Hazard's apparent finding that merchants, creditors, and landlords can and always will respond by readjusting quality and prices in a manner that leaves low-income consumers and tenants where they stood before the legal constraint was applied.

First, it appears improbable that landlords and merchants never possess a cushion of excess profit margins that can be drained before they must either manipulate prices and quality or cease operations. Hazard's assumption that the higher prices, interest rates and rentals charged the poor inevitably reflect higher costs of doing business with the non-affluent sector requires more verification than has been supplied. It apparently rests on the theory that in a competitive market "rational purchasers" will choose the best available bargain and thus drive prices downward toward costs. This appears wholly inapplicable in a process that thrives on the absence of "rational purchasers," one that, in fact, capitalizes on the lack of sophistication and weak bargaining power of buyers.

Legal actions often serve to slice off only that portion of the price that represents excess profits. In California, a recent appellate court decision invalidated certain late charges on interest payments as patently exorbitant and unrelated to the incremental expense of delayed collections.[145] The court found that the primary effect of these late charges was to provide an excess profit to the lender. Where these high profit margins do exist, limitations on effective interest rates, requirements of housing code compliance, etc., will not necessarily be reflected either in higher prices or rents or lowered quality but rather in reduced but reasonable profits.

Second, many merchants and creditors deal both with middle-class and low-income communities and can choose to respond to changes in the law by altering the terms of their contracts with middle-class customers, rather than the poor. To compensate for a rule cutting maximum effective interest rates for poor people from 50 percent to 20 percent, a creditor may elect to raise his charges for other borrowers from 10 to 15 percent. Or a car dealership, for example, that formerly derived a much higher rate of profit from sales to low-income, unsophisticated buyers than from sales to the affluent might retain its average profit level in the face of toughened fraud and unconscionability provisions by driving harder bargains with its middle-class customers. In either event, goods will be available to the poor at lower prices than in the past. Moreover, most adjustments made by merchants who deal with the general public will affect the larger, affluent segment of the population more than the poor. For example, assume the courts ban a collection technique used primarily against the poor, one which had the effect of reducing purchasing power in the poverty community by 5 percent. If Sears, Roebuck recoups its loss by raising general price levels by 1 percent, the poor still experience a net gain of 4 percent. The "cost" of adjusting to the new legal rule has been shifted largely to the affluent consumer.

Third, poverty lawyers do not necessarily lack either the foresight or skills to counteract undesirable consequences or evasive maneuvers which might follow an initial legal thrust. For instance, to insure that landlords do not abandon buildings, Legal Services attorneys sometimes have followed up housing code enforcement actions with legislative proposals for government subsidies to cover renovation costs. As another example, a new legal restriction on lending might be followed by a complete, or more likely partial, adjustment by lending institutions; this, in turn, might prompt a second response from consumer representatives, courts, legislatures and administrative agencies. Merely because the poverty lawyers' first move is partly neutralized through a market readjustment does not permanently foreclose their effectiveness; it only means they must conceive a second move.

Fourth, Professor Hazard may underestimate the significant loss of purchasing power attributable to operations that use fraud and slick sales techniques to palm off useless or defective merchandise and services at bloated prices. In the main, these are goods and services, such as lifetime dance lessons or fancy fire alarms, the low-income consumer does not need. Thus, the fact that vigorous legal action puts the seller completely out of business does not carry the same undesirable implications as housing code enforcement that forces landlords to abandon apartment buildings. Even where the goods or services are of value, they often can be obtained by the poor from legitimate dealers at a fraction of the cost.

Legal Services actions frequently have brought changes that hamper future schemes[146] as well as closing existing operations and recouping their clients' losses. Again, it would take empirical research to estimate both the total stolen from the low-income community by fraudulent business operations and the amount saved through the efforts of poverty lawyers. But it is not unreasonable to anticipate figures in the scores of millions of dollars.[147]

Fifth, it may be that some of the unintended consequences cited as harmful by Hazard and other critics are in fact beneficial at least in the long term. A good argument can be made that the poor would be better off if their supply of credit in fact were reduced (at least the ultra-high-cost loans permitted by time-price differentials, and the like). That outcome certainly may be preferable to continuation of a system that sharply curtails the purchasing power of their already inadequate dollar income. Similarly, housing code enforcement that takes dilapidated, unhealthy housing off the low-income market may, in the long run at least, benefit poor tenants by generating pressure for construction of new, improved, low-rent units.

In summary, without detailed empirical research, it is not possible to determine whether and how much the Legal Services Program has enhanced the purchasing power of the poverty sector's dollar income. Poverty lawyers have been able to persuade courts and legislatures to adopt legal rules which observers anticipated would lower effective price levels or improve product quality. But we lack the statistical data to verify to what extent they did. Nevertheless, there is reason to doubt the pessimistic expectations of Professor Hazard and others that business power and market forces will cancel out any legal constraints imposed on prices or other terms of a sale or rental.[148]

From studies in New York and Washington, it is not unreasonable to predict that the poor, at least in urban areas, probably must spend substantially more than the average consumer to obtain the same goods and services. Expressed in absolute dollars, that purchasing power gap probably amounts to billions of dollars in the nation as a whole. Obviously, if lawyers' actions pare even a few percentage points off the prices paid or contribute a marginal increment to the value received by the poor, the economic payoff is dramatic. Though we lack the hard data, it seems reasonable that the Legal Services Program has generated some unknown but sizable increase in the purchasing power of the low-income community.

2. The Equalization of Opportunity

Goods and services are not the only assets unequally distributed in American society. An intangible commodity, the opportunity to rise toward affluence, likewise is parceled out in uneven shares. Not only do some jobs pay too little to maintain a decent standard of living (unequal distribution of income), but for some individuals there is only a small chance of obtaining higher paying positions (unequal opportunity).

A. THE VALUE OF EQUAL OPPORTUNITY. There is good reason for setting forth the equalization of opportunity as a separate category of social-economic impact rather than merging it with the income distribution effects. In fact, there presently exists serious doubt that any causal relationship exists between balancing opportunities among all citizens and a larger quantity of goods and services for the low-income sector. The opportunity structure clearly affects who occupies which rungs on the economic ladder. There is some question whether it determines in any meaningful way the financial rewards for each rung.[149] To illustrate, when competitive disadvantages have been erased, an individual has a better chance to become president of the company, but if he nevertheless ends up on the assembly line his pay may be the same as if the president's job was unattainable from the start.

At first glance, this may seem a subtle point. However, in appraising the social-economic contribution of the Legal Services Program it is important to know the ultimate value of actions that equalize opportunity. Some observers, among them Professor Hazard, dismiss these moves as more or less irrelevant, since they presumably do not reach the fundamental income distribution question.[150]

It may be necessary to concede that the income structure does not mirror the opportunity structure (and quite possibly is unrelated). Yet equalization of opportunity can stand on its own as an important independent social value. It is especially important, in fact, to whomever occupies the bottom of the economic heap at a given moment. Apparently many persons prefer lower earnings coupled with possible upward mobility to a higher wage in a rigidly stratified economic system.[151]

Obviously, what we are talking about here is nothing more palpable than a human emotion—hope. But it is a form of hope with a price tag, measured by the willingness of people to give up a substantial quantity of goods and services today in return for some reasonable assurance that nothing bars them from a higher income in the future. With more research, it might someday be possible to calculate an economic value for mobility. We then could measure an "opportunity gap" in the sense we now refer to a "dollar income gap" and a "purchasing power gap." In the meantime, it is sufficient to know that to the extent Legal Services lawyers remove barriers to social-economic mobility, they supply something poor people value in the same way as food, clothing and shelter.

B. LEGAL ACTIONS AFFECTING OPPORTUNITY TO ATTAIN HIGHER IN-COME STATUS. Economic mobility appears to be related primarily to four factors: intelligence, family, race, and education.[152] Two of these, native intelligence and family status, are difficult to manipulate through law and legal processes and will not be discussed in this section.

1. Racial discrimination. Racial discrimination is the single most crucial —and least defensible—barrier to economic attainment. Some harsh statistics illustrate the extent of the problem.

—Negro incomes averaged only 50 percent of white incomes as recently as 1958.[153]

—A negro had twice as good a chance to earn under $3000 as a white man.[154]

—In 1962, 46.4 percent of negroes—and only 15 percent of whites—were in the two lowest paying occupation groups: common labor and the service trades.[155]

Discrimination—racial prejudice in action—bears the responsibility for these statistics. First, it has barred most nonwhites from the living environment and education that would equip them to compete for higher-status occupations.[156] Second, it has prevented those nonwhites who nevertheless had acquired the necessary education and traits from occupying these positions.[157] To counteract this biased treatment of minorities requires activation of a mechanism that can affect governmental and private decisions in housing, education, employment and elsewhere in society. History suggests that the crux of that mechanism is the law.

"You can't legislate morality" or "You can't eliminate prejudice through the law" are the common arguments against the use of the law to attack discriminatory practices.[158] Princeton sociologist Morroe Berger studied that issue in depth, focusing on the impact of school desegregation decisions because they represented a dramatic example of the use of legal restraints against discrimination by private persons.[159] Based on this research, Berger first makes the point that it is somewhat irrelevant to minorities whether the law eliminates prejudice as an internal attitude so long as it prevents the attitude from finding expression in an act of discrimination that harms them. He then concludes:

> There is much evidence, in the way the public has responded to the vast change in the legal structure since World War II, that civil rights laws, court decisions, and administrative actions substantially increase the proportion of people who retain their prejudices while reducing their discriminatory actions.[160]

Not satisfied with the proposition that prejudice is relatively inconsequential, Berger marshals evidence showing how the law modifies the underlying attitude as well as the overt discriminatory act.

> We have seen that the personality studies have found [extremely prejudiced] persons to be conformists of a kind, respecters of power, scorning the weak but toadying to the strong. One of the few constants in their behavior is submission to the symbols of power. Law, when it is backed by the full panoply of the state, . . . is just such a symbol. . . .

There is further agreement that intergroup contact under certain circumstances tends to reduce hostility, alter stereotypes, and ultimately reduce prejudice. . . . [L]aw is a particularly appropriate means by which to increase intergroup contact on an equal level. . . .

As an accomplished fact, law affects even those who oppose it. . . . Studies of public opinion show . . . that after the adoption of certain laws and policies there is a rise in public opinion favorable to these actions.[161]

Berger's evidence suggests the law can touch both the hand and the heart. Thus, lawyers who can help to enforce and change the law should occupy major roles in altering the decisions of school systems, governments, landlords and employers who handicap minority groups in their efforts at economic competition.

In several communities, Legal Services Agencies have ended *de facto* segregation of public schools[162] and elsewhere have promoted bilingual education for Spanish-speaking students.[163] In the field of employment discrimination, poverty lawyers have persuaded or compelled major businesses to adopt "affirmative action plans" to employ and promote a substantial proportion of minority group members, thus opening thousands of middle-class positions to low-income job seekers.[164] They also have filed challenges to written tests often used to avoid hiring minorities or promoting them in private and public agencies.[165]

Despite the examples described above, Legal Services lawyers have done much less to eliminate racial discrimination than to increase income for the entire poverty community. The most likely explanation is that few clients appear at neighborhood law offices complaining about discrimination in education or employment. These simply do not sound like concerns to take to a lawyer. In contrast, thousands seek help with welfare, consumer and housing problems—legal issues with ramifications for income distribution and purchasing power but seldom for equal opportunity. For this reason, most of the antidiscrimination cases have been brought by agencies like the Western Center on Law and Poverty and California Rural Legal Assistance. Lawyers in these organizations deliberately respond to community demands as well as issues that happen to be raised by individual clients requesting aid at poverty offices. Their numbers have been too few and their efforts too scattered to cause a full-scale breakthrough in equal opportunity for the minority poor. Yet they may have exposed the possibilities.

Ultimately, the upward economic mobility of a race or other segment of the population probably must be measured by the net movement of its members on the income ladder. Obviously, if more have climbed a rung than have fallen back, the group has progressed. The degree of progress is calculated by how many climbed how far. By this gauge, nonwhites have become slightly more mobile in recent years. From 1960 to 1969, the percentage of nonwhite males in the high status "professional, technical and managerial" occupational category rose by over one-third, from 7 to 11 percent of the total black labor force. In that same period, nonwhites also increased their employment in the top blue collar positions—craftsmen and foremen. In 1960, 10 percent of nonwhites were so employed; by 1969, this figure reached 14 percent. Meanwhile, the percentage stuck in low-paying farm labor jobs decreased from 14 to 7 percent and those hired as common laborers went down from 23 to 18 percent.[166]

With present data, it is not feasible to measure the Legal Services contribution to the improved economic opportunity for minorities. In fact, research may never be able to relate the breaking of social barriers, for instance in education, with a higher paying occupation that comes years later and after the intervention of many other factors. Nevertheless, the efforts of some poverty lawyers suggest the Program already has advanced equal opportunity for racial minorities somewhat and could make a much greater contribution in the future.

2. Educational inequality. The opportunity to obtain a satisfactory education is not entirely dependent upon race. It is also a function of the student's economic status and his residence. Economic status influences the extent of the student's education—how much schooling he will receive[167]; residence may determine the quality (and cost) of that education.[168]

Education through high school generally is provided at public expense to all interested students in the United States. As this country has become more industrialized, computerized and generally complex, entrance to many occupations requires a more advanced education than can be obtained in high school. Unless a job applicant has received the training, he is not qualified to even compete for the higher paying positions. In the face of this general need for higher education, only a few states offer cost-free education at college and technology institutes. As a result, students from economically deprived families are placed at a competitive disadvantage whether they are white or nonwhite.

The student's residence affects the quality of education primarily because of unequal expenditures by schools located in the same geographic area. During the academic year of 1968–69, the average allocation per pupil for students in Baldwin Hill, California was $577.[169] The average expenditure in Beverly Hills, just a few miles away—was $1231.[170] This suggests the Baldwin Hills students receive a lesser education, a handicap that will carry over into college acceptance figures, college performance, job placement, and lifetime income. Or consider Texas, where the wealthiest district expended $5334 per pupil while the poorest spent $264.[171]

What accounts for these gross inequities in school budgets? In most states, public education is financed primarily through local taxes. Each school district raises its own revenues from its own residents, and thus districts populated by wealthy families easily support generous school budgets while low-income districts strain to provide half as much.[172]

Our dependence on local school district taxation compounds the disadvantage of poverty. Those with the least to spend must pay the highest proportion of their income for education. And those with the greatest need for good schooling get the worst.

The school financing laws which perpetuate these inequities have come under attack in the courts. In *Serrano* v. *Priest,*[173] poverty lawyers persuaded the California Supreme Court to declare unconstitutional the school-funding system prevailing in the nation's largest state. Subsequently, other judges found that this pattern of educational financing denies residents of poor districts their right to equal protection of the law.[174]

3. The Achievement of Greater Personal Freedom from Actions of Public and Private Institutions

Beyond a decent income and an equal opportunity to succeed in the economic sphere, most people aspire to a large measure of personal freedom, the ability to make one's own basic decisions. In essence, this translates to an absence of arbitrary intrusions into an individual's life by other persons or institutions. This belief is deeply woven into the fabric of American ideology. But poor people in particular are subject to unilateral, irrational decisions by others. For no reason or for a bad one, they can lose a job, home, or welfare support overnight. Bureaucrats may dictate many details of their private lives, including who their friends are, how they may spend their money, whether they may have more children. Police may harass them, insult them, ban them from certain areas.

In part, poor people enjoy less personal freedom because of their heavy dependence on governmental assistance. The government giveth and the government taketh away. But their plight frequently is compounded by two other factors: weak bargaining position and racial prejudice.

In the private economic sector, the poor seldom possess the power to negotiate any form of job security or fair working procedures, because they are generally employed in unorganized industries with labor surpluses; their livelihood is at the whim of the boss.

For nonwhites, there is the interference of police officers, public housing managers or others who simply dislike or distrust minorities. These officials impinge on the freedom of blacks or Spanish-surnamed persons in ways they would never consider treating other citizens.

In this section, we consider what Legal Services lawyers can and have done to enhance the personal freedom of low-income citizens. This will entail examination of the guarantees for freedom in both the public and private sectors.

A. PUBLIC AGENCIES. Goods, services, and even opportunities, generally are provided to the poor through government and quasi-governmental agencies. Welfare departments, public housing authorities, the Social Security Administration, unemployment compensation boards, and scores of other local, state, and Federal agencies administer the transfer payments that supply half of the goods and services enjoyed by the bottom fifth of the population.[175] Poor people not only have a stake in the amount of goods and services distributed, a decision generally beyond the control of these agencies; they are also interested in the manner of distribution.

—Are the eligibility standards well advertised and applied uniformly?

—Is there undue interference with the privacy or life style of the recipients?

—Do the administrators apply all rules and policies without discrimination?

—Are the poor given adequate notice and a fair hearing before termination of their transfer payments?

—Do agency personnel treat the recipients with the respect due fellow human beings?

All of these questions involve matters within the control of the agencies charged with the responsibility of redistribution. A complex body of law, consisting of regulations, rules, and policies, has been formulated to deal with these questions by the agencies themselves. This special legal system has tolerated and sometimes promoted abusive, unfair, discriminatory procedures and practices. Some examples:

—"Midnight raids" on recipients by investigators seeking to unearth violations of welfare rules.[176]

—Denial of aid to applicants who fail to measure up to some arbitrary moral standard, that is, no member of family was ever arrested, no illegitimate children.[177]

—A quantity of detailed rules and regulations so onerous as to unduly constrict the daily lives of recipients.[178]

—Termination of welfare assistance or public housing tenancy for any reason before the recipient has an opportunity to refute the allegations at a hearing.[179]

Thus far, we have been discussing the practices of agencies primarily responsible for transfers of money, goods, and services to the low-income sector. But government bodies charged with provision of general public services—police protection, education, and so on—likewise are capable of mistreating individuals or groups that are poor. At this point, we are not concerned with decisions about the quantity of public services allocated to the poverty community. That is part of the distribution question discussed earlier.[180] Rather we are considering how public servants serve the less affluent of their "masters." Are police more likely to be brutal, discourteous or condescending toward poor people? Do schools arbitrarily discipline individual students or impose unnecessary, discriminatory restrictions? There is evidence that the answers to these and similar questions are in the affirmative in many cities.[181]

The fairness of governmental practices and procedures is not necessarily determined solely by the agency's own rules and regulations. There are statutes and constitutional principles as well that potentially bear upon the treatment of recipients. One hypothesis tested by the OEO Legal Services Program is whether these fundamental notions of fair play extend to welfare mothers, the unemployed, public housing tenants, and the other low-income clients of government programs.

In recent actions brought by poverty attorneys, courts have evidenced some willingness to impose due process requirements on public agencies. For instance, the Supreme Court held the Constitution requires welfare departments to grant recipients a hearing prior to terminating assistance and that under Federal regulations local housing authorities must give tenants notice and a hearing before evicting them from public housing.[182] Courts also have invalidated discriminatory eligibility criteria for public housing and other benefits[183] and expanded the rights of low-income persons in the judicial process itself.[184] However, the Supreme Court refused to stop people from the staffs of welfare departments from searching recipients' apartments without warrants.[185]

Thus far, it appears actions by Legal Services lawyers have produced reform of rules and procedures within government agencies, especially welfare departments and public housing authorities. But change in official rules and procedures does not always bring about fairer treatment for poor people. For the most part, the latter depends on millions of decisions by thousands of individual government employees, and influencing these patterns of conduct can be more difficult than rewriting an agency's rulebook. The central problem is obedience to official policy. A study of county-level welfare administration in rural Virginia uncovered widespread disregard of the letter and spirit of Federal and state regulations.[186] Welfare workers were abusive to applicants, misleading about eligibility and entitlement, and arbitrary in discontinuing aid.

Also in the interest of a fair appraisal, it should be noted that some other public agencies, especially police departments, have not yielded to actions brought by Legal Services lawyers. There is little evidence that either individual damage claims or broad-scale class action injunctions have reduced the level of police misconduct in those communities where it is a serious problem.

B.   PRIVATE INSTITUTIONS.   Government agencies are not the only institutions capable of arbitrary and arrogant treatment of the low-income sector. The present legal system allows employers, landlords and creditors to exercise enormous, and often unwarranted, discretionary power over vital aspects of the lives of the poor.

—Unless an industry is unionized, an employer usually can still take away a worker's job for any cause, or none, without even telling the employee why he is being fired.

—In most states a landlord can take away the tenant's shelter for any reason, or none, and in some states without any kind of hearing.

—Until recently an alleged creditor could take away most of a debtor's income, through garnishment, without even proving a debt is owed.

—Creditors also can harass a debtor unmercifully: contacting him at inconvenient hours, bothering his children, embarrassing him with his employer, and so on.

—Employers, landlords, and creditors have been known to disregard even the few protections that exist when dealing with people who lack legal counsel or an understanding of their rights.

To some extent the same fundamental notions of due process that limit governmental actions have been invoked against private institutions. The Supreme Court already has ruled that wages cannot be garnished until a hearing has been held.[187] In some jurisdictions, landlords no longer can evict tenants who report housing code violations.[188] In Georgia, evictions without a hearing recently were prohibited.[189] Injunctions have been granted against collection practices that invade a debtor's privacy or abuse his freedom. These cases and related developments[190] point toward a goal of fair play between economic classes in society. But as yet they remain only a beginning.

C. PERSONAL FREEDOM AND POVERTY. Due process, and its underlying notion of fair play, is comfortable home ground for the lawyer. The chances for success and the feeling of immediate personal gratification many derive are greatest when striving toward this goal. The mere presence of legal counsel almost guarantees more respect for the poor on the part of bureaucrats, landlords, and merchants. Beyond that, the fundamental principles of fair play are deeply imbedded in our legal system. Lawyers representing the poor frequently need only point out that procedures don't comply with constitutional requirements and judges will revamp the process.

The temptation among lawyers and social scientists is to fasten on this aspect of the legal profession's contribution to the social and economic betterment of the poor. It sounds like a legal assignment; it feels like lawyer work; it is reflected in a direct legal change. This may misplace the emphasis. Not that the poor do not want and deserve personal freedom and respect. But they could enjoy a perfection of fair procedures and respectful treatment, and still be "ill-housed, ill-clad, ill-nourished."[191] I suspect it would not be wise to conceive the lawyer's role that narrowly.

4. The Democratization of Government Agencies and Private Economic Institutions

A meticulous concern for fair procedures is possible, if admittedly not very probable, even in a dictatorship. But the sharing of power and decision-making authority is a trait unique to democracy. This sort of participation is the reverse side of personal freedom. In essence, freedom is the absence of interference by outside institutions in the individual's own decisions, while democracy is defined by the individual's ability to influence decisions of outside institutions.

The participation of the average citizen in politics once was limited to voting for major public officials and maybe an appearance at a public hearing on some proposal of special import. Now students, employees, parents, blacks, Mexican-Americans, the poor, and many others are demanding a louder voice in the decisions of most concern to their interests. Actually two levels of participation seem to be at issue. One is the opportunity to fully present the group's views to the ultimate decision-making body, whether it be a legislature, administrative agency, university faculty, or corporation board. The other is a role in the selection of the members of that body, which is an expression of a desire that the interest group be allowed to select some of its own to occupy voting seats on the decision-making panel. University students, for instance, have sought to place fellow students on administration committees, not merely to choose faculty members to represent their interests.

Low-income people have a special concern with the decisions of the agencies responsible for redistributing goods, services, and opportunity, and the poor possess the same right to participate in these decisions as the college students claim at a university. This the OEO has attempted to do. "Maximum feasible participation of the residents of the areas and members of the groups served" was a key clause in the Economic Opportunity Act.[192] And the poor did gain a voice in the local community action agencies established by OEO. Eventually, one-third or more of each CAA governing board was composed of representatives of the clients served.[193] But it was not a complete victory because the CAAs never achieved dominion over a substantial portion of the income or opportunity that was to be distributed to the poor.[194] Thus, participation in the administration of local CAAs was of limited utility.

Progress toward giving the poor an equivalent voice in other government agencies has not been encouraging. Some representation has been granted to tenant organizations in a few scattered public housing projects.[195] But the staffs of welfare departments and most other organizations responsible for transferring income and opportunity have seldom if ever been willing to share power with their clients. Moreover, if this kind of participation has been slow in coming to these agencies, it is unknown in other parts of government vital to the minorities and the poor: legislative bodies that make the basic allocation decisions; government agencies, like school boards and police departments, that dispense general government services[196]; and private business enterprises.[197]

The value of participation should not be overstated. It is easy to glamorize the idea of poor people helping to plan and administer the programs aimed at their welfare. Admittedly, participation in policy making offers rewards independent of anything it may accomplish. In fact, it is a fundamental tenet of this society that democracy has value above and beyond the objective results of its decisions.[198] That is why it has been listed as a separate social effect in this analysis of Legal Services impact. But there is precious little in the history of the OEO to suggest that the participation of the poor in the agencies of redistribution necessarily works miracles. It cannot affect the key problem—the amount to be redistributed. It may or may not produce sounder methods and procedures. Without more, the poor could find themselves to have gained power over nothing,[199] participation in yet another failure.[200]

Since the issues of prime concern to low-income people are resolved outside the OEO-funded community action agencies, it is important to appraise the capacity of Legal Services to magnify the voice of the poor in these vital areas of government. Their largest contribution probably has been to first-level participation—presenting the viewpoint of the low-income community to legislators, administrative bodies and the like. By 1972, over 50 legislative advocates were employed by Legal Services agencies. Appearing before committees, speaking to individual lawmakers in their offices, analyzing and drafting proposed bills, these representatives afford the low-income community at least a measure of participation in the legislative process.[201] In a similar way, poverty lawyers provide access to courts and also to administrative bodies.[202] Of course, in all these instances, the lawyers' presentation constitutes participation for the poor only to the extent that the professional advocate truly represents and is responsive to them. Thus, it is in this sense that the presence of poor people on Legal Services boards assumes special importance.

Poverty attorneys appear to have accomplished less in making it possible for the poor to participate in the selection of government decision-makers. However, they have not been completely inactive. Approximately 100,000 Mexican-Americans, literate in Spanish but not English, were enfranchised through a California Supreme Court decision.[203] Thus, this group, primarily poor, now can help choose the officials who govern them. In a different vein, poverty lawyers sometimes have negotiated arrangements with public housing authorities to place tenant representatives on the managing board[204] and have won citizen representation for the poor in urban renewal and model cities agencies.[205] And, outside of government, Legal Services attorneys have helped create business entities owned and run by the poor.[206] But the most enthusiastic advocate of Legal Services would have to concede that poverty lawyers have achieved only modest gains in giving the poor a larger say about who makes decisions in the legislature, the administrative agencies and the private economy.

5. The Peaceful Orderly Resolution of Grievances Held by Low-Income Groups

The four social-economic effects discussed thus far have redounded almost exclusively to the benefit of the primary clients of the Legal Services Program, the poor. The resolution of grievances, however, may offer as much to the affluent as it confers on the poor themselves. A society—any society—can tolerate only so much violence or it ceases to be civilized. And a democracy —any democracy—can tolerate only so much repression of violence or it ceases to be a free state. Thus, everyone has a stake in the peaceful, orderly resolution of grievances, great and small, held by anyone.

The poor are beset with problems. These range from fundamental issues like the distribution of goods and services to minor irritations over inadequate street-lighting, sidewalk maintenance, traffic light placement and tardy welfare checks. Whatever the source or depth of the various grievances, they tend to share one characteristic. American society seldom affords an effective, orderly method for resolving them. Too often the unresolved grievances merely accumulate until they fuel individual acts of violence or a public disturbance sparked by a single, often insignificant, incident. One of the basic causes of civil disorder is the fact that there exists no legal, peaceable mechanisms for redress of grievances,[207] or if a mechanism exists, it is available only to those with financial means.[208]

Normally, the lack of a formal grievance procedure does not harm the more privileged classes to the same degree it does the poor. The wealthy, and to a lesser but still substantial degree the middle class, can obtain redress through the exercise of informal power and influence. For example, a more privileged member of society subjected to police brutality often can obtain the dismissal or suspension of the offending officer and a more careful performance of police duties merely through the pressures he can exert. A poor man has no access to this kind of informal but very real power.[209] If he is brutalized by the police, society must provide a formal system for ascertaining the facts and taking corrective measures, or the wrong probably will go unrighted, but it will accumulate with a thousand unrighted wrongs, to produce widespread alienation and exacerbate the danger of violence. The same principle holds as to disputes between private parties if there is no formalized, effective, unbiased mechanism for settling disputes that is available to all. The side with the greater wealth, power, and influence invariably will prevail, and right or wrong, that side will prevail again and again until the consistent loser contemplates striking back with force against the system (or lack of system).

In part, this merely reiterates a rationale long ago articulated by the founders of the legal aid movement. Reginald Heber Smith foresaw social stability as a principal by-product of legal representation for poor people.[210] But the

OEO program has added a new dimension to this concept. Proponents of legal aid only envisioned defusing the personal grievances of individuals. The Legal Services Program, however, has explicitly undertaken to resolve community-wide issues as well, which probably contribute most to alienation and the risk of violence in the ghettos.

Virtually from its inception, the OEO Legal Services Program has been embarked on a unique and profoundly significant experiment. For virtually the first time in human history, a government has sought to develop peaceful means for accommodating class conflict and social change, in effect to rationalize and pacify a process that typically tears society asunder. The hope is to substitute advocacy, in its broadest terms, for violence in any form. The experiment seeks to encourage a full panoply of officially recognized forums for pursuing any social goals and full access to each of these forums for all individuals, groups and classes.

With their knowledge of the nation's policy-making apparatus—from courts to city planning commissions—and their advocacy skills, poverty lawyers appear to be especially qualified to use whatever peaceful modes of change that may exist. The results recounted thus far in this chapter suggest the Legal Services Program may be able to channel deeply felt community and class aspirations into orderly forums that produce results only protest, confrontation, and violent conflict formerly brought about.

However, it may be that the four fundamental social-economic ends discussed earlier in this chapter can be achieved only by means of violence and disorder. The Skolnick report to the National Commission on the Causes and Prevention of Violence[211] dissolved the myth that in "America there was no need—there never had been a need—for political violence" because "any sizable domestic group could gain its share of power, prosperity, and respectability merely by playing the game according to the rules."[212]

> [T]he proposition is false if it means that the established order is self-transforming, in that groups in power will always or generally share that power with newcomers without the pressure of actual or potential violence. The Appalachian farmer revolts, as well as tumultous urban demonstrations in sympathy with the French Revolution, were used by Jeffersonians to create a new two-party system over the horrified protests of the Federalists. Northern violence ended Southern slavery, and Southern terrorism ended radical Reconstruction. The transformation of labor-management relations was achieved during a wave of bloody strikes, in the midst of a depression and widespread fear of revolution. And black people made their greatest political gains, both in Congress and in the cities during the racial strife of the 1960's.[213]

Violence *can* be the means for obtaining a fair share of goods and services, equalizing opportunity, attaining personal freedom, and promoting participation. It can also be effective to highlight and even resolve lesser grievances.[214] But if that is the best our society can offer, the price of social change or social stagnation (depending on who wins out in the violent confrontation) may be too high. Thus, to the other desired effects of the Legal Services Program, we add another—peaceful, orderly movement toward the ends sought and peaceful, orderly resolution of the grievances held by the poor.

B. A Preliminary Evaluation of the Cost Effectiveness of Legal Services as an Antipoverty Program

To complete our evaluation of the social-economic impact of the OEO Legal Services Program it may prove helpful to go beyond identification of the principal effects. Obviously, the OEO officials who helped launch the experiment were misguided (or betrayed) if it merely diverted funds from other units that could have done more with those sums to reduce poverty. Thus, a further question becomes relevant: Is Legal Services a cost effective antipoverty strategy, especially as compared with other OEO programs?

Of necessity, this will be a limited inquiry.[215] We have neither the space nor the data to calculate in precise quantitative terms the total costs and total benefits attributable to Legal Services lawyers. Nevertheless, there is enough information to assemble rough estimates about certain critical inputs and outputs. And from these approximations we should be able to extract some valuable insights about the comparative cost effectiveness of the OEO Legal Services Program in the war on poverty.

In this section we are concerned with cost effectiveness in its simplest, most straightforward terms. Disregarded are the soft, noneconomic values a more sophisticated analysis would reveal. The costs referred to are simply the dollar amounts of the Federal outlays for a given program, not the social and political costs that might attend implementation of the program. Further, in describing the benefits, we are considering only the economic consequences, not the possible social or political gains. This admitted simplification is justified both because quantification is otherwise unfeasible and since at its core the most critical dimension of poverty is economic. There may be complex social, cultural, and political causes of poverty but the central fact of life for the poor is that they have fewer goods and services than other people.

At the same time, it should be recognized that this evaluation necessarily fails to take account of some of the most important benefits of the Legal Services Program, such as increased personal freedom, participation in decision making, and the equalization of opportunity. Thus, we actually are putting the Program through the toughest possible test of its cost effectiveness. A full appraisal would require the addition of a large, but presently unmeasured social dividend to the benefit side of the equation.

1. A Framework for Analysis

All Federal programs for the poor frequently are divided into two broad categories—cash and in-kind. As the names suggest, a cash program disburses money to its beneficiaries; an in-kind program distributes goods or services directly. The clearest example of a cash program is the welfare check. In-kind programs range from food programs through clothing and furniture allotments to charity hospitals.

The cost effectiveness of an in-kind program generally is judged on how much cheaper the commodity or service can be delivered through governmental channels than would be the case if recipients were merely furnished an equivalent amount of money with which to purchase those same goods and services on the open market. For example, would it be less expensive for the government to mass-produce (or mass-purchase) blankets and distribute them to poor people or to supply the recipients with enough money to purchase blankets at local stores?

Both methods of supplying legal assistance have been tried by OEO, and thus there is some fairly reliable statistical information on which a comparison of cost effectiveness can be based. Neighborhood law offices deliver legal help on an in-kind basis through attorneys whose salaries are paid and whose offices are supplied by the government. "Judicare," on the other hand, is in the nature of a cash transfer program allowing the recipients to "purchase" their legal assistance from private attorneys on the open market.[216]

In a study by the Bureau of Social Science Research, private attorneys participating in the Wisconsin Judicare program were found to charge $182.89 to "deliver" the average divorce as compared to an average cost of $41.53 for delivery of that same service through government salaried neighborhood lawyers located in similar rural areas. Bankruptcies were processed for $266.70 by Judicare but for $87.75 by salaried attorneys.[217] There are methodological problems with this study which cast some doubt on the precision of its figures. But the general scale of relative cost it portrays is consistent with an earlier comparison arrived at by dividing the total budget of competing programs by the total number of cases handled by these grantees. The result showed that services cost an average of $139 per case under Judicare and $48 through neighborhood law offices.[218]

This information suggests, first that government apparently can provide in-kind legal assistance less expensively—by a ratio of over 3 to 1—than this service can be purchased by poor people out of income transferred to them. Second, it indicates that salaried staff lawyers are a more efficient way of delivering legal services than compensated private counsel, at least in most circumstances.[219]

A tentative policy conclusion follows from these findings. Where government is attempting to transfer a pre-determined package of goods and services to the poor through a mix of cash payments and in-kind transfers, the price of the total package can be reduced if the legal services portion is delivered on an in-kind basis. Or, conversely, if the government has only a fixed number of dollars with which to purchase goods and services for the poor, they can buy a larger package by supplying legal assistance in-kind. (Many other goods and services, however, may be available on the open market at a price equal to or even cheaper than they can be furnished through government channels. In such cases, it makes good sense, speaking in economic terms at least, to merely transfer cash to the poor rather than make in-kind disbursements of these goods and services.)[220]

There are inherent limitations in the foregoing test of cost effectiveness. It assumes that prices on the open market accurately reflect the comparative value of various goods and services distributed to the poor. In effect, it focuses entirely on the "cost" side of the equation. One is provided with a ratio of budget costs to market prices, which is a good measure of comparative *efficiency* of competing Federal programs. However, this analysis does not supply sufficient information about the "benefit" side of the equation. Market prices may not take into consideration many of the more important social-economic effects of a given product or service. Its real value to the poor may be quite different from the fee paid by middle- and upper-class consumers. That is, assume the government were able to supply caviar with a market value of $3 for each Federal dollar expended. That would not necessarily indicate this was a better investment for the poor than $2 worth of beef that cost the government $1.

The more meaningful gauge of cost effectiveness takes into account the comparative impact of alternative Federal investments as well as their respective costs and efficiencies. There are at least three types of transfers the government can make to the poor: *consumer* resources, *opportunity* resources, and *redistribution* resources. *Consumer* resources are the material goods and services that provide immediate satisfaction of basic physical, psychological, and emotional needs. In this category falls food, housing, clothing, furniture and entertainment, among others (or equivalent cash income). It is the deprivation of such resources that constitutes income poverty, while the possession of ample supplies of these goods and services means affluence. Of course, OEO was never responsible for the government's major distribution of consumer resources to the poor, such as Social Security, public assistance, public housing and food stamps. But within the war on poverty itself there are several examples of consumer resource transfers. Many public job creation programs such as the Neighborhood Youth Corps merely involve Federal cash payments to low-income persons on a temporary basis for doing relatively menial tasks. Also, most of the services offered in OEO-funded Neighborhood Service Centers might otherwise have been purchased on the open market with the transfer of an equal amount of money, including housing relocation services, home-making services, many phases of consumer education, and marriage counseling.

Opportunity resources embrace goods and services such as tools, and job training and education designed to improve the individual's capacity to compete for a larger share of consumer resources. In theory, a dollar transferred to a poor person in this form today may ultimately enhance his earning capacity and thereby pay a dividend of several dollars worth of consumer resources sometime in the future. Examples from the poverty program include Headstart, Job Corps, and many manpower training efforts.[221]

Finally, the government can transfer *redistribution* resources to the poor. These have the potential for inducing some relevant decision maker to distribute more goods and services to the poor. Unlike *opportunity* resources, *redistribution* resources operate not on the individual poor person, but upon the distribution system itself. They are not designed to make the individual better able to compete for higher paying jobs and other income-producing positions in society, but rather to increase the rewards received in terms of consumer resources—for existing levels of skill and capacity. The prime examples of this type of investment during the war on poverty were community organizers and Legal Services lawyers.

An attorney, for instance, seeks to affect his client's stock of consumer resources whenever he sues for money damages (or even defends against such an action). Beyond that, of course, the attorney may initiate lawsuits or legislation to alter the income structure to channel more goods and services to his client on a continuing basis.[222] In any event, the lawyer's help is sought not because it fulfills any fundamental physical or psychological need, but because it may enhance the supply of the resources that do satisfy such needs.[223]

The benchmark for any antipoverty investment is the amount of consumer goods and services a poor person could purchase if the budget for that program were merely distributed directly in the form of cash. Unless it can be shown that a given program ultimately will generate more consumer goods and services for the poor than its own cost to the government, it is difficult to justify its inclusion in the OEO effort. After all, the Federal war on poverty was designed to "eliminate the paradox of poverty." Its programs were started because of the expectation that they would contribute more to that result than existing pure cash transfers like welfare. Accordingly, a government investment that reduces the income gap less than an equivalent amount of welfare does not seem to belong in OEO, although it might be entirely appropriate to some other program for the poor.[224] Conversely, any program which demonstrates a capacity to produce an ultimate increment of consumer resources substantially in excess of its own cost constitutes a sound antipoverty investment.

The cost effectiveness of programs can be assessed by comparing the dollar value of consumer goods and services received by the poor as a result of an antipoverty investment against the dollar cost of that antipoverty investment. As an example, assume a $25-thousand community organization effort whose sole contribution was to generate pressure on a city council to appropriate funds to purchase $50-thousand worth of blankets for occupants of a public housing project. The cost effectiveness ratio for this particular program would be calculated as follows:

$$\frac{\text{dollar value of consumer goods and services received by poor as a result of antipoverty investment}}{\text{dollar cost of antipoverty investment}} \quad \frac{\$50,000}{\$25,000} = \frac{2}{1}$$

This is the cost effectiveness ratio for the community organization program.

By this same analysis, a $25-thousand job training program that upgrades the skills of low-income workers sufficiently to increase their combined earnings by $5000 a year would have a four to one cost effectiveness ratio

$$\frac{\$100\text{-thousand (capital fund which produces }\$5\text{-thousand per annum at 5\% interest)}^{225}}{\$25\text{-thousand (cost of job training program)}} = \frac{4}{1}$$

cost effectiveness ratio for job training program

Accordingly, a government antipoverty agency with $25-thousand to invest apparently would be best advised to put its money in the job training program rather than the community organization effort.

Applying this approach to the major programs of OEO, it is apparent that any phase becomes suspect in economic terms unless it has a substantial, positive cost effectiveness ratio. Ordinarily, programs which distribute what are essentially *consumer* resources seldom will, and therefore the only way the OEO could justify such an investment would be to manufacture or purchase certain goods and services and deliver them to the poor at substantially lower cost than they could be bought on the open market. In stating this generalization, however, I am distinguishing sharply between OEO and other government benefit programs aimed at the low-income community. Cash transfers like welfare and in-kind transfers such as Medicare clearly are essential elements of the government's total strategy for dealing with poverty. But it is precisely because OEO was assigned a more ambitious mission than these other agencies and was given a comparatively small budget that its success depended on maximizing the return on its investments. For that reason, it appears OEO seldom should have been in the business of distributing consumer resources.

Opportunity enhancement resources like Headstart and job training are not easy to assess. Measuring their cost effectiveness entails complex calculations and problematical projections. As an example, the influence of a Headstart class for a four-year-old today on the possible increase in the goods and services he will receive during his working life will be difficult to demonstrate even in retrospect. Attempting to make the estimate while the student is still five or six years old is virtually impossible. However, the advantages an adult might gain from job training is, or at least should be, much more immediate and thus fairly easy to measure.

The fact that the benefits which opportunity resources provide the poor are difficult, and sometimes impossible, to forecast accurately obviously is not itself reason to exclude them from the antipoverty strategy. However, there are other factors that might give one pause. First, opportunity resources must ultimately generate very substantial dividends of consumer goods and services to justify their relatively high cost. Taking account of inflation, a Headstart student would have to earn $100–200 a year more each year over a 40-year job career to "break even" on the cost of his two years in Headstart. Moreover, as has been suggested before, if such programs only help the recipients to raise their own income at the expense of other low-income individuals, then from the viewpoint of reducing poverty itself, these resources might seem to be a questionable investment.

Redistribution resources appear to offer the antipoverty strategists the most tantalizing possibilities for a high payoff on the Federal investment. The gains in consumer goods and services will tend to come more quickly and to be more readily measured than those arising from a transfer of opportunity resource; the potential leverage also appears greater. Of course, to the extent the redistribution of consumer resources depends upon a court decision that changes basic allocations of income (i.e., the ruling that states could not deny welfare to children merely because a man was in the house), that structural change is reversible and the gains then achieved are subject to reduction or cancellation, usually by a legislative body.[226] Thus any such increase in the flow of consumer resources probably is best visualized as a revocable trust fund, one that requires constant attention and protection.

The rationale outlined above may suggest certain broad conclusions about the types of investments OEO should have emphasized. But our purpose is not to analyze in detail and compare other antipoverty efforts. Rather this discussion furnishes the background for consideration of the cost effectiveness of the Legal Services Program.

2. The Cost Effectiveness of the Legal Services Program

Appraising the cost effectiveness of the Legal Services Program is, in many ways, a more complex task than it is for most other programs of the war on poverty. Others, such as Headstart, are characterized by a relatively limited range of potential goals, means, and effects. A teacher employed in a Headstart program has a sharply defined function, enhancing the opportunity of the handful of students in one particular classroom. In no real sense can the instructor aspire to directly distribute income to those students, and clearly other poor persons are entirely outside the grasp of his helping hand. Moreover, except as he may influence the policies of the Headstart program in which he is employed, that teacher cannot expect to have any impact on the goals of personal freedom or increased participation in decision making.

A Legal Services lawyer, in contrast, has several options available to which his time and energies can be allotted. As suggested earlier in this chapter, he can choose among a variety of social-economic effects related to the cure or amelioration of poverty, some more important than others. A poverty attorney likewise can elect among several alternative strategies for accomplishing these results, some more effective than others (a subject to be discussed in detail in Chapter 9). The cost effectiveness of an individual Legal Services lawyer probably depends more on how well he selects his ends and means than it does upon his technical skill in implementing that decision, and the total cost effectiveness of the Legal Services Program is primarily a function of the sum total of these individual decisions.

To illustrate, assume a Legal Services lawyer has elected to devote most of his time to enforcement of child support orders against defaulting husbands and ex-husbands.[227] This attorney's actions probably would be counterproductive for the poor, for if the lawyer tries his case successfully, he will remove a low-income woman and her children from the welfare rolls and guarantee them a share of the salary of her low-income husband or ex-husband. This shifts the burden of supporting a part of the poverty community from the affluent taxpayers to the low-income male. The net result: a reverse redistribution of income—from the low-income community to the more affluent sectors of society.

At the other extreme are lawyers who devote a considerable percentage of their energies to legal actions that compel major shifts of income, opportunity, freedom or participation toward the poor. These efforts can be extraordinarily cost effective, sometimes in a single case earning or saving scores of millions for the poor at the expenditure of a few thousand dollars worth of the lawyers' time.[228] Some of the more dramatic examples include the case raising farmworker wages by $100 million annually; the welfare residency and "man in the house" cases increasing annual welfare income by $100–200 million; and cases halting reductions in Medicaid payments in New York and California involving over $200 million in each state.[229]

Of course, the choice is seldom so clear-cut as that between devoting time to a highly productive national test case with scores of millions of dollars at stake as opposed to a string of counterproductive child support enforcement prosecutions. Short of those two extremes, there are many degrees of cost effectiveness. Unfortunately, no studies have yet been performed which will tell us, with any degree of precision, the average costs and benefits characteristic of typical forms of legal action on behalf of the poor. However, it does not require any extended scientific inquiry to construct some reasonable hypotheses about the comparative cost effectiveness of cases undertaken on behalf of an individual client (and carrying potential benefit only for that client) as contrasted with those, usually more complex, undertakings that may touch many poor people who are not clients of the Legal Services lawyer.

Precisely because of his poverty, a poor person seldom has large sums at stake in any given case, at least as measured in absolute terms. A garnishment suit, for instance, that threatens 25 percent of a poor person's annual wages might involve $400 or $500. A landlord-tenant action seeking two months rent would typically place $150 to $200 in jeopardy. Most divorce cases (which account for almost 20 percent of the Legal Services caseload nationally) between low-income spouses involve little in the way of property, alimony, or child support payments. (Even more significantly, any asset or income transferred between the parties to this divorce litigation constitutes a transaction within the low-income class and no net gain or loss for the low-income sector.)

In addition, it is only rarely that any litigant, rich or poor, obtains 100 percent of his goal. This reduces the actual stakes even more. Yet it may cost as much to resolve a dispute realistically involving only $100 or $200 as one where the amount in issue is several times greater.[230]

Thus, it seems reasonable to anticipate that Legal Services will not be a particularly cost effective program to the extent that its collective lawyer resources are focused on cases whose benefits are confined to the individual client. The potential gains or losses in these suits appear too small to add up to a meaningful sum.[231] On the other hand, Legal Services apparently is an extraordinarily cost effective program to the extent its lawyers invest time in actions where the number of possible beneficiaries is large and the collective gains substantial. The cost-benefit potential becomes even more favorable where the goods and services distributed to the poor through legal action are of a type that may generate further economic dividends. Thus, a decision like *Serrano* v. *Priest*,[232] if it compels a redistribution of *opportunity* resources, may produce a future increment of consumer income that significantly exceeds the dollar value of the educational benefits initially transferred to the poor. To carry the analysis still further, legal actions which shift *redistribution* resources to the low-income community should in most circumstances be the most cost effective of all.

Certain qualifications must be made, however. Not every test case or legislative initiative succeeds. Legal Services lawyers have lost many decisions in the Supreme Court and lesser appellate tribunals. And several of these challenges involved millions in potential new benefits for the poor.[233] Thus, a lawyer's choice to devote time to high-leverage legal actions does not guarantee a maximum payoff for his efforts. Nor will the Program *necessarily* be highly cost effective as a whole merely because its attorneys collectively elect to concentrate on major reform efforts.

Another qualification must be added to the preliminary hypothesis that the Legal Services Program is cost effective to the extent its resources go into actions carrying possible benefits for many people. That is, it is apparent that to have any practical effect, legal changes must be disseminated to the client community and they must be enforced through lawsuits. Otherwise in many instances new rights simply will be ignored by government officials, businessmen, landlords, and the rest. These supporting activities presuppose the availability nationwide of lawyers committed to asserting rights on behalf of individual clients, without which most of the social-economic returns from major cases will seep away. Thus, in economic terms, this superstructure of attorneys represents a necessary fixed cost of effective change.

The question remains, to what degree have Legal Services lawyers focused their energies on the most cost effective alternatives, in contrast to those with less impact or a negative effect? In our present state of knowledge, a definitive answer to this question is impossible, but an informed appraisal is possible.

From its inception in 1965, through the end of 1972, the OEO Legal Services Program expended approximately $290 million.[234] On the benefit side, the 1969 minimum wage case already has produced about $300 million in added income for the poor, the 1969 welfare residency decision already has produced between $300 and $600 million added income for the poor, the 1968 man-in-house decision $400–$800 million, the 1969 and 1970 food stamp cases thus far have produced over $450 million in additional food allotments, the prior hearing case $200–$300 million. The California Medicaid suit saved $200 million in health services, the New York Medicaid case thus far has saved $367 million, and other actions undoubtedly have generated several millions in additional income.[235] Thus, a total dividend in excess of $2 billion actually has been received by the poor since the beginning of the Federal investment in legal services to the poor. Applying the more conservative cost effectiveness formula, one which makes no assumptions about the continuation of any benefits in the future, we find that benefits to the poverty community outweighed the cost of the program by a ratio of approximately 7 to 1.

$$\frac{\$2,000,000,000}{\$\ 290,000,000} = \frac{7}{1}$$

(cost effectiveness of Legal Services Program's first seven years)

To apply a more speculative formula, the increment in *annual* income generated by legal services actions is approximately $500 million.[236] Assuming that increment continues to be received in the future, the benefit conferred is equivalent to the trust fund required to produce that amount of annual income. This formula would then reflect:

$$\frac{\$10,000,000,000}{\$\ 290,000,000} = \frac{34}{1}$$

(cost effectiveness of investment in Legal Services Program during first seven years)

To place the cost effectiveness of Legal Services in perspective, it may prove worthwhile to project the impact of OEO were its other programs equally productive. During its first seven years, the budget of the legal arm of the war on poverty hovered between two and three percent of the total OEO appropriation.[237] Assume the validity of our hypothesis—that 3 percent of the OEO budget generated an annual dividend of $500 million a year in consumer income. A like return on the remaining 97 percent of OEO's investments would have yielded a $16 billion a year increment in goods and services for the poor. That, in turn, would have more than erased the entire income gap, the difference between what the poor actually receive as a class and what puts them over the hypothetical poverty line.[238]

The poverty income gap remains at about $10 billion,[239] but it by no means follows from the above comparison that had OEO sunk all its appropriations into Legal Services the gap would have been closed. Undoubtedly, the law of diminishing returns applies to the efforts of lawyers. At some point, more attorneys, more lawsuits, more legislative advocacy do not translate into further social-economic dividends. But I suspect that OEO could have enhanced its own total impact on the problem of poverty by allocating more of its budget to the Legal Services Program at the expense of reducing some of its less cost effective components.

3. Implications of the Appraisal of the Program's Cost Effectiveness

The analysis of cost effectiveness has offered some new perspectives for assessing the Legal Services Program and hopefully supplied some new insights. For one thing, it tends to provide context for debates about the contribution of the Program. Clearly, Legal Services lawyers have not "eliminated" poverty. But it is equally important to recognize that they have made an economic contribution far beyond their cost. That seems to be a more rational standard for judging performance than some expectation that the Program must cure all or it cures nothing, an attitude usually reflected in the complaint, "If we're spending millions on lawyers, why are people still poor?"

This approach may also introduce some precision, or at least a search for precision, into the consideration of several basic questions surrounding the administration of the Legal Services Program, and the decisions of its local agencies and their lawyers. How much money to invest in Legal Services; which kinds of cases to bring; how much time and effort is a given issue worth. In most instances, more data are needed to successfully employ this analytical tool. But it holds some promise for the more rational planning of Legal Services activity.

The apparent cost effectiveness of the Program likewise helps to explain why it has been under almost continual political bombardment. A bare handful of lawyers, scarcely a footnote in the Federal budget, has produced massive transfers of goods and services to the poor—some from the private sector and some from the public treasury. Some who felt they were involuntary transfer-ors of those goods and services have sought to eliminate the source of the advocacy that put the law on the side of the poor in certain phases of the economic contest. This has been particularly true of politicians who were caught cutting some illegal corners with benefits for the poor while trying to hold down public expenditures.

Finally, our preliminary evaluation of cost effectiveness suggests the Legal Services Program survived the most stringent test of its legitimacy as an antipoverty weapon. It probably could have been anticipated with confidence that lawyers would be able to advance the values of greater participation and more personal freedom for the poor. All they had to do was be available to match skill with skill in the courts, legislatures and administrative bodies, and win or lose, their actions meant far more participation in governmental deci-sion making than the poor had enjoyed in the past. Similarly, if lawyers experienced the same sort of successes on procedural issues as the ACLU had in the past, the poor would be freer from arbitrary interference with their personal freedom. These expectations have been fulfilled.[240]

But our findings also suggest that Legal Services lawyers have succeeded to a considerable extent in an area that might have seemed beyond their power —the economic dimension of poverty—where they produced dividends worth better than seven times the Program's total cost. In a sense, the millions of individuals helped with their personal crises, the expansions of personal free-dom and participation and equal opportunity were a bonus. At least it seems we need not quantify the impact in these other areas to sustain a conclusion that Legal Services attorneys have achieved a significant and measurable re-duction in poverty in the United States. And that may be one of the central lessons of the first seven years of the OEO Legal Services Program.

9: Toward Justice and Reform

The OEO Legal Services Program was not an end in itself. Properly conceived, any such government institution is merely a vehicle for realizing one or more societal goals. Thus, in looking to the future, it is not the OEO Legal Services Program itself that merits attention, but the accomplishment of the fundamental objectives that gave birth to the program.

I. THE FUTURE OF EQUAL JUSTICE

In earlier chapters passing reference was made that the demand for legal representation in the low-income sector far outstrips available resources. A University of Denver study used panels of attorneys to review reports of interviews with citizens of a poverty neighborhood, and they found that there were a total of 19,400 legal problems in a sample of 15,000 low-income households containing 40,373 individuals.[1] Projecting from this result to the national level, we can anticipate a total of over ten million legal problems among persons below the poverty line determined by OEO.

Experience under the Legal Services Program tends to support the results reported in the Denver survey. In San Francisco, which has a larger concentration of Legal Services resources per capita than most parts of the nation and thus comes closer to meeting the community's complete need, poverty lawyers currently handle over 30 cases a year per 1000 of *total* population.[2] In a nation of 210 million that projects to six million legal aid problems a year.

From this statistical evidence, it is apparent that to approach the goal of equal justice, capacity must be expanded from the present level of slightly over one million cases a year[3] to a minimum of six million. The manpower needs, therefore, are in the neighborhood of 12–15,000 full-time lawyers or their equivalent, which would entail an annual investment of over $350,000,000.[4] Will the American public make an investment of such magnitude? That, I submit, depends on how well several basic policy questions are managed, issues that have been largely unattended in the first seven years of Federal financing of legal assistance to the poor. These concerns fall roughly into two broad categories: (A) the provision of legal assistance, and (B) the design of dispute resolution machinery.

A. Equal Justice: Meeting the Need for Lawyers

Turning first to the question of legal assistance, there are fairly obvious issues for the future. Who is to receive subsidized legal services? How are the legal services to be financed? How are they to be delivered?

1. Who Is to Be Served?

By statute and philosophy the OEO Legal Services Program has been confined to the lowest income strata. Yet its lawyers soon learned there are millions of "near-poor" who cannot afford lawyers for many of their problems. It has been estimated that 112 million people fall in this hiatus between the client population presently eligible for government-subsidized legal assistance and those sufficiently affluent to employ a private attorney.[5] In recent years, these middle-class groups have begun to awaken to their own unfilled needs for legal assistance. Conferences have been held[6] and a lobbying organization formed.[7]

Thus far, most proposals for making lawyers available to the middle classes have emphasized private financing—usually through voluntary insurance plans or as part of a fringe benefits package for employees. But lacking government leadership and funding aid, progress has been slow. Moreover, it is not unlikely that a government subsidy will be necessary far up the income ladder if comprehensive help is to be available to all. There is ample precedent for this in the English scheme in which the government pays the difference between the lawyer's actual fee and the amount a litigant can afford.[8]

It is not my purpose here to explore the many difficult issues surrounding the provision of legal help to the middle classes. An excellent book—*Lawyers for People of Modest Means*[9]—has been devoted entirely to this topic. But I am suggesting that the Federal legal assistance program should broaden its coverage to embrace the nonpoor. Recent American history seems to favor programs, such as social security, which extend benefits to all, or nearly all citizens, rather than subsidizing only the poor. Perceived as a special dispensation for a relatively small minority of the population, a Federal legal services effort has a narrow political base. But as a program guaranteeing everyone access to the legal system, the Program in image and in reality becomes something in which the middle classes share a stake.

2. How Are Legal Services to Be Financed?

In a 1965 article,[10] Gerald Caplan and I surveyed a number of possibilities for permanent funding of legal services to the poor, including foundation grants, Federal and municipal revenues.[11] We leaned somewhat toward municipal government as the appropriate source of support in the long run. Subsequent history makes that choice appear dubious at best and disastrous at worst. In the same 1965 article, we asked whether local government would continue to feed dollars to an agency that inevitably would be biting the City Fathers' hands.[12] On the basis of several gubernatorial vetoes and the reaction of many local governments, it is difficult to be optimistic about the probable answer to that question.[13]

Actually, history has changed one of the basic premises upon which our recommendation of municipal funding was based. In 1965, OEO grants were viewed as seed money to implant programs that other resources would sustain on a permanent basis. Now, the assumption is directly opposite. The Federal role is presumed to be permanent by everyone (with the possible exception of some hopeful opponents of the Program). Moreover, while its travail in Congress cannot be ignored,[14] the Federal level has proven least susceptible to pressures from offended merchants, landlords, welfare administrators and government officials in general.

Dependence on state or local government financing of legal services suffers from another inherent drawback. Piecemeal, ad hoc decisions by 50 state legislatures or thousands of city councils and county supervisors will never produce a comprehensive nationwide system of government-subsidized representation. We have only to look at the experience with criminal representation of indigents. It is a decade since the Supreme Court announced the constitutional right to counsel in *Gideon* v. *Wainwright.*[15] Yet despite a heroic effort by the Ford Foundation-sponsored National Defender Project,[16] only a handful of states have installed a comprehensive government-financed defender program,[17] and 50 percent of the total funds committed to the representation of indigent criminal defendants are concentrated in only three of the 50 states of the Union.[18]

There is a further reason for turning to the Federal government to provide most of the financial subsidy for lawyers serving the lower economic classes. Other outlays needed for equal justice—more judges, courtrooms and the rest —presumably will continue to come principally out of state and local treasuries, for these traditionally are areas of local concern and local control. Legal assistance, on the contrary, has only infrequently been considered a responsibility of state or local governments. If the national government is to bear any part of the load, it makes some sense that Federal revenues and influence be concentrated where they will not intrude on what are viewed as state and local prerogatives.

And finally, the Federal government seems the logical source for a substantial part of the financing, because at that level of government, the total cost is put in perspective. A $360 million or even half-billion dollar Federal investment in legal assistance appears inconsequential alongside most expenditures designed to implement basic Constitutional goals. "To provide for the common defense" the national government spends over $70 *billion* annually,[19] and another $70 billion to "promote the general welfare."[20] Half a billion for the legal assistance necessary "to establish justice" would represent under one-twentieth of 1 percent of the nation's gross national product and only one-fifth of 1 percent of the Federal budget, less than $3 per person. Even with the other Federal expenditures on "Justice" added, the impact on Federal taxes is insignificant.

3. How Are Legal Services to Be Delivered?

The dispute over methods of delivering legal services has generally come down to two competing plans—salaried staff attorneys versus compensated private counsel (commonly called "Judicare"). OEO in fact has relied primarily on the former but experimented with the latter as well.[21] In Europe, the pattern is opposite. In those nations, private counsel, in most cases paid out of government funds, provides most of the legal assistance to the poor.[22]

American proponents of compensated private counsel cite two primary advantages *for the client:*

1. It allegedly eliminates discrimination against the poor in the delivery of legal services; that is, the poor can "employ" from the same pool of lawyers that serve the middle class, wealthy individuals, and commercial interests.[23]
2. The client has freedom of choice, that is, he can "employ" the attorney he prefers rather than being limited to the staff attorney who happens to be available when the client arrives at a neighborhood office.[24]

Many advocates of compensated private counsel also mention two advantages *for society:*

3. The reliance on private counsel as opposed to government salaried staff attorneys avoids "socialization of the legal profession."[25]
4. The reliance on compensated private counsel prevents the use of Federal funds for purposes of social reform.[26]

Proponents of the salaried staff attorney approach respond that freedom of choice is illusory to a ghetto resident far removed geographically and psychologically from the downtown areas where most high-caliber attorneys practice.[27] They likewise cast doubt on the availability of most competent private attorneys currently serving the middle and upper classes under any fee schedule likely to be approved by the government. At anywhere between $15 and $25 an hour, successful practitioners would have to look upon legal services work as a charitable effort, certainly not competitive with the $50 to $100 an hour they can earn with affluent clients.

The advocates for staff attorneys counter the "socialization of the legal profession" argument by stressing that the compensated private counsel system puts nearly every attorney in the nation on the Federal payroll. From the point of view of government power over the legal profession, they urge it is preferable to have relatively few attorneys dependent upon the Federal government for their full salary rather than every member of the profession counting on a Federal check for a substantial percentage of his income.

Finally, the social reform issue is merely turned around and made a disadvantage of the private counsel system. Proponents of the staff attorney approach accept the assertion that private lawyers will seldom produce reform, but argue this makes them less effective (and possibly less ethical) advocates of their clients' interests.[28]

This capsule summary of the seven-year-old debate about methods for delivering legal services does not fully define the issue for the 1970s and future decades. As we move further toward the goal of equal justice for all American citizens, some of the values asserted and concerns expressed by the advocates of compensated private counsel may become more relevant.

At present, legal counsel is provided to only a small fraction of those in the lower and middle classes who need the help, for the most part, by hiring on a full-time basis very few of the nation's lawyers. No threat of "socialization" there and no danger that the legal profession has become a docile arm of the government. But if the government should begin to subsidize the majority of the litigation and legal representation in this country,[29] we would have to make some basic choices about the sort of legal profession we want in the United States. If public-financed legal assistance is to reach into the middle classes and we rely exclusively on salaried staff attorneys, it is not unrealistic to foresee a time when 25 or 30 percent of the entire legal profession will be employees of government organizations (in addition to the 14 percent[30] that are already working for government as prosecutors, public defenders, county attorneys, or in some other way). At best, that is a different profession than the collection of independent practitioners to which we are accustomed. At worst, it is fraught with the mischief of government control and intimidation. I am not personally convinced that it would be impossible to maintain an independent legal profession capable of challenging judges, policies, and officials that threaten Constitutional rights and human values. But it certainly would be more difficult.

The choice of delivery systems also may affect the prospects for acquiring government appropriations that will match the need for legal assistance. Unlike the medical profession of a decade ago, the vast majority of lawyers currently embrace the notion of government payment for the services they render. However, there is a split within the ranks over delivery systems which seriously undermines the profession's lobbying strength in Congress. If "Judicare" adherents could be united with the coalition currently supporting neighborhood law offices, the resulting combination would be a potent force in the legislative halls. This factor alone justifies serious consideration of some accommodation between the staff attorney approach and the compensated private counsel system.

One tempting compromise is to divide responsibility between private counsel and salaried staff. Private lawyers could handle divorces, adoptions, and similar cases in which they probably possess as much expertise as full-time staff lawyers. Staff counsel then could concentrate on law reform, group representation, and most cases involving welfare, consumer, landlord-tenant or other problems where the dispute is between a poor person and some part of the affluent society. At first this appears to offer the best of both worlds. It relieves neighborhood law offices of the high-volume, low-impact work. (Family law problems account for 30 to 50 percent of the caseload of an average Legal Services Program.)[31] This frees salaried lawyers for activities which promise more social or economic benefits. At the same time, where private counsel have less expertise—welfare, in particular—or where they might be tempted to temper the vigor of their representation—in cases against interests who are present or potential clients of these attorneys—the poor can look to their own salaried staff lawyers.

Another compromise offers the poor even more of both worlds. Staff lawyers and a compensated private counsel system could exist side-by-side, with each individual client choosing whichever he thinks can better handle his particular problem. This approach, which currently is being attempted in Sweden and Canada,[32] offers the advantage of open competition, tending to keep lawyers in both systems at their peak. The principal danger is that adherents of one of the competing systems, probably the one that was proving least popular with clients, might choose to fight in the political arena rather than submit to consumer preference. If successful, such a lobbying campaign might produce rules that favored one of the delivery systems over the other, or provided rigid allocations of funds, or otherwise took the decision out of the hands of the client.

Quality of service and political issues aside, there is another test that any legal services delivery system must pass. That is, does it make sense economically? Measured against that standard, the mixed system is no bargain. It is precisely in those high-volume areas like divorce that cost comparisons most favor staff attorneys over compensated private counsel. In Chapter 8, we noted that a Judicare divorce costs the government *three to seven times* the price of a divorce delivered through staff attorneys.[33] The reasons are fairly obvious. First, the private lawyer charges 50–150 percent more per hour than the salaried attorney costs on an hourly basis. Secondly, the private office normally will have only two or three government-subsidized divorces at a time and thus cannot take advantage of economies of scale or systematize its handling of such cases. Finally, in most jurisdictions the bar fee schedule prescribes a flat minimum for divorces and many other legal matters. Even if an uncontested divorce takes only 15 minutes of a lawyer's time, for which he ordinarily would bill $15 or $20, he charges clients—including the government fund—the minimum divorce fee of between $200 and $400, depending on the jurisdiction. Thus, a government subsidy system pegged in any way to the prevailing fee system[34] will distort still further the payments to private attorneys.

Economic considerations do not necessarily dictate that we must abandon a mixed system of salaried staff attorneys and compensated private counsel formulated along the lines suggested above. It may be possible to negotiate fees downward and to abolish flat minimums. So-called closed panel plans could be encouraged, which channel all government subsidized business to lawyers agreeing to a sharply reduced fee schedule. Or individual law firms could be invited to bid for a government contract to provide representation in a certain category of cases or in a given geographic area at a flat charge.

Whatever the additional cost involved in incorporating private counsel into the delivery system, it may make sense politically. It is very probable that the added appropriations that the proponents of Judicare could generate through their political strength would exceed the increased expense of delivering some part of the legal assistance by this method. Accordingly, from the perspective of poor people, it appears likely they can expect more legal help if there is some participation of private attorneys even though the taxpayer ends up paying more than he would under a pure staff attorney system.

B. Equal Justice: The Implications of a Costless System

As Reginald Heber Smith documented in 1919, equal justice entails more than availability of government-subsidized lawyers for those unable to afford private counsel. Legal fees are only a part of the expense of resolving disputes in the courts, administrative agencies and similar decision-making bodies.[35] Many tribunals, particularly courts, also impose their own charges to help defray the operating costs of these institutions.[36] Included are filing fees, payments for service of process, jury costs, and other charges which must be paid to governmental agencies or functionaries. These can mount to several hundred dollars during the course of protracted litigation and even the costs for simple cases are more than the poor can pay. Beyond the lawyer's fee and government charges for use of the court system, there is another category of litigation expense. These are the payments that must be made to private persons: the compensation paid to a court reporter for preparing a transcript of a deposition or hearing, the fees charged by an expert witness, the bond often required to protect the financial interests of an opposing party and similar expenses.[37]

242 • AN ASSESSMENT

While courts may readily waive their own fees and, if necessary, could require lawyers to serve without compensation, to relieve the poor people of the litigation expenses that must be paid to court reporters, expert witnesses and other private persons presents special problems. For one thing, that ordinarily requires someone who can write a check on the public treasury, a difficult assignment for a judicial body.[38] Thus, low-income litigants may have to look to the legislatures rather than the courts for an assist in lifting this particular barrier.

Secondly, the possibilities for incurring expense in preparing a case for trial are almost limitless. How many depositions, for instance, are appropriate in a given case? Without some restraint, the financial strain on the government budget as well as the opposing party could become intolerable. Any adequate standard probably must take into consideration many factors: the seriousness and social-economic implications of the case, the cost of the litigation expense requested, its probable importance in development of the issues, and the accumulated cost of previously authorized publicly paid expenses in the case.[39]

Finally, certain of these costs are bonds designed to protect the financial position of the impoverished litigant's opponent.[40] Waiver of such bond requirements—which may run to thousands of dollars—often is essential if the poor man is to be able to seek an injunction, have a hearing, or pursue an appeal. However, this dispensation for the poor litigant deprives the opposing party of security to which he would be entitled in ordinary circumstances. Thus, unless the state supplies the affluent party with the bond the low-income party is unable to furnish, the court must choose between depriving the poor man of his day in court or the more affluent man of much needed protection against the risks of default, depreciation, and the like.

There will be a natural reluctance among both courts and legislators to remove the price tag from justice, because the full implications of that move are difficult to predict.[41] One of the imponderables, of course, is the amount of money that will have to be appropriated to absorb all of these expenses for low-income litigation. However, making litigation cost free for a segment of the population raises three other issues, less obvious but probably more important to judges and legislators.

1. If all costs of litigation are borne by the state, what will restrain the poor from prosecuting actions or raising defenses that are without merit?
2. If all costs of litigation for the poor are borne by the state, will they not possess unfair bargaining power against an opponent who must pay for his own lawyer and himself bear the other costs of litigation?
3. If litigation is provided free to the poor, what will prevent a deluge of cases which cost more to resolve than the amount at stake in the dispute?

Unless these concerns are resolved explicitly and forcefully, it seems unlikely the general public will enthusiastically support the goal of equal justice for the low-income community.

1. The Frivolous Suit or Defense

The fear of frivolous litigation frequently has been invoked as justification for charging court filing fees and similar costs. But in recent years, some courts have concluded that these financial tests are an inappropriate mechanism for sorting out the frivolous from the nonfrivolous. As Judge David Bazelon observed in *Thomson* v. *Mazo:*

> Any regulation which uses a financial hurdle simply to discourage suits, some of which might be taken in bad faith, is open to serious constitutional challenge, since it would appear to operate from the doubtful premise that the rich are less likely than the poor to maintain frivolous actions.[42]

But as the courts reject the financial filter because of its inherent unfairness, they need to develop substitute mechanisms for screening out nonmeritorious claims and defenses. Following the example of Federal courts in pauper's cases, it might be feasible to hold a brief hearing on the merits at the time the case is filed or to allow the judge to dismiss a case where he finds it clearly frivolous. The British rely on local committees composed of private solicitors to review any proposed step in government-subsidized litigation to determine whether further expenditures are justified. The standard applied is whether a private litigant of adequate means confronted with the same situation would expend his own funds on the proposed action.[43]

Experience with the Legal Services Program, on the other hand, suggests this problem may be exaggerated. Even when the financial expenses are borne by the state, litigation is by no means costless either to the low-income litigant or his Legal Services attorney. For the client, there is still the inconvenience of attending court, the dread of testifying, the travel cost to and from the courtroom, and for those that are employed, the days missed from work. These costs generally are sufficient to dissuade a poor person from filing a frivolous claim or raising an unmeritorious defense, since in either event he realizes the ultimate outcome will be defeat. To a Legal Services attorney, a frivolous case represents not only a waste of time that could be better spent on worthy suits and productive counseling but the probable embarrassment of a judicial tirade and a debit in his won-lost record. This ordinarily will lead the attorney to discourage his client from advancing dubious positions. With both the client and his attorney reluctant to take frivolous legal actions, the screening mechanism probably will be of marginal utility, excluding only a very small percentage of the law suits or defenses actually brought to the courts.

2. The Dilemma of the Disadvantaged Rich

This is a more realistic concern. Some legal services theorists have urged neighborhood lawyers to use their cost free status (at least costless to the client) as leverage in negotiations with opposing attorneys. In theory at least, a poor client can "afford" to have his legal services lawyer pour unlimited hours and energies into the preparation and trial of a relatively small (in economic terms) matter. His middle-class or even wealthy opponent must appraise the case not only in terms of how much money he has, but the value of what is at stake in the case itself. Clearly, such a litigant cannot afford to spend as much on attorneys' fees and other litigation costs as he stands to gain if successful, otherwise he will lose money even if he prevails.

There is little doubt that this theoretical bargaining disparity exists and that, potentially at least, the disadvantaged party is the rich litigant rather than the poor one. Using the government subsidy as a club, publicly financed attorneys and their clients could bludgeon many opponents into submission. The middle-class or well-to-do litigant might be compelled to surrender a solid case or a valid defense merely because he could not afford to bear the costs of endless discovery, lengthy trials, and interminable appeals.

Again, experience with the Legal Services Program suggests this may not be an important concern. Few self-supporting litigants have been forced to make unjust bargains. With so few attorneys to meet an overwhelming demand (caseloads generally are enormous, averaging about 500 per year), Legal Services lawyers of necessity ration scarce time sparingly among their many clients. Accordingly, they generally feel they can "afford" less time for a given case than could a private counsel who is billing someone for the other side of that same litigation. Scarcity, in other words, constrains the subsidized litigant and his Legal Services attorney in the same way the fee schedule and billable hours do the private lawyer and his client. It is not that clear what would happen were the supply of government financed counsel to be expanded dramatically.

Whether the fears are realistic or not, it is apparent that one of the primary sources of resistance to increased appropriations for legal services is the feeling that the public should not provide lawyers free of charge in any case where an unjust settlement might be exacted from a litigant who must depend upon his own funds to hire counsel.[44] Since this possibility exists in a majority of Legal Services cases, this policy would result in denial of an attorney to most low-income clients.

It simply is not rational to protect the affluent from possible injustice by denying the opportunity for justice to the poor. However, something of a positive nature must be done to eliminate the reality and appearance of the problem of the disadvantaged rich. The solution probably lies in the direction of government support, or at least government underwriting, of the cost of responding to the actions of a publicly financed attorney. At a minimum, the situation appears to mandate a statutory provision authorizing public payment of litigation costs for persons who are *successful* in contests against a party whose expenses were borne by the state. Of course, any such law increases still further the tax burden, as the treasury is now asked to absorb the cost of insuring equal justice for all parties in cases where the poor are sued or are suing.

This increased expense could be mitigated if the United States were to follow the example of England and allow the victorious party to recover his legal costs from the losing party as a matter of course.[45] As in Britain, the government also could obtain from the private litigant the salary of the Legal Services lawyer and associated expenses whenever the government supported party was successful.[46] If this step is not feasible, it may be necessary to write off the expense of protecting affluent litigants as a price to be paid for broad-scale political backing.

3. Accommodating the Meritorious, but Uneconomic, Dispute

Our present, predominately laissez-faire, justice system masks a central fact. The existing machinery for resolving legal controversies in the United States is too cumbersome and expensive to properly decide many, and possibly most, of the disputes that arise in this society.

To illustrate, let's take the typical $400 debt collection suit based on the purchase of a television. In most instances, the lawsuit presently is "resolved" at minimal cost. A creditor's attorney charges $30 or $40 for having his secretary type up a form complaint. The low-income debtor cannot afford to pay a lawyer, so he defaults; and the judicial system need allocate only $4 or $5 to the suit, the monetary value of the time it takes the clerk to call the case and the judge to say, "Judgment for the plaintiff. Next case." Thus, under current practice the case can be "decided" for between $34 and $45, about 10 percent of the amount at stake, a not unreasonable ratio. But examine how that economically feasible result was obtained—by depriving the low-income debtor of due process of the law.

Now let's take this same dispute and transpose it to a setting where lawyers and litigation expenses are paid by the state. If the debtor has any possible defense, and he generally will,[47] the defendant's attorney will want his client to have a fair chance at the trial. He will file extensive interrogatories, take depositions of the salesman, the credit manager and other possible witnesses, and utilize any other discovery devices which might yield evidence or leads to evidence. At the same time, the creditor's lawyer will have to spend hours drafting answers to the interrogatories, attending deposition hearings and possibly bolstering his own case by deposing the defendant and searching for other evidence. The trial probably will last at least one day and possibly two, and, very possibly, will take place before a jury.

Now, let's total the cost of resolving this dispute over an alleged $400 debt. The creditor's lawyer will charge his client $30 to $60 an hour for the five to ten hours of pretrial preparation, discovery, and so on, and at least $200 a day for the trial itself, for a minimum billing of $375 and more likely closer to $500. Thus, the moving party alone must absorb as much in legal expenses as he stands to gain should he succeed at trial. At best he breaks even, and he risks being out of pocket should he lose or be forced to settle at a negotiated figure. (Of course, as suggested in the previous section,[48] the creditor's dilemma could be ameliorated by publicly funding his lawyer's fees and litigation costs as well as the poor man's.)

The low-income litigant also has incurred costs, which we are assuming to be government-financed. In all probability, the debtor's counsel will spend more hours in discovery and pretrial preparation than the creditor's lawyer, merely because most of the evidence he needs is in the hands of adverse witnesses. Assuming the not unlikely expenditure of ten to twenty hours before trial and one or two days in court, the debtor's lawyer probably would devote between 18 and 38 hours to the case. Figuring his time at $12 an hour,[49] legal costs will total between $216 and $425. Yet that is only a part of the government expense for this hypothetical case. Assuming there are no hearings required other than the trial itself, that jury trial will cost the government approximately $700 a day.[50] Thus, by the time the trial is over and the jury returns its verdict, the public will have paid $1000 or more to resolve a $400 dispute. And if the legislature decides to subsidize the affluent litigant as well as the poor one, the minimum total charge to government rises above $1300. Faced with this possible expense, it might make more sense (and certainly be less expensive) for society merely to give the creditor a check for $400 and tear up the poor man's alleged debt.

It may be asked why the grossly uneconomic lawsuit is not a commonplace already, considering there are now over 2500 publicly supplied lawyers available to the poor. A partial answer to that question is that this kind of litigation does occur occasionally. But a more complete explanation is found in the fact that in 90 percent or more of the cases, the low-income debtor still does not have counsel and thus the contest never goes beyond the low-cost "judgment for the plaintiff" and a default stage. In the remaining few, it is too expensive for the creditor's attorney to take the claim to court against a tax-paid lawyer, so he settles for a figure very favorable to the debtor. Creditors can afford to negotiate these few cases at a loss because of the profit they are making from the other 90 percent. The uneconomic dispute will become a major issue only when government-subsidized counsel becomes widely available to low-income litigants and, moreover, probably only when the public offers to defray or at least underwrite the expenses of the affluent party as well.

It may be that society will decide the intrinsic value of peaceful settlement of grievances is ample in itself to justify expenditures that overshadow the amounts at stake. But that is not very probable if the process is consistently more expensive than the product. Less costly models do exist. Many countries employ some variety of people's court to handle common, lower level disputes.[51] The Cahns suggested neighborhood courts for the United States.[52] With better design and fairer procedures, the small claims court might be a usable approach.[53] There have been some experimental applications of compulsory arbitration to landlord-tenant and consumer credit disputes.[54] But these and other solutions must be appraised, tried out, and refined before they are installed. It is easy to design dispute-resolving institutions that are cheap. It is more difficult to make them both inexpensive and just.

C. Equal Justice for All—The Expanded Goal

From its inception, the legal aid movement has stood as the symbol of equal justice *for the poor.* The time has come to expand that mission. As reframed, the goal for government-subsidized legal assistance should be equal justice *for all.*

This represents something more than a semantic change. Legal aid attorneys and their supporters long perceived their role solely in terms of the lowest income classes. In most of the speeches and literature, the only defects in the American legal system that concerned them were associated with its treatment of the poor. The NLADA and its constituent organizations, for the most part, expressly avoided the problem of delivering justice to the near-poor and the middle classes. They likewise largely ignored legal aid's impact on other individuals and institutions in society. Because of its genesis as part of the war on poverty, the OEO Legal Services Program followed this same path.

Now, whether helpful to the poor or not, it appears probable that fundamental change in our machinery for resolving disputes will be on the legislative agenda, put there by the middle and upper classes. As taxpayers they will demand mechanisms that settle disputes fairly at prices substantially less than the sums at issue. As disputants they will ask for protection from frivolous claims and for subsidies when opposed by government-paid counsel. And at some point, labor and the middle classes probably will put in a claim for their own tax-supported legal assistance.

In sum, powerful constituencies are beginning to recognize they have a stake in improving the quality of justice in America. There is much to be said for harnessing them alongside the existing supporters of legal assistance for the poor. The resulting coalition promises to be very potent.

A broadened conception of the legal aid goal possesses obvious political advantages. But that is not the main reason for pursuing justice for all. It is simply a recognition that we have learned something in the fifty years since Reginald Heber Smith, Charles Evans Hughes, and the other founders of the movement first articulated its philosophy. The intervening time has shown that more ails our system of justice than its treatment of a small, impoverished segment of the population.[55] The deprivation of equality before the law extends well up into the middle class.[56] And our attempts to right the balance only for the poor tend to aggravate the disenfranchisement suffered by labor and middle-income groups.

As Congress and adherents of legal services ponder new arrangements for administering the government's legal assistance program, they might also profitably consider enlarging its mission and constituency as well. Specifically, the government should assume responsibility for the organization and subsidization of legal help for anyone unable to afford the entire cost of employing his own lawyer[57]; the underwriting of legal and litigation expenses for private persons opposed by publicly paid counsel; the development of economic yet just means for resolving disputes; and other measures calculated to further the cause of justice for every individual and all classes.

II. THE FUTURE OF REFORM

In coming years, many forces will converge to shape the lawyer's role in the advancement of the economic and social interests of the poor. The first seven years of the OEO Legal Services Program hinted at the potential contribution that could be made. But those years also previewed some of the political pressures that in the future may undermine the lawyer's power to help the poor.[58]

Considering the political uncertainties, it would be foolhardy to predict whether poverty lawyers will accomplish more in the next seven years or, for that matter, the next seventy, than they did from 1966 through 1972. During most of those first years, at least they were committed, albeit imperfectly, to the "law reform" priority. There is no guarantee antagonistic political forces will not compel abandonment of that thrust or even dismantle the Program itself. In the face of such risks, it is only possible to articulate what seems an optimal role for lawyers in the antipoverty effort. The political gods will rule whether anything like it ever comes to pass.

There are two dimensions to our design for socially productive legal services. First, there is the question of what lawyers do, the functions to which they commit their time. Second, how are they to be organized, that is, what systems and institutions will best facilitate meaningful, responsive social-economic impact?

A. An Overview of the Strategies Available to the Lawyer

Thus far, most debate about the proper goals and methods of Legal Services lawyers has proceeded at the level of sloganeering. (I admit to being one of the participants.) "Law reform," "individual services," "test cases," "the power of the caseload," "economic development," "community organization" and "legislative advocacy" are all mentioned. (Obviously, many of these strategies actually overlap.) Too often proponents line up behind one or the other of these positions without making any deep analysis of other possibilities. The tendency is to write off all other approaches as insignificant and champion the chosen slogan as "the solution" to the problems of the poor. I submit it is doubtful there is any "the solution." A lawyer's role will not be optimized by searching for some utopian remedy but by gaining an accurate appreciation for all the available techniques and a proper blending of these.

The most popular current panacea is based on the notion that Legal Services lawyers should "redistribute power to the poor." Like most of the other slogans, this thesis suffers from a certain vagueness. It also alarms the more conservative forces in the nation, perhaps unnecessarily.[59] It is a useful concept only if we demystify the glamour word—power. In so doing we are likely to find it embraces "law reform," "legislative advocacy," "test cases," and some of the other more accepted strategies mentioned earlier.

At the outset it should be noted that the common element in any successful antipoverty action undertaken by a Legal Services lawyer is the social or economic significance of the case he is pursuing. The most artfully conceived and executed legal stratagem will have negligible impact if employed to secure benefits only for a single client or a few individuals. Only by allocating substantial resources to cases with more general impact can an individual legal services lawyer or the entire Program make a meaningful contribution to the reduction of poverty. (See pages 230–233, *supra.*) Viewing the social and economic effects described in Chapter 8 as ends to be sought, in the following sections we will be concerned with means which lawyers might use to achieve those ends.

1. The Decision Making Process

What is power? In the present context, at least, I submit it is nothing more mysterious than the capacity to cause others in society to make decisions favorable to your interests and desires. Obviously, a given individual or group can be powerful with one decision maker, say an employer, and ineffectual with another, the state legislature, for instance. One's total power therefore can be visualized as the sum of his capacity to affect the choices of various decision makers multiplied by the impact of these decisions on his life.[60]

In the broadest sense, all lawyers in fact are in the business of influencing others in society to make decisions that are relevant to their clients' interests. These others are found not only in government but among employers, merchants, landlords, and credit companies in the private sector. Among them, these people make up all the basic determinations: they allocate money income;

set prices, rents and quality; structure economic opportunity; make procedural rules; and establish levels of participation in the various decision making processes.

Basically there are three ways one can gain a favorable decision. One can persuade the other person directly; one can get someone with power over the other person to issue an order; or, one can replace the other person with someone who holds a favorable view. Assume some tenants desire their landlord to make essential repairs on their apartments. They could meet with the owner and attempt to persuade him to make that decision. (I am using the term persuasion in its broadest sense to encompass not only rational argument but any leverage the tenants might have available to bargain for the needed repairs.) Failing that, the tenants could seek a court order compelling the landlord to repair the defects. And if this measure were not feasible or it was ineffectual, they could form a co-op and attempt to purchase the property from the owner.

These methods can be applied in the public sector and to governmental decision making as well. Take the case where a group of welfare mothers wants to ensure payments will not be terminated before the recipient has an opportunity for a hearing. They could meet with the public assistance administrator and seek to persuade him to revise the agency regulations to provide for a prior hearing in termination situations. If he refuses, they could approach the legislature with a proposed statute guaranteeing that right, an enactment which would be binding on the welfare administrator. Or, third, through a variety of political means, they could seek to displace the official who refuses to comply with the request.

In the political arena the pattern is similar. An interest group desiring reform can seek to persuade existing congressmen or legislators to enact those changes. In some instances they can compel reform through other branches of government, that is, through the judiciary. But ordinarily, if they are unable to convince existing members of the legislative body, the only recourse is to replace them with a new set of lawmakers more favorably inclined to the group's position. In a democracy, that transfer of power normally takes place through elective politics. Throughout history it has often occurred through riot and revolution, however.

2. Influencing Decisions through Persuasion

The first reality that confronts the lawyer representing poor people in the United States is that for all practical purposes only two of the fundamental strategies for affecting decisions are available to his clients. It is seldom they are in a position to displace the decision maker. They lack the dollars to buy out a landlord, merchant, employer, or anybody else in the private sector. And they lack both the dollars and the votes to unseat congressmen, presidents or administrators whose policies they dislike. Nor do they pose a reasonable threat to do so. (Even if this option were available, the lawyer's role would be minimal, since the attorney has no special part in elective politics.)

Once one considers the other two methods of affecting decisions, the lawyer and his special skills become more relevant. Both depend on persuasion, either of the primary decision-maker or some other institution possessing the power to order the primary body to act.

When an individual or group attempts to persuade a decision maker in the public or private sector, they can employ rational or emotional argument; offer some objective "reward" for making the desired decision; or, threaten some objective sanction unless a favorable decision is rendered. The incentives may be economic—more business, more money, more jobs, more anything that offers some ultimate dollars-and-cents gain. They may be social or psychological—the esteem of one's colleagues, even a party invitation. Or they may be political—more votes, more campaign work, and the like. The sanctions fall in the same categories and usually are merely the converse of the incentives.[61]

In practice, these three methods of persuasion usually are blended into one presentation or negotiation. However, not all three are appropriate for every institution. Courts, in particular, specifically ban consideration of most kinds of inducements or sanctions. But legislators, for instance, are open to the incentive of campaign support or the threat of opposition, as well as appeals based on the merits, yet cannot accept bribes. Similarly, an employer is more apt to come forward with increased wages on the basis of promises of greater productivity or threat of a strike than because he is convinced in his heart that workers should receive a larger share of the business earnings. And a merchant will be more likely to be motivated to lower prices because a consumer group promises to throw more business his way, or conversely, threatens to picket his store than because the members make him believe that it is immoral to charge all the traffic will bear.

Similarly, when seeking to affect the actions of a primary decision maker through some sort of instruction or order obtained from a secondary decision maker, the same three options are usually appropriate. That is, the secondary decision maker may be susceptible to argument or to the promise of reward or the threat of sanction.

In the succeeding sections, we examine how these various inducements and decision making bodies interrelate in the context of social reform for the poor.

B. An Appraisal of Alternative Strategies Available to the Legal Services Lawyer

We are now in a position to examine the specific means through which poverty lawyers can pursue their clients' major social and economic goals. As hinted above, the options are much wider than the defense of individual lawsuits, the primary role envisioned in the legal aid movement. We will discuss the following principal alternatives:

1. Influencing private decisions through persuasion of private decision making institutions;
2. Influencing public and private decisions through:
    a. persuading the judiciary to modify the legal structure;
    b. persuading legislative bodies to modify the legal structure;
    c. persuading executive agencies to modify their formal regulations or their individual decisions;
    d. enforcement of existing laws by the judicial or executive branch;
3. Influencing private decisions through substitution of economic entities controlled by or committed to the poor.

For some readers, present and former Legal Services lawyers in particular, the discussion on the next several pages (to page 267) may be superfluous. In essence, it is an untraditional, yet elementary, examination of some rather traditional lawyer functions. But for those less familiar with what attorneys do in American society, this discussion should provide some basis for comparing the value of various legal tools that can be used to reduce poverty.

1. Influencing Private Decisions through Persuasion of the Private Decision Making Institutions

It already has been observed that many, if not most, of the decisions that determine the social and economic standing of the poor are made by private individuals and private organizations.[62] In these instances, governmental institutions are brought in, if at all, only because they may indirectly modify the conduct of the primary decision maker, whether he be an employer, landlord, merchant, or creditor. The more direct and obvious method is to sit down with the private party and convince him to decide in a manner favorable to the poor. If a ghetto appliance store is overcharging, meet with the manager and persuade him to lower prices. If a landlord is failing to maintain apartments in habitable condition, negotiate a promise from him to make repairs. And if a firm does not hire a substantial percentage of minority workers, convince management to institute an affirmative action plan for employment of more minority group members.

Merely stating these examples suggests the limitations inherent in this direct approach. It is easy to send a delegation of consumers off to confer with a merchant. It is not so realistic to anticipate they will come out of the meeting with an agreement to reduce prices or alter sales practices, for an amorphous group of low-income consumers seldom brings many chips to the bargaining table, nor do impoverished debtors, tenants or nonunion employees. Their stock of incentives, sanctions and persuasive skills generally is limited.

Where does the Legal Services lawyer fit into this process? He represents three things to the poor when they approach the private decision maker. First, he is, or should be, a professional at persuasion, trained and experienced in negotiating and familiar with the protocol, language, and subtleties of middle-class business deals. Whatever can be won through rational argument, the attorney should be able to secure on behalf of his delegation of clients. At the least, he can neutralize the businessman's expertise and the specialized jargon of profit margins, pricing policies, vacancy rates, the many explanations that make lower prices, housing code compliance, or better wages "impossible, even though I'd like to."

Second, the lawyer's knowledge and advice often is vital to properly deploy the limited repertoire of rewards and sanctions available to the low-income consumer, tenant, debtor, or employee. Boycotts, picketing and rent-withholding typically constitute the only negotiating leverage possessed by community organizations. All of these techniques are restricted by complex, technical legal restrictions. Picketing, for instance, usually requires an official permit and the number, location, and activities of picketers are closely regulated.[63] Withholding rent likewise must be done in compliance with certain statutory procedures to be effective. Thus, without legal advice, low-income groups are hard pressed to offer a viable inducement to important private decision makers, such as merchants, landlords, creditors, and employers.

Finally, the attorney sometimes possesses some bargaining capital unique to his profession. Whether it is even mentioned at the negotiating session, most participants recognize the lawyer may take his cause to the courts if his clients remain dissatisfied with the settlement offered. As a matter of fact, serious negotiations about social change often are not even started until after a lawsuit has been filed. Clearly, the litigation option is not always available. But where a lawsuit is even a remote possibility, a businessman generally will bend somewhat at the bargaining table in order to avoid going to court. He fears the expense, possible bad publicity and potential courtroom defeat in the same way he is threatened by loss of revenue from a boycott, rent-withholding or picketing.[64]

At the outset of this section, it was mentioned that negotiating with the critical private decision makers themselves was the most obvious as well as the most direct method of affecting practices in this area. Actually, because of their training, members of the legal profession often overlook this means to achieve social change. There is another reason this obvious, direct path is not utilized more frequently by Legal Services advocates. To negotiate change with a private individual or organization, a proponent ordinarily must possess something that can be bartered for the new policy.[65] And, as I have said, a poor person seldom can wield rewards or sanctions that make any difference to merchants, landlords, creditors, or employers.

2. Influencing Public and Private Decisions through Persuasion of Government Institutions with Power to Control Behavior of Others

Lawyers frequently find themselves attempting to influence one decision maker by petitioning another decision maker that has some power over the first. For instance, they may seek to amend a welfare department practice by going to a court for an order ruling the department's actions illegal. In many instances, the route will be even more indirect, involving several stages between the lawyer's actions and the desired decision somewhere in society. The lawyer may find it necessary to petition the court for an order directing an administrative agency to enforce a rule that will cause a landlord or a merchant or someone else in the private sector to behave in a certain manner that will benefit the lawyer's client. In the next four sections we consider three institutions—the courts, the legislature, and the executive branch—that ordinarily operate indirectly on other decision makers. (In the first three sections, lawyers seek to modify existing legal rules or policies; in the fourth, they seek to enforce compliance with the existing law.)

A. INFLUENCING PUBLIC AND PRIVATE DECISIONS THROUGH PERSUADING THE COURTS TO MODIFY THE LEGAL STRUCTURE. One place where unfavorable patterns of decision can be changed is the courts. The antique notion that "judges only find law, they don't make it" has been exposed as false by astute studies of the judicial process and the actions of the courts themselves.[66] As a lawyer and political scientist, Victor Rosenblum, concluded in his book, *Law as a Political Instrument,* "The choice of judicial doctrines—all of which are legally correct—is sufficiently broad and significant to make the law that judges find actually the equivalent of 'made laws'."[67]

The courts are capable of making meaningful changes whether the underlying legal rule is part of the common law (created by a judge), statutory (enacted by the legislature) or a regulation (promulgated by an executive agency). The judiciary also can devise and promulgate new rules to govern conduct where none presently exist.

1. *Reforming common law rules.* The common law is relevant to poverty, for it is an integral part of the legal system that currently distributes the nation's goods and services, including the purchasing power of dollar income received by the poor. The price they pay for major purchases and the quality of those goods is intimately related to whether the courts will cut outrageous prices as unconscionable; whether the courts will void unreasonable contracts imposed on a take-or-leave-it basis; and whether the courts will prohibit evasion of usury laws through time and price differentials. In many states, these are all issues for the common law. Similarly, the value of the poor man's housing dollar will be influenced by whether the common law gives him a right to withhold rent if the landlord is failing to maintain the apartment in a livable condition.

The common law, of course, is entirely judge-made. Often the judicial figure who first created a given rule or principle was born several centuries ago. His name, political philosophy and passions are buried in antiquity. But age does not guarantee validity. There is nothing more divine behind any judge-made rule than the soundness of the policy and reasoning of the individual judge who created it. The doctrine of *stare decisis* (the duty to follow earlier decisions of the same question) purports to place restraints on courts who might desire to discard existing common law rules and the policies behind them. But Edward Levi, in a classic analysis of legal reasoning,[68] places *stare decisis* in perspective.

> Where case law is considered, and there is no statute, [the judge] is not bound by the statement of the rule of law made by the prior judge even in the controlling case. The statement is mere dictum, and this means that the judge in the present case may find irrelevant the existence or absence of facts which prior judges thought important. It is not what the prior judges intended that is of any importance; rather it is what the present judge, attempting to see the law as a fairly consistent whole, thinks should be the determining classification. In arriving at his result he will ignore what the past thought important; he will emphasize facts which prior judges would have thought made no difference. It is not alone that he could not see the law through the eyes of another, for he could at least try to do so. It is rather that the doctrine of dictum forces him to make his own decisions.[69]

The common law, as Levi demonstrates, is a dynamic structure. It is always changing, constantly evolving. "The process is one in which the ideas of the community and of the social sciences, whether correct or not, as they win acceptance in the community, control legal decisions."[70]

The tragedy of the common law and the poor is that the lower economic classes have been virtually excluded from that process. Appellate courts respond only to the extent that lawyers bring clients, arguments, and social policies to their attention through acutal cases filed or defended—and appealed. Lawyers are to the building of the common law what the vote is to legislative law-making, the citizen's key to participation. Without access to counsel, the poor have been disenfranchised in a vital part of the nation's law-creation machinery. Given that fact, it is not surprising that the common law that evolved over the past 200 years discriminates against the low-income community.

2. Reshaping statutory law. Statutes are enacted by legislatures, but more often than not, the "statutory law" is "made" by the courts. For instance, the nation's primary antitrust legislation, the Sherman Act, is only a few lines of vague language. Thousands of court decisions later, the words of the act are of relatively minor importance. What counts are the judge-made rules that have been layered on the thin statutory foundation. New kinds of business arrangements are continually added to the list of prohibited practices while others are removed. New standards are developed; new economic theories introduced; current market factors taken into account. All of this is happening without any further congressional enactment. It is the courts who are "making" the antitrust laws, and they have been for decades.

What is true of antitrust law is valid, more or less, for almost every other statute that is passed by any legislative body in the United States. The greater the degree of ambiguity[71] in statutory language the more legislative power— for that's precisely what it is—the legislature has delegated to the courts. For some idea of how vague a statute can be, consider an enactment of vital interest to the poor. The Uniform Commercial Code as adopted by the legislatures of many states contains a provision making contracts unenforceable if they are "unconscionable."[72] In several jurisdictions where this code was passed, there were no preexisting common law rules barring unconscionable contracts. Thus, the legislature has introduced a true change in the law of the state. But at the same time, the elected lawmakers left what is by far the most important legislative task, the definition of unconscionability, entirely to the courts. Is a sales contract "unconscionable" where the only questionable element is a price two or three times higher than the reasonable value of the merchandise?[73] Is a relatively less onerous contract rendered "unconscionable" when it is obtained by high pressure tactics practiced on unsophisticated customers?[74] These are among the questions still to be answered, in other words, the areas yet to be legislated in most of the states that enacted the unconscionable contract section of the UCC.[75]

Beyond its power to interpret legislative language, a court can affect practices that are anchored to existing statutes in several other ways. First, some Federal and state statutes unfavorable to the poor may be unconstitutional. Legislative bodies largely responsible to middle-class voters and wealthy contributors are prone to enact statutes that deny equal protection, as well as due process and other constitutional rights, to the poor. A good example is the residency requirement for receipt of welfare which was described in earlier chapters. The Supreme Court found these statutes unconstitutional under the Equal Protection clause of the 14th Amendment,[76] in effect holding that the legislature's desire to protect the pockets of its middle-class voters and wealthy contributors was not a constitutionally permissible reason for creating otherwise arbitrary eligibility categories for transfer payments.[77] Other common statutes that have been successfully challenged on constitutional grounds include: wage garnishment prior to judgment,[78] denial of hearing prior to termination of welfare payments[79] and the requirement of payment of court fees to file divorce.[80]

Second, state and local legislation unfavorable to the poor may be inconsistent with Federal statutes or administrative regulations. For example, many of the transfer payment programs, public assistance in particular, are joint Federal, state, and local ventures. The Federal government is more liberal in its laws, policies and interpretations than many of its governmental partners, and it is not uncommon for state and local bodies to enact laws that partially defeat the legislative intent of Federal legislation. Already the Supreme Court has overturned 19 state statutes that denied welfare to dependent children where an alleged "substitute father" was present in the home.[81] This was decided on the grounds that these state statutes were inconsistent with the purposes of the Federal legislation establishing the program of Aid to Families with Dependent Children.[82]

3. *Affecting administrative conduct.* Courts can affect administrative regulations and policies much as they exercise power over statutes. Administrative provisions may be unconstitutional; they may contravene Federal law; they may be inconsistent with the statute under which they were promulgated; and they too are subject to interpretation by the judiciary. Any one of these grounds can be used as the basis for judicial intervention to rewrite administrative rules. And Legal Services lawyers have used all of them to overturn or modify regulations that impinged on their clients.[83]

4. *An assessment of the courts' capacity to influence decision making.* In seeking to refashion private and public conduct through judicial action, an attorney must take account of the appellate court's decision making process. There are at least four considerations that, in varying degrees, determine a judge's choice between an old rule and a new rule.

—*The reported opinions of other courts* regarding analogous factual situations, in effect, the prior statement of the controlling legal rule. By sophisticated reasoning a good advocate often can limit the decisions and language that support the "old" rule and emphasize the decisions and language that show a trend toward the "new" rule. Moreover, he can often show that other respectable jurisdictions already have adopted the "new" rule.

—*The facts of the particular case* that is before the court may or may not expose the controlling rule to be capable of producing hardship or, at the least, results that run contrary to its purported purpose. "Hard" cases do not necessarily make bad law but they do tend to make new law.

—*Empirical data* about the actual operation of the rule—not as it affects this particular client in this particular case, but as it harms or helps the entire segment of the population most concerned. This empirical data may be brought into the case through the testimony of expert witnesses at trial,[84] a "Brandeis" brief on appeal[85] or the judge's own reading of pertinent information from sources in the social sciences.

—*The judge's own predispositions*—his basic economic and political philosophy, his open-mindedness, his sensitivity to suffering, even his attitude toward the role of a judge.[86]

The advocate for change thus confronts a relatively malleable situation.

Within bounds, his own lawyering skills will determine the outcome. Of the four critical inputs, he sometimes can control one—the particular case that is brought before the court—at least where he is filing an affirmative class action and can select the named plaintiffs whose special situations will constitute the facts of the case. Beyond that, the attorney has real influence over two other factors. Through the perceptive analysis of prior court opinions and the persuasive introduction of empirical data, he can expose the frail legal foundation of the old rule and establish the sound policy basis for the new rule. It is even sometimes possible to determine the fourth input, the judge himself, by choosing when and where to file a case or appeal. But ordinarily, and this is especially true at the appellate level, selecting the judge is often beyond the control of the advocate. The court in which a case will be heard, complete with its peculiar set of attitudes, prejudices, and predispositions, is a given.

In a jurisdiction and during an era favored with judges sympathetic to change, reform through the courts may well be the most effective strategy available to the poor. Certainly in the Warren years, the U.S. Supreme Court made law that generated many of the social-economic effects described in Chapter 8. (Of course, not every court in every state is such a willing instrument of change.) But for the poor, the judiciary does offer certain inherent advantages, particularly when contrasted with the legislative branch.

The poor represent a small minority of the population in the United States. This simple fact, although a blessing for the country as a whole, is a problem for those who are living in poverty. They don't have enough votes to elect change and they lack the money to buy change.[87] Courts, even appellate courts, are not wholly immune to political considerations either. But objective facts and rational argument play a larger role in judicial deliberations than they do in the legislative chambers. Judges violate their oath if they count the votes for or against a proposed change in the law; a legislator violates his oath, or at least his pledge to his constituents, if he fails to count those votes. By design, the courts are the forum of reason; the legislature the forum of power. And while we can only hope the poor will be more often right than in error, they certainly are more often right than powerful.

The courts possess other theoretical advantages. In our tripartite system of government the executive and legislative branches are the implementors of majority will; the judiciary alone is the guardian of minority rights. This is not entirely a defensive posture. Admittedly the role, guardian of minority rights, is a shield not a sword. But a shield can be carried and courts certainly have moved forward when necessary. In some respects courts have become, in fact always were, the legislature of the minority. Only the minorities have changed. Where initially the judiciary may have been intended to secure the propertied few against the depredations of the propertyless rabble controlling the legislature,[88] they now sometimes seem to have become the protectors of the propertyless few against the oppression of the affluent majority.

In recent years, the courts, especially the Federal courts, have begun to be the promoters of equality as well as the guardians of the minority. "Equal protection of the laws" has come to mean something not only to the racial minorities but to others who frequently do not fare well with Congress and state legislatures. Law-making bodies dominated by an affluent majority have a weakness for passing legislation that discriminates against the non-affluent minority. Sometimes the statutes omit the poor from certain rights and benefits the rest of the population enjoys. On other occasions, uneven treatment follows from a desire to hold down tax expenditures, or to promote a certain moral code, or to favor particular commercial interests. When they petition a legislature, the poor confront a body largely indifferent to equality. But when they carry their cause to the courts, the poor find a forum dedicated to that principle.

The courts, however, cannot make all the changes the poor desire. Although many statutes, for example, are phrased ambiguously, and are subject to interpretation, others, such as statutes establishing tax rates, are so specific that the court cannot bring about meaningful change through "interpretation" no matter how badly it wants to. (But bear in mind that much of the law relevant to purchasing power and other matters of interest to the poor is not statutory but solely common law.)

The courts cannot appropriate public funds. Nor can they directly compel the legislature to appropriate public funds. Many of the problems facing the poor can only be solved through an allocation of more tax monies to certain programs. Consequently, courts tend to be more successful in the effectuation of rights that do not involve public money, for instance, the rights of accused criminal defendants. (But the importance of this limitation should not be overstated. As a practical matter, sometimes courts do make changes that impel the appropriation of additional funds for the poor, such as prohibiting residency requirements and "the man in the house" decisions.)

The courts tend to make changes slowly. Not only does each appellate decision come only at the end of a lengthy process, but judges generally only move the law enough to decide the facts of that particular case and ones closely similar. A legislature on the other hand ordinarily writes with much bolder strokes—when it can be energized.

These limitations on judicial power apply to all courts. They are some of the reasons an advocate for the poor might discard reform through the judiciary for other strategies of change in certain circumstances. But the most important consideration in that decision has not been mentioned as yet. The predispositions of the individual judges who compose a specific appellate court are the single most crucial and unchanging input influencing that court's decisions. Judges vary in their conception of the judiciary's "right" to "change" old rules —whether those rules are common law or statutory in origin. They also have different political leanings and favorite economic theories. The poor and the racial minorities were blessed for over a decade because the United States Supreme Court was willing to reconsider prior rulings, and generally was more sympathetic to their cause than were most legislative bodies.

But no court is a forum for all seasons—or all cases. A good lawyer, for the reasons given above, must assess the predispositions of the appellate courts in his jurisdiction as well as their power to effect the changes his clients seek. He should compare the court's attitude and power with that of the state legislature; he must determine its responsiveness to the poor in contrast with that of other competing decision makers. He may well decide to forego court action in favor of another approach. But for reasons cited earlier, the lawyer is still likely to find the courts more receptive to the kinds of changes the poor need than most other important decision making bodies in society.

B. INFLUENCING PUBLIC AND PRIVATE DECISIONS THROUGH PERSUADING LEGISLATIVE BODIES TO MODIFY THE LEGAL STRUCTURE. With some notable exceptions, most of the decisions that affect the distribution of income and other interests vital to the poor are susceptible to legislative control. A new statute can prohibit certain conduct, overpricing by merchants or termination of welfare without a hearing, for example. Conversely, the written law can encourage other actions by offering rewards, financial or otherwise. The difficult questions for Legal Services are whether lawyers have any special contribution to make in the process of legislative change and whether that role is proper.

Of course, there has never been any dispute over the lawyer's role as a legislative draftsman. Legal aid lawyers were preparing legislative proposals beneficial to the poor long before anyone conceived of a Legal Services Program.[89] Nor does testimony before a legislative committee represent anything new.[90] But drafting legislation and testifying before committees seldom is enough to gain passage of a bill favorable to the poor.

As an alternative, therefore, some have proposed that Legal Services lawyers should organize the poor into a more cohesive, effective political force. This raises a serious question—whether organizing the poor is a worthwhile expenditure of the time of lawyers. Those that serve the poor are few in number and on the whole comprise the most expensively educated professional group available to the poverty community. Their training has been specialized but not in the theory or practice of organizational techniques. Other, less costly personnel probably can organize the poor at least as well. Moreover, no amount of organization of the poor in itself will produce substantial legislative change. As I have said, the poor remain a relatively small minority and thus cannot compel change in the legislative arena by the weight of their numbers. What they need is someone who can translate their limited political power into effective persuasion of elected decision makers. In part, this may be a lawyer's proper role.

1. Defining the lawyer's function in influencing the legislative body.
How does a relatively impotent minority group like the poor move a legislative
body to enact laws favorable to its interests? The pattern obviously differs from
state to state and statute to statute. But some of the key elements of the process
can be identified.

Proponents of legislative change usually must first create a broad base of
support for their proposal. General public opinion sometimes can be mobilized
behind legislation benefiting the poor through a dramatic event or media
exposé.[91] The base of support also can be broadened by forming coalitions with
middle-class groups.[92] In a basically middle-class society, it is crucial, wherever
possible, to link proposals to middle-class issues that benefit middle-class
people and are backed by middle-class citizens. Finally, the public may be
compelled to support change because of decisions like *Serrano* v. *Priest* which
render existing law illegal, unworkable or irrational.[93] If a constituency for
change has been created by a lawsuit, a coalition, a shift in public opinion, or
a combination of these, the next step usually is to cultivate legislative spokesmen.[94] Unless at least one legislator is pushing the proposal personally, it has
only a slim hope of passage. In order to persuade someone to undertake such
an assignment, it frequently is necessary to offer back-up help in the form of
research, speechwriting and similar aid.[95]

With the groundwork laid, the persuasion of individual legislators can begin
in earnest. Letters, telegrams, personal visits, research documents, opinion
polls, formal committee presentations, well-prepared floor speeches, all are
part of this process.[96] They are to legislative advocacy what the trial, the
written brief and oral argument are in the judicial context. However, the
message can be much broader than the facts and rational argument conveyed
to courts. Legislators will appraise the proposal in terms of constituent support
and public image as well as the objective merits. As observed earlier,[97] elected
lawmakers unlike judges are in the business of counting votes and implementing "popular" change.

As is obvious from even this cursory examination, legislative advocacy is a
time-consuming task requiring the exercise of highly developed talents and the
possession of specialized knowledge. Among the functions that must be performed are:

—*legislative strategy,* planning the overall campaign and making adjustments in the strategy as new developments occur.
—*public relations,* working with the media, keeping them informed, issuing
 press releases and otherwise improving the public image of the proposed
 change.
—*negotiations,* lining up support from middle-class organizations, legislators, and other necessary allies, negotiating, within limits, exchanges of
 support and modifications in the proposal.

—*representation,* acting as the principal public advocate for the legislative campaign, including testifying before legislative committees, giving speeches to middle-class audiences, and holding press conferences.[98]

—*legislative drafting,* translating the aims of the proponents into suitable statutory language.

—*speech writing,* preparing speeches and testimony to be delivered by legislators, public spokesmen, affiliated organizations, and other supporters of proposed legislation.[99]

All of these functions require traits, knowledge, and skills with which lawyers especially are expected to be familiar. An attorney by training and experience generally possesses sophisticated understanding of the legislative process; a knowledge of the existing law as well as the proposed change and how they both fit into the entire legal system; experience in negotiating with other individuals and groups; a special skill in persuading others to support his cause through oral argument; a wide range of "contacts" with opinion makers—especially in the media and government; and, carefully honed drafting skills.

Because lawyers have the qualifications necessary to press legislation, the poor, as well as others, look to them to plan, persuade, negotiate, and manage a legislative campaign. However, the lawyer is not the ultimate authority on fundamental decisions about aims and objectives; control should remain with the organization for which he is acting as counselor. He should only advise.

2. *Assessment of reform through government-subsidized legislative advocacy.* If reform through the courts depends upon the vagaries of judges, legislative reform is even more subject to the attitudes of members of the legislative body (and the voters and political contributors who support them). As conservative as many appellate courts are, they do not necessarily resist change any more strenuously than do the state legislatures. If it is within the power of both the judiciary and the legislative branch to enact a new legal rule, a lawyer would have to ponder seriously whether to invest time and energy in a legislative campaign before exhausting his opportunities in the courts.

Admittedly, reform through the judiciary requires the expenditure of a great deal of time—drafting pleadings, conducting hearings and trials, preparing briefs, and all the rest. But legislative reform usually absorbs even more time and energy.[100] Admittedly, change in the courts is a long drawn-out process. But, except in rare instances, legislative action takes much longer. The task is difficult—to translate an idea into a respectable opinion; and from a respectable opinion into a broadly supported proposal; and from a broadly supported proposal into a legislative mandate. The entire process ordinarily will take several years.

We earlier mentioned the most telling handicap borne by legislative advocates representing the poor. That is the inherent political weakness of the poverty community. They do not possess a healthy stock of inducements which can be employed to steer legislative decisions in their direction.

The upper classes have money, a commodity that Jess Unruh calls the "mother's milk of politics." Every legislator who bucks their desires risks drastic cuts in his campaign treasury. Compliance, however, will fatten the fund. The middle classes and labor possess some money and the vast majority of the votes. But in American society, the poor are short of both, and under ordinary circumstances a legislative proposal in their behalf is doomed unless somehow it earns the support or at least the tolerance of these other classes who wield rewards and punishments prized by most elected lawmakers.

The direct action techniques rarely succeed in the legislative arena. Picketing, boycotts, sit-ins, and strikes are relatively effective when practiced on certain business enterprises or a welfare department. After all, the low-income community represents a major constituency to ghetto merchants and public assistance administrators. These tactics pose a real threat of inconvenience, lost business, and so on, often sufficient to induce policy shifts by these minor decision makers. But in the arena of legislative politics, a legislator typically would rather ignore a sit-in or picket line than risk alienating the other classes, the source of his campaign funds or voting support.

But with all its difficulties and limitations, legislative reform is often the best, and sometimes the only, route open to the poor in their pursuit of social justice. At a minimum, it appears low-income people deserve the technical help that will give them a measure of participation in this influential law-making process.[101] However, it is precisely here that the Legal Services role becomes most controversial. The current administration, in fact, has attempted to sharply circumscribe legislative advocacy by poverty lawyers.[102]

Opposition to Legal Services lawyers providing advocacy in the legislative arena apparently is based on the feeling that it is improper for government funds to be used to affect the decisions of government legislators.[103] This is perceived as some sort of conflict of interest. And a new dimension is added when *Federal* funds and *state* lawmakers are involved. This exhumes the spectre of Washington intermeddling in state government.

These notions are inaccurate. The Legal Services Program is not a government agency influencing government legislation or a group of Federal authorities insinuating themselves into state and local affairs. A Legal Services lawyer represents a private client and his interests, not the government, Federal or otherwise. The fact the attorney's salary is paid from public funds is an inevitable incident of the poverty of his clients. But it does not alter his loyalties or duties, which are the same as any member of the legal profession serving any private individual able to pay a fee.[104] Thus, it is really the poor person, not a government agency, who seeks to persuade the legislative body with the aid of legal counsel. And it is this client rather than a Federal official who strives to reform local law.

In Chapter 8, we cited the peaceful resolution of individual and class grievances as one of the principal effects of the Legal Services Program. It is very doubtful this end could be served if Program lawyers were to be barred from the decision making body with the greatest power to remedy serious problems. For this reason as well, then, society as a whole has a stake in the continued availability of government-subsidized legislative advocates for the poor.

Setting aside any of the social-economic consequences of legislative advocacy, the elemental goal of achieving equal justice appears to demand that Legal Services lawyers undertake this form of representation. The attorney's function has long embraced advocacy before legislative bodies. Private counsel continually work the corridors, the hearing rooms and chambers of law-making power on behalf of their paying clients. Denying the poor access to similar representation in this vital forum deprives them of any opportunity for justice equal to that received by the affluent.

Edward Wright, the ABA president chiefly responsible for drafting the present Code of Professional Responsibility, was questioned about this in the Senate.

SENATOR CRANSTON. . . . [D]o clients have a right under the code to expect their attorneys to pursue any lawful objectives through any lawful means?

MR. WRIGHT. I think the answer is yes, Senator.

SENATOR CRANSTON. Thank you. Is urging a change in the law through the passage of legislation the pursuit of a lawful objective through legal means?

MR. WRIGHT. Yes, sir.

SENATOR CRANSTON. Are clients who can afford to pay attorneys entitled to have their attorneys seek changes in statutes in the legislatures or before Congress?

MR. WRIGHT. . . . The answer would be yes, sir. . . .

SENATOR CRANSTON. One final question. Are the provisions of the code intended to extend its duties and protections to every client irrespective of whether he can pay for a private attorney?

MR. WRIGHT. Absolutely.[105]

Consequently, when a client's only reasonable chance is in the legislature, his lawyer apparently is duty bound to pursue that remedy.[106]

Another ethical provision imposes on lawyers a duty to seek legislative changes needed to improve the legal system.[107] Were a policy enacted that would exclude Legal Services attorneys from that forum, it would cause these members of the legal profession to disregard the ethical requirements of their calling. It likewise would make them "half-lawyers" and consign their clients to half of a right to counsel.

C. INFLUENCING PUBLIC AND PRIVATE DECISIONS THROUGH PERSUADING EXECUTIVE AGENCIES TO MODIFY THEIR FORMAL REGULATIONS OR THEIR INDIVIDUAL DECISIONS. The agencies and departments responsible for implementing governmental policy wield enormous influence over the lives of the poor. As dispensers of government benefits such as welfare, education, medical care, public housing, and the like, their impact is direct and obvious. As regulators of private conduct—public utility rates, sales and trade practices, fair hiring programs, housing code compliance, labor-management relations, and so on—agencies and departments indirectly and subtly manipulate the earnings structure, net purchasing power, and economic opportunity in ways that can help or hinder the poor. True, the major allocations and priorities tend to be set by legislators and in some circumstances by judges. But executive personnel make thousands of choices every day, and their collective impact on social, political and economic patterns is substantial.

The executive departments and administrative agencies operate under relatively broad guidelines issued by the legislative and judicial branches. If their written regulations, prevailing policies, or individual decisions harm the poor, it may be possible to seek relief in the courts or legislature as described in the previous sections. But more often than not, outside intervention is either not feasible, ineffective, or uneconomic. The alternative is to influence the agency's own decision making process directly. There are two basic approaches.

1. The persuasion of the official or officials responsible for the regulation, policy, or decision. Sometimes agencies provide for a relatively formal procedure at which evidence and argument can be offered. Examples are hearings held before CAB decisions on airline routes are made, before the FCC makes license renewals and before public utility commissions set rates. (Of course, if there are no formal procedures, it is necessary to go outside established channels or create new mechanisms to gain an effective hearing.)

Whether a formal hearing or merely an informal request to the responsible official, the initial appeal is to reason, using rational argument and empirical data. Often a "brief" is submitted and oral testimony is taken in the form of the experiences of two or three clients who accompany the lawyer to the official's office or testify at a hearing. Usually, lingering in the background, there is an implicit threat of possible court action should the official prove intransigent. But the aim is to induce the agency itself to make the change, not to impose that decision through a judicial decree.[108]

If rational argument fails, the poor can attempt to focus outside pressure on the responsible agency. This approach is similar to legislative reform. The issue is dramatized; media coverage is asked for; middle-class organizations are asked publicly to support the cause. The poor attempt to convert public opinion into concrete, firm demands for change. Only in this instance the pressures are aimed at an executive department or administrative agency rather than a legislative body.

The advantages and disadvantages, the possibilities and limitations of rational argument and outside pressure in the context of an executive agency closely parallel the experience with similar techniques in the courts and legislatures. If there is a significant difference, it is that poor people form a large segment of the constituency of some types of agencies. This is seldom true of a legislative body. Thus, organized public assistance recipients, for instance, ordinarily have more leverage in dealing with a welfare administrator than they do with Congress or state lawmakers.

2. *The creation of a decision making process that allows the poor to participate in the formulation of regulations, policies and decisions that affect their lives.* Permitting the poor to participate in decisions that affect their lives may be the more lasting solution and the most difficult to bring about. But it is not impossible to imagine a county welfare board on which some of the members are selected by welfare recipients or a housing code enforcement agency managed by a council that includes tenant members. There already are public housing authorities that share at least some of their powers with tenant councils.[109] This same principle is involved in the move toward decentralization of public school administration in several cities.[110] But as yet most government agencies have successfully resisted any restructuring of the decision making process that would give their consumers a meaningful role. And generally, the larger and more powerful the agency, the less likely that the poor are sharing in policy formation.

D. INFLUENCING PUBLIC AND PRIVATE DECISIONS THROUGH ENFORCEMENT OF EXISTING LAWS BY THE JUDICIAL OR EXECUTIVE BRANCH. It is too easy to assume that behind every social evil lurks an evil law. In actuality, the substance of the legal structure is sometimes admirable, and the problem is that these rules are not enforced, in part because the poor are denied lawyers and access to the courts. (Of course, this shortage of lawyers and denial of access to the courts in themselves represent an inequitable distribution of resources attributable in good measure to defects in the existing legal structure.)

There are many existing legal rules which if fully enforced would increase the purchasing power of the dollar income received by the poor. For instance, they are daily victims of outright fraud: used television sets sold as new and at the prices of new sets and misrepresentations about the price or performance of goods. Even under existing law, these purchases frequently can be cancelled or at least can be reformed to give the buyer fair value for his dollar. Yet some merchants, especially among firms who cater to the poor, continue to engage in these patently illegal practices because they know that only a small percentage of their customers will be in a position to challenge them in the courts. The businessmen know they can afford to settle at a loss with this handful as a cost of doing business and still take home a larger profit than they could earn if they adhered to legitimate sales techniques. In addition, statutes and common law rules exist, which, if enforced, would protect the poor from arbitrary conduct by bureaucrats; unsafe working conditions; dilapidated apartments; and hundreds of other social ills.

Laws are not enforced on behalf of the poor for several reasons. First, the poor often are unaware of the existence of these provisions.[111] They have been conditioned by prior experience to doubt the existence of rules favorable to their interests. Second, they frequently are discouraged from asserting legal rights by the threat of economic retaliation.[112] This practice is so common among employers and slum landlords that the terms "retaliatory discharge" and "retaliatory eviction" have earned a place in the law books. Third, the remedy for illegal action, a court suit for instance, sometimes is too time-consuming for the individual to bother asserting his existing rights. Underlying all these other factors is the shortage of lawyers and the inaccessibility of the courts. Until there are about 12,000 to 15,000 lawyers provided to serve the poor, as opposed to the 2600[113] now available to them, it will be impossible to approach the goal of enforcing the existing legal rights of each individual poor person.

In the meantime, it is possible to maximize the effect of a few lawyers. The assertion of established defenses in individual lawsuits which have been brought against clients who happen to wander into a neighborhood law office is not always the most economic utilization of limited legal resources. Affirmative class actions brought on behalf of everyone whose existing rights are threatened by a given landlord, credit company, or government agency frequently are more effective and efficient.[114] This tactic also nullifies any attempt to settle with a few individuals and profit from the hundreds whose cases are not defended.

Another worthwhile approach in appropriate circumstances is to persuade responsible government agencies to enforce existing rules. This is an easier assignment than convincing them to modify their present policies and regulations. Many prosecutors' offices have power to move against consumer fraud; some states have labor codes and bureaus charged with enforcing those provisions; most cities have housing code enforcement divisions. Lawyers sometimes can activate these agencies on behalf of their clients by presenting a well-documented "case"—a series of affidavits, for instance, proving a pattern of abuse—to the right officials. On other occasions, it may require the pressure of an exposé in the press or a politician's interest. But the power and effectiveness of an aroused government enforcement agency often warrants the commitment of a lawyer to the cause.

3. *Influencing Private Decisions through Substitution of Economic Entities Controlled by or Committed to the Poor*

In our overview of methods for influencing policy formulation, replacing the present decision maker was listed as one of three fundamental alternatives. In the public sector, this ordinarily means electing a new executive or legislative body. Since campaign politics are outside the realm of legal services or antipoverty activity, this approach does not merit discussion here. But the private sector is another matter.

The poor, as one of the grievances already discussed, receive too little income from the economy and pay too much for goods and services. One cure is to replace some of the present decision making institutions—merchants, landlords, employers—with new forms that will upgrade the earnings and purchasing power of the poverty community. Three categories of private entities are capable of providing the lower economic groups with more leverage in the private market: (1) Organs of production or distribution owned by poverty organizations; (2) consumer organizations composed of low-income persons; and (3) organs of production and distribution (usually nonprofit) *not* owned by the poor but committed to their economic betterment.

A.   ORGANS OF PRODUCTION OR DISTRIBUTION OWNED BY LOWER ECONOMIC GROUPS.   In recent years, this approach has appeared in the guise of "Black Capitalism."[115] The basic concept is to create new economic entities—financed by the government and the white establishment—that are owned and operated by blacks. In theory, these new businesses contribute to the marketplace and receive profits, salaries, and wages for their black owners, black managers, and black employees. In effect, black capitalism represents a redistribution of income-producing wealth to an ethnic group. In the long run, this redistribution of income-producing wealth should generate an increase in the share of goods and services that group receives from the economy.

Black capitalism may or may not prove a boon to the *poor*. The terms "black" and "poor" are not synonymous. Only one-quarter of the poor are black[116] and "only" one-third of the blacks are poor.[117] It is entirely possible that black capitalism could help middle-class blacks without substantially alleviating the poverty of the rest; or even to help the black poor without touching the lives of the remaining 75 percent.

Yet these considerations do not detract from the *potential* value of capitalism for the poor. For the past two centuries, American lawyers have played a leading role in creating and guiding business institutions which dominate our system of production and distribution. In the present era of government financing, regulation, subsidization, and taxation of business, attorneys have become even more essential in both the formation and maintenance of these organizations. There is no inherent reason that lawyers serving the poor cannot use their ingenuity to create economic institutions of, by, and for the lower economic classes. At the same time, the lawyer's role is not paramount. Accountants, market analysts, financial experts, experienced businessmen in general have at least as much to contribute.

Four factors are important in evaluating just how effective this approach can be as a means of helping the poor.

1.   The amount of income-producing resources that are redistributed.   In former years little capital was available for economic entities owned and controlled by the poor in general or blacks in particular.[118] Only the allocation of huge amounts of government or private funds for this purpose can bring about meaningful results. Assuming a 10 percent return on invested capital, it would take a $2 billion transfer of income-producing wealth to generate even a $200 million-a-year increase in annual profit income for the poor—the approximate annual gain in welfare income that resulted from just two Supreme Court decisions.[119] (Of course, to the extent these new business entities employed poor persons and paid them more than they otherwise would earn, an additional amount in the form of wage income would accrue.) At the same time, there is nothing at the moment to suggest that investments on that scale are contemplated.

2. *The extent to which the businesses are owned by the poor themselves.* One problem is to devise a form of business organization that will guarantee that ownership and control repose with poor people. Nothing will have been accomplished if middle-class persons who happen to be of the same race as many of the poor are the only beneficiaries of a program designed to help the poverty community. And the gain is marginal where the only ones aided are the nearly poor and the barely poor. Cooperatives owned by employees or consumers are among the forms of organization in which low-income groups can retain ownership and control. However, the policy of providing assistance to individual businessmen holds less promise for poor people.

3. *The extent to which the businesses created do not compete with businesses owned by other low-income individuals and groups.* The market for any product or service is essentially finite. A newly created business almost invariably will be competing with other producers or distributors of the same goods, and most profits earned by the new enterprise will come at the expense of the income received by existing businesses. If these existing companies are owned by upper-income or middle-income individuals, this results in a redistribution of profit income from the affluent to the poor. But if the market entered by the newly formed business is dominated by marginal enterprises, there may only be a reallocation of income *among* low-income individuals rather than a net redistribution to the low-income class. Thus, if black capitalism is implemented unimaginatively, it could result merely in some increase in the earnings of poor blacks at the cost of further impoverishment of poor whites (or other low-income blacks). This suggests that wherever feasible the poor should be encouraged to channel their ventures into the production or distribution of new products and services or into fields that are dominated by middle-class and upper-class organizations.

4. *The economic strength and success of the entities formed.* Businesses that fail do not better the economic standing of their owners. Considering that most small businesses do not survive,[120] there is a high risk the owners, manag-

ers and employees will merely be spilled back into poverty. This suggests that the new entities probably should be of fairly good size; they should be well financed and generously supported by expert advice. It also may indicate that there are inherent limitations to this approach as a means of increasing the distribution of goods and services to the poor.

    B. CONSUMER ORGANIZATIONS COMPOSED OF LOW-INCOME PERSONS. Business organizations owned by the poor redistribute goods and services by increasing the share of dollar income, specifically profit income, earned by low-income groups. Consumer organizations of various types, in contrast, can modify the distribution pattern by enhancing the purchasing power of the dollar income received. These organizations include buying clubs, tenant unions, some types of credit unions, and so-called consumer action agencies. *Buying clubs* amass the purchasing power of the poor to buy food and other commodities at a discount for their members; they also make it feasible for members to purchase at less expensive stores outside the ghetto. *Tenant unions* and *consumer action agencies* rely on the coercive power of collective action to bargain for lower rents and prices, improved conditions and quality, better terms and broader guarantees. *Credit unions* pool the financial resources of many low-income citizens as well as other individuals and loan money to their members on more favorable terms and at substantially less cost than other sources of credit available to the poor.

Although the various kinds of consumer organizations utilize different strategies, they share the common goal of obtaining more purchasing power for the poor. They likewise are plagued by similar theoretical and practical limitations.

—Consumer organizations cannot increase the dollar income obtained by the low-income classes. Therefore, they can only make the poor less poor, but they will still remain poor.

—Tenant unions and consumer action agencies are difficult to organize and especially difficult to keep organized because of the transient character of the low-income population, the infrequent appearance of dramatic issues, and other factors.[121]

—Tenant unions and consumer action agencies typically suffer from comparatively weak bargaining power. Unlike labor unions, they do not possess a large stable of legally recognized and protected sanctions to deploy in their "collective bargaining" efforts, and they are more susceptible to retaliatory action, such as eviction. In addition, consumer action agencies, in particular, seldom control the market to the degree a labor union does. That is, a labor organization generally represents all of the employees of a business enterprise, or at least through reciprocal arrangements can control all of the workers. It is seldom a consumer action organization can manipulate all—or even a majority—of the customers of such a business.

Under ordinary circumstances, the lawyer's role is not central to the creation and operation of consumer organizations since they are less complex and their affairs less subject to governmental regulations and policies than the business enterprises discussed in the preceding section. The community organizer, rather than the lawyer, must carry the load. However, a major exception to this generalization arises when a tenant union or consumer action group moves to exert pressure on a landlord or merchant. The attorney's skills as negotiator, his advice about the legality of boycotts, picketing, and other bargaining techniques, his ability to defend against evictions, injunctions, and other legal maneuvers can make him a critical resource for the consumer organization.[122]

C. ORGANS OF PRODUCTION AND DISTRIBUTION COMMITTED TO ECONOMIC BETTERMENT OF LOW-INCOME PERSONS. Members of the middle and upper class have established organizations, usually nonprofit, to provide lower prices and cheaper rents for the poor, along with higher quality housing.[123] Low-income representatives may sit on the governing body and a special effort may be made to hire low-income employees. But the individual receives his primary dividend as a consumer of the organization's products and services, rather than as an owner of its assets. In effect, these enterprises pass on to the low-income consumer the excess profit less altruistic owners formerly derived through exploitive practices along with any legitimate profit income an ordinary firm would have charged. It is a true increase in the goods and services received by lower income groups.

Because of greater business experience and financial resources, these middle-class organizations sometimes find it easier than poverty groups to obtain the funding to undertake expensive business operations. This is especially true for ambitious projects like the renovation of existing slum housing, the construction of new low-income housing, and the larger credit union operations.

As more Federal financial support becomes available for the construction of housing of all types, the poor gain a stake in the existence of organizations that can capture a substantial share of that Federal support and direct it to the building of low-income housing as opposed to middle-income or even luxury housing.[124] These nonprofit organizations are important to the poor also because they place low-income housing under the control of individuals more likely to offer them quality shelter at a reasonable price than is the typical slum landlord.

Lawyers serving the poor can help to create these nonprofit housing corporations and supply valuable advice when they apply to the Federal government for financial support for a zoning variance, or to negotiate with various local government agencies, among other activities. Further, attorneys can seek to insure significant participation by low-income individuals in policy formulation, management, and employment in these companies.[125]

C. A Revised Structure for Antipoverty Advocacy

The needs of the poor for advocacy emerge as something much more than the common image of the lawyer as a courtroom performer. We have identified several types of decision makers that together determine the structure of poverty. They appear at all levels—local, state, and national—and in both the private and public sectors. As we have observed, each responds to a different pattern of arguments and inducements. And each demands a different set of persuasive skills.

1. Staffing for Reform

As we found the goal of equal justice would be served by broadening the client base, the antipoverty mission profits from expanding our concept of the advocacy function. And one of the implications of this is clear. The resources afforded the poor should include personnel possessing all the pertinent abilities, working as a team capable of drafting legislation and speeches, negotiating with public and private agencies, planning legislative campaigns, and so on, as well as conceiving and carrying out litigation.

Possibly lawyers could perform all these functions. But they need not. We already have spoken of the uses of para-professionals to lower the cost of resolving disputes.[126] For reasons of both economy and effectiveness, the roster of reform personnel also could easily include nonlawyers. Several elements of the legislative advocacy process, in particular, can be allocated to other specialists. Speech-writing, media relations, bill-watching and similar roles actually fall within the expertise of nonlegal occupations. Thus, an expanding concept of antipoverty advocacy leads naturally to a revised staff roster, augmenting attorneys with other relevant specialists.

2. An Antipoverty Structure

In what was perceived by many at the time as a revolutionary proposal, Edgar and Jean Cahn in 1965 advanced the notion of a neighborhood law office that would articulate and advocate the common concerns of a compact ghetto community. Eight years later, that suggestion seems almost tame, and even a bit naïve. (But only in retrospect and with the advantage of hindsight, I hasten to add.) The "war" for which the Cahns wished to provide a "civilian perspective" never became more than a skirmish. And the invisible forces that predestine poverty for a sizable percentage of our population trace far beyond the community institutions that raised their ire.

An appreciation for the many levels and complexities of decision making suggests an even more drastic change must be made in the design of the efforts of the Legal Services Program to overcome poverty. Thus far, the primary responsibility for that role has reposed with the neighborhood law offices.

True, as discussed in Chapter 7, neighborhood lawyers are supported by a collection of national backup centers, a clearinghouse, several publications, and a recruitment program.[127] Yet most of the resources and responsibility remain in the local offices.

The first seven years of the OEO Legal Services Program indicate the more influential decision makers are not located where the poverty lawyers are—in the neighborhoods, nor even in the local communities. The real power to refashion the structure of poverty exists with government and private decision makers at the state, regional, and especially the national levels. From the perspective of maximizing reform, the future appears to call for a substantial redesign of the Legal Services Program. Instead of recruiting, training, and providing backup centers and other agencies solely for the purpose of "supporting" neighborhood law offices, a comprehensive reform structure should be devised.

What might this structure look like? There would be an alignment of priorities and resources to enable the program to more effectively influence the more important decisions which determine the distribution of income, opportunity, fairness, and participation in this society. In other words, there should be a reorientation to enlarge capacity to affect decision making at the national and state level, where billions are at issue, even if this must be done at the expense of somewhat reducing the ability to influence neighborhood institutions where the stakes tend to be in the hundreds or thousands of dollars. The main ingredients might include: (1) a large national advocacy staff equipped to represent the poor at the Federal level, and closely coordinated with (2) a group of national research centers capable of providing in-depth long-range research in the law and social sciences pertaining to relevant problem areas, which in turn are well coordinated with (3) a system of state and metropolitan advocacy centers designed to represent the poor, especially state and city-wide organizations of the poor, before legislatures, administrative agencies, and courts.

The national, state, and metropolitan centers would be staffed by teams composed of lawyers and other specialists. Of course, they should remain accountable by being closely tied to poverty organizations and being governed in part by representatives of the poor. The centers also should coordinate with local Legal Services agencies. But the primary responsibility for advocating major causes would be placed with the advocacy centers rather than neighborhood law offices.

D. Establishing an Antipoverty Agenda for the Future

The first seven years of the Legal Services Program offered a time for testing the poverty lawyer, an opportunity to unlimber his muscles, to measure his reach and sort strengths from weaknesses. In these last two chapters, we have essayed many of these exploratory moves, their impact, and potential. The future, I suspect, will not be marked so much by discovery of new goals, tactics, and techniques as, hopefully, the more rational and focused development of proven measures.

With a somewhat more sophisticated notion of the social-economic impact of certain decisions (see Chapter 8) and the strategies for affecting those decisions (Section II, this chapter), it makes sense to contemplate a major planning element for the national advocacy. Ideally, the team would include economists, sociologists, political scientists, systems analysts, and lawyers. Meshing these diverse disciplines, it should be possible to produce a master set of possible priorities. Alternative targets for change can be ranked on the basis of comparative economic, social, and political benefits and costs, and estimates of legal feasibility. General strategies for achieving these priorities likewise can be plotted. The preliminary analysis of social-economic effects outlined in Chapter 8 and the strategies considered in this chapter suggest some of the choices available to the national planning unit.

At present there is some limited planning taking place at the existing backup centers. This planning falls short of the comprehensive effort I am advocating on three counts. First, at best it is but a minor, almost ad hoc function of these centers. Second, to the extent there is advance planning, it tends to be performed exclusively by lawyers and to focus entirely on the question of legal feasibility. In other words, the staff of a national backup center surveys the subject area assigned to determine what issues seem most "ripe" for change in the courts and elsewhere. They are equipped neither by background nor inclination to assess the comparative social and economic benefits of other alternative targets. Third, and most important, the planning function, such as it is, has been spread among a dozen centers, each of them confined to a specific subject area such as welfare, housing, consumer, or juvenile problems. Thus, no single staff has taken an overall look at the costs, benefits, and feasibility of possible actions in all subject areas. Missing is the broader perspective that might yield new insights and a national, and probably a drastically different, ranking of priorities.

I am not suggesting that this national planning team impose its priorities on the attorneys helping the poor directly. The planners are not to become a "general staff" for the Legal Services Program, handing out marching orders to a corps of foot-soldier attorneys. Compliance with the priorities and recommended strategies should be entirely voluntary. Obviously, there is no problem with encouraging poverty lawyers to be on the lookout for cases which implement the national plan. But the ABA Code of Professional Responsibility, political considerations, and common sense all appear to condemn any ban on bringing cases or engaging in other activities which fall outside the suggested priorities.

Such a ban contravenes the Code because it jeopardizes the integrity of the relationship between the attorney and the client, which guarantees that the lawyer will pursue any lawful end by any legal means that implements the best interests of his individual client.[128] The Code would be violated, for example, if a lawyer were prohibited from filing a test case merely because the national planning unit concluded that this particular issue could be handled better through legislative advocacy.

Even were it ethical, enforcement of national priorities through negative strictures would constitute political suicide. In one bold stroke, it would realize the worst fears of bar leaders, the most terrifying demagoguery of conservative politicians, and the recurring nightmare of the powerless poor. Gone would be the professional advocate, duty bound to implement his clients' interests and desires. In his stead would be the servant of government bureaucrats whose handling of lawsuits is dictated, depending upon your perspective, by "social workers," "radicals," or "the man."

The findings reported by a national planning unit are best conceived as a critical and basic input, but not the end product of the total priority-setting process. The data about objective costs and benefits should be judged in the light of the expressed subjective preferences of clients and the insights of the Legal Services lawyers helping them. Moreover, the ultimate goals and resource allocations for metropolitan, state, and national advocacy centers should be set only while working with representatives of the poverty community.

If priorities and strategies cannot, as an ethical or political matter, be enforced, is the planning effort worth the investment? It clearly is. There are hundreds of Legal Services lawyers interested in contributing to the elimination of poverty. It is not unreasonable to expect that many of them would be willing to consider a national plan. Without compulsion in any form, many of the priorities and recommended strategies would be implemented. Possibly more important, the plan would provide both the incentive and beginning point for the development of meaningful regional and local planning efforts that combine the insights of social scientists, poverty lawyers, and community organizations.

Without presuming to prejudge the outcome of a sophisticated, interdisciplinary, multilevel planning process, it may be useful to suggest some hypotheses about the future direction of antipoverty advocacy. I think it not unreasonable to anticipate that a better grasp of the structure of poverty would lead to a rechanneling of resources to some areas that are now largely neglected. As an example, the billions of dollars taken out of the poverty community through the existing tax structure—especially regressive social security, property, and sales levies—deserve special attention from advocates for the poor. Even negligible relief in percentage terms can yield hundreds of millions to poor people, whether they are wage earners or live on government transfer payments. Through a combination of litigation,[129] legislation,[130] and other strategies, advocacy centers have a reasonable opportunity to affect tax rate decisions. Certainly the extraordinary payoff seems to make this a worthwhile investment of the Legal Services Program.

Also concerning taxes, the localized nature of the present system for raising taxes and distributing government services at the local level tends to worsen the condition of individual poverty. *Serrano* threw a spotlight on the tip of the iceberg—educational financing. Under the surface floats a discriminatory system that allows residents of wealthy residential areas to pay less of their income in return for more and better services across the board. The poor generally need more police protection, garbage collection, street maintenance, and other government help than they are getting. Certainly they need to see a smaller percentage of their income taxed for these benefits. Again billions are at stake. And again there is a fair opportunity for success. Yet the current specialization of legal services within the national law reform centers[131] discourages a concerted, sustained consideration of this pervasive issue.

Augmenting the income of low-paid wage earners also may be pointed out, as a result of the planning process, to be a high ranking item on the Legal Services agenda. It is not unlikely that advocates can make a difference through broadening the coverage of minimum wage laws or extending collective bargaining rights to new classes of employees or changing eligibility rules for unemployment compensation and public assistance to embrace the seasonally unemployed worker.

Government programs, especially in the housing field, have made hundreds of millions of dollars available, often through programs created primarily for the poor. Nevertheless, how much actually goes to low-income owners and tenants—as opposed to middle- and upper-income groups—may be determined by the quality and quantity of legal representation available to the contesting classes. Here again the possibilities are enticing, especially in attempting to persuade Federal agencies to promulgate regulations that give priority to the primary intended beneficiaries—the poor.

Earlier—in Chapter 8—we commented on the comparative dearth of activity aimed at eliminating employment discrimination. Significantly, in 1972, when two Legal Services agencies for the first time undertook a planning effort to establish priorities, equalization of employment opportunity emerged as the highest ranking goal.[132] This outcome—and the value low-income citizens place on economic mobility[133]—indicate equal job opportunity might receive a generous allocation of Legal Services resources under any comprehensive plan.

Another tantalizing new field is found in certain long-neglected private transfer programs, especially employee pension funds. The potential leverage is tremendous. It is estimated these funds hold $135 billion in trust for the nation's workers. Yet because of legal loopholes and dubious practices, a congressional study found only about a quarter of the intended, and expectant, beneficiaries collect even one dime of their pensions.[134] Even minor litigation victories in this area would yield hundreds of millions to the elderly poor.

Consumer problems and landlord-tenant relations, however, do not appear to be logical areas for increased attention. True, they account for the largest amount of the purchasing power deficit suffered by the poor. Yet these two fields already absorb a substantial percentage of Legal Services resources. Here the real need is not for more time and lawyers, but for sophisticated empirical research—to identify with precision the legal means that can be used to reduce net prices and improve quality.

Other families of issues may be recommended for deemphasis as a result of a rationalized planning effort. Any investigations into the objective costs and benefits of a legal program is apt to expose the marginal payoff from cases that merely expand procedural rights or enhance fair treatment, especially for a small minority of the poor. Not surprisingly, creating new procedural rights for prison inmates rated last in a recent ranking by the community representatives and poverty lawyers who were setting priorities in one of the local planning processes mentioned earlier.[135]

Admittedly, the foregoing paragraphs describe merely the broad, tentative outlines of an agenda for future reform on behalf of the poor. Yet two salient observations can be made. First, for the most part, the highest ranking priorities are not ones that would emerge from an analysis of the individual problems most frequently brought to the neighborhood lawyer by his clients. Not too many poor people will appear on the doorstep of the office pleading for the attorneys to lower taxes or to get the litter out of the streets. It even is relatively unusual for a low-income client to think of taking his employment or wage problems to a lawyer. It is not because these issues do not exist or that poor people do not care about them. It is simply that you have to be fairly sophisticated to understand how an invisible pattern of external decisions, public and private, envelops your life. And it takes even more sophistication to realize that a lawyer may be capable of manipulating some of those decisions in your favor.

The second pattern that can be deduced from our tentative agenda reinforces an earlier observation. On the whole, the solutions to these problems are not found in the ghetto. They are at the national, state, and community level. Taking any of our highest priorities, the most pervasive and profound decisions are made by institutions located miles or, more often, hundreds of miles from the neighborhood law office.

If the full-scale planning effort came up with findings approaching those of our tentative list, the implications would be clear: Not only should more resources be allocated to new substantive goals, but additional lawyers should

278 . AN ASSESSMENT

be distributed to new roles as well. In other words, not only would lawyers be concerned with the implications of local tax laws, but more would be assigned to national, state, and metropolitan advocacy centers than have been in the past. Where the neighborhood facility is best equipped to deal with the local welfare worker, merchant, or landlord, the most vital decision makers are in Washington, the state capitols, the corporate headquarters, union offices, banks, and so on. The ghetto resident can be effectively linked with these centers of power only by affording them effective counsel at these locations.

Lest these recommendations be perceived as radical suggestions, it should be remembered that other interests in American society already have their advocates in place at every one of these levels. Major law firms, state capitol lobbyists, Washington counsel, and all the rest constitute a mammoth national advocacy system for business, labor, and others in society. Litigation, legislative advocacy, and lobbying administrative agencies are among their principal activities.[136] Simply to right the balance somewhat, low-income people require a much expanded capacity at all three levels: Federal, state and metropolitan. The general practitioner is no longer the universal prototype for the American legal profession. There is no valid reason to so limit the services available to the poor.

III. THE MERGER OF JUSTICE AND REFORM

The Legal Services Program became possible because of a partnership between constituencies harboring differing visions of its primary mission. The Program survived through three years of a Democratic administration and five years of Republican rule in part because it deliberately served both these conceptions. But underneath, at an almost subliminal level, a more profound change was taking place. The ideologies, the supporters, the personnel of the legal aid movement and the neighborhood lawyer movement fused. For this, the Program owes more to its enemies than any deliberate stratagem. The political cauldron forged links that time and mutual persuasion may never have produced.[137]

In retrospect, the mingling of philosophies was predictable. Young neighborhood lawyers exposed to waiting rooms full of clients naturally identified with the goal of making legal assistance available to every individual poor person, and legal aid leaders became believers in reform when they saw the results achieved by the talented newcomers to their movement.

However, in recent years, changes have been taking place outside the Legal Services Program and its primary constituencies, trends that threaten to slow down, if not reverse, its momentum. It must be remembered that the Program was started during a Presidential administration that generally favored reform of the kind generated by Legal Services lawyers. A war on poverty had been declared and actions, at least peaceful ones, that gave poor people more money, more opportunity and more rights seemed praiseworthy. But during the Republican years, the social and economic effects brought about by Legal Services attorneys have become less and less popular with the national administration. More money for poor people seems antithetical to the Nixon policies.

Thus, the problem of survival has entered a new phase: Will the Federal treasury continue to finance advocacy that consistently and inevitably produces social and economic results the current government finds offensive? In other words, when the poor man's causes fall into disfavor, will the advocates for those causes also succumb?

Though an imminent question as of the writing of this book, this actually is an inherent issue for any legal assistance program in any country in the long run. After all, how often can one expect the goals of the government in power to coincide, nearly precisely, with the aspirations of the poor. (In the United States, apparently about four years out of every century.) Accordingly, unless advocacy of major causes as well as minor ones is accorded a protected status independent from the desirability or undesirability of its social and economic impact, such advocacy is doomed. Reform, as such, though a noble goal, simply is not a viable justification for a program over the long term.

Yet the model clearly is available, as is the philosophical underpinning. The model is that of the legal profession sworn to defend unpopular clients and causes; the philosophical justification is found in the goal of equal justice—that is, truly *equal* justice. For equal justice, in fact anything approaching that goal, requires that the poor be afforded advocates possessing both the right and the capacity to raise the same fundamental issues about the allocation of income, opportunity, rights and power as those with funds have done since the beginning of the Republic.

Some commentators have been thrown off the track by the "traditional" legal aid society as it actually performed through most of this century. They drew the inference that since society attorneys rarely, if ever, undertook test cases or engaged in legislative advocacy, these activities were not part of the "services" considered *legitimate* by the "traditional" legal assistance movement. As Professor Hazard describes it, "traditional Legal Aid" was confined to "individual cases . . . centered on the routine disorders of daily life—domestic discord, trouble with creditors and landlords, and involvements with the police, welfare agencies and other organs of government." Purportedly, "traditional legal aid" shunned cases that might provide a "bridge between broad social grievance (e.g. bad housing, racial discrimination, expensive credit, chronic unemployment) and social reform."[138]

It is true, as we observed in Chapter 1, that the primary motivation of the legal aid movement was the expansion of due process justice, and especially the capacity to handle Professor Hazard's "routine disorders of daily life." Moreover, because they were short of resources, imagination or courage (and possibly all three), the performance of most legal aid societies seldom strayed beyond that narrow definition of justice. Yet, the vision of what is permissible, appropriate and even laudable was never so limited.

Reginald Heber Smith devoted an entire chapter of *Justice and the Poor* to the appellate litigation and legislative advocacy undertaken by pioneer legal aid societies.[139] Smith justified those actions on fundamental grounds of equality and justice. Writing about appellate work, he argued:

> In cases wherein new important points of law and matters of general legal or social interests are involved, it is essential that legal aid organizations should be able to carry the issue through to the highest court for its decision.
>
> Just as the legal aid organizations are necessary to secure to the individual poor person his day in court, so they are necessary to secure his hearing on appeal. But the latter is more than a question of individual justice; on it may depend the right to protection and redress of countless other persons similarly situated."[140]

Smith also endorsed legislative campaigns directed against "broad social grievances." Expensive credit, one of the evils Hazard felt legal aid never touched, became cheaper because of legislative advocacy by Smith's own organization in Boston.[141] Employment conditions were improved in a series of statutes promoted by legal aid lawyers in New York,[142] and the harshness of wage garnishment was eased in Cleveland.[143] As Smith explained, legislative advocacy seemed an essential tool for the achievement of justice.

> It early became apparent, . . . that if [legal aid societies] were to be effective in their fight against injustice, they must . . . take a part in the formulation of remedial legislation. They saw cases of injustice which the law was powerless to redress because of the inadequacy of certain provisions or the lack of proper laws framed to meet the changed conditions.
>
> It is apparent that the legal aid organizations have taken up the burden of trying, through remedial legislation, to keep the law equal. . . .[144]

In the face of these clear pronouncements by the founder of the philosophy of legal aid, it would have been remarkable if the leaders of the "traditional" movement had not readily embraced and defended the reform mission. Admittedly, the primacy of that goal marked a departure from legal aid performance and even its philosophy. But once Legal Services lawyers scored an early round of test case victories, they punctured the myth that the substantive law was unbiased.[145] In so doing, they undercut the rationale for emphasizing "individual disorders" at the expense of major litigation or legislative advocacy. Smith himself explicitly recognized that the "fairness of the substantive law . . . is the *requisite foundation* for an equal administration of justice."[146] With the foundation demonstrably disintegrating underfoot, legal aid's own logic dictated a shift in program priorities. In effect, reform has become a prerequisite of justice. Thus it is no longer feasible for knowledgeable constituents of legal aid to ignore the indispensability of substantive change.

Apparently several observers and politicians outside the legal aid movement failed to grasp the philosophical transformation that overtook the movement and its establishment bar supporters during the last half of the 1960s. Not fully comprehending the interdependence of a fairer distribution of substantive rights and an equal administration of justice, critics sought to create a schism between the timid pre-OEO legal aid societies they understood and the vigorous poverty lawyers whose continued favor with the ABA they cannot fathom.[147] Typical were the comments of Vice President Agnew in a recent article appearing in the *American Bar Association Journal.*

> (T)he legal services program has gone way beyond the idea of a governmentally funded program to make legal remedies available to the indigent and now expends much of its resources on efforts to change the law on behalf of one social class —the poor.[148]

The article approved "reforming the law to rectify old injustices or correcting the law where it has been allowed to be weighted against the poor" but in the next breath condemned efforts which "redistribute societal advantages and disadvantages, penalties and rewards, rights and resources." This attempted distinction, which also underlies Professor Hazard's major thesis,[149] appears specious. For what is the law but a mechanism that allocates "societal advantages and disadvantages, penalties and rewards, rights and resources?" To change the former is to redistribute the latter. (And sometimes even to enforce the law on behalf of the formerly disenfranchised is to reallocate societal advantages and disadvantages and all the rest.) A Legal Services lawyer would be hard pressed to redistribute anything without convincing a judge or other decision making institution that the law needed to be changed "because it has been allowed to be weighted against the poor" or at least that existing law which is favorable to the poor ought to be enforced. Conversely it is impossible to reform the law "to rectify old injustices" without generating the sort of societal redistributions the critics apparently abhor.

In order to curtail social and economic effects they find undesirable, without appearing to disenfranchise the poor, critics have proposed two modifications in the Federal Legal Services Program. One is to give the Federal government itself the responsibility for advocating the major causes of the poor, to be accomplished by transferring law reform resources and authority from poverty lawyers to Federal employees.[150] The second approach is to make the poverty lawyers "accountable" to state and local government or the local bar association.[151] (Accountability apparently is a code-word for government or bar association screening of causes and cases before they are undertaken.)

As grounds for these drastic measures, it first is claimed that the discretion allowed poverty lawyers must be checked because they disregard their client's interest in pursuit of "their own individual theories of how society should be structured." This allegation bears examination at two levels. First, there is the matter of accuracy. Legal Services attorneys have handled over 4 million clients and thousands of appellate cases in the past seven years. Yet critics have been unable to cite a single case in which a Legal Services lawyer has been disciplined for choosing to pursue a test case at the expense of a favorable settlement for his client even though this constitutes a clear ethical infraction. Yet I know of many instances where poverty attorneys have settled what were promising test cases.

But even assuming that it was fairly common that clients' interests were being disregarded, the remedies prescribed seem wholly inappropriate. To turn control over to government or a local bar association is not calculated to increase client input and power. In fact, that step moves in the opposite direction. In actuality, the goals poverty lawyers pursue are not their own theories about how society should be structured but objectives that will improve economic and social conditions for their low-income clients. If abuses exist, the remedy is to strengthen the client community's role in policy making and priority setting. The other course—government or bar association control either of the purse or of the case selection—simply vitiates the influence of the poor entirely. At the worst, a poverty lawyer might err because of innocent misconceptions about the desires of his clients. But at least the client's economic and social betterment will be uppermost in his mind. The government or bar association, on the other hand, will be examining a proposed action from the viewpoint of its potential impact on interests diametrically opposed to the poor. Thus, under the guise of preventing imagined abuses, this approach curtails the influence of the poor rather than enhancing it. In fact, it robs them of the right to pursue remedies unpopular with powerful elements in society.

But the critics' objections go deeper. In their perception, the Legal Services Program "transfers great power in community affairs from elected officials."[152] In the more neutral terms of our earlier analysis, the Program has given the poor the wherewithal to participate in decision making in our society.[153] Or as Reginald Heber Smith wrote in 1919, "The significance of [law reform] is that it denotes the presence of an organization that can speak for an estate in the community which by reason of its own limitations is inarticulate."[154] But the critics demand that this "great power in community affairs" must be brought under community control, hence the suggested transfer of law reform responsibility to Federal employees and the screening of major causes by governments or local bar associations.

Refined to the essence, the issue is who is to decide which lawful objectives are to be pursued by what legal means—the clients and their lawyers, on the one hand, or government officials on the other. With responsibility for all significant actions reposing in the Federal headquarters, the Legal Services Program would resemble an arm of the Department of Justice—filing only those lawsuits and seeking only those reforms that suited the philosophy and political aims of the administration then in power.

"Accountability" to governments or bar associations would have similar effects and poses the same issue. Are legal services to the poor to be essentially client-actuated or are they to be controlled by others? This apparently is not a problem when only relatively minor disputes are involved. No serious objection has been made to poverty lawyers when they defend simple eviction cases, negotiate consumer debts and the like without clearance from above. But when the stakes are raised, so are the claims that public financing imposes a duty not shared by other lawyers, a responsibility to pursue only those legal objectives that square with the governing caste and to use only those lawful means that will least inconvenience those interests.

The genius of the Legal Services Program has been its ability to raise issues of value to clients irrespective of the preferences of government officials or others in society. Like other members of the legal profession, its attorneys can seek to persuade judges, legislators and similar decision makers about the merits of proposals that may or may not please the majority of citizens. Notice that this does not mean they unilaterally can make changes that benefit the poor at the expense of the affluent. Poverty lawyers—whether part of a specialized unit or a neighborhood office—merely advocate; they do not decide. Thus, the implication that they have been delegated power to restructure society to suit their own ideology or that of the poor[155] is fallacious. A judge or some other conservative decision maker must be convinced that any proposed policy is necessary or at least desirable. When the issue reaches this decision making body, the nonpoor have a substantial input, through their own lawyers and other advocates. That should be enough. To allow government, a bar association, or any other body to screen or discourage antipoverty cases or proposals before they are asserted is much more insulting than telling low-income persons those petitions will be denied. As a practical matter, it is not only disagreeing with what the poor have to say, it is denying them the right to say it— at least in any useful way in any meaningful forum.

It may be, as the current administration apparently fears, that the distribution of income, opportunity, power and the rest is altered significantly by the existence of lawyers serving the poor. It may also be true that the present administration prefers the allocations that would prevail if the poor had only limited advocacy in the courts, legislative chambers, or elsewhere in society. But that would be a false distribution of society's rights and resources, and in a very real sense an unfair one. For it depends on the poor being silent, or at least unheard, in the places the distributional decisions are being made. Rea-

284 • AN ASSESSMENT

sonable men may differ about what is an equitable distribution of the national income: should the poor have five percent or fifteen; the rich twenty-five percent or forty? But it is difficult to contend any allocation is fair if it is predicated on denying equal justice to a sizeable segment of the population. The fact that equal justice may inevitably produce reform is not sufficient grounds for rendering it less equal or less just, even for those who abhor the reforms.

And so, America's poor await a verdict. Properly perceived, it is one that involves the quality of justice they receive as much as their chance to enjoy a better life. Are they to be entitled to equal justice only when their causes are minor or consonant with the philosophy of the ruling political party? Or will they be able to pursue any legal objective through any lawful means in keeping with the ideals of the legal profession? In the long run this ultimate question will be answered by the American public. The response most certainly will be the measure of the poor man's opportunity for justice in this nation and his right to seek better conditions through the orderly processes of the law. It may also determine, in large part, the quality of American democracy in the last quarter of the Twentieth Century.

Appendix I: Comparative Statistical Data

A. Income Distribution in the United States

Table I-1: Share of Money Income Received by Family Units—By Income Rank and Income Group: 1955 to 1970

[A family unit is two or more people living in the same dwelling unit and related to each other by blood, marriage, or adoption. A single person unrelated to the other occupants in the dwelling unit or living alone is a family unit by himself.]

FAMILY UNITS INCOME RANK[1]	PERCENT OF TOTAL INCOME 1960	1965	1970	LOWEST INCOME (dollars) 1960	1965	1970	INCOME GROUP	SHARE OF TOTAL MONEY INCOME (percent distribution) 1955	1961	1965	1970
							Total	100	100	100	100
Lowest tenth	1	1	2	(NA)	(NA)	(NA)	Under $1,000	1	1	(Z)	(Z)
Second tenth	3	3	3	1,500	1,870	2,700	$1,000–$1,900	3	2	1	1
Third tenth	5	5	5	2,640	3,000	4,000	$2,000–$2,999	6	4	3	1
Fourth tenth	7	6	6	3,700	4,200	5,500	$3,000–$3,999	9	5	3	2
Fifth tenth	8	8	7	4,000	5,500	7,000	$4,000–$4,999	11	7	4	3
Sixth tenth	9	9	9	5,500	6,670	8,600	$5,000–$5,999	13	10	6	3
Seventh tenth	11	11	11	6,275	8,000	10,045	$6,000–$7,499	15	14	11	7
Eighth tenth	13	13	13	7,200	9,220	12,010	$7,500–$9,999	15	19	19	12
Ninth tenth	16	16	17	8,593	11,200	15,000	$10,000–$14,999	14	19	26	27
Highest tenth	27	28	27	11,000	14,680	20,000	$15,000 and over	13	19	27	44

NA Not available.

Z Less than 0.5 percent.

[1] Ranking based on size of money income before taxes.

SOURCE: *Statistical Abstract of the United States, 1972* (Washington: U.S. Government Printing Office, 1972), Table 529.

B. Income Distribution in Other Nations

Table I-2: Income Distribution Estimates—Percentage Shares in Total National Income Going to Population Groups of Different Income Levels in 44 Countries

	Poorest 20%	Poorest 60%	Middle 40–60%	Highest 20%	Highest 5%
ntina	7.00	30.40	13.10	52.00	29.40
ia	4.00	26.60	8.90	59.10	35.70
il	3.50	22.70	10.20	61.50	38.40
na	10.00	36.00	13.00	48.50	28.21
on	4.45	27.47	13.81	52.31	18.38
	12.00	35.00	12.00	43.00	23.00
e	5.40	27.00	12.00	52.30	22.60
mbia	2.21	15.88	8.97	68.06	40.36
a Rica	6.00	25.40	12.10	60.00	35.00
omey	8.00	30.00	12.00	50.00	32.00
dor	6.30	42.60	26.10	41.80	21.50
alvador	5.50	23.60	11.30	61.40	33.00
on	2.00	15.00	7.00	71.00	47.00
ce	9.00	34.10	12.30	49.50	23.00
	8.00	36.00	16.00	42.00	8.00
	2.00	16.00	8.00	68.00	34.00
l	6.80	38.80	18.60	39.40	11.20
y Coast	8.00	30.00	12.00	55.00	29.00
ica	2.20	19.00	10.80	61.50	31.20
n	4.70	31.10	15.80	46.00	14.80
ya	7.00	21.00	7.00	64.00	22.20
non	3.00	23.00	15.80	61.00	34.00
a	0.11	1.78	1.28	89.50	46.40
gasy	7.00	23.00	9.00	59.00	37.00
co	3.66	21.75	11.25	58.04	28.52
cco	7.10	22.20	7.70	65.40	20.60
	12.00	35.00	12.00	42.00	23.00
ria	7.00	23.00	9.00	60.90	38.38
stan	6.50	33.00	15.50	45.00	20.00
ma	4.90	28.10	13.80	56.70	34.50
	4.04	17.10	8.30	67.60	48.30
ppines	4.30	24.70	12.00	55.80	27.50
lesia	4.00	20.00	8.00	65.00	60.00
gal	3.00	20.00	10.00	64.00	36.00
a Leone	3.80	19.20	9.10	64.10	33.80
n Africa	1.94	16.27	10.16	57.36	39.38
n	5.60	29.30	14.30	48.10	17.10
am	10.70	37.00	14.74	42.40	15.40
an	4.50	29.00	14.80	52.00	24.10
ania	9.75	29.25	9.85	61.00	42.90
dad & Tobago	3.60	18.52	9.16	57.00	26.60
sia	4.97	20.57	9.95	65.00	22.44
zuela	4.40	30.00	16.60	47.10	23.20
bia	6.27	26.95	11.10	57.10	37.50
ges	5.6	26	12	56	30

CE: 9 *Development Digest* 27 (October 1971), Table 1.

C. Government Expenditures for the Low-Income Population

Table I-3: Families Below and Above Low Income Level, by Type of Income and Sex of Head: 1970

TYPE OF INCOME		ALL FAMILIES			FAMILIES WITH MALE HEAD			FAMILIES WITH FEMALE HEAD		
		Total	Below low income level	Above low income level	Total	Below low income level	Above low income level	Total	Below low income level	Above low income level
Total families	1,000	51,948	5,214	46,734	45,998	3,280	42,718	5,950	1,934	4,016
Percent		100.0	100.0	100.0	100.0	100.0	100.0	100.0	100.0	100.0
Earnings		91.0	64.7	93.9	92.7	70.5	94.4	77.8	54.7	89.0
Wages or salary		85.8	53.7	89.3	87.1	55.1	89.6	75.2	51.4	86.6
Nonfarm self-employment		12.3	11.0	12.5	13.3	15.3	13.2	4.5	3.7	5.0
Farm self-employment		5.3	8.4	4.9	5.7	12.6	5.1	2.1	1.3	2.5
Income other than earnings		64.4	67.3	64.1	62.5	61.4	62.6	79.3	77.3	80.3
Soc. Sec. and Government railroad retirement		19.9	29.7	18.8	17.7	34.5	16.5	36.2	21.7	43.2
Dividends, interest, and rent		41.8	13.3	45.0	43.7	16.7	45.8	27.1	7.5	36.6
Public assistance income		6.0	29.5	3.4	3.4	16.9	2.3	26.6	50.9	14.8
Other transfer payments [1]		16.4	9.3	17.2	16.6	11.7	17.0	14.7	5.2	19.3
Private pensions, alimony, annuities		9.4	8.8	9.5	8.0	4.9	8.2	20.9	15.4	23.6
No income		0.3	3.3	—	0.1	2.0	—	1.8	5.5	—
Total income	mil. dol.	576,934	11,528	565,406	539,967	7,438	532,529	36,967	4,090	32,877
Mean income	dollars	11,106	2,211	12,098	11,739	2,268	12,466	6,213	2,115	8,186
White	dollars	11,495	2,084	12,308	11,986	2,132	12,641	6,773	1,970	8,375
Negro	dollars	7,442	2,531	9,479	8,726	2,825	10,045	4,526	2,307	7,178

Nonfarm self-employment	7.2	1.0	7.5	7.6	1.5	7.7	1.9	0.2	2.1
Farm self-employment	1.3	0.1	1.3	1.3	0.1	1.4	0.5	0.1	0.5
Income other than earnings . . .	11.4	50.5	10.6	10.0	41.2	9.6	31.6	67.4	27.2
Soc. Sec. and Government railroad retirement	3.3	18.7	3.0	2.9	21.9	2.6	9.8	12.8	9.4
Dividends, interest, and rent . .	3.7	2.1	3.7	3.6	2.8	3.6	4.9	0.8	5.4
Public assistance income . . .	0.9	21.7	0.4	0.4	9.8	0.2	7.9	43.3	3.5
Other transfer payments [1] . .	2.0	3.8	2.0	1.9	4.8	1.9	3.0	2.0	3.1
Private pensions, alimony, annuities	1.5	4.3	1.5	1.2	2.0	1.2	6.0	8.4	5.7

— Represents zero.

[1] Unemploy. and workmen's comp., gov. employee pensions, veterans' payments.

SOURCE: *Statistical Abstract of the United States, 1972* (Washington: U. S. Government Printing Office, 1972), Table 546.

D. Profile and Income of Legal Community

Table I-4: Lawyers—Selected Characteristics: 1954 to 1970

CHARACTERISTIC	1954	1957	1960	1963	1966	1970 Total	1970 In cities with population— Less than 200,000	1970 In cities with population— 200,000—499,999	1970 In cities with population— 500,000 or more
All lawyers[1]	241,514	262,320	285,933	296,069	316,856	355,242	172,030	41,075	142,137
Lawyers reporting[2]	221,600	235,783	252,385	268,782	289,404	324,818	159,291	37,411	128,116
In cities with population:[3]									
Less than 200,000	105,709	111,543	115,453	124,092	135,515	159,291	159,291	(X)	(X)
200,000–499,999	30,651	33,001	37,388	39,279	41,205	37,411	(X)	37,411	(X)
500,000 or more	85,240	91,239	99,544	105,411	112,684	128,116	(X)	(X)	128,116
Male	216,564	229,433	245,897	261,639	281,336	315,715	155,356	36,428	123,931
Female	5,036	6,350	6,488	7,143	8,068	9,103	3,935	983	4,185
Year of birth:									
1904 and earlier	83,582	76,479	69,017	60,346	52,026	42,454	22,050	4,545	15,859
1905–1914	58,526	59,491	59,327	58,055	56,378	52,956	25,524	5,557	21,875
1915–1924	54,793	60,235	62,704	63,566	63,944	63,077	32,784	7,565	22,728
1925–1934	19,100	36,225	57,082	70,692	76,651	79,679	39,276	9,518	30,885
1935 and later	19,100	36,225	1,891	14,345	38,559	85,980	39,403	10,126	36,451
Not reported	5,599	3,353	2,364	1,778	1,846	672	254	100	318
Education:									
Attended college	171,687	191,198	211,711	232,617	256,823	296,572	145,556	33,984	117,032
College degree	107,617	122,767	146,359	168,179	194,120	238,213	114,081	26,997	97,135
Attended law school	194,273	214,019	233,600	253,250	276,327	314,453	153,094	36,391	124,973

Federal	9,040	12,458	13,045	15,113	16,284	18,710	5,234	1,591	11,885
State	3,561	4,000	4,316	6,486	7,416	9,293	5,444	1,332	2,517
City or county	8,678	7,787	8,260	7,715	7,580	7,800	5,438	690	1,672
Judicial	7,903	7,910	8,180	8,748	9,712	10,349	7,392	997	1,960
Federal	621	769	599	707	800	878	363	145	370
State or county	5,041	5,056	5,301	5,712	6,823	7,548	5,672	660	1,216
City	2,241	2,085	2,280	2,329	2,089	1,923	1,357	192	374
Private practice	189,423	188,955	192,353	200,586	212,662	236,085	119,5C7	27,166	89,412
Individual	127,389	122,389	116,911	113,127	113,273	118,963	62,377	12,529	44,057
Partner	51,668	54,966	60,709	70,064	78,544	92,442	48,6S7	11,285	32,460
Associate [5]	10,366	11,600	14,733	17,395	20,845	24,680	8,433	3,352	12,895
Salaried	16,648	21,054	25,198	29,510	33,222	40,486	15,453	5,562	19,471
Private industry	15,063	18,911	22,533	26,492	29,405	33,593	12,372	4,806	16,415
Educational inst	1,351	1,504	1,798	2,100	2,717	3,732	2,092	435	1,205
Other private employ	234	639	867	918	1,100	3,161	989	321	1,851
Inactive or retired	6,581	7,661	10,887	12,024	14,881	16,812	11,353	1,502	3,957

X Not applicable.

[1]Includes lawyers not reporting and an adjustment (subtraction) for duplications.

[2]Includes duplications: 1954, 4,440; 1957, 4,506; 1960, 4,504; 1963, 5,918; 1966, 6,787; 1970, 8,834.

[3]1954–1957, 1950 Census of Population; 1960, 1960 Census of Population; 1963 and 1966 unofficial estimates, of *Editor & Publisher Yearbook;* and 1970, 1970 Census of Population.

[4]In some cases, if more than 1 subentry was applicable the individual was tabulated in each.

[5]Lawyers employed by individual practitioners or partnerships.

SOURCE: *Statistical Abstract of the United States,* 1972 (Washington: U. S. Government Printing Office, 1972), Table 258.

Table I-5: Law Firms—Selected Data: 1967
[Money figures in millions of dollars]

ITEM	All firms, total	FIRMS OPERATED ENTIRE YEAR, WITH RECEIPTS OF—			SELECTED STATES				
		Under $25,000	$25,000–$100,000	$100,000 and over	Calif.	Ill.	N.Y.	Pa.	Tex.
ALL FIRMS									
Number	143,069	88,032	42,893	10,811	13,416	8,458	23,040	6,600	7,016
Sole practitioners[1]	121,930	85,116	34,413	1,922	11,397	7,146	19,979	5,756	5,993
Partnerships[1]	21,139	2,916	8,482	8,887	2,019	1,312	3,061	844	1,023
Receipts	6,334	1,046	1,998	3,187	733	450	1,150	311	282
Sole practitioners[1]	2,853	1,009	1,490	335	323	183	450	140	128
Partnerships[1]	3,481	38	510	2,852	410	267	700	171	154
FIRMS WITH PAYROLL									
Number	69,891	29,195	28,875	10,785	6,637	3,838	9,728	3,231	3,446
Receipts	5,230	530	1,421	3,183	613	374	965	259	234
Payroll	1,172	162	266	722	143	85	245	58	50
Paid employees[2]	201,699	33,772	57,642	105,567	21,576	12,940	35,723	10,539	8,999
With 4 or more employees:									
Number	11,862	236	3,087	8,341	1,356	699	1,715	606	530
Receipts	3,114	4	203	2,856	390	238	662	169	135
Payroll	753	2	54	684	100	60	183	39	30
Paid employees . .	118,435	1,096	14,699	99,639	14,052	8,314	24,623	6,758	4,939

[1]Includes corporations.
[2]For week including March 12.

E. Dimensions of Civil Legal Assistance—1959, 1965 and 1971

Table I-6: Dimensions of Civil Legal Assistance—1959, 1965 and 1971

	1959[1]	1965[2]	1971[3]
TOTAL BUDGET	$2,084,125	$5,375,890	$77,272,710
SOURCE OF BUDGET:			
Government	143,031	*	60,848,725
Community Chest	1,148,245	2,469,373	3,767,262
Bar Association	264,032	891,823	2,275,412
Other	528,817	1,994,694	10,371,311
NUMBER OF LAWYERS	292	*	2,534
TOTAL CASES	447,096	426,457	1,237,275
TYPES OF CASES:			
Family	42%	*	36.6%
Economic	28%	*	15.9%
Housing	15%	*	14.4%
Administrative	*	*	11.2%
Other	15%	*	21.9%
DISPOSITION OF CASES:			
Referred	22%	*	17.0%
Advice Only	54%	*	42.0%
Litigated	6%	*	17.0%
Service without Court Action	13%	*	17.3%
Administrative	*	*	2.2%
Withdrawn	*	*	4.5%
Partial Service	5%	*	*

*Figures not available

SOURCES: 1. BROWNELL, LEGAL AID IN THE UNITED STATES, Supplement (Rochester: Lawyers Co-operative, 1961), pp. 37, 44, 47, 62.
2. 1966 SUMMARY OF PROCEEDINGS of the 44th ANNUAL CONFERENCE (Chicago: NLADA, 1966) pp. 46–47.
3. 1971 STATISTICS OF LEGAL ASSISTANCE WORK (Chicago: NLADA, 1972), pp. iv–v; 1–22.

Appendix II: Analysis of Clearinghouse Review

The following summary was compiled from the September 1967 through October 1972 issues of the *Clearinghouse Review* (with the exceptions of April, August, September, October, November, December, 1969; October and December, 1970; March, July and October, 1971). This publication reports the more significant test cases for which pleadings, memoranda or briefs have been received from Legal Services Agencies. All of these materials, along with thousands of other unreported items, are maintained in files at Northwestern Law School, ready for retrieval on request of any poverty lawyer confronted with an analogous problem.

The following summary is based on an analysis of the cases reported in the *Clearinghouse Review*. The analysis included an identification of the Legal Services agencies responsible for these legal actions and the number and types of such cases for each agency.

Statistical Summary

Total Number of Legal Services Agencies with Cases Reported in *Clearinghouse Review* 279
Total Number of Reported Cases in *Clearinghouse Review* 2,050
Agencies with 1–3 reported cases 152
Agencies with 4–10 reported cases 80
Agencies with 11–20 reported cases 24
Agencies with 21 or more reported cases 23

Types and Numbers of Cases Reported

Agriculture	5	Insurance	5
Bankruptcy	14	Juveniles	114
Civil Procedure	11	Legal Services	14
Civil Rights	18	Licenses	3
Consumer	159	Mental Health	29
Criminal	72	Migrants	57
Day Care	1	Military	5
Domestic Relations	14	Municipal Services	7
Drivers Licenses	22	Police Practices	19
Education	121	Prisons	54
Elderly	1	Public Utilities	36
Employment	98	Selective Service	3
Environment	30	Social Security	10
Federal Jurisdiction	5	Unemployment Compensation	46
Food Programs	52	Urban Renewal	2
Health	99	Voting	31
Housing	347	Welfare	430
In Forma Pauperis	46	Women's Rights	7
Indians	60	Workmen's Compensation	3

Notes

Chapter 1:   The Legal Aid Movement and the Goal of Equal Justice

1.   *Slade v. Valley National Bank, Glendale,* 93 S. Ct. Rptr. 445 (1972).
2.   MAGNA CARTA, cap. 40.
3.   Note, *The Right to Counsel in Civil Litigation,* 66 Columbia L. Rev. 1322–1324 (1966) See also Maguire, *Poverty and Civil Litigation,* 36 Harvard L. Rev. 361 (1922–1923).
4.   Statute of Henry VII, 1495, II Hen. VII, c.12.
5.   EDGERTON and GOODHART, LEGAL AID (Oxford: Oxford University Press, 1945) at pp. 7–9.
6.   English Legal Aid and Advice Act, 12 and 13 Geo. VI, Ch. 51.
7.   SMITH, JUSTICE AND THE POOR (New York: Carnegie Foundation, 1919) at p. 6. See also Silverstein, *Waiver of Court Costs and Appointment of Counsel for Poor Persons in Civil Cases,* 2 Valparaiso L. Rev. 21 (1967).
8.   *Id.* at p. 6.
9.   "We the people of the United States, in order to . . . establish justice, . . . and secure the blessings of liberty to ourselves and our posterity, do ordain and establish this Constitution for the United States of America." PREAMBLE, UNITED STATES CONSTITUTION, 1789.
10.   SIXTH AMENDMENT, UNITED STATES CONSTITUTION.
11.   A short-lived legal aid experiment was started in the District of Columbia and some Southern states during the early Reconstruction period by the Freedmen's Bureau. Beginning in late 1865, private attorneys in these jurisdictions were retained by the Bureau to represent destitute blacks in criminal and civil cases. For a fascinating account of legal aid under the Freedmen's Bureau, consult Westwood, *Getting Justice for the Freedman,* 16 Howard L. J. 492 (1971). This first legal aid program was aborted, and largely forgotten by the public with the demise of its parent, the Freedmen's Bureau, in 1868. *Id.* at p. 497.
12.   MAGUIRE, THE LANCE OF JUSTICE (Cambridge: Harvard University Press, 1928) at p. 18. This entire book is devoted to an account of the first 50 years (1876–1926) of the New York Legal Aid Society, an institution that evolved out of the German Legal Aid Society in 1890.
13.   SMITH, *op. cit., supra,* n. 7, at p. 134–135.

14. *Id.* at p. 135, 136.
15. *Id.* at p. 136.
16. *1962 Summary of Conference Proceedings,* NLADA, p. 13. In 1962 there were 143 Legal Aid facilities with paid staff and 93 offices with volunteer staffs. On the defender side there were a total of 110 organizations: 92 public, 11 private and seven private/public.
17. In fact, several books have been written on this subject. See, e.g., MAGUIRE, *op. cit., supra,* n. 12; BRADWAY and SMITH, GROWTH OF LEGAL AID WORK IN THE UNITED STATES (U.S. DEPT. of Labor, Bull. No. 607, 1936); BROWNELL, LEGAL AID IN THE UNITED STATES (Lawyers Coop. Publ. Co., 1951); SUPPLEMENT (1961).
18. SMITH, *op. cit., supra,* n. 7.
19. *Id.* at pp. 11, 12.
20. *Id.* at p. 147.
21. *Id.* at p. 152.
22. *Id.* at p. 192.
23. *Id.* at p. 152.
24. *Id.* at pp. 245–46.
25. *Id.* at p. 249.
26. *New York Times,* January 4, 1920.
27. Address, "The Relation between Legal Aid Work and the Administration of Justice" by Reginald Heber Smith, 45 ABA Reports 217, 226 (1920).
28. Smith, *Interest of the American Bar Association in Legal Aid Work,* 205 THE ANNALS 108, 109 (1939).
29. This action required an amendment to the ABA Constitution. It passed without debate. BRADWAY, THE WORK OF LEGAL AID COMMITTEES OF BAR ASSOCIATIONS (Baltimore: Lord Baltimore Press, 1938) at p. 13.

    Smith reports that Chief Justice Taft and former ABA President Elihu Root, the "dean of the American Bar," were prepared to give speeches supporting creation of a standing committee on legal aid. "Since the action was taken without debate, neither Mr. Taft nor Mr. Root spoke, and so legal aid literature was deprived of two statements that in all probability would have been classic." (Smith, *op. cit., supra,* n. 28, at p. 109.)
30. The National Association of Legal Aid Organizations (NALAO) was formed in Cleveland in 1923. The first informal national meeting of legal aid organizations actually took place ten years earlier in Pittsburgh. *Id.* at p. 108. In 1912, this informal group met in New York and formed a "National Alliance of Legal Aid Societies." The National Alliance met in 1914 and 1916 but discontinued during World War I, to be resurrected in 1923 as the NALAO. Bradway, *National Aspects of Legal Aid,* 205 THE ANNALS 101 (1939).
31. BROWNELL, *op. cit., supra,* n. 17, at p. 27.
32. *Id.* at p. 168. This represented a 140 percent increase from the $226,079 available at the beginning of the decade.
33. BROWNELL, *op. cit., supra,* n. 17, at p. 168.
34. *Id.* at p. 234. Nationally, the funds available to legal aid dropped from $596,941 in 1932 to $481,756 in 1933. *Id.* at p. 168.

35. *Id.* at p. 168.
36. *President's Annual Report,* National Legal Aid Association, 33rd Annual Conference, at p. 1 (October, 1955).
37. *Ibid.*
38. See BROWNELL, *op. cit., supra,* n. 17, at p. 29.
39. See, e.g., Marden, *Legal Aid, The Private Lawyer and the Community,* 20 Tenn. L. Rev. 757 (1949); BROWNELL, *op. cit., supra,* n. 17, at p. 29.
40. 12 and 13 George VI, Ch. 51.
41. The controversy surrounding the English plan is described at pp. 34–36, *infra.*
42. BROWNELL (1961 SUPPL.) *op. cit., supra,* n. 17, at p. 68. "The most dramatic fact to emerge from this review of the past decade is that there are now, at the end of it, nearly three times as many Legal Aid and Defender offices . . . as there were at the beginning." *Id.* at p. 10.
43. NLADA *Conf. Proc. op. cit., supra,* n. 16, at p. 13.
44. *Ibid.* The 1962 figure was $3,465,403.
45. Carlin and Howard, *Legal Representation and Class Justice,* 12 UCLA L. Rev. 381, 410 (1965).
46. Brownell reported average staff attorney salaries ranged between $5124 and $5958 in 1959, depending on the size of the society. In that same year, average salaries for staff directors ranged from $6091 to $9877. BROWNELL (1961 SUPPL.), *op. cit., supra,* n. 17, at p. 48.
47. In 1959, the caseload varied from 466 to 2533 per attorney. Brownell found an inverse correlation between the size of the caseload and the percentage of cases litigated. "On the average in 1959, staff lawyers in the offices which went to court in more than 6 percent of their cases, handled just over 900 cases a year. The caseload per attorney increased by nearly 40 percent in those offices in which the court work accounted for less than 6 percent but more than 3 percent of case closings, and by 70 percent when fewer than 3 percent of the cases were disposed of by court work." *Id.* at pp. 50–51.
48. CARLIN, HOWARD, and MESSINGER, CIVIL JUSTICE AND THE POOR (New York: Russell Sage Foundation, 1966) at p. 50.
49. SMITH, *op. cit., supra,* n. 7, at pp. 257, 261.
50. SMITH and BRADWAY, LEGAL AID WORK IN THE UNITED STATES (1926), Preface.
51. Speech to the Fifth Open Meeting on Legal Aid Work, Annual Convention, American Bar Association (September 29, 1941).
52. Vance, *The Historical Background of the Legal Aid Movement,* THE ANNALS (March, 1926).
53. BRADWAY, THE WORK OF LEGAL AID COMMITTEES OF BAR ASSOCIATIONS (1938), at p. viii.
54. Speech entitled "Legal Aid Societies, Their Function and Necessity," Annual Convention, American Bar Association (1920).
55. BROWNELL, *op. cit., supra,* n. 17, Foreword at p. iv (1951).
56. *Id.* at p. 257.
57. *Id.* at p. xiii.
58. A typical expression of this sentiment appears in JUSTICE AND THE POOR.

"It is not of chief importance whether the legal aid organizations win or lose their appeals; the prime consideration is that our common law system should have a fair chance to work itself out by having points . . . fairly argued, not from one, but from both points of view." SMITH, *op.cit., supra,* n. 7, at p. 207.

59. SMITH, *op.cit., supra,* n. 7, at pp. 13–14, 15.

60. BROWNELL, *op. cit., supra,* n. 17, at p. 158, quoting the Standards of the National Legal Aid and Defender Association enacted in 1948. Emphasis supplied.

61. *Id.* at p. 159.

62. See Chapter 8, especially pp. 196–224, for a discussion of the social-economic potential of various types of legal actions.

63. Interview with Junius Allison, former executive director of National Legal Aid and Defender Association, January, 1973.

64. Speech to Annual Legal Aid Conference, Baltimore, Maryland (1941).

65. BROWNELL, *op. cit., supra,* n. 17, at pp. 167–168.

66. See, Cappelletti and Gordley, *Legal Aid: Modern Themes and Variations,* 24 Stanford L. Rev. 347 (1972). See also, Pelletier, *English Legal Aid: The Successful Experiment in Judicare,* 40 U. Col. L. Rev. 10 (1967); and Pelletier, *Legal Aid in France,* 42 Notre Dame L. Rev. 627 (1967); MATTHEWS and OULTON, LEGAL AID AND ADVICE (London: Butterworths, 1971); Ginsburg, *The Availability of Legal Services to Poor People and People of Limited Means in Foreign Systems,* 6 Int'l Lawyer 128 (1972).

67. NLADA *Conf. Proc., op. cit., supra,* n. 16, at pp. 13–22.

68. SMITH, *op. cit., supra,* n. 7, at p. 176.

69. "The Fourth period, consisting of the last four years up to 1918, constitutes the most remarkable chapter in the entire history. . . . The most important fact in this last period is that the prevailing type of organization shifted to that of the publicly controlled, publicly supported bureau." *Id.* at p. 147, 148.

70. *Id.* at pp. 184–185.

71. *Id.* at pp. 246.

72. "There is no justification for saying that justice should be denied if a person cannot pay the price fixed. No one would claim that the only persons entitled to protection are those who are able to defray the cost of that protection by paying the judge and clerk their salaries, the jurors their fees, and by renting the courtroom. The cost of justice is variously estimated. In Massachusetts the expense to the state of a civil jury trial has been fixed at $248.89 per day. The Public Defender in Los Angeles has reported that the salaries, fees, and overhead expenses in a criminal jury trial amount to $200 per day. The daily cost of the Philadelphia Court of Common Pleas is about $150. The expense of a jury trial in the Chicago Municipal Court is not less than $75 per day. Any serious proposal to restrict the use of the courts to only such persons as could defray these expenses is inconceivable. Justice is not merchandise; it cannot be granted or withheld according to the purchasing power of the applicant. It is the affirmative duty of the state, at public expense, to do all that is needful to secure justice to everyone. In the main this is perfectly

recognized. The state does afford all that is necessary with the exception of the attorney. As this omission is fatal in certain cases, the argument concludes that the state must administer its justice better by supplying the attorney in such cases." *Id.* at p. 183.

73. Address, "The Relation of Legal Aid to the Municipality" by Ernest L. Tustin, 45 ABA Reports 236, 240 (1920).

Throughout his speech, Tustin emphasized the role of government sponsored legal aid in the acculturation process, closing with:

> The relief that the new bureau is bringing to hundreds of applicants is already establishing a bond of sympathy between the extreme poor, the foreigner and the city Government.
> We believe that there is no department of our great municipalities which will so work for the Americanization of the foreigner, the alleviation and quieting of the unrest among the poor and the ignorant, as a well-established municipal legal aid bureau. It is worth all the costs to have a place where the poor, the misunderstood and the ignorant can get their troubles out of their systems; a forum where they can consult someone in authority who will hear their woes, which to them are very great and very real, and where they may obtain sympathy, help and relief. [*Id.* at p. 246.]

74. Address, "Legal Aid Societies, Their Function and Necessity" by Charles E. Hughes, 45 ABA Reports 227, 232 (1920).

75. William Howard Taft, "Forward," *Legal Aid Work,* THE ANNALS, Vol. CXXIV, at p. iv (1926).

76. Norton, "The Problem of Financing Legal-Social Work," *Law and Social Welfare,* THE ANNALS, Vol. CXLV, part 1, at p. 146 (1929).

77. SMITH, *op. cit., supra,* n. 7, at p. 184, n. 1.

78. SMITH, *op. cit., supra,* n. 7, at p. 186.

79. See p. 10, *supra.*

80. BROWNELL, *op. cit., supra,* n. 17, at p. 97.

81. Lenvin, *Legal Aid: A Study of its Goals, Problems, and Relation to the War on Poverty* (An unpublished Senior Essay; Barnard College, 1966), at p. 31.

82. BROWNELL, *op. cit., supra,* n. 17, at p. 97.

83. Washington Rev. Stat. Tit. 2, para. 2.50 (1961), and Chap. 93, SESSION LAWS OF 1939. Summers was a member of the ABA's Standing Committee on Legal Aid at the time he drafted this statute. It was designed as the first step in the implementation of a proposal of the Standing Committee that state bar associations undertake to obtain public and private funds to operate comprehensive legal aid systems in their jurisdictions. Under the Committee recommendation, the public financing was to come from state and local, rather than Federal, government. "The county or city may grant money for legal aid, but the establishment and supervision of legal aid offices will be intrusted to the state bar, . . ." SMITH, *op. cit., supra,* n. 28, at p. 112.

84. *Report,* Legal Aid Committee of the Association of the Bar of the City of New York (1937) at p. 223.

85. *Id.* at p. 224.

86. Sec note 6, *supra*.
87. *Guild Report,* 10 Lawyers Guild Review 24 (1950).
88. The Lawyers' Guild itself was under constant attack during this period as an alleged communist front. In 1953, the Attorney General attempted unsuccessfully to list the Guild as a "subversive organization." Lenvin, *op. cit., supra,* n. 81, at p. 34.
89. Storey, *The Legal Profession Versus Regimentation: A Program to Counter Socialization,* 37 ABA Journal 100, 101, 103 (1951).
90. 78 ABA Reports 243 (1953).
91. Marden, *op. cit., supra,* n. 39, at p. 761.
92. 75 ABA Reports p. 93 (1950). The resolution of the ABA General Assembly adopted upon recommendation of the Resolutions Committee provided in pertinent part as follows:

> . . . WHEREAS, the legal profession will not be free and independent if it is dependent upon government handouts or subsidies; and WHEREAS, the existence of the National Legal Aid Association and the ever-increasing number of privately financed local legal aid societies throughout the country provide a solid basis of experience and organization for administering legal aid without government intervention; now therefore, be it RESOLVED (1) That it is the primary responsibility of the legal profession, . . . as an expression of its devotion to the ideal of equal justice for all, and in order to forestall the threat to individual freedom implicit in growing efforts to socialize the legal profession, to assume . . . the leadership in establishing and maintaining adequate organized legal aid facilities in all parts of the country. (2) That legal aid facilities should be established and maintained so far as possible as a privately supported community service and, in any event, without governmental control or influence over their operation. [*Assembly Proceedings,* 75 ABA Reports 93–95 (1950).]

This resolution, incidentally, was one of only four recommended for passage by the Resolutions Committee at the 1950 convention. The other three required establishment of a committee "to study communist tactics, strategy and objectives . . . as they relate to the obstruction of proper court procedure and law enforcement;" to encourage imposition of loyalty oaths on all present and future members of the bar; and, to urge Congress to pass the Internal Security Act of 1950. *Id.* at pp. 93–95. All were adopted by the General Assembly.

93. See pp. 238–39, *infra.*

Chapter 2: *The Neighborhood Lawyer Experiments and the Goal(s) of Equal Justice*

1. Interview with William Pincus, New York, New York, September, 1968. Further background on the Ford Foundation role can be gleaned from Pincus, *Programs to Supplement Law Offices for the Poor,* 41 Notre Dame Lawyer 887 (1966).

2. Interview with Edgar and Jean Cahn, San Juan, Puerto Rico, October 31, 1968.
3. *Ibid.*
4. *Ibid.*
5. *Ibid.*
6. Mobilization for Youth, Certificate of Incorporation, dated January 12, 1960.
7. Vera Foundation, *A Proposal to Set Up a Legal Unit for Mobilization for Youth,* dated May, 1968, at pp. 1–3.
8. *Id.* at pp. 2–3.
9. One of Mrs. Wickenden's early memoranda illustrates the underlying thesis of her position—that court action could and should be used to modify the structure of welfare assistance. In a six-page document dated February 25, 1963 and entitled, "Poverty and the Law: The Constitutional Rights of Assistance Recipients," she urges:

> Many critics of the contemporary social scene, including lawyers and others dedicated to the role of law in the democratic process, have recently expressed their concern over the mounting evidence that poverty itself constitutes a barrier to equal treatment under law. . . .
>
> Recently, however, a new concern has arisen among lawyers, social workers, and others interested in protecting the constitutional rights of all Americans regardless of their economic or social status. This is the standard of law enforcement to persons *because* of their poverty, especially if that poverty is reflected in dependence upon tax-supported benefits such as public assistance. . . .
>
> Nowhere is the role of the federal law in assuring equal access to federally-aided benefits more evident than in the category of Aid to Families with Dependent Children (AFDC) authorized by Title IV of the Social Security Act.. . . .
>
> Many efforts have been made by state legislatures to circumvent federal requirements for equal access to these benefits and federal interpretation of these requirements has itself developed somewhat greater precision as a consequence. For example, a law passed in Georgia in 1951 denying assistance to 'more than one illegitimate child of a mother' was ruled out of conformity with the provisions of the Social Security Act and the Federal Constitution on the grounds that denial of assistance to a child who met all the other eligibility requirements of the state solely because of the legal circumstances of his birth was discriminatory and constituted an "unreasonable classification". . . .

The memorandum then lists a series of potential legal issues in the welfare field and concludes:

> Welfare policies have rarely been challenged in the courts by individuals or groups who feel that their rights have been abridged. The very poverty of those who depend upon assistance makes this impractical and organizations have not interested themselves in this area to the same extent as in questions of racial or religious discrimination. Organizations interested in welfare policy have typically sought to exert their influence at the point of legislative or administrative decision rather than seeking court review of such policy.
>
> Nevertheless, the possibilities for legal remedy do exist in the appeals procedure and in the courts, both federal and state. This memorandum has been written [with the thought that it might encourage lawyers] and others interested in

assuring the protections of the Constitution to all groups in the population to consider these possibilities.

10. Memorandum to members of the Policy Committee, MFY Legal Services Unit, from Ed Sparer dated March 4, 1964, at p. 2.

11. *Id.* at p. 3.

12. *Ibid.*

13. Sparer, "Poverty Law and Social Welfare," unpublished memorandum dated January 11, 1964.

14. *Id.* at p. 12.

15. *Statement of Basic Policy for Supervisory Committee,* MFY Legal Services Unit, May 15, 1964.

16. Now a Federal District Court Judge.

17. Petition to Appellate Division of Supreme Court of New York First Judicial Department, at p. 3. Under a unique provision of the New York law, all corporations providing legal services, including those providing services to poor people, must receive specific authorization from the appellate courts and continue to operate under the supervision of those courts. Accordingly, the petition to the court and the court order authorizing practice by the corporation controlled the scope of activities and the circumstances under which the service could be provided.

18. There were three abstentions.

19. *Proposal* prepared by Community Progress, Inc., dated January 24, 1964, at pp. 2–3.

20. *Id.* at p. 3.

21. *Id.* at p. 4.

22. *Id.* at p. 8.

23. *Id.* at p. 40.

24. See p. 129, *infra,* for examples of the continued life of this concept.

25. See pp. 151–54, and 157–60, *infra,* for examples of situations where the issue of "social worker" control of Legal Services hung over deliberations about legal services.

26. Interview with Gary Bellow, Los Angeles, California, August, 1968.

27. See pp. 32–34, *infra,* for a discussion of the content of this law review article, and pp. 40–43, *infra,* for a discussion of the role this article played in the political evolution of the National Legal Services Program.

28. Proposal to Ford Foundation and HEW, from United Planning Organization, dated August 10, 1964.

29. Interview with Gary Bellow, Los Angeles, California, August, 1968.

30. Judicial Council committees can include persons other than Federal judges.

31. Undated letter to author from Howard C. Westwood, Esq., received in February, 1972.

32. Interview with Gary Bellow, Los Angeles, California, August, 1968.

33. Undated letter, *op. cit., supra,* n. 31.

34. Interview with Gary Bellow, Los Angeles, California, August, 1968.

35. See pp. 42–45, *infra.*

36. These included Westwood, who occupied the powerful position of chairman

of the Policy Committee; Alfred Scanlon of Shea & Gardner; Timothy Atkeson of Steptoe & Johnson; James Fitzpatrick of Arnold & Porter; and James Stoner.

37. These included William Bryant (the lawyer responsible for the landmark case of *Mallory* v. *United States,* 354 U.S. 449 (1957) who is now a Federal District Judge); Fred Evans of Thompson & Evans; and Shelley Bowers.

38. This criterion reflected the continuing influence of the 1964 New Haven proposal.

39. This criterion implemented the Wickenden-Sparer emphasis on structural change.

40. *Report of NLSP Policy Committee to Board of Directors,* dated December 10, 1964, at pp. 6–7.

41. *Id.* at pp. 7–11.

42. *Id.* at p. 13.

43. *Report of NLSP Policy Committee to Board of Directors,* dated January 4, 1965, at pp. 4–8.

44. *Id.* at pp. 8–9.

45. *Report of NLSP Policy Committee to Board of Directors,* dated December 10, 1964, at pp. 1–3.

46. *Report of NLSP Policy Committee to Board of Directors,* dated January 4, 1965, at p. 4.

47. The factors to be taken into consideration in deciding whether to represent a group were:

> (a) The size of the group. . . .
> (b) The relative poverty of the individual members of the group. . . .
> (c) The probable expense of representation in addition to the attorney's fee—court costs, supersedeas bonds, printing of briefs and other litigation expenses can dissipate quickly the funds accumulated by a group to pursue their interests in the courts. The more extensive the litigation contemplated by the group the more probable it will be that litigation expenses will absorb all or most of the funds which the group could be expected to contribute as a fee for a private attorney.
> (d) The time and effort required to provide adequate representation in the particular matter—the more complex and novel the legal and factual issues involved, the more time and effort will be required of an attorney representing the group and the less likely the group will be able to afford to pay a fee which will provide reasonable compensation to a private attorney.
> (e) The potential monetary recovery—some actions which a group of indigents might desire to pursue could involve a suit for damages, compensatory or punitive; others might contemplate only injunctive relief or a similar remedy which would not result in a substantial monetary gain to the litigants. As the probability of a substantial monetary recovery increases, private counsel will become more ready to accept the case without an advance fee or with a minimal advance fee because of a possibility of receiving a substantial contingent fee. [Staff study to NLSP Board of Directors, dated June 2, 1965, at pp. 1–3.]

Representation of groups, however, was at this stage a sufficiently delicate matter that the NLSP Board of Directors required all requests for service by groups of poor people to be submitted to the Board for a determination whether representation by NLSP lawyers was appropriate under the foregoing criteria.

48. Interview with Gary Bellow, Los Angeles, California, August, 1968.

49. See, *Proposal for NLSP Training Program*, submitted by Howard University Law School, dated December 15, 1964.

50. One of these memoranda was prepared by a second-year Georgetown Law student, Constance Pearson, and developed the theories upon which the constitutionality of residency statutes for receiving welfare could be challenged.

51. Even during the 18-month gestation period, the article, in its several draft forms, was an influential force in the history of the National Legal Services Program. See pp. 40–42, *infra.*

52. Cahn and Cahn, *The War on Poverty: A Civilian Perspective,* 73 Yale L. J. 1317 (1964).

53. *Id.* at pp. 1324–25.

54. *Id.* at pp. 1321–22.

55. *Id.* at pp. 1322, 1324, 1328.

56. *Id.* at p. 1322.

57. In describing the activities of their model neighborhood law office, the Cahns ranged far beyond the central thesis of *a civilian perspective.* The Cahns pointed out nine characteristics of a neighborhood law firm.

    1. The neighborhood law firm should be readily available to its potential clients. This meant that even a medium-sized city should have "several offices scattered throughout the target neighborhoods, each of which would be manned by a person trained to perform an initial interviewing, screening, and referral function." (*Id.* at p. 1350)

    2. A neighborhood law firm should counsel clients before they enter into leases or installment contracts which might bind them to unfair and unfavorable deals. (*Id.* at p. 1338)

    3. The neighborhood law firm should educate poor people about their rights under the law. As the Cahns saw it, neighborhood lawyers "must not only assert rights; . . . [they] must also create a widespread consciousness of such rights within the community." (*Id.* at p. 1338)

    4. Neighborhood law firms should assist in the formation and legal representation of associations and organizations of poor people. This could "include the incorporation of a block, neighborhood, or community organization; retained 'house counsel' to safeguard the interests of the community and to keep officials and private parties dealing with the community under continuous surveillence." (*Id.* at p. 1339)

    5. A neighborhood law firm should attempt to clarify the law where it is vague, uncertain or destructively complex and adversely affects the poor. (*Id.* at p. 1341)

    6. A neighborhood law firm should attempt to reform legal rules and administrative practices that appear susceptible to attack or that appear unconstitutional or invalid. (*Id.* at p. 1336)

    7. A neighborhood law firm should act as a voice for the poor in pressing

claims and righting grievances which appear, at first glance, to be nonlegal. The Cahns pointed out, quite correctly, that a lawyer's role is not limited to the courtroom.

> [T]he assumption that the problems which beset the poor are not "legal" is frequently based on an artificially narrow conception of "law" . . . . [T]he lawyer's function is essentially that of presenting a grievance so that those aspects of a complaint which entitle a person to a remedy can be communicated effectively and properly to a person who can provide a remedy. . . . [I]t is altogether possible that for many a remedy is available if the grievance is properly presented—even though the decision-maker may be a school board, principal, welfare review board, board of police commissioners, or urban renewal agency. (*Id.* at p. 1336)

8. A neighborhood law firm should draw in other specialists to treat the psychological and social problems of clients. Because visiting a lawyer does not carry the stigma of mental, physical or social weakness "lawyers are often presented with problems which call for the services of a psychiatrist, or family counselor or social worker, but which never would have been brought to such professionals voluntarily." (*Id.* at p. 1334)

9. Underlying all of its other functions, the neighborhood law firm should increase the economic and political power of its poverty neighborhood vis-à-vis the rest of the community. (*Id.* at pp. 1346, 1347, 1348, 1349)

Chapter 3: Birth of the Federal Program

1. The first explicit statutory mention of the OEO Legal Services Program appeared in the 1966 amendments to the Economic Opportunity Act. These amendments, enacted November 8, 1966 as Public Law 89–794, contained the following language.

> In carrying out sections 204 and 205 (the community action sections of the Act), the Director shall carry out programs . . . which provide legal advice and representation to persons when they are unable to afford the services of a private attorney, together with legal research, and information as appropriate to mobilize the assistance of lawyers or legal institutions, or combinations thereof, to further the cause of justice among persons living in poverty. . . . [Sec. 211–1 (b), Economic Opportunity Amendments of 1966, Public Law 89–794, November 8, 1966, 80 Stat. 1472]

Prior to the passage of the 1966 amendments, legal services grants were made pursuant to the general authority of the community action provisions of the Act. Congress expressly recognized that the original community action language was broad enough to encompass financial aid for legal assistance programs. As stated in the 1965 Senate Report:

> The listing of activities in section 205 (a), of course, is not intended to exclude other types of activities related to the purpose of community action programs, such as legal services for the poor. . . . In order to make this absolutely clear, the committee has also included an amendment (enacted in October, 1965) to this

section which would indicate that programs are to be conducted in fields including 'but not limited to' those which are specifically enumerated. [S. Rept. No. 599, 89th Cong., 1st Sess. at p. 9]

2. Actually a plan to undertake a coordinated drive against poverty was on the drawingboard during the Kennedy administration. However, it had not yet reached the stage of public exposure or specific legislative proposals. The history of the Kennedy plan is related in LUNDQUIST, POLITICS AND POLICY (Washington: Brookings Institution, 1968).

3. The development of the War on Poverty legislation is described in detail in LUNDQUIST, *op. cit., supra,* n. 2; MOYNIHAN, MAXIMUM FEASIBLE MISUNDERSTANDING (New York: Free Press, 1969); and, WEEKS, JOB CORPS: DOLLARS AND DROPOUTS (Boston: Little Brown and Co., 1967).

4. See pp. 14–19, *supra.*

5. See pp. 13–14, *supra.*

6. Interview with Edgar and Jean Cahn, San Juan, Puerto Rico, October 31, 1968.

7. Quoted in Cahn and Cahn, *The War on Poverty: A Civilian Perspective,* 73 Yale L. J. 1317, 1337 (1964).

8. Interview with Edgar and Jean Cahn, *op. cit., supra,* n. 6.

9. Interview with Gary Bellow, Los Angeles, California, August, 1968.

10. Interview with Gary Bellow, Los Angeles, California, August, 1968; interview with Edgar and Jean Cahn, San Juan, Puerto Rico, November 1, 1968.

11. *Ibid.*

12. Interview with Lowell Beck, Washington, D. C., August, 1968. Beck subsequently became executive director of Common Cause and is currently the deputy executive director of the ABA.

13. *Ibid.*

14. *Ibid.*

15. *Ibid.*

16. *Ibid.*

17. Memorandum to Richard Boone from Dr. Edgar Cahn, dated November 27, 1964.

18. The Boston program was not discussed in Chapter 2 because it, unlike the other HEW-Ford Foundation sponsored programs, was a traditional legal aid program operated through a pre-existing legal aid society and representing no new philosophy.

19. Interview with John Murphy, Washington, D.C., August, 1968.

20. *Ibid.*

21. Interview with William McCalpin, St. Louis, Missouri, June, 1968; interview with John Cummiskey, Grand Rapids, Michigan, August, 1968.

22. Interview with John Murphy, Washington, D.C., August, 1968.

23. *Ibid.*

24. U.S. Department of Health, Education and Welfare, *The Extension of Legal Services to the Poor,* November 12–14, 1964, at pp. 76–77 (hereafter HEW Report).

25. *Id.* at pp. 87–88. Notice the flavor of the 1964 CPI "social-legal" team proposal.
26. *Id.* at pp. 94, 95, 98.
27. Interview with John Murphy, Washington, D.C., August, 1968.
28. HEW Report, *op. cit., supra,* n. 24, at pp. 102–03.
29. *Id.* at p. 103.
30. *Ibid.*
31. Interview with Theodore Voorhees, Philadelphia, Pennsylvania, August, 1968.
32. *Ibid.*
33. *Resolution,* Executive Committee, National Legal Aid and Defender Association, December 16,1964.
34. Interview with John Cummiskey, Grand Rapids, Michigan, August, 1968.
35. Interview with William McCalpin, St. Louis, Missouri, June, 1968.
36. *Ibid.*
37. *Chicago Daily News,* November 18, 1964.
38. *Ibid.*
39. *Ibid.*
40. Interview with Lewis Powell, Richmond, Virginia, March, 1969.
41. Memorandum to Messrs. Powell, Early from Don Hyndman, November 19, 1964 (underlining and numbering of points by Lewis Powell).
42. Interview with William McCalpin, St. Louis, Missouri, June, 1968.
43. Interview with William McCalpin, St. Louis, Missouri, June, 1968; interview with John Cummiskey, Grand Rapids, Michigan, August, 1968; interview with Bert Early, Chicago, Illinois, August, 1968.
44. Interview with Edgar and Jean Cahn, San Juan, Puerto Rico, November 1, 1968.
45. *Ibid.*
46. Interview with John Cummiskey, Chicago, Illinois, February, 1969.
47. Interview with Edgar and Jean Cahn, San Juan, Puerto Rico, November 1, 1968.
48. Interview with John Cummiskey, Grand Rapids, Michigan, August, 1968; interview with William McCalpin, St. Louis, Missouri, June, 1968.
49. Interview with Edgar and Jean Cahn, San Juan, Puerto Rico, November 1, 1968.
50. Interview with John Cummiskey, Grand Rapids, Michigan, August, 1968; interview with William McCalpin, St. Louis, Missouri, June, 1968.
51. Interview with Edgar and Jean Cahn, San Juan, Puerto Rico, November 1, 1968; "A rather lengthy conversation [at the December 28 meeting] convinced me that it was necessary that our plans . . . build upon cooperation and coordination with legal groups already working in this field." *Status Report,* from Jean Camper Cahn to Dick Boone, dated January 29, 1965.
52. *Staff Report, Meeting Between Representatives of the American Bar Association and the U.S. Office of Economic Opportunity,* December 28, 1964.
53. See pp. 138–40, *infra,* for discussion of "National Emphasis" programs and their place in the War on Poverty.

54. See pp. 32–33, *supra.*
55. As late as November 27, 1964, Edgar Cahn conceded he had only a tenuous commitment from Shriver for "greater OEO involvement and activity in the area of legal services for the poor." Memorandum to Richard Boone from Dr. Edgar Cahn, dated November 27, 1964.
56. Memorandum to ABA Standing Committee on Lawyer Referral, from William McCalpin, December 29, 1964, at p. 2.
57. *Ibid.*
58. Speech of Lewis Powell, ABA House of Delegates, New York City, August 14, 1964, at p. 17.
59. *Id.* at pp. 18–19.
60. *Id.* at p. 19.
61. Interview with William McCalpin, St. Louis, Missouri, June, 1968.
62. *Brotherhood of Railroad Trainmen* v. *Virginia ex rel. Virginia State Bar,* 377 U.S. 1 (1964).
63. Interview with Lewis Powell, Richmond, Virginia, March, 1969.
64. Interview with William McCalpin, St. Louis, Missouri, June, 1968.
65. For an excellent book-length treatment of the American Medical Association's anti-Medicare campaign, see HARRIS, A SACRED TRUST (New York: The New American Library, 1966).
66. *Id.* at p. 46.
67. Interview with Lewis Powell, Richmond, Virginia, March, 1969.
68. *Ibid.*
69. Interview with Edgar and Jean Cahn, San Juan, Puerto Rico, October 31, 1968.
70. *Ibid.*
71. Letter to Bert Early from Lewis Powell, dated January 24, 1965.
72. *Ibid.*
73. Interview with Lewis Powell, Richmond, Virginia, March, 1969; interview with John Cummiskey, Grand Rapids, Michigan, August, 1968; interview with William McCalpin, St. Louis, Missouri, June, 1968.
74. Interview with Edgar and Jean Cahn, San Juan, Puerto Rico, November 1, 1968. The Cahns were so confident they already had prepared a congratulatory telegram for Shriver's signature thanking the ABA for its endorsement of the Legal Services Program. In a January 29, 1965, memo Jean Cahn recommended that CAP "[h]ave Mr. Shriver to agree to issue a congratulatory telegram on February 8 in response to the ABA resolution of February 7." (To make this seem less set up Al Friendly, Managing Editor of the Washington Post, is being asked down to New Orleans to cover the Conference so it will be no problem in having the necessary information to send such a telegram without giving a clue to any of the inside politicking that produced the results.)
75. Memorandum, "Procedure for Expansion of Legal Services Resolution" (undated).
76. Interview with John Cummiskey, Grand Rapids, Michigan, August, 1968.
77. Remarks of William McCalpin to Special Meeting of Committee and Section Chairmen at New Orleans, Louisiana, February 7, 1965.

78. Interview with John Cummiskey, Grand Rapids, Michigan, June, 1968; interview with Lewis Powell, Richmond, Virginia, March, 1969.
79. Interview with John Cummiskey, Grand Rapids, Michigan, August, 1968.
80. Interview with Lewis Powell, Richmond, Virginia, March, 1969.
81. See pp. 137–38, *infra*, for a description of the OEO administrative structure.
82. See pp. 22–23, *supra*, for a description of Mrs. Cahn's experience with the Community Action Agency in New Haven.
83. Interview with Edgar and Jean Cahn, San Juan, Puerto Rico, October 31, 1968.
84. Interview with Edgar and Jean Cahn, San Juan, Puerto Rico, October 31, 1968. As some indication of how sudden and unexpected this resignation was, the author, at that time deputy director of Neighborhood Legal Services in Washington, D.C., was scheduled to meet with Mrs. Cahn about a proposed training grant for NLSP lawyers in the early morning of April 1, 1965. Upon arrival I was advised by her small staff that as of that date Mrs. Cahn was no longer at OEO.
85. Interview with Lowell Beck, Washington, D.C., August, 1968.
86. Mr. Downs later became the deputy regional director for all OEO programs in the Great Lakes region.
87. In 1966 Terris left OEO for the President's National Crime Commission and subsequently became a private attorney and chairman of the Democratic Party in the District of Columbia.
88. Rauh is the son of labor lawyer and Democratic Party leader Joseph Rauh.
89. Interview with Bruce Terris, Washington, D.C., August, 1968.
90. Interview with William McCalpin, St. Louis, Missouri, June, 1968.
91. Interview with John Cummiskey, Grand Rapids, Michigan, August, 1968.
92. Interview with Bruce Terris, Washington, D.C., August 1968.
93. Interview with Lewis Powell, Richmond, Virginia, June 1969.
94. Westwood, a senior partner in Washington's largest law firm, will be remembered as one of the major figures in the development of the Washington, D.C., Neighborhood Law Office Program. See pp. 28–29, *supra*.
95. Letter from Howard Westwood to Lewis Powell, dated July 28, 1965.
96. Address by Sargent Shriver to the Conference of Bar Presidents, ABA Annual Meeting, Miami, Florida, August 1965.
97. Letter from Howard Westwood to author, dated January 13, 1972.
98. Interview with E. Clinton Bamberger, Jr., Baltimore, Maryland, December, 1968.
99. Letter to Lewis Powell from Howard Westwood, dated August 20, 1965.
100. A few years later, Shestack was one of the founders of a new initiative in the American Bar Association, the Section on Individual Rights and Responsibilities and in 1969 and 1970 served as chairman of that Section.
101. Interview with Jerome Shestack, Philadelphia, Pennsylvania, August, 1968.
102. Interview with E. Clinton Bamberger, Jr., Baltimore, Maryland, December, 1968.
103. See Chapter 5, *infra*.

Chapter 4: Development of Legal Services Organizations

1. See Chapter 5, *infra.*
2. Interview with E. Clinton Bamberger, Jr., Baltimore, Maryland, December, 1968.
3. *Ibid.*
4. Edson was bright, hard-working, and an uncontrollable punster. His concentrated energy expressed itself through constant pacing, darting in and out of offices, and general fretting. He soon acquired the office nickname of "Fidget," but his drive was to stand him in good stead when he became chief of operations for the Legal Services Program a year later. (Edson now is a partner in a Washington law firm specializing in housing and urban development.)
5. Known to Bamberger as an easy-going, "nice guy," Hettleman became the toughest and probably the most effective negotiator on the entire staff. (When Hettleman left in mid-1966, he became chief-of-staff to the Baltimore mayor.)
6. Mrs. Long was a Depression baby named after one of FDR's New Deal programs, the National Industrial Recovery Administration. (When she left the Legal Services staff two and one-half years later, she was made the Civil Rights Coordinator for AID.)
7. Mrs. Fisher's manner caused every bar association lawyer she met to assume that she was a member of the legal profession. (Upon leaving the Legal Services staff, Mrs. Fisher entered law school and is now a lawyer in California.)
8. Miss Yanow (now Mrs. Earl Johnson, Jr.) was the most experienced political hand on the staff. Her one-month assignment ended more than two years later. (She subsequently became a Legal Services lawyer in California and now works for a U.S. Senator.)
9. Mrs. Chayes remained on the Legal Services staff until her death in February, 1973. At that time she was the only original staff member still working at OEO's Office of Legal Services.
10. Greenawalt is now a partner in a Wall Street law firm.
11. Stocks later succeeded me as deputy director of the Legal Services Program and subsequently became director of the National Bar Foundation.
12. McGee is now a law professor at UCLA.
13. Mitchell was the only one of the entire staff other than myself who had been involved previously in providing legal services to the poor. (Mitchell is now director of the Legal Services Program in the Trust Territories of the South Pacific.)
14. Cordell appeared to possess the right mixture of Southern accent, Southern sympathies and egalitarian commitment necessary to handle the old South. In order to erase any latent feelings of racial superiority we brought Cordell to Washington and assigned him to work on a detailed, technical research and writing job with one of the brightest young blacks in OEO, a woman with a Ph.D. from one of the Ivy League schools. (Cordell has returned to private practice.)

15. Barvick turned out to be a born administrator, and the patient, firm negotiator that the complacent Great Plains lawyers required. (Barvick is now a law professor at the University of South Carolina.)

16. A former Justice Department attorney who had supervised Wilson rebuked us, "That man is going to be the first Negro member of the U. S. Tax Court if you leave him where he is." (Wilson later became vice president of a predominantly black college in Mississippi.)

17. See pp. 116–17, *infra.*

18. See Chapter 6, *infra,* for a discussion of relations between the Legal Services Program and the remainder of the OEO administration.

19. Memorandum from "Earl" to "Clint," entitled "Some Priorities for Fiscal 1966" dated November 10, 1965. The full text of the memorandum follows:

> I suggest that we should have some fairly well defined priorities—in terms of types of programs, geographic areas, kinds of communities, etc.—which we want to see funded during this fiscal year. This means, as I see it, that in addition to general promotional efforts designed to stir up interest in all communities to begin thinking about legal services programs, we should address special effort to encourage the development of certain programs. This will allow us to focus our own efforts and those of the supporting organizations such as ABA, NLADA and Young Lawyers' Committee.
>
> It should lead to earlier development and funding of these programs. If we can get a number of *successful* programs operative, programs embodying different features and in different areas of the country, we can use these to sell both the organized bar and OEO on further expansion.
>
> I think we might usefully consider the following priorities for our promotional effort during fiscal 1966.
>
> 1. I would favor concentrating on urban areas during fiscal 1966 with only such effort devoted to promotion in rural areas and with migrant groups as would be necessary to start a few scattered experimental programs. For one thing, the rural areas will be much harder to reach. Moreover, our notions as to what kind of legal program is worth funding in rural areas are not sufficiently developed to warrant investment of much money in these areas.
>
> 2. I think we should attempt to fund programs in all of the top 10 cities (population) during fiscal 1966.
>
> 3. With regard to urban areas not within the top 10, I think we should concentrate promotional effort on those which have evidenced substantial interest in developing meaningful programs.
>
> 4. I think we should make sure that among the *urban* programs developed, each of the following features are embodied in one or another of the programs:
>
>   a. Some organized on a neighborhood basis.
>
>   b. Some at least partially based on "manning" the points in the system where the poor come in contact with the law, i.e., landlord-tenant court, welfare board hearing, etc.
>
>   c. Some with a separate "trial and appeal" staff which handles only the trial and appeal cases which have broad legal significance with other lawyers handling all the "routine" cases.
>
>   d. Some with neighborhood offices manned with skeleton staff which handles only simple matters and refers to large central staff all cases entailing litigation or substantial representation of another sort.

e. Some with at least a portion of the city represented on the basis of referrals to private counsel compensated out of a fund (like Durham plan).

5. I think that among the few rural programs we do fund, there should be at least one which embodies each of the following features:

a. Lawyer "rides circuit" from community center to community center, with regular office hours at each place.

b. Lawyer makes "home calls" or "farm calls" on basis of requests telephoned to his centrally located office.

c. Lawyer has "lawyermobile" in which he holds office hours on a regular schedule at different ports in the countryside.

d. The lawyer has a central stationary office in the major town in the trading area but maintains office hours during evenings and on Saturdays and Sundays when rural poor can feasibly come to town to see him. This might be quite feasible in a fairly substantial town (10,000–25,000) which serves a large surrounding rural area. The farmers and their hands come to town regularly on Saturdays to buy groceries, etc., and could visit the lawyer at the same time.

6. I think we should attempt to get many of the supportive research and publication programs promoted and funded this year since this should lead to an upgrading of the services provided by all legal service organizations, including otherwise unimproved and unexpanded traditional legal aid societies.

The foregoing are merely some offhand thoughts on priorities. Certainly, we could and should refine, modify, and add to the list. The essential point is that unless we define our priorities somewhat, there is a substantial danger that we will spread our own efforts and the available funds too thin.

20. See pp. 48–49, *supra.*

21. See pp. 45–47, *supra,* for a report of the HEW conference which revealed the low regard of neighborhood lawyers for existing legal aid staff members.

22. Address, NLADA Annual Meeting by E. Clinton Bamberger, Jr., *1965 Summary of Proceedings of the 43rd Annual Conference* (November 16–19, 1965) at pp. 17–22.

23. 1965 NLADA *Conference Proceedings, id.* at pp. 39–41 (November, 1965).

24. Address, NLADA Annual Meeting, by Earl Johnson, Jr., *id.,* at pp. 29–34.

25. *Id.* at pp. 45–46.

26. *Proceedings,* National Conference of Bar Presidents, February 19–20, 1966, at pp. 25–26.

27. Theodore Voorhees, Address to Toledo Bar Association, Toledo, Ohio (April, 1966).

28. Interview with Junius Allison, Chicago, Illinois, July 1968.

29. See Chapters 6 and 7 for discussion of the causes and consequences of OEO's predisposition and the Legal Services Program's resolution of the local control-national standards issue.

30. See pp. 108–12, *infra.*

31. See pp. 117–21, *infra,* for a discussion of the development of national policy on this issue.

32. See pp. 112–13, *infra,* for discussion of the attempt to impose a national means test on all Legal Services agencies.

33. See p. 107, *infra*, for a discussion of OEO policy on this issue.
34. See p. 107, *infra*, concerning the national policy on this issue.
35. See pp. 140–48, *infra*.
36. For discussion of ABA role in policy making, see pp. 106–16, *infra*.
37. See pp. 123–24, *infra*, for discussion of the major issues involved in this controversy.
38. For detailed appraisal of state and local bar associations, see Pye and Garraty, *The Involvement of the Bar in the War Against Poverty*, 41 Notre Dame Lawyer 860 (1966).
39. Some aspects of this controversy are described in an article by a former director of the Winston-Salem Legal Services Program. "Although seldom articulated by some members of the bar with any specificity, laymen on the governing boards of legal aid programs was regarded as the unauthorized practice of law." Moize, *OEO's Legal Services Programs In North Carolina: Ethical and Allied Considerations*, 4 Wake Forest Intramural L. Rev. 194, 196 (1968).
40. "At a meeting of representatives of OEO, the Legal Aid Society of Forsythe County and the Council of the North Carolina State Bar in March, 1967, a compromise in the form of New Articles of Association for the Legal Aid Society of Forsythe County was approved. . . . [T]he Forsythe Plan was specifically approved as a model for legal services to be funded by OEO in North Carolina." *Id.* at pp. 197–198. The author was present at this meeting and monitored the negotiations throughout. Much of the account of this dispute is based on personal recollection.
41. Since the downtown office was soon stocked with the best young lawyers in the Program, this was not much of a concession.
42. 42 U.S.C. §2834.
43. *Stanislaus County Bar Association v. California Rural Legal Assistance, Inc.* (Cal. Super. Ct., Stanislaus Cty., No. 93302, Jan. 1, 1967) 2 Poverty Law Reporter, para. 8100.05.
44. *Troutman v. Shriver*, 273 F. Supp. 415 (M.D. Fla. 1967).
45. *In re Community Legal Assistance, Inc., Application for Charter* (Pa. Ct. of Common Pleas, C.P. No. 4, No. 4968, June 30, 1966), The Legal Intelligencer (Phil.), Vol. 155, No. 1.
46. *Touchy v. Houston Legal Foundation*, 417 S.W. 2d 625 (Tex. Civ. App., 1967).
47. *Harrison v. United Planning Organization* (D.D.C., Civ. No. 2282–65, Dec. 21, 1965).
48. *Troutman v. Shriver*, 417 F. 2d 171, 172 (5th Cir., 1969).
49. *Harrison, op. cit., supra*, n. 47.
50. *Stanislaus County Bar, op. cit., supra*, n. 43.
51. *Touchy, op. cit., supra*, n. 46, affirming dismissal by 165th Judicial Court of Harris County, Texas. This dismissal was reversed and the case reinstated for trial by the Texas Supreme Court, 432 S. W. 2d 690 (1968). At the trial, the judge withdrew the case from the jury and entered judgment for the Legal Services Program. This decision was sustained on appeal, thus apparently concluding almost five years of litigation against the Houston Legal Founda-

tion. *Scruggs* v. *Houston Legal Foundation,* 475 S. W. 2d 604 (Tex. Ct. App., 1972).

52. This holding was sustained on appeal in *Troutman* v. *Shriver,* 417 F. 2d 171 (5th Cir., 1969).

53. *In re Community Legal Assistance, op. cit., supra,* n. 45. This decision was upheld on appeal. *Community Legal Services, Inc.,* 43 D. and C. 2d 51 (1967).

54. N.Y. Judiciary Law §495 (McKinney, 1968) bars the practice of law by corporations and voluntary associations. An exception is made, however, for "organizations organized for benevolent or charitable purposes, or for the purpose of assisting persons without means in the pursuit of any civil remedy, whose existence, organization or incorporation may be approved by the Appellate Division." See Botein, *The Constitutionality of Restrictions on Poverty Law Firms: A New York Case Study,* 46 New York L. Rev. 748 (1971).

55. *In Matter of Community Action for Legal Service, Inc.,* 26 App. Div. 2d 354, 362, 274 N. Y. S. 2d 779, 788: "All the proposals are deficient . . . in not prohibiting entirely and without evasive qualification political lobbying, and propagandistic activity."

56. *Id.* at pp. 354–363, 274 N. Y. S. 2d at p. 779, 789.

57. Order, *Matter of Community Action for Legal Services, Inc.* (App. Div. 1st Dept.). However, two years later in 1970 the court imposed some relatively stringent rules on group representation and lobbying. Botein, *op. cit., supra,* n. 54, at p. 749. These rules were challenged in *Young Lords* v. *Superior Court,* 328 F. Supp. 66 (S.D.N.Y., 1971).

58. The essential ingredients for the Florida migrant settlement were:
(1) Several counties were eliminated from coverage (although 80 percent of the original client community was located in the remaining six counties).
(2) The funds were transferred from the original grantee headquartered in Tampa to a new entity spun off by the Miami Legal Services agency.
(3) The local bars were given substantial representation on the board of this new organization. (However, this representation fell short of the majority control sought by these associations.)

59. See pp. 146–49, *infra.*

60. *Resolution,* Board of Governors, Tennessee Bar Association, April 30, 1966.

61. See pp. 122–23, *infra.*

62. See pp. 89–90, *supra.*

63. Memorandum from Earl Johnson, Jr., to Clint Bamberger dated April 1, 1966, regarding "Al Cohn's presentation at University of Florida Law School reunion."

64. See pp. 17–19, *supra,* for earlier bar opposition to "Judicare" type programs.

65. See note 1, Chapter 3, *supra,* for full excerpt from the 1965 Senate Report which stated that the original community action title authorized Federal grants for programs of "legal services for the poor."

66. See p. 92, *supra.*

67. ". . . WHEREAS, The Tennessee Bar Association believes that new and expanded legal aid programs and organizations can be developed, consistent with the rules

and programs formulated by the OEO and within the traditional high ethical standards of the bar of Tennessee; . . .

NOW, THEREFORE, BE IT RESOLVED, that the Board of Governors of the Tennessee Bar Association hereby endorses and supports the Legal Services Program of the Office of Economic Opportunity . . .

BE IT FURTHER RESOLVED: . . . That each local bar association is urged to take action . . . for the establishment of new or expanded legal aid programs . . . within the framework of the provisions of the Economic Opportunity Act of 1964. . . .

[T]hat the policy of this Association as enunciated by a resolution adopted by its Board of Governors on April 30, 1966, be and the same is hereby rescinded, and that the principles expressed in this resolution be hereafter considered as the policy of this association. [*Resolution,* Board of Governors, Tennessee Bar Association, November 11, 1966, published in Tennessee Lawyer, Vol. 15, No. 4, at pp. 2–3.]

68. By June 30, 1967, Miami, Jacksonville, Tampa, Daytona Beach, Gainesville, and Fort Pierce had received grants.

69. See p. 90, *supra.*

70. The text of the resolution reads in pertinent part as follows:

WHEREAS the legal profession has long been conscious of the need to aid those who cannot afford the cost of securing adequate legal representation;

And WHEREAS, despite the efforts of existing legal aid programs, large numbers of Americans have not had such representation;

And WHEREAS equal justice under the law requires that all citizens be entitled to adequate legal counsel;

And WHEREAS the American Trial Lawyers Association and its 25,000 members constitute a large part of the lawyers of America now engaged in serving the needs of the poor and upon whose professional resources any meaningful program of legal services to the poor must necessarily draw;

And WHEREAS the American Trial Lawyers Association believes that legal services can be extended to the poor without interrupting or destroying the essential client-attorney relationship;

And WHEREAS the American Trial Lawyers Association is aware of the many Federal programs that are now rapidly expanding into the field of legal services, and that it is the responsibility and duty of the American Trial Lawyers Association as rapidly as possible to aid in the development and implementation of such programs in cooperation with the Legal Services Programs of the U. S. Office of Economic Opportunity;

And WHEREAS the American Trial Lawyers Association is concerned that the formulating and carrying out of a program for the extension of legal services to the poor, preserves important traditional rights and values of the people, including, among others:

A.   that the private, privileged nature of communications between a citizen and his attorney be preserved;

B.   that the attorneys representing citizens, whether poor or rich, maintain independence from government influence or control;

C.   that the quality of legal service provided for the poor not be inferior, but of high quality;

D.   that any system of referral of lawyers be a fair and impartial one;

E.   that, so far as possible, each client have an opportunity freely to select the attorney of his choice and the attorney, in turn, freely select his client;

F.   that the programs instituted allow for as much flexibility as possible so that each is designed to respect and meet peculiar needs of local areas;

G.   that a fair system be devised under which all attorneys will participate and not place the burden on just a few, both as to legal referral systems and as to the direction of the programs in local communities;

H.   that the programs shall not apply to cases where "fees" for legal services can be provided through private sources, whether because they generate fees as in contingent fee cases, or where a fee is provided by statute or administrative rule or otherwise;

And WHEREAS the office of the Legal Services of the Office of Economic Opportunity of the United States Government indicated a desire to have the American Trial Lawyers Association represented on National Advisory Committee to the Legal Services Program so as to bring the experience and talent of our membership to bear in the formulation of policy;

Now, BE IT RESOLVED that the Board of Governors of the American Trial Lawyers Association hereby establishes a permanent Committee on Legal Services to the Indigent, empowered to carry out the intent of this resolution, with proper staff and financial aid, and empowered to cooperate with the OEO Legal Services Programs, arrange for representation on its National Advisory Board, and to provide for cooperation and participation by the American Trial Lawyers Association, and its local affiliates, in the implementation of local programs so as to provide the benefits of such programs throughout the nation.

71.   Interview with Lowell Beck, Washington, D.C., dated August, 1968.

72.   Birmingham, Alabama, was one of the few new agencies funded in 1968.

73.   *Analysis of Fiscal Year 1966 Grantees* (unpublished) prepared by OEO Legal Services Staff (August, 1966). Some of these statistics were presented to the House Committee. See Economic Opportunity Act Amendment of 1967, *Hearings,* Committee on Education and Labor, U.S. House of Representatives, Ninetieth Congress, First Session (June 20, 1967), Pt. 2, at p. 914.

74.   Economic Opportunity Act Amendments of 1967, *Hearings, op. cit., supra,* n. 73, at p. 1002.

75.   *Analysis, op.cit., supra,* n. 73.

76.   Obviously, if the planning and processing of grants were programmed over several years, OEO would be in a far better position to work out details of agency structure and design that must be ignored or disregarded in the hurried pace of mass-production grant-making. Even more important, with the luxury of time Legal Services staff could stimulate competing applicant groups from the same community. This, in turn, would make possible selection of sponsors and design features best calculated to implement the full mission of the OEO Program in each community.

For an analysis concluding that quality of local grantees is determined primarily by the aspirations and philosophy of the sponsoring group, see Finman, OEO *Legal Services Programs and the Pursuit of Social Change: The Relationship Between Program Ideology and Program Performance,* 1971 Wisc. L. Rev. 1001.

77. *Analysis, op. cit., supra,* n. 73.

78. Two situations accounted for most of the nonlegal aid fundings. In many areas, especially the sparsely settled region, no charitably financed organization existed. Here there was obviously no choice. But in a surprising number of major urban centers, the local bar or Community Action Agency shunned an old-line society in favor of alternative institutions. Washington, D.C., Philadelphia, San Francisco, New Orleans, Miami, Seattle, Boston and Detroit all founded brand new legal assistance agencies, most with local bar support. In Los Angeles and New York both existing societies and competing organizations received grants.

Ironically, the bypassed legal aid societies were some of the largest, most influential elements in the legal aid movement. However, they also were located in large cities plagued by huge concentrations of poverty. This meant OEO could afford to allocate more time to foster high quality sponsors for these grants. In some cases, the Legal Services staff actually made it clear the existing legal aid society was not an acceptable entity for Federal funding. But there were more important factors operating in some of these large cities than the active role played by OEO. Political complexities, large minority communities, and the relative sophistication of the bar associations combined to create intense pressure favoring revised institutional arrangements. Bar leaders themselves frequently recognized the limitations of board and staff personnel in the existing legal aid society. They perceived it an easier task to · participate in the construction of a substitute agency than to displace the present administration. Thus, even though new legal assistance organizations were created in the majority of our largest population centers, in most of these cities the establishment bar continued to be a significant if not dominant influence in these operations.

79. For example, in 1967 when Senator Murphy sought to prohibit Legal Services suits against government agencies, scores of state and local bar associations joined with the ABA to resist this incursion. In an especially helpful action, the law partners of a crucial California congressman turned him around on the issue. Significantly, those lawyers were board members in a below-par legal aid society.

80. Without the help of the ABA intra-bureaucratic lobbying, it is probable that the Legal Services budget would have suffered along with the rest of OEO. It was one of the few program areas within OEO to maintain its 1967 level after the total agency appropriation stagnated.

One commentator argues that the ABA intervention was counterproductive in budget negotiations. This position is premised on the fact that the organized bar never received all it asked. Pious, *Policy and Public Administration: The Legal Services Program in the War on Poverty,* 2 Politics and Society 376 (1971). In the face of OEO's dire financial situation, it would have been extraordinary if the agency leaders had granted the doubling of the Legal Services Program which was sought by the ABA. The only way to comply would have been to terminate grantees in other program areas with the consequent firing of thousands of grantee personnel. Nevertheless, OEO consistently raised the Legal Services budget to keep pace with increased costs even though most other programs were absorbing significant cuts. In fiscal 1968, in particular, vigorous ABA lobbying pressured the Agency to raise its allocation for legal services from $33 million to $38 million (plus $4 million for research, training and experimental grants).

81. See, e.g., Finman, *op. cit., supra,* n. 76 and Pious, *op.cit., supra,* n. 80.

82. This survey of evaluators covered over 100 Legal Services grantees. Twenty-three percent of the evaluated programs were governed by boards that were classified as "Supports law reform and/or other controversial actions"; 48 percent fit the category "Indifferent to law reform and/or other controversial actions"; and 29 percent were "Against law reform and/or other controversial actions." This finding is based on questionnaires completed at the request of the author by more than 20 of the most experienced legal services evaluators. The questionnaires report the evaluators' appraisals of 110 separate Legal Services Agencies during the period 1967–69. A basic compilation of these questionnaires and several correlations of various factors are maintained in files at the University of Southern California Law Center and the Russell Sage Foundation.

83. Even if the Legal Services staff were so disposed and possessed sufficient time to closely examine motives and where necessary to negotiate for substitute sponsors in local communities, the prior experiments had not provided anything approaching a specific formula. What could be imposed on local applicants beyond a vague commitment to do something about poverty, a guarantee incidentally that almost every agency made in its grant proposal? Was that duty discharged by a promise to create social-legal teams to "rescue" poor people from poverty? Or was it a willingness to keep the Community Action Agency in check, to provide a "civilian perspective" for the war on poverty? Or did it entail a vigorous effort to revise the legal structure that discriminated against the poor in the distribution of goods, services and opportunity? How about the newly emerging prescription, "economic development"? There was no blue litmus test. Several expanded legal aid societies and bar-sponsored agencies attained significant social-economic gains for the poor while some newly created organizations had minimal impact.

Chapter 5: The Policy-Making Process in the Legal Services Program

1. See Chapter 7, *infra,* especially pp. 164–67 for the grant-makers' problems in affecting the actual output of the recipient of a grant.

2. See pp. 58–59, *supra.*

3. Interview with E. Clinton Bamberger, Jr., Baltimore, Maryland, December, 1968.

4. *Ibid.*

5. *Ibid.*

6. For the nature of these concerns, see pp. 135–37, *infra.*

7. *Introduction to the Development of a Legal Services Program* (draft of Legal

Services Guidelines) at p. 5 (Nov. 10, 1965). The full text of the proposed guidelines read:

> To qualify for funding, a program must be one that is developed, conducted and administered with the maximum feasible participation of residents of the areas and members of the groups served. This is a most fundamental principle—that the people to be served should themselves have something to say about the services they need and the manner in which those services should be provided. The aim of the Economic Opportunity Act is not only to help the poor but to help the poor help themselves. Meaningful participation of the residents of the areas served may be secured in several possible manners. Among the means to ensure this participation are:
> a. Representation on the policy-making body and appropriate advisory boards,
> b. Use of existing and neighborhood organizations and the creation of new representative neighborhood organizations for advice on program policy,
> c. The provision of meaningful opportunities for residents, either as individuals or in groups, to protest or to propose additions to or changes in the ways in which a program is being planned or undertaken,
> d. Employment, to the maximum extent feasible, of residents of areas being served on jobs created as part of the program.
> There is no national standard for compliance with the provision that the poor must be represented. As stated by Sargent Shriver at the American Bar Association's Annual Meeting in August, 1965;
> > Our statute requires maximum feasible participation of the poor in all aspects of antipoverty programs. We intend to carry out the mandate of Congress on this. But to do so does not require the imposition of inflexible and arbitrary quotas. We have already financed legal service programs approaching this requirement in a variety of ways. We believe in flexibility. But flexibility cannot become a euphemism for evasion of our statutory duty.

8. Italics mine.
9. In funding the Houston Legal Aid Foundation, this concept of representation of the poor was actually put into effect.
10. All of the discussion from the November 11, 1965 meeting of the National Advisory Committee that is quoted here and in the following pages is taken from an unpublished transcript of those proceedings.
11. *Guidelines for Legal Services Programs* (1966) at p. 11 (hereinafter referred to as *Guidelines*). The full section as redrafted reads:

> The Economic Opportunity Act requires that community action programs be:
> ... *developed, conducted and administered with the maximum feasible participation of residents of the areas and members of the groups served.* ... Sec. 202 (a) (3)
> The Act commits the Nation and the Office of Economic Opportunity to a purpose and a plan that require more than help for the poor. We must involve the impoverished people themselves in the formulation and operation of programs to alleviate poverty. The poor will not only be helped but must help themselves. The Act requires that programs for legal assistance, like all components of community action programs, be developed, conducted and administered "with the

maximum feasible participation of the residents of the areas and members of the groups served."

Policy for legal assistance programs must be formulated with the participation of the "residents of the areas and members of the groups served." As explained in the preceding section of this pamphlet, the legal services program will have in most instances an autonomous policy-making board separate from the governing body of the community action agency. The poor must be represented on the board or policy-making committee of the program to provide legal services, just as they are represented on the policy-making body of the community action agency.

The board members who represent the poor need not be poor themselves. However, if they are not "residents of the areas and members of the groups served" then they must be truly representative of those residents and groups. This essential quality may be assured by truly democratic selection by the poor. There should neither be a requirement that the residents of the area must select lawyers nor any other arbitrary restriction.

OEO does not require a fixed proportion of the people to be served or their representatives on the policy-making board. As Sargent Shriver, the Director of OEO, stated at the Annual Meeting of the American Bar Association in August 1965:

Our statute requires maximum feasible participation of the poor in all aspects of antipoverty programs. We intend to carry out the mandate of Congress on this! But to do so, does not require the imposition of inflexible and arbitrary quotas. We have already financed legal service programs approaching this requirement in a variety of ways. We believe in flexibility. But flexibility cannot become a euphemism for evasion of our statutory duty.

The representation of the people to be served should be sufficient to assure that the concerns of people in poverty will be articulated and considered.

Additional effective participation of the residents of the areas may be provided by advisory councils already existing under community action agency sponsorship or such councils formed for this specific purpose. OEO encourages this additional involvement. This participation is not likely to be effective without the necessary support to articulate the decisions of these advisory councils and a requirement that the policy-making board must consider and act upon the suggestions of the advisory councils. Some board members of legal services programs should attend the meetings of the advisory councils. Staff should be provided to prepare formal resolutions adopted by the advisory councils, to report these actions to the board, and to inform the advisory councils of the actions of the board. [*Guidelines,* at pp. 10–14.]

12. That honor was reserved for the "informal" policy discouraging "Judicare" programs. See pp. 117–21, *infra.*

13. Interview with E. Clinton Bamberger, Jr., Baltimore, Maryland, December, 1968. Also based on author's personal recollection of conversations.

14. In New York, Philadelphia, and a few other large cities, legal aid societies served clients earning as much as $5000 to $5500 for a family of four.

15. To relieve the tension at a particularly hot moment, Shestack jested, "We've come a long way to hear a new verse, 'Partridge on a fair fee'." The committee divided evenly on groans versus laughs.

16. My research has not turned up a transcript of the January 4, 1966, meeting. It is entirely possible the tape was never transcribed. Accordingly, the above account is based on my own recollection of the meeting.

17.   The full text of the guideline provision reads:

> The legal services program, like all other OEO efforts, directs its attention and the community's resources to the needs of those afflicted and disadvantaged by poverty. OEO will not provide funds for programs to provide free legal assistance for individuals or organizations who can afford to employ private counsel. The standard should not be so high that it includes clients who can pay the fee of an attorney without jeopardizing their ability to have decent food, clothing and shelter. This is a program of legal assistance for the poverty stricken.
>
> The eligibility criteria should include such factors as income, dependents, assets and liabilities, cost of a decent living in the community, and an estimate of the cost of the legal services needed.
>
> No standard should be inflexible. Allowance should be made for the provision of assistance in cases of unusual hardship which may be caused, for instance, by lengthy periods of unemployment or illness. To avoid abuse, such discretion should be vested only in supervisory personnel and should be subject to review by the policy-making board.
>
> Programs should not provide free legal advice in fee-generating cases, such as contingent fee cases or other cases in which a fee provided by statute or administrative rule is sufficient to retain an attorney. The test should be whether the client can obtain representation. When a case generates a fee sufficient to employ competent private counsel, the client should be referred under an appropriate lawyer referral system. If the fee is not sufficient to attract a private lawyer, the client may be eligible for the assistance of the OEO-funded program. [*Guidelines,* at pp. 19–21.]

18.   One earlier draft, for instance, contained the following language:

> It is desirable that representation be provided for organizations of the poor such as credit unions, cooperatives, and block clubs. Such representation may include helping such organizations to start, to advise them concerning the organization's objectives, and to represent them in litigation. The proposal should show cognizance of the kinds of organizations to be served and the kinds of problems of such organizations to be handled. In some areas, the statutes, administrative regulations, or case law is either unclear or is detrimental to the interests of the poor. The proposal should consider the role of the legal service program in defining or changing such law. This may include judicial challenge to particular practices and regulations, studies of whole areas of the law in advance, research into conflicting or discriminatory applications of laws or administrative change. In addition, the proposal may include research into such questions as the legal problems of the low income community and their relationship to the individual community problems. [*Tentative Guidelines for Legal Services Programs,* at pp. 8–9 and 10–11 (June, 1965).]

19.   Bruce Terris, who had become an NAC member (as designee of the Attorney General), had been especially active in the preparation of earlier drafts of the *Guidelines.* He was a very active participant at both those meetings. Yet even he did not bring this omission to the attention of the committee or the Legal Services staff. In a five-page undated memorandum Terris sent to Bamberger in November, 1965, he outlined 16 specific criticisms of the Wolf-Bamberger-Johnson draft of the *Guidelines,* yet made no mention of the omission of any reference to law reform or representation of groups.

20. Pye, *The Role of Legal Services in the Antipoverty Program,* 31 Law and Contemporary Problems 211, 228–230 (Winter, 1966).

21. *Guidelines,* at pp. 21 and 23.

22. "The continuing and wider acceptance of this responsibility among members of the legal profession is indispensable if the Legal Services Program is to accomplish its overall objectives:

> *First:* To make funds available to implement efforts initiated and designed by local communities to provide the advice and advocacy of lawyers for people in poverty.
>
> *Second:* To accumulate empirical knowledge to find the most effective method to bring the aid of the law and the assistance of lawyers to the economically disadvantaged people of this nation. OEO will encourage and support experiment and innovation in legal services proposals to find the best method.
>
> *Third:* To sponsor education and research in the areas of procedural and substantive law which affect the causes and problems of poverty.
>
> *Fourth:* To acquaint the whole practicing bar with its essential role in combating poverty and provide the resources to meet the response of lawyers to be involved in the War on Poverty.
>
> *Fifth:* To finance programs to teach the poor and those who work with the poor to recognize problems which can be resolved best by the law and lawyers. The poor do not always know when their problems are legal problems and they may be unable, reluctant, or unwilling to seek the aid of a lawyer. [*Guidelines,* at pp. 2–3.]

23. See pp. 80–82, *supra,* for a description of measures undertaken by the organized bar in support of the Legal Services Program.

24. Even the most explicit and fundamental of the *Guidelines* were not completely sacrosanct. In Houston, Texas, and Chattanooga, Tennessee, after much introspection the Legal Services staff funded programs without requiring representation of the poor on the policy-making board. The Houston decision was mitigated by establishment of a unique experiment with poverty community advisory boards who were given their own ombudsman to check on agency policy and execution as well as guaranteed access to the board and staff. However, the Chattanooga grant was made merely to gain a foothold in this important Southern community even at the sacrifice of normal standards.

25. Interview with E. Clinton Bamberger, Jr., Baltimore, Maryland, December, 1968.

26. The full text of this memorandum reads as follows:

> To fund this program on its present scale is to invite every Bar in the country to submit similar programs. Although some may regard this system as ideal, I feel there are possible inherent difficulties.
>
> a. There may be some question as to how diligently a private attorney will press cases for indigents out of whom he will earn a few hundred "judicare" dollars a year, where their interests conflict with those of clients who pay him thousands or tens of thousands of dollars a year.
>
> b. It is difficult, if not impossible, for a group of autonomous private practition-

ers to build a strategy for change in the law or even to accumulate the experience which would indicate what changes are needed.

c. It is difficult, if not impossible, for autonomous private practitioners to be coordinated with CAA services and other social services in the community or participate effectively in community organization.

d. Many lawyers who might participate in the program because of the opportunity for financial gain may not be philosophically attuned to the cause of the poor. I don't know the attitudes of Wisconsin lawyers. Generally, I do know that in talking to lawyers in other areas of the country, I have been appalled at what they have regarded as adequate legal service to the poor: advising a poor man charged with crime to confess if they learn he is guilty; advising a tenant or debtor with good defenses that he should pay up or suffer eviction or repossession.

e. Private attorneys will not have the opportunity to build up expertise in the kinds of cases of most relevance to the poor since presumably no single attorney will handle that many of these cases. Nor are they likely to participate in any lengthy training sessions to become familiar with these legal frills.

f. There is no provision for representation of groups of indigents

I would suggest that the following course of action be followed:

After appropriate modification in the content of this program, fund it only for a multi-county rural area in Wisconsin. It could be contracted out from the CAA in that area to a State Bar created non-profit corporation with poor on the Board. Simultaneously, or nearly simultaneously, fund similar programs in a medium-sized city (Durham, North Carolina) and an urban area or part of an urban area (we do not have any of these yet as far as I know) in another section of the country. Consideration should be given to funding these all as demonstration grants. In any event, build a heavy evaluation component into each. I think we can justify this restriction on the size of the program on the grounds that we cannot afford to expend 5% of our total national allocation on a very experimental model.

Zona proposes that we defer until we have several "judicare" type proposals in hand and then choose the best two or three to fund. It seems to me this alternative has certain dangers. We must decide now, I think, whether we are going to sink over $750,000 in any one of these two or three we are going to fund. Moreover, pressure, legitimate pressure, will build up as we sit on the "judicare" proposal. If we do send a consultant to perfect the program, we will be pretty much committed to funding it at its present scale. [Memorandum on "Application for Legal Services Program, Wisconsin State Bar, Judicare," to Bamberger from Johnson, dated January 7, 1966.]

27.   As Emery Brownell, Director of the National Legal Aid and Defender Association, has said:

The most striking fact to emerge . . . is that both an office and a salaried lawyer are essential for adequate service. Busy lawyers cannot give the necessary time to the kind of troubled and confused client who come to Legal Aid; . . . . On an average, the volunteer committees reach fewer than one-third as many who need legal aid as do the Legal Aid offices which have an unpaid legal staff, and the volunteer-staffed offices reach but two-fifths as many as do the offices with salaried lawyers.

Brownell, Legal Aid in the United States (Rochester: Lawyers Cooperative Publ. Co., 1951) at p. 117.

28. Bamberger, speech to National Conference of Bar Presidents, Chicago, Illinois, February 8, 1966.

29. Typical of the public statements made by organized bar leaders about the Judicare issue are the comments of John Cummiskey, chairman of the ABA Standing Committee on Legal Aid and Indigent Defendants and NLADA Washington counsel, Howard Westwood, at the October, 1966, NLADA meeting.

> MR. CUMMISKEY: . . . I think we should draw a distinction between urban areas and rural areas, because I think we all agree that in urban areas the concept of the modified English system is not really as sound as the concept of the staff Legal Aid Office.
>
> In the United States we have developed almost 100 years of experience in the use of the Legal Aid Society staff attorney concept. It has been successful in meeting a great many of the requirements that we have had. We have not been able to do nearly as much as we want, but the concept has been successful and accepted, and we just kept on betting on a winning horse.
>
> MR. WESTWOOD: It was nearly ten years ago in the District of Columbia when it was first recommended by a group that had been sponsored by the Bar Association that there be an extension of organized legal aid to cover the whole field.
>
> There was a group in the Bar there who were very enamored of what we now call judicare, and considerable studies were made of the respective costs of the two ways of going about it.
>
> It was quite apparent that if you were to assume a comparable scope of service through making some payment to the private attorney in private practice, that there was just no comparison as to costs. Cost of the judicare approach would be very much greater than that of the organized legal aid approach.
>
> Now, there are additional aspects of it which are not to be ignored, and I think with the legal services projects that OEO has been funding, if we begin to get practical experience with them, particularly in the large centers, we can see the point that I have in mind very clearly, that there are not just incidental but very important phases of an organized legal aid operation with a regular staff and doing things on a law office basis, that can be accomplished which simply could not effectively be done under judicare as it is known in England or with some modifications applied to this country.
>
> I am speaking of such things as community education. We barely scratch the surface in that area.
>
> . . . There is the other aspect that I have particularly in mind is what Earl Johnson referred to as law reform.
>
> The thing that can be done; we are finding this in Washington, and I am sure you are finding this in other of the larger cities. We are finding that by taking the resources that you have available, when you have a considerable group working together full-time on an organized basis, you can begin to get to some of the roots of the problems in this area and to devise means for their solution in a broad way instead of simply handling each individual case as it comes along.
>
> Again, judicare as it is advocated by so many lawyers, and as we know it, generally speaking, in England, makes no provision for that kind of thing. And it cannot.

30. See pp. 108–12, *supra.*
31. Interview with E. Clinton Bamberger, Jr., Baltimore, Maryland, December, 1968.
32. *Resolution,* Florida State Bar Association, dated March 19, 1966.
33. For instance, in February, 1966, the San Francisco Bar Association drafted a resolution to present to the ABA House of Delegates requiring local bar control of Legal Services programs. The San Francisco contingent was dissuaded from introducing this resolution by the personal intervention of ABA president-elect Orison Marden and Legal Aid Committee chairman John Cummiskey. Interview with E. Clinton Bamberger, Jr., Baltimore, Maryland, December, 1968.
34. See p. 89, *supra.*
35. Several Indian reservations and two or three rural programs were located in areas so remote it was impossible to enlist any significant number of lawyers to serve on their boards.
36. Speech by E. Clinton Bamberger, Jr., to Florida State Bar Association Convention, Hollywood Beach, Florida (June 16, 1966) at pp. 7–9.
37. Memorandum to Legal Services Staff from Earl Johnson, Jr., dated August 18, 1966.
38. "A lawyer . . . may cooperate . . . with . . . legal services activities . . . provided that his independent professional judgment is exercised in behalf of his client without interference or control by any organization or other person." AMERICAN BAR ASSOCIATION, CODE OF PROFESSIONAL RESPONSIBILITY, Disciplinary Rule 2–103 (D).
39. "Various types of legal aid offices are administered by boards of directors composed of lawyers and laymen. A lawyer should not accept employment from such an organization unless the board sets only broad policies and there is no interference in the relationship of the lawyer and the individual client he serves." Ethical Consideration 5–24, ABA CODE, *op. cit., supra,* n. 38.
40. "A basic tenet of the professional responsibilities of lawyers is that every person in our society should have ready access to the independent professional service of a lawyer of integrity and competence. . . .

    "History is replete with instances of distinguished and sacrificial services by lawyers who have represented unpopular clients and causes. Regardless of his personal feelings, a lawyer should not decline representation because a client or a cause is unpopular or community reaction is adverse." Ethical Consideration EC 1–1, EC 2–27, ABA CODE, *op. cit., supra,* n. 38.
41. "In certain areas of legal representation not affecting the merits of the cause or substantially prejudicing the right of a client, a lawyer is entitled to make decisions on his own. But otherwise the authority to make decisions is exclusively that of the client and, if made within the framework of the law, such decisions are binding on his lawyer." Ethical Consideration 7–7, ABA CODE, *op. cit., supra,* n. 38.
42. "The duty of a lawyer both to his client and to the legal system is to represent his client zealously within the bounds of the law . . . In our government of laws and not of men, each member of our society is entitled to have his

conduct judged and regulated in accordance with the law, *to seek any lawful objective through legally permissible* means; and to present for adjudication any lawful claim, issue, or defense." Ethical Consideration 7–1, ABA CODE, *op. cit, supra,* n. 38.

43. "A lawyer shall not permit a person who recommends, employs, or pays him to render legal services for another to direct or regulate his professional judgment in rendering such legal services." Disciplinary Rule DR 5–107 (B), ABA CODE, *op. cit., supra,* n. 38.

44. See Chapters 6 and 7 of JOHNSON, AND STILL LOVE JUSTICE (to be published by Public Affairs Press).

    James Lorenz, first director of California Rural Legal Assistance, probably the single most controversial Legal Services Agency in the country, told the author in 1968 that the most steadfast and helpful support for the right of his staff lawyers to undertake class actions and to sue government agencies came from establishment, generally conservative lawyers on the CRLA board of trustees. Lorenz said that on these issues he would rather count on conservative lawyers who generally feel an absolute commitment to the profession's ideals than on liberal non-lawyers who sometimes waver before an onslaught from public figures, preferring to temporize the agency's actions in order to reduce the political risks.

45. See Chapter 4, note 82, *supra.*

46. See Chapter 7, *infra,* especially pp. 170–71.

47. Smith and Clifton, "Income of Lawyers, 1965," 55 ABA Journal 562 (1969).

48. MILLER, RICH MAN, POOR MAN (New York: Crowell, 1971) at p. 16.

49. See Chapter 6, *infra,* for description of the ABA role in bureaucratic survival of the Program. See Chapters 6 and 7 of JOHNSON, *op. cit., supra,* n. 44, for description of organized bar assistance in thwarting political attacks launched against the Program.

50. See Chapter 4, *supra,* for description of ABA and NLADA efforts in aid of the OEO campaign to create and expand local Legal Services organizations.

51. See pp. 25–27, *supra.* During 1966 and 1967, many OEO-funded Community Action agencies continued to press their delegate Legal Services projects to make a heavy commitment of lawyer resources to these multi-disciplinary teams.

52. Two independent studies undertaken in the mid 1960s sought to measure the impact of intensive application of social resources to "cure" problem individuals. The results were negative, failing to show statistically significant improvement attributable to the expensive programs. See MEYER, et al., GIRLS AT VOCATIONAL HIGH (New York: Russell Sage, 1965), especially at p. 207, and BROWN, THE MULTI-PROBLEM DILEMMA (Metuchen, N.J.: Scarecrow, 1968), especially at p. 151.

53. New entities run by poor people who lacked any business background were not likely to appear good risks for Small Business Administration (SBA) loans when competing with established firms run by experienced, often successful, businessmen. But even if organizations owned by the poor captured all of SBA's funds, this was not enough to make a substantial dent in the poverty

problem. (The total SBA budget for 1967 was $504 million.) Nor were other sources of government support a meaningful alternative in 1967. The Economic Development Administration, like most community development agencies, operated on a trickle down theory. Thus, EDA funds were reserved primarily for major projects like dams and bridges. The 1968 Housing Act was not even on the horizon. Richard Nixon and his advocacy of "Black Capitalism" had yet to make an appearance. (Even as late as 1972, and despite President Nixon's rhetoric on behalf of "Black Capitalism," money for economic development by low-income individuals and groups was almost nonexistent.)

54. See pp. 268–70, *infra*.

55. "One anonymous House Democrat said that . . . 'Extremist groups . . . have seized [community organization] as a forum for dissent.' " DONOVAN, THE POLITICS OF POVERTY (New York: Pegasus, 1967) at pp. 70–71.

   At an earlier stage in OEO's development, the term "community action" translated roughly as "community organization." But by 1967 the word had begun a transformation toward the meaning of local political control. See p. 166, *infra*.

56. None of this interferes, of course, with the representation of groups and organizations by Legal Services lawyers, nor does it argue against the proposition that poor people generally are more effective in both the political and private spheres when associated in groups rather than when operating as individuals. See pp. 252–54, *infra*.

   The point is simply that there were not enough Legal Services lawyers—even assuming all were skilled community organizers—to mount the massive organizational campaign which alone could produce meaningful improvement in the poverty problem through the application of pressure by organizations composed of low-income individuals.

57. For a discussion of these techniques, see pp. 249–68, *infra*.

58. See pp. 23–24, *supra*.

59. For some examples of such changes, see pp. 254–66, *infra*.

60. Ethical Considerations 8–1; 8–2, ABA CODE, *op. cit., supra*, n. 38.

61. See Chapters 6 and 7 of JOHNSON, *op.cit., supra*, n. 44, for description of ethical defense of law reform by OEO and ABA leaders.

62. See pp. 34–35, *supra*.

63. *Transcript*, January 4, 1967, meeting of National Advisory Committee of the OEO Legal Services Program, at p. 201. The decision to introduce such a resolution at the January meeting actually was made the night before at a private gathering of representatives of the organized bar on the NAC and their close advisors. I was at the meeting and spoke of the staff's concerns about the course the Program was taking primarily because of caseload problems. However, it was NLADA's Washington counsel, Howard Westwood, who again made a decisive move in Legal Services history, suggesting not only the resolution, but who should make and second it.

64. *Transcript, id.* at p. 204.

65. A subcommittee was set up to determine the best way to free Legal Services

resources for activities calculated to have a major impact on poverty. It was chaired by Bamberger and staffed by a consultant, John Murphy, who had organized the HEW Legal Services Conference over two years earlier. See pp. 44–48, *supra.* By this time Murphy was a law professor at Georgetown University.

66. *Proceedings* of the Harvard Conference on Law and Poverty (March 17, 18 and 19, 1967) at pp. 1, 3.

67. *Id.* at p. 4.

68. See Economic Opportunity Act Amendments of 1967, *op. cit., supra,* Chapter 4, n. 73, at pp. 912–914.

69. S. Rep. No. 563, 90th Cong. 1st Sess. (1967) at p. 40.

70. See pp. 164–68, *infra,* for a discussion of the problems of focusing the energies of local projects on the chosen goal. See also pp. 168–71, *infra,* for an example of support for law reform among leaders of organized bar.

Chapter 6: "Up the Bureaucracy": Preserving Policy and Program Integrity within the OEO Administration

1. See pp. 22–23, *supra,* for details of this incident.

2. See pp. 41–43, *supra.* It may not be overstatement to conclude that the single act of firing Jean Cahn did more than anything else to turn the national Legal Services Program toward an alliance with the organized bar and away from assimilation into the multi-service teams.

3. See pp. 24–25, *supra,* for account of the dispute that clarified the policy-making supremacy of the advisory committee to the MFY Legal Services unit.

4. See pp. 29–31, *supra,* for discussion of the extensive role of the NLSP board.

5. See, e.g., pp. 124–26, *supra.*

6. These percentages pertain to that portion of the Economic Opportunity budget administered by OEO itself. In each year, a substantial proportion of the funds appropriated under the Economic Opportunity Act were transferred to the Labor Department and other Federal agencies for operation of antipoverty programs delegated to those agencies.

7. Section 201, Economic Opportunity Act of 1964.

8. Subsequent amendments increased this "local share" requirement to 20 percent and eventually 30 percent.

9. William Bozman, CAP's longtime deputy director, stated that CAP spent its first two and one-half years "worrying about" program structure rather than program content. Conversation with William Bozman, Washington, D.C., February, 1968.

10. See pp. 152–53, *infra,* for a discussion of the weaknesses of administration by CAP generalists compared with administration by specialists.

11. Interview with E. Clinton Bamberger, Jr., Baltimore, Maryland, December, 1968.

12. *Ibid.*

13. In a meeting in May, 1966, CAP deputy director William Bozman conceded that he was more concerned that Legal Services would be too successful and absorb $80 million during its first fiscal year than that it would fail to meet its goal of $20 million in grants.

14. These levels of review included the CAP analyst for the community involved, the CAP regional director, the overall OEO regional director and his deputy, the headquarters general counsel's office, the headquarters civil rights director, the headquarters CAP deputy director, the headquarters CAP director, and the OEO deputy director.

15. All of the discussion from the November 11, 1965 meeting of the National Advisory Committee that is quoted here and in the following pages is taken from an unpublished transcript of that meeting.

16. Memorandum to Mr. Kelly, acting CAP director, from Clint Bamberger, dated December 6, 1965. The permanent CAP director, Theodore Berry, was on leave at the time of this reorganization.

17. These internal management directives were called CAP Analyst Memos.

18. *Transcript* of March 6, 1966, meeting, National Advisory Committee, at pp. 102–103.

19. Letter to Sargent Shriver from Theodore Voorhees, dated March 8, 1966.

20. Interview with E. Clinton Bamberger, Jr., Baltimore, Maryland, December, 1968.

21. Memorandum to Mr. Berry from E. Clinton Bamberger, dated April 20, 1966.

22. See pp. 94–95, *supra.*

23. In many respects the *de facto* administrative structure differed sharply from the formal written procedures and flow charts. For instance, although the regional Legal Services personnel theoretically were selected jointly by the director of Legal Services and the regional OEO director and reported to both, all of them in fact were recruited by the Legal Services office and felt their primary allegiance to the national Legal Services Program rather than the regional office. Thus, despite the official bureaucratic relationships, the regional Legal Services staffs tended to function as extensions of the headquarters office and to adhere to Legal Services policy as opposed to CAP policy. This, of course, enhanced the potential for conflict between Legal Services and CAP personnel at the regional level.

    In two regional offices the Legal Services staff was able to negotiate on a strictly personal basis a degree of actual independence which contradicted the official dogma requiring subordination to CAP personnel. Operations in these offices ran smoothly and internal friction was minimal. Unfortunately, the remaining regional offices, including all of the larger ones, were in constant tension. As CAP policy and Legal Services policy began to diverge more and more, especially as Legal Services focused on law reform, the number of substantive conflicts increased. In several instances, only the existence of the requirement of approval by the national Legal Services director preserved the integrity of program policy. On one occasion, for instance, the regional OEO director in the Great Lakes Region (Chicago office) unilaterally made two

Judicare grants that had been expressly rejected by both regional and headquarters Legal Services staff. These grants were nullified in one of many tests of strength that seemed inherent in the hybrid administrative arrangements under which the Program labored.

24. DONOVAN, THE POLITICS OF POVERTY (New York: Pegasus, 1967) at p. 72.
25. See pp. 143–45, *supra,* for Shriver's candid disclosure of his management philosophy to the National Advisory Committee.
26. DONOVAN, *op. cit., supra,* n. 24.
27. The research phase of the McKinsey study was completed in a few months and consisted of interviews with a relatively small sample of staff members in OEO's Washington headquarters and at one or two regional offices. None of the Legal Services personnel in the headquarters office was included in this survey and only one regional staff member was interviewed.
28. McKinsey and Company Management Study of OEO, Chapter 2, p. 3; Chapter 4, pp. 1, 2–4.
29. *Id.* at Chapter 3, p. 8; Chapter 4, p. 10.
30. Interview with Theodore Jones, former OEO regional director, Chicago, Illinois, August, 1968.
31. *Transcript,* May 19, 1968, National Advisory Committee meeting, at pp. 178–179.
32. Letter to Sargent Shriver from Edwin C. Kepler, dated May 26, 1967.
33. Conversation with Richard Nahstoll, Hawaii, August, 1967.
34. Conversation with Orison Marden, Honolulu, Hawaii, August, 1967.
35. *Ibid.*
36. MR. BAMBERGER: Jerome Shakespeare has written a poem.
MR. SHESTACK: It should have been read earlier. It is just kind of an introduction to the earlier discussion, which is:
"A report known as McKinsey We feel is extremely flimsy. It threatens service, Makes lawyers nervous, And throws the staff in a frenzy."
Clint has his own version.
MR. BAMBERGER: I have a less acceptable version. "A book by Kinsey Took sex out of bed. A report by McKinsey Made lawyers see red."
And I have another one, directed to the same subject matter and to you, which I'll read to you privately.
MR. SHRIVER: It is almost as complicated as sex, I agree.
VOICE: But not as much fun.
Transcript, National Advisory Committee meeting, September 21, 1967, at pp. 92–93.
37. The discussions from the September 21, 1967, meeting of the National Advisory Committee which are quoted here and on the following pages were taken from an unpublished transcript of that meeting.
38. House Education and Labor Committee, *H. Rept. No. 866,* 90th Congress, First Session (1967) pp. 24–25.
39. Conversation with Damon Holmes, Washington, D.C., March, 1969.
40. Letter to Sargent Shriver from William T. Gossett, dated October 28, 1967. Italics mine.

41. White House Statement of the President on the Office of Economic Opportunity, Press Release, San Clemente, California (August 11, 1969). A year later, in 1970, the Legal Services Program went through a replay of the 1967 regionalization controversy. Again, the Program and its supporters prevailed, but only after a prolonged public dispute that culminated in the firing of the Legal Services director, Terry Lenzner. See Chapter 8 of JOHNSON, *op. cit., supra,* Ch. 5, n. 44.

Chapter 7: *Implementing National Goals: Affecting the Management of Local Organizations*

1. "[Federal grant programs in the field of social welfare] multiplied from thirty to four hundred, while expenditures [rose] to more than $20 billion annually from 1961–1968." Pious, *Policy and Public Administration: The Legal Services Program in the War on Poverty,* 2 Politics and Society 376 (1971).

2. The evaluator's survey revealed that 75 percent of agencies whose staff director favored reform rated good or better in law reform performance and 45 percent were excellent or superior. On the contrary, among agencies led by directors who opposed reform only 6 percent scored good or better in law reform performance, none were found excellent or superior, and 81 percent were rated poor. Grantees with directors indifferent to reform produced *no* rankings of good or better and 68 percent were poor in law reform performance. Incidentally, 63 percent of the staff directors supported reform, 15 percent opposed, and 22 percent were indifferent.

3. This difference in management philosophy was one of the factors contributing to the determination of the Legal Services staff to maintain, and, if possible, expand its autonomy within the OEO bureaucracy. See Chapter 6, *supra.*

4. *Transcript,* National Advisory Committee meeting, November 11, 1965, at p. 205.

5. See pp. 130–32, *supra,* for the rationale behind the selection of this particular management goal.

6. See p. 132, *supra,* for an account of the National Advisory Committee deliberations concerning problems of caseload and the law reform goal of the Legal Services Program.

7. Quoted in Law in Action, Vol. 2, No. 9 (December 1967) at pp. 3, 21.

8. "Legal Services Program of the Office of Economic Opportunity," *Hearings* before the Subcommittee on Employment, Manpower and Poverty, U. S. Senate, Committee on Labor and Public Welfare, 91st Congress, First Session (Nov. 14, 1969) at p. 90.

9. Letter from John Robb to Edward L. Wright, July 7, 1969, at pp. 1, 4–5.

10. These excerpts are from the version of this speech published under the title, *A Conservative Rationale for the Legal Services Program* in 70 W.Va.L. Rev. 350–362 (1968).

11. "A legal services board . . . would violate the Canons if . . . it attempted to screen certain kinds of individual cases to determine whether the project

attorney should pursue a certain remedy on behalf of his clients in those cases. . . . [T]he leading decision upholding . . . the corporate form of organization for legal aid societies . . . stressed the fact that the Legal Aid Society itself was not the lawyer for the client; that the society was merely the vehicle for furnishing a lawyer to a client; and that . . . 'the lawyer owes the same fidelity as if the client was able to pay for proper fee. . . . If the board of directors inserted itself into the decision-making process about the course of action to be followed by a staff attorney . . . , it would be violating the personal relationship between the staff attorney and his client. The board, rather than the staff attorney, and hence a corporation, rather than an individual lawyer would be practicing law." Director's column, Law in Action, Vol. 2, No. 8, at p. 2 (November, 1967) at p. 2.

12. Based on a survey of evaluators. See Chapter 4, note 82, *supra*.

13. Evaluators reported that boards opposing law reform selected staff directors with an opposing view in only 16 percent of their choices. *Ibid.*

14. In the North Central region there were so few local Legal Services agencies that the regional Legal Services staff could spend enough time with each grantee to establish a high correlation between progress toward the Program's goals and these very real monetary rewards and sanctions. Consequently, in that region, substantial improvements were made in many marginal agencies through employment of the monetary incentive feature of the evaluation process. Unfortunately, a majority of the regional offices, and especially the larger ones, were so understaffed that they simply were not in a position to use evaluation reports to make the Legal Services goals financially relevant to the employees and staff of the local agencies. (This feature of evaluations is but another phase of the independent system of incentives for agency staffs that the Legal Services Program sought to institute to counterbalance the system of rewards and punishment that could be manipulated by local agency boards. See pp. 176–78, *infra*, for a discussion of other aspects of this system.)

15. This attempt to rationally allocate the limited Legal Services funds often brought our staff into conflict with regional CAP. When OEO sustained an approximate 10 percent cutback in overall funds in fiscal 1968, we proposed to allocate the reduction on the basis of quality (or lack thereof). But CAP officials in several regions resisted. They argued that the Legal Services Program should follow the general CAP pattern of reducing on a straight percentage, across-the-board basis. This was just another example of the issues that tended to divide the Legal Services staff and the remainder of the OEO bureaucracy. As a practical matter, CAP resistance to budget allocations on the basis of quality performance did not prevent the Legal Services staff from accomplishing many transfers from poor quality to high quality programs. But it did make this task much more difficult.

16. See pp. 164–67, *supra*, for a discussion of some of the more important management powers that rest solely with the local agency board or by delegation in the staff director of the local agency.

17. Of the 13 issues published between April, 1967 and July, 1968, the front page

story in fully nine centered around some major law reform action. Moreover, on other pages there were 88 stories about law reform efforts.

18. See pp. 180–82, *infra.*
19. See p. 164, *supra,* for an earlier discussion of the importance of the power to hire and fire Legal Services staff attorneys.

Recruitment is especially critical because should an imaginative attorney inadvertently be hired by a conservative grantee it is difficult for the agency administration to suppress even his most controversial efforts on behalf of clients whose best interests are served by class actions, test cases, legislative advocacy and the rest.

20. Memorandum to Clint Bamberger from Earl Johnson, dated November 12, 1965.
21. Interview with John Robb, Albuquerque, New Mexico, June, 1968.
22. Notes of meeting with Reginald Heber Smith Fellows, February, 1968, Philadelphia, Pennsylvania.
23. See p. 192, *infra,* for a discussion of this development.
24. Compilation of questionnaire returns from Reginald Heber Smith Fellows (1969).

The impact of the Fellows also can be judged from the testimony of evaluators and local agency administrators. A sampling of directors of agencies to which members of the charter class were assigned reveals universal admiration, albeit sometimes grudging. One agency head, for instance, observed that the Fellows have far more background in the relevant law and are generally far superior to persons recruited directly from law school. A Chicago director characterized the program as a "recruiting bonanza." Another director testified that their "set-the-world-on-fire" enthusiasm soon infected his entire staff. The month-long training session afterwards also added to the effectiveness of the lawyers in moving local agencies to advocate law reform more aggressively. Several agency directors noted that the Fellows were familiar with imaginative legal theories and current trends in law reform litigation that were unknown to staff attorneys.

It is apparent the Reginald Heber Smith Program attracted talent that otherwise would not have been available to local Legal Services agencies, even those agencies which were disposed to employ lawyers of that calibre and commitment. Almost two-thirds of the Fellows responded that without the Reggie program they either definitely would not have entered the legal services field or "possibly, but it would have been much more difficult."

25. This departure from orthodox bureaucratic behavior has been the subject of some criticism. See, e.g., Blumenthal, *The Legal Services Corporation: Curtailing Political Interference,* 81 Yale L. Journal 231, 238–259 (1971).
26. "When dealing with human institutions, the whole at times may prove greater than the sum of its aggregate parts. The Legal Services Program is a case in point." Philadelphia: Auerbach Associates, *Final Report to OEO Legal Services Program* (October 31, 1971) at p. 6–1.

Chapter 8: The First Seven Years: Testing the Potential of Legal Services to the Poor

1. See pp. 11–14, *supra,* for discussion of this goal.
2. See pp. 34–35, *supra,* for an analysis of the competing concepts of the proper role of lawyers in the reduction of poverty.
3. See pp. 235–36, *infra,* for a discussion of the current relationship between resources and need.
4. Admittedly, other groups also have developed an interest in the activities of the Legal Services Program as it has grown and especially as its lawyers have had some success against powerful elements in society. Thus, in a sense, there are a number of what might be called "involuntary constituencies" or "counter constituencies," including several state governors, thousands of landlords and creditors, welfare administrators, etc. Also, in the peripheral sense that he is affected by most government programs, the average citizen and taxpayer is a "constituent" of the Legal Services Program.

    The goals of the "counter constituencies" are not considered in this evaluation of the Legal Services Program because they tend to merely be the antithesis of the aspirations of the Program's supporters and recipients.

    For evaluation purposes, we are only considering the goals of constituencies whose primary allegiance, in terms of the Legal Services Program, is to the best interests of the clients of that Program.
5. *1966 Summary of Conference Proceedings,* National Legal Aid and Defender Association (Chicago, 1966) at p. 46. In the same year, the combined budget of all criminal defense organizations was $6,343,149. *Ibid.* As it is, there was a 23.5 percent increase in the civil legal aid budgets between 1964 and 1965, and a 28.4 percent increase in defender budgets in that same year. *Id.* at p. 47.
6. Johnson, *The OEO Legal Services Program,* 14 Catholic Lawyer 99 (1968).
7. *1971 Statistics of Legal Assistance Work,* National Legal Aid and Defender Association (Chicago, 1972) at p. iv. This OEO contribution supplied 72.8 percent of the financing for civil legal aid.
8. Estimate by Philip Murphy, former deputy executive director, NLADA.
9. Johnson, *op. cit., supra,* n. 6.
10. Interview with Constance Dupre, Office of Legal Services, OEO, December 21, 1972.
11. *Ibid.*
12. *1966 Summary, op. cit., supra,* n. 5, at p. 46.
13. *1971 Statistics, op. cit., supra,* n. 7, at pp. iv and v.
14. In 1959, percentages were 28 percent "economic" cases; 15 percent property; 42 percent family law; and 15 percent "other," BROWNELL, LEGAL AID IN THE UNITED STATES (Rochester: Lawyers Coop. Publ. Co., 1961) at pp. 35–37. By 1971 the figures were 15.9 percent consumer or employment; 11.2 percent welfare and other administrative; 14.4 percent landlord-tenant and other housing; 36.6 percent family law; and 21.9 percent miscellaneous. *1971*

Statistics, op. cit., supra, n. 7, at p. iv. The drop in family law cases is more significant than it appears. OEO reversed the restrictive policies toward divorce that typified most legal aid societies. This move could well have caused the family law percentage to increase dramatically, but for an even more pronounced rise in other kinds of cases, such as welfare, seldom handled by the societies.

15. In 1965, the average salary of legal aid society attorneys, most of whom had more than ten years experience, was approximately $6,500. (Estimate of Philip Murphy, former deputy executive director of the National Legal Aid and Defender Association.) This estimate is consistent with the salaries reported by Brownell in 1959. He found staff attorneys at that time averaged $5282 in smaller cities and $5958 in larger ones. *Id.,* at p.48. It likewise is consistent with NLADA *Summary of Data on Legal Aid Offices* (1964), which reported average salaries of $3900 for staff attorneys in cities of 100–250,000 population and $7504 for those in cities over 750,000. In 1967, the average salary of OEO funded attorneys was $9500. *Hearings, Economic Opportunity Act Amendments of 1967, Committee on Education and Labor,* U.S. House of Representatives June 20, 1967, Part 2, at p. 914.

16. See for instance, Note, *Neighborhood Law Offices: The New Wave in Legal Services for the Poor,* 80 Harvard L. Rev. 805 (1967).

17. See p. 179, *supra.* Jerome Shestack, National Advisory Committee member, and partner in one of Philadelphia's largest law firms, testified to this. In addition to holding a cocktail party to honor the charter class of Reginald Heber Smith Fellows, he circulated their biographical sketches to senior partners in his firm. The response, "When can we interview these prospects?"

18. Membership on a law review editorial board usually is restricted to the upper 10 or 20 percent of a law school class.

19. In 1959 Brownell reported 6 percent of legal aid cases involved litigation. BROWNELL, *op. cit., supra,* n. 14, at p. 44.

20. *1971 Statistics, op. cit., supra,* n. 7, at p. iv.

21. OEO has not maintained statistics regarding appeals. Thus, the 1000 appeals per annum is an estimate, but an extraordinarily conservative one. It was derived as follows: In early 1967 statistics on appeals were collected for purposes of congressional testimony. 93,000 persons had applied for service and 72 appeals had been filed. Thus, even in these early days, before the law reform emphasis was implemented and before many of the 93,000 cases had matured to the appellate stage, a ratio of one appeal for every 1300 applicants was established. Applying that modest ratio to the nearly 1.3 million applicants served in 1971 yields 1000 appeals.

   In all probability, the actual statistic is much higher than this minimal estimate. An informal survey of five typical Legal Services agencies revealed they averaged over one appeal per attorney during 1972. With over 2600 lawyers currently employed in the Program this projects to a national total of approximately 3000 appeals each year.

22. It is difficult to establish this sort of negative fact conclusively. However, Philip Murphy, former deputy executive director of the NLADA reported no

legal aid case had reached the U.S. Supreme Court and there appears to be no reference to such a case in the many histories and surveys of the legal aid movement. Moreover, the staff of the New York Legal Aid Society, the oldest and largest, reported that agency had not appealed to the Supreme Court at any time before 1966.

23. *Supreme Court Docket,* POVERTY LAW REPORT (Chicago: CCH, 1968—).

24. Compilation of questionnaires from Legal Services Evaluators.

25. Auerbach Associates, *op. cit., supra,* Chapter 7, n. 26, at pp. 1–2.

26. Among the leaders of the organized bar and legal aid movement interviewed during the preparation of this book were Lewis Powell (former ABA president), Theodore Voorhees (former NLADA president), Maynard Toll (former NLADA president), John Cummiskey (former legal aid chairman), John Robb (former legal aid chairman) and Howard Westwood (former NLADA Washington counsel).

27. "Apart from semantics the only real problem that I could see in those days [1965] was the 'poor on the board' problem. At first Ken Pye and I resisted it for NLSP. . . . It turned out well for NLSP in the early days and I became a supporter of the idea. . . ." Undated letter from Howard Westwood to Earl Johnson, at p. 8.

28. Among the communities initiating meaningful legal assistance programs for the first time under OEO sponsorship were Chattanooga, Tennessee; Daytona Beach, Florida; Tulsa, Oklahoma; Fort Pierce, Florida; Charleston, South Carolina; and Charlotte, North Carolina.

29. As of 1969, only 99 Legal Services attorneys—6 percent of the total—were located in all the states of the Deep South. PIVEN and CLOWARD, REGULATING THE POOR (New York: Pantheon, 1971) p. 319.

30. See p. 74, *supra.*

31. LEVITAN, THE GREAT SOCIETY'S POOR LAW: A NEW APPROACH (Baltimore: Johns Hopkins, 1969) at p. 186.

32. The author was sent a complete draft for comment in spring, 1968, while he was still director of the OEO Legal Services Program. This draft did not differ from the printed text of the book in any substantial way.

33. See pp. 126–28, *supra.*

34. These figures are derived from a tabulation of questionnaires from Reginald Heber Smith Fellows, incorporated in a 1969 OEO evaluation of that program.

35. See pp. 167–82, *supra.*

36. These figures are derived from a tabulation of questionnaires from participants in training programs of the National Institute for Education in Law and Poverty, incorporated in a 1969 OEO evaluation of that program.

37. Based on a compilation of questionnaires from Legal Services evaluators. See Chapter 4, note 82. It should also be noted that the Legal Services Program appears to benefit from a "whole exceeds the sum of its parts" phenomenon and thus the ratings of individual agencies may understate the total law reform activity of the entire program. (see p. 184, *supra.*)

38. Seventeen of 27 agencies with 11 or more staff attorneys were rated "good" or better in law reform effectiveness. *Ibid.*

39. Analysis of *Clearinghouse Review,* Appendix II.

40. Another commentator, Richard Pious, argues that the Legal Services Program has not been any more active than legal aid in bringing about law reform. He asserts "the successes of the Legal Aid movement in law reform and institutional reform match anything the projects have done in overhauling the practices of welfare bureaucracies or promotion of legislation." Pious, *Policy and Public Administration: The Legal Services Program in the War on Poverty,* 2 Politics and Society 376 (1971). For this interesting conclusion, he relies on some references to legislative and appellate court activities in earlier literature concerning legal aid. SMITH, JUSTICE AND THE POOR (New York: Carnegie Foundation, 1919), at p. 39; see, e.g., Wismer, *Lobbyists for the Poor,* 225 THE ANNALS 172 (1936); and Abrahams, *Legal Aid and Preventive Law,* 16 Legal Aid Briefcase 68 (1958), cited in notes 84 and 85 of Pious, *id.* at p. 388.

     It is true that legal aid philosophy approved of test cases and legislative advocacy. (See pp. 280–81, *infra.*) But legal aid lawyers seldom engaged in those activities. Pious concludes that since legal aiders occasionally dabbled in law reform, that is the same as the OEO Program's rather extensive commitment to those activities. That seems to be the equivalent of saying a Boeing 747 is no better air transport than a hot-air balloon because they both fly. Apparently ignored by Pious is the quantum difference between a handful of appeals taken by legal aid lawyers during an 89-year history and the thousands filed *each year* by poverty attorneys; apparently no cases taken to the United States Supreme Court in those 89 years versus the more than 200 taken and the 73 won on the merits in seven years of the OEO Program; and an infrequent legislative proposal contrasted with scores of bills enacted each year through the Legal Services effort. (See notes 21–23 and 34–39, *supra.*)

41. *Congressional Record,* Vol. 113, pt. 21, at pp. 27871, 27872, reporting Senate floor debate on October 4, 1967. This speech accompanied Senator Murphy's surprise introduction of an amendment which would have barred "any action against any public agency of the United States, any State, or any polical subdivision thereof." The Murphy amendment was defeated on a roll-call vote, 52–36. See *id.* at p. 27873. Vigorous lobbying activity prevented this measure from being introduced in the House of Representatives.

42. These legislative campaigns are described in Chapters 6 and 7 of JOHNSON, *op. cit., supra,* Ch. 5, n. 44. In the course of the battle in 1969 the ABA Board of Governors passed a resolution that "reaffirms its position that the Legal Services Program should operate with full assurance of independence of lawyers . . . to render services . . . in cases which might involve action against government agencies *seeking significant changes.*" (Emphasis supplied.)

43. All these instances are discussed *id.* at Chapters 6 through 9.

44. Hazard, *Social Justice Through Civil Justice,* 36 U. Chicago L. Rev. 699 (1969).

45. Much of the rhetoric, the theoretical discussions and the practice of the

campaign against poverty in the 1960s may have been based on an invalid premise. It is what noted economist Paul Samuelson terms the *fallacy of composition* [see SAMUELSON, ECONOMICS (New York: McGraw-Hill, 1973) at p. 14]: the assumption that what is true for the part is true for the whole. Applying this logical principle to the antipoverty effort, it is the assumption that by compensating for the competitive weaknesses of the individual poor person—educational deficiencies, lack of motivation, racial barriers, etc.,— and placing him in a middle-class job, we have reduced the number of poor persons in the nation. The idea behind many antipoverty efforts—Job Corps, Headstart, and so on—was to repeat that process enough times with enough people so that eventually there would be no more poor people. But that is where the fallacy of composition enters in. It is not necessarily true that improving the competitive status of the individuals who presently are poor will necessarily reduce poverty in the nation as a whole. There is a good chance that in most instances this strategy merely allows more of the present poor to get jobs that otherwise would go to present members of the working class or the middle class and sends some present working-class and middle-class individuals tumbling into poverty.

Visualize a ladder with many rungs—a $1000-a-year rung, a $2000 rung, a $3000 rung, and on up the ladder. Each rung is full of people. The smarter, tougher, better ladder-climber you are, the higher up the ladder you stand. Now let's imagine we give a special course in the latest techniques of ladder climbing to those on the bottom three rungs. As a result, several of them become better ladder-climbers than some of the people on the $4000 rung, the $5000 rung, and even the $6000 rung. They set out to climb to those higher rungs. Often they succeed and—as individuals—are no longer part of the "low-rung" world. But all this effort has *not* solved the "low-rung" problem. As these individuals climbed up and took over spots on the $4000, $5000, and $6000 rungs, the individuals who had occupied these spots were pushed down to the $1000, $2000, and $3000 rungs. Thus, the number of individuals on the lower rungs remained the same and the "lower rung" problem was just as grave.

Now, admittedly, the real economic world is not that simple. There probably is *some* elasticity on the working-class and middle-class rungs of the ladder. Possibly some more people can be squeezed in on those rungs without displacing those who are already there. But it may be naïve to suppose that there is an inexhaustible supply of openings for computer programmers, skilled electronics workers, teacher aids, among others, just because society might be able to train almost an unlimited number of people for those jobs. Poverty as a societal phenomenon—rather than an individual challenge— may be a problem of moving the rungs up the ladder rather than transferring individuals between the rungs. This view is held by economist Lester Thurow. See especially, Thurow, *Education and Economic Equality*, 28 The Public Interest 66 (1972).

46. Undated letter from Howard Westwood to Earl Johnson, at p. 8.
47. With 5 percent of the world's population, the United States has 44 percent

of its automobiles, 32 percent of its trucks, and 29 percent of its railroad mileage. The United States also produces 35 percent of the world's electricity, 60 percent of natural gas, and 25 percent of its steel, coal and oil. INFORMATION PLEASE ALMANAC (New York, 1971) at p. 112.

48. MILLER, RICH MAN, POOR MAN (New York: Crowell, 1971) at p. 16.

49. In 1966, the upper quintile received 43 percent of the nation's before-tax income and 41 percent of the after-tax income. *Ibid.*

50. In 1965, the lowest tenth among family units included all such units with annual incomes below $1870 and as a group received one percent of the nation's money income. U.S. DEPT. OF COMMERCE, STATISTICAL ABSTRACT OF THE UNITED STATES, 1972 (Washington: Government Printing Office, 1972) Table 529, at p. 324.

51. Haley, "Changes in the Distribution of Income in the United States," in SCOVILLE, PERSPECTIVES ON POVERTY AND INCOME DISTRIBUTION (Lexington: D.C. Heath, 1971) at p. 19.

52. "In 1935, the poorest fifth of the families and individuals received only 4 percent of the income. Their share rose to 5 percent in 1944 and has remained at about that level since." MILLER, *op. cit., supra,* n. 48, at p. 50.

53. "The lessening of inequality seems to be confined to those groups within the top half of the income distribution, with no great change in the income share of and no change in the inequality within the bottom half. The lowest one-fifth got 4.1 percent of income in 1935, 5.0 percent in 1947, and 4.6 percent in 1962. Lampman, "Income Distribution and Poverty," from GORDON, ed., POVERTY IN AMERICA (San Francisco: Chandler, 1965) at p. 105.

54. In 1964, the Council of Economic Advisers estimated $3000 was needed for a family of four to maintain a minimal standard of living. All families below the figure were "poor." Council of Economic Advisers, "The Problem of Poverty in America," in SCOVILLE, *op. cit., supra,* n. 51, at p. 67.

55. Orshansky, *Recounting the Poor—A Five Year Review,* Social Security Bulletin, Vol 24, No. 4. (April 1966) at p. 23.

56. OFFICE OF ECONOMIC OPPORTUNITY, THE POOR 1970: A CHARTBOOK (Washington: U.S. Government Printing Office, 1971) at p. 3. In 1972, it was raised again, to $4200 a year for a nonfarm family of four. OEO Digest, Vol 3, No. 4 (December 1972) at p. 8.

57. There is a constant stream of propaganda to the effect that America's poor are very well off by comparison with citizens of other countries. The point is often made that no matter how high we raise our economic ladder, there will always be a bottom rung and those who occupy that rung will still complain they are poor. It is certainly true that the standard of poverty has been moving upward constantly as our perception of minimal tolerable living standard is raised (and more often as a result of inflation.) But the conclusion that poverty is entirely relative and therefore can never be eliminated is not well drawn. The relevant comparison is not between poor people here and the destitute multitudes in other countries, but between the poor and the affluent segments in our own society. It is not unreasonable to anticipate that as long as the bottom 20 percent of America's population receives only 5 percent of

this nation's goods and services, they will always feel poor. They will feel, correctly so, that they are not sharing fairly in the nation's affluence. That would be true even if our gross national product were to climb to four or five times its present level so that a member of the bottom fifth would have as much shelter, food, transportation, entertainment, and so on as the *average* American does now.

58.   "Isn't it enough that the *amount* of income received by the poor has gone up substantially? Why be concerned about their share as the critical factor? . . . Arnold Toynbee . . . notes that minimum standards of living have been raised considerably . . . but he observes that this rise has not stopped us from 'demanding social justice,' and the unequal distribution of the worlds goods . . . has been transformed from an unavailable evil to an untolerable injustice.' " MILLER, *op. cit., supra,* n. 48, at p. 46.

A comparative study of income distribution in various countries reveals the United States actually affords its bottom fifth a smaller share of the national product than the average nation. On the other hand, the remaining 80 percent of our population split the rest of the economic pie more equitably than most. See "Income Distribution in Other Nations," Appendix I-B.

59.   See e.g. MILLER and ROBY, THE FUTURE OF INEQUALITY (New York: Basic Books, 1970).

60.   If the median income (the figure which divides the upper and lower halves of all receiving income) were over $10,000 (as it was in 1972), then according to those who accept this criteria, poverty would not be eliminated until each income unit received at least $5000 per annum.

61.   In 1964, the poverty income gap stood at $15.6 billion. STATISTICAL ABSTRACT, *op. cit., supra,* n. 50, Table 541, at p. 330.

62.   See, e.g., "Schemes for Transferring Income to the Poor," in SCOVILLE, *op. cit., supra,* n. 51, at p. 182.

63.   See pp. 205–06, *infra.*

64.   Of course, even a laissez-faire economy is structured by law, principally directed toward preserving free and open competition among private individuals and economic units. So, in that sense, political rules affect the distribution of goods and services even in a laissez-faire system. However, in the ideal situation, the rules do not favor any participant nor does the government intercede in any way on behalf of any individual or class.

65.   In 1967, the total of all taxes paid was 28 percent of the GNP. LAMPMAN, ENDS AND MEANS OF REDUCING INCOME POVERTY (Chicago: Markham, 1971) at p. 94. According to figures from "The Economic Report of the President, 1973" the total of Federal, state and local expenditures now amounts to 32 percent of the GNP.

66.   A 1966 study at the University of Michigan concluded that Federal income taxes in 1965 reduced inequality by 17.7 percent. OKNER, INCOME DISTRIBUTION AND THE FEDERAL INCOME TAX (Ann Arbor: Institute of Public Administration, 1966).

67.   The Federal personal income tax varies from 14 percent of taxable income for those in the lowest brackets to 70 percent of taxable income for those in the highest. Internal Revenue Code. 26 U.S.C. §1 (1970).

68. "The personal and corporate income taxes levied by the federal government, then, supply the major progressive elements in the over-all tax system. All other federal taxes and the state and local taxes taken together have a regressive effect which tempers the progressivity of the federal income taxes." LAMPMAN, *op. cit., supra,* n. 65, at p. 99.

69. When all taxes were considered, in 1965 those receiving the bottom fifth of personal income paid 22 percent of that income in taxes. The middle and upper-middle classes, earning between $3300 and $10,000 paid between 24 percent and 26 percent of their income in tax. *Id.* at p. 102. Another study based on data from Ohio reflected even less progressivity in the effective tax rates. Those with incomes under $2000 paid 34.2 percent of their income in Federal, state and local taxes; those earning $3000 to $3999 actually paid a slightly lower rate, 33 percent; and the middle class—those between $5000 and $7499—paid substantially less, 29 percent. Those earning $10,000 or over were taxed at a 38.9 percent rate. Batchelder, "Palliatives: Transfer from Peter to Paul," THE ECONOMICS OF POVERTY (New York: Wiley & Sons, 1966) at p. 137.

70. In 1965, the upper fifth of income earners, those who received more than $11,000, paid only 33 percent of their income in Federal, state and local taxes. LAMPMAN, *op. cit., supra,* n. 65, at p. 102. Exclusive of the upper 5 percent who paid at a 42 percent rate, the remainder of the upper quintile saw 29 percent of their income taken in Federal, state and local taxes. *Ibid.*

71. Columbia professor Paul Dodyk has made an interesting suggestion for modifying Federal income tax laws to mitigate the regressivity of other Federal, state and local levies. "Refunds of excess taxes paid or withheld have been with us since the inception of the Federal income tax, as has the notion of allowing deductions from income or credits against tax for tax payments to other jurisdictions. All that is required is to adapt these techniques to repay to taxpayers all tax payments—Federal, state or local—that have the result of reducing after-tax incomes to a level below those minimum standards necessary for a decent and healthful existence." Dodyk, *The Tax Reform Act of 1969 and the Poor,* 71 Columbia L. Rev. 758, 777 (1971).

72. "The term 'transfer' [means] a receipt of either money or goods or services for which less than a full quid pro quo payment was made, on service delivered, by the recipient in the current period. . . . The largest part of the transferring is done by public agencies, but a not insignificant amount is done by employers and employees via insurance benefits." LAMPMAN, *op. cit., supra,* n. 65, at pp. 103, 104.

73. In 1970, these farm subsidies amounted to $5831 million, compared to a total Federal expenditure on public assistance of $7621 million in that same year. Library of Congress, Legislative Reference Service, based on *The Budget of the United States Government;* Dept. of HEW, Social Security Bulletin (December, 1970).

74. The redistributive effects of tax subsidies are analyzed in Dodyk, *op. cit., supra,* n. 71. It has been pointed out that as a result of tax and ordinary subsidies, "[e]verybody—well, almost everybody—in this country is on wel-

fare . . ." MILWAUKEE COUNTY WELFARE RIGHTS ORGANIZATION, WELFARE MOTHERS SPEAK OUT (New York: Norton, 1972) at p. 17.

75. Various types of transfers in the United States in fiscal 1967 amounted to $132 billion, over one-sixth of the Gross National Product. LAMPMAN, *op. cit., supra,* n. 65, at p. 104.

76. The "pre-transfer poor"—the 25 percent of the population who would be below the poverty line but for transfer income . . . received $49.2 billion of these transfers. *Id.* at p. 107–08.

77. *Id.* at p. 109.

78. In 1967, 31 percent of families whose head was employed in agriculture were officially classified as "poor." By contrast, only 3 percent of those families whose head was employed in manufacturing were poor. LAMPMAN, *op. cit., supra,* n. 65 at p. 84.

79. "Of the three million [poor] families headed by a man under age 65 . . . half were 'fully employed' in terms of time spent on the job. Seven out of 10 of these men were white and so presumably not subjected to discrimination in the hiring hall." Orshansky, *"The Shape of Poverty in 1966,"* in SCOVILLE, *supra,* n. 51, at pp. 80–81.

80. *Id.* at p. 81.

81. For instance, bar associations and medical associations perform similar functions for lawyers and doctors as unions do for industrial workers.

82. *Williams* v. *Wirtz,* 2 Law in Action, No. 7, pp. 1, 10 (October 1967). In this action, California Rural Legal Assistance sought and was granted injunctive relief blocking the importation of braceros. The case was subsequently settled by an agreement between the Department of Labor and CRLA's clients, American farm workers. Under the terms of the agreement, the Department of Labor would screen the applications from growers for bracero certification with the full care that the law requires. Among other requirements, under the law, the grower must make reasonable efforts to recruit domestic workers.

83. *Alaniz, et al.,* v. *Wirtz, et al.,* Civ. No. 47807 (ND Cal., 1967). As a consequence of a settlement with the U.S. Department of Labor pursuant to this lawsuit, 5000 foreign workers were kept out of the labor market, thus preserving $2,250,000 in wages for American workers. CRLA *Annual Report to OEO,* submitted September 1969, at p. 23.

84. In 1966, the Bureau of the Census reported that 47 percent of craftsmen were union members and this group received 31 percent higher wages than nonunion craftsmen. In that same year, 49 percent of semiskilled workers were unionized and their annual earnings were 56 percent greater than the unorganized. MILLER, *op. cit., supra,* n. 48, at pp. 217, 219.

85. *Riviera* v. *Division of Industrial Welfare,* 71 Cal. Rptr. 739 (1968) ordering $.25 an hour wage increase for 200,000 California farmworkers. *Los Angeles Times,* Feb 16, 1973, at Editorial Page.

86. Legal Services cases seeking to expand coverage of minimum wage legislation include *Roebuck* v. *Florida Dept. of Health and Rehabilitation Services,* CA No. 1841 (ND Fla-1972)—seeking coverage for mentally retarded workers, and *Jontberg* v. *U.S. Dept. of Labor,* CA DKT 13–113 (D ME)—seeking coverage for patients of state hospitals.

87. Many economists charge that the net impact on occupations covered by such laws is to reduce employment by the amount that individual wages rise. See e.g. Brozen, *The effect of statutory minimum wage increases on teen-age employment*, 13 J. Law and Economics 109. (1970)

88. It should be remembered, however, that the Legal Services impact on the earnings structure is an entirely different matter from its effect on economic mobility. See notes *162–64, infra*, and accompanying text for description of some of the Program's activity in furtherance of better employment opportunities for minorities and the low-income sector.

89. In 1962, the lowest fifth of the population received approximately $25 billion in income, of which $10 billion consisted of transfer payments. LAMPMAN, *op. cit., supra*, n. 53, at p. 110.

   By 1970, 67.3 percent of families below the poverty line received transfer income in some form and this accounted for 50.5 percent of total income received by these poor families (all but 4.3 percent of the transfer being governmental in origin). U.S. DEPT. OF COMMERCE, *op. cit., supra*, n. 50, Table 546, at p. 333. For low income families headed by females, transfers provided 67.4 percent of their income and 77.3 percent received such transfers. *Ibid.*

   Although most transfer income going to the poor derives from government sponsored programs, they did receive some transfers from private sources, in fact, amounting to over 6.4 percent of their total income in 1970. The private transfers embraced dividends, interest and rent (2.1 percent of total income received by the poverty community) and private pension, alimony, and annuities (4.3 percent of poverty community income). However only 13.3 percent of the poor received any dividends, interest or rent and only 8.8 percent received any private pension, alimony, or annuity income. *Ibid.*

90. In 1965, 20 percent of the poor received public assistance which accounted for 13 percent of all income received by everyone below the poverty line and 60 percent of the income received by those who actually were on public assistance. MILLER, *op. cit., supra*, n. 48, at pp. 135–136. At that time Federal expenditures totalled approximately $2.4 billion. *Id.* at p. 133. Total public assistance expenditures (Federal, state and local) were $5.4 billion in 1965. Statistical Abstract, U.S. DEPT. OF COMMERCE, *op. cit., supra*, n. 50, Table 486, at p. 299.

   By 1970 the proportion of poor families on public assistance had increased by 50 percent—to 29.5 percent and this source provided 21.7 percent of the total income received by the poor, an increase of more than 50 percent in the five-year period. U.S. DEPT. OF COMMERCE, *op. cit., supra*, n. 50, Table 546, p. 333. For poor families headed by females, public assistance supplied 43.3 percent of their total support and 50.9 percent of such families were receiving this form of aid. Total expenditure for public assistance had reached $14.4 billion by this time and rose to $18.6 billion in 1971. *Id.*, Table 452, at p. 279.

91. In 1965, 34 percent of poor households received some form of Social Security. Twenty-two percent of all income going to the poverty community was derived from this source. MILLER, *op. cit., supra*, n. 48, at p. 134. Approxi-

mately 4.7 billion was transferred to the poor through this mechanism. *Id.* at p. 133.

By 1970, there had been a slight decrease in the population of low-income families receiving Social Security (29.7 percent) and the proportion of income derived from this source by the poverty sector (18.7 percent), perhaps accounted for by more liberal benefits moving many elderly persons over the poverty line. U.S. DEPT. OF COMMERCE, *op. cit., supra,* n. 50, Table 546, p. 333.

By 1971, Social Security payments to the poor had risen to $7.7 billion. *Id.,* Table 549, at p. 335.

92. In 1966, $200 million was transferred to the poor in the form of unemployment compensation. *Ibid.,* Table 549, at p. 335. This represented less than 1 percent of the total income received by the poverty sector. By 1971, unemployment compensation payments had trebled, contributing $600 million to the poverty sector. *Ibid.*

In 1970, the category of "other transfer payments," composed primarily of unemployment compensation, workmen's compensation, employee pensions, and veteran's payments, accounted for 3.8 percent of the total income received by poor families. Of these families, 9.3 percent received at least some income from one of these transfer programs. *Ibid.,* Table 546, at p. 333.

93. By 1970, 33.7 percent of poor families had no transfer income (39.6 percent of families headed by males and 20.7 percent of families headed by females) either from governmental or private sources. *Ibid.,* Table 546, at p. 333. This included the 3.3 percent of poverty units who had *no* income (2 percent of families headed by males and 5.5 percent of families headed by females). *Ibid.*

94. "Federal aid for public assistance originated with the Social Security Act of 1935, which authorized federal grants-in-aid based on state and local government expenditures for the programs. The establishment of a program depends on state implementation. Each state has a great deal of control over the number of recipients and virtually total control over the size of payments in its public assistance programs." Collins, "Public Assistance Expenditures in the United States," in SCOVILLE, *op. cit., supra,* n. 51, at p. 268.

95. Of course, in either case the gain in transfer income *might* be offset somewhat by a decrease in earned income if some marginal employees decided to stop working because they became eligible for welfare or the welfare income they might receive was raised to the point that it almost equalled their present wages.

96. Many of the restrictive eligibility rules are described in PIVEN and CLOWARD, *op. cit., supra,* n. 29, at pp. 126–145.

97. Typical of the substitute parent rule employed by 19 states as late as 1967 was Alabama's. AFDC payments were denied to children when an able bodied man cohabited with their mother, even if the man was not legally obligated to support the children or whether he in fact did so or not. For a full discussion of substitute parent rules see the opinion of Chief Justice Warren in *King* v. *Smith,* 392 U.S. 309, 88 S. Ct. 2128, 20 L. Ed. 2d 1118 (1968).

98. The most common residency requirement was that persons were not eligible

to receive public assistance until they resided in a state for one year. See, *e.g.,* Conn. Gen. Stat. Rev. §17–2d (1966); D.C. Code Ann. §3–203 (1967); Pa. Stat., Tit. 62, §432(6) (1968).

99. The Supreme Court struck down Alabama's substitute parent rule, note 97 *supra,* because it was inconsistent with the Social Security Act:

> We believe that Congress intended the term "parent" in §406 (a) of the Act, 42 U.S.C.A. §606 (a), to include only those persons with a legal duty of support. *King* v. *Smith, supra,* at 392 U.S. 324

The ruling also invalidated similar provisions in eighteen other states.

100. The generally stated purpose in imposing a one-year residency requirement for the receipt of public assistance was to keep indigents from migrating to a state solely to take advantage of its public assistance program. The Supreme Court held this to be an impermissible purpose on an equal protection theory in *Shapiro* v. *Thompson,* 394 U.S. 618, 89 S.Ct. 1322, 22 L. Ed. 2d 600 (1969).

101. These estimates were reported in *The New York Times,* May 19, 1968, at p. 32; April 22, 1969, at p. 1; June 3, 1969, at p. 28.

Two of the leading welfare theorists give test cases considerable credit for the entire surge of public assistance income to the poor in the late 1960s and early 1970s.

"There is no way of measuring the exact impact of these major legal reforms on the welfare rolls; all that can be said is that it has been considerable. Persons knowledgeable in the public welfare field generally believe that at least 100,000 persons annually had been denied aid because of residence laws. Attorneys and welfare rights organizers in the South estimated tens of thousands of families were denied aid under employable-mothers rules. Once such rules were weakened or abandoned, approval rates rose, and the rolls grew. . . . The effect of this continuous and much publicized course of litigation was startling: in Mobile, for example, the caseload rose from 1700 to 3100 (an increase of 82 percent) in the brief period between June 1966 and February 1969." PIVEN and CLOWARD, *op. cit., supra,* n. 29, at p. 309.

Public assistance income increased by $4.5 billion from 1967 to 1971 and the number of recipients by almost six million, with most of these increments in AFDC. U.S. DEPT OF COMMERCE, *op. cit., supra,* n. 50, Table 486, at p. 299. Legal Service lawyers are given even more credit for this development by another observer in Liebman, *Book Review,* 85 Harvard Law Review 1682 (1972).

Some observers disagree with the conclusion that liberalizing eligibility standards in welfare programs raises the total income transferred to the poor. They argue that any increase in the number of individuals participating in the program will be counterbalanced by a commensurate reduction in the payment schedule, thus leaving the total distribution at the original level. The result of loosening eligibility criteria, in other words, is merely to slice the welfare pie into more but smaller pieces rather than expanding the size of the pie itself.

This thesis does not appear to square with the facts. It is true there are jurisdictions where a sudden surge in welfare rolls has prompted cutbacks in individual benefit schedules. On a national level, however, the net impact of changes in eligibility rules has been a simultaneous sharp increase in both numbers of recipients and levels of payments. In the year immediately following the residency decision, the combination of favorable court decisions and active assertion of welfare rights produced a 17 percent rise in recipients of a single Federal assistance program—Aid to Families with Dependent Children (AFDC). Yet the welfare pie did not remain constant. In fact, as the chart reveals, the average benefit actually rose moderately at the same time as the number of beneficiaries was moving upward dramatically. The cumulative effect was enough to increase the total welfare budget by 20 percent in that single year. [Department of HEW, *Advance Copy of Selected Tables from Public Assistance Statistics* (July 1970).]

Table 1. AFDC Recipients and Payments, 1964 through June 1970

Year	Average monthly number of recipients	Child participation rate per 1,000[a]	Average monthly payment	Total expenditure
1964	4,118,000	45	$30.30	$1,496,525,000
1965	4,329,000	47	31.65	1,644,096,000
1966	4,513,000	49	34.15	1,849,886,000
1967	5,014,000	55	37.40	2,249,673,000
1968	5,705,000	63	41.25	2,823,841,000
1969	6,706,000	75	44.10	3,546,668,000
1970, January-June	7,912,000	—	46.35	—

a. Number of children participating per 1,000 children in total population under 18.

STEINER, THE STATE OF WELFARE (Washington, D.C.: Brookings Institution, 1971), p. 32.

One explanation for this result is found in the way welfare is financed and budgeted. Over half the funding is supplied by the Federal government on an open-ended basis. Whatever the state and local authorities appropriate, the national treasury will match. The state and local governments, in turn, divide their share of the burden on some fixed formula. These governments set the benefit levels and eligibility criteria. But once they do, any one is entitled to assistance if he fits the category defined. Thus, the total has a built-in flexibility. Unlike public housing, for instance, where a fixed resource exists and only a limited number of applicants will be accepted, welfare aid is paid to whomever qualifies. In fact, Federal regulations prohibit state and local governments from arbitrarily denying public assistance to needy individuals who satisfy the general eligibility requirements. ["In denying AFDC assistance . . . on the basis of this invalid regulation, Alabama has breached its federally imposed obligation to furnish aid to families with dependent children . . . with reasonable promptness to all eligible individuals. . . . 42 U.S.C. § 602(a) (9). . . ." *King* v. *Smith*, 392 U.S., 309, 354 (1968).]

Local and state governments are further encouraged to be relatively liberal in both benefits and eligibility standards by the fact they can "purchase" two dollars of welfare for only one dollar of their own funds. Actually, since state and local bodies generally divide this expense, either of them can "buy" welfare at a still lower cost, with the Federal treasury and the other levels of government bearing the bulk of the burden.

102. Total public assistance payments were $7.8 billion in 1967. By the end of 1971, as a result of the broadening of eligibility rights, the assertion of existing rights and higher benefit schedules, this had more than doubled to $17.7 billion per year. U.S. DEPT. OF COMMERCE, *op. cit., supra,* n. 50, Table 486, p. 299.

103. In 1968, the poverty income gap was almost $11 billion. *Ibid.,* Table 541 at p. 330. This percentage reduction in the income gap is calculated on the basis of the "minimum standard of living definition of poverty." See pp. 196–98, *supra.*

104. The total annual income received by the bottom quintile in 1968 was approximately $30 billion.

105. For a concise presentation of this view, see Tobin, "The Case for an Income Guarantee," in SCOVILLE, *op. cit., supra,* n. 51, pp. 289–293. In 1969, President Nixon adopted the "income floor" approach. In "Proposals for Welfare Reform," the President stated: "I propose that the federal government pay a basic income to those American families who cannot care for themselves in whichever state they live. The income floor for a family of four would be $1600." SCOVILLE, *id.* at pp. 302–310. However, this 1969 proposal was not adopted as the 92d Congress adjourned in October, 1972.

106. Lampman has stated that even the adoption of Nixon's modest proposal would add $3 billion to the cash transfers to the poor. LAMPMAN, *op. cit., supra,* n. 65, at p. 162.

107. Typical of regulations of this type was the scheme employed by Maryland. A limit of $250 per month was imposed upon the benefits which any one family receiving public assistance under the AFDC program could receive. See Md. Manual of Department of Public Welfare, pt. II, Rule 200, Sched. A, p. 27.

108. This practice is especially significant since it permits local authorities to maintain politically popular recipients at an adequate standard of living without doing the same for unpopular ones. If the blind and disabled could not receive an adequate stipend unless an equal income were provided the equally needy children of dependent mothers, there would be stronger public support for higher benefit levels generally.

109. The Social Security Law was amended in 1967 to prohibit states from paying less than the minimum standard of need determined as of January 1, 1967, to AFDC recipients. 42 U.S.C. §402 (a) (23) (1970).

New York then enacted a provision which called for the payment of a flat grant of $100 per year to each AFDC recipient in New York City for "special" needs, such as clothing. 1969 N.Y. Stats. c. 184. This replaced the previous system of allowing each individual's need to be determined separately. As a result, the welfare bill for New York City was cut $40,000,000 from the amount paid using the standards in effect on January 1, 1967.

110. In *Dandridge* v. *Williams,* 397 U.S. 471, 90 S.Ct. 1153, 25 L. Ed. 2d 491 (1970), the Court upheld the Maryland maximum grant regulation: ". . . the Constitution does not empower this Court to second guess state officials charged with the difficult responsibility of allocating limited public welfare funds among the myriad of potential recipients." *Id.* at p. 487.

In *Rosado* v. *Wyman,* 397 U.S. 397, 90 S. Ct. 1207, 25 L. Ed. 2d 442 (1970), the court upheld the New York flat grant rule. The court held: "Providing all factors in the old equation are accounted for and fairly priced and providing the consolidation on a statistical basis reflects a fair averaging, a State may, of course, consistently with §402 (a) (23) redefine its method of determining need." *Id.* at p. 419.

111. *Morris* v. *Williams,* 63 Cal. Rptr. 689 (1967), where the California Supreme Court found that regulations pursuant to the Medi-Cal program, which sought to reduce minimum coverage for recipients of public assistance and sought to eliminate certain services entirely, were invalid as violative of California statutes.

112. The regulations struck down by the court sought to cutback state expenditures by $211 million. The decision of the court restored the cutback. 63 Cal. Rptr. 689, 697 (1967).

113. "Neither food stamp programs nor commodity programs exist in over one-third of our poorest countries." *Hearings on Senate Resolution 281.* Senate Committee on Labor and Public Welfare (1968) at p. 14.

114. "The Secretary [of Agriculture] has returned more than one billion dollars to the Treasury in the last ten years—money which could have been spent on alleviating hunger." Clancy and Wyse, *Feeding the Hungry,* 5 Harvard Civil Rights—Civil Liberties L. Rev. 440, 446 (1970).

115. 2 CCH Poverty Law Reporter para. 9114 (1968). Among these cases was *Jay* v. *USDA,* 2 CCH Poverty Law Reporter para. 10,790 (ND Tex, Dec. 30, 1968), in which the District Court held that the purpose of the legislation was to feed the poor not merely help the farmer and ordered the program implemented in the 109 Texas counties that had refused to participate. Similar victories were scored in California, Missouri and other states. Soon most were falling in line.

As reported in a recent study, "Under pressure from OEO and the Senate Poverty Subcommittee, the Department of Agriculture . . . began a project designed to insure that a food assistance program would be available in each of the thousand counties with the lowest per capita income." SEGAL, FOOD FOR THE HUNGRY: THE RELUCTANT SOCIETY (Baltimore: Johns Hopkins Press, 1970) p. 52.

116. Not only were all but eight of the 1000 poorest counties brought into the program, but so was most of the rest of the nation. "As of January 1970, the food programs were operating in 2,731 of the 3,049 counties in the country and in 25 independent cities." *Id.* at p. 52.

117.   From 1967 to 1971 various forces—including the Legal Services lawsuits—
        combined to increase the number of "participating areas" from 838 to 2027,
        the number of food stamp recipients from 1,832,000 to 10,567,000 and the
        Federal investment in food stamps from $296 million to $2.7 billion. U.S.
        DEPT. OF COMMERCE, *op. cit., supra,* n. 50, Table 133, p. 87.

118.   Successful cases to require local government to enlarge school lunch pro-
        grams were filed in Chicago [*Stogner* v. *Page,* Civ. No. 69C 1338 (ND Ill.,
        1970)]; Detroit [*Kennedy* v. *Detroit Board of Education,* Civ. No. 33, 367 (ED
        Mich., 1970)]; Milwaukee [*Gully* v. *Board of Schools of Milwaukee,* Civ. No.
        69C468 (ED Wis., 1970)]; Pueblo, Colorado [*Ayala* v. *District 60 School
        Board of Pueblo, Colo.,* Civ. No. C-2067 (D. Colo., 1970)]; and Modesto,
        Calif. [*Shaw* v. *Governing Board of Modesto City School Dist.,* 310 F. Supp
        1282 (ED Cal., 1970)]. These and other similar suits are credited with helping
        to prod Congress to improve and enlarge the school lunch program in 1970.
        Note, *The National School Lunch Program, 1970: Mandate to Feed the Chil-
        dren,* 60 Geo. L. Journal 711, 712–713 (1972). For further discussions of the
        school lunch program see Note, *Feeding the Hungry,* 5 Harvard Civil Rights
        —Civil Liberties L. Rev. 440 (1970) and Comment, *The National School
        Lunch Program,* 119 U. Pa. L. Rev. 372 (1970).

119.   See, e.g., Merson, *Municipal Services—Hawkins* v. *Town of Shaw,* 48 Denver
        L.J. 286 (1971); Ratner, *Inter-Neighborhood Denials of Equal Protection in the
        Provision of Municipal Services,* 4 Harvard Civil Rights—Civil Liberties L.
        Rev. 1 (1968); Comment, *Equal Protection in the Urban Environment: The
        Right to Equal Municipal Services,* 46 Tulane L. Rev. 496 (1972).

120.   See, e.g., Comment, *Educational Financing, Equal Protection of the Laws and
        the Supreme Court,* 70 Mich L. Rev. 1324 (1972); Ratner, *op. cit., supra,* n. 119.

121.   *Serrano* v. *Priest,* 5 Cal. 3d 584, 487 P. 2d 1241 (1971); *Rodriguez* v. *San
        Antonio School Dist.,* 337 F. Supp 280 (W D Tex 1971) revd. U.S. Supreme
        Court Bulletin B 1663 (1972–73) decided March 21, 1973; *Van Dusartz* v.
        Hatfield, 334 F. Supp. 870 (D. Minn. 1971); *Robinson* v. *Cahill,* 118 N. J.
        Super 223, 287 A 2d 187 (1972). For a discussion of the economic and
        educational dimensions of school financing, see COONS, *et al.,* PRIVATE
        WEALTH AND PUBLIC EDUCATION (Cambridge: Belknap Press, 1970) and
        WISE, RICH SCHOOLS, POOR SCHOOLS: THE PROMISE OF EQUAL EDUCA-
        TIONAL OPPORTUNITY (Chicago: Univ. of Chicago Press, 1968). For a dis-
        cussion of the implications outside the educational field see the articles and
        cases cited in note 119.

122.   This center founded in 1968 at the University of California, Berkeley, bears
        the full title "National Housing and Economic Development Law Project."
        The staff of the Project has produced a multivolume guide to Federal housing
        programs, subsequently published by Prentice-Hall, and has assisted many
        local Legal Services agencies to apply for funds on behalf of local community
        groups.

123.   Among the local Legal Services agencies that have helped poverty groups to
        obtain government funds are the Cleveland Legal Aid Society, California
        Rural Legal Assistance, the Navajo Legal Services Program (Dinebeina

Nahilna Be Agaditahe), the San Francisco Neighborhood Legal Assistance Foundation, and the St. Louis Legal Aid Society.

124. Some of the more interesting examples of this phase of legal services work: The Cleveland Legal Aid Society aided a community-based organization in the Hough area (a run-down black ghetto) to obtain $8 million in funds, most in the form of government-subsidized loans, to construct low-rent housing and over $2 million for another low-rent project elsewhere in the city. The Cleveland Legal Services lawyers also played a key role in obtaining the government financial assistance that permitted community organizations to create and control a shopping center containing a supermarket and 16 other businesses, to start a $125,000 restaurant and to purchase two "McDonald's" franchises. (Interview with Burt Griffin, Cleveland, Ohio, February 2, 1973.)

In the meantime, CRLA has aided community groups to build Federally financed housing for migrants in several areas of the state. Near Watsonville, CRLA attorneys also assisted the creation of a strawberry cooperative owned and operated by 35 farmworker families. A total of $215,000 in grants and loans have been obtained for the cooperative since 1969. The average income of the 35 families has almost tripled—to $10,000 per annum. (Interview with David Madway, Director, Economic Development Section, National Housing and Economic Development Law Project, University of California, Berkeley, California, January 26, 1973.)

Other examples are described in *Application for Refunding (Economic Development Component),* National Housing and Economic Development Law Project, dated July 1, 1972, at pp. 3–15.

125. An excellent analysis of the factors which led to this result may be found in Note, *Consumer Legislation and the Poor,* 76 Yale L. Journal 745 (1967).

126. "The survey disclosed that without exception low-income market retailers had high average mark-ups and prices. On the average, goods purchased for $100 at wholesale sold for $255 in the low-income market stores, compared with $159 in general market stores." Federal Trade Commission, *Economic Report on Installment Credit and Retail Sales Practices of District of Columbia Retailers,* (1968) p. 2.

127. CAPLOVITZ, THE POOR PAY MORE (New York: Free Press of Glencoe, 1963). The study shows that merchants located in New York City sell durable goods to low-income purchasers at higher prices than the same goods would have sold for in the general market. The main reasons for the higher prices were the high risk of doing business with the poor and the merchants' willingness to use illegal and/or unethical marketing prices.

128. Note, *op. cit., supra,* n. 125, at p. 756.

129. CAPLOVITZ, *op. cit., supra,* n. 127, at pp. 28–29. A common sales device is to advertise products for extremely low prices to attract customers. Once inside the store, the customer can be persuaded to buy less merchandise at a slightly higher price. The problem here is that the higher eventual price does not represent increased quality but, rather, the customer often buys refinished products as "new."

130. See CAPLOVITZ, *op. cit., supra,* n. 127, at pp. 142–154 for a description of the

most common sales practices used to deceive the low-income consumer. The classic case involving these practices is *Leon A. Tashof,* FTC 168, CCH Trade Reg. Serv., para. 18,606.

131.   This practice has been made illegal in many states. See e.g., Cal. Civil Code, Section 1803.4. And yet the practice continues. See *Morgan v. Reasor Corp.,* 69 C. 2d 881, 73 Cal. Rptr. 398, 447 P. 2d 638 (1968).

132.   Courts have been forced to resort to varied doctrines in order to circumvent the effects of such agreements. A finding of fraud is common [e.g., *Norman v. World Wide Distributors, Inc.* (Super. Ct. of Pa. 1963), 195 A.2d 115]. A finding of "usury" is another example [*Matthews v. Aluminum Acceptance Corp.* (Mich. App.Ct., 3d Div., 1965), 137 N.W.2d 280]. But in most situations in the past these practices have been allowed to continue.

133.   CAPLOVITZ, *op. cit., supra,* n. 127, at pp. 147–150.

134.   See e.g., *Uni-Serv. Corp. v. Commr. of Banks,* 349 Mass. 283, 207 N.E.2d 906 (1965). For a discussion of the time-price differential in the context of modern installment sales, see Warren, *Regulation of Finance Charge in Retail Installment Sales,* 68 Yale L. Journal 834 (1959).

135.   "Studies have shown that as much as 35 percent of low-income households, compared to 14 percent of other households, shop for food outside of chain or discount stores. . . . A consumer survey . . . in Detroit found that inner-city chains had prices 3 to 5 percent higher than their counterparts in the suburbs and concluded that because many of the poor had to shop in corner groceries, . . . they paid from 20 to 40 percent more for their groceries." SEGAL, *op. cit., supra,* n. 115, at p. 32.

136.   Minorities sometimes find themselves paying the same rent as whites for less housing or higher rents for identical or worse housing. As reported by the Riot Commission:

> In Detroit, whites paid a median rental of $77 as compared to $76 among non-whites. Yet 27 percent of nonwhite units were deteriorating or dilapidated, as compared to only 10.3 percent of all white units.
> [I]n four areas of [Newark, New Jersey] nonwhites with housing essentially similar to that of whites paid rents that were from 8.1 percent to 16.8 percent higher. . . . This condition prevails in most racial ghettoes. [REPORT OF THE NATIONAL ADVISORY COMMISSION ON CIVIL DISORDERS (New York: Bantam ed., 1968) at p. 471.]

137.   Wald, *Law and poverty: 1965* (Washington: OEO, 1965) p. 13. Minorities find an especially high percentage of their income taken up with rental payments. The Riot Commission found that in Cleveland 33.8% of non-whites paid 35 percent of their income or more on rent while only 8.6% of whites spent this much on this item in their budget. In Kansas City, 40 percent of nonwhite and 20 percent of whites devoted 35 percent or more of their income to rent. REPORT OF THE NATIONAL ADVISORY COMMISSION ON CIVIL DISORDERS at p. 471.

138.   "In 1960, there were 3,684,000 urban slum housing units. Of these 1,173,000 were 'dilapidated urban units' by the standard definition used in the 1960

census. The remaining 2,511,000 were urban housing units lacking some or all plumbing facilities. In this urban slum housing, at least 12.5 million people lived." HUNTER, THE SLUMS: CHALLENGE AND RESPONSE (New York: Free Press, 1968) p. 32.

139. Some of the primary handicaps the low-income consumer brings to the marketplace are catalogued in Note, L. J., *op. cit., supra,* n. 125 at pp. 748–752.

140. See e.g., *Imperial Discount Corp.* v. *Aiken,* 38 Misc. 2d 187, 238 NYS 2d 269 (1963) disallowing a pyramid of extra expense charged defaulting debtor as unconscionable; *Jefferson Credit Corp.* v. *Marcano,* 302 NYS 2d 390 (1969) denying the seller's attempt to collect on an automobile that fell apart and invalidating the clauses waiving such defense on grounds this conduct was unconscionable as practiced on uneducated, Spanish-speaking customers; *Jones* v. *Star Credit Corp.,* 59 Misc. 2d 189, 298 NYS 2d 264 (Sup. Ct. 1969) holding gross overcharging itself is unconscionable conduct. And in *Fairfield Credit Corp.* v. *Donnelly,* 158 Conn. 543, 264 A 2d 547 (1969), waivers of defense clauses were held unenforceable.

Certain collection practices have been curtailed. *Fuentes* v. *Shevin,* 407 U.S. 67 (1972) (prejudgment replevin of goods purchased on installment); *Snaidach* v. *Family Finance, Corp.,* 395 U.S. 337 (1968) (prejudgment garnishment of wages); *Adams* v. *Egley,* 40 U.S. Law Week 2456 (SD Cal. 1972) (prejudgment repossession). See also cases collected in *Coercive Collection Tactics—An Analysis of the Interests and Remedies,* 1972 Wash. U.L.Q. 315 (Winter, 1972).

Retaliatory evictions have been ruled illegal [*Edwards* v. *Habib,* 397 F 2d 687 (DC Cir. 1968); *Dickhut* v. *Norton,* 173 N.W. 2d 297 (Wis Sup. Ct. 1970)] and tenants have been authorized to place rental payments in escrow pending compliance with housing codes [*DePaul* v. *Kauffman,* 272 A2d 500 (Pa. Sup. Ct. 1971)], to withhold rent entirely [*Bonner* v. *Beechem,* 1 Pov. L. Rept., para. 2225.26 (Colo. Co. Ct., Denver, No. 2–76984, Feb. 20, 1970)] or to pay a reduced rent (*Morbeth Realty Corp.* v. *Rosenshine* 323 NYS 2d N.Y. City Civ. Ct. 1971). Tenants also have been authorized to make repairs themselves and deduct the cost from rent [*Marini* v. *Ireland,* 56 NJ 130 (1970)]. An implied warranty of habitability has been imposed in some jurisdictions [see *Lemle* v. *Breeden,* 462 P 2d 470 (Haw. Sup. Ct. 1969)] and breach of that warranty can result in money damages (*Grigsby* v. *Rabb,* Cal. Munic. Ct., No. 226505, June 12, 1969, 1 Pov. L. Rept., para. 2105.19) or reduction of rent [*Mease* v. *Fox,* 200 NW 2d 791 (Iowa Sup. Ct. 1972)].

141. See e.g., Hazard, *op. cit., supra,* n. 44, at p. 707 and STERNLIEB, THE TENEMENT LANDLORD (New Brunswick: Rutgers, 1966).

142. "While a *selective* program of [housing code] enforcement may be expected to increase rents in the 'target area,' a *comprehensive* program of enforcement will not increase rents charged in Slumville [a hypothetical low-income housing area] provided that there are a significant number of lukewarm families who refuse to pay more for standard units than they paid for 'inferior' units." Ackerman, *Regulating Slum Housing Markets on Behalf of the Poor: Of Housing Codes, Housing Subsidies and Income Redistribution Policy,* 80 Yale L. Journal 1093, 1108 (1971).

The Ackerman article, over 100 pages in length, describes a variety of hypothetical slum markets in which comprehensive code enforcement will yield improved housing conditions without raising rents or closing units.

143. Hazard, *op. cit., supra,* n. 44, at p. 707.

144. See pp. 204–05, *supra.*

145. See, e.g., *Clermont* v. *Secured Investment Corp.,* 25 Cal. App 3d 766 (1972), which held it was illegal to impose certain standard "late charges" on debtors who were tardy with their loan payments. This widespread practice netted millions of dollars of unearned income for lending institutions in California, especially mortgage brokers, over and above legal interest charges. The *Clermont* case is one of a series brought by the Western Center on Law and Poverty challenging various practices of the mortgage broker industry.

146. In Miami, for instance, proceedings against a vocational school were accompanied by legislative action to tighten regulations of such organizations.

147. Virtually every Legal Services agency of any size has closed or curtailed some major rackets. In Chicago, portrait studio and modeling school swindles were put out of business. In Miami, a phony half-million-dollar vocational school was shut down. In Washington, D.C., a multimillion-dollar home improvement racket was stopped and through poverty lawyers' efforts the owners were convicted of civil fraud. The Austin, Texas, program likewise put an end to a multimillion-dollar home improvement scheme. In each of these cities, it took a time-consuming, well-coordinated effort usually involving class action, legislative advocacy, and so on, to accomplish the result.

148. It is reported that in ancient Rome a creditor was entitled by law to imprison a defaulting debtor, to enslave and even kill him [Durant, Caesar and Christ (New York: Simon and Shuster, 1944) at p. 22]. One can almost hear an advocate for the creditors of Rome addressing the Senate as it considers a reform that would limit the remedies to imprisonment and loss of one hand:

> Friends, Romans, Countrymen, if you pass this pernicious law you will be injuring all the plebeians in Rome. For if those who have money to lend cannot extract the last full measure they will be unable to collect their debts from the poor. And if they cannot collect their debts, why should they lend money? And if those with money will not lend it, will not the plebeians be unable to borrow?
> A Senator: But Hazardus, may not the plebeians prefer to be alive and poor, rather than dead and poor? And may not those who have money prefer to lend it at some risk rather than have it rust in the cellar?
> Hazardus: Et tu, Brutus?

See also pp. 261–62, *infra.*

149. Some of the limited literature on this question is summarized in Windham, Education, Equality and Income Redistribution (Lexington: D. C. Heath, 1971): "It was usually assumed that education, especially if it was equally available to all, would reduce income inequality by equalizing the abilities of individuals. Henry George, for one, doubted this assumption. In his view educational inequalities were results and not primary causes of income differences." *Id.* at p. 6. See also, Cheswick, *The Average Level of Schooling and the Intra-Regional Inequality of Income: A Clarification,* 58

Amer. Econ. Rev. 495 (1968); Mineer, *Investment in Human Capital and Personal Income Distribution,* 66 Found. Pol. Econ. 281 (1958). For a recent, provocative study concluding that educational equality will not equalize income, see JENCKS, INEQUALITY (New York: Basic Books, 1972).

150.　See Hazard, *op. cit., supra,* n. 44, at pp 707–08.

151.　"Men who see little opportunity for improvement in their own economic status, or, at least, that of their children, have greater inducements than those anticipating advancements in status to organize a union to raise wages or to vote for a party that advocates higher taxes for the wealthy. . . . It follows from these unproved but plausible considerations that high rates of mobility permit extant differences in rewards to persist and even to grow." BLAU and DUNCAN, THE AMERICAN OCCUPATIONAL STRUCTURE (New York: Wiley and Sons, 1967) p. 440.

152.　*Id.* at pp. 206–208.

153.　MILLER, *op. cit., supra,* n. 48. As reported in a major study of occupational mobility, "[T]he general conclusion is that the American occupational structure is largely governed by universalistic criteria of performance and achievement, with the notable exception of the influence of race." BLAU and DUNCAN, *id.* at p. 291. The problems of employment discrimination are surveyed in Note, *Minority Workers and the Continuing Effects of Racial Discrimination—The Limits of Remedial Treatment,* 58 Iowa L. Rev. 143 (1972).

　　　　". . . the incidence of poverty among Negroes rose between 1950 and 1962 from 2 to 2½ times the white rate." Batchelder, "Poverty: The Special Case of the Negro," in SCOVILLE, *op. cit., supra,* n. 51, at p. 119.

154.　Kentucky was the only Southern state in which the average income of the Negro reached 60 percent of the white average, dropping as low as one-third in Mississippi and South Carolina," MILLER, *op. cit., supra,* n. 48, at p. 98.

155.　In 1962, the Department of Labor's projection of these figures for 1972 was 14.3 percent for whites and 41.7 percent for nonwhites. Marshall, "Economic Conditions of Negro Workers," in SCOVILLE, *op. cit., supra,* n. 51, at p. 140.

156.　Educational statistics for whites and nonwhites account in part for the fact that negroes are under-represented in the higher paying jobs. In 1965, 11.8 percent of non-whites had not finished the fifth grade. Only 24.4 percent had completed high school and the median number of years spent in school by nonwhites was 10.5. By contrast, only 2.7 percent of whites failed to finish the fifth grade, 36.8 percent had finished high school and all whites spent a median of 12.3 years in school. *Id.* at p. 148.

157.　Even when nonwhites had the same educational background as whites, they do not get equal paying jobs. In 1961, whites with four years of high school earned an average salary of $6390 as opposed to $4559 for nonwhites. Whites with four years of college earned $9315 on the average while nonwhites earned only $7875. *Id.* at p. 147.

158.　See BERGER, EQUALITY BY STATUTE (New York: Doubleday, 1968) at p. 216.

159.　Berger points out that in 1942, before the school desegregation cases, only 2 percent of Southern whites favored desegregation. In 1956, two years after

Brown, 14 percent of whites in the South favored desegregation. By 1963, this figure had risen to 30 percent. *Id.* at p. 230.

160. *Id.* at 223–224. A similar conclusion is reported in MAYHEW, LAW AND EQUAL OPPORTUNITIES (Cambridge: Harvard Press, 1968) at pp. 282–283.

161. *Id.* at pp. 226–230.

162. *Johnson* v. *Inglewood Board of Educ.,* LA Sup. Ct. #973669 (1969): *Soria* v. *Oxnard School Dist.,* 328 F. Supp. 155 (S.D. Cal. 1971). The Oxnard school board sought a stay of the desegregation order. This request was denied by the Ninth Circuit on August 21, 1972 and by the U.S. Supreme Court on September 24, 1972.

163. See e.g., *Diana* v. *California State Board of Education,* No. C-70 37 RFP (N.D. Cal. 1970) requiring I.Q. placement tests to be given in both English and Spanish.

164. As an example, CRLA filed a lawsuit against the Imperial Irrigation District charging discriminatory employment practices [*NAACP, et al.* v. *Imperial Irrigation District,* Civ. No. 70-302-GT (S.D. Cal. March 31, 1972]. They then negotiated an agreement for an affirmative action plan in which the District promised to eliminate discriminatory testing requirements and to hire only minority applicants until certain target percentages are reached.

165. The San Francisco Legal Services Agency challenged written tests required for firemen in that city, *Western Addition Community Organization, et al.* v. *Alioto, et al.,* 340 F Supp. 1351 (N.D. Cal., 1972). A similar challenge was made by various bay area Legal Services agencies against tests required by certain labor unions [*DeLeon* v. *Operating Engineers,* Civ. No. C-71 898 RFP (N.D. Cal., 1971).] See, generally, Cooper and Sobol, *Seniority and Testing Under Fair Employment Laws: A General Approach to Objective Criteria of Hiring and Promotion,* 82 Harvard L. Rev. 1598 (1969); Note, *Employment Testing: The Aftermath of Griggs* v. *Duke Power Company,* 72 Columbia L. Rev. 900 (1972).

166. According to the 1970 Census, nonwhite families had a median income of $6308 versus $3161 in 1960 while white families had a median income of $9961 in 1970 and $5893 in 1960. Thus, the income of nonwhites increased by 99.6 percent during the decade while white income only rose 69 percent. "General Social and Economic Characteristics," U.S. BUREAU OF THE CENSUS, CENSUS OF POPULATION (Washington: U.S. Government Printing Office, 1972) at pp. 1–355, 1–377–78.

167. In 1960, the West Virginia county with the highest unemployment rate (17.1 percent) and the next to lowest median family income in the state also had the highest high-school dropout rate (47.3 percent). For those counties with an unemployment rate of 6 percent or less, the dropout rate was below the state average. Aside from the cost of attending school, students with a low family income drop out for two main reasons: (1) a high level of education is not expected of him; (2) he generally finds school difficult and leaves to escape failure. Gibbard, "Poverty and Social Organization," in FISHMAN, POVERTY AMID AFFLUENCE, (New Haven: Yale University Press, 1965) pp. 61–62.

168. Residence is determinative, to a great extent, of the quality of one's education because of the system of financing public education by the local property tax. See notes 169–74, *infra,* and accompanying text.

169. *Serrano* v. *Priest,* 5 Cal. 3d 584, 594, 487 P. 2d 1241, 96 Cal.Rptr. 601, 607 (1971).

170. *Ibid.*

171. The Texas statistics are reported in Comment, *op. cit., supra,* n. 120, at p. 1326, fn. 8.

172. For the 1969–1970 school year in California, school districts spent as much as $2586 per pupil in elementary classes and as little as $407 per pupil. This disparity is due chiefly to the difference in the assessed valuation of real property in the low- and high-budget school districts. *Serrano, op. cit., supra,* n. 169, at pp. 607–608. Since commercial and industrial property ordinarily is taxed also, school districts encompassing large business districts or heavy industrial concentrations sometimes enjoy a tax windfall.

173. *Ibid.*

174. The Texas scheme of financing public education by local property tax revenues was attacked successfully in *Rodriguez* v. *San Antonio Independent School District,* 299 F.Supp. 476 (1969). However, this decision was reversed by the Supreme Court, U.S. Supreme Court Bulletin B 1663 (1972–73), decided March 21, 1973. Similar cases were brought in New York, *Spona* v. *Board of Education of Lakeland Central School, District No. 1, Town of Yorktown,* CCH Poverty Law Reporter, para. 15, 138 (1972); and Kansas, *Caldwell, et al.,* v. *Kansas,* CCH Poverty Law Reporter, para. 16,079 (1972).

   See e.g., Goldstein, *Interdistrict Inequalities in School Financing: A Critical Analysis of Serrano* v. *Priest and Its Progeny,* 120 U. Pa. L. Rev. 504 (1972).

175. See note 88 and accompanying text, *supra.*

176. An Oakland social worker lost his job for refusing to participate in a mass unannounced search of welfare recipients' homes early on a Sunday morning. This was common practice as late as 1963. The worker was eventually reinstated when the policy was declared unconstitutional in *Parrish* v. *Civil Service Commission,* 66 Cal. 2d 260 (1967).

   See, generally, Reich, *Midnight Welfare Searches and the Social Security Act,* 72 Yale L. Journal 1347 (1963).

177. A New Jersey law which provided aid for legitimate but not illegitimate children was not held to be in violation of the equal protection clause of the Fourteenth Amendment. *New Jersey Welfare Rights Organization* v. *Cahill,* CCH Poverty Law Reporter, para. 1200.35 (1971).

178. One observer has identified certain common characteristics of welfare agencies:

    > . . . the elaborate complexity of determining eligibility and especially of budgeting (including both the determination of need and the amount of assistance to which the recipient is entitled); the low visibility, for the recipient of the agency decision-making processes and of appeal opportunities and procedures; the comparative powerlessness, from the recipient's viewpoint, of the line social worker—the person with whom he must deal—in the decisions made about his assistance grant; the linkage of financial assistance to other services so that the aid recipient also

automatically becomes a client who, at least partly at the discretion of the agency, may become the object of other services (for example, counseling and psychiatric treatment); and review and surveillance of the recipient's expenditure of aid funds beyond that necessary to establish eligibility and detect possible fraud. [Briar, "Welfare From Below: Recipients' Views of the Public Welfare System," in TEN BROEK, THE LAW OF THE POOR, (San Francisco: Chandler, 1966) pp. 59–60.]

179. No hearing at all was required for a state to terminate the benefits of a welfare recipient until 1969. In *Goldberg* v. *Kelly,* 397 U.S. 254 (1970), a Legal Services case, the Supreme Court held that a "fair hearing" must be held before benefits were terminated. The procedural due process to be afforded to the recipient included the rights to appear personally, to be represented by counsel, to offer evidence and to confront and cross-examine witnesses.

180. See p. 205, *supra.*

181. See, generally, *Report of the National Advisory Commission on Civil Disorders,* 302–303 (N.Y. Times ed., 1968); THE PRESIDENT'S COMMISSION ON LAW ENFORCEMENT AND THE ADMINISTRATION OF JUSTICE, TASK FORCE REPORT: THE POLICE, 145–146 (1967); Condlin, *Citizens, Police, and Polarization: Are Perceptions More Important Than Facts?,* 47 J. Urban Law 653 (1969–70); Note, *Lawless Law Enforcement,* 4 Loyola L.A.L. Rev. 161 (1972).

182. See *Goldberg* v. *Kelly, supra,* n. 179, for the requirement of a hearing prior to the termination of welfare benefits.

In 1967, HUD made it a requirement that tenants in Federally assisted public housing be given written notice of the reasons for eviction and the opportunity for a conference to rebut those reasons. See *HUD Circular 2–7-67.* In *Thorpe* v. *Housing Authority of City of Durham,* 393 U.S. 268, 89 S.Ct. 518 (1969), the Court held that this requirement was a valid exercise of the rule-making powers given to HUD by the Housing Act of 1937, as amended in 42 U.S.C. §§1401, 1408, 1410(a). See also, Note, *Eviction of State's Tenants Necessitates a Limited Hearing According to the State Action Doctrine of the Fourteenth Amendment,* 21 Buff.L. Rev. 524 (1972); Weintraub, Kohn and Hollingsworth, *The Mixed Blessings of Escaleria: New Vistas of Due Process for Public Housing Tenants in Termination of Tenancy,* 17 N.Y.L.F. 1 (1971).

183. In *Tucker* v. *Norwalk Housing Authority,* CCH Poverty Law Reporter, para. 2735.13 (1972), a Federal district court in Connecticut held that a local housing authority could not automatically exclude applicants who had previous criminal records or a history of poor housekeeping habits.

In *Thomas* v. *Housing Authority of City of Little Rock,* 282 F. Supp. 575 (1967), a Federal district court in Arkansas held that the local housing authority's policy of automatic rejection of applicants with illegitimate children was unconstitutional on an equal protection theory. However, the court held that the housing authority could take the fact that an individual applicant had illegitimate children into account on a case-by-case basis (*Id.* at p. 581).

In *Buttle* v. *Municipal Housing Authority for the City of Yonkers,* 53 F.R.D. 423 (1971), the court granted a preliminary injunction against the authority's policy of refusing applications of those on public assistance, unless the local welfare agency would co-sign the lease, on the ground that the plaintiffs had shown that they had probable success at trial of proving that such policy violated their rights under the due process and equal protection clauses of the Fourteenth Amendment (*Id.* at pp. 427–29).

184. The procedure used in the typical landlord-tenant suit is different from ordinary civil procedure. In the District of Columbia, a number of cases have been brought seeking to afford the tenant discovery rights, the right to counsel and the right to have a transcript provided. On a more basic level, the summary nature of the proceeding itself is under attack. See Roisman, *Tenants and the Law: 1970,* 20 Amer. U. L. Rev. 58, 72 (1970–71).

In *Boddie* v. *Connecticut,* 401 U.S. 373, 91 S.Ct. 781 (1971), the court held that the state must show a "countervailing state influence of overriding significance" before access to the courts can be denied to poor women who wish to seek divorces but cannot pay the court fees (at p. 377). In this case, Connecticut could show no interest and, therefore, the imposition of court fees which acted as a barrier to access to the courts was a denial of due process (at U.S. 381).

185. The Supreme Court held that required home visits by social workers were not "unreasonable" searches and that, therefore, no warrant was required by the Fourth Amendment. *Wyman* v. *James,* 400 U.S. 309, 91 S.Ct. 381 (1971).

186. In discussing the welfare boards of three rural counties in Virginia, Mashaw has stated: "The attitudes held by a number of these rural board members display a startling indifference to legal requirements. By and large they do not feel compelled to follow state or federal policy in situations where they consider the policy unsuited to 'local conditions.' " Mashaw, *Welfare Reform and Local Administration of Aid to Families with Dependent Children,* 57 Va. L. Rev. 818, 826 (1971).

187. In *Snaidach* v. *Family Finance Corp.,* 395 U.S. 337, 89 S.Ct. 1820, 23 L.Ed.2d 337 (1969), the Court held that Wisconsin's statute allowing the debtor's wages to be frozen before a trial on the merits did not meet the procedural due process requirements of the Fourteenth Amendment.

188. Eviction for reporting the landlord to the local housing or health authorities for violation of health and safety ordinances has been termed "retaliatory eviction." By statute, the following states have recognized the defense of retaliatory eviction to any action sought by a landlord to recover possession of the tenant's premises within a specified time period after the tenant has made such a report to local authorities: California, Connecticut, Illinois, Maine, Maryland, Massachusetts, Minnesota, New Jersey, Rhode Island. CCH Poverty Law Reporter, para. 2325.70 (1972). The appellate courts in the District of Columbia arrived at the same result through judicial interpretation. *Edwards* v. *Habib,* 397 F.2d 687 (D.C. Cir., 1968) app. den. 393 U.S. 1016 (1969).

189. *Sanks* v. *Georgia,* 401 U.S. 144 (1971). The Supreme Court dismissed the appeal brought by the Atlanta Legal Aid Society but primarily on the basis the Georgia legislature had rescinded the statute which had allowed landlords

to evict tenants without a hearing and which required tenants to post a bond equal to double the rent likely to be due at the conclusion of a court proceeding if they wanted to challenge the eviction.

190.   In *Brown* v. *Southall Realty Company,* 237 A. 2d 834 (1968), the District of Columbia Court of Appeal held that a lease made for an apartment which the landlord knew was in such a state of disrepair as to be uninhabitable according to the local housing authority was a void contract and the lease could not support an action for eviction for nonpayment of rent. In *Diamond Housing Corp.* v. *Robinson,* 257 A.2d 492 (1969), the same court held that a tenant who successfully invoked the *Brown* defense to an action for eviction could not be immediately evicted thereafter because the landlord wishes to terminate the tenancy. The tenant became a tenant at sufferance and was entitled to 30 days notice before the landlord could recover possession of the premises. For less promising trends see DeFeis, *Abuse of Process and Its Impact on the Poor,* 46 St. John's L. Rev. 1 (1971).

191.   Obviously, there are several instances where an action that enhances personal freedom simultaneously produces a transfer of goods, services or opportunity as well. Banishment of prejudgment garnishment, for instance, precludes an arbitrary, unilateral disturbance of the debtor's property. But it also probably will reduce the amount of income transfer from debtor to creditor by some unknown figure. And two leading commentators on the public welfare system credit the court decisions that created new procedural rights with increasing public assistance income even more than cases that removed eligibility barriers.

> All in all, then, the legal assault on welfare departments contributed to the collapse of restrictions, partly by overturning major exclusionary statutes, but perhaps more importantly by instituting procedural safeguards that hampered the arbitrary exercise of discretion by relief officials. Rather than devote themselves to the difficult and time-consuming task of defending their decisions, welfare functionaries more often acquiesced, with the result that more people got on the rolls and they were not so likely to be terminated capriciously. [PIVEN and CLOWARD, *op. cit., supra,* n. 29, at p. 314.]

192.   42 U.S.C. §2781 (a) (4) (1970).

193.   In order to insure "maximum feasible participation," the Economic Opportunity Act which authorized the creation of Community Action agencies was amended to require that: ". . . (2) at least one-third of the members [of the governing board of the agency] are persons chosen in accordance with democratic election procedures adequate to assure that they are representative of the poor in the area served." 42 U.S.C. §2791 (b) (2) (1970).

194.   In 1967, the total of all "welfare" expenditures in the United States by public agencies was $99.7 billion. In 1968, the total was $112 billion. LAMPMAN, *op. cit., supra,* n. 65, at p. 110.

    In 1967, the Community Action Program of OEO, over which the poor had some direct control, received $805 million. In 1968, the CAP received $866 million. LEVITAN, *op. cit., supra,* n. 31, at p. 123.

By examining the above figures, it can be seen that the CAP administered less than 1 percent of all social welfare expenditures.

195. In Michigan, by statute, any city with over one million in population must create a board of tenants' affairs if it has one or more public housing projects within its boundaries. CCH Poverty Law Reporter, para. 2720.05 (1972). See also Hirshen and Brown, *Public Housing's Neglected Resources: The Tenants,* City, Vol. 6, No. 4 (1972) at p. 15 for a description of other experiments in tenant participation in public housing policy.

196. In analyzing why school boards, through selection of textbooks, deemphasize the achievements of blacks, Carmichael and Hamilton point out that over 76 percent of school board members in one survey were business and professional men, while this group represented only 15 percent of the population. In the same sample, only 3 percent of the board members were laborers. CARMICHAEL and HAMILTON, BLACK POWER (New York: Vintage, 1967) at p. 10, note 3.

One reason for the low level of representation of the poor in elected policy-making bodies is gerrymandering. Carmichael and Hamilton point out that 60 percent of the population of Manhattan is black but that blacks do not hold anywhere near 60 percent of the seats on the City Council representing Manhattan.

Another method of denying representation is to create large council districts which include both whites and blacks. In this case, a black cannot be elected because whites will vote en masse against him. Los Angeles, with large council districts did not elect a black councilman until 1963. *Id.* at p. 16.

197. In Harlem, the only large department store is owned by whites. Only one bank is owned by blacks, the others being branches of major downtown banks. In addition, most of the residential and commercial property is owned and controlled by people who live outside of Harlem. CLARK, DARK GHETTO (New York: Harper & Row, 1965) at pp. 27–28.

198. In discussing the independent democracy values of the Community Action Program, Levitan has said:

> . . . [W]hile it cannot be claimed that participation by the poor automatically improved the quality or quantity of services offered to them and their neighbors, it undoubtedly made these services more satisfying. There is ample evidence to show that doing things for people is not an effective way of helping them. A regard for basic democratic concepts also dictates that people have a say in society's efforts on their behalf. [LEVITAN, *op. cit., supra,* n. 31, at pp. 115–116.]

199. For a discussion of the limited economic and social payoff from participation of the poor in the Community Action agencies, see KRAMER, PARTICIPATION OF THE POOR (Englewood Cliffs: Prentice-Hall, 1969) at pp. 260–73.

200. For a contrary appraisal of the objective gains from representation of the poor on CAA boards, see LEVINE, THE POOR YE NEED NOT HAVE WITH YOU (Cambridge: M.I.T. Press, 1970) at pp. 161–67.

201. See pp. 260–65, *infra.*

202. See pp. 264–65, *infra.* For a discussion of various mechanisms for affording beneficiaries some participation in the operation of government programs, see Tomlinson and Mashaw, *The Enforcement of Federal Standards in Grant-in-Aid Programs: Suggestions for Beneficiary Involvement,* 58 Va. L. Rev. 600 (1972).

203. *Castro* v. *State of California,* 2 Cal.3d 223, 85 Cal.Rptr. 20, 466 P.2d 244 (1970). The court held that the provision of the California Constitution making the ability to read English a requirement for voting was unconstitutional as applied to the plaintiffs. Automatic disqualification for those not literate in English was a denial of equal protection. The plaintiffs in this case had access to Spanish language newspapers and periodicals and, therefore, had the necessary political information to make the decisions required of a voter.

204. See e.g., Hirshen and Brown, *op. cit., supra,* n. 195.

205. The Model Cities Act directs the Secretary of HUD to "emphasize local initiative in the planning, development and implementation" of local programs to insure "prompt response to local initiatives" by the Federal government. 42 U.S.C. §3303 (b) (1), (2) (1970).

    In Philadelphia, the Area-Wide Council was a local group organized to represent the poor in the implementation of the Model Cities Act. The group was to have substantial representation on the board of directors of the corporations which would administer the specific program in the area. In 1969, the City and HUD changed the program so as to lessen the representation of Area-Wide Council without consulting local people.

    In *North City Area-Wide Council* v. *Romney,* 428 F.2d 754 (1970), the Third Circuit held that such a change in program could not be made without local citizen participation. The court did not decide, however, on the exact amount of representation the local citizens should have in the program.

206. See Finman, *OEO Legal Services Programs and the Pursuit of Social Change: The Relationship Between Program Ideology and Program Performance,* 1971 Wisc. L. Rev. 1001. The author describes the activities of five unnamed Legal Services agencies and includes accounts of the attempts to form private business entities served and run by the poor and the necessary follow-up work done by the agencies to serve the new corporations.

207. In 1968, the Kerner Commission reported:

    > We are convinced, on the record before this Commission, that the frustration reflected in the recent disorders results, in part at least, from the lack of accessible and visible means of establishing the merits of grievances against the agencies of local and state government, including but not limited to the police. [REPORT OF THE NATIONAL ADVISORY COMMISSION ON CIVIL DISORDERS, 291 (Bantam ed., 1968).]

208. The Kerner Commission recommended that the poor use the courts as means of redress but also recognized the problem that the poor seldom get into court:

    > . . . through the adversary process which is at the heart of our judicial system, litigants are offered meaningful opportunity to influence events which affect them

and their community. However, effective utilization of the courts requires legal assistance, a resource seldom available to the poor. [*Id.* at p. 292.]

209.   Speaking to the general problem of the poor's lack of informal power, the Kerner Commission said:

> ... middle class citizens, although subject to many frustrations and resentments in dealing with the public bureaucracy as ghetto residents, find it relatively easy to locate the appropriate agency for help and redress. If they fail to get satisfaction, they can call on a variety of remedies—assistance of elected representatives, a friend in government, a lawyer.
> ... On the other hand, the typical ghetto resident ... [is] unable to break down his problems in ways which fit the complicated structure of government. [*Id.* at p. 285.]

210.   See pp. 12–13, *supra.*

211.   SKOLNICK, THE POLITICS OF PROTEST (Washington: U.S. Government Printing Office, 1969).

212.   *Id.* at p. 6.

213.   *Id.* at p. 11.

214.   In discussing violence as a political instrument, Skolnick states: "Collective violence by powerless groups acts as a 'signaling device' to those in power that concessions must be made or violence will prevail." *Id.* at p. 259.

215.   Some of the possible complications attending this type of analysis are suggested, in part, by the variety of concepts which might be used, and even more by the variety of perspectives from which the analysis might be conducted. The perspective we will use here is that of the poor: what is the cost effectiveness of the legal assistance program from their point of view. But conceivably, we could be looking at the Program's cost effectiveness from any *one* of several additional perspectives: the Legal Services lawyer, the judicial system, the taxpayer, etc.

The evaluation concept used here is somewhat different than the conventional cost/benefit calculations used by economists. Their evaluation concept runs into technical difficulties in the case of programs such as Legal Services that essentially affect the *distribution* of income rather than the total *amount* of income. One would like to argue that transferring a dollar of income from a rich man to a poor man increases the total welfare of society, but economists will tell you that *there is no rigorous way to even establish* that such transfers are beneficial (i.e., that the rich man derives less utility from an extra dollar than a poor man does), much less *measure* the amount of the benefit. We would try to support the notion of differential utility here, or could point to the benefits of decreased crime, increased political stability, and the like, which might result from such transfers of money, but I do not choose to elaborate such arguments here. I will only point out that society has apparently made a decision supporting the value of such redistributive transfers, and that this decision is evident in all the welfare legislation which already exists. For further discussion of this issue, see Thurow, *Toward a Definition of Economic Justice,* 31 The Public Interest (1973).

216. See pp. 117–18, *supra*.

217. These statistics are found in GOODMAN and FENILLAN, ALTERNATIVE AP-
PROACHES TO THE PROVISION OF LEGAL SERVICES FOR THE RURAL POOR:
JUDICARE AND THE DECENTRALIZED STAFF PROGRAM (Washington:
Bureau of Social Science Research, 1971) at p. 141.

> Judicare bankruptcies cost seven and one-half times as much as Pine Tree Legal
> Assistance [Maine] bankruptcies and nearly six times as much as they do under
> Upper Peninsula Legal Services [Michigan]. . . . Divorces are nearly five times as
> costly as they are under Upper Peninsula Legal Services and close to seven times
> the cost of those handled by Pine Tree Legal Assistance. [*Id.* at p. 143.]

218. In 1967, staff attorneys were delivering legal representation at $48.39 per case.
Judicare was costing $139.01 per case. *Hearings on H.R. 8311*, Committee
on Education and Labor, U.S. House of Representatives, (90th Cong., 1st
Sess., June 20, 1967) at pp. 914–915.

219. The disparity between the per case cost of a staff attorney versus a compensated private counsel delivery system can be explained by a combination of
factors: (1) staff attorney programs deliver services at approximately $10 to
$15 per attorney hour (including all expenses from the attorney's own salary,
space rental, secretaries, and so on), while the average hourly rate charged
by private attorneys is in the $30 to $50 range. (In many communities, the
minimum fee schedule set by the local bar is $30 or more, and Sacramento
County, California, for instance, has a $50 *minimum*. ABA STANDING COM-
MITTEES ON ECONOMICS OF LAW PRACTICE, MINIMUM FEE SCHEDULES
(Chicago: ABA, 1970) pp. 36–51.) The usual *minimum* hourly rate is $30 in
California, Illinois, and Michigan and $40 in Texas. *Id.* at pp. 52, 54. This
factor alone accounts for a 100 percent to 200 percent cost differential. Even
the "Wisconsin Judicare" program which held its private lawyers to $16 to
$20 per hour at various times during its experimental period, still was deliver-
ing services at an hourly charge of 20 to 25 percent above salaried staff
agencies.

(2) Staff attorneys can produce more service in a given hour because they
soon develop expertise in many of the common legal problems of the poor.
Thus, the typical Legal Services lawyer can draw on prior research and
experience to solve in an hour a case that might require three or four hours
of library time for the average private attorney.

(3) Staff attorney offices can produce more services in a given hour because
they can utilize various management and organizational techniques to reduce
time required of the lawyer per case in the more common categories of legal
problems. Because of volume, they can utilize forms, paraprofessionals, systems, and so on, not feasible for the general practitioner. For instance, one
staff attorney can handle an entire docket of routine divorce trials in a
morning, but if those same cases were scattered among several private lawyers, all would be sitting in the courtroom piling up billable hours to be
charged to the government.

Thus, staff attorneys generally require fewer hours to dispose of the average poverty case and cost less for each hour they do devote to the case. The combination is enough in and of itself to account for a dramatic difference in cost per case. One other element should be mentioned, however. Private attorneys generally charge flat minimum rates for certain kinds of cases and legal work, irrespective of how little time they require. In many jurisdictions, a divorce costs at least $300 to $400 even if it only takes an hour of the lawyer's time. A bankruptcy will cost at least $250 to $300 no matter how little time it takes. And a court appearance will be billed at a minimum of $150 to $500 even if the case is resolved in an hour or two. *Id.* at pp. 36–51. As a result, these matters generally are priced at a mark substantially higher than a straight hourly charge system would produce. This further skews the cost-effectiveness ratios in favor of salaried staff counsel.

220.   There still may be other sound policy reasons for preferring in-kind distribution of certain goods and services even if the cost is the same or higher than prevailing market prices. Society may desire to insure that the poor receive some essential items such as medical assistance, shelter or a minimal diet. Through the in-kind approach, we avoid the risk that recipients will spend cash disbursements on other, less important (to society) products. In addition, the need for some services is so unpredictable and the expense so great when the need arises that ordinary cash transfer cannot cover the bill. The most obvious example is the medical aid entailed by any serious illness. It is unreasonable to expect a poor family to bear that burden out of their welfare check. It probably makes more sense to supply this form of assistance on an as needed, in-kind basis irrespective of the economic factor.

221.   The Job Corps was established to train youths between the ages of 14 and 22 from disadvantaged backgrounds to become employable. 42 U.S.C. § 2711 (1970).

    The Headstart program was designed to accustom preschool children to an education environment in order to have them adjust better to a school environment when they got older. The primary goal here was to prepare the children of the poor to take advantage of their formal education as soon as it began without the usual nonproductive period of adjustment to school. 42 U.S.C. § 2809 (a) (1) (1970).

222.   See pp. 198–211, *supra.*

223.   There are some antipoverty programs that have multiple effects. Many forms of education, for example, simultaneously qualify as consumer resources and opportunity resources because they serve immediate basic psychological needs (intellectual enjoyment, among others) at the same time that they provide knowledge and develop traits that will facilitate access to higher income positions than otherwise would be possible. Much of education is an end in itself as well as a means to the end of economic mobility. Similarly, medical assistance may make a poor person feel better; it also may remove a physical or mental disability that has made him unemployable. In the first instance, doctors serve as a consumer resource; in the second, they qualify as an opportunity resource.

224.   Obviously, in marginal cases, services which fail the cost-effectiveness test may be worthwhile because of factors like convenience. See n. 220, *supra.*

225. This capital fund entry merely indicates that the job training program has had an effect similar to the creation of a $100,000 trust fund for the workers who were trained. It would take a fund of that size to produce enough interest to pay them their salary increment each year. Obviously, to make this formula fully accurate, it would be necessary to discount the future increments of annual income, which would mean that a somewhat smaller capital fund would be sufficient to yield the current value of future earnings.

226. These *redistribution* services tend to have little independent value. If they fail to generate additional consumer resources for the poor, their own existence seldom provides a consolation prize. This contrasts with government investments in an educational program, for instance. It may or may not justify its cost in terms of its eventual economic benefits. But at least the students can derive stimulation and enjoyment from the learning experience itself. This is rarely true of lawyers and other redistribution resources.

227. This is not an unreasonable assumption. The Washington, D.C. Legal Aid Society, for instance, has processed thousands of such cases.

228. For example, one of the most expensive of all the litigations undertaken by Legal Services lawyers was the series of cases against the welfare residency requirements. In total, 25 challenges to welfare residency statutes were filed in over 20 jurisdictions. Most of these had produced injunctions barring enforcement of local residency requirements long before the ultimate Supreme Court decision in *Shapiro* v. *Thompson, op. cit., supra,* n. 100. However, most of these cases utilized pleadings and research obtained from the national welfare center and local Legal Services agencies that already had filed. Consequently, no major commitment of time was involved except for the three challenges that went all the way to the Supreme Court: Connecticut, Pennsylvania, and the District of Columbia. Interviews with key attorneys in these three cases suggest that no more than 2½ lawyer man-years were devoted to all stages of preparation, litigation, and appeal of all three cases. Even at an average of $30,000 per lawyer man-year (including staff and support costs), the three principal cases only entailed a total cost of $75,-000,000. Of course, realistically, the cost side of the equation must embrace more than the expenses directly associated with the test cases themselves. Any such legal change will lie fallow unless poor people are educated to assert their new rights, and lawyers must be available to enforce the new rules with individual court suits. Thus, a full analysis must take account of these education and enforcement services. Although with existing data it is impossible to identify or measure the Legal Services resources committed to support the residency decision, a rough estimate places the outer parameters at about $200,000. (That assumes that 10 percent of the resources going into welfare cases—the latter make up 3 to 4 percent of the Legal Services caseload—were devoted to enforcement of the residence cases. That is a generous estimate considering the hundreds of other issues in that field.)

Combining litigation, education and enforcement expenses, an investment in the neighborhood of $300 thousand generated an annual income increment of $100–$200 million for the poor. Granting our rough approximations of the variables, the cost-effectiveness ratio works out to be:

$$\frac{\$3,000,000,000 \ (=\text{capital fund required to generate } \$150 \text{ million annual income at } 5\% \text{ interest})}{\$1,300,000 \ (=\text{estimate of legal services resources committed to litigation, education and enforcement of decision during initial period plus the capital fund required to provide } \$50,000 \text{ per year in continuing education and enforcement support})} = \frac{2307}{1}$$

(cost effectiveness of welfare residency decision)

To adopt a more conservative approach and only recognize the increased income actually received by the poverty community through mid-1972, the calculations reveal:

$$\frac{\$300,000,000-\$600,000,000 \ (\text{additional welfare income attributable to removal of residency barrier—1969–72})}{\$400,000 \ (\text{estimate of Legal Services resources committed to litigation, education and enforcement of residency decision in 1969–72})} = \frac{750-1500}{1}$$

(cost effectiveness of welfare residency decision)

Sometime we may possess the data to refine both the cost and benefit estimates in the above equations, but I seriously doubt that the definitive figures when carried to the last penny will detract significantly from the scale of cost effectiveness portrayed—something between 750 to 1 and 2300 plus to 1.

229. The estimate for the minimum wage case is a projection from data reported by the *Los Angeles Times.* (See n. 85 *supra.*) The estimates for the welfare residency and "man in the house" cases were made by HEW. (See n. 101 *supra.*) The estimate for the New York Medicaid case came from the Center on Social Welfare Policy formerly located at Columbia Law School and for the California Medicaid case see the court decision (n. 111, *supra*).

The decisions requiring a hearing prior to termination of welfare apparently generate a dividend well in excess of $100 million a year. See e.g., *Goldberg* v. *Kelly, supra,* n. 179. The California welfare department estimated that a 1972 case that enforced this requirement in California will increase public assistance payments in that single state by $25 million a year. *(Los Angeles Times,* December 19, 1972 at p. 3.) Some authorities suggest *Gold-*

berg and other procedural decisions probably accounted for much of the $4½ billion welfare expansion in the late 1960s and early 1970s. See note 101 *supra*.

230. See pp. 245–47, *infra*.

231. However, caution must be exercised in classifying a given case as one which benefits only that client. Frequently, Legal Services lawyers by standing ready to take individual cases of a given type actually "enforce" a better code of conduct by businessmen or administrators, thus benefiting all customers or recipients.

232. See n. 121, *supra*.

233. In *Dandridge* v. *Williams* and *Rosado* v. *Wyman*, n. 110, *supra*, the Supreme Court refused to declare maximum welfare grants, regardless of family size, unconstitutional and allowed New York City to cut its welfare bill by $40,-000,000 by averaging costs instead of appraising needs on a case-by-case basis. Thus, despite the cost of this litigation and the effort involved in climbing the appellate ladder all the way to the Supreme Court, the two decisions failed to increase income for the poor.

234. The annual budgets for operating programs of the OEO Legal Services Program from its inception in October, 1965 (during fiscal year 1966) through June 30, 1972, are as follows:

FY 1966	$20 million	FY 1970	$50 million
FY 1967	$25 million	FY 1971	$55 million
FY 1968	$38 million	FY 1972	$61 million
FY 1969	$42 million	TOTAL	$291 million

235. See notes 85, 101, 112, 115–17, 124, 145, 147, 191, and 229, *supra*. There are many other examples of large amounts of income which have been channelled to poor people in various states through Legal Services cases, for instance, *Boddie* v *Wyman*, ordering upstate New York to increase grants by $13 million *annually* to reach levels in downstate New York; *Rodriguez* v. *Powell*, requiring Texas to give AFDC Aid to relatives (other than mother) who cared for dependent children, yielding $14 million a year in additional assistance; before reversal of *Rosado* v. *Wyman*, notes 110 and 233, *supra*, in the U.S. Supreme Court, a court in Texas followed the lower court case, resulting in the distribution of $30 million of additional benefits over the several months *Rosado* was pending.

236. It is relatively easy to list another $400 million in increased *annual* income brought about by Legal Services actions comparable to the welfare residency case. The California case raising minimum wages 25¢ an hour meant $100 million a year to farmworkers. See note 85, *supra*. HEW estimates the man-in-the house case, brought under the auspices of the OEO-funded Columbia Center on Social Welfare Policy (the national welfare backup center), was responsible for an increase of $150 to $300 million a year in welfare benefits. See note 101, *supra*. A series of food stamp cases conceived and coordinated by the Columbia Center and implemented by Legal Services programs in over 23 states, increased food stamp distributions by over $150 million a year (estimate by Center for Social Welfare Policy). The Supreme Court decision

requiring a hearing prior to welfare termination has meant another $100 million per annum to the low-income sector. See note 229, *supra*. And a miscellany of other lawsuits and legislative changes probably have generated scores of millions in annual income for the poor, e.g., actions cited in note 235, *supra*, the decisions barring prejudgment garnishments, and the cases collected in note 140, *supra*. In a more speculative vein and looking to the future, *Serrano* v. *Priest*, should it be confined only to California and compel a mere 10 percent shift in educational funding in that state, will transfer over $400 million a year in educational benefits to the lower income districts (or reduce taxes for existing benefits in those districts by a like amount). If similar decisions are rendered in other states, as much as a billion dollars a year of educational services (or tax reductions) might be redistributed to the poor.

In addition to cases calculated to increase benefits, Legal Services lawyers frequently have prevented the loss of existing income. The most dramatic examples of this were the Medi-Cal case won by California Rural Legal Assistance in 1967, when the attorneys of that program enjoined a $200 million a year reduction in government-financed medical benefits for the poor and a similar case in New York halting a $190 million a year reduction in that state's Medicaid program which was enacted by the legislature in 1971.

237. The total OEO budgets from fiscal year 1966 through fiscal year 1972, that is, July 1, 1965 through June 30, 1972, are compared with the total Legal Services budget during these same years in the following chart:

	OEO	LSP	LSP as % of OEO
FY 1966	$1,500 million	$20 million	1.3%
FY 1967	$1,700 million	$25 million	1.5%
FY 1968	$1,900 million	$38 million	2.0%
FY 1969	$1,900 million	$42 million	2.2%
FY 1970	$1,900 million	$50 million	2.6%
FY 1971	$1,900 million	$55 million	2.9%
FY 1972	$1,900 million	$61 million	3.2%
TOTAL	$12,700 million	$291 million	2.3%

238. See pp. 196–97, *supra*. This "income gap," of course, is the one based on the "minimum standard of living" definition of poverty.

239. The income gap was estimated to be about $10 billion in 1971. See STATISTICAL ABSTRACT, *op. cit.*, *supra*, n. 50, Table 541, at p. 330.

240. See pp. 216–21, *supra*.

Chapter 9: Toward Justice and Reform

1. Sykes, *Legal Needs of the Poor in the City of Denver*, 4 Law and Society Review 255, 262–64 (1969). The diagnosis of problems requiring legal assistance was made by a panel of attorneys.

2. *1971 NLADA Statistical Report*, at pp. 3–3a. Redwood City, California re-

ported an even higher figure: 37 cases per 1000 which projects to over 7,700,000 cases per year nationally.

3. See pp. 188–89, *supra.*

4. In 1972, the budget for the OEO Legal Services Program and its administrative support within the agency approximated $70 million or $60 per case. At this rate, six million cases would cost $360 million.

5. "As a rough characterization, however, people of moderate means [those unable to afford private attorneys for most matters and yet ineligible for free legal aid] might be thought of usefully, in terms of income, as those earning between $5,000 and $15,000 a year. . . . In 1963, 60 percent of the nation's families—a total of approximately 28 million family units—had family incomes of more than $5,000 but less than $15,000." CHRISTENSEN, LAWYERS FOR PEOPLE OF MODERATE MEANS (Chicago: American Bar Foundation, 1970) at p. 5, n. 4. As of 1970, 58.5 percent of all families remained in this $5,000 to $15,000 bracket. UNITED STATES DEPARTMENT OF COMMERCE, STATISTICAL ABSTRACT OF THE UNITED STATES, 1972 (Washington, D.C.: U.S. Government Printing Office, 1972) Table 523, p. 322.

6. On April 27 29, 1972, a group of labor unions, consumer organizations, and bar association representatives gathered in Washington, D.C., for a National Conference on Prepaid Legal Services, attended by 325 conferees. The panels and discussions are reported in *Transcript of Proceedings,* National Conference on Prepaid Legal Services (Chicago: American Bar Association, 1972). This was followed by a conference on July 21–22, sponsored entirely by union and consumer groups and aimed specifically at creating an action arm. See note 7, *infra.*

    In 1969 and 1971, smaller conferences were held on the same general subject matter at UCLA. See *Prepaid Legal Services: Proceedings of A Conference on the Development of Prepaid Legal Services* (Los Angeles: UCLA, 1972).

    A newsletter reporting recent developments in this field also began publication in 1972. See *Group Legal Services News,* published by Pension Services, Inc., New Orleans, Louisiana.

    In the course of the discussion at the April 27–29 conference, Helen Nelson, president of the Consumer Federation of America, sounded the theme of the middle-class consumer-oriented movement when she said: "Access to legal services has become too important to be left to lawyers." *Transcript, Id.* at pp. 411–12.

7. At a conference on July 21–22, an amalgam of unions, consumer, senior citizens, and ethnic organizations formed a National Consumers Center on Legal Services. Designed to promote, coordinate, evaluate, organize and fund legal services plans for middle-income groups, the organization also will "carry on non-partisan legislative activity to further above goals." *Group Legal Services News,* Vol. 1, No. 6, 19728 at pp. 1–3.

    Elements of this coalition introduced legislation in Congress designed to allow unions to bargain for legal services as a permissible fringe benefit in their negotiations with management. This bill, H.R. 13938, amends "Section 302

(a) of the Labor-Management Relations Act to permit employer contributions to trust funds established for the purpose of defraying the costs of legal services." On April 27 and May 16, 1972, the proposal was the subject of testimony before the House Special Subcommittee on Labor. *Hearings on H.R. 13938,* Special Subcommittee on Labor, Committee on Education and Labor, U.S. House of Representatives, 92nd Cong., 2nd Sess. The original bill died but in 1973 it was reintroduced and enacted with minor amendments.

During the course of the hearings on this legislation, Congressman Frank Thompson suggested the future might hold the possibility of a Federal role in the provision of legal assistance to middle classes.

> Now we have a great middle class of working people . . . [who] don't go to lawyers oftentimes when they should . . . for a whole spectrum of legal services. I see eventually some participation by the Federal Government in legal services programs for these people. [*Id.* at p. 7.]

8. This feature is described in Pelletier, *English Legal Aid: The Successful Experiment in Judicare,* 40 U. Colo. L. Rev. 10, 31–33 (1967). In actuality there is an upper limit on this sliding scale which effectively excludes most persons with incomes above the median from governmental assistance no matter how expensive their legal problem.

9. CHRISTENSEN, *op. cit., supra,* n. 5. An earlier book discussing this general subject is CHEATHAM, A LAWYER WHEN NEEDED (New York: Columbia Univ. Press, 1963).

10. Caplan and Johnson, *Neighborhood Lawyer Programs: An Experiment in Social Change,* 20 U. Miami L. Rev. 184–91 (1965).

11. The past seven years also have uncovered other alternative systems for financing legal services not considered in our 1965 piece. One of these new approaches, prepaid legal insurance, is especially relevant for the secondary target group—labor and the middle class. With the actuarial experience gleaned from current experiments it should become feasible to develop a comprehensive system of prepaid legal insurance analogous to Blue Cross-Blue Shield in the medical field. For reasons of cost to be explored later in this section (see pages 240–41, *infra*), it may be necessary to couple this insurance method of financing with a salaried staff attorney or closed panel group plan. [Salaried staff attorneys are evaluated at pages 238–41, *infra.* "Closed panels" of private attorneys are appraised in Zimroth, *Group Legal Services and the Constitution,* 76 Yale L. Journal 966 (1967).]

Moreover, the prepaid plan is an answer only for persons of at least moderate means, not the poor or the lower-middle class, since participants must be in a position to pay a substantial premium. At the same time, it is not out of the question that government, in conjunction with private insurance companies, might evolve a comprehensive insurance plan with the government paying all or part of the premium based on a sliding scale related to participants' income.

12. *Id.* at pp. 187–88.

13. See Chapters 6 and 7 of JOHNSON, AND STILL LOVE JUSTICE, to be published by Public Affairs Press.

14. See Chapters 7 and 8 of JOHNSON, *op. cit.,supra*, n. 13.
15. 372 U.S. 335 (1963).
16. The National Defender Project gave out grants totalling over $5 million during the period from 1964–1971. The purpose was to stimulate and experiment—to promote nationwide coverage of locally financed and operated criminal defense systems.
17. A recent survey indicated 12 states offer complete or nearly complete coverage in all courts. Allison and Phelps, *Can We Afford to Provide Trial Counsel for the Indigent in Misdemeanor Cases?* 13 William and Mary L. Rev. 75, 84 (1971)
18. "[T]hree states with 21 percent of this country's population provide more than one-half of all state appropriations for indigent defense." Note, *Dollars and Sense of an Expanded Right to Counsel,* 55 Iowa L. Rev. 1249, 1265 (1970)
19. In 1970, the Federal government allocated $76.6 billion for national defense. NEW YORK TIMES ENCYCLOPEDIA ALMANAC, 1972 (New York: New York Times, 1972) at p. 650.
20. In 1970, the Federal government spent over $72 billion on the general welfare: health ($12.9 billion), income security ($43.7 billion), education ($17.3 billion), housing ($2.9 billion) and veteran's benefits ($8.6 billion). *Id.* at p. 122.
21. See pp. 230–34, *supra,* for a cost-benefit comparison of these alternative means of providing legal assistance.
22. See, e.g., Cappelletti and Gordley, *Legal Aid: Modern Themes and Variations,* 24 Stanford L. Rev. 347 (1972); Ginsberg, *et al., The Availability of Legal Services to Poor People and People of Limited Means in Foreign Systems,* 6 Int'l. Lawyer 128 (1972).
23. "The English system as it has found expression in American 'Judicare' offers considerable promise for the future. . . . [I]t represents a method by which all lawyers may be brought into the legal aid process, which is not achieved in the more conventional programs." Pelletier, *op. cit., supra,* n. 8, at p. 43.
24. "The use of private practitioners coupled with freedom of selection personalizes what is essentially a social welfare benefit, giving both the lawyer and the legal aid client the feeling they are acting independently of governmental control. . . . Individual choice in social welfare programs served to maintain the personal dignity of the recipient, making the service appear less an act of charity." *Id.* at p. 14.
25. "[T]he legal profession is clinging to the brink of the most serious threat ever posed to the independency and individuality and strength of the profession . . ." Bethel and Walker, *Et Tu Brute,* 1 Tenn. B. Journal 11, 25 (1965).

> Lawyers who believe that this nation must maintain an independent legal profession in order to preserve a democratic system of government in the United States have spoken out loudly and strongly in bar association circles in the halls and offices of Congress, and in the Executive Department in Washington. These lawyers have been assisted by a section of the American Bar Association, the

Section of General Practice, and by a newly-formed group, "Lawyers for Judicare." [Fendler, *Utilization of Legal Manpower to Assist the Poor (Legal Aid)*, 25 Ark. L. Rev. 203, 204 (1971).]

26.   A national conference of 79 private practitioners in 1969 arrived at a consensus statement of principles on government financial legal assistance. After advocating compensated private counsel as the vehicle in all communities except large metropolitan centers, the statement said:

> Any program of free legal services should be restricted to customary legal services to the individual and should not include advocacy for social reform or influencing legislation. [National Conference of General Practitioners, *First Report* (1969).]

27.   See pp. 119–20, *supra.*

28.   See, e.g., Green and Green, *The Legal Profession and the Process of Social Change: Legal Services in England and the United States,* 21 Hastings L. Journal 563 (1970).

29.   At present, the British government finances legal assistance in approximately 50 percent of litigation occurring in English courts. Pelletier, *op. cit., supra,* n. 8, at p. 34

30.   THE AALS STUDY OF PART-TIME LEGAL EDUCATION (Washington: AALS, 1972) at p. 224.

31.   The national average for family law problems is 36 percent. *1971 NLADA Statistical Report,* at p.iv.

32.   On July 1, 1973, Sweden put into effect a new Legal Aid Law (Rättshjälpslag) which provides that persons may receive assistance in civil cases either from a private law firm or a "Public Law Office." In either situation, the government will pay that portion of the lawyer's cost as well as other expenses of litigation which the client is unable to afford. It is anticipated that Public Law Offices, employing fully licensed attorneys and "representative with a law degree," will be opened in most cities and towns in Sweden. For further information about the new Swedish system, see, CAPPELLETTI, GORDLEY and JOHNSON, TOWARD EQUAL JUSTICE: A COMPARATIVE STUDY OF LEGAL AID IN MODERN SOCIETIES (to be published by Giuffrè, Milan, Italy).

33.   See pp. 224–26, *supra.*

34.   Wisconsin Judicare, for instance, pays 80 percent of the minimum bar fee schedule for legal work. In England the government subsidizes at 90 percent of the prevailing fee schedule for some cases and 100 percent for others.

35.   SMITH, JUSTICE AND THE POOR (New York: Carnegie, 1919) at pp. 20–30.

36.   See Silverstein, *Waiver of Court Costs and Appointment of Counsel for Poor Persons in Civil Cases,* 2 Valparaiso L. Rev.21 (1967) for a discussion of the historical origins and the extent of such court fees.

37.   Note, *Litigation Costs: The Hidden Barriers to the Indigent,* 56 Georgetown L. Journal 516 (1967–68) and Willging, *Financial Barriers and the Access of Indigents to the Courts,* 57 Georgetown L. Journal 253 (1968–69) contain a complete catalog and discussion of these litigation expenses. See also, Moore, *Relief of Indigents from Financial Barriers to Equal Justice in American Civil Courts,* Institute for Research in Poverty (U. of Wisc., July, 1971).

38.   A few judges have held that the judicial branch possesses the inherent power

to compel the legislature to appropriate funds necessary for the effective functioning of the courts. See, e.g., *Commonwealth ex rel Carroll* v. *Tate,* 442 Pa. 45, 274 A.2d 193 (1971). Whether this is truly a feasible approach is open to serious question. See Hazard, et al., *Court Finance and Unitary Budgeting,* 81 Yale L. Journal 1286 (1972). The authors of another law review comment concluded their analysis of *Tate* with the warning: "The administration of justice, like the provision of all governmental services, is inescapably and ultimately in the hands of the electorate; it is their decision whether they will suffer an outmoded system of justice." Comment, *State Court Assertion of Power to Determine and Demand Its Own Budget,* 120 U. Pa. L. Rev. 1187, 1209 (1972).

39. See pp. 245–47, *infra,* for a more detailed treatment of the closely related issue of articulating criteria for allocating legal and dispute resolution resources.

40. So-called supersedeas bonds may be required before a preliminary injunction is granted or in some cases to protect a property owner until a hearing can be held, or bonds are even more frequently required from the losing party pending an appeal. See Silverstein, *op. cit., supra,* n. 36.

41. At the same time, there are urgent reasons to tear down the obstacles that deny tens of millions of American citizens access to the courts. As the late Justice Harlan, the leading conservative spokesman on the Court in recent years, argued in *Boddie* v. *Connecticut:*

> . . . Perhaps no characteristic of an organized cohesive society is more funda-mental than its erection and enforcement of a system of rules defining the various rights and duties of its members, enabling them to govern their affairs and defi-nitely settle their differences in an orderly, predictable manner. . . . Within this framework, those who wrote our original Constitution, in the Fifth Amendment, and later those who drafted the Fourteenth Amendment recognized the centrality of the concept of due process in the operation of this system. Without this guarantee that one may not be deprived of his rights, neither liberty nor property, without due process of law, the State's monopoly over techniques for binding conflict resolution could hardly be said to be acceptable under our scheme of things. Only by providing that the social enforcement mechanism must function strictly within these bounds can we hope to maintain an orderly society that is also just. . . . [401 U.S. 371, 374–75 (1971).]

42. *Thompson* v. *Mazo,* 421 F. 2d 1156, 1160 n.11 (D.C. Cir., 1970).

43. "The Area and Local Committees are charged under the provisions of the Act with applying a twofold 'legal test' to each application for legal aid. First, the applicant must have reasonable grounds for initiating, defending, or being a party to the proceedings. This requirement is met when the committee feels there exists a legal case or defense that is likely to be successful, assuming the facts as stated by the applicant to be true. The second part of the test examines the reasonableness of the application, and asks 'whether a man of moderate means (sufficient to afford the costs of the litigation but not in a position to waste money) would embark on litigation relying on his own means.' " Pelle-tier, *op.cit., supra,* n. 8, at p. 29.

44. In 1971, the U.S. House of Representatives actually passed an amendment to

the Legal Services Corporation Act requiring the Federal government to pay state and local governments for costs incurred in successfully defending cases brought by Legal Services attorneys. This provision was deleted in the House-Senate conference. However, it was indicative of the strong sentiment for extending some protection to the parties opposed by publicly subsidized litigants. In 1973, the House enacted a similar provision, evidencing a continuing concern with this issue.

45. Pelletier, *op.cit., supra,* n.8, at p. 32.

46. In 1965–1966, almost 40 percent of the total cost of legal assistance was derived from a combination of recoveries from opposing parties and partial fees from assisted parties. *Id.* at p. 34.

47. Caplovitz found that fully 45 percent of consumer debtors had a claim of fraud or other possible legal defense. See CAPLOVITZ, DEBTORS IN DEFAULT (New York: Bureau of Applied Social Science Research, Columbia University, June, 1970) Vol. 2, Ch. 4.

48. See pp. 244–45, *supra.*

49. This estimate is made by dividing 2000 working hours a year into $25,000 (a fairly typical average cost per Legal Services attorney, including his own salary, secretarial support, space costs, equipment, supplies, and so on).

50. This estimate is for California Superior Courts. A recent study performed for the judiciary in California estimated the cost of a trial (excluding jury fees) at $730.00 per day. Judicial Council of California, A STUDY OF ARBITRATION IN THE JUDICIAL PROCESS (San Francisco, 1973), p. 22.

The economics of the hypothetical case we have constructed from typical characteristics of the American judicial system and legal profession are consistent with an empirical study recently conducted in Italy.

> While in large cases the average incidence of costs upon the parties is as low as 8.4 percent, the figures rise to between fifty-one and sixty percent in cases of less than 1,600 dollars; they jump to 170 percent in cases of less than 160 dollars —clearly an unbearable economic burden. [Cappelletti, *Social and Political Aspects of Civil Procedures—Reform and Trends in Western and Eastern Europe,* 69 Mich. L. Rev. 847, 873 (1971).]

A recent study in Germany showed the same pattern:

Amount in controversy	Fees (Court and Lawyers)
from 200 DM	336 DM
1,500 DM	1,676 DM
10,000 DM	5,568 DM

Bauer, *Legal Aid and Legal Insurance,* Studi in Memoria Carlo Furno (Milan: Guiffrè, 1973), at p. 93.

51. See e.g., SHEININ, PEOPLE'S COURTS IN THE USSR (Moscow: Foreign Languages Publishing House, 1959).

52. We propose a neighborhood tribunal with at least four auxiliary arms: a neighborhood arbitration commission, a panel of hearing referees with independent investigative resources, a youth division run and administered by youth, a referral bureau (modelled after the English Citizens' Advice Bureau) and possessing power

to summon and initiate Grand Jury investigations. Each of these institutions would be manned primarily by neighborhood inhabitants—trained and appropriately selected to fulfill their respective duties as officers of the "court." Such a neighborhood court system might well come into being as decentralized arbitration, fact finding and conciliation branches of the small claims court, magistrates court, domestic relations court, juvenile court and landlord-tenant court. We are not proposing the replication in miniature of every specialized municipal court—but rather we are suggesting the delegation of certain arbitration, conciliation, fact finding, and hearing functions to locally based and locally responsive tribunals. [Cahn and Cahn, *What Price Justice?*, 41 Notre Dame L. Rev. 927, 950 (1966).]

53. The perversion of the small claims court into a collection agency for creditors is the thesis of Moulton, *The Persecution and Intimidation of the Low-Income Litigant as Performed by the Small Claims Court in California*, 21 Stan. L. Rev. 1657 (1969). The difficulties confronting unassisted low-income litigants are outlined by a judge in Murphy, *D.C. Small Claims Court—The Forgotten Court*, 34 D.C. Bar Journal 14 (1967). See also, Note, *Small Claims Courts*, 34 Colum. L. Rev. 932 (1934); Olson, *The Establishment of Small Claims Courts in Nebraska*, 46 Neb. L. Rev. 152 (1967).

54. See, e.g., McDermott, *Arbitrability: The Courts vs the Arbitrators*, 23 Arbitration Journal, 18 (1968). An attempt to utilize arbitration for consumer disputes was established in Philadelphia in 1969. This experiment was largely unsuccessful. Small Claims Study Group, *Little Injustices: Small Claims Courts and the American Consumer* (Mimeo, March, 1972) at pp. 90–93.

55. See pp. 241–47, *supra.*

56. See, e.g., Lefkowitz, *The Non-Availability of Legal Services to Persons of Moderate Means*, 27 Record of Association of Bar of New York 144 (1972) at pp. 144–52.

57. In the case of middle-class litigants, the government subsidy should be limited to the difference between the lawyer's fee and the contribution the litigant can afford to make.

58. See, e.g., Address of the Vice President of the United States to the National Governor's Conference, February 23, 1972. The theme of this and similar speeches to the Texas State Bar and the Mayors' Conference are captured in an article in the American Bar Journal:

> . . . [T]he legal services program has gone way beyond the idea of a governmentally funded program to make legal remedies available to the indigent and now expends much of its resources on efforts to change the law on behalf of one social class —the poor. We are not discussing merely reforming the law to rectify old injustices or correcting the law where it has been allowed to be weighted against the poor. We are dealing, in large part, with a systematic effort to redistribute societal advantages and disadvantages, penalties and rewards, rights and resources. . . .
> . . . Through the imaginative use of ever-expanding constitutional concepts, the legal services program has seized upon the idea of the law and the lawsuit as an offensive weapon to redress an alleged imbalance created by the political processes. . . .

> . . . [W]ithout some form of control at the top, you have a Federal Government
> project using public monies purportedly for public purposes but actually for
> whatever purpose the individual lawyer deems worthwhile. As it operates now,
> it is a public project but without public direction or public accountability. . . .
> [Vice President Agnew, *What's Wrong with the Legal Services Program,* 58 ABA
> J. (September, 1972) at pp. 930–32.]

Responses to this article have appeared in the Journal. See, Klaus, *Legal
Services Program: Reply to Vice President Agnew,* 58 ABA J. 1178 (1972) and
Falk and Pollak, *What's Wrong with Attacks on the Legal Services Program,
Id.* at p. 1287.

In late January, 1972, Vice President Agnew, acting on complaints from
local officials in Camden, summoned poverty lawyers to a meeting in his
office. Despite objections from the OEO Legal Services director, Fred
Speaker, the Vice President not so subtly pressed for a compromise of the
pending lawsuit against the city's urban renewal program. For a description
of these events, see JOHNSON, *op. cit., supra,* n. 13.

59.   See n. 58, *supra,* and pages 281–84, *infra.*

60.   For an excellent summary discussion of various definitions of "power" see
ROSE, THE POWER STRUCTURE (New York: Oxford Press, 1967) at pp.
43–53. The definition incorporated in this chapter closely parallels several
cited by Rose.

> . . . C. Wright Mills, for example, "Power has to do with whatever decision men
> make about the arrangements under which they live . . . in so far as such decisions
> are made, the problem of who is involved in making them is the basic problem
> of power." Or Bertrand Russell's definition: "The production of intended effects
> by some men on other men." Or Lasswell and Kaplan: "*Power* is participation
> in the making of decisions. . . . The making of decisions is an interpersonal process:
> the policies which other persons are to pursue is what is decided upon. Power is
> participation in the making of decisions is an interpersonal relation. . . . [*Id.* at
> p. 50.]

61.   Power, in essence and stripped of its mystical connotations, then is simply the
possession of incentives, sanctions, and persuasive abilities that will motivate
the conduct of relevant decision makers in the private and public sectors. If
I as an individual possess many rewards to dangle, many "swords" to rattle,
or a fluent tongue, I am powerful. If I have none of these, I am weak.

62.   Other important decisions are governmental at the source. For instance, and
especially, the many issues surrounding transfer programs are purely government decisions. The ultimate behavior to be influenced is that of governmental officials and employees, not private citizens.

63.   The legal problems attending picketing and other phases of a boycott are
described in Comment, *The Consumer Boycott,* 42 Miss. L. Journal 226,
(1971).

64.   For instance, Legal Services lawyers obtained an agreement from a major
public utility to initiate a strong "affirmative action" program to employ and
promote more Mexican-Americans. Throughout the negotiations, the threat
of a possible lawsuit was kept in the background.

65. For example, Legal Services lawyers in Cleveland negotiated favorable "collective bargaining" leases on behalf of a tenant organization by employing the threat of rent withholding.

66. See, e.g., CARDOZO, THE NATURE OF THE JUDICAL PROCESS (New Haven: Yale Univ. Press, 1921); Douglas, *Stare Decisis*, 49 Columbia L. Rev. 735 (1949); Llewellyn, *The Rule of Law in Our Case-Law of Contracts*, 47 Yale L. Journal 1244 (1938).

67. ROSENBLUM, LAW AS A POLITICAL INSTRUMENT (New York: Random House, 1955) at p. 8.

68. LEVI, AN INTRODUCTION TO LEGAL REASONING (Chicago: Univ. of Chicago, 1948).

69. *Id.* at pp. 2–3.

70. *Id.* at p. 6.

71. As Levi points out, statutes are inherently ambiguous:

> [Ambiguity] is not the result of inadequate draftsmanship, as is so frequently urged. Matters are not decided until they have to be. For a legislature perhaps the pressures are such that a bill has to be passed dealing with a certain subject. But the precise effect of the bill is not something upon which the members have to reach agreement . . . [T]here is a related and an additional reason for ambiguity. As to what type of situation is the legislature to make a decision? Despite much gospel to the contrary, a legislature is not a fact finding body. There is no mechanism as there is with a court, to require the legislature to shift facts and to make decisions about specific situations. There need be no agreement about what the situation is. The members of the legislature cannot force each other to accept even a hypothetical set of facts. The result is that even in a non-controversial atmosphere just exactly what has been decided will not be clear. [*Id.* at pp. 30–31.]

72. "If the court . . . finds the contract . . . to have been unconscionable . . . the court may refuse to enforce the contract . . . or . . . so limit the application of any unconscionable clause as to avoid any unconscionable result." Section 2–302 (1) of the Uniform Commercial Code.

73. Some courts have held a price can be so out of line as to be unconscionable. "The question which presents itself is whether or not . . . the sale of a freezer unit having a retail value of $300 for $900 ($1439.69 including credit charges and $18 sales tax) is unconscionable. . . . The court believes it is." *Jones* v. *Star Credit Corp.*, 59 Misc. 2d 189, 298 NYS 2d 264, 266 (Sup. Ct. 1969).

74. See, e.g., *Williams* v. *Walker-Thomas Furniture Co.*, 350 F.2d 445 (D.C. Cir. 1965).

75. There are, of course, limitations on the power of the courts to affect law that has a statutory base. First, there are the words of the statute itself. Unlike rules made by judges that can be discarded entirely and replaced with new words, statutory language is fixed. In the name of interpretation courts can expand or contract the meaning of the terms used, but they cannot change the words of the underlying rule itself. Levi contends there is still another limitation that means judges cannot, or at least should not, be as free to change law that is embodied in legislation.

> [It] seems better to say that once a decisive interpretation of legislative intent has been made (by a court), and in that sense a direction has been fixed within the gap of ambiguity, the court's interpretation of legislation is not dictum. The words it uses do more than decide the case. They give broad direction to the statute. [LEVI, *op.cit., supra* n. 68, at p. 32.]

Thus, adopting Levi's observation, courts not only are bound by the statutory words but also by earlier judicial interpretations of those terms. Without attempting an exhaustive examination of the question, it appears judges have always behaved much the same toward prior judicial constructions of legislative language as they have toward earlier formulations of common law rules.

76. *Shapiro* v. *Thompson,* 394 U.S. 618 (1969).

77. "We recognize that a state has a valid interest in preserving the fiscal integrity of its programs. . . . But a state may not accomplish such a purpose by invidious distinction between classes of its citizens. The saving of welfare costs cannot justify an otherwise invidious classification." *Id.* at 631.

78. *Snaidach* v. *Family Finance Corp.,* 395 U.S. 337 (1969). See also *Fuentes* v. *Shevin,* 40 Law Week 4692 (1972).

79. *Wheeler* v. *Montgomery,* 397 U.S. 280 (1970).

80. *Boddie, op. cit., supra,* n. 41.

81. *King* v. *Smith,* 392 U.S. 309 (1968).

82. "A significant characteristic of public welfare programs during the last half of the 19th century in this country was their preference for the 'worthy' poor. . . . The most recent congressional amendments to the Social Security Act . . . corroborate that federal public welfare policy now rests on a basis considerably more sophisticated and enlightened than the 'worthy person' concept of earlier times. . . . [I]t is simply inconceivable . . . that Alabama is free to discourage immorality and illegitimacy by the device of absolute disqualification of needy children." *Id.* at 320, 324–26.

83. See, e.g., *Thorpe* v. *Housing Authority of City of Durham,* 393 U.S. 268 (1969).

84. See, e.g., Rose, *Social Scientist as Expert Witness,* 40 Minn. L. Rev. 205 (1956) and Clark, *Social Scientist as Expert Witness in Civil Rights Litigation,* 1 Social Problems 5 (1953).

85. So-called because Mr. Justice Brandeis, while still an attorney, pioneered in the use of social information in appellate briefs, beginning with *Muller* v. *Oregon,* 208 U.S. 412 (1908).

86. See, e.g., Grossman, "Social Backgrounds and Judicial Decision-Making," from GROSSMAN, et al., SOCIAL SCIENCE APPROACHES TO THE JUDICIAL PROCESS: A SYMPOSIUM (New York: DeCapo Press, 1971).

87. > The various factors that are combined to give any group its power can be divided into four closely interrelated categories: (1) wealth, (2) numbers, (3) leadership and organization, and (4) strategic position. Upon examination, each of these turns out to be a vastly complex area in itself.
> The importance of wealth as a source of power is quite obvious. Over the course of centuries the wealthier groups in any nation have always been among the dominant forces, if not *the* dominant ones.
> In addition to its direct value as a means of persuasion and compulsion, wealth

has the great advantage of providing the wherewithal to obtain other sources of power. To win followers, build an organization, and achieve strategic positions costs money. Generally speaking, the more money available for these purposes, the better the job that can be done.

Even to a small group, numbers are essential. An individual in isolation is weak, and it is only as a number of individuals get together that the possibilities of power emerge. . . . When disputes are settled by peaceful rather than by violent means, 'counting noses' is a widely used technique.

Numbers can also provide access to other sources of power. They can provide a source of wealth, if only through dues payments or tithes. They provide the raw materials for organization and leadership.

Only through organization can the full advantage of wealth or numbers be exploited. [GROSS, THE LEGISLATIVE STRUGGLE (New York: McGraw-Hill, 1953) at pp 143–45.]

88. The Supreme court performed this protective role for the propertied interests in admirable fashion throughout most of American history, striking down many Congressional enactments favored by the majority of the public. The shift began in the late 1930s when, partially in response to President Roosevelt's "court-packing" effort, the Court retreated, emasculating the Constitutional doctrine—substantive due process—that it had used to thwart many of Roosevelt's economic reforms.

89. SMITH, *op. cit., supra,* n. 35, at pp. 200–201.

90. *Id.* at pp. 205–206.

91. The purpose is obvious: To transpose the proposal from a minority petition into a majority demand. Public interest can be engaged in several ways. Among them:

—initiating a newsworthy event that highlights the most dramatic evils of the present situation. Depending on the issue and the social context a lawsuit or a demonstration will be more or less effective for this purpose.

—inducing the media to conduct their own investigation and exposé of the present situation. The CBS-TV documentary on "Hunger" in 1969 is an example of the public impact that can be made through this type of exposé.

—distributing a book, pamphlet, or report that will alarm and educate readers —especially opinion-makers—about the problem. Ralph Nader's attack on auto safety standards is a classic example in a long line of successful "muckraking" books that produced enough public outcry to force legislative change.

—persuading a substantial proportion of opinion-makers to issue public statements, to make speeches to various meetings of middle-class organizations, and to otherwise "talk up" the problem and the proposed solution.

Issues are by no means equal in the inherent drama that makes for easy capture of public interest. Some conditions—like visible, nauseating hunger amid agricultural surplus—simply have more punch than others of equal seriousness to the poor.

92. Many laws the poor are seeking to enact will be helpful to large numbers of middle-class citizens as well. Consumer protection laws and landlord-tenant reform are prime examples. Middle-class consumers are victimized, albeit

generally to a lesser degree, by many of the sales and collection practices that plague the poor. Middle-class tenants often find themselves legally impotent in dealing with their landlords, too. Of course, to the extent that a proposal touches only peripheral interests of the middle-class organization, there will be difficulty in persuading the organization's leadership to supply anything more than nominal support. They will not be anxious to expend their own political capital on anything less than issues vital to their own constituency.

There also will be situations in which support of a middle-class organization can be "brought along" only with substantial concessions regarding the scope and nature of the proposal itself. This will be true especially when the interests of the middle-class and the poor coincide only partially. Alliance then becomes a delicate political question for the political strategist. Should the poor be satisfied with a limited remedy this time out and hope to go all the way the next time around? Or should they forego an increased chance of passage for the continued purity of their proposal? Or is there some way of using the middle-class support—as far as it goes—without reducing the other momentum behind their full proposal? This kind of decision entails a sophisticated knowledge of the political terrain, a precise weighing of many ponderables along with a few imponderables, and some value judgments about the worth of various alternative pieces of legislation.

93.   *Serrano* v. *Priest* ruled the prevailing school financing scheme unconstitutional in California, forcing California lawmakers to consider a more equitable, or at least different, system. And the welfare residency decision fomented pressure from many sources to abandon the balkanized public assistance system by removing barriers to migration of recipients. The day after the residency decision, California Senator George Murphy, ordinarily an ardent "states righter," introduced legislation to "federalize" the national welfare system. Both President Nixon (*New York Times,* April 23, 1969, p.1; August 1, 1969, p. 1) and HEW Secretary Finch (*New York Times,* April 22, 1969, p. 1) stated the court's action "compelled" a substantial revamping of that system, and support for welfare reform suddenly crystallized throughout the Congress.

A survey of state welfare directors after *Thompson* revealed that because of the residency decision they now favored Federal welfare standards (*New York Times,* April 22, 1969, p.1). A Taxpayers Committee to Federalize Welfare sprung up and began a newspaper advertising campaign in support of nationalization of welfare and 90 percent Federal financing of the system (*New York Times,* April 28, 1969, p. 38). Other political leaders such as Mayor Lindsay (*New York Times,* May 27, 1969, p. 1) and Governor Rockefeller (*New York Times,* May 27, 1969, p.61) echoed the same theme. And in a virtually unanimous vote the National Governor's Conference passed a resolution urging Federalization of welfare costs (*New York Times,* September 3, 1969, p.1).

The welfare residency decision probably accomplished more than any lobbying effort that might have been mounted by the Welfare Rights Organization, or other recipient groups. It took away one of the essential logical premises behind the old Federal-state-local relationship, the sanctity of state boundaries. States no longer could restrict the intake of new welfare recipients. The Court compelled Congress and the President to face up to the fact that the welfare system was a national system. It also forced a confrontation with some of the more obvious inequities. It was easy to ignore the fact that Mississippi ADC families only received $33.00 per month per family unit, while New Yorkers received $197.00 per month and Californians $179.00, when movement between those states was difficult because of residency requirements. [Figures for 1965: STATISTICAL ABSTRACT OF THE UNITED STATES, 1972 (Washington: U.S. Government Printing Office, 1972) p. 302, Table 302.] After the *Thompson* case, California and 39 other states could not allow Congress to continue its indifference to that problem.

Obviously, these experiences cannot be replicated with every piece of legislation that might help the low-income community. It is not often that an integral logical prerequisite for an entire statutory structure is open to constitutional attack. But there may be parallels in both welfare and the private sector.

As court cases and minor administrative changes broaden the various eligibility categories for welfare, the system becomes more and more akin philosophically and in actuality to a negative income tax or guaranteed annual income. This may ease the transition to one of these more progressive approaches to income maintenance. Any rationale for continuing the old system will have eroded.

Some welfare reformers have advocated that existing systems can be changed through a concerted campaign of massive litigation (Cloward and Piven, *A Strategy to End Poverty*, Nation, May 2, 1966, at pp. 510–517.) By raising every possible issue in hundreds or thousands of cases, the system can be overwhelmed and will be forced to yield ground until it breaks down completely and the legislature is forced to enact fundamental changes. This approach may underestimate the ingenuity and determination of the existing systems and overestimate the potential resources of the Legal Services Program or any other source of lawyer manpower available to the poor.

With respect to the private sector, the existing low-income housing situation remains tolerable for the slumlords only because of certain legal principles that may be eroded through court action. The common law rules that allow owners to collect rent on apartments that violate the housing code constitute the legal underpinning of the entire economy of slumlordism. If those rules were changed in the courts, housing codes would be enforceable for the first time. Profits would tumble. Slumlords—and the powerful financial interests behind them—might be compelled to lobby for more government aid for low-income housing. Moreover, society as a whole would be forced to confront the hypocrisy of the present situation where housing codes are enacted in order to salve our collective conscience but then are not enforced, thus perpetuating the slum owner's profits.

94. A piece of controversial legislation rarely makes it through a legislative body without the special advocacy of one or more individual legislators. A bill can

be dropped or be smothered at any of several stages of the committee review, between committees, or on the floor.

95.   An advocate for the legislation must pick able legislators with as much influence as possible but who are not overcommitted to other duties. His primary tools of persuasion with the legislator consist of whatever political power the sponsoring groups represent, the likely public relations and political gain that will accrue to a spokesman for this particular cause, and the assistance the advocate can offer to the legislator.

96.   Various means of persuasion are described or evaluated in the following: GROSS, *op.cit., supra*, n. 87, at pp. 260–262; ROSE, *op.cit., supra*, n. 60, at pp. 377–78 (research reports); Kefauver and Levin, *Letters That Really Count*, from KATZ, PUBLIC OPINION AND PROPAGANDA (New York: Holt, Rinehart and Winston, 1964) at pp. 220–226; Cartwright, *Public Opinion and Democratic Leadership*, from KATZ, *supra*, at pp. 226–230; MILBREATH, THE WASHINGTON LOBBYISTS (Chicago: Rand McNally & Co, 1963) at pp. 209–214; SCOTT and HUNT, CONGRESS AND LOBBIES (Chapel Hill: Univ. of North Carolina, 1966) at pp. 60–85.

97.   See pp. 258–59, *supra*.

98.   The public spokesmen may or may not be associated with the groups most interested in passage of the legislation.

99.   This kind of talent and knowledge does not come cheap. Is it any wonder that political scientists stress that one of the primary advantages enjoyed by wealthy interests in the legislative contest is their ability to afford technicians, usually called lobbyists, who can maximize the impact of their existing economic strength? GROSS, *op.cit., supra*, n. 87, at pp. 223–233. For an excellent book documenting the significant contribution of talented legislative advocates on behalf of public interest legislation, see BARDACH, THE SKILL FACTOR IN POLITICS (Berkeley: Univ. of California Press, 1972). And for a discussion of why lawyers play such a prominent role in legislative advocacy, see JOHNSTONE AND HOPSON, LAWYERS AND THEIR WORK (New York: Bobbs-Merrill, 1967), pp. 106–08.

100.   Hazard takes another view, claiming litigation is impractical because it is an expensive, time-consuming process. "It is difficult to imagine a more expensive way to redistribute income than by litigation. (It is difficult to imagine doing almost anything in a more expensive way then by litigation.)" Hazard, *Social Justice Through Civil Justice*, 36 Univ. Chicago L. Rev. 699, 709 (1969).

Yet the discussion of cost-effectiveness in Chapter 8, *supra*, suggests the opposite is true. Litigation, at least that aimed at achieving meaningful gains for many people, turns out to be a bargain. See pp. 230–34, *supra*. Possibly Hazard's statement should be rephrased to read: Litigation is the most expensive way to do anything—except for all the rest.

101.   "The supreme obligation of government to improve the machinery of public participation in the political process requires that government take bold, affirmative steps to afford all our citizens an opportunity to be heard in the legislatures of the land, not only through their votes, but also through their

lobbies. Public subvention of lobbying activity . . . is a sound policy which could do much to expand the frontiers of social justice in the United States." Note, *The Poor and the Political Process: Equal Access to Lobbying,* 6 Harvard Journal on Legis. 369, 392 (1969).

102. When the Administration introduced its version of legislation to transfer the Legal Services Program to a new National Legal Services Corporation, its draftsmen inserted a provision that Legal Services "attorneys shall refrain from undertaking to influence the passage or defeat of any legislation . . . by representation to [legislative] bodies, their members or committees, unless such bodies . . . request that the attorney make representation to them." *Hearings,* Subcommittee on Employment, Manpower and Poverty, U.S. Senate Committee on Labor and Public Welfare, 92nd Congress, First Session, on S.1305, pt. 5, at p. 1682.

103. It is a criminal offense to use Federal funds to influence *Federal* legislation. 18 U.S.C. 1913. But see Engstrom and Walker, *Statutory Restraints on Administrative Lobbying: "Legal Fiction,"* 19 Journal of Public Law (1970), pp. 89–103.

104. "A lawyer shall not permit a person who . . . pays him to render legal services for another to direct or regulate his professional judgment in rendering such legal services." Disciplinary Rule 5–107 (B), ABA Code of Professional Responsibility.
     See, also, Ethical Considerations 5–1, 5–21, 5–23, 5–24, and Disciplinary Rule 5–105 (A).

105. *Hearings,* Economic Opportunity Act Amendments of 1971, Subcommittee on Employment, Manpower and Poverty, U.S. Senate, Part 4, at pp. 1500–01 (May 11, 1971).

106. "In our government of laws and not of men, each member of our society is entitled . . . to seek any lawful objective through legally permissible means." Ethical Consideration 7–1, ABA Code, *op. cit., supra,* n. 104.

107. "If a lawyer believes that the existence or absence of a rule of law, substantive or procedural, causes or contributes to an unjust result, he should endeavor by lawful means to obtain changes in the law." Ethical Consideration 8–2 ABA Code, *op. cit., supra,* n. 104.

108. A discussion of the present status and future prospects of formal advocacy in the administrative context is found in Gellhorn, *Public Participation in Administrative Proceedings,* 81 Yale L. Journal 359 (1972).

109. Tenant participation experiments in Boston, St. Louis, Philadelphia, and Michigan are described in Hirshen and Brown, *Public Housing's Neglected Resource: The Tenants,* City, Vol. 6, no. 4, (1972) at p. 15.

110. See, e.g., ALTSHULER, COMMUNITY CONTROL (New York: Pegasus, 1970); *cf.,* Kline and LeGates, *Citizen Participation in the Model Cities Program,* 1 Black Law Journal 44 (1971).

111. "A recurrent theme throughout the findings was that people were not aware of many of their rights. Only with the most 'conventional' kinds of problems, those that involved a status change or the use of a legal instrumentality, did a substantial proportion of the sample seek assistance—legal or otherwise."

Levine and Preston, *Community Resource Orientation Among Low-Income Groups,* 1970 Wisconsin L. Rev. 80, 109 (1970).

112. See p. 207, *supra.*

113. See p. 188, *supra.*

114. For instance, in 1968, the Chicago Legal Aid Bureau brought an affirmative class action against a door-to-door portrait firm on behalf of all customers deceived by certain questionable sales practices. The ultimate judgment restored thousands of dollars to scores of plaintiffs and put the portrait concern out of business.

115. BLAUSTEIN and FAUX, THE STAR-SPANGLED HUSTLE (Garden City: Doubleday, 1972); HADDAD and PUGH, eds., BLACK ECONOMIC DEVELOPMENT (Englewood Cliffs: Prentice-Hall, 1969); CROSS, BLACK CAPITALISM (New York: Atheneum, 1969).

116. According to the 1970 Census, about 27 percent of all poor families are black. See Table 95, *General Social and Economic Characteristics,* U.S. BUREAU OF THE CENSUS, CENSUS POPULATION: 1970 (Washington: U.S. Government Printing Office, 1972).

117. According to the 1970 Census, 29.8 percent of Negro families and 35.0 percent of all Negro persons were below the poverty line in 1969. Table 95, *id.* at p. 1–400.

118. The Small Business Administration made a total of $504 million of loans in 1967. Had *all* these funds gone to minority businesses—and hardly any did —it would have been a drop in the bucket. By 1971, SBA made loans totalling over $1 billion, but only 19 percent, $197 million, went to minority businessmen. BLAUSTEIN and FAUX, *op. cit., supra,* n. 115, at p. 200. That is less than the Federal loan guarantee voted to one major corporation—Lockheed. *Id.* at p. 252.

119. See pp. 203–04, *supra.*

120. "All private and Government studies indicate that about two-thirds of all businesses started to fail within the first five years. Failure rates for small businesses have been estimated as high as 80 percent." BLAUSTEIN and FAUX, *op. cit., supra,* n. 115, at pp. 256–57.

121. These problems and their effects—small, ineffectual, and frequently short-term organizations—are discussed in KRAMER, PARTICIPATION OF THE POOR (Englewood Cliffs: Prentice-Hall, 1969), pp. 225–237, 248–253.

122. See pp. 252–54, *supra.*

123. These middle-class groups frequently take the form of nonprofit private corporations qualified for Federal interest subsidies to build and operate low-rent housing under Section 236 of the Housing and Urban Development Act of 1968. See 1 Pov. L. Rept., para 2805.

124. In 1970, $2.5 billion was spent by the Federal government on credit subsidies primarily for construction of low and moderate income housing (public and private). U.S. DEPT. OF COMMERCE, *op. cit., supra,* n. 5, Table 618, p. 390. Most of these subsidy programs are outlined in 1 Pov. L. Rept., para. 2805.

125. As of 1972, the Cleveland Legal Aid Society had the largest unit devoted to the creation and operation of economic organizations benefiting the poor.

Consisting of six lawyers aided by law students and business advisors, this unit has set up a multi-million dollar housing development corporation, a coop supermarket and several other businesses.

126. See p. 247, *supra.*
127. See pp. 176–82, *supra.*
128. ABA Code, *op.cit., supra,* note 106.
129. See pp. 254–60, *supra.*
130. See pp. 260–65, *supra.*
131. As described earlier, see pp. 180–82, *supra,* the national reform centers are divided among various areas of the law, that is, welfare law, consumer law, housing law, and the like.
132. These agencies were California Rural Legal Assistance (CRLA) and the Long Beach Legal Aid Foundation. In both cases, the planning process involved Legal Services lawyers, poverty community representatives and board members.
133. See pp. 211–12, *supra.*
134. National Senior Citizens Law Center, *Litigation as a Tool for Private Pension Reform,* 6 Clearinghouse Review 593 (1973).
135. This was the result reported for a relatively sophisticated team planning effort undertaken by the Long Beach Legal Aid Foundation. The outcome of a comparable CRLA exercise supported this finding.
136. For a description of the wide-ranging activities of a major component of this system, see GOULDEN, THE SUPERLAWYERS (New York: Weybright & Talley, 1972).
137. See JOHNSON, *op.cit., supra,* n. 13, Chapters 6–9, for an account of the political attacks that periodically were made against the Legal Services Program in the years from 1967–1973.
138. Hazard, *op. cit., supra,* n. 100, at p. 701.
139. SMITH, *op. cit., supra,* n. 35, Ch XXI.
140. *Id.* at pp. 206–207.
141. "In 1916 the (Boston) Society secured the passage of a law limiting the rate of interest on small loans to three percent per month. . . ." *Id.* at p. 201.
142. *Id.* at p. 203.
143. *Id.* at p. 202.
144. *Id.* at pp. 200, 204.
145. See pp. 256–57, *supra.*
146. SMITH, *op. cit., supra,* n. 35 at p. 205.
147. See, e.g., Hazard, *op. cit., supra,* n. 100; Agnew, *op.cit., supra,* n. 58.
148. Agnew, *id.* at p. 930.
149. Hazard, *op. cit., supra,* n. 100, at pp. 720–21.
150. Agnew, *op. cit., supra,* n. 58, at p. 932.
151. *Ibid.*
152. *Id.* at p. 932.
153. See pp. 219–21, *supra.*
154. SMITH, *op. cit., supra,* n. 35, at p. 205.
155. Agnew, *op. cit., supra,* n. 58, at p. 932

Bibliography

A. Books

1. THE SOCIAL, POLITICAL AND ECONOMIC DIMENSIONS OF POVERTY

ALTSHULER, COMMUNITY CONTROL (New York: Pegasus, 1970)

BATCHELDER, THE ECONOMICS OF POVERTY (New York: Wiley & Sons, 1966)

BLAU and DUNCAN, THE AMERICAN OCCUPATIONAL STRUCTURE (New York: Wiley & Sons, 1967)

BOWEN, et al., THE AMERICAN SYSTEM OF SOCIAL INSURANCE (New York: McGraw-Hill, 1968)

BRITTAIN, THE PAYROLL TAX FOR SOCIAL SECURITY (Washington: Brookings, 1972)

BUDD, INEQUALITY AND POVERTY (New York: Norton, 1967)

CAPLOVITZ, DEBTORS IN DEFAULT (New York: Bureau of Applied Social Science Research, Columbia University, 1970)

CAPLOVITZ, THE POOR PAY MORE (New York: Free Press of Glencoe, 1963)

CARMICHAEL and HAMILTON, BLACK POWER (New York: Vintage, 1967)

CLARK, DARK GHETTO (New York: Harper & Row, 1965)

COONS, et al., PRIVATE WEALTH AND PUBLIC EDUCATION (Cambridge: Belknap Press, 1970)

CRADDOCK, et al., SOCIAL DISADVANTAGEMENT AND DEPENDENCY (Lexington: D. C. Heath, 1970)

EDELMAN, POLITICS AS SYMBOLIC ACTION: MASS AROUSAL AND QUIESCENCE (Chicago: Markham, 1971)

ELMAN, THE POORHOUSE STATE: THE AMERICAN WAY OF LIFE ON PUBLIC ASSISTANCE (New York: Random House, 1966)

FISHMAN, POVERTY AMID AFFLUENCE (New Haven: Yale University Press, 1965)

GLADWIN, POVERTY: USA (Boston: Little, Brown, 1967)

GOOD, THE AMERICAN SERFS: A REPORT ON POVERTY IN THE RURAL SOUTH (New York: G. P. Putnam, 1968)

GOODWIN, DO THE POOR WANT TO WORK? A SOCIAL PSYCHOLOGICAL STUDY OF WORK ORIENTATIONS (Washington: Brookings, 1972)

GORDON, ed., POVERTY IN AMERICA (San Francisco: Chandler, 1965)

HUNTER, POVERTY: SOCIAL CONSCIENCE IN THE PROGRESSIVE ERA (New York: Macmillan, 1904)

HUNTER, THE SLUMS: CHALLENGE AND RESPONSE (New York: Free Press, 1968)

JENCKS, INEQUALITY (New York: Basic Books, 1972)

LAMPMAN, ENDS AND MEANS OF REDUCING INCOME POVERTY (Chicago: Markham, 1971)

LARNER and HOWE, eds., POVERTY: VIEWS FROM THE LEFT (New York: William Morrow, 1968)

MARGOLIS, THE INNOCENT CONSUMER VS. THE EXPLOITERS (New York: Trident Press, 1967)

MILLER, RICH MAN, POOR MAN (New York: Crowell, 1971)

MILLER and ROBY, THE FUTURE OF INEQUALITY (New York: Basic Books, 1970)

MILWAUKEE COUNTY WELFARE RIGHTS ORGANIZATION, WELFARE MOTHERS SPEAK OUT (New York: Norton, 1972)

NETZER, ECONOMICS OF THE PROPERTY TAX (Washington: Brookings, 1966)

OFFICE OF ECONOMIC OPPORTUNITY, THE POOR 1970: A CHARTBOOK (Washington: U. S. Government Printing Office, 1971)

OKNER, INCOME DISTRIBUTION AND THE FEDERAL INCOME TAX (Ann Arbor: Institute of Public Administration, 1966)

O'NEIL, THE PRICE OF DEPENDENCY: CIVIL LIBERTIES IN THE WELFARE STATE (New York: E. P. Dutton, 1970)

PARKER, THE MYTH OF THE MIDDLE CLASS (New York: Liveright, 1972)

RAINWATER, AND THE POOR GET CHILDREN (Chicago: Quadrangle Books, 1960)

REPORT OF THE NATIONAL ADVISORY COMMISSION ON CIVIL DISORDERS (New York: Bantam ed., 1968)

ROACH and ROACH, eds., POVERTY (Baltimore: Penguin, 1972)

ROSE, THE POWER STRUCTURE (New York: Oxford Press, 1967)

SANFORD, et al., HOT WAR ON THE CONSUMER (New York: Pitman, 1969)

SCHULTZE, THE DISTRIBUTION OF FARM SUBSIDIES (Washington: Brookings, 1971)

SCOVILLE, PERSPECTIVES ON POVERTY AND INCOME DISTRIBUTION (Lexington: D. C. Heath, 1971)

SEGAL, FOOD FOR THE HUNGRY: THE RELUCTANT SOCIETY (Baltimore: Johns Hopkins Press, 1970)

SELIGMAN, PERMANENT POVERTY: AN AMERICAN SYNDROME (Chicago: Quadrangle Books, 1968)

SELIGMAN, ed., POVERTY AS A PUBLIC ISSUE (New York: The Free Press, 1965)

SHEPPARD, POVERTY AND WEALTH IN AMERICA (Chicago: Quadrangle Books, 1970)

SKOLNICK, THE POLITICS OF PROTEST (Washington: U.S. Government Printing Office, 1969)

STEIN, ON RELIEF: THE ECONOMICS OF POVERTY AND PUBLIC WELFARE (New York: Basic Books, 1971)

STEINER, THE STATE OF WELFARE (Washington: Brookings, 1971)

STERNLIEB, THE TENEMENT LANDLORD (New Brunswick: Rutgers, 1966)

STONE and SCHLAMP, WELFARE AND WORKING FATHERS: LOW-INCOME LIFE STYLES (Lexington: D. C. Heath, 1971)

TAWNEY, EQUALITY (London: George Allen and Unwin, 1952)

THUROW, POVERTY AND DISCRIMINATION (Washington: Brookings, 1969)

TIFFANY, et al., THE UNEMPLOYED: A SOCIAL-PSYCHOLOGICAL PORTRAIT (Englewood Cliffs: Prentice-Hall, 1970)

WAXMAN, ed., POVERTY: POWER AND POLITICS (New York: Grosset and Dunlop, 1968)

WILL and VATTER, eds., POVERTY IN AFFLUENCE: THE SOCIAL, POLITICAL AND
ECONOMIC DIMENSIONS OF POVERTY IN THE UNITED STATES (New York: Har-
court, Brace & World, 1965)

WINDHAM, EDUCATION, EQUALITY AND INCOME REDISTRIBUTION (Lexington: D.
C. Heath, 1971)

WISE, RICH SCHOOLS, POOR SCHOOLS: THE PROMISE OF EQUAL EDUCATIONAL
OPPORTUNITY (Chicago: University of Chicago Press, 1968)

2. *THE LEGAL SYSTEM AND ITS RESPONSE TO POVERTY*

AMERICAN ASSOCIATION OF LAW SCHOOLS, STUDY OF PART-TIME LEGAL EDUCA-
TION (Washington: AALS, 1972)

AMERICAN BAR ASSOCIATION SPECIAL COMMITTEE ON EVALUATION OF ETHICAL
STANDARDS, CODE OF PROFESSIONAL RESPONSIBILITY (Chicago: ABA, 1969)

AMERICAN BAR ASSOCIATION STANDING COMMITTEE ON ECONOMICS OF LAW
PRACTICE, MINIMUM FEE SCHEDULES (Chicago: ABA, 1970)

BRADWAY, THE WORK OF LEGAL AID COMMITTEES OF BAR ASSOCIATIONS (Baltimore: Lord Baltimore Press, 1938)

BRADWAY and SMITH, GROWTH OF LEGAL AID WORK IN THE UNITED STATES (U.S.
Dept. of Labor, Bull. No. 607, 1936)

BROWNELL, LEGAL AID IN THE UNITED STATES (Rochester: Lawyers Coop. Publ.
Co., 1951); SUPPLEMENT (1961)

CAPPELLETTI, GORDLEY AND JOHNSON, TOWARD EQUAL JUSTICE: A COMPARA-
TIVE STUDY OF LEGAL AID IN MODERN SOCIETIES (to be published by Guiffrè,
Milano)

CARDOZO, THE NATURE OF THE JUDICIAL PROCESS (New Haven: Yale University
Press, 1921)

CARLIN, HOWARD and MESSINGER, CIVIL JUSTICE AND THE POOR (New York:
Russell Sage Foundation, 1966)

CHEATHAM, A LAWYER WHEN NEEDED (New York: Columbia University Press,
1963)

CHRISTENSEN, LAWYERS FOR PEOPLE OF MODERATE MEANS (Chicago: American
Bar Foundation, 1970)

DOWNIE, JUSTICE DENIED: THE CASE FOR REFORM OF THE COURTS (New York:
Praeger, 1971)

EDGERTON and GOODHART, LEGAL AID (Oxford: Oxford University Press, 1945)

GOULDEN, THE SUPERLAWYERS (New York: Weybright and Talley, 1972)

GROSSMAN, et al., SOCIAL SCIENCE APPROACHES TO THE JUDICIAL PROCESS: A
SYMPOSIUM (New York: DeCapo Press, 1971)

JOHNSON, AND STILL LOVE JUSTICE (To be published by Public Affairs Press)

JOHNSTONE and HOPSON, LAWYERS AND THEIR WORK (New York: Bobbs-Merrill,
1967)

LEVI, AN INTRODUCTION TO LEGAL REASONING (Chicago: University of Chicago,
1948)

MAGUIRE, THE LANCE OF JUSTICE (Cambridge: Harvard University Press, 1928)

MATTHEWS and OULTON, LEGAL AID AND ADVICE (London: Butterworths, 1971)

OFFICE OF ECONOMIC OPPORTUNITY, THE POOR SEEK JUSTICE: LEGAL SERVICES IN
ACTION (Washington: U.S. Government Printing Office, 1967)

ROSENBLUM, LAW AS A POLITICAL INSTRUMENT (New York: Random House, 1955)
SHEININ, PEOPLE'S COURTS IN THE USSR (Moscow: Foreign Languages Publishing House, 1959)
SMITH, JUSTICE AND THE POOR (New York: Carnegie Foundation, 1919)
SMITH and BRADWAY, LEGAL AID WORK IN THE UNITED STATES (1926)
TEN BROEK, THE LAW OF THE POOR (San Francisco: Chandler, 1966)
WASSERSTEIN and GREEN, eds., WITH JUSTICE FOR SOME: AN INDICTMENT OF THE LAW BY YOUNG ADVOCATES (Boston: Beacon, 1970)

3. APPRAISAL OF LEGAL SERVICES AND OTHER ANTIPOVERTY PROGRAMS

ALBERTS, A PLAN FOR MEASURING THE PERFORMANCE OF SOCIAL PROGRAMS (New York: Praeger, 1970)
BAUER, SOCIAL INDICATORS (Cambridge: MIT Press, 1966)
BERGER, EQUALITY BY STATUTE (New York: Doubleday, 1968)
BLAUSTEIN and FAUX, THE STAR-SPANGLED HUSTLE: WHITE POWER AND BLACK CAPITALISM (Garden City: Doubleday, 1972)
BLUMROSEN and BLAIR, ENFORCING EQUALITY IN HOUSING AND EMPLOYMENT THROUGH STATE CIVIL RIGHTS LAWS (Newark: Rutgers Law School, 1972)
BROWN, THE MULTI-PROBLEM DILEMMA (Metuchen, N.J.: Scarecrow, 1968)
CROSS, BLACK CAPITALISM (New York: Atheneum, 1969)
DONOVAN, THE POLITICS OF POVERTY (New York: Pegasus, 1967)
DORFMAN, MEASURING BENEFITS OF GOVERNMENT INVESTMENTS (Washington: Brookings, 1965)
ECKSTEIN, ed., STUDIES OF THE ECONOMICS OF INCOME MAINTENANCE (Washington: Brookings, 1967)
GOODMAN and FENILLAN, ALTERNATIVE APPROACHES TO THE PROVISION OF LEGAL SERVICES FOR THE RURAL POOR: JUDICARE AND THE DECENTRALIZED STAFF PROGRAM (Washington: Bureau of Social Science Research, 1971)
HADDAD and PUGH, eds., BLACK ECONOMIC DEVELOPMENT (Englewood Cliffs: Prentice-Hall, 1969)
KAHN, STUDIES IN SOCIAL POLICY AND PLANNING (New York: Russell Sage Foundation, 1969)
KERSHAW, GOVERNMENT AGAINST POVERTY (Chicago: Markham, 1970)
KRAMER, PARTICIPATION OF THE POOR (Englewood Cliffs: Prentice-Hall, 1969)
LEVINE, THE POOR YE NEED NOT HAVE WITH YOU (Cambridge: MIT Press, 1970)
LEVITAN, THE GREAT SOCIETY'S POOR LAW: A NEW APPROACH (Baltimore: Johns Hopkins, 1969)
MAYHEW, LAW AND EQUAL OPPORTUNITIES (Cambridge: Harvard Press, 1968)
MEYER, et al., GIRLS AT VOCATIONAL HIGH (New York: Russell Sage Foundation, 1965)
MOYNIHAN, MAXIMUM FEASIBLE MISUNDERSTANDING (New York: Free Press, 1969)
PIVEN and CLOWARD, REGULATING THE POOR (New York: Pantheon, 1971)
ROSSI and WILLIAMS, EVALUATING SOCIAL PROGRAMS: THEORY, PRACTICE AND POLITICS (New York: Seminar Press, 1972)
TULLOCK, PRIVATE WANTS, PUBLIC MEANS (New York: Basic Books, 1970)
WEEKS, JOB CORPS: DOLLARS AND DROPOUTS (Boston: Little, Brown & Co., 1967)

4. *GENERAL*

BARDACH, THE SKILL FACTOR IN POLITICS (Berkeley: University of California Press, 1972)

GROSS, THE LEGISLATIVE STRUGGLE (New York: McGraw-Hill, 1953)

HARRIS, A SACRED TRUST (New York: The New American Library, 1966)

KATZ, PUBLIC OPINION AND PROPAGANDA (New York: Holt, Rinehart & Winston, 1964)

LUNDQUIST, POLITICS AND POLICY (Washington: Brookings, 1968)

MILBREATH, THE WASHINGTON LOBBYISTS (Chicago: Rand McNally, 1963)

NEW YORK TIMES ENCYCLOPEDIA ALMANAC–1972 (New York: New York Times, 1972)

PRESIDENT'S COMMITTEE ON LAW ENFORCEMENT AND THE ADMINISTRATION OF JUSTICE, TASK FORCE REPORT: THE POLICE (1967)

SAMUELSON, ECONOMICS (New York: McGraw-Hill, 1973)

SCOTT and HUNT, CONGRESS AND LOBBIES (Chapel Hill: University of North Carolina, 1966)

UNITED STATES BUREAU OF THE CENSUS, CENSUS POPULATION: 1970 (Washington: U.S. Government Printing Office, 1972)

UNITED STATES DEPARTMENT OF COMMERCE, STATISTICAL ABSTRACT OF THE UNITED STATES, 1972 (Washington: U.S. Government Printing Office, 1972)

B. *Congressional Hearings, Government Reports, Statutes, Etc.*

Congressional Record, Vol. 113, October 4, 1967

Connecticut General Statute, Rev. Section 17–2 (1966)

Department of Health, Education and Welfare, *Social Security Bulletin,* December, 1970

District of Columbia Code Annotated §3–203 (1967)

Economic Opportunity Act of 1964, §201

Federal Trade Commission, *Economic Report on Installment Credit and Retail Sales Practices of District of Columbia Retailers*

Housing and Urban Development Act of 1968, §236

Maryland, *Manual of Department of Public Welfare*

Office of Economic Opportunity, *Guidelines for Legal Services Programs*

Pennsylvania Statute, Title 62, §432(6) (1968)

Uniform Commercial Code §2–302(1)

U. S. Constitution, Preamble, Fourth Amendment, Sixth Amendment

U. S. Department of Health, Education and Welfare, *The Extension of Legal Services to the Poor,* November 12–14, 1964

U. S. Department of Health, Education and Welfare, *Advance Copy of Selected Tables from Public Assistance Statistics* (July, 1970)

U. S. Department of Housing and Urban Development, *HUD Circular 2–7–67*

U. S. House of Representatives, *Hearings,* Economic Opportunity Act Amendments of 1967, Committee on Education and Labor, 90th Congress, 1st Session (June 20, 1967)

U. S. House of Representatives, *Hearings on H.R. 8311,* Committee on Education and Labor, 90th Congress, 1st Session (June 20, 1967)

U. S. House of Representatives, *Hearings on H.R. 13938*, Special Subcommittee on Labor, Committee on Education and Labor, 92nd Congress, 2nd Session (1971)

U. S. House *Report No. 866*, Committee on Education and Labor, 90th Congress, 1st Session (1967)

U. S. Senate, *Hearings on Senate Resolution 281*, Senate Committee on Labor and Public Welfare (1968)

U. S. Senate, *Hearings*, Subcommittee on Employment, Manpower and Poverty, Committee on Labor and Public Welfare, 91st Congress, 1st Session (November 14, 1969)

U. S. Senate *Hearings*, Subcommittee on Employment, Manpower and Poverty, Senate Committee on Labor and Public Welfare, 92nd Congress, 1st Session.

U. S. Senate, *Hearings on the Economic Opportunity Act Amendments of 1971*, Subcommittee on Employment, Manpower and Poverty, Senate Committee on Labor and Public Welfare (May 11, 1971)

U. S. Senate *Report No. 563*, 90th Congress, 1st Session (1967)

Washington Rev. Stat. Title 2 (1961)

Washington Session Laws of 1939

White House *Statement of the President*, Press Release, San Clemente, California, August 11, 1969

18 U.S.C. § 1913

26 U.S.C. § (1970)

42 U.S.C. §402 (a) (23) (1970)

42 U.S.C. §602(a) (9)

42 U.S.C. § 2711 (1970)

42 U.S.C. § 2781 (a) (4) (1970)

42 U.S.C. §2791 (b) (2) (1970)

42 U.S.C. §2809 (a) (1) (1970)

42 U.S.C. §2834

42 U.S.C. §3303 (b) (1), (2) (1970)

42 U.S.C. §606 (a)

1969 N.Y.Stats. c. 184

C. Articles

Abrahams, *Legal Aid and Preventive Law*, 16 Legal Aid Briefcase 68 (1958)

Abrahams, *Twenty-five Years of Service: Philadelphia's Neighborhood Law Office Plan*, 50 ABA J. 728 (1964)

Ackerman, *Regulating Slum Housing Markets on Behalf of the Poor: Of Housing Codes, Housing Subsidies and Income Redistribution Policy*, 80 Yale L. J. 1093 (1971)

Agnew, *What's Wrong with the Legal Services Program*, 58 ABA J. 930 (1972)

Allison and Phelps, *Can We Afford to Provide Trial Counsel for the Indigent in Misdemeanor Cases?* 13 William and Mary L. Rev. 75 (1971)

Bethel and Walker, *Et Tu Brute*, 1 Tenn. B. J. 11 (1965)

Blumenthal, *The Legal Services Corporation: Curtailing Political Interference*, 81 Yale L. J. 231 (1971)

Botein, *The Constitutionality of Restrictions on Poverty Law Firms: A New York Case Study*, 46 New York L. Rev. 748 (1971)

Bradway, *National Aspects of Legal Aid,* 205 The Annals 101 (1939)

Burstein, *Legal Aid in Juvenile Court,* 20 Legal Aid Briefcase 139 (Apr. 1962)

Cahn and Cahn, *Power to the People or the Profession?* 79 Yale L. J. 1005 (1970)

Cahn and Cahn, *The War on Poverty: A Civilian Perspective,* 73 Yale L. J. 1317 (1964)

Cahn and Cahn, *What Price Justice, The Civilian Perspective Revisited,* 41 Notre Dame L. Rev. 927 (1966)

Caplan and Johnson, *Neighborhood Lawyer Programs: An Experiment in Social Change,* 20 U. Miami L. Rev. 184 (1965)

Cappelletti, *Social and Political Aspects of Civil Procedures—Reform and Trends in Western and Eastern Europe,* 69 Mich. L. Rev. 847 (1971)

Cappelletti and Gordley, *Legal Aid: Modern Themes and Variations,* 24 Stanford L. Rev. 347 (1972)

Carlin and Howard, *Legal Representation and Class Justice,* 12 UCLA L. Rev. 381 (1965)

Cheswick, *The Average Level of Schooling and the Intra-Regional Inequality of Income: A Clarification,* 58 Amer. Econ. Rev. 495 (1968)

Clancy and Wyse, *Feeding the Hungry,* 5 Harvard Civil Rights–Civil Liberties Law Rev. 440 (1970)

Clark, *Legal Services Program—The Case Load Problems or How to Avoid Becoming the New Welfare Department,* 47 J. Urban L. 797 (1969–70)

Cloward and Piven, *A Strategy to End Poverty,* Nation 510 (May 2, 1966)

Comment, *Educational Financing, Equal Protection of the Laws and the Supreme Court,* 70 Mich. L. Rev. 1324 (1972)

Comment, *Equal Protection in the Urban Environment: The Right to Equal Municipal Services,* 46 Tulane L. Rev. 496 (1972)

Comment, *Legal Services Survey Report,* 49 Neb. L. Rev. 877 (1970)

Comment, *State Court Assertion of Power to Determine and Demand Its Own Budget,* 120 U. Pa. L. Rev. 1187 (1972)

Comment, *The Consumer Boycott,* 42 Miss. L. J. 226 (1971)

Comment, *The National School Lunch Program,* 119 U. Pa. L. Rev. 372 (1970)

Condlin, *Citizens, Police, and Polarization: Are Perceptions More Important Than Facts?* 47 J. Urban Law 653 (1969–70)

Cooper and Sobol, *Seniority and Testing Under Fair Employment Laws: A General Approach to Objective Criteria of Hiring and Promotion,* 82 Harv. L. Rev. 1598 (1969)

DeFeis, *Abuse of Process and Its Impact on the Poor,* 46 St. John's L. Rev. 1 (1971)

Dewey, *What Happened in Albuquerque,* 28 Legal Aid Briefcase 227 (1970)

Dodyk, *The Tax Reform Act of 1969 and the Poor,* 71 Colum. L. Rev. 758 (1971)

Douglas, *Stare Decisis,* 49 Colum. L. Rev. 735 (1949)

Duniway, *Poor Man in Federal Courts,* 18 Stan. L. Rev. 1270 (1966)

Dworkin, *The Progress and Future of Legal Aid in Civil Litigation,* 28 Modern L. Rev. 432 (1965)

Engstrom and Walker, *Statutory Restraints on Administrative Lobbying: "Legal Fiction"* 19 J. Pub. Law 89 (1970)

Falk and Pollak, *What's Wrong with Attacks on the Legal Services Program,* 58 ABA J. 1287 (1972)

Fendler, *Legal Profession and the Anti-Poverty Program,* 8 New Hampshire B. J. 172 (1966)

Fendler, *Utilization of Legal Manpower to Assist the Poor (Legal Aid),* 25 Ark. L. Rev. 203 (1971)

Finman, *OEO Legal Services Programs and the Pursuit of Social Change: The Relationship Between Program Ideology and Program Performance,* 1971 Wisc. L. Rev. 1001 (1971)

Fox, *Providing Legal Services for the Middle Class in Civil Matters: The Problem, the Duty and a Solution,* 26 U. Pitt. L. Rev. 811 (1965)

Frankel, *Experiments in Serving the Indigent,* 51 ABA J. 460 (1965)

Gaines, *The Right of Non-Property Owners to Participate in a Special Assessment Majority Protest,* 20 UCLA L. Rev. (1972)

Gellhorn, *Public Participation in Administrative Proceedings,* 81 Yale L. J. 359 (1972)

Ginsburg, *The Availability of Legal Services to Poor People and People of Limited Means in Foreign Systems,* 6 Int'l. Lawyer 128 (1972)

Goldstein, *Interdistrict Inequalities in School Financing: A Critical Analysis of Serrano v. Priest and Its Progeny,* 120 U. Pa. L. Rev. 504 (1972)

Green and Green, *The Legal Profession and the Process of Social Change: Legal Services in England and the United States,* 21 Hastings L. J. 563 (1970)

Greenfield, *Coercive Collection Tactics—An Analysis of the Interests and Remedies,* 1972 Wash. U. L.Q.1 (Winter,1972)

Guild Report, 10 Lawyers' Guild Rev. 24 (1950)

Hannon, *Law Reform Enforcement at the Local Level: A Legal Services Case Study,* 19 Journal of Public Law 23 (1970)

Hannon, *Leadership Problems in Legal Services Programs,* 4 Law & Soc. Rev. 235, (1969)

Hannon, *Legal Services and the Community Action Program: Oil and Water in the War on Poverty,* 28 Legal Aid Briefcase 5 (1969)

Hazard, et al., *Court Finance and Unitary Budgeting,* 81 Yale L. J. 1286 (1972)

Hazard, *Law Reforming and the Anti-Poverty Effort,* 37 U. Chi. L. Rev. 242 (1970)

Hazard, *Social Justice Through Civil Justice,* 36 U. Chi. L. Rev. 699 (1969)

Hirshen and Brown, *Public Housing's Neglected Resources: The Tenants,* City, Vol. 6, No. 4, p. 15 (1972)

Horowitz, *Equal Protection Aspects of Inequalities in Public Education and Public Assistance Programs for the Poor,* 15 UCLA L. Rev. 787 (1968)

Hughes, *Legal Aid Societies, Their Function and Necessity,* 45 ABA Reports 227 (1920)

Income of Lawyers, 1965, 55 ABA Journal 562 (1969)

Johnson, *A Conservative Rationale for the Legal Services Program,* 70 W. Va. L. Rev. 350 (1968)

Johnson, *Legal Aid and Social Reform,* 4 Dialogue 56 (1971)

Johnson, *Refutation and Endorsement: A Reaction to Hannon's Analysis of the Murphy Amendment and the Bar,* 28 Legal Aid Briefcase 257 (1970)

Johnson, *The OEO Legal Services Program,* 14 Catholic Lawyer 99 (1968)

Kelso, *What Lawyers Can Do Towards Eliminating the Causes of Poverty,* 25 Bus. Law. 1303 (1970)

Kergis, *Law Firms Could Better Serve the Poor,* 55 ABA J. 232 (1969)

Klaus, *Legal Services Program: Reply to Vice President Agnew,* 58 ABA J. 1178 (1972)

Klauser, *Legal Assistance in the Federal republic of Germany,* 20 Buff. L. Rev. 583 (1971)

Kline and LeGates, *Citizen Participation in the Model Cities Program,* Black L. J. 44 (1971)

Lampman, *Expanding the American System of Transfer to Do More for the Poor,* 1969 Wisc. L. Rev. 541 (1969)

31 Law and Contemporary Problems 211 (Winter, 1966)

Lefkowitz, *The Non-Availability of Legal Services to Persons of Moderate Means,* 27 Record of Association of Bar of New York 144 (1972)

Legal Aid Services Abroad, 21 Legal Aid Briefcase 120 (1963)

Legal Services Survey Report, 49 Nebr. L. Rev. 877 (1970)

Lempert, *Strategies of Research Design in the Legal Impact Study,* 1 Law & Soc. Rev. 111 (1966)

Levine and Preston, *Community Resource Orientation Among Low-Income Groups,* 1970 Wisc. L. Rev. 80 (1970)

Liebman, *Book Review,* 85 Harv. L. Rev. 1682 (1972)

Llewellyn, *The Rule of Law in Our Case-Law of Contracts,* 47 Yale L. J. 1244 (1938)

Maguire, *Poverty and Civil Litigation,* 36 Harv. L. Rev. 361 (1922–23)

Marden, *Equal Access to Justice: The Challenge and the Opportunity,* 19 Wash. & Lee L. Rev. 153 (1962)

Marden, *Legal Aid, The Private Lawyer and the Community,* 20 Tenn. L. Rev. 757 (1949)

Martin, *Legal Aid in Ontario,* 10 Can. B. J. 473 (1967)

Mashaw, *Welfare Reform and Local Administration of Aid to Families With Dependent Children,* 57 Va. L. Rev. 818 (1971)

Masotti and Corsi, *Legal Assistance for the Poor,* 44 J. Urban Law 483 (1967)

Mattis, *Financial Inability to Obtain an Adequate Defense,* 49 Nebr. L. Rev. 37 (1969)

McDermott, *Arbitrability: The Courts vs the Arbitrators,* 23 Arbitration Journal 18 (1968)

Merson, *Municipal Services—Hawkins v. Town of Shaw,* 48 Denver L. J. 286 (1971)

Mineer, *Investment in Human Capital and Personal Income Distribution,* 66 Found. Pol. Econ. 281 (1958)

Moise, *OEO's Legal Services Programs in North Carolina: Ethical and Allied Considerations,* 4 Wake Forest Intra. L. Rev. 194 (1968)

Moore, *Relief of Indigents from Financial Barriers to Equal Justice in American Civil Courts,* Inst. for Research in Poverty (U. of Wisc., 1971)

Moulton, *The Persecution and Intimidation of the Low-Income Litigant as Performed by the Small Claims Court in California,* 21 Stan. L. Rev. 1657 (1969)

Murphy, *D.C. Small Claims Court—The Forgotten Court,* 34 D.C. B. J. 14 (1967)

Norton, *Law and Social Welfare,* Annals, Amer. Acad. Pol. & Soc. Science, Vol. CXLV, pt. 1, p. 147 (1929)

Note, *A Statistical Analysis of the School Finance Decisions: On Winning Battles and Losing Wars,* 81 Yale L. J. 1303 (1972)

Note, *Beyond the Neighborhood Office—OEO Special Grants in Legal Services,* 56 Geo. L. J. 742 (1968)

Note, *Consumer Legislation and the Poor,* 76 Yale L. J. 745 (1967)

Note, *Dollars and Sense of an Expanded Right to Counsel,* 55 Iowa L. Rev. 1249 (1970)

Note, *Employment Testing: The Aftermath of Griggs v. Duke Power Company,* 72 Colum. L. Rev. 900 (1972)

Note, *Eviction of State's Tenants Necessitates a Limited Hearing According to the State Action Doctrine of the Fourteenth Amendment,* 21 Buff. L. Rev. 524 (1972)

Note, *Feeding the Hungry,* 5 Harv. Civil Rights-Civil Liberties L. Rev. 440 (1970)

Note, *Lawless Law Enforcement,* 4 Loyola L.A. L. Rev. 161 (1972)

Note, *Minority Workers and the Continuing Effects of Racial Discrimination—The Limits of Remedial Treatment,* 58 Iowa L. Rev. 143 (1972)

Note, *The National School Lunch Program, 1970: Mandate to Feed the Children,* 60 Geo. L. J. 711 (1972)

Note, *Neighborhood Law Offices: New Wave in Legal Services for the Poor,* 80 Harv. L. Rev. 805 (1967)

Note, *New Public Interest Lawyers,* 79 Yale L. J. 1069 (1970)

Note, *Persecution and Intimidation of the Low-Income Litigant in Calif. Small Claims Court,* 21 Stan. L. Rev. 1657 (1969)

Note, *The Right to Counsel in Civil Litigation,* 66 Colum. L. Rev. 1322 (1966)

Note, *Rural Poverty and the Law in Southern Colorado,* 47 Denver L. J. 82 (1970)

Note, *Small Claims Courts,* 34 Colum. L. Rev. 932 (1934)

Note, *The Poor and the Political Process: Equal Access to Lobbying,* 6 Harv. J. on Legis. 369 (1969)

OEO Digest, Vol. 3, No. 4, p. 8 (Dec., 1972)

Olson, *The Establishment of Small Claims Courts in Nebraska,* 46 Nebr. L. Rev. 152 (1967)

O'Neil, *Of Justice Delayed and Justice Denied: The Welfare Prior Hearing Cases,* 1970 Supreme Court Review, p. 161.

Orshansky, *Recounting the Poor—A Five Year Review,* Social Security Bull. Vol. 24, No. 4, p. 23 (April, 1966)

Pelletier, *English Legal Aid: The Successful Experiment in Judicare,* 40 U. Colo. L. Rev. 10 (Fall, 1967)

Pelletier, *Legal Aid in France,* 42 Notre Dame L. Rev. 627 (1967)

Pincus, *Programs to Supplement Law Offices for the Poor,* 41 Notre Dame Lawyer 887 (1966)

Pious, *Policy and Public Administration: The Legal Services Program in the War on Poverty,* 2 Politics and Soc. 376 (1971)

Preloznik, *Wisconsin Judicare,* 25 Legal Aid Briefcase 91 (1967)

Pye, et al., *Legal Aid—A Proposal,* 47 (N.C. L. Rev. 528 (1969)

Pye and Garraty, *The Involvement of the Bar in the War Against Poverty,* 41 Notre Dame Lawyer 860 (1966)

Ratner, *Inter-Neighborhood Denials of Equal Protection in the Provision of Municipal Services,* 4 Harv. Civ. Rights-Civ. Lib. L. Rev. 1 (1968)

Reich, *Midnight Welfare Searches and the Social Security Act,* 72 Yale L. J. 1347 (1963)

Report of the Standing Committee on Legal Aid Work, 45 ABA Report 380 (1929)

Roisman, *Tenants and the Law: 1970,* 20 Amer. U. L. Rev. 58 (1970–71)

Salant, *Legal Aid in Israel,* 21 Legal Aid Briefcase 127 (1963)

Schmertz, *Indigent Civil Plaintiff in the District of Columbia, Facts and Commentary,* 27 Fed. Bar. J. 235 (Summer, 1967)

Silver, *Imminent Failure of Legal Services for the Poor: Why and How to Limit the Caseload,* 46 J. Urban Law 217 (1968)

Silverstein, *Eligibility for Free Legal Services in Civil Cases,* 44 J. Urban Law 549 (1967)

Silverstein, *Waiver of Court Costs and Appointment of Counsel for Poor Persons in Civil Cases,* 2 Valparaiso L. Rev. 21 (1967)

Smith, *Interest of the American Bar Association in Legal Aid Work,* 205 The Annals 108 (1939)

Smith, *The Relation Between Legal Aid Work and the Administration of Justice,* 45 ABA Reports 217 (1920)

Social Scientist as Expert Witness, 40 Minn. L. Rev. 205 (1956)

Social Scientist as Expert Witness in Civil Rights Litigation, 1 Soc. Prob. 5 (1953)

Stohr, *The German System of Legal Aid: An Alternative Approach,* 54 Calif. L. Rev. 801 (1966)

Storey, *The Legal Profession Versus Regimentation: A Program to Counter Socialization,* 37 ABA J. 101 (1951)

Stumpf, *Law and Poverty: A Political Perspective, 1968,* Wisc. L. Rev. 694 (1968)

Stumpf, *The Legal Profession and Legal Services: Exploitation in Local Bar Politics,* 6 Law & Soc. Rev. 9 (1971)

Sykes, *Legal Needs of the Poor in the City of Denver,* 4 Law & Soc. Rev. 255 (1969)

Symposium: *Group Law Practice,* 18 Clev. Marshall L. Rev. 1 (1969)

Symposium: *Legal Needs of the Poor,* 66 Colum. L. Rev. 248 (1966)

Symposium: *A Legal Service Program for West Virginia,* 70 W. Va. L. Rev. 277 (1968)

Taft, *Legal Aid Work,* Annals, Amer. Acad. Pol. & Soc. Science, Vol. CXXIV, p. iv (1926)

Tennessee Lawyer, Vol. 15, No. 4, p. 2 (1966)

Toll and Allison, *Advocates for the Poor,* 52 Judicature 321 (1969)

Tomlinson and Mashaw, *The Enforcement of Federal Standards in Grant-in-Aid Programs: Suggestions for Beneficiary Involvement,* 58 Va. L. Rev. 600 (1972)

Tustin, *The Relation of Legal Aid to the Municipality,* 45 ABA Reports 236 (1920)

Vance, *The Historical Background of the Legal Aid Movement,* Annals, Amer. Acad. Pol. & Soc. Science (March, 1926)

Voorhees, *Legal Aid: Past, Present and Future,* 56 ABA J. 765 (1970)

Wald, *Law and Poverty: 1965,* Prepared as a working paper for the National Conference on Law and Poverty, Washington, D.C. (June, 1965)

Warren, *Regulation of Finance Charge in Retail Installment Sales,* 68 Yale L. J. 834 (1959)

Weintraub, Kohn and Hollingsworth, *The Mixed Blessings of Escaleria: New Vistas of Due Process for Public Housing Tenants in Termination of Tenancy,* 17 N.Y.L.F. 1 (1971)

Wells, *Legal Services for the Poor,* 49 Mass. L.Q. 273 (1964)

Westwood, *Getting Justice for the Freedman,* 16 How. L. J. 492 (1971)

Widiss, *Legal Assistance for the Rural Poor. An Iowa Study,* 56 Iowa L. Rev. 100 (1970)

Willging, *Financial Barriers and the Access of Indigents to the Courts,* 57 Geo. L. J. 253 (1968–69)

Willging, *Litigation Costs: The Hidden Barriers to the Indigent,* 56 Geo. L. J. 516 (1967–68)
Wismer, *Lobbyists for the Poor,* 225 The Annals 172 (1936)
Young, *Legal Aid in Scotland,* 21 Ala. L. Rev. 191 (1969)
Zimroth, *Group Legal Services and the Constitution,* 76 Yale L. J. 966 (1967)

D. Miscellaneous Sources

1. NEWSPAPER ARTICLES
Chicago Daily News, November 18, 1964
Group Legal Services News, Vol. 1, No. 6, 1972
Los Angeles Times, December 19, 1972; February 16, 1973
New York Times, January 4, 1920; May 19, 1968; April 22, 1969; April 23, 1969; April 28, 1969; May 27, 1969; June 3, 1969; August 1, 1969; September 3, 1969; December 19, 1972

2. PUBLISHED REPORTS
Auerbach Associates, *Final Report to OEO Legal Services Program,* October 31, 1971
Harvard Conference on Law and Poverty, *Proceedings,* March 17–19, 1967
Judicial Conference of California, *Annual Report* (1972)
McKinsey and Company, *Management Study of OEO*
National Conference of Bar Presidents, *Proceedings* (February 19–20, 1966)
National Conference on Prepaid Legal Services, *Transcript of Proceedings* (1972)
National Legal Aid and Defender Association, *President's Annual Report,* 33rd Annual Conference, October, 1955
National Legal Aid and Defender Association, *1962 Summary of Conference Proceedings*
National Legal Aid and Defender Association, *1965 Summary of Proceedings of the 43rd Annual Conference* (November 16–19, 1965)
National Legal Aid and Defender Association, *1966 Summary of Conference Proceedings*
National Legal Aid and Defender Association, *1971 Statistics of Legal Assistance Work*
Prepaid Legal Services, *Proceedings of a Conference on the Development of Prepaid Legal Services* (Los Angeles: UCLA, 1972)
Small Claims Study Group, *Little Injustices: Small Claims Courts and the American Consumer* (1972)

3. MEMORANDA AND LETTERS
American Bar Association, memorandum, "Procedure for Expansion of Legal Services"
Bamberger, memorandum to Mr. Berry, April 20, 1966
Bamberger, memorandum to Mr. Kelly, December 6, 1965
Cahn, memorandum to Mr. Boone, November 27, 1964
Cahn, Jean Camper, *Status Report to Dick Boone,* January 29, 1965
Gossett, letter to Mr. Shriver, October 28, 1967
Hyndman, memorandum to Messrs. Powell and Early, November 19, 1964
Johnson, memorandum to Mr. Bamberger, "Application for Legal Services Program, Wisconsin State Bar, 'Judicare,' " January 7, 1966

Johnson, memorandum to Mr. Bamberger, "Some Priorities for Fiscal 1966," November 10, 1965

Johnson, memorandum to Mr. Bamberger, November 12, 1965

Johnson, memorandum to Mr. Bamberger, "Al Cohn's Presentation at University of Florida Law School Reunion," April 1, 1966

Johnson, memorandum to Legal Services Staff, August 18, 1966

Kepler, letter to Mr. Shriver, May 26, 1967

McAlpin, memorandum to ABA Standing Committee on Lawyer Referral, December 29, 1964

Mobilization for Youth Legal Services Unit, *Statement of Basic Policy for Supervisory Committee,* May 15, 1964

National Legal Aid and Defender Association, *Resolution,* December 16, 1964

Neighborhood Legal Services Program (Washington, D.C.), *Report of Policy Committee to Board of Directors,* December 10, 1964

Neighborhood Legal Services Program (Washington, D.C.), *Report of Policy Committee to Board of Directors,* January 4, 1965

Neighborhood Legal Services Program (Washington, D.C.), *Staff Study to Board of Directors,* June 2, 1965

Office of Economic Opportunity, *Staff Report,* Meeting with Representatives of the American Bar Association, December 28, 1964

Powell, letter to Mr. Early, January 24, 1965

Robb, letter to Mr. Wright, July 7, 1969

Sparer, *Poverty Law and Social Welfare* (unpublished memorandum), January 11, 1964

Sparer, memorandum to members of the Policy Committee, Mobilization for Youth Legal Services Unit, March 4, 1964

Voorhees, letter to Mr. Shriver, March 8, 1966

Westwood, letter to Mr. Powell, July 28, 1965

Westwood, letter to Mr. Powell, August 20, 1965

Westwood, letter to author, January 13, 1972

Westwood, undated letter to author, received February, 1972

Wickenden, *Poverty and the Law: The Constitutional Rights of Assistance Recipients,* February 25, 1963

4. *UNPUBLISHED REPORTS, PAPERS, ETC.*

California Rural Legal Assistance, *Annual Report to the Office of Economic Opportunity,* September, 1969

Community Progress, Inc., *Proposal,* January 24, 1964

Florida State Bar Association, *Resolution,* March 19, 1966

Legal Aid Committee of the Association of the Bar of the City of New York, *Report* (1937)

Lenvin, *Legal Aid: A Study of its Goals, Problems, and Relation to the War on Poverty* (unpublished Senior Essay; Barnard College, 1966)

National Conference of General Practitioners, *First Report* (1969)

National Housing and Economic Development Law Project, *Application for Refunding (Economic Development Component),* July 1, 1972

Neighborhood Legal Services Program (Washington, D.C.), *Proposal for Training Program* by Howard University Law School, December, 1964

Office of Economic Opportunity, *Tentative Guidelines for Legal Services Programs* (June, 1965)

Office of Economic Opportunity, *Introduction to the Development of a Legal Services Program* (Draft of Legal Services Guidelines), November 10, 1965

Office of Economic Opportunity, Legal Services Program, National Advisory Committee, *Transcript of meeting,* November 11, 1965

Office of Economic Opportunity, Legal Services Program, National Advisory Committee, *Transcript of meeting,* March 6, 1966

Office of Economic Opportunity, Legal Services Program, National Advisory Committee, *Transcript of meeting,* January 4, 1967

Office of Economic Opportunity, Legal Services Program, National Advisory Committee, *Transcript of meeting,* September 21, 1967

Office of Economic Opportunity, Legal Services Program, National Advisory Committee, *Transcript of meeting,* May 19, 1968

Office of Economic Opportunity, Legal Services Staff, *Analysis of Fiscal Year 1966 Grantees* (unpublished, August, 1966)

Tennessee Bar Association, *Resolution,* Board of Governors, April 30, 1966

Tennessee Bar Association, *Resolution,* Board of Governors, November 11, 1966

U. S. Department of Health, Education and Welfare, *Analysis of Impact of Supreme Court Decisions* (1970)

Vera Foundation, *A Proposal to Set Up a Legal Unit for Mobilization for Youth,* May, 1968

5. SPEECHES

Bamberger, speech to annual convention, National Legal Aid and Defender Association, Scottsdale, Arizona, November 18, 1965

Bamberger, speech to the National Conference of Bar Presidents, Chicago, Illinois, February 8, 1966

Bamberger, speech to the Florida State Bar Association Convention, Hollywood Beach, Florida, June 16, 1966

Johnson, speech to annual convention, National Legal Aid and Defender Association, Scottsdale, Arizona, November 18, 1965

Lashley, speech to the Annual Legal Aid Conference, Baltimore, Maryland, 1941

Powell, speech to the American Bar Association House of Delegates, New York City, August 14, 1964

Rutledge, speech to the Fifth Open Meeting on Legal Aid Work, American Bar Association Annual Convention, September 29, 1941

Shriver, speech to the Conference of Bar Presidents, American Bar Association Annual Meeting, Miami, Florida, August, 1965

Voorhees, speech to the Toledo Bar Association, Toledo, Ohio, April, 1966

Index

ABA. *See* American Bar Association.

AFDC. *See* Aid to Families with Dependent Children.

AMA. *See* American Medical Association.

ATL. *See* American Trial Lawyers.

Abbott, Lyman, 12

Accountability, 282, 283

Ackerman, Bruce, quoted, 354 n. 142

Affluent, the, 243–245

Agnew, Spiro, 378 n. 58; quoted, 281, 282, 377–378 n. 58

Agriculture Department, 205, 350 n. 115. *See also* Food stamp program.

Aid to Families with Dependent Children (AFDC), 257, 303 n. 9, 349–350 n. 107, n. 109; and Alabama, 346 n. 97, 347 n. 99, 348 n. 101, 380 n. 82. *See also* Welfare assistance.

Alabama, 99; and AFDC, 346 n. 97, 347 n. 99, 348 n. 101, 380 n. 82

Alaska, the Program in, 100

Albuquerque (N. Mex.), bar association vs. lawyers, 85; Community Chests and test cases, 193

Allison, Junius, 45, 48–49, 74

Ambiguity, 256, 379 n. 71

American Bar Association (ABA), and the British system, 18–19; Canons of Ethics, 25, 124–125, 131; Code of Professional Responsibility, 124–125, 264, 274–275, 327 n. 38–43 (quoted, 131, 385 n. 104, n. 106, n. 107); General Assembly, 19, 302 n. 92; and the goal of justice, 12; House of Delegates, 58–64; and the national

American Bar Association (*cont.*)
Program, 43–70, 80, 81, 94; and Judicare, 118–119; and *Justice and the Poor*, 7; and law reform, 170; and local bar association protests, 88–89; and national policy, 105–126; and the OEO budget, 319–320 n. 80; and regionalization, 153–161; Resolutions Committee, 302 n. 92; Section on Individual Rights and Responsibilities, 311 n. 100; Standing Committee on Legal Aid, 7–8, 18–19, 55, 298 n. 29, 301 n. 83; and test cases, 193; Young Lawyer Section, 61

American Medical Association (AMA), fight on Medicare, 57

American Trial Lawyers (ATL), Committee on Legal Services to the Indigent, 318 n. 70; and NAC, 318 n. 70; and the Program, 95–98; resolution, 317–318 n. 70

Antipoverty advocacy, 272–273

Appeals, 13–14, 189, 280, 337–338 n. 21, n. 22, 339 n. 40. *See also* Litigation.

Area-Wide Council, 363 n. 205

Arizona, and test cases, 193

Association of the Bar of the City of New York, 7, 17

Atkeson, Timothy, 305 n. 36

Atlanta (Ga.), regional office in, 138

Auerbach Associates, quoted, 189–190, 335 n. 26

Austin (Tex.), regional office in, 138; swindles in, 355 n. 147

Austria, 14